For Eloise

Peter Harbison

14 Oct. 2004

MORE LASTING THAN BRASS

Caroline Haring White in 1883

More Lasting than Brass

A Thread of Family from Revolutionary New York
to Industrial Connecticut

Members of the
Haring, Herring, Clark, Denton, Phelps, White, Griggs, Judd
and Related Families

by
Peter Haring Judd

with a foreword by
Alan Taylor

Newbury Street Press & Northeastern University Press
Boston, Massachusetts
2004

Published by
Newbury Street Press, Boston,
special publications imprint of the
New England Historic genealogical Society
and
Northeastern University Press, Boston

Library of Congress Cataloging-in-Publication Data
Judd, Peter H.
More lasting than brass : a thread of family from Revolutionary New York to industrial Connecticut / by Peter Haring Judd, members of the Haring, Herring, Clark, Denton, Phelps, White, Griggs, Judd and related Families ; with a foreword by Alan Taylor.
p. cm.
Includes bibliographical references and index.
ISBN 1-55553-626-3 (cl. : alk. paper)
1. Herring family. 2. New York (State)—Biography. 3. Connecticut—Biography. I. Title.
CT274.H48J84 2004
929'.2'0973—dc22   2004006848

Printed and bound by Edwards Brothers, Inc., Lillington, North Carolina. The paper is EB Natural, an acid-free sheet.

Manufactured in the United States of America

To

Caroline Haring (White) Griggs
"C.H.W.G."

San Rafael, California, 1875–Waterbury, Connecticut, 1969

custodian and preserver

&

Alicia Mai Matsumoto

Little River, California, 1988–

her great-great-great-granddaughter, and the future

As the long train
Of ages glide away, the sons of men,
The youth in life's green spring, and he who goes
In the full strength of years, matron and maid,
And the sweet babe, and the gray-headed man,—
Shall one by one be gathered to thy side,
By those, who in their turn shall follow them.
      —William Cullen Bryant, *Thanatopsis*

CONTENTS

FIGURES

FOREWORD

by Alan Taylor

In *More Lasting than Brass,* Peter Haring Judd offers a distinctive marriage of history and genealogy that magnifies their individual strengths. From history he recovers the social and economic context that gives meaning to the shifting concerns and constraints of successive lives. Genealogical inquiry permits Judd to connect the present to the past through a sequence of lives, each a way station of change and a measure of continuity. History enables us to see Samuel Haring or Julia Phelps Haring as exemplars of social mobility and class formation characteristic of their generations, while, as individuals, they give personalities to otherwise abstract concepts. Especially for the late nineteenth and early twentieth centuries, Judd draws on a rich collection of family letters and photos. Of course he supplements them with the staples of informed genealogy (and social history): vital, probate, and census records. But he also resourcefully probes into such distinctive and productive corners as corporate, sanitarium, and private academy documents. Finally, in deft prose, he narrates the rise and fall of a family fortune in a manner that reveals the key stages in the intertwined history of American capitalism and the life cycle of families.

Judd begins with the American Revolution, illuminated from the perspective of middle-class folk rather than the great generals and national statesman ordinarily celebrated as the Founding Fathers. Here the protagonists are John Haring and James Clark—local rather than national leaders. A politician in the lower Hudson Valley, Haring served in New York's Provincial Congress and a couple of terms as a back bencher in the Continental Congress. A junior officer in the New York militia, Clark endured the military defeats that lost New York City to the British in 1776. Thereafter the Haring and Clark families lived on the front lines of the most persistent and important theater of the war: the bloody, contested, and plundered no-man's-land between Washington's army at West Point and the British headquarters in the city. By their stubborn endurance through deprivation, destructive raids, bitter defeats, and Benedict Arnold's treason, Haring and Clark personified the larger Revolution, which succeeded as much through the tenacity and patience of common people as by the occasional strokes of political and military fortune associated with great leaders.

Military victory rewarded ambitious men of middling means with new opportunities, both in the city and on the frontier. Upon the British evacuation of 1783, John's brother-in-law Abraham Herring (the surname anglicized by the "city cousins") moved into heavily damaged New York City to prosper as a trader, exploiting the commercial vacuum left by the departing Loyalist merchants. John's eldest son, Samuel Haring, preferred the settlement frontier of upstate New York, then a fertile forest recently and violently wrested from the Iroquois Indians, who had sided with the defeated British and Loyalists. James Clark and his family similarly moved northwest, away from crowded Ulster County, settling new farms in the Finger Lakes Region. There, in 1797 Samuel Haring married Sarah Clark, daughter of James and Deborah (Denton) Clark. As a rural merchant, Samuel Haring benefited from the appreciating real estate and expanding wheat cultivation wrought in combination by the rapid settlement of upstate New York and by the swelling demand in Europe for American produce. Bushels of wheat and barrels of flour flowed from thousands of new farms down the Mohawk and Hudson Rivers via Albany to New York City, where urban merchants, including Abraham Herring, organized and dispatched cargos in sailing ships that crossed the Atlantic. Prospering as a rural storekeeper, Samuel and Sarah Haring moved up the mercantile chain to Albany and later to New York City, becoming grocers. They found a noisy and dirty but booming city, swelling with immigrants, especially from Ireland.

In politics the Clarks and Harings favored the victorious republican interest of Governor George Clinton and of President Thomas Jefferson, pitting them against the fading Federalist interest of John Jay and Alexander Hamilton. As reward for his politics, Samuel Haring reaped an army officer's commission for a new conflict with the British empire: the War of 1812. In this blundering war, American junior officers suffered more frustration and command incompetence than had their fathers in the revolution—and they bore it with far less fortitude. Instead of glory, Samuel Haring's reward was a debilitating illness that affected the rest of his life. American diplomats rescued the beleaguered republic by securing a surprisingly honorable peace treaty at the end of 1814.

The second generation after the Revolution weathered a transition from a mercantile to an industrial form of capitalism, which made vast new fortunes for the nimble—but traumatic bankruptcies for those wedded to older forms of enterprise. The unfortunate included Thomas Herring, son of Abraham, undone by the stressful succession of the embargo of 1807–1809, War of 1812–15, and postwar depression. Demobilized by peace, his cousin Samuel Haring also struggled, as an Albany merchant. But wealth awaited those who could exploit the transportation revolution, especially in New York State, which spawned both the steamboat and the celebrated Erie Canal during the first quarter of the nineteenth century. The railroad followed during the 1840s. In combination, the three developments promoted an economic integration that connected the seaport city to the Great Lakes, promoting a massive expansion of settler agriculture and an equally great expansion of the urban population. Samuel's and Sarah's sons, John Samuel Haring and James Demarest Haring, thrived in New York City as flour merchants, able to ride out occasional trade depressions thanks to their sterling credit rating.

In 1846 James Demarest Haring married well, to Caroline Eliza Phelps, the daughter of a successful New York City importer from a distinguished Connecticut family. The marriage represented an alliance of Yankee-Puritan tradition with the commercial vibrancy of the booming metropolis. Thriving young entrepreneurs sought the prestige of an old family connection, cross-pollinating cultural continuity with economic innovation. This mixture also drove the city's mid-century cultural aspiration manifested in grand new opera houses, theaters, libraries, colleges, mansions, stone churches, grand hotels, and art collections of European masters. Once a vibrant but homogenous city of middle-class striving and brick buildings, New York became a more complex megalopolis with new money adopting an aristocratic style.

The age also made a sharper distinction between commerce and politics, as the former became a full-time profession that merchants avoided. In contrast to the political engagement and fervor of his father and grandfather, James Demarest Haring avoided public contentions, including any service during the Civil War (though he was then suffering from tuberculosis). Fully attentive to business, he left an estate that helped support his daughter.

In 1868 death claimed both James and Caroline Eliza, leaving their legacy largely to their daughter Julia Phelps Haring. She found consolation and social polish in a grand tour by steamship to, and railroad across, old Europe. Returning, she married, however, in mid-America—the heartland of the ongoing economic integration of the continent with the northeastern centers of capital and transportation. If families of status and means looked to Europe for style, they continued to rely on internal agriculture and railroad development for profits. The Haring family's trade provided a connection with Minneapolis, an emerging center for milling wheat into flour. From a city of brick and stone, Julia moved to a newer, smaller city of wood.

In Minneapolis she became engaged to George Luther White, the son of a Yankee inventor and entrepreneur, who made a fortune in the metalware industries of Waterbury in Connecticut. Endowed with capital, young George was also cursed with tuberculosis, which led him to the clear, cold air of Minneapolis. With family money, he opened an office that sold sewing machines, then a new invention. In 1874 marriage brought together the new money of manufacturing with the older money of mercantile commerce manifest in the Phelps and the Haring families. For their honeymoon, the newlyweds crossed the continent by railroad—the technological instrument of a transcontinental economy and nation. From the railroad car windows they saw survivors of the Indian peoples dispossessed by that process of nation building.

After spending a winter in sunny Marin County, California, George felt cured of his tuberculosis. In 1875 the couple returned to live in Waterbury, a small industrial city with cultural pretensions, attested by the ownership of almost one piano per household. Julia devoted herself to family and to genealogical research, creating a notebook that served as a major source for this book, more than a century later. George prepared to inherit and run his father's factories, which made metal button backs and strawboard (cardboard). This status placed the family in the top rank of Waterbury society. The city hosted an array of factories united by some mechanical manipulation and combination of metals, producing hinges, nails, buckles, clasps, pins, paper clips, buttons, lamps, brass wire, watches, and clocks. Attentive to technological possibility, Waterbury manufacturers began to make parts for cameras and electrical equipment during the 1880s.

As the generation of inventor-founders passed away, ownership passed on to their sons, who managed complex arrays of superintendents, engineers, and workers. Father White retired in 1892 and died a year later, leaving two companies to George. The new generation of Yankee owners generally avoided politics except to vote Republican to preserve the economic status quo in the state and nation. The Waterbury elite invested more energy in transforming the architecture at the city center, replacing wooden frame houses with stolid Italianesque structures in stone and brick.

Days at the family factory were crowded and noisy, but retreat by carriage to the family meant a large, comfortable house on the hillside that was the "best" part of town, tended by Irish servants. The children went to private schools, culminating in Yale for the boys. Finding purpose in their families, wealthy women felt isolated when husbands died and children matured into marriage.

Within this realm of privilege matured the eldest daughter of George and Julia: Caroline Haring White (born in 1875). At age twenty-one she emulated her mother with a grand tour by steamship and by chaperone to Europe—the social orbit depicted in the novels of Henry James. Caroline delighted in Europe where, she observed, "'the people all seem happier and not so driven-to-death" (p. 297). But duty returned her to Waterbury and marriage to a driven American man of business. By design a European tour "finished" a wealthy young woman for an elite marriage. In 1902, aged twenty-six, she married Robert Foote Griggs, a widower, aged thirty-three, Yale graduate, and business associate of her father. Like the Whites, the Griggs family had deep, seventeenth-century roots in Puritan New England and ties to Waterbury's nineteenth-century industrialization.

The couple remained in Waterbury attending to the traditional roles of husband-businessman and wife-mother. Rather than manage a factory, Griggs became a stock broker, opening his own small firm, which soon became the largest in town. This shift represents the further ramification of American capitalism in a new century, as the growth of capital required more elaborate financial institution to facilitate greater liquidity.

No longer a weak republic on the margins of European empires, the United States had become by economic and territorial expansion a global power, trading with the world and receiving its emigrants. In 1898, by crushing the overmatched Spanish, the United States acquired an overseas empire including Puerto Rico, Cuba, and the Philippines. By 1900 Waterbury had multiplied to 75,000 inhabitants, a third of them immigrants from Ireland, Italy, Russia, and Poland. They worked for long hours (fifty-four per week) at low wages (less than $10 per week) in loud, stuffy factories making immense profits in most years for the owners. The First World

War proved especially good for Waterbury business, as the factories filled orders for shell cases, cartridge clips, buckles, and buttons. And security sales boomed at the firm of Robert F. Griggs & Company. More surprising, Waterbury factories, despite their distance from raw materials, continued to thrive during the postwar 1920s.

Robert and Caroline raised a new generation trained in good manners, refined speech, elegant dress, European travel, and friends of the appropriate class. In Connecticut, elite parents expected college for their sons—preferably Yale—but never for their daughters. Upon graduating from a private academy in 1925, daughter Carol (the author's mother) made her own chaperoned coming-of-age tour of Europe, the third generation to do so. Her life seemed so far to fall into all the expected patterns, with marriage to follow.

Upon returning to America in 1926, however, she suffered a mental breakdown characterized by paranoia, self-mutilation, and resistance to treatment—especially when sent away to a sanitarium in 1927. Diagnosed as manic-depressive, she gradually improved, winning release to her mother's care in 1930. After a recuperative mother-daughter tour of Europe, she received and accepted a proposal of marriage from Stuart Edwards Judd. A Yankee-Puritan descendant, Judd was the reserved son of a Waterbury stockbroker who had also founded a factory, known as the Mattatuck, which produced furniture and typewriter parts. A graduate of Yale, Stuart had deviated only by further study at the new Harvard Business School. Despite her psychological travails, Carol had married up to family expectations. The newlyweds settled in West Hartford, where Stuart worked in a brokerage firm.

In addition to Carol's illness, the family coped with a succession of other setbacks. Her father suddenly died of a cerebral hemorrhage in late 1927. Her grandmother followed to the grave in early 1928. In late 1929 the infamous stock market crash reduced, but did not cripple, the family fortune, which had been conservatively invested. Alcohol, however, took a heavier toll. In early 1930 brother Haring White, another Yale graduate, married well but manifested an alcoholism unaffected by Prohibition. During Carol's wedding at year's end, Haring made a drunken scene that roiled the family and alienated his own wife—soon compounded and completed by her discovery of his adultery. Divorced and frozen out of Connecticut society, Haring chose exile to California—that great refuge for the disreputable—especially when sustained by inherited money.

In 1931 Carol gave birth to her first child, the author, Peter Haring Judd, with a second son following two years later. In 1934 the worsening depression cost Stuart Judd his brokerage job, obliging his retreat to Waterbury to manage the Mattatuck factory. The strain of the move contributed to a recurrence of Carol's manic-depressive cycle and a six-month stint in another sanatorium. Breast cancer followed, leading to hospitalization and death in 1940. She was thirty-four.

Seeking relief in work, Stuart Judd poured his energies into guiding the Mattatuck, building profits and making a small fortune during the 1940s and early 1950s, when another world war and a cold war again bolstered Waterbury manufacturing with government orders. In 1944 his surprising marriage to the family housekeeper named Edna offended grandparents and marginalized the couple within Waterbury society. Seeking a social escape, the family moved to a wooded suburb—the aptly named Woodbury—as so many other Americans did during the 1950s.

But neither work nor suburbia could provide Stuart with a haven from a spiral of economic and family troubles. Edna succumbed to her own mental illness, which led to their divorce in 1958. At work, the Waterbury factories, in general, and the Mattatuck, in particular, confronted workers newly organized into national unions and ready to challenge ownership. An old-school paternalist, Stuart disliked confrontation and sought to cooperate with the union, but he could not avert a bitter strike in 1956. A compromise settlement failed to halt the firm's steady loss of business, workers, and profits to German and Japanese competition. The reeling firm suffered a further blow in 1962, when a stroke disabled Stuart Judd, who lost the power of speech. Obliged to take charge, Peter Judd sold the firm at a depreciated value in 1963, terminating his family's century-long engagement with manufacturing in Waterbury. Temporarily rescued by a resourceful new owner, the Mattatuck later fell victim to a further development of American capitalism: the growth of conglomerate, multinational corporations without local roots. Purchased by such a corporation in 1988, the Mattatuck was closed two years later and left to rot—as were most Waterbury factories during the 1970s and 1980s. The industrial revolution lay in Connecticut ruins, unable to compete on the new, global stage of American capital.

Avoiding a narration of relentless celebration, Judd tells this family saga with refreshing honesty and acuity. Despite, or perhaps because of, the material comfort enjoyed by the family, many young members experienced profound stress in early adulthood. For example, Judd writes of his mother, her siblings, and her parents: "Given the psychological troubles that each of the children had in abundance, and though there was a genetic origin for some, the family dynamics may have involved paternal disparagement of the sons (Bobby's self-esteem suffered in later life), and overcompensating—perhaps enveloping—maternal affection for Haring and Carol, contributed to later troubles" (p. 406). Such penetrating observations never taste of betrayal because Judd suffuses the overall story with such affection. Humanely empathetic to all, he details the psychological toll of family life, as well as the triumphs of love in a narrative of America's transformation from rebellious colonies to global power and its domestic costs.

ALAN TAYLOR is the author of *William Cooper's Town* (1995), winner of the Pulitzer Prize for that year, and *American Colonies* (2001).

PREFACE

Quid Aere Perennius?

This book presents the history of a single strand of a family, seven generations that spanned nearly the first two hundred years of the republic. It begins with people born under the British flag in New York City and the Hudson Valley and carries the family story to their twentieth-century descendants in industrial Connecticut.

Manhattan, the Hudson River Valley, and its Mohawk tributary are the settings for the first half of the book. The stories in the second half of the book unfold primarily in and about Waterbury, Connecticut, a once dynamic manufacturing center in west-central Connecticut. The question posed by the title of this preface, "What is More Lasting than Brass?" is inscribed above the entrance to Waterbury City Hall, designed by Cass Gilbert and completed in 1915; it speaks to the spirit and hopeful pride that made that city the self-proclaimed "Brass Capital of the World."

The division of the narrative into two parts corresponds generally to the involvement of individuals in the dominant economies of their times. The families of the earlier period were supported by commercial trade, largely in commodities, whereas those of the Waterbury period were supported by manufactures. Such in broad terms is the social and economic context.

This is also a human story, which reveals men and women responding to surroundings and circumstances, marrying, raising families, coping with illnesses, choosing paths to follow, completing ventures or having them cut short by mortality. Many speak in their own voices, in letters. For many we have likenesses, some captured in the early days of photography. We have the awesome privilege of looking at whole lives, whose beginning, middle, and end are laid out for us to reflect upon.

The narrative begins in the Revolution with two families whose children were to be later joined in marriage. John Haring, his wife and first cousin, Mary Herring, their children and kin, were in the thick of a near civil war during the Revolution in the lower Hudson Valley, in lands crossed and re-crossed by opposing armies and their forage parties. Young James Clark, from New Windsor, just north of the Hudson Highlands,

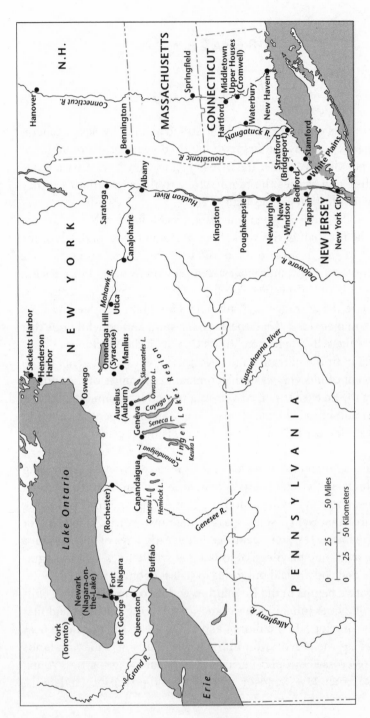

1. New York State and the Connecticut River Valley

joined other Ulster militia, who answered the call to defend Manhattan in 1776. He was in the rear guard that pushed off from Fulton Landing at dawn in the evacuation that saved the American cause after the Battle of Brooklyn. Three years later he married Deborah Denton in the house of George Clinton, the general who led the Ulster troops in 1776 and had then become the first governor of New York. She survived him to live on in Ballston Springs near Saratoga, which had by then become a vacation destination of the prosperous middle classes, the Revolution and its trials in an almost unrecognizable past.

Their children, Samuel Haring and Sarah Clark, were the heirs of the society and economy the American Revolution had opened—they enjoyed more mobility, access to former Indian lands in New York and further west, and buoyant commercial activity stimulated by steady improvements in transportation. Married in a log church by the stream that flows from Lake Owasco, their destiny took them back down the Hudson Valley of their parents to Manhattan, and, later, to Albany. During these years Herring and Kip relatives were also active in trade up and down the Hudson, the Mohawk and across the Atlantic; the story of Abraham Herring, his sons Elbert and Thomas, and the family reveals the ups, and in Thomas's case, the downs of merchant life at the time, a divorce, as well as longevity and distinction in the city. In the second great national event in which members of this family line were engaged, Samuel Haring served as a Captain in the Thirteenth U.S. New York Regiment in the northern campaigns near Lake Ontario in 1812 and 1813. Sarah Haring gave birth to eleven children, and had responsibility for raising three who were under age at their father's death in 1831. She was aided by her eldest surviving daughter, Catharine Teller Haring, "Kate," who lived separated from her husband in New York City until she married for a second time, a Kip second cousin.

Samuel and Sarah's second youngest son, James Demarest Haring, a minor when his father died, joined his older brother in a flour broking business on Peck Slip and later on Front Street in Manhattan. He married Caroline Eliza Phelps, daughter of a fruit importer with a long family history in New England. Thus a Dutch family, with New Amsterdam heritage, was joined to one whose English Puritan ancestors had arrived in Massachusetts Bay Colony. Their sole surviving daughter was seventeen when her parents died, within four months of each other, in 1868.

The life of this daughter, Julia Phelps Haring, is the bridge between the New York and Hudson Valley world of her childhood and the society created by Connecticut manufacturers in the mid-nineteenth century. Julia met her future husband, George Luther White, in Minneapolis—such can be the circuitous route of a life's path—where George had gone for clean air to heal a tubercular lung. The couple lived long lives in Waterbury, where George's father had been one of the country lads with a mechanical bent who had come to the city and involved himself in the emerging economy of factories—he designed fixtures for oil lamps, button back machinery, and operated a straw board and paper business. George carried on these ventures, invested in growing Waterbury businesses, and used his prosperity for comfortable travel.

George and Julia's eldest child and daughter, Caroline Haring White, "Carrie," married Robert Foote Griggs, whose father and grandfather had established factories in Waterbury. Her husband saw the possibilities offered by the popularity of equities for investment, and he became a stockbroker. Their daughter, Carolyn White Griggs, "Carol"—my mother—married Stuart Edwards Judd, the son of a man who had started his life in business as a bank teller and whose investments in a metal-working factory supported his family handsomely through the 1920s. Stuart devoted the prime of his life to that factory, called the Mattatuck after the Indian name for Waterbury. He carried it on against the tide of economic changes that shortly would leave a city built around factories and the employment they offered with little of either.

I was a child and youth in the latter years of this account, and thus a participant-observer, a witness. I was also briefly a participant in what became the last involvement of the family in manufacturing when I sold the Mattatuck in 1963 after Stuart's disabling stroke. I saw the end of the industrial economy that the country lads had created in Connecticut in the early nineteenth century. I also saw the demise of most of the social structures, residences, and work places that they and their heirs established.

Others have told the story of working people and the immigrant groups that made up a vital part of Waterbury's life. My perspective is that of the families who created the manufacturing economy and kept it going until the 1960s. I am surely one of the last to be able to record the story, based on what I observed in my childhood and youth. That a place has changed drastically is a stimulus to chronicle what was, one of the inspirations that impelled me to develop this chronicle. It is a history of a family that becomes a family memoir.

In this narrative I have taken a similar approach to that used in my *The Hatch and Brood of Time* (1999), a history of closely related family members covering about five generations. The earlier book began and ended earlier than the present account, 1720s to 1880s versus, roughly, 1776 to the early 1960s (with an afterword carrying on to near the present). The only threads common to both histories are the marriage of Caroline Eliza Phelps with James Demarest Haring in 1846 and the childhood of their daughter, Julia Phelps Haring, which is treated in a few pages of the earlier book. My aim then and now is to present the lives of individuals in the context of the times and places in which they lived and to portray their social and economic circumstances—to put them in American and regional frames. As a historian I tie the narrative to personal and cultural documents. The material could well be made into a historical novel, but I leave imaginings to a reader stimulated by fact. As a genealogist I use methodologies of that discipline to verify personal events and relationships. The footnote thrives still in genealogical writing, and I encourage the reader to follow my sources—references often tell stories of their own.

Many figures in these pages "speak" in their own words. Julia and Carrie, her daughter, saved letters, an archive covering almost a hundred years from the 1860s. Most were written from elsewhere, resorts in the south and New England, ocean liners, and hotels in England and the continent before and after the Great War. Julia's Aunt Kate (Catharine Teller [Haring] Kip) wrote warmly to her then newly orphaned niece to comfort her, and as the last of the Harings in her generation, put Julia in touch with memories of the grandparents and great-grandparents she had never known. Julia had a suitor, later a distinguished physician in New York City, who wrote her warmly (and with misplaced hope of her affection) and recorded his youthful delight in the singers and musicians from Europe who in the 1870s were attracting the interest of the American upper middle classes. From public collections there are Haring and Herring letters from the eighteenth and early nineteenth centuries, few of which have ever been cited, much less published. My own archive includes letters from my father, Stuart Judd. With newspaper references, these give a vivid picture of the ugly labor relations at his factory in the mid-1950s and of his often-harrowing personal life. Carol Griggs Judd, my mother, died at the age of thirty-four. She left journals of European trips and was an enthusiastic letter writer. The record of her treatment for manic-depressive psychosis in a private clinic survives and provides an insight into the young woman's condition and treatment.

Genealogical and biographical material arranged in a modified *Register* format and pertaining to the Haring, Herring, Clark, Denton, Phelps, White, Griggs, and Judd families will be made available on the Web site of the New England Historic Genealogical Society: www.NewEngland-Ancestors.org. Footnote citations of "Genealogical and Biographical Notes" refer to these documents. Those seeking detailed personal information about families treated in the narrative will find it here.

I have mentioned the leading characters in this narrative, but the reader will find numerous others whose lives are no less a part of this family's history. As a young man Stuart Edwards Judd, my father, collected the works of the poet Edwin Arlington Robinson. A verse from one of Robinson's poems is appropriate to this inquiry into lives long gone.

> There were faces to remember in the Valley of the Shadow,
> There were faces unregarded, there were faces to forget;
> There were faces of grief and fear that are a few forgotten ashes,
> There were sparks of recognition that are not forgotten yet.
> For at first, with an amazed and overwhelming indignation
> At a measureless malfeasance that obscurely willed it thus,
> They were lost and unaccompanied—until they found
>   themselves in others,
> Who had grasped that they were groping where dim ways were perilous.
> —E. A. Robinson, *The Valley of the Shadow*

ACKNOWLEDGMENTS

Help from many quarters went into this work. First I must acknowledge the fine repositories that exist in New York City, where the bulk of my research was done: the Irma and Paul Milstein Division of United States History, Local History, and Genealogy at the Research Division of the New York Public Library, on Forty-second Street, with its superb collection of New York City material and other local histories; the New York Genealogical and Biographical Society, with abundant and unique New York City material, extensive genealogies and local histories, and open shelves—a haven for days of intensive research; the New-York Historical Society, with its unique manuscript collections and, in recent years, accommodating library hours; the Museum of the City of New York, holding Jones family papers that led me to a better understanding of the tensions in that family in the Revolutionary War period. Outside of New York, I should mention the resources of the Sterling and Beinecke Libraries at Yale University; the library and Web site of the New England Historic and Genealogical Society, Boston; the Connecticut State Library; and Baker Library at the Harvard Business School, where I consulted nineteenth-century credit reports of the R. G. Dun & Co. Collection. The Mattatuck Museum in Waterbury, Connecticut, has extensive and largely unique collections of which I made full use—my particular thanks to Assistant Curator Raechel Guest and to the Mattatuck's director, Marie Galbraith. Warm thanks to the helpful custodians of all the collections I visited numerous times in the course of my research. I used, albeit remotely, the Peter Smith Papers held by the Special Collections Research Center, Syracuse University, available on microfilm at NYPL—I salute their custodianship of materials that add greatly to our understanding of merchant life in the early republic. The library of the Reform Club in London yielded contemporary guides to late-nineteenth-century European spas, the volumes sturdy and intact, survivors of the Blitz. The archivists at Jesus College Cambridge and at the University College Archives provided timely responses to my inquiries. The Library of Congress in its American Memory Web site provides easy access to historic maps and town and city panoramas that have added greatly to this volume, the former from the Geography and Map Division, the panoramas from its Prints and Photographs Division.

Acknowledgments

There are numerous individuals whose help I acknowledge. The late E. Haring Chandor, of New York, a descendant of Abraham Herring, his father, Elbert (the owner of the family farm in the Bowery) and the Harings of Tappan, provided me with precious family records. Rev. George Razee, first cousin-in-law, shared with me photograph albums and other material from the Griggs family. Rita Hollenga of the office of the Collegiate Church on John Street in New York shared invaluable birth and death records form the early Dutch Reformed churches in New York; Jane Cuccurullo, Secretary, Green-wood Cemetery, provided me with information on the burials in the Elbert Herring plot and a guide to its location on a matchless June day. Stefan Bielinski introduced me to the Albany Project and helped locate the early residence of Samuel Haring in that city. Paul Donovan, Law Librarian of the Supreme Court of Vermont, provided an essential link to discover the bankruptcy of Thomas Herring.

I am grateful to those with whom I talked about family members and who subsequently have died: Elizabeth Wade White, her brother H. Wade White, Patty (Spencer) Day, and Alfred Bingham. My grandmother, Caroline Haring White Griggs, the Carrie who is an important figure in the book, told me about the family when I was a boy and young man; it was she who saved the letters that provide the family record for a hundred years from the mid-nineteenth century. Orton Camp Jr. knows more about Waterbury and its people than I ever shall and led me on a tour of the Wilfred Griggs and other buildings that remind of the heyday the later pages in this narrative describe.

Thanks also to my cousins, Elizabeth Gay (Griggs) Dorn and Caroline Comfort Dorn for information bout their families. Kenneth Hewes Barricklo gave me a tour of New Windsor and Newburgh, which greatly aided my sense of the lands where the Clark family lived during the Revolution. My friend Dr. C. Christian Beels helped me understand the nature of Carolyn White Griggs's illness and the treatments that were in use in the 1920s. My friends Emilie de Brigard and Phyllis La Farge Johnson read portions of the book. Harry Macy, of the NYGB, and Robert Anderson, of the Great Migration Project, provided key information on the Clark and Herring families. Walter C. Krumm did similarly in connection with the Denton family and Hermine Williams with the Kirkland family.

John Tormey transcribed most of the family letters several years ago. He told me he "fell in love with" Julia, and he certainly could transcribe accurately her episodic letters, full of thoughts dashed off in empty corners of the stationery. David P. Chandler read every word of early drafts on his then frequent visits to the city; the blue ink of his pen showed me repeatedly where I could tighten a sentence, break one apart, emphasize more a certain point. Thanks also to Laura Kozachek for diligent proofreading and invaluable assistance with indexing.

Chris Hartman, of Newbury Street Press, and Brenton Simons, of NEHGS, have strongly supported this project; Robert Gormley, of Northeastern University Press, added his encouragement.

In ways that only he and I know, Thomas Kozachek, my editor, was a true collaborator on this project. Credit to him for clean sentences and consistent citations. Much of our work together was done by e-mail, which made the work closer and more immediate than it would have been in former days. The fact that with all its detail, the preparation of this book has been a joy, can be attributed to his assistance.

Peter Haring Judd

ABBREVIATIONS

Citations

ANB	*American National Biography.* New York: Oxford Univ. Press, 1999.
Budke	George Henry Budke Collection, Manuscripts Division, NYPL.
BC-34	"Historical Miscellanies," vol. B.
BC-38	"Tomb-stone Inscriptions, Rockland Co., N.Y.," vol. 2.
BC-58	"The Van Houten Family, Genealogical Note-book No. 1."
BC-70	"Historical Miscellanies," vol 1.
BC-85	"Miscellaneous Manuscripts."
Clinton Papers	Clinton, George. *Public Papers of George Clinton, First Governor of New York, 1777–1795–1801–1804.* 8 vols. Albany, N.Y., 1899–1914.
CSL	Connecticut State Library.
DAB	*Dictionary of American Biography.* New York: Scribner's and Sons, 1928.
DNB	*Dictionary of National Biography.* London: Smith, Elder, 1885–1901.
EAR	*Encyclopedia of the American Revolution.* Edited by Mark Mayo Boatner III. Bicentennial ed. New York: David McKay, 1974.
Enc. Brit.	*Encyclopedia Britannica.* 11th ed. Cambridge, 1910–11.
ENCNYC	*The Encyclopedia of New York City.* Edited by Kenneth T. Jackson. New Haven: Yale Univ. Press, New York Historical Society, 1995.
JHW MSS	Julia Haring White Manuscripts, in possession of the author.

MCCNYC	*Minutes of the Common Council of the City of New York, 1784–1831.* 19 vols. New York: City of New York, 1917.
NEHGS	New England Historic Genealogical Society.
The New Grove	*The New Grove Dictionary of Music and Musicians.* Edited by Stanley Sadie. 20 vols. London: Macmillan, 1980.
NYGB	The New York Genealogical & Biographical Society.
NYPL	New York Public Library.
NYSL	New York State Library.
NYT	*New York Times.*
PSP	Peter Smith Papers, 1767–1851. Microfilm, 12 reels, NYPL. Original papers at the Special Collections Research Branch, Syracuse University.
Record	*The New York Genealogical and Biographical Record* (1870–).
Waterbury VS	Office of Vital Statistics, City of Waterbury, New Haven Co., Conn.

Names

CGJ	Carolyn White (Griggs) Judd
CWG	Carolyn White Griggs [Judd]
CHW[G]	Caroline Haring White [Griggs]
CTHK	Catharine Teller (Haring) Kip
EWW	Elizabeth Wade White
GLW	George Luther White
GMT	George Montgomery Tuttle
JPH	Julia Phelps Haring [White]
JHW	Julia Phelps (Haring) White
PHJ	Peter Haring Judd
RFG	Robert Foote Griggs Jr.
SEJ	Stuart Edwards Judd Jr.

I

LAND AND REBELLION IN THE HUDSON VALLEY

The banks of Hudson's river are for the most part rocky cliffs. . . . The passage through the highlands affords a wild romantic scene for sixteen miles through steep and lofty mountains: the tide flows a few miles above Albany, the navigation is safe, and performed in sloops of about forty or fifty tons burden, extremely well accommodated to the river: about sixty miles above New-York the water is fresh. . . .

—William Smith Jr., *The History of the Late Province of New-York from Its Discovery to the Appointment of Governor Colden in 1762*

The advantages of this river for penetrating into Canada and protecting the Southern colonies . . . must be very apparent to every judicious observer of the maps of the inland parts of North America.

—*The History of the Province of New-York from the First Discovery to the Year 1732*

Children of the Revolution

On 8 October 1797 in central New York Sarah Clark and Samuel Haring were married in a forest clearing near Owasco Outlet, a stream that runs from the lake by that name. She was seventeen, he a day short of his twenty-first birthday. Their lives in the world they inherited would take them to Albany and New York City, but at the time of their marriage they were settlers in the recently opened up Indian lands of central New York. Sarah and Samuel were children of men who had participated in the military and civil struggles in New York during the Revolution. They were born in the war, children of the Revolution, and thus of the first generation to live their entire lives in the independent country.

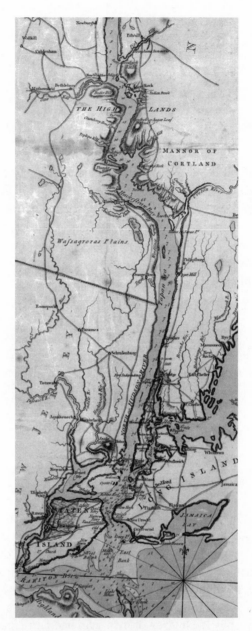

2. The lower Hudson. From "A Topographical Map of Hudsons River" (London, Wm. Faden, 1777).

Library of Congress, Map Collection

The marriage of a Haring son and a Clark daughter in a hamlet on the Genesee trail connected two distinct traditions of early American settlement and manners. The Harings came from the Netherlands and New York, the Clarks originally from England and New England. The Haring-Clark union also brought together two strains of Calvinism: the Dutch Reformed (from the Confession of Dort) and the Presbyterianism of the Westminster Catechism, which the Clarks adopted after leaving Congregational Connecticut Colony. The marriage, with its ethnic and religious mixing reveals the increasing openness of American society in the post-Revolutionary years.

The Hudson Valley was home to both the Haring and Clark families in the eighteenth century, and despite their differences, the two families did share the yeoman political culture of the settlements on the west bank of the river. The Harings had been settled by the Tappan Zee and in New York City since the seventeenth century. The Clarks settled Bedford in Westchester County from Connecticut, and three generations later in the mid-eighteenth century Sarah Clark's grandfather ventured into trade and farming near the Hudson, above the highlands. Men and women of both families were deeply involved in the Revolution, in the actions in and around New York City and in Orange and Ulster Counties.

The social and economic conditions in which these young people were to live their lives were shaped in large part by the successful resolution of the struggle against British domination. The settlement on Owasco Outlet, where they were married, to cite one particular, had only come into existence after the Revolution, a consequence of which was the opening up of Indian lands to European settlement. New York was the scene of more military and civil conflicts than any of the thirteen original states. The fathers of Samuel and Sarah were deeply engaged—John Haring in Manhattan and southern Orange County in the lower Hudson Valley and James Clark in Ulster north of the highlands and in the actions of 1776 in and around Manhattan. The actions of their generation created the new conditions of American life. The stories of their involvement with the Patriot cause illuminate the Revolution in New York from different perspectives of family background, social position, and geography. Before returning to the young couple making their way in the new republic, it will prove instructive to consider the experiences of their families during the Revolution.

The Harings

John Haring, Samuel's father, was the great-great grandson of Jan Pietersen Haring, who arrived in Nieuw Amsterdam as a child in the 1630s. Fifty years later Jan Pietersen's family was one of a number of farming families who settled away from English-dominated Manhattan on a tract they purchased from the Tappan Indians near the west bank of the Hudson, where it widens to form the Tappan Zee. The Tappan Patent granted by the royal governor gave the Dutch farmers land enough for themselves and for their children. Under their cultivation the land provided for the families' needs and yielded surplus crops to be sold in the city.

The Harings multiplied, and family members in the next two generations continued to be prominent in what came to be designated under British rule as the southern part of Orange County (now Rockland). Peter Haring, John's grandfather, and Abraham, his father, each in their time served for years in the Provincial Assembly. Because that body met in Manhattan, the Haring men became familiar with the commercial world of New York. As Firth Haring Fabend observed in her study of the seventeenth and eighteenth century Harings,

> The historical significance of the political experiences of farmer-politicians like the Haring[s] . . . were twofold. On the local level by participating in governments in their own communities they were exposed to the demands of public office, formed attachments to local prerogatives, and experienced the pluralism toward which the society was gradually moving. On the provincial level, their close involvement meant in the daily affairs of the colony provided [them] . . . with a valuable education in negotiations, conflict management, and cooperation with men of diverse interests. Most important, exposure to politics reinforced such men in a tradition of resistance to royal authority that their sons and grandsons would jealously guard when their constitutional rights and prerogatives were threatened by authority.[1]

John, born in 1739, was conversant with the Dutch society of Tappan and, to a greater degree than his forebears, with commercial and political circles in New York. "Like most ambitious men of the day, John Haring had several sources of income, for he had received enough education to

---

1. Firth Haring Fabend, *A Dutch Family in the Middle Colonies, 1660–1800* (New Brunswick, N.J.: Rutgers Univ. Press, 1991), 183.

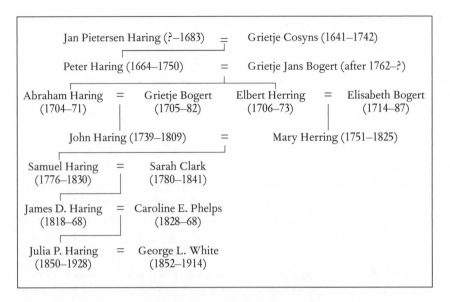

3.   Jan Pietersen Haring descent to Julia Phelps Haring

qualify both as a surveyor and as a lawyer," and, to judge by his letters, he was fluent in English.[2] Like his forebears, John Haring was a devoted member of the Dutch Reformed Church, becoming one of the original trustees of Queen's (later Rutgers) College, established in 1766 to train ministers for the church and, according to the second charter, for the "education of youth in the learned languages, liberal and useful arts and sciences." He was supported by the Coetus party of the Dutch Church, one of whose aims was the education and ordination of ministers in America.[3]

In 1769 John Haring stood for his ailing father's seat in the Provincial Assembly. When he lost the election to the Anglican faction that sup-

---

2. Ibid., 200. He "attended school in New York City." *Biographical Directory of the American Congress, 1774–1927* (Washington, D.C.: GPO, 1928). Surveying, in this period, was a profession of some distinction, as attested to by the fact that both George Washington and George Clinton, of New York, were surveyors. Fabend, *Dutch Family*, 201, cites the following sources for Haring's survey activity: "Records of the Supreme Court of New York County," Division of Old Records, 39 Chambers Street, New York; field book of John Haring and S. Metcalfe for a survey of Man of War Ridge (1771); Bayard-Campbell-Pearsall Papers, Orange Co., box 3, NYPL.

3. Franklin Burdge, *A Notice of John Haring, a Patriotic Statesman of the Revolution* (New York, privately printed, 1878), unpaginated. The opposition, or Conferentie, party, maintained that all ministers must be ordained in Amsterdam; John Haring's position in this controversy was an indication of his ability to challenge an established orthodoxy.

ported the royal governor, he petitioned to have the vote reversed on the grounds of fraud. The petition was denied, and Haring was fined costs by the Governor's Council. This brush with the powers-that-be may well have contributed to his resentment of the royal administration.[4]

John's marriage to his first cousin, Mary Herring, in 1773, at the advanced age of thirty-four, broadened the circle of influential families in the city to whom he—and Samuel after him—was connected. Mary was the daughter of John's uncle, Elbert Herring (1703–73), who as a youth came to New York as a bolter (sifter) of flour and anglicized the family name to Herring as he rose in prominence in the English city. He expanded the family holdings to create a farm of over a hundred acres in the Bowery, at his death the second largest farm on the island. Elbert Herring had sixteen children by two wives. Six of his daughters married men from well-known families in the city: George Brinkerhoff, a member of the Mayor's Council before the Revolution; Cornelius Roosevelt, of the merchant family; Samuel Jones, an eminent member of the bar before and after the Revolution; John De Peyster, of the prominent merchant family; Samuel Kip, of the family who owned Kip's Bay on the East River and who later succeeded to the mansion; and Gardner Jones, a prominent physician in New York City after independence.[5] In their time Sarah and Samuel were part of this large extended family. It was Mary Herring's young brother Abraham, a merchant with interests in the city, upriver, and to the west, who became an influential example for Samuel. All of these families supported the Patriot cause and fled when the British forces occupied Manhattan in late summer 1776. They returned with children born during the war and re-established themselves in the city after the British evacuation.[6]

John Haring had some preferment under the Crown when, in 1774, he was appointed judge of the Court of Common Pleas of Orange County.[7] This did not make him a supporter of the royal government, however, for

---

4. Fabend, *Dutch Family*, 188–89; William Smith, *Historical Memoirs from 16 March 1763 to 25 July 1778*, ed. William H. W. Sabine (New York: The Arno Press, 1969), 65.

5. See "Haring," Genealogical and Biographical Notes, in Peter Haring Judd, *The Hatch and Brood of Time: Five Phelps Families in the Atlantic World, 1720–1880* (Boston: Newbury Street Press, 1999), 360–61.

6. The most notable to return and prosper was Samuel Jones, who resumed his position of prominence in the bar and became the first controller of the state of New York.

7. The appointment is dated 29 March 1776, in *Letters Patent*, BC-85.

at the Yoast Mabie house in Tappan on 4 July 1774 he was one of the signatories of the Orangetown Resolutions, which warned that "however well disposed we are towards his majesty, we cannot see the late acts of Parliament imposing duties upon us, and the act for shutting up the port of Boston, without declaring our abhorance of measures so unconstitutional and big with destruction." This was a position that presaged the Revolution, uncannily on the date of the later Declaration: "It is our unanimous opinion that the stopping of all exportation and importation to and from Great Britain and the West Indies would be the most effectual method to obtain a speedy repeal."

John Haring was one of the five (including his brother-in-law, Gardner Jones) appointed to "correspond" with like-minded colonists in New York City.[8] A further step towards rebellion came when proponents of a vigorous position against British governance convened a congress in New York to supersede the authority of the New York Provincial Assembly. Haring subscribed to this overtly subversive action and was elected as a delegate from Orange County.[9] The battles of Lexington and Concord on 19 April 1775 increased the tempo of political protest in New York, where, in August, the Provincial Congress elected Haring chairman of the committee formed to appoint officers in the militia.[10] The Orange County electors then sent him to the First Continental Congress, sitting at Carpenters' Hall in Philadelphia.[11]

In September Haring became a member of the Committee of Safety of the New York Congress—in a sense the executive committee of the group which still included those uncertain as to whether to embrace a complete break with Britain.[12] On 16 December he was unanimously elected president pro tem of the Provincial Convention—briefly successor to the Congress—in which capacity, as Fabend notes, he was "in effect the head of

---

8. Peter Force, *American Archives, Fourth Series* . . . (Washington, D.C.: St. Clair Clarke and Peter Force, 1843), 1:566 (hereafter cited as Force), also transcribed in David Cole, *History of Rockland County, New York, with Biographical Sketches of Its Prominent Men* (New York: J. B. Beers, 1884), 27.

9. Cole, *History of Rockland County*, 30.

10. Donald F. Clark Collection, NYHS, 530.

11. Haring took his seat on 14 Sept. 1774. *Letters of Delegates to Congress, 1774–1789, August 1774–August 1775*, ed. Paul H. Smith (Washington, D.C.: Library of Congress, 1976), 1:xxix–xxx.

12. John Haring to Brigadier Gen. Wooster, 16 Sept. 1775, Emmet Collection, NYPL MSS Div.

the revolutionary government in New York."[13] Throughout May 1776, as Washington and the troops prepared defenses against British invasion, John Haring was continually in New York at meetings of the Provincial Congress.[14] In late May he joined with John Jay and John Morin Scott, two of the leading attorneys in the city who sided with the rebel cause, to consider the Continental Congress's Resolutions of 15 May supporting independence.[15] Their recommendation to the New York Congress was "to adopt such Government as shall, in the opinion of the Representatives of the People best conduce to the happiness and safety of their constituents in particular and America in general."[16] The die was cast for the Revolution in New York.

In August 1776 Haring was appointed brigade major by the New York Congress and continued as chairman of its Committee of Safety,[17] which operated as the executive arm when the Congress was not in session.[18] Shortly afterwards the British attacked the rebels on Long Island and invaded Manhattan—among the opposing forces was Ulster militiaman James Clark, father of Haring's future daughter-in-law.

With Manhattan closed off, Haring returned to Tappan, which also became a refuge for the Kip, de Peyster, and Jones in-laws, among others. John Morin Scott left a glimpse of the crowded conditions there in his request for leave to visit his wife, who was in "Tappan with her whole family, in one room . . . overwhelmed with distress, and continually in tears, not knowing how to dispose of all that are dear to her except myself."[19] Manhattan, the lower Hudson Valley, the lands to the east and west including the once prosperous farming communities of south Orange County and adjacent Bergen County, New Jersey, were subjected to more

---

13. Force 4, 1:418; Cole, *History of Rockland County*, 31; Fabend, *Dutch Family*, 203.

14. Force 4, 1:1000 ff.

15. Force 4, 1:1338.

16. Force 4, 1:1351.

17. *Calendar of Historical Manuscripts relating to the War of the Revolution in the Office of the Secretary of State* (Albany, 1868), 628.

18. *Clinton Papers*, 4:44.

19. "I have a light skiff that rows with four oars, which will be the most expeditious way of going to her, and I promise you, unless accidents should happen, not to sleep till I return. I shall set off in an hour, if I do not receive your orders to the contrary." John Morin Scott to William Heath, 6 Oct. 1776, Cole, *Rockland*, 39. John Morin Scott (1730–84), a Presbyterian lawyer and associate of William Smith, was also a member of the Provincial Congress. *DAB*, s.v. "Scott, John Morin."

destruction than any other area of the colonies during the war. It was within this so-called "neutral ground"—meaning no one side dominated—that John Haring spent the war years, with his life and his family's livelihood on the line.

The signs of war were evident in the little stone Dutch Reformed Church in Tappan when Samuel Haring, John and Mary's second child, was baptized on 3 November 1776. The church was then occupied by men wounded in the battles of Long Island and Harlem Heights. John Haring, an elder of the church, had helped arrange this improvised hospital care.[20] The celebration of the birth of this first son was tempered by the evidence of the devastating defeats the Patriot cause had suffered in the previous weeks.

Clarks: From Connecticut to the Hudson Valley

James Clark, Sarah's father, was in the fourth generation from William Clark (whose parents are not known) who was one of twenty from Stamford on Long Island Sound who established a new settlement in the "Hopp ground," about twelve miles northwest of the town.[21] In May 1682 the General Court of Connecticut did "grant [the settlers] the priveledg of a plantation, and doe order that the name of the town be henceforth Bedford."[22] The proprietors possessed an area of six square miles, divided into house and meadow lots and awarded by lottery.

Like other Connecticut towns, Bedford was governed with a high degree of local autonomy, and town officers were elected. In 1700, however, a long-standing challenge by the Province of New York was resolved by a royal edict transferring Bedford to Westchester, where much of the county was governed by owners of large tracts of land who permitted only leaseholds and who exercised virtually feudal authority over their tenants.[23] The church established by the original settlers was Presbyterian, not Congregational, as in other Connecticut towns at that period, an indi-

---

20. Clinton to Haring, 30 Aug. 1776; Haring to Clinton 12 Sept. 1776, *Clinton Papers*, 1:329, 345–46.

21. See "Clark," Genealogical and Biographical Notes.

22. *The Public Records of the Colony of Connecticut from May 1678–June 1689*, ed. J. Hammond Trumbull (Hartford, 1859), 101.

23. Ibid., 83, 101; *The Public Records of the Colony of Connecticut from August 1689 to May 1706* (Hartford, 1868), 195, 263, 270, 328, 335.

William Clark (d. before 1696/97) = —?—

Nathan Clark (ca. 1672–after 1828) = —?—

Jehiel Clark (ca. 1711–86) = Lydia —?

James Clark (1756–1814) = Deborah Denton (1762–1843)

Sarah Clark (1780–1841)   William Clark (1786–1836)

‖   ‖

Samuel *Haring* (1776–1831)   Mary Bogart (1793–1871)

– Mary Clark (1813–82) = John Samuel *Haring* (1810–60)

– William Clark (1822–?) = Rosamond Michael

– Helen Clark (1834–?) = George A. *Phelps* Jr. (1834–1916)

4.   Clark connections with Harings and Phelpses

cation of the doctrinal disputes that may have stimulated the move and setting the stage for the alliance of this branch of the family (including James
and his father) with other Presbyterian families on the west bank of the
Hudson who supported the Patriot cause in 1775 and after.[24] William's
son, Nathan (ca. 1672–after 1738) was born and died in Bedford, alone in
that descent to remain in the same place for his entire lifetime.[25]

The family lands in Bedford, however, were too circumscribed to contain a growing family with an increasing taste for worldly success, and
James's father, Jehiel Clark (Nathan's fourth son, born ca. 1711–12),
decided to seek his fortune elsewhere. Unlike his forebears, who were
driven by religious zeal to leave their homes, Jehiel was inspired by the
prospect of commercial opportunity. He was in his late thirties when, in
the late 1740s or early 1750s, he moved to New Windsor, on the west bank
of the Hudson, then in the southernmost section of Ulster County (now in

24. J. Thomas Scharf, *History of Westchester County New York, including Morrisania, Kings Bridge,
and West Farms* (Philadelphia, 1888; reprint, Camden, Maine: Picton Press, 1982), 25.

25. *Town of Bedford, Westchester County, New York: Historical Records, Minutes of Town Meetings,
1680–1737* (Bedford, N.Y., 1966), 1:44, 62, 73, 76, 89–90, 10, 112. See also "Clark," Genealogical
and Biographical Notes.

Orange County). "The people of Ulster having long enjoyed an undisturbed tranquility, are some of the most opulent farmers in the whole colony," wrote William Smith in 1751 of the sparsely populated county.[26] For Jehiel, however, from landlocked Bedford, this was a leap into a different society and economy. His new situation offered opportunities for trade as well as farming.

New Windsor was a landing above the Hudson Highlands where farmers brought their grain to warehouses by the river. From there traders shipped them by sloop to New York City. Jehiel Clark and Arthur Smith (also from Bedford) purchased a large piece of property in New Windsor in 1751. Their strip of land ran from the river inland, part of a patent that had been issued to Francis Harrison in 1716.[27] The purchase involved over £500, and how Jehiel Clark, a younger son, could have acquired such a sum is not evident from surviving records. He had inherited twenty-four acres of land from his father when he was a small child, but somehow at age forty had been able, with Smith, to amass this sum. By virtue of his purchase he had become part of a community whose commercial highway was the river.

On the 1783 New Windsor map made by Simeon De Witt, an intersection of roads to the south of Murderer's Creek is marked "Clark's." It was probably Jehiel's New Windsor homestead. (This is within the limits of present-day Cornwall-on-Hudson, where there is a Clark Street at approximately the same location.) Many years later Katherine (Clark) Fowler, Jehiel's daughter, deposed that in the winter of 1776–77 her brother James "came to a place called Eleses [Ellison's?] Woods where they were quartered for winter and were engaged in building Sheveau de freezes. This Encampment was about three miles from my fathers residence. During this Encampment my brothers aforementioned [were] frequently at home to visit us . . ."[28] The military camp—"a short distance

26. Smith, *History*, 315.

27. Office of the Clerk, Ulster Co., Kingston, N.Y., Land Records, Book FF:272–75; cited in E. M Ruttenber, *History of the County of Orange with a History of the Town and City of Newburgh* (Newburgh, N.Y.: E. M. Ruttenber and Son, 1875), 132. As often occurred in connection with land granted by patent, the boundaries were inaccurate or nonexistent, and therefore the size of the lot was undefined. In this case the deed provided that Charles Clinton was to determine its bounds.

28. Clark, James; Clark, Deborah, Pension Application File W 16907, Records of the Department of Veterans' Affairs, RG 15, National Archives, Washington, D.C. (hereafter cited as James Clark Pension Application).

from the Ellison house"—consisted of about eighty acres on Plum Point, which forms the north bank of Murderer's Creek at its confluence with the Hudson.[29] From Plum Point to Pollepel's Island close to the opposite bank, south of present-day Beacon, New York, is a distance of about 4,000 feet. (It was there that *chevaux-de-frise* were being prepared in 1776 and 1777, to be placed across the river to impale British warships heading upstream.)[30]

According to a family history, Jehiel Clark later purchased one hundred and forty acres of land in Balmville, in the northern section of Newburgh, paying 17*s* 6*d* New York currency per acre for a narrow tract "on the Hudson river, and extended back."[31] This is probably the property to which Ruttenber, the historian of New Windsor and Newburgh, refers when he writes that the "old Arthur Smith and Jehiel Clark farms were about half-way to Marlborough [on the river north of Newburgh]."[32]

It was probably at New Windsor that James Clark was born on 17 August 1756—there is only a family record. He was the fifth of the six children of Jehiel Clark and his wife Lydia, whose surname we do not know. Their first child was Samuel, born sixteen years before, under whom the younger man would serve in the militia during the war.

New Windsor

In 1724 two entrepreneurs from Queens, Judge Joseph Sackett and his brother-in-law, John Alsop, purchased the central portion of the "Chambers-Southerland Patent," on the west bank of the river. There, at a land-

---

29. Edward M. Ruttenber, *History of the Town of New Windsor, Orange County, N.Y.* (Newburgh, N.Y.: Historical Society of Newburgh Bay and the Highlands, 1911), 72.

30. Lincoln Diamant, *Chaining the Hudson: The Fight for the River in the American Revolution* (New York: Carol Publishing Co., 1989), 124–28.

31. Edgar W. Clark, *History and Genealogy of Samuel Clark, Sr. and His Descendants from 1636–1882—256 Years* (St. Louis, 1892), 57.

32. Ruttenber, *History of the County of Orange*, 182. When Smith drew up his will five years later, Jehiel Clark, "farmer," was a witness. Like Jehiel he had come from a Bedford family, and the will included a bequest to a brother living there. *Ulster County, N.Y. Probate Records in the Office of the Surrogate and in the County Clerk's Office at Kingston, N.Y.*, vols. 1 and 2 combined (New York, 1906; reprint, Rhinebeck, N.Y.: Palatine Transcripts, Arthur C. M. Kelly, 1980), 20:472. The will, dated 17 March 1756, was proved on 22 Nov. 1757. The names of Arthur Smith, Leonard Smith, his brother, and Arthur Smith—presumably his father—appear in Bedford records. *Town of Bedford: Historical Records*, 4:22, 72, 153.

ing that would become New Windsor, they built a wharf and a storehouse and maintained a regular freight and passenger service by sloop to and from New York City.[33] Most trade was carried on using these slow-but-sturdy sloops to carry produce to New York City and dry goods north.[34] Others followed the men from Queens. William Ellison had a store and a sloop that sailed to and from his New York City dock on the North River as early as 1732. Ellison's son, John, who had a store on Little Queen Street in the city as well as one in New Windsor, built a handsome house overlooking the river in the mid-1750s.[35]

Sackett's son established a flatboat ferry service for people, horses, and cattle to Fishkill, whose landing was upstream across the river. Farmers brought their produce to New Windsor, where it could be stored before being shipped south and where they could purchase goods sent up from the city. The population was tiny: there were only 1,669 souls in the whole of Ulster County in 1726, of which fewer than a hundred lived in the southernmost Highlands Precinct.[36]

The Sacketts and others mostly of English origin formed "The Proprietors of New Windsor" in 1749 to sell lots and develop a village. Charles Clinton, "clerk and surveyor," laid out the township plot and prepared a map showing the lot divisions for potential buyers.[37]

The potential for development had improved with regular ferry service from Fishkill, which was becoming a popular route for the increasing number of migrants from Connecticut and Westchester taking the overland journey to lands in the Susquehanna Valley. This ferry traffic made

33. Charles H. Weygant, *The Sacketts of America, their Ancestors and Descendants 1630–1907* (Newburgh, N.Y.: 1907), 30–31. Judge Joseph Sackett (1680–1755), of English Kills, Newtown, married in 1706 Hannah Alsop (1690–1773), daughter of Capt. Richard Alsop, sister to John Alsop. John Alsop is said to have been located in New Windsor prior to the 1724 purchase, but later removed to New York City. Joseph Sackett Jr. lived in New Windsor and was one of the proprietors when the development company was formed in 1749. Ibid., 51.

34. Ruttenber, "The County of Ulster," in *The History of Ulster County, New York*, Alphonso T. Clearwater, ed. (Kingston, N.Y.: W. J. Van Deusen, 1907), 26, 28; Samuel W. Eager, *An Outline History of Orange County* (Newburgh, N.Y.: S. T. Callahan, 1846–47), 600.

35. Ruttenber, "The County of Ulster," 28–29. Eager, *Orange County*, 614.

36. *The Documentary History of the State of New York,* ed. E. B. O'Callaghan (Albany, 1850), 3:584.

37. "Owners of the village plot in 1749 were of English origin, from Long Island: Ebeneezer Seely, Brant Schuyler, Henry Case, Vincent Mathews, Michael Jackson, Daniel Everet, Evan Jones, Hezekiah Howell, Joseph Sackett Jr., James Tuthill, and John Sackett." Eager, *Orange County*, 614. The Clinton homestead at Little Britain was west of the limits of the town plot.

New Windsor a way station, not by any means as important as Albany, but helpful to the provision trade at the landing. The first sale by the proprietors, in September 1749, was a "store-house, dwelling house, barn and lot."[38]

By the late 1750s the settlement's streets were lined with houses and "store houses," wharves to which farmers brought produce from the interior by wagon, and a riverfront animated by sloops and the activities of loading and unloading. There was a glass-making business in the village in 1754. Until the Revolution, most of "the foreign business of the county was done through New Windsor." Later, however, economic activity in Newburgh would eclipse that of its southern neighbor.[39]

The most prominent family settled just inland from New Windsor was that of Charles Clinton (1690–1773), who disposed of his estate and left Ireland in 1730 with a group of other Presbyterian "dissenters" to the Anglican ascendancy.[40] His son, George (1739–1812) became the leading opponent of royal authority in Ulster. John Haring was George's exact contemporary and a close associate when Clinton became the first governor of the independent state of New York. James Clark would be married in his house during the war.

Little Britain, the name Charles Clinton chose for the new settlement, was about three miles from New Windsor. There he built a mill, taught himself and practiced the profession of land survey (just as John Haring did), and bought and sold property. In time he became comparatively wealthy. (The term "yeoman" is often applied to both him and his son, George Clinton, because their wealth came from their abilities, not manorial privilege.) The Clintons' manner and way of life contrasted with the

---

38. Ruttenber, "The County of Ulster," 24–26.

39. Eager, *Orange County*, 614.

40. Charles Clinton was descended from a family in Ulster, Ireland, that had been involved in the civil conflicts that embroiled the British Isles in the seventeenth century. His father supported the victorious William of Orange in the late 1680s and was awarded an estate in Longford in the center of Ireland. The family were Presbyterians, however, "dissenters," who felt discriminated against in the increasingly Anglican dominance. A man of enormous determination, Charles Clinton put the estate out to lease in 1729, and, with four hundred other dissenters chartered a ship headed for Pennsylvania. After a five-month passage with numerous deaths—including two of his children and ninety of the passengers—the ship landed at Cape Cod. John P. Kaminski, *George Clinton: Yeoman Politician of the New Republic* (Madison, Wis.: Madison House, 1993), 11–12.

feudal pretensions of the landlords on the east bank of the river, the so-called "lords of the manor"—a difference that would influence later political developments. George followed in his father's footsteps as an independent and became the leader of the west bank, yeoman farmer, and Dissenter interests.

The Ulster in which the Clintons and Clarks lived was sparsely settled by the river, had a ragged and dangerous western frontier, and land ownership in fee simple. Leaders like the Clintons lacked aristocratic pretensions, and many inhabitants were Presbyterians. Distrust of Anglican and aristocratic pretence in provincial New York and the authority of the royal governor came easily. During the war a British officer termed Ulster "a Nursery for almost every Villain in the Country."[41] Jehiel Clark and his sons might have been proud to be so considered, as all supported the Patriot cause. In Newburgh, on 28 July 1775, he and sons Samuel (35), Lewis, Daniel, Jehiel, and James (20), signed the Oath of Allegiance, a pledge effectively committing them to take arms against the Crown.[42] The Newburgh Committee of Safety and Observation, which oversaw the oaths, had been organized in January 1775, well before Lexington and Concord. By the spring of 1776 the committee was effectively the local government of Newburgh and New Windsor.[43]

Both James Clark and his brother, Samuel, joined "Newburgh's Own," a militia unit authorized by the New York Provincial Congress, officially the Fourth New York Militia Regiment.[44] Samuel Clark began service as captain, James as a sergeant; they were later promoted to major and lieutenant respectively. The companies nominally consisted of about eighty

41. John Vaughan, on the *Friendship*, off Esopus, Friday, 17 Oct. [1777], *London Gazette*, 23 Dec. 1777, quoted in George W. Pratt, "An Account of the British Expedition above the Highlands of the Hudson River and of the Events Connected with the Burning of Kingston in 1777," *Collections of the Ulster Historical Society*, vol. 1, 107–74 (Kingston, N.Y., 1860), 189.

42. The ages of three of the sons are not known, but presumably they were older than James. Ruttenber, *History of the County of Orange*, 135–36.

43. Albert Gedney Barratt, "The Fourth New York Regiment in the American Revolution," *Record* 59 (1928): 225, 260; Ruttenber, *History of the County of Orange*, 135–36. Weigand's Tavern, a log building on Broad Street where the Newburgh Committee of Safety met, became a marshalling point for the militia in the course of the many alarms over the next years.

44. A chronicle of the activities of this regiment made from the often sketchy records available (and without citation of sources) may be found in Barratt, "The Fourth New York Regiment," 351–60.

men, including one captain, two lieutenants, one ensign, four sergeants, four corporals, one clerk, one drummer, one fife, and privates.[45]

The four militia regiments raised in Ulster formed a brigade under George Clinton, who was appointed a brigadier general by the New York Congress and charged with the defense of the stretch known as the Highlands, where the Hudson flowed through high ground for about sixteen miles on both sides, described later by James Fennimore Cooper as a "succession of confused and beautifully romantic mountains, with broken and irregular summits, which nature had apparently once opposed to the passage of the water."[46]

Had the British controlled these mountains, they would have held the key to the upper Hudson Valley, which opened out with no such natural obstacles all the way to Albany. Defense of the Highlands was key to the success of the Patriot cause in New York. In early 1776 men from Ulster militia units built fortifications overlooking the river from high ground in preparation for a British assault. By early summer, however, it was evident that the first British move in New York would be to seize Manhattan. The Clarks and other Ulster militiamen went downriver to its defense.

The British Assault New York

The British army and fleet evacuated Boston in June 1776, unwilling to brave Washington's artillery on Dorchester Heights. They re-assembled in Halifax, Nova Scotia, to prepare for an assault on New York City and the Hudson Valley. The strategy was to seize the port and its magnificent harbor and ultimately to drive up the Hudson to split the rebellious colonies in two. The British navy and army were experienced in combined and amphibious operations, and the seizure of the city and the Hudson Valley seemed a sure thing. In July 1776 three hundred ships appeared in New

---

45. Each militiaman on duty was to be supplied with "a good Musket or Flintlock, Bayonet or Tomahawk, a Blanket and a Knapsack, and every six men with a Pot or Camp Kettle." The pay system stipulated "that one penny per mile be allowed to each Non-commissioned Officer and Private during their march for subsistence money, and one days pay for every twenty miles between their respective homes and rendezvous, going and coming." Resolution of New York Convention, 7 Sept. 1776, Force 5, 2:671. In fact, however, there were inadequate arms and supplies, pay was uncertain, and service in many cases was short-lived and given reluctantly.

46. Ibid.

York harbor bearing 32,000 British and Hessian troops.[47] Against them were the small Continental Army and militia units from up and down the coast, all under Washington's command. Farmers and artisans with scant military training faced an experienced and professional army and navy in overwhelming force. The effort set in motion by London was unprecedented in the British Empire, evidence of the importance seen in regaining control of the colonies.

In response to the call from Washington in Manhattan for more troops, nineteen-year-old James Clark and other Ulster men "left Newburgh about the first of April 1776" for duty to the south, as his sister Elizabeth recalled.[48] Samuel Clark was then "implyed in Carying & Quartering troops" to Fort Montgomery in the Highlands in his sloop, the *Speedwell*, but would later join in the defense of Manhattan.[49]

When the huge British forces appeared in the harbor, Washington put his forces on the alert. On 15 July he ordered General Clinton, in Ulster, "to take measures of securing the passes in the Highland, lest they [the British and Tory allies] have designs of Seizing them and have a force concealed for that purpose."[50] Clinton already had "heard from the cannon signals" that the enemy had arrived. He ordered three militia regiments into the forts and left other units in the frontier settlements to defend them against Indians. He reported to Washington that "the Men turn out of their Harvest Fields to defend their Country with surprising alacrity. The absence of many of them however at this Time when their Harvests are perishing for want of the Sickle will greatly distress the Country."[51]

---

47. Christopher Ward, *The War of the Revolution*, ed. John Richard Alden, 2 vols. (New York: Macmillan, 1952), 1:209.

48. James Clark Pension Application.

49. Samuel Clark was issued a voucher at Fort Montgomery for services done "for the Congress" on 14 July 1776 by order of Col. Jonathan Hasbrouck. *Clinton Papers*, 1:499–500. Barratt states, without citing his source, that "During the first two weeks in July 1776 Col. Hasbrouck's militia and other troops, were carried to Ft. Montgomery and quartered in the sloop *Speedwell*, owned by Samuel Clark and Benjamin Lewis," and that Samuel was also engaged in the transport of troops in August 1776." He was paid twenty-four shillings per day for sixteen days. Barratt, "The Fourth New York Regiment," 230.

50. Washington to John Hancock, in New York, 14 July 1776. *The Papers of George Washington: Revolutionary War Series*, vol. 5, ed. W. W. Abbot and Dorothy Twohig (Charlottesville: Univ. Press of Virginia, 1993), 304 (hereafter cited as *GW, Rev. War Ser.*).

51. From Brig Gen. George Clinton, at Fort Montgomery, 15 July 1776. *GW, Rev. War Ser.*, 5:319–20.

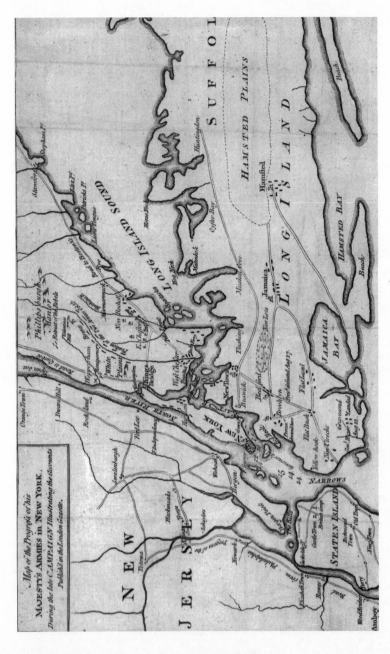

5. "Map of the Progress of His Majesty's Armies in New York" (*London Gazette*, 1776)

Library of Congress, Map Collection

The British took over Staten Island as the staging area for their next moves. Well aware that an attack on Manhattan was imminent, on 8 August Washington ordered Clinton to join him with troops, including Captain Samuel Clark's company, in the regiment commanded by Col. Levi Pawling. There were 368 men available for duty in the regiment at the beginning of the campaign, 1,600 in the five Ulster regiments that formed the brigade.[52] These and other units from New York constituted about one seventh of the force that Washington had available to him in and near the city—9,000 troops in total by mid-April, 19,000 at the outbreak of fighting in late August, "the larger part raw recruits, undisciplined and inexperienced in warfare, and militia, never to be assuredly relied upon."[53]

Amid the foreboding, there were high spirits at the promise of adventure. Abraham Leggett, who served in the Ulster regiment, a lad two years younger than James Clark, recalled how he felt that summer. He had been working as a blacksmith in "Pokipsey," and when the news came that "the British Fleet and large army was at Statten Island . . . I then with several others Formed ourselves in a company under the command of Barnardus Swartwout [part of the Ulster regiment] all Volunteers—." The "Time began to appear Very Interesting," to the young apprentice, as very likely it did to nineteen-year-old James Clark, who probably had never been in the city before. "[W]e march'd off in High Spirits. . . ."[54]

The Ulster regiments assembled at Kingsbridge, at the northern end of Manhattan, where the Boston Post Road crossed into Westchester on "Kings Bridge" over Spuyten Divil Creek. This was "a most important pass," Gen. Charles Lee reported to Washington after a survey of the island, "without the command of which We cou'd have no communication

---

52. Henry F. Johnston, *The Campaign of 1776 around New York and Brooklyn* (Brooklyn, N.Y.: Long Island Historical Society, 1878), 128.

53. Ward, *The War of the Revolution*, 207.

54. Abraham Leggett (1755–1842) was born in West Farms, Westchester Co., N.Y. As a youth he apprenticed to a blacksmith in New York City. In February 1776, after the outbreak of hostilities, he walked the eighty-three miles to Poughkeepsie from West Farms to work on two frigates being built there by order of the Continental Congress. He joined the Ulster regiment under the command of Col. Barnardus Swartwout, which was sent to Brooklyn the day of the evacuation and, as his narrative shows, he was involved with the last troops to be taken off on the morning of 30 August. *The Narrative of Major Abraham Leggett of the Army of the Revolution, Now First Printed from the Original Manuscript*, ed. Charles I. Bushnell (New York: privately printed, 1865), 10.

with Connecticut."[55] It was the only way to cross to the mainland on foot. If the enemy seized it, the Patriots on the island would be trapped.[56]

Manhattan, surrounded by water on all sides and with only this one bridge to the mainland, was highly vulnerable to a British naval force, which could rapidly move troops and firepower. Despite the near impossibility of the task, Washington and the Congress were determined to defend the city because of its strategic and symbolic value. They believed that if the city were abandoned without a fight, supporters of the Patriot cause everywhere would be disheartened and the cause itself would be in danger of collapse. Picks and shovels were put to hard use as the troops built redoubts at the southern tip of the island and at strategic points along the two rivers. The largest of these were the forts on the heights opposite the New Jersey Palisades (later Washington Heights), where cannons could command the river. Washington also chose to station a large force on the heights to the east of the village of Brooklyn, from which an enemy could bombard lower Manhattan. To man these defenses required a risky dispersion of forces.[57]

The Attack Comes on Long Island

On 22 August 1776, 15,000 British troops moved from Staten Island through the Narrows in flatboats and transports to occupy the Dutch villages on the flat lands at Jamaica Bay. They were soon joined by 5,000 Hessians.[58] Five days later a British column surprised and outflanked the American defenses on the heights. The battle at Flatbush Pass (within present-day Prospect Park) was a bloody defeat for the Patriots. A second British column ran into tough resistance as it followed the edge of the harbor in an attempt to cut off the Americans defending the heights. A few hundred resolute Marylanders resisted this column with considerable loss

---

55. Charles Lee to Washington, 29 February 1776. *GW, Rev. War Ser.*, 3:39.

56. E. Wilder Spaulding, *His Excellency George Clinton: Critic of the Constitution* (New York: Macmillan, 1938), 59–60.

57. Ward, *War of the Revolution*, 1:206. These were the Brooklyn Heights; the present-day term refers to what was then the village of Brooklyn, at the edge of the river.

58. On the Battle of Long Island see the standard source, Johnston, *The Campaign of 1776 around New York and Brooklyn*. Modern summaries are found in Ward, *War of the Revolution*, and John J. Gallagher, *The Battle of Brooklyn 1776* (New York: Sarpedon, 1995).

of life at the Cortelyou House, by Gowanus Creek. Their actions delayed the British advance and saved the American army from being encircled. Nevertheless, the cost to the Americans in killed, wounded, and captured was high. By nightfall the 7,000 men that Washington had on Long Island were essentially defenseless and could have been overwhelmed if the British had pushed.

In a decision that has puzzled commentators ever since, the British General Howe held his forces back over the next two days. This allowed Washington to send reinforcements, among them James Clark, in his brother's company.[59] Abraham Leggett was also among the reinforcements and must be allowed to speak for James. The "Two armies [were] close in View of Each other, and for three Days the Rain fell in Torrents so that we could not Cook," he recalled, a consequence was that he was "Brought to Eat Raw Pork."[60]

Then followed a feat of arms that saved the American army, Washington's reputation, and possibly the Revolution. Taking advantage of Howe's delay, and employing a clever subterfuge, Washington set in motion an evacuation. On the foggy night of 29 August, the American units left campfires alight and proceeded to the landing on the East River closest to the city (later the Fulton Ferry landing). Fortunately, the army included fishermen and sailors from Marblehead and Salem who skillfully ferried the troops across the foggy river, known for its strong tides. In all, 9,000 were evacuated without loss of life. Samuel Clark's company was assigned to the rear guard, an exceedingly dangerous role. Leggett can again speak for James Clark and his fellows:

---

59. Neither Col. Pawling's nor Samuel Clark's company is listed among the forces defending the Heights prior to 27 Oct. Samuel Clark's sister and son stated in the pension application that James was in the Battle of Long Island, and Samuel's son placed his father as being one of the last to leave in the evacuation. James Clark Pension Application.

60. *The Narrative of Major Abraham Leggett*, 11–12; also quoted in Thomas W. Field, *The Battle of Long Island*, Memoirs of the Long Island Historical Society, vol. 2 (Brooklyn, N.Y., 1869), 500–501. Leggett's account states that he "crowsed to the Island" with Capt. Swartwout on 29 Aug., but his narrative states that he was on duty there for two days before the foggy night of the evacuation; he must have crossed two days earlier. *Narrative of Major Abraham Leggett*, iii–vii. Bernardus Swartwout (1761–1824) was the son of a prominent merchant of New York. He went into the brick and lumber business in NYC with his father and was an original member of the Society of the Cincinnati, as was Leggett. Ibid., 32.

The night was Foggy & Very Dark . . . Early in the morning yet Very Dark we was Paraded under the Report that we was to attack the Enemy in there Lines we was Led around we now not where till I saw the old Stone Church of Brooklyn [Dutch Reformed]—then an Officer Riding by Says, a Groce mistake—we was ordred to wheel about and Reman the lines, which we did—a dangerous attempt—There we Remaned Till Some Time after—we then formed the Rear Gard we was ordred forward, still expected to meet the enemy. Till we found ourselves at the Ferry and the army all cross'd . . . we then was order'd to Choak up the Street with waggons and carts to Prevent the Light Horse from Rushing Down upon us—at this time no boats—I Prepar'd myself to Swim the River flood tide But Fortunately Two Battoes Struck this Shore—by this Time there was but a few of us left—we all Hurried on Board and Shoved off—the Enemy Rush'd Down on the Hill and Comenced a Brisk fire. Fortunately no one was Hurt in our Boat—the other Boat had four wounded—we Remaned in the Town Two days then our Capt. march'd us up the Island to near King's Bridge . . .[61]

Samuel Clark was "injured and bleeding" in the action.[62] The units regrouped at the Kingsbridge encampment.

Manhattan Invaded

The next move in the British assault came on 15 September in another well-executed amphibious operation. Under cover of massive cannon fire from warships far more powerful than the scanty shore batteries, a flotilla of flatboats loaded with redcoats crossed the East River from Newton Creek and landed at Kip's Bay on the East River, then overlooked by the Kip family mansion—vacated by Samuel Kip, his wife Ann (Mary Haring's sister) and their children, who took refuge with other Haring-Herring relatives in Tappan. (Kip's Bay was at the eastern end of present-day Thirty-fourth Street.)

The Connecticut troops on duty at Kip's Bay, aware of a general and disorderly retreat north from the settled part of the island, left their posts and joined those fleeing north along the Post Road on the east and Bloom-

---

61. *The Narrative of Major Abraham Leggett*, 11–12; also quoted in Field, *The Battle of Long Island*, 2:500–501.

62. James Clark Pension Application.

ingdale to the west.[63] British troops then occupied the city and were to hold it for seven years.

The Americans assembled that night on Harlem Heights (on the west side of the island, about as far north as the present 135th Street). Early the next morning, while reconnoitering the British lines, a company of Connecticut Rangers under Lieut. Col. Thomas Knowlton came up against Hessian pickets. A bloody series of skirmishes ensued, lasting some four hours, in which the Americans caused the British to retire. Samuel Clark and his company took part in the battle and later buried the dead, including the heroic Knowlton.[64]

George Clinton described the fierce give-and-take in his account of the morning encounter:

On Monday Morning about 10 o'clock a Party of the Enemy consisting of Highlanders, Hessians, The Light Infantry & Grenadiers of the English Troops, Number uncertain, attacked our Advanced Party, commanded by Col. Knolton [sic] at Matje David's Fly; they were opposed with spirit, & soon made to retreat to a clear Field, south west of that about 200 Paces where they lodged themselves behind a Fence covered with Bushes. Our People attacked them in Turn & a reinforcement with 2 Field Pieces being ordered in they caused them to retreat a Second Time leaving 3 Dead on the spot. We pursued them to a Buckwheat Field, on the Toop [sic] of a high Hill, distant about 400 Paces, where they received a very Considerable Reinforcement with some Field Pieces, & made a stand there; a very brisk Action ensued, at this Place which continued about Two Hours. Our People at length worsted them a third Time, caused them to fall back into an Orchard, from thence across a Hollow, & up another Hill not far distant from their own Lines. A large Column of the Enemy's army being at this Time discovered to be in

---

63. "They could not see or expect any Assistance from the Troops above as yᵉ were all retreating. Officers and Men had Expected that that their Retreat would be cut off unless they could fight their way through them we [ ] thout [sic] very dangerous and precarious. In such a Situation it was not reasonable to expect that they could make any vigorous Stand. The men were blamed for retreating and even flying in these Circumstances, but I image the fault was principally to the General Officers in not disposing of things to give the men a rational prospect of Defense and a Safe retreat should they engage the Enemy. And is probable that many Lives were saved. . . ." Benjamin Trumbull, *Journal*, 15–16 Sept. 1776, in *The American Revolution: Writings from the War of Independence* (New York: Library of America, 2001), 222, originally published in *Collections of the Connecticut Historical Society* (Hartford: Connecticut Historical Society, 1899), 7:193–96.

64. According to Clinton's account. Clinton to Dr. Peter Tappen, King's Bridge, 21 Sept. 1776, quoted in Ward, *War of the Revolution*, 1:144.

Motion, and the Ground we then occupied being rather disadvantageous, a
Retreat, likewise without bringing on a Genl. Action which we did not think
prudent to Risk, rather insecure, Our Party was therefore ordered in, & the
Enemy was well contented to hold the last Ground we drove them to.

The casualties were heavy:

Colo. Knolton, a brave Officer, & 15 Privates killed . . . enemy: upwards of
Sixty killed & violent presumption of 100 . . . that night I commanded the
Right Wing of our advanced Party or Picket on the Ground the Action that
began off which Col° Pawling [of which the Clarks were a part] & Col°
[Isaac] Nicoll's Engineers were part and next day I sent a Party to bury our
Dead. They found but 17 . . . [and] found about 60 places where enemy dead
lay. . . .[65]

The foray was tonic to morale after the ignominious retreat of the preceding day. It was the first time in and around New York that the Patriots
had seen the backs of the enemy. "I consider our success in this small
Affair at this Time almost equal to a Victory," Clinton added, "It has animated our Troops & gave them new spirits & erased every bad impression
the Retreat from Long Island &c. had left on their minds. They find they
are able with inferior Numbers to drive the Enemy & think of nothing
now but Conquest."[66]

Once again the British under Howe did not press their advantage. The
two armies faced each other without serious incident for nearly a month. It
was during this lull that Elizabeth Clark, the brothers' sister, and Elizabeth, Samuel's wife, came to see them in Kingsbridge, probably traveling
the over sixty miles from New Windsor on foot, as there was considerable
danger from enemy warships on the river. And they surely brought food
and warm clothing for the men. The lull was coming to an end, though,
for "whilst on our visit," Elizabeth recalled, "the British attacked Fort

---

65. Clinton, at Kingsbridge, 18 Sept. 1776, *Clinton Papers*, 1:352–53. In today's Manhattan the battle
began at about 106th Street and West End Ave.; after the first skirmish the Rangers retreated along
the present Claremont Avenue to 125th and Broadway ("The Hollow Way"); the Buckwheat Field
was on the southward-facing slope between 116th Street and 120th Street, including where Columbia Teachers College now stands. A more detailed designation of present day locations of the battle
is found in Bruce Bliven Jr., *Battle for Manhattan* (New York: Henry Holt, 1956), 86–98; see also
Johnston, *Campaign of 1776*, 244–56; Ward, *War of the Revolution*, 1:71.

66. George Clinton, at Kingsbridge, 18 Sept. 1776, *Clinton Papers*, 1:351.

Washington. I heard the firing and our brothers advised us to leave for home which we did."[67] (The firing may have been between enemy warships on the river and Fort Washington; the successful British assault of the fort did not take place until nearly a month after the units had left Kingsbridge for White Plains.)

In yet another well-executed amphibious operation, on 12 October, Howe landed his troops at Throgs Neck on the Westchester shore of Pelham Bay. Abraham Leggett, then at home, remembered that "when I Got there I saw the whole River from Hellgate to Flushing Bay Cover'd with Crafts Full of Troops, and my unkels Family moving off. . . ."[68]

To avoid being trapped, the Patriot troops had to leave Kingsbridge. This meant forced marches north with what supplies their wagons could carry. Speed was essential, as Howe and his troops intended to trap the Americans in Manhattan and southern Westchester. Washington's order of the day for 21 October offered encouragement in the face of this dismal prospect: "The Army will do their duty, with equal duty and zeal whenever called upon, and that neither dangers, difficulties or hardships will discourage Soldiers, engaged in the Cause of Liberty, and commending for all that Freemen hold dear and valuable."[69]

The division under General William Heath, of which Clinton's brigade and the Clarks' company were a part, "began its march from Kingsbridge about 4 o'clock on the afternoon of 21 October and arrived at Chatterton's Hill on the west side of White Plains about four the next morning,"[70] meaning that most of the march was in darkness with consequent confusion and disorder. Private James Clark may have had a similar experience to that of Private Joseph Plumb Martin who abandoned equipment to lighten the load.

> I told my messmates that I *could not* carry our kittle any further. They said they *would* not carry it any further. Of what use was it? They had nothing to cook and did not want anything to cook with . . . I sat it down in the road and one of the others gave it a shove with his foot and it rolled down against the fence, and that was the last I ever saw of it. When we got through the night's

---

67. James Clark Pension Application.

68. *Narrative of Major Abraham Leggett*, 13.

69. General Orders, Headquarters, Harlem Heights, 21 Oct 1776. *GW, Rev. War Ser.*, 7:24.

70. *GW, Rev. War Ser.*, 7:4.

march we found our mess was not the only one that was rid of their iron bondage.[71]

When he reached White Plains, Martin "was so beat out before morning with hunger and fatigue that [he] could hardly move one foot before the other."

In order to delay the enemy, Washington chose to make a stand at White Plains, the Westchester County seat, and where the eastward road link to Connecticut, vital for supplies from New England, met the west and north roads to Dobb's Ferry on the Hudson and to the Highlands.[72]

The Americans took positions on high ground and watched the British parade in their finery on the plain. The Third Ulster Regiment, under Col. Rodolphus Ritzema, was one of the units that defended Chatterton's Hill by the Bronx River on 28 October, the principal action of what came to be called the Battle of White Plains.[73] The British and Hessians succeeded in taking the hill, but again Howe did not press his advantage.

The other Americans, including the Clarks' unit, watched anxiously. "Our lines were manned all night in consequence of this [fear of attack]," wrote George Clinton, "and a most horrid night it was to lie in cold trenches. Uncovered as we are, drawn by fatigue, making redoubts, flashes [fleches], abatis and lines . . ." Exposure to the cold and wet was wasting the troops. "This I am sure of, that I am likely to lose more in my brigade by sickness occasioned by extra fatigue and want of covering, than in the course of a active campaigns is ordinarily lost in the most severe actions."[74] "We continued some days, keeping up the old system of starving," Private Martin recalled, giving a sense of what it must have been like for the common soldiers. "A sheep's head which I begged of the butchers who were killing some for the 'gentleman officers' was all the provision I had for two or three days."[75]

The Patriot army was dissolving. "Militia are deserting in great numbers," Philip Schuyler reported. "General Washington advises that if they

---

71. Joseph Plumb Martin, *Private Yankee Doodle* . . . ed. George F. Scheer (Hallowell, Maine, 1830; Boston: Little, Brown, 1962), quoted in *GW, Rev. War Ser.*, 7:54, 7:24.

72. *GW, Rev. War Ser.*, 7:24.

73. *GW, Rev. War Ser.*, 7:51–52.

74. *Clinton Papers*, 1:399–401, quoted in *GW, Rev. War Ser.*, 7:59.

75. *Yankee Doodle*, 50–52, quoted in *GW, Rev. War Ser.*, 7:54.

are not absolutely wanted, to dismiss them as he fears they will distress us as such as they have him by eating our provisions and doing no service."[76] Washington was "surprised and shocked to find both officers and soldiers, straggling all over the Country under one idle pretence or other, when they cannot tell the hour, or minute the Camp may be attacked . . ."[77] The enemy was gaining recruits as "ours are daily decreasing by sickness, deaths and desertions."[78] Washington himself admitted to the Continental Congress that the army was in a state of dissolution.[79] Yet again Howe did not press an attack. Instead he broke camp to turn his attention to Fort Washington on the heights of Northern Manhattan, which had been left defended (and was to fall to British attack on 16 November). Washington and a remnant of his army headed for Dobb's Ferry, where they crossed the river to New Jersey. He and the small army evaded British pursuit and ended up by Christmas on the Delaware, near Trenton.

At White Plains, James Clark was among those taken sick "of a bilious fever." According to his sister, he returned to New Windsor and their father's house, "where he remained sick a Short time and in which illness I nursed him." When he recovered, "[h]e again returned to camp where after a Short time the Company came to a place called Eleses Woods [Ellison's Woods, near the house of Col. Thomas Ellison, overlooking the river][80] where they were quartered for winter and were engaged in building Sheveau de freezes. This Encampment was about three miles from my fathers residence. During this Encampment my brothers aforementioned frequently [were] at home to visit us."[81] He and his fellows experienced a bitterly cold winter; as attested by young Abraham Leggett: "In December we had Very Cold weather and Seven Snow Storms—all this Time we was in Tents—we had to build Chimneys with Sods and Stone at one End of the Tents . . ."[82]

---

76. Philip Schuyler to Horatio Gates, 30 Oct. 1776. Force 5, 2:1299, quoted in *GW, Rev. War Ser.*, 7:55.

77. General Orders, Headquarters, White-Plains, 31 Oct. 1776. *GW, Rev. War Ser.*, 59.

78. *GW, Rev. War Ser.*, 7:71.

79. Washington to Hancock, 6 Nov. 1776. *GW, Rev. War Ser.*, 7:96.

80. A painting of the Col. Thomas Ellison house is in the house built by him for his son, John Ellison, now maintained by New York State as the Knox Headquarters House by the Silver Stream, New Windsor.

81. James Clark Pension Application.

82. *Narrative of Major Abraham Leggett*, 14.

The year 1777 was crucial for the Hudson Valley north of the highlands, though the defeat of the British strategic plan came about through Burgoyne's surrender rather than from defensive works, which, as it turned out, were permeable. When James Clark's fulltime service was up, he remained on the rolls of the militia as a sergeant (later lieutenant) in his brother's company, "Newburgh's Own," for the remainder of the war. The fiercest action in which Ulster militia participated was the unsuccessful defense of Fort Montgomery on 6 October 1777. A British fleet had moved upriver in a diversion to relieve pressure on Burgoyne, whose army near Saratoga faced a large Patriot force. Troops from the warships successfully stormed Fort Montgomery in an approach from the rear. The casualties were heavy on the American side, with two hundred and fifty killed, wounded, and captured. In the rotation of the militia units to defend the fort the Clark company was not then assigned to Montgomery, which may have spared the Clark brothers' lives.

This British naval foray was the first and only test of the *chevaux-de-frises*, built with such effort, and it proved them ineffective. "On Monday evening we sailed from fort Montgomery, having first entirely demolished it, and blown up the magazine," wrote one of the attacking party. The next day "we weighed, got through the Cheveau de Frize, and proceed[ed] up the river." According to this officer, New Windsor and Newburgh "appeared totally deserted by the inhabitants."[83]

As the fleet proceeded north, most of the militia on the west bank was on a forced march to Kingston, which was clearly the British destination. At 9 A.M. on 15 October, George Clinton spied from the New Windsor shore through the fog "30 sail, eight large square rigged vessels among them, and all appear to have troops on board." He added "My troops are parading to march for Kingston." He left men of Hasbrouck's regiment, of which the Clarks were then a part, "as a guard along the shore."[84] Because many militia had been assigned to the forts and individuals were serving with the northern army then facing Burgoyne, Clinton could only call on about one thousand men. By the time the column arrived near Kingston

---

83. Extract of a "Letter from Esopus," Oct. 16, Rivington's *New York Gazette*, 27 Oct. 1777, in Pratt, "An Account of the British Expedition," 141.

84. George Clinton, headquartered in New Windsor, to the Council, 9 A.M. on 16 Oct. 1779, quoted in Pratt, "An Account of the British Expedition" 1:130–31.

the soldiers were exhausted by the long, hasty march and in no condition to fight.[85]

The British warships began to shell the town. On 16 October they landed troops. It was then that the British commander Col. Vaughan wrote that Ulster, with Kingston at its heart, was "a Nursery for almost every Villain in the Country."[86] His troops torched a hundred houses. George Clinton and his men could see it all but could do nothing.[87] However, unbeknownst to the triumphant Vaughan, Burgoyne and his army at Saratoga were surrounded, the very next day surrendering to the rebels. This stunning defeat soon resonated across the seas and brought the French to the aid of their enemy's enemy. It was the turning point of the war.

The burning of Kingston was all the British had to show for their strategic plan to split the colonies by occupying the Hudson Valley. By November 1777 the Hudson Valley was peaceful, and there were no more threats to the Highlands, though that was not expected at the time. The war was not over for James Clark or his brother, as construction of defensive works continued. In April 1778 one hundred men under Samuel Clark were detailed to New Marlborough (west of Newburgh) to cut logs for the boom that would place the great chain across the river at West Point; other militia worked on Highland forts. Their skills had improved since the first forts. Chastellux, a French military engineer, visited West Point in November 1780 and commented with wonder on the quality of the works "built by a people, who six years ago had scarcely ever seen a cannon."[88] However, neither the forts nor the chain had to be tested in battle.

---

85. Ibid., 131, 137–38.

86. "Col. John Vaughan on Board the *Friendship*, off Esopus, Friday 17 Oct [1777] 10 O'Clock Morning," *London Gazette*, 23 Dec 1777, quoted in Pratt, "An Account of the British Expedition," 189.

87. Barratt, "The Fourth New York Regiment," 254. William Smith visited Col. Johannis Hardenbergh at home in Rosendale two months later and learned that he "censured Geo. Clinton much & blamed him for the Desolation of Esopus. Says 24 hours was loitered away by him & 500 men at his House who might have saved Kingston." Entry of 3 Jan. 1778, Smith, *Historical Memoirs*, 281–82. An insight into how lawlessness accompanied the civil war in the area is found in another remark by Hardenbergh that day, "All the inhabitants of Orange below the mountains greatly displeased by the Conduct of one Johnson of Kakiata to whom Mr. Clinton has given 60 or 70 Rangers who plunder both Whig & Tory & convert all to their private Emolument. Mr. Clinton supports him tho' he may disapprove of his conduct." This Hardenbergh was probably the father of Johannis Hardenbergh Jr., who commanded the Newburgh Regiment in 1779 and after.

88. Chastellux, *Travels*, 2:91, quoted in *Encyclopedia of the American Revolution*, ed. Mark Mayo Boatner III, Bicentennial ed. (New York: David McKay, 1974), 530.

A Wedding in the Governor's House

It was in George Clinton's house that twenty-three-year-old Lieutenant James Clark was married on 20 June 1779. His bride was Deborah Denton, from Newburgh, then seventeen. The service was performed by the Reverend John Close, the Presbyterian minister at Newburgh since 1773 and the chaplain of its militia.[89] It was a signal honor to be married in the house of the state's governor and Ulster's most prominent Patriot, evidence to his respect for the Clark family.

Deborah Denton's grandfather, Nehemiah, like Jehiel Clark, had immigrated to the Hudson Valley in the 1750s, in his case from Jamaica, Long Island. The Dentons arrived in Massachusetts Bay, moved to Wethersfield and then to Stamford. From there they crossed the sound to Long Island, where for several generations they lived at Hempstead, later Jamaica. Like the Clarks, they were Presbyterians. Several members of the family removed to the Hudson Valley.[90] Nehemiah built a gristmill in Newburgh on what came to be called Denton's Creek, which flowed into the Hudson north of the town (in the district later called Balmville).[91] His son Nehemiah, Deborah's father, was in Newburgh during the Revolution, declared "exempt" (too old or incapacitated) for militia service in 1778 and 1779.[92] In 1777 he supplied barrels to be used for the army, but there is no record of his having signed the oath administered by the Com-

89. George Clinton was on the committee that called Close to the congregation. Ruttenber, *History of the County of Orange*, 295–96. John Close (1737–1813) graduated from the College of New Jersey in 1763. Ruttenber, *History of the County of Orange*, 298; Bolton *Westchester County*, 3:516. After the fall of the Highland forts in early 1777, Clinton moved his family to a house away from the river for security reasons. It was here that the ceremony was held. The governor was probably present to honor the young couple, as there is a break in his official correspondence from Kingston, where, as governor, he usually resided in those days.

90. Walter C. Krumm, "Who Was the Rev. Richard Denton?" *Record* 117 (1986): 163–65, 211–18; "Descendants of the Rev. Richard Denton," *Record* 120 (1989): 10–17, 159–64, 93–97, 222–24; 121 (1990): 22–24, 144–49, 221–23; 122 (1991): 37–44, 168–69, 215–28. See "Denton," Genealogical and Biographical Notes.

91. Ruttenber, *History of the County of Orange*, 213.

92. Daniel Denton, James Denton, Samuel Denton, and Thomas Denton were also declared exempt in these years. Barratt, "The Fourth New York Regiment," 222. James Denton and Nathaniel Denton served in the Newburgh village militia. Ibid., 221.

Richard Denton (1603–1662/3)	=	—?—
Nathaniel Denton (1628–bef. 1690)	=	*poss.* Sarah —?
Nathaniel Denton Jr. (1653–?)	=	Deborah Ashman (?–after 1685/6)
Nehemiah Denton (ca. 1704–ca. 1770)	=	Deborah ___ (ca. 1731/2–?)
Nehemiah Denton (ca. 1732/3–1825)	=	Sarah Flewelling (1734–1776)
Deborah Denton (1762–1843)	=	James Clark (1756–1814)

6.   Richard Denton descent to Deborah Denton

mittee of Safety and Observation.[93] A James Denton did sign the oath and served in the militia. Two members of the family, however, refused to sign. It is a pointed reminder that political allegiances did not respect blood, religious, or economic lines, even in Ulster. These yeoman farmers ultimately fled to Canada.[94]

The first child born to Deborah and James Clark was the Sarah who married Samuel Haring, born in 1780. Over the next twenty-five years Deborah would bear ten more children.

John Haring's war

John Haring was thirty-seven in 1776, well established as a leader in his native Tappan and in surrounding southern Orange County, and strongly identified with the Patriot cause locally. He was a participant in the intricate political struggles of 1775–76 in New York City in which Patriots took over the governance of the province. Though for a time he held the title of brigade major from the New York Congress, his involvement in the

---

93. William Paulding reported to George Clinton on 28 May 1777 that he received from Nehemiah Denton 47 Barrrels. *Clinton Papers*, 2:192–93. In the Revolution, Daniel Denton of Ulster County refused to take the oath supporting the rebel cause and was "carried beyond the enemy's lines." John J. Nutt, comp., *Newburgh, Her Institutions, Industries and Leading Citizens* (Newburgh, N.Y., 1891), 723.

94. Ruttenber, *History of the County of Orange*, 136.

war was as a civilian leader in and around Tappan, where a civil war was waged between Loyalists and Patriots and which was scoured by foragers of both armies. Tappan, or Orangetown—to use its official English name—was the site of four encampments by the Continental Army, which brought John Haring into direct relationship with Washington and his generals. During the war he and Mary were surrounded by family members in refuge from British-occupied New York. Mary Herring's widowed mother owned the house two doors from the manse where John Haring lived, across from the church. The families of Mary's sisters, Ann (Herring) Kip, Elizabeth (Herring) de Peyster, and Sarah (Herring) Jones, from New York City, spent the war years in Tappan. "Even in this urban and cosmopolitan branch of the Haring family," according to Firth Haring Fabend, "Tappan retained its value as the symbolic center of family life, and it was to Tappan, when trouble came, that the family repaired."[95] In that first wartime winter it was hardly a secure retreat.

John Haring's wartime experience offers an insight on the war from the perspective of a mature civilian leader from the heavily Dutch settlements in the lower Hudson Valley, giving contrasting perspective on the war from that of James Clark in Manhattan and in Ulster.

In southern Orange County in the fall and winter of 1776, Loyalists were emboldened by the British success around New York. After White Plains, a British force under Cornwallis had crossed the Hudson at the Palisades in pursuit of Washington, expecting to catch him, but the "fox" eluded them and, with the remnant of the Continental Army, by late December was encamped on the Pennsylvania side of the Delaware River. Nothing then seemed more unlikely than the success of the struggle begun at Lexington and Concord. John Haring was well known and was certain to be imprisoned and tried as a traitor if Tappan fell completely into Tory and British hands.

The immediate situation was fraught. "The southernmost part of this country is ravaged by the enemy, plundering the friends of the country of their property, and disarming them, at Orange Town. Some of them are flying to the country, others flying for that protection to the enemy which we do not afford them." So Brigadier General Alexander McDougall reported to the New York Congress that December. Without help, "[t]hey will all, or the greatest part of them, submit to the enemy; and if this event

---

95. Fabend, *Dutch Family*, 99.

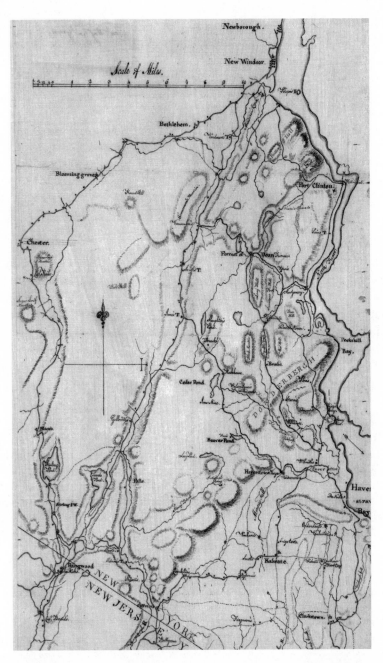

7. Orange County, New York. Surveys by R. Erskine, 1778, 1779.

Library of Congress, Map Collection

33

takes place, they will greatly aid the enemy in crossing the mountains, to show the sincerity of their submission . . . For these reasons, as well as for the honour of the State, it is absolutely necessary that three or four hundred men should be posted at Orange Town."[96]

John Haring that same month passed on a report from neighbors that

the King's troops, our cruel and merciless enemies, have last Saturday been in Orange Town, have taken some prisoners, and robbed others. The English troops and the Tories make great havoc; the latter insult and abuse the Whigs in a matter not to be born with. Part of the Militia of Bergen County are now taking up arms against us, and unless we get assistance, the Southern part of Orange County will be laid waste. [97]

"[P]rocure us protections" was Haring's plea to George Clinton.

General Heath, upriver in Haverstraw, reported the situation on the New Jersey–New York boundary to Washington: "I find the inhabitants in the utmost distress . . . the Tories are joining the enemy and insulting and disarming the Whigs, stripping of their cattle, effects, etc. Complaints, petitions, etc., are continually presented for relief; and the greatest complaints are from Orange Town, Clarks Town and the neighborhood of Hackensack."[98] Washington was miles away, by the Delaware, had few troops, and was in no position to help. A militia commander conveyed the extent of civil conflict:

The country from Tappan is all in arms. On Sunday they were called together, and had King's arms and ammunition delivered among them. Whether there is any of the enemy's regular troops below, about Fort Lee and English Neighborhood [Bergen County, New Jersey], I cannot find out, and I really think my party insufficient to take part at Tappan; but our friends are so distressed thereabouts that I think it indispensable duty to attempt supporting them. My people are now almost unfit for duty on account of their clothes,

---

96. Alexander McDougall, in Haverstraw, to the Provincial Congress, 9 Dec. 1776, *Journals of the Provincial Congress, Provincial Convention, Committee of Safety and Council of Safety of the State of New-York, 1775–1776–1777*, 2 vols. (Albany, 1842), 1:315.

97. John Coe, John Smith, John Coleman, Derick Vanderbilt, Johannes Vanderbilt, and Theodore Polemus to Brig. Gen. George Clinton, 8 Dec. 1776, enclosed in letter from John Haring to Clinton of same date. Cole, *Rockland*, 52–53.

98. William Heath, in Haverstraw, to Washington, 11 Dec. 1776, Cole, *Rockland*, 54.

and so much marching; so that I really do not think they can stay after the middle of the month.[99]

There was some relief, when, on 12 December, General Heath made a quick foray through Tappan "with so much secrecy and dispatch that the inhabitants had no knowledge of my coming," a show of force which momentarily confounded the Tories.[100] The food supply was short and all that could be spared for Tappan was thirty barrels of flour—the full barns of the Dutch farmers had been plundered bare.[101]

A few days later George Clinton went to Tappan himself, "Accompanied by some of my Officers & a small Detachment of Light Horse." He found the enemy (regular troops), "few in number," and on his approach they and the "principal tories," alarmed by Heath's show two days before, had fled by the bridge and the river, leaving their stores to be confiscated. He recommended that a regiment be stationed in Tappan.[102] This was all well in concept, but the militia were in no condition to fight. Col. William Allison of the militia reported of his men that "many . . . [of] their families [are] in a suffering condition and, therefore, doubt not, but you will have the whole discharged . . . soon." Rations were insufficient: "We have been Exceedingly disappointed about beef, and no salt for what Little we have had; we have this morning procured 2 or 3 small cattle which may serve about two days; but are doubtful whether a full supply can possibly be had, should we Ly here any Time."[103] In reply, Clinton could send no help. "[I]f you cant provide for them I must let them Return Home. I cant think of asking them to continue & suffer."[104] Later, in response to the militiamen's departures, Clinton urged Col. Allison "for Heaven's sake, for the sake of your Bleeding country, keep your Men together a few Days longer; dont let them basely Desert so honorable a Cause & Suffer our Enveterate & Cruel Enemy to plunder & distress our Friends."[105]

---

99. William Malcolm, in Clarkstown, to Heath, Cole, *Rockland*, 54.

100. Heath, in Hackensack, to Gen. Washington, 15 Dec. 1776, Cole, *Rockland*, 55.

101. A. Hawkes Hay, in Haverstraw, to Heath, 15 Dec. 1776, Cole, *Rockland*, 56.

102. Clinton to the New York Provincial Convention, 17 Dec. 1776, *Clinton Papers*, 1:469–70.

103. William Allison, in Tappan, to Clinton, 20 Dec. 1776, *Clinton Papers*, 1:475.

104. Clinton, in Paramus, to Allison, 20 Dec. 1776 *Clinton Papers*, 1:476.

105. Clinton, in Ramapo, to Allison and John Hathorn, *Clinton Papers*, 1:505.

Early in January John Haring described to Clinton an unsuccessful foray and unauthorized plunder. "[N]inety hearty men," drawn from three militia regiments, and "and about a dozen from the Orange Town militia" had assembled at Tappan. Starting at ten at night "Col. Allison at the head of about 100 men, marched into Schraalenburgh [across the New Jersey boundary], but as he found the traveling excessive bad, and the weather Very Cold, he returned without Getting any new information." Allison's party came across the militia under Capt. Robert Johnston "busy in plundering"—an example of the indiscriminate warfare going on in the area. "Johnston's Conduct has much displeased the inhabitants of this place, and I am afraid that it will make them backward in Going a scouting for they are enemies to plundering. Thus are matters managed. . . ."[106]

"[B]y the best accounts I can Get," Haring continued, "I am inclined to think that there are about 300 of the enemy at the Bridge [over the Hackensack River]; the three regiments stationed here about 400 men, besides which there is one Company from this place on duty but none from Haverstraw present yet come down. Our men complain much that they have no rum allowed them when they are on fatigue; if you have any to spare pray send it."

Such was the confusion of what amounted to civil war. John Haring here reveals the role he was playing under dangerous conditions with a grasp of both the military and political situation. He was clearly a respected adviser to Clinton, who shortly requested him to confer with him at Ramapo regarding the disposition of Tories that had been arrested.[107]

In February 1777 Haring, "expecting soon to remove out of the Colony of Orange," resigned the office of brigade major awarded him by the Provincial Congress.[108] However, the move out of the county did not occur, and he and the family remained in Tappan for the duration of the war. He may have resigned because he was serving as a political leader and source of intelligence in Tappan, not as a militia officer. Shortly after Haring's resignation, on 20 April, George Clinton was elected the first governor of the newly created state of New York; he retained his commission as general in charge of the Highlands' defense.

---

106. John Haring, in Orangetown, to Clinton, 3 Jan. 1777, *Clinton Papers*, 1:523–25.

107. Clinton, at Ramapo, to Haring, *Clinton Papers*, 1:539.

108. Haring to the Provincial Congress, *Calendar of Historical Manuscripts relating to the War of the Revolution in the Office of the Secretary of State* (Albany, 1868), 629.

Tappan and its surrounding country continued to be scavenged by foraging parties on both sides. "The Continental troops, in passing through this part of the country last summer and fall, committed great devastation on many of the inhabitants well affected in the cause, by burning their fences, destroying their grain and corn, and taking away their property without making any compensation whatever," wrote John Coe, of the Tappan Committee of Correspondence. Local residents were forced to care for the sick and bury the dead at their own expense.[109] A British foraging party that passed through Tappan and nearby towns came off with "some little booty . . . amounting to some horse, about 400 head of cattle and the same quantity of sheep, together with twenty milch cows, which"—the British commander seemed to find entertainment in the raid—"afforded a seasonable refreshment to the squadron and the army (amongst whom they were all distributed) without costing either them or the government a shilling)."[110]

The warfare and dangers did not interfere with the expansion of the Haring-Herring families. The Rev. Samuel Verbryck, who had baptized Samuel Haring and was his godfather, baptized a dozen more children in this extended family, including three more to Mary Haring, two to Elizabeth Herring and John De Peyster, one to Ann Herring and Samuel Kip, and four to Sarah Herring and Gardner Jones. Abraham Herring and Elizabeth Ivers, his wife, spent the war years in Stratford, Connecticut, but brought their first child, Elbert, born in July 1777, to be baptized in Tappan a year later. He was to live to ninety-eight and carry the memories of the Revolution to the Centennial year.[111] Mary Herring would bear ten children over twenty-one years, from 1775 to 1796.

---

109. John Coe, Esq., Deputy Chairman, Committee of Safety, Tappan, to the Provincial Convention, 3 May 1777, *Journals of the Provincial Congress*, 1:477.

110. Referring to a raid of 11 Aug. 1777. *The American Rebellion: Sir Henry Clinton's Narrative of his campaigns 1775-1782*, ed. William B. Wilcox (New Haven: Yale Univ. Press, 1954), 71.

111. *Baptism Record of the Tappan Reformed Church, Tappan, Rockland County, N.Y. 1694–1899*, ed. Arthur C. M. Kelly (Rhinebeck, N.Y.: privately printed, 1998), records 2529, 2496, 2563, 2596, 2611, 2634, 2672, 2875, 2691, 2717, 2260 "The World's Oldest Lawyer: Hon. Elbert Herring's Remarkable Career; In his Ninety-Eighth Year, Reminiscences of New York in 1790, A Judge in 1805," *New York Herald*, 5 April 1875. Samuel Verbryck, minister at Tappan from 1750 to 1784, was buried at the Tappan cemetery. "Church Yard of the Reformed Church of Tappan, Rockland County, N.Y.," *Bergen County New Jersey Tombstone Inscriptions*, 2:24046, BC-38.

Although the British remained on Manhattan, after the failures of 1777, the Patriots in and around Tappan had the upper hand over now discouraged Loyalists. As the new state became politically organized, John Haring was appointed the first judge of the Orange County Court of Common Pleas in January 1778.[112] In May he was made one of the "Justices of the Courts of Oyer and Terminer and General Gaol Delivery in and for the County of Orange," which made him one of the chief legal representatives of the state in that county.[113] He was also a de facto local government executive. As such he was an advocate on issues of local concern to the new state government, as shown in a letter in which he requested from Clinton a waiver of the state's prohibition of the sale of wheat outside its borders.[114]

The military threat was not over, and John Haring was an important source of intelligence on enemy actions. In late September 1778 he was in Harington Township (named for the family and a home to relatives), across the New Jersey line, probably with militia forces preparing to resist an impending British action. Cornwallis had assembled a force of regulars at Newark to make a sweep up the Hackensack valley to seize ripened crops and rally Tories. On the twenty-fifth Haring sent word of the British moves to Thomas Smith, commanding at Haverstraw, with a request for assistance. He had learned on "good authority . . . that the enemy have already Seventeen field pieces at the liberty pole, they daily recive reinforcements from Newyork and have actually part of their army near the New Bridge [over the Hackensack River]; their intention is to march thro' this place your way. This Intelligence or the Chief part thereof we have from a Creditable woman who has been among the enemey, she has seen

---

112. Appointment dated 21 Jan. 1778. S. C. Hutchins, *Civil list and Constitutional History of the Colony and State of New York* (Albany, 1869), 102.

113. 28 May 1778. *Minutes of the Committee and of the First Commission for Detecting and Defeating Conspiracies in the State of New York, December 11, 1776–September 23, 1778 with collateral documents to which is added Minutes of the Council of Appointment, State of New York, April 2, 1778–May 3, 1779.* (New York: Collections of the New-York Historical Society for the Year 1925, 1924), 20. John Haring was re-elected to a one-year term on 17 Oct. 1778, 53.

114. Haring, in Orangetown, to George Clinton, 13 May 1778. *Clinton Papers,* 3:300. Local farmers had requested permission to exchange their wheat for Connecticut salt ("the Quantity of salt they want is about 50 Bushels and they are to give 10 Bushels of wheat for 3 of salt"). Haring recommended that the governor permit this exchange for the sake of about twenty families for whose "attachment to the Cause of Liberty" he could vouch.

the above number of field pieces." "Inform the General Officers," he wrote, "that unless they send us Speedy relief they will not have Occasion to send or give any, on our account, as it is not worth while for us to think of maintaining our Ground much longer." In a postscript marked, "8 O'Clock in the Evening," he added, "This moment some women and Children are coming up the road and Give an alarm; they say the enemy take women and Children and Commenced their old practice of burning. J. H."[115]

On 28 September the enemy "made their appearance at Tappan with a large Body Commanded by Cornwallis in Person." On this day occurred one of the bloodiest atrocities of the war. On a farm that belonged to a Haring relative, a detachment of over a hundred Continentals under Colonel Baylor of Virginia was surprised and overwhelmed by one of Cornwallis's detachments, their presence betrayed by a Tory spy. British regulars proceeded to bayonet "in a most inhuman manner a number of the Light Horse and militia who had surrendered themselves prisoners...."[116] "[T]he attack was so sudden," wrote Dr. James Thacher, who talked with survivors, "that they were entirely defenseless, and the enemy immediately commenced the horrid work of slaughter; their entreaties and cries for mercy were totally disregarded by their savage foes. It has been well ascertained that the British soldiers were ordered by their inhuman officers to bayonet every man they could find, and gave no quarter."[117]

---

115. John Haring, Gilb't Cooper, in Harington Township, to Thomas Smith, in Haverstraw, 25 Sept. 1778, *Clinton Papers*, 4:86–87.

116. Appeal to Gov. George Clinton from multiple signatories, 18 Oct. 1778, *Clinton Papers*, 4:169–72; Adrian C. Leiby, *The Revolutionary War in the Hackensack Valley* (New Brunswick, N.J: Rutgers Univ. Press, 1960), 171–76.

117. James Thacher, *A Military Journal During the American Revolutionary War, from 1775 to 1783, Describing Interesting Events and Transactions of this Period, with Numerous Historical Facts and Anecdotes.* (Boston: Richardson and Lord, 1823), 169. When the massacre occurred James Thacher (1754–1844), surgeon, was in charge of a military hospital in Albany; he spent the winter of 1779–80 with the Continental Army in Morristown and was with the army on its two encampments in Tappan in 1780. *Encyclopedia of the American Revolution*, s.v. "Thatcher, James." Sir Henry Clinton, the British commander-in-chief made light of this, one of the notorious atrocities of the war. "I had the satisfaction to find that the move had not proved altogether fruitless, Lord Cornwallis having by one of his detachments surprised and carried off almost an entire regiment of the enemy's light cavalry and a few militia." *American Rebellion*, 105.

After this outrage, which offended every sense of honor, as the Americans had asked for quarter, "they turn'd their Cruelties to Women and Old men, whome they treated with every kind of Brutality their Perfidiousness could invent; and from thence extended their Depredations within a quarter of a mile of Clarkstown and Continued every day since to display in and about this State the most wanton Scenes of Cruelty. . . ."[118]

Two years into the conflict, Tappan and nearby lands presented a ravaged landscape. It is a story that can only be glimpsed through the surviving documents, but after a century in which similar and worse depredations are familiar from news photography, it can easily be imagined. The Revolution is often taught as a series of battles—the experiences of those who lived in Tappan and the "neutral ground" tell a different story. John Haring and his family had to cope with continual devastation and civil chaos during the war years.

The winter of 1779–80 was notoriously severe, as the Continentals camped at Morristown were aware. The Hudson was ice-bound, and streams froze for weeks, during which time the mills could not operate. "The Hard Winter of 1779, made a very deep impression on my mind," recalled one Newburgh resident years later. "We were fourteen days without bread. Owing to the severity of the weather, the mills could not run much of the time, and then they did run it was on flour for the army . . . Wheat was so plentiful that the horses were fed with it; but we could not get flour . . . For forty days that winter the water did not drop from the eaves. It snowed almost every day."[119]

In July 1780 Patriot prospects brightened with the landing of French troops at Newport. The Continentals encamped twice in Tappan as Washington maneuvered north of the city, crossing the river twice, to make the enemy doubt his intentions and to forestall any attempt on their part to attack the American allies. However, the arrival of the army in Tappan in August was accompanied by foraging as devastating as that done by the enemy. John Haring reported to the commander-in-chief that his fellow inhabitants were "filled with apprehensions of being brought to a Starving condition. Fences are wantonly destroyed and consequently Cornfields, buckwheat, Orchards, meadows, &c, &c are laid waste, and we know not where it will end." Washington replied immediately:

---

118. *Clinton Papers*, 4:169–72; Leiby, *The Revolutionary War*, 171–76.

119. Recollection of James Donnelly in 1838, quoted in Ruttenber, *History of the County of Orange*, 169.

It has long been my endeavor as much as in my power to prevent the troops from omitting depredations of any kind whatsoever on the inhabitants. That there should be cause of complaint from the well-affected is an additional aggravation. You may be assured that the most pointed orders have been issued to the army on this subject since we came to this ground, and the strongest recommendations used to the officers that they may be carried into execution.[120]

The army decamped from Tappan on 25 August to move about northern New Jersey then upriver to keep the enemy guessing as to its intentions. According to Dr. Thacher the move was possibly to "to procure a supply of provisions, and forage from the inhabitants between the lines, which otherwise would go to supply the want of the enemy."[121]

The troops returned in late September under General Nathanael Greene, while Washington was in Hartford meeting with the Comte de Rochambeau, commander of the French army in America, to plan operations. In a general order, Greene ordered abuses of property of the Tappan farmers to stop,

And for this purpose the Camp and Quarter guards are to confine every person detected in either removing or burning fencing stuff; and as it frequently happens that there are numbers of soldiers standing round a fire made of fencing though none will acknowledge or inform who made it such therefore as are standing by it shall be considered as the Authors unless they point out the Persons and shall be confined and punished accordingly.[122]

---

120. Haring, in Orangetown, to Washington, 11 Aug. 1780; Washington, in Orangetown, to John Haring, 11 Aug. 1780, *The Writings of George Washington from the Original Manuscript Sources, 1745–1799, June 12, 1780–September 5, 1780,* ed. John C. Fitzpatrick (Washington, D.C.: GPO, 1937), 19:358–59.

121. The sick were left in his charge. A gentle forage on their behalf was not well received. "Feeling myself authorized to take a small supply from the inhabitants for immediate necessity, I required from a Dutchman four sheep from his farm as he was offended and made some opposition, I was obliged to force them from him, giving a receipt, that he might recover a compensation from the public." Entries of 25 and 28 Aug. 1780 in James Thacher, *A Military Journal During the American Revolutionary War, from 1775 to 1783, Describing Interesting Events and Transactions of this Period, with Numerous Historical Facts and Anecdotes* (Boston: Richardson and Lord, 1823), 249–50; *The Writings of George Washington,* 19:423 ff., 20:5–72.

122. General Orders, HQ, Orangetown Thursday, 21 Sept. 1780, Nathanael Greene, *Writings of George Washington,* 20:75–76.

André

Then came Arnold's treachery. Washington rejoined his staff at the house of Beverley Robinson on the east bank of the Hudson on 25 September to find that Arnold, in command at West Point, had fled under suspicious circumstances. Washington sent an express to Greene at Tappan: "You will also hold all the Troops in readiness to move on the shortest notice. Transactions of a most interesting nature and such as will astonish You have just been discovered."[123]

In contact with Major John André, an intelligence officer on the British commander's staff, Arnold had sold himself and his knowledge of West Point and the fortifications of the highlands to the British. In flight, he boarded the aptly named British sloop *Vulture* and was taken to New York. André was captured in civilian clothes by "Cow-boys," marauders who preyed on travelers in the no man's land a few miles from the British lines. They delivered André to a Continental officer, and once his identity was recognized, he was sent to Tappan to be tried as a spy.

André's court martial under General Greene took place in the Tappan Church a few steps from the Manse where the Harings lived. During the trial André was confined in the nearby Yoast Mabie house, where John Haring had signed the Orangetown Resolutions. Maria Haring, the eldest child, nearly six at the time, recalled in old age that Washington had sent André food from his table, and that her father had brought him a blanket when he was moved to the church after the guilty verdict. ("Maria was a favorite with the officers about the headquarters of Tappan, and her father's house was their constant resort," her nephew reported. "She had frequently sat upon the knees of General Washington, Greene and Putnam while they were being entertained at meals. . . .")[124] On the fatal day "[a]t an early hour in the morning." Maria recounted,

> Preparations were being made at home to witness André's execution. My brother, Samuel, was a child of four years and repeatedly entreated Father to take him along. At last, Father called him to his knee and said 'My child, this man can now talk and act like others, soon he will be in eternity, where either happiness or misery awaits him.' This was too impressive for even such a little child, and he replied, 'Oh! Papie, I don't want to go.'

123. Washington to Greene, 25 Sept. 1780, ibid., 20:85.

124. Ambrose T. Secor recorded the recollections of his great-aunt, Maria Haring (1775–1868), eighty years after the event; notes transcribed in Budke, BC-70.

Her father permitted her to go with him, and they "secured a good position." "When the moment approached," Maria recounted,

A mounted officer, Captain John Stagg, who was stationed immediately in front and near the gallows, but in the rear of the guard which surrounded it, invited me to a seat on his horn in front of him, and Father placed me there, from which position I had a full view of that awful scene.[125] More than eighty years have passed since that event and my recollection of it is as clear and vivid as were my earliest impressions, and will so remain until my dying day.

Major André walked between guards to the place of execution which was on the side of the hill in sight of our house. A wagon drawn by horses was driven before him and carried his coffin which was painted black. It was stopped directly under the gibbet which was made of stout poles with a cross pole at the top. He mounted the wagon and stood upon the coffin, and, after the noose was adjusted and he had blindfolded himself with his own handkerchief and his arms had been bound with another, the wagon was quickly drawn from beneath him and he swinging back and forth, very far at first and his feet almost touched the ground. His open grave was close by. We did not remain long afterward as Father was anxious to go home for he was very sorrowful. André's quiet manner and gentle bearing had softened toward him the hearts of nearly every spectator it seemed, for tears were freely shed by both men and women, of whom there was an immense multitude. Father always spoke of him afterward as a young man of rare accomplishments, and mild disposition, and a gallant officer, who was more unfortunate than criminal, and I believe Washington expressed himself in nearly the same language.[126]

John Haring was elected to the state senate from Orange County in 1781. He was one of the majority of "new men" then elected to that body, one of the "plain men" of the type exemplified by George Clinton.[127] John Kaminksi, in his study of political New York during and after the Revolu-

---

125. John Stagg (1758–1803) began as a Captain in the N.Y. Militia, and served in the Continental Army as a major, private secretary to Washington at Valley Forge, and chief clerk for eight years to President Washington. He was an original member of the Society of the Cincinnati. William Nicholas Puffer, "Contributions to the History of the Stagg Family," *Record* 9 (1878): 86.

126. Julia Phelps Haring (1851–1928), daughter of Maria Haring's nephew, James Demarest Haring (1819–68), remembered the story she learned from her father differently: Maria watched atop the shoulders of a black woman servant. JHW MSS.

127. Edward Countryman, *A People in Revolution: The American Revolution and Political Society in New York, 1760–1790* (New York: W. W. Norton, 1981), 245.

tion, termed Clinton the "idol of the country yeomen," one who "exemplified the new era of opportunity." It was to Clinton that "a host of rising young lawyers, merchants, militia officers, and men from the lesser branches of aristocratic manorial families flocked."[128] John Haring was one of these, and in the state senate and Continental Congress to which he was again elected after the war, he can be considered a "Clintonite."

He took his seat at the temporary capital of Poughkeepsie on 1 October 1781 in a session that was still underway when the news came of the Yorktown victory late that month. The incredible had come about with the surrender of the large British army at the height of the Empire's power. Cornwallis, the scourge of southern Orange and the Jerseys had been humiliated. The rebels had won.

It took over two years more for the British to evacuate New York, which they did on 25 November 1783. After the British evacuation, John Haring moved his family from desolated Tappan to Manhattan, where he built a house in rural Greenwich, near the corner of the later Bleecker and Christopher Streets. They would remain there for five years, and young Samuel would get a taste of life in Manhattan.[129]

The Harings were now much in contact with the wider family. The Kip, de Peyster, and Gardner Jones families had returned to Manhattan from Tappan; Samuel and Cornelia (Herring) Jones and their children returned from the family estate in Oyster Bay, Long Island, where they had spent the war under British occupation; Abraham and Elizabeth (Ivers) Herring returned from Stratford, Connecticut, and Abraham rapidly established himself as a merchant in the city. All of these relatives were part of the rebuilding of a city that had been depopulated and devastated during the seven years of British occupation. With the peace, John and his brothers-in-law completed their work as executors of the Elbert Herring estate, after a delay of ten years, in which Abraham Herring, the youngest son, played an important role. All of these closely related families remained in New York for the rest of their lives in comfortable circum-

---

128. John P. Kaminski, "New York: The Reluctant Pillar," in Stephen L. Schechter, ed., *The Reluctant Pillar: New York and the Adoption of the Federal Constitution* (Troy, N.Y.: Russell Sage College, 1985), 49.

129. BC-34:91 (includes receipts for materials).

stances. Only John and Mary Haring returned to New Jersey and New York lands across the river after their five years in the city.

The independent New York that these families inherited was home to the Continental Congress, and John Haring was elected to the first postwar session on 11 April 1785. He was also actively involved in the resolution of boundary disputes and land claims that dated from before the Revolution.[130] In 1785–86 he was one of the commissioners appointed to resolve the Cheesecocks boundary dispute in Orange County (concerning land in the Ramapo River valley, often called the Clove). In the hearings he saw firsthand the legal skills of Alexander Hamilton and Aaron Burr, the opposing attorneys.[131] His brother-in-law, Samuel Jones, again a leader of the New York Bar, as he had been before the Revolution, was a fellow commissioner.

Both Haring and Jones also served on the commission agreed upon by Massachusetts and New York to resolve the former's claims on western New York lands. The commissioners developed an ingenious solution to the dispute: Massachusetts gave up its claim for the western lands but was given permission to sell them. The purchaser was Oliver Phelps, who became one of the private developers of the lands, offering smaller parcels for sale to homesteaders. Many of those passing through the clearing in central New York where Samuel and Sarah were married ten years later were on their way west, attracted by the developers' offers.[132] Thus Haring, Jones, and their fellow commissioners contributed to what was shortly to become a massive immigration of (mostly) New Englanders to central and western New York.

Then came a political watershed. At the New York Federal Constitution Ratifying Convention meeting in Poughkeepsie in June 1788 Haring,

---

130. *The Law Practice of Alexander Hamilton: Documents and Commentary,* Julius Goebel Jr., Joseph H. Smith, eds. (New York: Columbia Univ. Press, William Nelson Cromwell Foundation, 1980), 3:442–50; *Biographical Directory of the American Congress,* 200–201; H. James Henderson, *Party Politics in the Continental Congress* (New York: McGraw-Hill, 1974), 354–58, 395. *Journals of the Continental Congress, 1774–1789,* Gaillard Hunt, ed. 34 vols. (Washington: United States Government Printing Office, 1923; reprint, New York: Johnson Reprint, 1968), 1784 and 1785 entries, vols. 26 and 28.

131. *Papers of Aaron Burr,* NYHS microfilm, 26:625 ff. *The Law Practice of Alexander Hamilton,* 3:450–67.

132. *The Law Practice f Alexander Hamilton,* 1:563–78; *Journal Continental Congress,* 32:231; Burdge, *A Notice of John Haring.*

a delegate from Orange County, was in the large minority intending to vote against acceptance of the United States Constitution.[133] Governor Clinton had strenuously opposed the ratification, in part on the grounds that it would drain the state of its lucrative customs duties, but more importantly because he felt that a strong executive could reassert the kind of authority that the Revolution had banished from the state. Haring followed his lead. When it became clear with the New Hampshire vote that the majority of the other states ratified the Constitution, New York could not realistically stay out. Clinton, a realist, led the majority in an affirmative vote. Samuel Jones—who had previously held Clinton's anti-ratification position—framed the final motion to approve. Haring let others speak for his position at the convention, but it can be inferred that he too feared the assertion of a central state authority. His anti-Federalist position took him out of the political swim in the state despite his closeness to Clinton, and from then on he devoted himself primarily to private pursuits away from Manhattan.

For some years he lived "in some affluence" in the Ramapo area of Bergen County, where he was a sales agent for the General Proprietors of Eastern New Jersey.[134] By 1796 he had moved to Teaneck, New Jersey, where he became an elder of the church at Schraalenbergh (where Samuel and Sarah briefly rejoined him in 1801).[135] In 1803 he and Mary had rejoined the Tappan Church—for all the decayed condition of the village, the church where the Harings had worshipped over a hundred years continued to attract.[136]

John Haring was a prominent actor on the New York stage before, during, and after the Revolution. He fostered the Patriot cause—the "Cause of Liberty" as he put it—and helped keep it alive under difficult and dangerous circumstances. He had worked with and knew from close contact every key figure in New York City and State, and Washington and his

---

133. *The Debates in the Several State Conventions for the Adoption of the Federal Constitution as Recommended by the General Convention at Philadelphia of 1787*, ed. Jonathan Elliot (Philadelphia: J. B. Lippincott, 1881), 412–13; Burdge, *A Notice of John Haring*.

134. Reginald McMahon, *Ramapo: Indian Trading Post to State College* (Mahwah, N.J.: Ramapo College of New Jersey, 1977), 24–27; BC-34:70ff.

135. Adrian C. Leiby, *The United Churches of Hackensack and Schraalenburgh New Jersey, 1686–1822.* (River Edge, N.J,: Bergen County Historical Society, 1976), 249; Burdge, *A Notice of John Haring*.

136. Cole, *Reformed Church in Tappan*, 155.

generals during their Tappan encampments. His support of the Revolution
and astute leadership in local politics during trying times are clear from
the surviving correspondence and his participation in local and state politics. Yet in detailed histories of the period his name is only mentioned in
passing. In part this must be due to the absence of an archive of his papers,
such as exist for many of his contemporaries. The documents that he must
have accumulated over the course of his career would be of immense value
to historians, as would a memoir or family letters. If these still exist, they
have not come to light. His withdrawal from political life in New York
after the ratification of the federal constitution is certainly another reason
for his relative obscurity. What is evident in the account of his war years
that can be assembled from the extant records is that he was a person characterized by persistence, courage, independent judgment, and intelligence.
He must have been a beacon of strength for the residents of Tappan and its
neighbors.

Vitality did not return to the people and land of Tappan after the Revolution—the world of the Dutch yeoman farmer was all but destroyed. It is
little wonder that Samuel Haring chose to go elsewhere. Tappan and surrounding farms became, in the words of the Boston writer, Lydia Maria
Child, a "stagnant social pool," a depressed backwater. At the time of her
visit in the 1840s, it had just begun to stir with the arrival of the New York
and Erie Railroad, which built a terminal north of the Slote. Child was
drawn to the place by the story of André. She found at

> [t]he foot of the eminence where the gallows had been erected . . . an old
> Dutch farm house, occupied by a man who witnessed the execution, and
> whose father often sold peaches to the unhappy prisoner . . . Everything
> about this dwelling was antiquated. Two prim pictures of George III and his
> homely queen, taken at the period when we owed obedience to them . . . An
> ancient clock which has ticked uninterrupted good time on the same ground
> for more time than a hundred years . . .
>
> [I]t has never been my lot to visit scenes so decidedly bearing the impress
> of former days, as this Dutch country, [which for] a century produced no vis-
> ible change in theology, agriculture, dress, or cooking . . . The same family
> lived on the same homestead, generation after generation. Brothers married,
> and came home to fathers to live, so long as the old house would contain
> wives and swarming children; and when home and barn were both overrun, a
> new tenement of the self-same construction, was put up, within a stone's
> throw.

When Child visited, the railroad was beginning to ripple "the surface of the stagnant social pool," dividing "orchards, pastures and gardens; but in many cases cut right through the old homesteads."[137]

A century and a half later the railroad was gone. The long jetty at the outlet of Tappan Slote, which had been used to dock the barges to transfer freight cars, is now a park, occupied on a sunny day by walkers and fishermen. The meadow on the hill where André was hung is now a small green surrounded by comfortable houses. The past is more palpable in the center of Tappan. Although the present church replaced the square, peaked structure topped with its weathercock early in the nineteenth century, it stands amid the graveyard whose stones tell of Harings—Abraham Haring, John's father, most prominently. Across from the church is the Manse where John Haring lived during most of the Revolutionary War years and where Samuel could not face going to the execution. John Haring's grave is separate from other Harings, in a newer cemetery on a hill beyond the Manse. Yoast Mabie's house and tavern, where the Orangetown Resolutions were drawn up and signed and André was imprisoned is now "The Old '76 House," a pleasant place for lunch and dinner, but, for this visitor, haunted by the story of the handsome young officer partaking of John Haring's kindness in his last meals. Down the road and across a stream is the De Windt house, built in 1700 by a prosperous trader, where Washington stayed during the encampments at Tappan. It stands on ground that is shielded from nearby roads and houses, making it easier to imagine the farmhouse as it was and the bustle that attended the commander-in-chief.

Clarks Move North and West

The Clarks left New Windsor soon after the Revolution. Attracted by good agricultural land free of hostile Indians, Samuel and James Clark moved their families to near Saratoga, then lightly populated. This move to more expansive lands was a fruit of the independence for which they fought and coincided with the significant economic development of the area. In the 1790s the therapeutic qualities of its springs made Ballston and neighboring Saratoga fashionable resorts.

Samuel Clark became a prominent and prosperous citizen, with a house set on six hundred acres that became the first county courthouse. It must have been with pride and local notoriety that this veteran of the 1776

---

137. L. Maria Child, *Letters from New York* (New York: C. S. Francis, 1843), 173–74.

actions defending New York and the Hudson Highlands cast his vote for Washington as a presidential elector in 1792.[138] He rose in the ranks of the militia to be a general by the War of 1812. He had taken good advantage of the opening up of the western lands, and in 1823 his estate included "lands and tenements lying in the Counties of Saratoga, Sullivan, Seneca and Madison."[139]

James Clark remained near his brother until about 1796, when he and the family moved to lands further west.[140] He may have accompanied his nephew, Samuel's son, Jehiel[5] Clark, who founded Clarksville, a nearby settlement, rival to Hardenbergh's Corners, where Samuel then lived. This move brought James and Deborah Clark's seventeen-year-old daughter Sarah closer to Samuel Haring, whom she would soon meet.[141]

Hardenbergh's Corners

The land by Owasco Outlet where Sarah Clark and Samuel Haring were married had been cleared four years before by John L. Hardenbergh— baptized Johannes Leonardus in the Dutch Reformed Church. There he built a cabin and constructed a log dam to power a gristmill, which could grind up to twelve bushels of corn daily.[142] He called the place Harden-

---

138. For this and other details of his career see "Clark," Genealogical and Biographical Notes.

139. Will Book, 6:16, Saratoga Co., N.Y.; personal communication from Office of the County Historian, Saratoga Co., Dec. 1999.

140. In 1786 James Clark was a lieutenant in the Albany County Militia; in 1791 and 1792 he was a captain in the militia of the newly created Saratoga County. *Military Minutes of the Council of Appointment of the State of New York 1783–1821*, ed. Hugh Hastings (Albany: 1901), 1:113, 196. In 1797 James Clark was replaced as captain in Saratoga County Militia, and the next year noted as "moved away." Loc. cit., 1:387, 1:403.

141. Land Records, OG:266, Township 8, Lot 75 (2 March 1798), Cayuga Co., N.Y.

142. Henry Hall, *The History of Auburn* (Auburn, N.Y.: Dennis Brothers, 1869), 43. Joel H. Monroe, *Historical Records of a Hundred and Twenty Years, Auburn, N.Y.* (Geneva, N.Y., 1913), 12, 15. In a recent analysis of the origins and development of the city of Auburn, Scott Anderson considers John L. Hardenbergh an outstanding early leader, who committed himself to the community and reinvested the money he made there. His widow and son were respected members of the town in the next generation. Though he cites no sources for many of these comments, it is clear from the text he was acquainted with Hardenbergh's file books and other documents held by the Cayuga County Historical Society at Auburn. Scott Anderson, "Entrepreneurs and Place in Early America: Auburn, New York, 1783–1880" (Ph.D. diss., Syracuse Univ., 1997), 113.

bergh's Corners, and it was well located for commerce on the trail that led to the Genesee country further west. Most who settled there or passed through on their way further west came on bateaux from Albany, ascended the Mohawk River, and after portages, left the waterways at Old Fort Schuyler, where they picked up the ever-widening trail that eventually became the Albany Turnpike. A few of the early residents of Harden-bergh's Corners came through the Susquehanna Valley to the south. The Old Genesee Trail led west to the good farming country of the Genesee, the destination of many homesteaders.

According to Scott Anderson's recent study of the town of Auburn, which sprang from this modest settlement, Hardenbergh was a "leather-stocking hero of large proportion and gentle humor." He was a Revolu-tionary War veteran and had taken up the land bounty in this part of the Military Tract as his reward.[143] The "Colonel," as he was called from his later militia title, had been with the Second New York Continental Regi-ment in both battles at Saratoga, served with the Sullivan expedition against the Iroquois (when he first saw this part of the country), spent the Valley Forge and Morristown winters with the army, was at West Point when Arnold's betrayal was discovered, was at Tappan when Major André was tried and hung, and was at Yorktown for Cornwallis's surrender to Washington.[144] He was the same age as John Haring, whom he knew and admired, as he named a son for him. He almost certainly knew James Clark from his wartime service in Ulster County. In 1797, the year of the Clark-Haring marriage, Hardenbergh was fifty-one, "tall and robust,"

---

143. Anderson, "Entrepreneurs and Place," 86–87.

144. Hardenbergh was a fourth-generation descendant of a Dutch family that had settled near Eso-pus (Kingston) early in the eighteenth century. His great-grandfather, Johannes, was the principal owner of a vast tract of land purchased from the Indians for the sum of £60 and recognized by a royal patent in 1707. This was the famous Hardenbergh Patent of Ulster County, estimated to have been from one and a half to two million acres, extending west and south into the watershed of the Delaware River. The owners benefited little from their possession in colonial times, as it remained largely uninhabited. Myrtle Hardenbergh Miller, *The Hardenbergh Family: A Genealogical Compila-tion* (New York: American Historical Co., 1983), 26–30. "[After the Revolution] the family retained large tracts which were leased on a variety of terms, through chiefly for life and in perpetuity." David Maldwyn Ellis, *Landlords and Farmers in the Hudson-Mohawk Region, 1790–1850* (Ithaca, N.Y.: Cornell Univ. Press, 1946), 61.

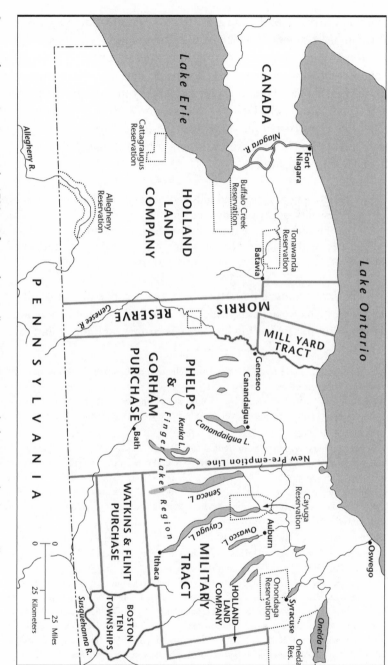

8. Land tracts in New York, 1790s. After Anderson, "Entrepreneurs and Place in Early America."

with a swarthy complexion and struck a "commanding figure on horse-back in his regimentals which he wore on military occasions."[145]

Hardenbergh must have recognized the extraordinary potential for the land he settled when he surveyed what became the New Military Tract. It comprised about 1.5 million acres acquired by the state from the Onondaga and Cayuga tribes in 1784–88.[146] Simeon De Witt, surveyor-general of New York, instructed the surveyors (his cousin Moses De Witt, the chief, assisted by the Hardenbergh brothers, Abraham and John) to lay out the lots in a uniform pattern:

> [T]he crossing of creeks and hills and ridges or mountains of note—or even the inequality of ground may be omitted provided you sketch them on the maps. The principle use that I shall make of your returns will be to [lay] that country on the map of the state with assurance and to give the boundaries of lots . . .[147]

This was a radical departure from the practice in almost all previous surveys of American lands, which hitherto had used metes and bounds and laid out boundaries following streams, ridges, and other natural bound-

---

145. Miller, *Hardenbergh Family*, 318. A biography of John Leonard Hardenbergh (1748–1806) is included in *The Journal of Lieut. John L. Hardenbergh of the Second New York Continental Regiment from May 1 to October 3, 1779 in General Sullivan's Campaign against the Western Indians*, Collections of Cayuga Historical Society, vol. 1 (Auburn, N.Y.: Cayuga Historical Society, 1879).

146. This discussion of the Military Tract is based on Richard H. Schein, "Framing the Frontier: The New Military Tract Survey in Central New York," *New York History* 74 (1993): 5–28. See also the same author's, "A Historical Geography of Central New York: Patterns and Processes of Colonization on the New Military Tract, 1782–1820" (Ph.D. diss., Syracuse Univ., 1989), from which "Framing the Frontier" was derived. See also Anderson, "Entrepreneurs and Place." The "New" was used to distinguish it from the previously established tract of military bounty lands in the Adirondacks, the Old Military Tract.

147. Simeon De Witt to Moses De Witt, 1 Sept. 1791, De Witt Family Papers, box 2, Arents Research Library, Syracuse University, quoted in Richard H. Schein, "Unofficial Proprietors in Central New York," *Journal of Historical Geography* 17 (1991), 151. Simeon De Witt (1756–1834) was born in Wawarsing, Ulster Co. His maternal uncle was James Clinton, whose son, later governor, was named for the De Witt family. Simeon De Witt assisted Robert Erskine, geographer to the Continental Army, and succeeded him at his death in 1779. In 1784 he was appointed surveyor-general for New York State, in which position he served for fifty years. He made a comprehensive map of New York State in 1802. *DAB*, s.v. "De Witt, Simeon." The relationship of Moses De Witt (1772–94) to Simeon is noted by William Heidt Jr., *Simeon De Witt, Founder of Ithaca, N.Y.* (De Witt Historical Society of Tompkins County, 1968), 2; Robert S. Rose, "The Military Tract of Central New York" (master's thesis, Syracuse Univ., May 1935).

aries.[148] The New Military Tract surveyors did, however, put notes on their maps regarding "navigability of streams, tree cover, soil, slopes, suitability for meadows, existence of old Native American fields, brooks and general judgment as to the quality of the land," so a judgment could be made as to quality.[149]

Over the course of three seasons the surveyors laid out twenty-eight townships, each about 9.7 square miles, divided into lots of six hundred acres; both townships and lots were strictly rectangular in shape (hence De Witt's "corners"). The veterans were eligible for one or more lots: a private received five hundred acres from the state plus one hundred from the federal government; a lieutenant, as Hardenbergh was when he left active service, received 1,200 acres. A number of lots in each township were reserved for schools, churches, and roads. Fifty acres in each were set aside as "surveyors' lots," their sale paying for the cost of the survey.[150]

The townships were famously named for great men from classical antiquity: Cato, Scipio, Brutus, Pompey, Ovid, Marcellus, Lysander, Homer, Muntius, Hector—later additions were Locke, Dryden. "How these classical names happened to be peppered over New York without any pertinent association, has occasioned much discussion," commented the state historian, Alexander Flick. Amusement too, he could have added—contemporaries lampooned the use of such names and attributed

---

148. "The surveying method which had been in use for wild lands, used irregular natural boundaries. Rivers, ridge lines, blazed trees and boulders . . . allowed pioneers the freedom to avoid poor acreage and select only premium parcels for ownership . . . the result was oddly shaped land units, little development of more marginal tracts, and constant land disputes." This was "anathema" to land developers and caused them to look with favor on the rectilinear method. William Wyckoff, *The Developer's Frontier: The Making of the Western New York Landscape* (New Haven: Yale Univ. Press, 1988), 25.

149. Schein, "Framing the Frontier," 15; The New Military Tract—so-called because a smaller tract had been set aside earlier in the Adirondacks—is seen by Schein as "at once an answer to the pressing political-economic demands of a fledgling nation-state, a framework for colonization by an expanding American populace, and a symbol of a new American order." Ibid., 6; The pattern of equal sized, rectilinear lots was the embodiment of equality and was later used by Jefferson to map the American Midwest and New York City in 1811. It came to have "transcendent meaning . . . and it was used to proclaim rational, egalitarian, pragmatic ideals for the new nation." Ibid., 26.

150. These "surveyors' lots" of fifty acres each were typically purchased by speculators many of whom bought them in quantities. Anderson lists a number of those who did so, most of them merchants from Albany and New York, "smart money," as he terms it. "Entrepreneurs and Place," 60–61.

it to the whim of the Simeon De Witt.[151] Hardenbergh's Corners fell within the township of Aurelius, named for Sextus Aurelius Victor, a Roman historian, whom the emperor Constantine made consul.[152]

Few veterans actually occupied the plots awarded to them as bounty; they sold them to others or passed them on to relatives as may have been done by John Haring to Samuel. It had taken years to make the allocations, and, as most were not willing to start up again in a new place, they sold their lots to former officers—merchants who were interested in speculation, not homesteading.[153] (Anderson's examination of the purchasers of 1,823 lots revealed that only 189 were taken by the soldiers who earned them or by heirs or family.)[154] Hardenbergh was an exception. With his knowledge of the terrain, he chose a lot by a flowing stream to provide power for the mills that would attract users and encourage people to settle nearby.[155] Owasco Lake lies at a higher elevation than the neighboring Finger Lakes, and water flows north in a stream called the Owasco Outlet. The lots Hardenbergh chose were astride a crossing of this stream where Indians earlier had made a crossing place with stones and which was a nexus of their trails. The stream powered the saw and gristmill he built there, which made it a center for commerce.[156]

Hardenbergh was a promoter, an "unofficial proprietor" as a recent study termed him, in that he was not selling lots but stood to gain from increased business and a rise in the value of his land from those purchasing

151. Alexander C. Flick, *New York Place Names* (*History of the State of New York*, vol. 10, 1937; reprint, New York: Columbia Univ. Press, 1937), 315.

152. Hall, *History of Auburn*, 33.

153. Schein, "Unofficial Proprietors," 149.

154. Anderson, "Entrepreneurs and Place," 40. Samuel Haring, although his father was a veteran, purchased his piece.

155. Hardenbergh and Moses De Witt acquired great influence in the course of the survey. They hired from among the few residents in the areas, they patronized the inns and were recognized for their knowledge of the land and the advice they could give concerning the quality of the lots. They also pursued their own interests. Moses De Witt identified the most desirable lots on his map, typically mill sites and good agricultural land. He later chose to develop the site that became Ithaca, on Lake Cayuga. The cluster of promising sites on Owasco Creek, where Hardenbergh was to settle, also figure on his map. Richard H. Schein, "Unofficial Proprietors," 152.

156. Anderson, "Entrepreneurs and Place," 87, notes, "As settlers converted this thoroughfare into the Old Genesee Road, nudging it to conform to the lot boundaries in 1791, and in 1795, relocating it as the New Genesee Turnpike and coursing it directly through 47, it assured Hardenbergh of constant traffic through his property."

nearby.[157] The site was located on the road from Albany, which by 1795 had been cleared to a thirty-foot width and soon would extend across the northern shores of the Finger Lakes to the rich agricultural lands of the Genesee. Along it thousands of emigrants traveled west in search of cheap land, and this road (and the successor Genesee Turnpike and Seneca Turnpike) remained the principal east-west route until the opening of the Erie Canal thirty years later.[158] Hardenbergh's Corners became the center of the town of Auburn, which in later years became a railroad and manufacturing center.

In the year of the wedding, Samuel had been in Hardenbergh's Corners for over two years, since he was nineteen, very probably referred to Hardenbergh by his father. Hardenbergh sold him his first lot, which was extremely well sited, with frontage on the creek and adjacent to Hardenbergh's mills and the Genesee Turnpike. (The friendship between Hardenbergh and John Haring must have had much to do with this.) Jehiel Clark's Clarkville was nearby, a less successful commercial center at the time than Hardenbergh's. Presumably in the traffic between the settlements Samuel met Sarah Clark. The young man was already somewhat established. He had the means—probably supplied by his father—to buy a well-situated lot, and he bought additional properties nearby. Years later he would sell these properties at much higher prices, which helped him to sustain his business and family in New York.

Although Samuel had been living as a homesteader for a couple of years, he evidently had another ambition, a clue to which was his identification as "Samuel Haring, merchant" in the indenture by which James and Deborah Clark conveyed land to him after the marriage.[159] This was a pretentious occupational description for one so young—he reached his majority the day after the ceremony—but it was perhaps justified by the favorable prospects for the property he had acquired and his observation of trade at the Corners. It did reveal the direction he would take, and he was no doubt inspired by his maternal uncle, Abraham Herring, who had by then established trade up and down the Hudson and to and from England. Abraham in these years had trading partners in locations west of Albany, including Old Fort Schuyler (later Utica), where another of his nephews had established himself. The route Samuel would have taken

---

157. Schein, "Unofficial Proprietors."

158. Monroe, *Historical Records*, 20. Much later this became roughly State Route 5 today.

159. See note 141, above.

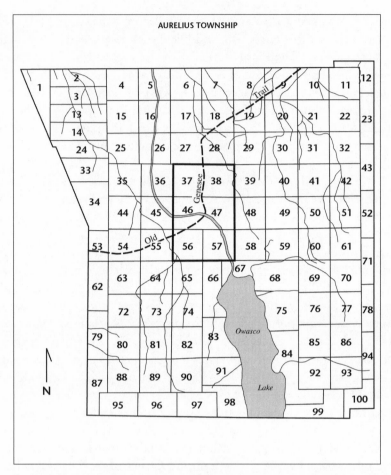

8. Aurelius Township, 1792. After "Map of Township Aurelius,"
    State Archives Series A0273, Survey Maps of Lands in New York
    State, New York State Archives

    The town of Aurelius was formed from the lots outlined in bold. Samuel
    Haring owned land in Lots 47, 57, and 18.

from the family home in the lower Hudson Valley would have been
upriver to Albany and west through Fort Schuyler, where he would have
observed trade such as that practiced by his uncle, grains to the New York
City, manufactured goods up the river and west along the Mohawk.

A New Beginning in the Wilderness

Hardenbergh was a devout member of the Dutch Reformed Church (as was John Haring), and in addition to the mills he built a log church at the Corners, the first Dutch Reformed Church in western New York. Ten families of Dutch background from Gettysburg, Pennsylvania, who had traveled up the Susquehanna Valley to settle nearby, joined Hardenbergh in founding the church.[160] It was likely in this log church that Samuel and Sarah were married on 8 October 1797. It is likely, too, that the minister who joined them was twenty-four-year-old Rev. Peter Labagh, then on a mission to western New York, later a well-known Dutch Reformed missionary in Kentucky. There was a strong Haring connection, as he had been ordained to ministry less than two years before in the Tappan Church.[161]

The covenant of marriage in the Dutch Reformed service at the time of the young couple's wedding was a sober text. It reminded the couple of the perils and uncertainties of life, the prevalence of sin ("Whereas married persons are generally, by reason of sin, subject to many troubles and afflictions . . ."), the certainty of God's assistance, and the married state as an institution of God. The words of the service assured them of "the certain assistance of God" and that the married state is "an institution of God, which is pleasing to him."[162]

In terms that must have resonated in that forest clearing where domestic and wild animals were essential for food, *Genesis* reminded the young couple that God ordained that "man should have dominion over the beasts of the field, over the fish of the sea, and over the fowls of the air." The service also set out the three reasons why God had "instituted the action" of

---

160. The settlers from Pennsylvania arrived in 1793 according to Hall, *History of Auburn*, 50, in 1795 according to W. N. Dailey, *The History of Montgomery Classis R. C. A.* (Amsterdam, N.Y.: Recorder Press, 1916), 10; *Journal of Lieut. John L. Hardenbergh*, 16.

161. Labagh's aim in the near-wilderness was to advance the cause of his church, and in later years he was noted for his missionary work in Kentucky and became the subject of a biography. Labagh was born on 10 Nov. 1773 at New York City, ordained at the Dutch Reformed Church, Tappan, on 21 July 1796, and died on 25 Oct. 1858. John A Todd, *Memoir of Rev. James Labagh, D. D., with Notes of the History of the Reformed Protestant Dutch Church in North America* (New York, 1860), 36, 44, 211.

162. *The Constitution of the Reformed Dutch Church in the United States of America with an Appendix Containing Rules and Orders from the General Synod from 1794 to 1815* (New York: George Forman, 1815), 123 ff.

marriage: for companionship ("each faithfully assist the other in all things that belong to this life, and a better"); to ensure the proper raising of children ("in the true knowledge and fear of God, to his glory and their salvation"); and to instill respect for sexual limits ("[t]hat each . . . avoiding all uncleanness and evil lusts, may live with a good and quiet conscience.")[163] With such injunctions from the two-hundred-year-old Calvinist tradition, Samuel and Sarah began married life.

Samuel and Sarah were heirs to the Revolution, part of the first generation to come of age in the new nation. At Hardenbergh's Corners they had already seen some of its characteristics: the movement of people west, the availability of cheap land, the profits that could be made developing it, the quickening of trade in goods and crops.

Only fifteen years before, Washington had reminded his newly independent fellow citizens that they had been "placed in the most enviable condition," that they were "the sole Lords and Proprietors of a vast Tract and Continent, comprehending all the various soils and climates of the World, and abounding with all the necessaries and conveniences of life." Americans were "from this period, to be considered as the Actors on a most conspicuous Theater, which seems to be peculiarly designed by Providence for the display of human greatness and felicity." They were "not only surrounded with every thing which can contribute to the completion of private and domestic enjoyment, but Heaven has crowned all its other blessings, by giving a fairer opportunity for political happiness than any other Nation has ever been favored with."[164]

It was in this "most conspicuous Theater" that Samuel and Sarah would live their lives, but the working out of their destinies would largely be a pursuit of the means to secure "private and domestic enjoyment." As Gordon S. Wood concluded from his study of the Revolution and its aftermath, the new country

> . . . would find its greatness not by emulating the states of classical antiquity, not by copying the fiscal-military powers of modern Europe, and not by producing a few notable geniuses and great-minded men. Instead, it would dis-

---

163. Ibid.

164. Washington, "Circular to the States," Head Quarters, Newburgh, 8 June 1783. *Writings of George Washington*, 26:485–86.

cover its greatness by creating a prosperous free society belonging to obscure people with their workaday concerns and their pecuniary pursuits of happiness—common people with their common interests in making money and getting ahead.[165]

Samuel striving to become a merchant is one of those with "workaday concerns and pecuniary pursuits" The post-Revolutionary society offered opportunities to make money and have a more comfortable manner of life, and it was towards those ends he would strive.

In pursuit of their domestic felicity Samuel and Sarah became city folk, emulating his grandfather, Elbert Herring, Uncle Abraham Herring, and, perhaps, the father who lived in New York City for a time after the Revolution. They would live their lives in the cosmopolitan society of New York and in an Albany invigorated by the immigration of Yankees. Not long after their marriage Samuel and Sarah, too, took the turnpike east to return to Albany and the Hudson Valley.

Samuel's maternal uncle, Abraham Herring, and his son Thomas already had established trade in rapidly developing New York west of Albany, and it is to that part of the family we turn to next, before returning to Sarah and Samuel making their way.

---

165. "A new generation of Americans was no longer interested in the revolutionary dream of building a classical republic of elitist virtue out of the inherited materials of the Old World . . . No doubt the cost that America paid for this democracy was high—with its vulgarity, its materialism, its rootlessness, its anti-intellectualism. But there is no denying the wonder of it and the real earthly benefits it brought to the hitherto neglected and despised masses of common laboring people. The American Revolution created this democracy, and we are living with its consequences still." Gordon S. Wood, *The Radicalism of the American Revolution* (New York: Alfred A. Knopf, 1992), 369.

II

MERCHANTS IN A VAST EMPIRE

The whole province is contained in two narrow Oblongs, extending from the City East and North, having Water Carriage from the Extremity of one, and from the Distance of one hundred and sixty miles of the other . . . This is one of the strongest Motives to the Settlement of a new Country, as it affords the easiest and most speedy Conveyance from the remotest Distances and at the lowest expense. . . . there is scarce a Farmer in the province that cannot transport the Fruits of a Year's Labour to some convenient Landing, where the Market will be to his Satisfaction, and all the Wants from the Merchant, cheaply supplied; beside which, the Boat shall steal into the Harbour of New-York. . . .

—William Smith Jr., *The History of the Province of New-York, from the First Discovery to the Year 1732*

The potential for European-style land and economic development in central New York in and near the Mohawk Valley attracted the energies of Samuel Haring's uncle, Abraham Herring. By the late 1790s, Herring was well established in New York City and Albany as a trader, helping to facilitate the flow of commodities and dry goods between the city and the Mohawk Valley. With his son Thomas he imported goods from across the Atlantic.

The Mohawk Valley also presented Abraham's contemporaries and younger relatives with the means to make their fortunes. Peter Smith (1768–1837), born in the Haring-Herring heartland of Tappan, after an apprenticeship with Abraham Herring, moved to the Mohawk Valley at the age of twenty in pursuit of prosperity. By the late 1790s he had helped transform Old Fort Schuyler, a fording place on the Mohawk, from a trading post to the flourishing town of Utica, and possessed extensive lands nearby. James S. Kip, Abraham's nephew and Samuel's first cousin and nearly exact contemporary, had been drawn to the possibilities in and near

Old Fort Schuyler through the family connection. He became one of Utica's substantial citizens—a trader, landowner, and manufacturer.[1]

Abraham and Thomas Herring corresponded with Smith from the early 1790s to 1830, leaving a rich archive, preserved by Smith's son, touching on family matters as well as business.[2] These letters let us glimpse into their affairs and personalities. Thomas in particular was a warm friend of the morose and withdrawn Smith, often commenting on the latter's behavior and encouraging visits. These voices may be heard within the context of Smith's growing success in New York City and State.

The careers of Abraham Herring, a grown man in 1776 (a Patriot forced to flee New York City), and of Smith, a boy during the war, were almost entirely made in the new republic. Independence released great energies in New York State. New transportation technology, which made intensive use of natural harbor and river systems, was rapidly and eagerly exploited. This in turn had hastened European-style settlement in the former Indian lands, which had been reorganized into lots for speculative sale. The Herrings were not "new men"—they had a family background in commerce from colonial times—but they were individuals who seized and realized the opportunities opening up before them with results unprecedented in the family history—including wealth for Abraham and a dizzying fall for his son, Thomas, who after prosperous beginnings became bankrupt and, in quiet later years, dependent on his father. We see in this family both the successes and failures that accompany a proclivity for risk taking.

Trade on the Hudson-Mohawk Rivers was "a barometer of local, state and national growth," David Maldwyn Ellis has written. "To the Hudson River landings in colonial days came the wheat, flour, potash, and barreled

---

1. M. M. Bagg, *The Pioneers of Utica* (Utica, N.Y.: Curtiss and Childs, 1877), 17. Peter Smith (1768–1837) was born near Tappan, N.Y., son of Gerrit P. and Wyntje (Lent) Smith. He married Elizabeth Livingston in 1792, by whom he had six children. The most prominent of his children was the abolitionist Gerrit Smith (1797–1874). *ANB*, s.v. "Smith, Peter." See also Florence Van Rensssalaer, *The Livingston Family in America and Its Scottish Origins*, arranged by William Beer (New York: privately printed, 1949), 313.

2. *Peter Smith Papers, 1767–1851*, microfilm, reels 1–2, NYPL (hereafter cited as PSP). Smith's original papers are at the Special Collections Research Branch of the Syracuse Univ. Library. See also *Guide to the Microfilm Edition of the Peter Smith Papers, 1763–1850* (Glen Rock, N.J.: Microfilming Corporation of America, 1974). The correspondence from the Herrings is among the largest in the archive: there are 125 letters from Thomas in the collection, 22 from Abraham, and 13 from his eldest son, Elbert. Extensive portions of the correspondence are illegible due to the poor condition of the original documents.

meats of the farms fronting the river. After the Revolution wagons and later canal boats laden with cereals and lumber brought through the Mohawk gateway the products of central and western New York."[3] Between 1790 and 1807 foreign trade made startling gains as wars in Europe caused its nations to buy grains from abroad. America was "Britain's bread basket." In 1791 the value of U.S. exports was $19 million. Ten years later it was $94.11 million, and in 1807 it rose to $105.35 million. Much of this came from New York State. The competition was so intense to purchase grain that "runners went to Albany to outbid local merchants."[4]

In 1800 John Maude, an English traveler curious to learn about the prosperity in Albany and to the west, visited Alexander and James Kane, traders in the Mohawk Valley, and like Abraham Herring, correspondents of Peter Smith. He was astonished by the profits they had made over the fall and winter. They told him that

> Thirty-four thousand bushels of Wheat, which were bought on average at one dollar and fifty cents per bushel, fifty-one thousand dollars, [were] sold at New York for one dollar and ninety-three and three quarters cents, sixty-five thousand eight hundred and seventy five dollars. They took also, in Potash two thousand five hundred barrels, worth on average, twenty-five dollars per barrel, sixty-two thousand five hundred dollars. So that in these two ready money articles alone, they turned over upwards of one hundred and twenty thousand dollars [equivalent to about $1.666 million today].[5]

Such profits were also to be had in the family. Seven years later Abraham's son Thomas in New York expected to turn $10,000 in April to $300,000 by the autumn, in part from his Mohawk Valley accounts.[6]

---

3. David Maldwyn Ellis, *Landlords and Farmers in the Hudson-Mohawk Region, 1790–1850* (Ithaca, N.Y.: Cornell Univ. Press, 1946), 1.

4. Ibid., 77–78.

5. John Maude, *Visit to the Falls of Niagara in 1800* (London: Longman, Rees, Orme, Brown, and Green, 1826), 30, entry of 3 July 1800. A "Lieut. Kip" had been one of the passengers with Maude on the sloop from New York City to Albany, headed for Utica. This is almost certainly James S. Ibid., 3–4, entry of 21 June 1800.

6. "My [   ] sales in April are $10,000 & by close of the year with life & health & peace will probably make $300,000 [   ], a small portion of this sum travels the Mohawk, my trade of late has taken another direction . . ." Thomas Herring, in New York City, to Peter Smith, in Peterboro, 8 Sept. 1807, PSP, reel 1.

Washington saw the potential of the Mohawk Valley as a trade and emigration route west when, in July 1783, with Governor George Clinton and Alexander Hamilton, he spent nineteen days on horseback along the river west of Albany. The tour impressed him "with the possibility of using the Mohawk Valley as the approach to the great uncharted and uninhabited interior of the continent."[7] Opening up a safe water route west attracted the energies of Philip Schuyler, the Revolutionary War general, and others in the new state. The "natural focus of Albany policymakers throughout much of the early history of the state was to gain control of access routes to transportation," a key part of which was the area in and around Old Fort Schuyler, later called the "Gateway to the West."

There were few white men west of the Mohawk when Washington made his visit. The Indians were much reduced as a result of the flight of many west and to Canada after the Revolution—in 1792 only 720 Oneidas lived in their homelands north of Old Fort Schuyler. In the view of Christopher Colles, an early promoter of the water connection that became the Erie Canal, Indian lands were "waste and unappropriated lands," ready for development.[8] By force and guile the state eased the way for purchasers and developers such as Peter Smith and James S. Kip. Investors and speculators re-shaped the land to serve the purposes of a culture of "development." It was organized it into lots for private ownership and connected to the Hudson Valley and the Atlantic by roads and canals.

By the late 1790s Durham boats began to replace the bateaux that had been used on the Mohawk and lakes for decades. The Durhams were "heavy-duty transport vessel[s] patterned (and named) after the earlier Pennsylvania ore boats used by George Washington in 1776 to cross the Delaware to attack Trenton." They would be used extensively in the course of Samuel's service on Lake Ontario in 1813. At sixty feet, the Durham was twice as long as the bateau and had many times the capacity—about twenty tons of cargo versus the one and a half of a bateau.[9] In shape it was "not unlike a canal scow, being low and open, fitted with a walking board along the gunwale, and with a mast that could be raised when required."[10] In these vessels farmers and traders in new settlements

---

7. T. Wood Clarke, *Utica for a Century and a Half* (Utica, N.Y.: Widtman Press, 1952), 14.

8. Ibid., 11.

9. "Heading West: 200 Years Ago: Inland Navigation in the 1790s," brochure with maps (Albany: New York State Library, ca. 1992).

10. Durham boats on the Mohawk. As depicted in Christian Schultz, *Travels on an Inland Voyage* (1810).

in the west could ship grain in bulk. The Durhams meant more business in Albany and New York, more shipping on the Hudson, more clerks, warehousemen, grocers, and merchants.

Passage was improved on the Mohawk in 1796 when the Western Inland Lock Navigation Company, formed by private investors headed by Philip Schuyler of Albany, deepened the channel of the river and built a canal with locks at Little Falls, making conveyance of the larger boats possible.[11] The mile-long canal around the falls was, according to a recent business history, "perhaps the most important mile long water way ever constructed . . . now the back country serving New York directly by water became larger than that supplying Philadelphia." This led to New York's future dominance over other eastern seaboard ports.[12]

At Albany grains from Durham boats were transferred to sloops for the journey downriver, and westward-bound emigrants outfitted themselves and signed on passage. In 1800 John Maude counted forty-five sloops based in Albany and an equal number in New York City handling

---

10. Bagg, *Pioneers of Utica*, 21. The boats were propelled "by means of long poles thrust into the river and pushed from the shoulders of men, who walked from end to end of the boat." There were five or six hands to a boat and they "considered themselves fortunate when they made ten miles in one day, but were often half a day in proceeding only a few rods."

11. Clarke, *Utica*, 14.

12. Thomas B. Cochran, "An Analytical View of Early American Business," in Joseph R. Frese, S. J., and Jacob Judd, eds., *Business Enterprises in Early New York* (Tarrytown, N.Y.: Sleepy Hollow Press, 1977), 11.

freight and passengers on the river. "Albany," he predicted, "will probably increase and flourish beyond any other City or Town in the United States."[13]

Traders and Entrepreneurs

The other crucial ingredient for rapid development was the trader-entrepreneur. Old Fort Schuyler was located in a low and swampy place where travelers forded the Mohawk. Ballou's Creek flowed into the river at that point, forming a lagoon, which was useful for mooring boats. It was a resting place on the journey and a transfer point for those going on by land along the Genesee Trail.[14] The settlement remained essentially a landing and fording place until the road to the west was improved in the mid-1790s, but Peter Smith saw its potential as a trading spot.[15]

11. Peter Smith

Peter Smith Papers,
Special Collections Research Center,
Syracuse University Library

Smith was born near Tappan, near the Haring country cousins, and in his early teens he came to the city as an apprentice to Abraham Herring, then importing upcountry grains to the city and shipping dry goods north. After a brief apprenticeship, Smith went off on his own for a few years, selling "books and library provisions, canes and snuff boxes," and, because of his interest in acting, theatrical materials, which he soon ceased to sell due to religious scruples. He was a man of internal conflicts and, later, morbid self-scrutiny, qualities exposed in letters he received from Thomas Herring.[16]

---

13. Maude, *Visit to the Falls of Niagara,* 17–18.

14. The fort was termed "Old" to distinguish it from Fort Schuyler, at what would become Rome, upstream and the last navigable point on the river, which was named for Colonel Peter Schuyler, father of Revolutionary War general, Philip Schuyler. By the end of the Revolution that fort had been renamed Fort Stanwix.

15. Bagg, *Pioneers of Utica,* 5–7.

16. *ANB,* s.v. "Smith, Peter."

Smith early sought a larger field for his ambitions, and in 1788, at the age of twenty, no doubt inspired by what he had learned from Abraham's interests in the region, opened a trading post at Little Falls. This location was well chosen, since traffic had to slow at that point—crew, passengers, and freight had to be portaged for a mile or so around the falls, and Indian traders from the north gathered there to sell furs.[17] John Jacob Astor (1763–1847), a recent immigrant from Germany and then at the start of his legendary business career, met Smith at Little Falls while cultivating sources for the furs he sold in the city and abroad. Astor, only five years Smith's elder, saw that he had kindred trading interests and made him his agent. Seeing a better opportunity to establish himself at a new settlement, Smith moved in 1789 to Old Fort Schuyler, which was barely inhabited at that point. He built a log house and set up a trading post with supplies for the fur trade.[18]

Smith and Abraham Herring remained in close touch. In a letter of 1793 (sent with an "Indian chief"), Abraham reported that Astor had just been to call and sent Smith the wishes that reflect the personal warmth that characterized his and his son's twenty-seven-year correspondence: "Mrs. Herring joins in compliments to you and Mrs. we expect her with you when you come down."[19] Over the coming years the Herrings would be frequently in the north on business, and they and their wives exchanged visits with the Smith family.

Astor and Smith had "ardent youth and boundless energy," as Smith's son later recalled. He described them as journeying "on foot from Schenectady to Old Fort Schuyler with their packs on their back, stopping here and there to pick up furs at the Indian settlements along the way."[20] Smith had an agreement in which he provided Astor with a dependable source of furs, and Astor supplied trade goods and marketed the furs, an

---

17. Gerrit Smith to W. B. Astor, 26 May 1843, quoted in Kenneth Wiggins Porter, *John Jacob Astor, Business Man*, 2 vols. (Cambridge: Harvard Univ. Press, 1931), 1:37.

18. John Denis Haeger, *John Jacob Astor: Business and Finance in the Early Republic* (Detroit: Wayne State Univ. Press, Great Lakes Books, 1991), 50.

19. Abraham Herring, in New York City, to Smith, 4 March 1793, PSP, reel 1.

20. Bagg, *Pioneers of Utica*, 18; Gerrit Smith to W. B. Astor, 26 May 1843, Haeger, *John Jacob Astor*, 37; Porter, *John Jacob Astor*, 1:37

arrangement which continued for many years.[21] Astor is reputed to have sold furs in Europe at a 1,000 percent mark-up.[22]

When the fur trade declined in the mid-1790s, Smith began to speculate in land. In 1794, with Astor and William Laight, Smith bought what was known as the Charlotte River and Byrnes Patents in the Mohawk Valley, lands formerly owned by Sir William Johnson (1715–74).[23] These patents were not without certain legal entanglements, and Smith and his co-owners had to lobby state officials with their interest. Here too there was a link to Abraham Herring in New York, who reported that he had met the "old Governor" (George Clinton) and told him "you [Smith] should not be cheated by those who came forward for the title" He dispatched his lawyer son, Elbert, to file a formal notice on his friend's behalf.[24]

While the purchase of the former Johnson lands presented some difficulties, other acquisitions were uncomplicated by conflicting claims, and Smith "acquired a large fortune over the years by shrewd procedures in land transactions, both with Astor and alone, handling over the years about 500,000 acres altogether."[25] By subdividing these tracts and offering lots for sale to individuals of modest means this activity—albeit conducted by a wealthy elite—contributed to the democratization of land use in New York State in the post-Revolutionary years.[26]

The description of Smith's appearance by M. M. Bagg, whether he was writing from someone's recollection or to add color to his proud centennial narrative, seems apt. He was "[e]xcessively plain in his dress and equipage and frugal in all his ways." Along with that "keen and penetrating"

---

21. Haeger, *John Jacob Astor*, 51.

22. *ANB*, s.v. "Smith, Peter."

23. Johnson was the Crown's agent in western New York and its representative to the Iroquois. After the Revolution, the state confiscated the lands from Johnson's Tory heirs and made them available for purchase in large tracts. Unbeknownst to Smith and his colleagues, however, Johnson had given "rights" to the land to a number of individuals, and when they emerged with competing claims, no land could be sold until the matter was resolved by the legislature in 1802. Ibid.

24. A. Herring, in New York, to Smith, in Old Fort Schuyler, 28 April 1797, PSP, reel 1. Clinton had left the office in April 1795; he was succeeded by John Jay. Clinton would be re-elected again and serve April 1801–April 1804.

25. Biographical note, *Microfilm Guide to the Peter Smith Papers*.

26. Ellis, *Landlords and Tenants*, 45.

hawk eye, he is said to have been short and stout, with a curved nose.[27] According to one biographer, Smith "from the outset demonstrated respect for the Indians"—and became fluent in their language. On one occasion he addressed the Oneida nation in its native tongue. Another view could be that he took advantage of them. To circumvent a law that prohibited the purchase of lands from the Indians at the time, he negotiated a lease of 999 years with the Oneidas and named the village where he later built a house Peterboro and the township Smithfield, both, of course, for himself.[28] With the Oneida lands in the hands of European-minded developers, the east-west transportation route used by those heading west was secure. Old Fort Schuyler, where Smith had his store and house until the early 1800s, became the key transfer point between the water route and the Genesee Turnpike west.[29]

Thomas Herring knew where Smith's acquisitive passion lay: "Land, Land is your hobby, an acre of land will weigh as much as two dollars of Dry Goods," was his apt characterization of his friend's interest.[30] Smith made a fortune and gave away large sums to religious causes in the 1820s. He left an estate of $400,000 (equivalent to about $5.6 million today) and large tracts of land to his son, Gerrit Smith (1797–1874), who used his profits to sponsor abolitionist causes, including John Brown's raid.[31]

The other early settler at Old Fort Schuyler closely connected to the Herrings was James S. Kip (New York, 1766–Utica, 1831), Abraham's nephew. Though he played a smaller role in the region than Smith, he was also an entrepreneur who made the most of opportunities he perceived in and around the settlement. In 1794, at the age of twenty-eight, he arrived at Old Fort Schuyler to stay with Peter Smith. In early November news

---

27. Bagg, *Pioneers of Utica*, 17.

28. *ANB*, s.v. "Smith, Peter."

29. "The lease included Augusta in Oneida Co. and the towns of Stockbridge, Smithfield, Fenner, and northern Cazenovia in Madison County. Smith named his first son Peter Schenandoah after his alleged 'friend.' The 1795 state treaty with the Oneidas allowed for the purchase of Smith's leased tract. In the end Smith later paid the state to obtain title to 22,300 acres of these 'former Oneida land.'" Laurence M. Hauptman, *Conspiracy of Interests: Iroquois Dispossession and the Rise of New York State* (Syracuse, N.Y.: Syracuse Univ. Press, 1999), 45; see also 32.

30. T. Herring, in New York, to Smith, in Peterboro 8 Sept. 1807, PSP, reel 1.

31. *DAB*, s.v. "Smith, Gerrit."

came to Abraham that James was severely ill. Fearing the worst, Abraham wrote Smith, requesting that he assist James's brother John (Johannes) should the former die. James recovered, however, and later took over Smith's house when the latter moved up market.[32]

Within days of James's arrival in what later became the commercial center of Utica, he bought four hundred acres, sold a portion to buy another lot, which included the site of the old fort, and there built a small store and established a landing on the river.[33] According to Bagg, from there he "strove to divert commerce from Mr. Post and other rivals, who were located a little higher on the stream." He also built a potashery and was "a considerable manufacturer."[34] In his early days he was in partnership with Abraham Herring.[35] It was not as easy a business relationship as the Herrings had with Smith—"I will thank you to speak to J. Kip and get him to assert himself for me," Abraham wrote Smith before the partnership dissolved.[36] Six years later Thomas Herring expressed his annoyance that Kip was not paying interest on funds owed to the Herrings.[37] Thomas evidently found his cousin a spendthrift. When James was in New York at the Kip mansion after his father's death, Thomas confided to Smith, "The

32. A. Herring, in New York, to Smith, 14 Nov. 1794, PSP, reel 1. James S. (the middle initial probably for Samuel) was the son of Ann Herring and Samuel Kip, who had spent the war years in Tappan and after the British evacuation resided in the family mansion at Kip's Bay, which Samuel Kip had inherited. Frederic Ellsworth Kip and Margarita Lansing Hawley, *History of the Kip Family in America* (Montclair, N.J.: privately printed, 1928), 408; Bagg, *Pioneers of Utica*, 34–35; Clarke, *Utica*, 15, 17.

33. The original European purchasers of the lands that included Old Fort Schuyler in 1772 were Philip Schuyler, Gen. John Bradstreet, Rutger Bleecker, and John Morin Scott; it was surveyed in 1786. Bagg, *Pioneers of Utica*, 3; Kip's first purchase was lot 96 from the Bradstreet heirs, "In the center of what is now the city of Utica." He sold a fraction of that and bought lot 93. Ibid., 34, Clarke, *Utica*, 29.

34. Bagg, *Pioneers of Utica*, 34. The original store was at "the eastern end of Main Street [within the original four hundred acre purchase] . . . and embraces at this day a very valuable portion of the city, extending from a few feet east of Broadway, to a little west of the line of Cornelia Street, and extending back from the river some three miles." The account is in Kip and Hawley, *Kip Family*, 408, appears to be based entirely on Bagg.

35. Notice of dissolution of partnerships between James S. Kip and Abraham Herring, [Albany] *Centinel*, 27 Feb.–13 April 1798.

36. A. Herring, in New York, to Smith, in Old Fort Schuyler, 11 Sept. 1797, PSP, reel 1.

37. T. Herring, in New York, to Smith, in Utica, 17 Oct. 1803, PSP, reel 1.

major [Kip] is still here, says he cannot get [funds] to carry him home. I asked him how much he wanted. He replied $2000. What in the name of heaven do you want so much for, I asked. Why Eliza wants nearly $1000 for family uses."[38] However, the Herrings kept in close touch with him and reported news, visits to New York, deaths in the family, and sales of Kip land in Manhattan.

When the Genesee Road was opened up in 1797, Old Fort Schuyler was in "the same relation to Western and Northern New York that St. Louis held to California at the time of the gold rush in 1849. It was here that land-hungry emigrants, disembarking from the Durham boats, procured their Conestoga wagons and loaded them with supplies, to start on the original trek west."[39] The settlement was incorporated in 1798 as Utica, named for the ancient Carthaginian port city, another witness to classical pretensions in central New York. In the new century it became a boomtown, with its population tripling between 1800 and 1810.[40]

As he grew older, Kip was "ambitious to shine in other spheres," and he sought recognition in militia service, becoming Major Kip. Bagg wrote that "Sheriff [an office to which he was elected in 1804] or Major Kip as he was indifferently called, was portly in person, somewhat pock-marked, and wore glasses."[41] In a sign of the maturing of the local economy, Kip became the first president of the newly created Utica Bank (1811). In politics he was a "warm partisan," and Bagg relates a story in which Kip attacked an election rival by waving a cowhide to force him to dismount his horse. The two fought with their fists so severely that the opponent had to draw the blood from the bruises with a beefsteak. There was justice, however, as Kip lost the election. Kip was a "generous liver and bountiful provider and 'given to hospitality'" (which may well be the centennial historian's polite way of saying he was a heavy drinker). In 1812, as a presidential elector, he cast his vote for De Witt Clinton in the election won by James Madison.[42]

---

38. T. Herring, in New York, to Smith, in Utica, Oct. 1804, PSP, reel 1.

39. Clarke, *Utica*, 17, 22.

40. Ellis, *Landlords and Farmers*, 81.

41. Jacob Judd, ed., *Correspondence of the Van Courtlandt Family of Courtlandt Manor, 1800–1814* (Tarrytown, N.Y.: Sleepy Hollow Restorations, 1978), 575; Kip and Hawley, *Kip Family*, 408–11.

42. Bagg, *Pioneers of Utica*, 35–36. The vote for Clinton is noted in *Correspondence of the Van Courtlandt Family*, 575; Kip and Hawley, *Kip Family*, 408–11.

Kip outsmarted himself as the Erie Canal was being built:

> When the canal was constructed, Mr. Kip was anxious to save his garden and
> grounds. Accordingly, he induced the commissioners to run the line where
> they did, instead of south of the building as they had intended to do. The con-
> sequence was, that, they were forced to bring the channel so close to the rear
> of his house as to greatly injure its beauty and value, and to interfere with its
> comfortable use, by the intrusion of water into the cellar. Thus the plan of
> being made richer by the canal, as he probably would have been, had the orig-
> inal been adhered to, [had the contrary effect and] he was severely damaged.
> This circumstance tended to discourage and embitter Mr. Kip, but did not, as
> some have thought, lead to his removal from the place . . .[43]

James S. Kip died in Utica in 1831, at the house of his son-in-law.[44]

Neither Kip nor Smith seemed to enjoy the fruits of their efforts in creating a new community or accumulating personal wealth. In later years
Kip was bitter and litigious. His first wife died in 1811, and Bagg comments cryptically that a second marriage "was not so fortunate."[45] After
making his fortune, Peter Smith became "concerned about the state of his
soul, and after the death of his first wife, his religious concerns mounted to
a near obsession." He had been a man of personal as well as religious
peculiarities for much of his life. Now in his later life, in spite of his financial successes, he grew morose, claiming that he was "trouble to himself
and a vexation to those about him."[46]

The Herrings were early aware of Smith's tendency to harshness.
When Smith's daughter, Cornelia, suffered a nervous collapse in Newark,
where she had been sent to school, Thomas was summoned to assist her.
He wrote her father frankly that "as her mind is very strong & improved
for a girl of her age though at the time very irritable & her feelings are
extra sensible—I presume she has been worried by the manner of your
[ ] which at times has been harsh and apparently without affection." He
added to the rebuke—from which the friendship survived for another

---

43. Bagg, *Pioneers of Utica*, 36–37.

44. Kip and Hawley, *Kip Family*, 411.

45. Bagg, *Pioneers of Utica*, 37.

46. Biographical note, *Microfilm Guide to the PSP; ANB*, s.v. "Smith, Peter."

twenty years—"You must pardon my frankness."[47] He later urged Smith to visit his family (with whom Cornelia was then living). "To visit us in New York," he wrote, in a manner suggesting he had a tough case to deal with,

> might appear like persecution but I cannot think that you would find such a visit otherwise than agreeable for you have frequently regretted that no society in which you found yourself was knit together with divine friendship. Come hither and make a proof of its efficacy. At any rate, this [conjunction?] of circumstances & the wishes of our families conspire in demanding the residence of your Cornelia among us. In our family she will learn nothing but patience, economy and virtue—Postpone this business no longer. The period of Childhood is the loveliest period of initiation.[48]

Thomas's letter reveals the warmth and sentiment of the Herring family circle as much as it reflects Smith's peculiarities.

Washington warned the citizens of the new nation, with its ample and productive lands, rational system of government, and "unbounded extension of Commerce," that if they "should not be completely free and happy, the fault will be entirely their own."[49] The admonition may as well been aimed at Smith and Kip, men who had gained worldly goods from the bounty of the continent but ended their lives dissatisfied and angry.

---

47. Thomas had received "a line from Mrs. Woodbridge at Newark . . . begging me to visit her immediately. . . . To remove your anxiety however before I go on in a recital of her malady I would have you understand that she is at our house at present well & apparently as collected as ever—When I arrived at Newark the family in which she was domesticated told me that three days before she suddenly complained of a lightness & pain in the head; & imputed it to her sitting in a room where was a close stove highly heated. Mrs Woodbridge hearing of her ailing went up into her bedroom to enquire into her illness that suitable remedies might be applied, but was quite impressed at Cornelia's manner and addressing her. Her eyes seemed wild, her language incoherent & her manner expressing, while at the same time there was little or no fever and no general symptoms of illness . . ." Cornelia came to live in the Herring household, and later letters report her improved condition. T. Herring, in New York, to Smith, in Utica, 3 April 1800, PSP, reel 1. Cornelia Smith later married Capt. John Cochrane, M.D. *The Livingston Family in America*, 313.

48. T. Herring, in New York, to Smith, in Utica, 18 May 1802, PSP, reel 1.

49. Washington, "Circular to the States," Head Quarters, Newburgh, 8 June 1783, *The Writings of George Washington from the Original Manuscript Sources, 1745–1799*, ed. John C. Fitzpatrick, Jan. 1, 1783–June 10, 1783 (Washington, D.C.: GPO, 1938), 26:485–86.

Abraham Herring, Merchant

In September 1776, when the British occupied New York, Abraham Herring, the inspiration to these pioneers of Utica and an example to young Samuel, was twenty-one and already in business. He and his sisters were heir to their father's considerable estate, which consisted mainly of Manhattan lands. It had not been distributed in the three years between Elbert's death and the British invasion, perhaps because several children were still minors. It was to remain in limbo until after the British evacuation.

Abraham left the city when the British arrived in September 1776 to find refuge in Stratford, Connecticut—unlike his Kip, De Peyster, and Gardner Jones in-laws who gathered in Tappan.[50] In that same month, according to a family record, he married there Elizabeth Ivers, and it may be that it was because of her and her father, Thomas Ivers, that he had gone to Stratford. We know from the records of Christ Episcopal Church, Stratford—one of the earliest-established Anglican churches in colonial Connecticut—that two children born to Thomas and Hannah Ivers, younger than Elizabeth, were baptized there in the 1760s.[51] While we do not know what Thomas Ivers was doing in Stratford, in New York City after the Revolution he established a rope works at Corlears Hook on the East River,[52] suggesting that he had been familiar with supplying the needs of ships, which he could have done before the war in Connecticut. Abraham, later a trader and merchant, may have met him and his family under such circumstances early in his career. Thomas Ivers was strongly attached to the patriot cause, as evidenced by his election to the Common Council of New York City immediately after the evacuation. Shortly thereafter he was awarded confiscated Tory lands in the city.[53]

According to the family record, the Herring-Ivers marriage was solemnized by the then rector of Christ Church—the Ivers family church—on

---

50. See "Haring-Herring," Genealogical and Biographical Notes. The marriage of Abraham Herring to Elizabeth Ivers in Stratford and the birth of three sons there are evidenced by a family record of uncertain origin.

51. The records of the Rev. Mr. Edward Winslow list baptisms of children of Thomas and Hannah Ivers in Stratford, Anne, in 1761 and Thomas in 1763. Christ Church, Stratford, Records, 1:72. Personal communication from Mary Lawrence, church historian, 2 Jan. 2003.

52. *New York City Directory* (1792). William Ivers, possibly a brother, is also listed as a rope maker at the site.

8 September 1776.[54] In later years Abraham and Elizabeth were devoted members of the Reformed Dutch Church into which he had been born, but in the year of the Declaration of Independence, ironically, these two Patriot families were joined by the Rev. Mr. Kneeland, who was soon to be placed under house arrest for his Tory sympathies.[55] The first children of the marriage were born in Stratford—Elbert, named for his paternal grandfather, in 1777, and Thomas, named for his maternal grandfather, and his twin, George, presumably named for Washington, in 1780. Elbert's long life nearly spanned the centenary of the republic; in venerable old age he recalled to visitors the sounds of gun wagons from his early childhood.

At the time of Abraham's move to Connecticut, many in Stratford (which included the boundaries of the later Bridgeport) were actively engaged in the war. The city's coastal location made it a center for privateers and the contraband brought off British-occupied Long Island in "fast rowing boats." In their turn, British and Loyalists raided the Connecticut coastal settlements, most notoriously in 1779, when regulars burned Fairfield and New Haven.[56] It seems likely that Abraham, throughout his life a successful and indefatigable trader, participated in this illicit exchange of goods on the Patriot side.

By 1780, however, Abraham was in great need, as he put it—perhaps with a touch of exaggeration, appropriate for such an appeal—in a memorial to the Connecticut General Assembly, a consequence of "early, sincere, and warm attachment to the American cause." He described his situation, in the third person, as "obliged to quit his habitation and real estate near that city within the enemies lines and ever since resided and is

---

53. Thomas Ivers was made a member of the newly organized New York City Common Council immediately following the British Evacuation and was present at its first meeting on 10 Feb. 1784 and on subsequent meetings through 16 March 1784. MCCNYC, 1:1–2; he was awarded forfeited DeLancey lands in the Out-Ward after the evacuation. *Report of Committee of Forfeiture for the Southern Distinct of the State of New York*, 24 Dec. 1787, in Alexander Clarence Flick, *Loyalism in New York during the American Revolution* (New York: Columbia Univ. Press, 1901), 239.

54. See "Thomas Ivers," Genealogical and Biographical Notes.

55. E. Edwards Beardsley, *The History of the Episcopal Church in Connecticut from the Settlement of the Colony to the Death of Bishop Seabury* (New York: Hurd and Houghton, 1874), 1:317. Kneeland died under arrest in 1777.

56. Samuel Orcutt, *A History of the Old Town of Stratford and the City of Bridgeport Connecticut* (Fairfield: Fairfield County Historical Society, 1886), 1:382, 400.

thereby reduced with his family to indigent and distressed circumstances."
There is credibility in this description in that the selectmen of Stratford
supported him in a petition that accompanied his appeal, "Esteem[ing] him
a Gentleman of Reputation and good Character and Reputation, who as
far as we know, has ever acted the part of a Sincere and warm Friend to the
Liberties and Independence of the Unites States of America." He sought
permission to return to the city to "take up an advantageous and convenient opportunity of disposing of about fifteen hundred pounds worth of
real estate lying within the enemies lines." The selectmen supported his
proposal to the assembly on the basis of his promise to invest the proceeds
from the sale "in such goods as might if imported here be beneficial to
these States as well as to himself in reducing the distresses of his family."
There was one more favor—that he "might be excused from Drafts and
Taxes which he is not able to bear without reducing his family to Absolute
Poverty and Distress."

The committee appointed to deal with the matter approved Abraham's
"request for Importing the Avails of his Estate upon the Conditions &
under the Restrictions & Directions pointed out & under proper Regulations." He was to "invest the avails in clothing for the army under the
direction of Brig Gen. Gold Silleck Silliman."[57] Young Abraham, even in
his "distress," had an appetite for commerce and an ability to persuade
others. He and the family had integrated themselves into the Yankee community, and he had probably proved his bona fides in the privateering
trade. The ingenious deal in which he agreed to use proceeds from the sale
to purchase clothing for the army apparently never took place, however,
as there is no further record in Connecticut and no transfers of the Elbert
Herring lands until after the Revolution.[58]

---

57. Resolution, Oct. Session 1780, Connecticut Assembly, *The Public Records of the State of Connecticut from May 1780 to October 1791, Inclusive*, comp. Charles J. Hoadly (Hartford, 1922), 3:413. Frederick Gregory Mather, *The Refugees of 1776 from Long Island to Connecticut* (Albany, 1913), 671,
930–33.

58. In the same year, Samuel Kip, Abraham's brother-in-law, husband to Ann Herring, also an heir
to the Elbert Herring estate, petitioned Gov. George Clinton to return from Tappan to the family
farm in Manhattan on the grounds that the owner of the house where he was living wanted to re-
possess it and his own infirmity. Petition of Samuel Kip, in Orangetown, to Gov. George Clinton, 27
April 1780, *Clinton Papers*, 5:657. There is no record of what action, if any, the governor took or if
Samuel Kip returned to the family mansion at Kip's Bay before the evacuation.

A reference in a letter from Thomas Jones of West Neck, a fervent Loyalist who fled the country after Yorktown, seems to implicate Abraham Herring as a Patriot raider. Thomas was the cousin of Samuel Jones, who was married to Abraham's sister Cornelia. In December 1782, when it was clear that the British would soon be evacuating Long Island and New York, Thomas, in London, wrote his sister, in West Neck, that he was "Apprehensive that what things left at fort Neck may be in Danger from the rebel Whale Boatmen (especially if Herring should have the place), I have ordered Ed. Stanton to fetch them down to New York and sell them." The connection between "Herring" and "rebel Whale Boatmen" seems to refer to Abraham at Stratford, where many whale boat raids originated. Thomas revealed his antagonism to his cousin and the Harings/Herrings when he urged his sister that "father's will should be in your care as next in line . . . It should be kept in a safe place least [sic] it should fall into the hands of the rebells whose Interest it might be to destroy it," and warned her not to trust the document "with Sam Jones or any of that family. I have particulars and substantial reasons for using this precaution." He explained in a subsequent letter that he feared his being a Loyalist exile would prompt Samuel Jones, an attorney who opposed the Loyalists in the family, to attempt to have his father's will declared invalid.[59]

Abraham and Elizabeth took their first born, Elbert Herring, to be baptized in Tappan a year after his birth. The Rev. Samuel Verbryck presided, as he had for Samuel Haring's baptism. The child's godparents were Samuel Kip, uncle by marriage (father of James S.), and Elizabeth Herring, maternal aunt, wife of John De Peyster. As we have seen, both of their families had taken refuge in Tappan from occupied New York.[60] It cannot have been an easy journey with the baby through the "neutral ground" in Westchester, across the river and to a Tappan disturbed by civil strife. The church of their fathers asserted its strong influence over the family.

---

59. Since "Herring" and "Haring" were often used interchangeably, another possibility is that it referred to John Haring, whose prominence might give him a claim on the Jones estate. However, the reference to whaleboats would seem to connect the reference to Abraham Herring across the Sound in Stratford. Thomas Jones, in London, to Mrs. David Richard Floyd, at West Neck, Long Island, 18 Dec. 1782; second letter, 4 Nov. 1783, Jones Papers, Museum of the City of New York.

60. Elbert Herring was baptized at Tappan on 9 June 1778, with Samuel Kip and Elizabeth Herring as godparents. The record (2529) lists his birth date as 8 July [1777]. *Baptism Record of the Tappan Reformed Church, Tappan, Rockland County, N.Y. 1694–1899*, ed. Arthur C. M. Kelly (Rhinebeck, N.Y.: privately printed, 1998), 121. Samuel Verbryck (1721–84) served as pastor 1750–84. Ibid., 48.

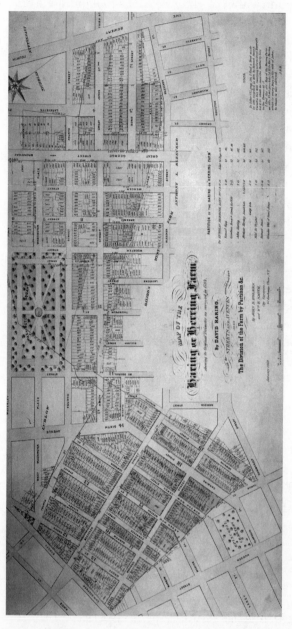

12. Map of the Haring, or Herring, Farm. By David Haring (1784), John B. Holmes, and William V. Smith (1869).

The farm extended from the Bowery eastward to what became Christopher Street near its junction with Hudson Street. Its bounds included part of what became Washington Square, in the center. Elbert Herring's heirs who received portions of the property were his sons Nicholas and Abraham, sons-in-law Samuel Jones and Gardner Jones, Samuel Kip, and John Haring. The properties were later divided and incorporated into the 1811 street grid of the city.

E. Haring Chandor, New York City

78

When Abraham Herring returned to the city, the first order of business was to settle the 1773 estate of his father. The Elbert Herring farm extended from the Bowery, near the junctions of present-day Great Jones and Cornelia Street—named for Samuel Jones and Cornelia Herring, his brother-in-law and wife, respectively—across Washington Square Park, to Christopher Street. On 13 April 1784—just five months after the evacuation—the executors sold the entire farm in the Bowery, about a hundred acres, to Abraham Herring for £7,515 (equivalent to about $841,000 today). In the next month the lots were distributed to the eight heirs.[61] Abraham's share was two lots worth £800, one of which he shortly sold.[62] For Abraham, amicable division of the property meant good relations with his sisters and their Haring, Kip, De Peyster, and two (unrelated) Jones husbands, each of whom became prominent people in the city and state. (Samuel Jones later became the first controller of the state, Gardner Jones a leading physician in post-Revolutionary New York.) Somehow during his years as a refugee, Abraham had come into money; one can speculate that it had to do with privaterring and trade across the Sound, but there is no record. The money established him in business of the reviving port city, with his father-in-law Thomas Ivers, and his Kip, Gardner Jones, and de Peyster in-laws very much a part of the society created by the victorious Patriots.

Abraham was listed in the first city directory in 1789 at 42 Water Street, by the East River piers, with his occupation listed as "flore"—he was trading in flour, just as his father had as a youth, probably purchasing grain and flour upriver and selling it in the city. In the 1790 census his household (the counting house comprising the offices and a domestic establishment) included three slaves, a large number for a young city man. There were

---

61. In a draft typescript apparently intended for later publication, Budke, BC-58, provided a detailed account of the initial 1784 division of the Elbert Herring estate based on his examination of the conveyances, citing New York City conveyance Lib. 41:193, 41:149, 42:199, 46:401, 41:367, 42:03, 48:98, 49:145, and 64:263. His typescript includes citations of the heirs' later disposition of their lots. The executors of the Elbert Herring estate were his wife, Elisabeth, son Nicholas, son-in-law Samuel Jones, and brother-in-law Petrus Bogert, and by codicil, sons-in-law John De Peyster Jr. and John Haring (*Abstracts of Wills N.Y. Co.*, 29:27; N.Y. Co. Surrogates Court, New York, N.Y., 8:151–53). The will of Elizabeth Herring was proved on 30 June 1787 (*Abstracts of Wills N.Y. Co.*, 4:40–41; N.Y. Co. Surrogates Court, New York, N.Y., 40:19).

62. The original vellum of Samuel Kip's release of his claim to his brother-in-law, Abraham Herring, is in New York City Deeds, 1784, NYHS.

twelve in the household for the slaves to serve (three males over sixteen, four under sixteen, and five females). Apprentices may account for the two older men beside Abraham in the household.[63] He was denoted in the 1791 directory by the prestigious denotation "mer" (merchant).

By 1798 his counting house was at 192 Pearl, in the heart of the mercantile community, and he was in the "Dry Goods trade," meaning manufactured goods of all descriptions and grains. The Herring trade by then reached across the Atlantic. "I have rec^d letters from Thomas in London from whom I have rec^d a firm apportionment of goods," Abraham reported in 1797, requesting Smith to send a note "by the first opportunity. . . I am in great want of cash to remit my Son in London as he has given Bills for the Goods sent out and which he must receive from me or else."[64] Two months later he mentioned the value of the goods that Thomas had bought. "Bills to amount to 9000.00 or 10,000 [about $126,000–$130,000 today] for which I have to pay by the 1st July therefore after all the cash you can spare [   ] will be very acceptable. I know you will from former experiences do all you can for me." As always he adds a personal note, "I expect to see you at my house sometime this summer, but as to business, rather dull but cash state do. [the same]."[65] The process of international trade—which still depended on balancing accounts between traders—brought forth another anxious letter to Smith:

> On 9th Instant I rec^d a letter from Son Thos in London in the greatest distress owing to my Bills just then being [   ] Protested and begging of me on receipt his to remitt him £4000. . . .[   ] to keep him from prison. I must [   ] beg of you to do all you can for me on your own [   ] and by all means if you are able to procure what is due me from A & Condry neither of which have paid me a Shilling.[66]

All worked out well, and Thomas was home in May 1798, with news from a Europe riled by the tension between post-Revolutionary France and England, which would limit trade. "I have the pleasure of informing you I am home a few days since from Liverpool after a passage of 40 days," Thomas wrote Smith.

---

63. *Heads of Families at the First Census of the United States Taken in the Year 1790, New York* (Baltimore: Genealogical Publishing Co., 1976).

64. A. Herring, in New York, to Smith, in Old Fort Schuyler, 30 March 1797, PSP, reel 1.

65. A. Herring, in New York, to Smith, in Old Fort Schuyler, 8 May 1797, PSP, reel 1.

66. A. Herring, in New York, to Smith, in Old Fort Schuyler, 11 Sept. 1797, PSP, reel 1.

With respect to political information what we brought has been detailed at length in papers. It was generally believed that [   ] attacks on England, yet all seemed in perfect tranquility. In consequence of the late move of the French Directory insurance had greatly risen & I think few goods will be sent this spring. Papa informed me you had written me.[67]

When in the 1810s the Herrings began to deal in sugar, their business extended from the Mohawk to the West Indies and, in peacetime, to Liverpool.

The Pearl Street address showed that, at forty-three, Abraham was well established. When Thomas joined him in the business, the establishment became Herring & Co., which endured through the early 1800s.[68] In later years Abraham had addresses both in New York City and Albany. He lived in the latter city in 1798 and 1799, as we know from the baptisms of two of his children in the Albany Reformed Dutch Church. It was in those years that Samuel and Sarah Haring were also in Albany.[69]

Abraham took on some civic responsibilities in the city. On 5 May 1788 the Common Council appointed him to serve as one of the commissioners of the Alms House & Bridewell—another commissioner appointed at the same time was John Stagg, the former officer who had held Abraham's niece, Maria Haring, on the pummel of his horse to watch the execution of André eight years before—surely a topic of reminiscence.[70] The same year he was appointed one of the four managers of the lottery; this was renewed in 1795, and the bond he posted in connection with that position was released on 13 June 1798.[71] He was also appointed inspector of elections for the Second Ward, on 6 April 1802, and, on 16 May 1803, an assessor in connection with improvements being made to Pine Street.[72]

"I purpose associating myself with my Father in Business," Thomas wrote Smith in 1802 (though previous letters had included many matters

---

67. T. Herring, in New York, to Smith, in Old Fort Schuyler, 26 May 1798, PSP, reel 1. On 11 Dec. Abraham Herring reported that his son was again off to England and again appealed for help in getting what was owed him from "Frisbie."

68. New York City directories, 1789–.

69. See "Herring," Genealogical and Biographical Notes.

70. MCCNYC, 1:368. Matters to do with the Alms House brought to the attention of the council by the commissioners in 1790 are found in 1:552, 524.

71. MCCNYC, 1:530, 589; 2:136, 449.

72. MCCNYC, 3:87; 3:282.

in which the son spoke on his father's behalf). He proceeded to provide an illuminating glimpse of how well the business was doing. "Providence has again smiled in our territory—This spring profits add Five Thousand dollars to our Capital."[73] It was a mark of his prosperity that in 1806–8 Abraham could keep a separate residence at 44 Broadway, the most fashionable street in the city. Herring & Co. remained on Pearl Street until 1812 and in later years moved uptown from Pearl to Pine Street, to Wall, to Maiden Lane.[74]

In 1800 Thomas reported to Smith that "[he] was travelling up as you traveled down the Mohawk River,"[75] and later wrote that he would soon return.[76] This travel had a purpose—to dun customers for payment. In 1801 Abraham reported, "Tho[s] left town upwards of a fortnight ago on a collecting trip." (Young Elbert, Thomas's elder brother, termed a similar upriver trip, "a dunning expedition.") "I hope for success as every nerve is now strained by the payments I have made and have to make for 60 to 90 days."[77]

The Herrings frequently visited Utica and Smith's house, "The Castle," at Peterboro. "Our parents and *three sisters*" are at Albany, Thomas once warned Smith, "intending to spend some time at the Castle in Peterboro. Haply this may reach you before the annunciation!"[78] After one visit Thomas confessed that "I cannot wean myself from the attraction for . . . the western country . . . I could pitch my tents for life in Oneida. My friends ridicule this favorite *penchant*." But he concluded that he could not leave the city, "except in the dull times of the year . . . Business survives under my care, dies on my absence." The Herrings had bought property in Utica that they found difficult to sell, and Thomas added "Pray assist us in the disposal of our farm in Utica. What an incalculable benefit it wd be to us!"[79]

---

73. T. Herring, in New York, to Smith, in Utica, 17 July 1802, PSP, reel 1.

74. With his cousin, William G. Jones, son of Gardner Jones and Sarah Herring, "Herring & Jones, merchants & sugar refiners" were sequentially on Pine and Wall Streets and on Maiden Lane from 1813 to 1815. *New York City Directory* (1813).

75. Herring, in New York, to Smith, in Utica, 3 April 1800, PSP, reel 1.

76. Herring, in New York, to Smith, in Utica, 6 May 1800, PSP, reel 1.

77. A. Herring, in New York, to Smith, in Utica, 12 July 1801; Elbert Herring, in New York, to Smith, in Utica, 2 July 1803, PSP:1.

78. T. Herring, in New York, to Smith, in Peterboro, 10 July 1807, PSP, reel 1.

79. T. Herring, in New York, to Smith, in Utica, 7 May 1801, PSP, reel 1.

Thomas Herring's dunning and collecting and Abraham's frequent worries about not having enough cash, were part of merchant life in which goods were bought and sold on good faith, but the credit that made that possible had to be leveraged by a cash reserve. The more cash on hand the larger the purchases on credit, meaning potentially higher profits. Thomas's appeal to Smith to find a buyer for the Utica farm was made in the interest of his father's health. With a sale that would raise $5,000: "[H]is credit would soon make him rich, & his ease of mind restore his health which breaks very fast." (The tonic of cash must have come through in one way or another as Abraham lived for another thirty-six years.)

With cash on hand a merchant could take advantage of any upturn in business. "Business commenced at a very early period this spring and is now at its highest pitch," Thomas reported in 1801. "Nothing but the want of money [cash] could prevent my claiming it for 5000 . . . But I am fairly pledged and my flights interest be but along the ground."[80]

By the 1800s Thomas refers to bank checks being used for payment rather than the traditional reconciling of credits and debits between merchants. The Herrings' relationship with Smith was so close than on occasion Abraham signed a check leaving the amount and payee to be completed by Smith. One blank check was to be completed at Smith's option for "three to four thousand dollars." Such wide discretion reveals noteworthy mutual trust.[81]

In politics the Herrings were Republicans, of the party in New York led by George Clinton, nationally by Jefferson and in opposition to the Federalists, who had strong support from any similarly well-to-do. Thomas was pleased in April 1801 that Clinton had succeeded the Federalist, John Jay, as governor. "The election of Coll. Clinton welcomed on & it is confidently believed that the whole Republican ticket will be returned for the Assembly—"[82] In a postscript, probably seeking to draw his correspondent out, Thomas referred to "someone" who had asked him "if Peter Smith could be depended on as a Republican! What can this mean? I replied that your Politicks were moderate, and as far as I could discover leaned to the

---

80. T. Herring to Smith, 23 April 1801, PSP, reel 1.

81. T. Herring to Smith, 26 Feb. 1802, PSP, reel 1. This check was to Berent Bleecker of Albany, who twenty-seven years later wrote in support of a war pension for Samuel Haring. Another check was to made out to "Kelley." T. Herring, in New York, to Smith, in Utica, 18 May 1802, PSP, reel 1.

82. T. Herring, in New York, to Smith, in Utica, 23 April 1801, PSP, reel 1.

present Republican interest."[83] The west bank heritage of independence remained strong, even among these men who were "monied elite."

Sally & Plato

It must have been on one of his frequent trips north to visit Smith and on "dunning" expeditions that Thomas Herring met Sarah—"Sally"—Kirkland whom he married on 22 November 1799 at his family's Dutch Reformed Church in New York City.[84] She came from Paris, a town near Utica, in Oneida County, where her father, the Rev. Samuel Kirkland, had lived since before the Revolution carrying out his mission to the Oneida Indians. The family lived in a house ("The Mansion") that remains today, near Hamilton College in Clinton, New York. Thomas and Sally had celebrated their twentieth birthdays during the year.[85] Three days after the marriage young Thomas left for England on business, as Abraham reported to Smith,[86] leaving his new bride in the city. After his return in the spring he charged that "Sally Herring" had broken her matrimonial vows "between the day of the voyage and the return" with "certain company" in the city, and he petitioned the chancery court to dissolve the marriage and that he be "freed from all obligations by a sentence or decree of this honorable court."[87]

---

83. T. Herring, in New York, to Smith, in Utica, 26 Feb. 1802, PSP, reel 1.

84. *Marriages from 1639 to 1801 in the Reformed Dutch Church, New York,* Collections of the New York Genealogical and Biographical Society (New York, 1890 et seq.), 9:277. "On Friday last 22, Thomas Herring to Miss Sally Kirkland of Paris, Oneida County." N.Y. *Spectator,* 28 Nov. 1799. Joseph Gavit, *American Deaths and Marriages—November 1784–1829,* microfilm, NYSL, NYGB. See "Haring-Herring," Genealogical and Biographical Notes.

85. Sarah Kirkland (1779–1848) was the daughter of the Rev. Samuel Kirkland (1744–1808) and his first wife, Jerusha Bingham (1748–88); Elfrieda A. Kraege, *The Kirtland-Kirkland Families: 1600s–1800s, with a Few Twentieth-Century Items* (New York: privately printed, 1979), 92. There is no reference to a marriage to Thomas Herring in this compilation. I am indebted to Hermine Williams, of Clinton, N.Y., for providing me with information on this Kirkland family. Samuel Kirkland trained for the ministry at Eleazar Wheelock's school in Lebanon, Connecitcut, and began his mission to the Oneidas in the mid-1760s. In 1775 he was successful in having the Oneidas declare neutrality in the coming struggle with Britain. He founded the Oneida Academy in 1793, which became Hamilton College in 1812. *DAB,* s.v. "Kirkland, Samuel."

86. A. Herring, in New York, to Smith, in Old Fort Schuyler, 11 Dec. 1799, PSP, reel 1.

87. The petition was prepared by his first cousin, Samuel Jones Jr. *Thomas Herring* vs. *Sally Herring,* filed 2 July 1800, BM 1337, New York Co. Clerk's Office, Division of Old Records, Chancery Court, State of New York.

A commentary to the affair is provided in a letter to the bride, written that May, from her sister, Eliza Kirkland, which Thomas intercepted (and later sent to Smith).[88] Eliza wrote of "Plato," her name for a man both sisters knew who appeared willing to act on Sally's behalf to allow her to separate from her husband. "I sent for Plato and read your letters," Eliza wrote,

—oh sister. What a task for me; he was cruelly divided. He knew not what to say or where to rest. He condemns your acting openly in violation of all laws, but if private revenge you are bent upon—he will eagerly be the medium of your mari's suspicions. You shall have my patronage, and any services included from that ceremony—which you require—I renounce him, yield him to your consuming blushes—but when you return him, let him be as when I gave him—Do not corrupt his morals, or lessen his sensibility—neither cloud his reason on the mists of love, or abate his ardor in friendship; do not pervert his judgment for he thinks well of me—

"Plato" was probably aptly nicknamed, as it seems that the affair between him and Sally was at that point probably more of "intellect" and sensibility than sensual and that it was Sally who sought to press the breach with Thomas into public view. Eliza, too, was drawn to "Plato" and developed a pastoral vision of the three together, showing she had taken Virgil (or derivative fiction) to heart—and also revealing what may have been her own thwarted feelings for him:

I shall never visit Boston unless forcibly dragged thither nor any place save this, unless Plato will take us both to the Appalachian Mountains whither He often says He will go, and if we chuse we may accompany him. Twould be an outrageous affront to all civilized people—but I would not hesitate a moment, and you I believe are not less airy nor less a votary than myself. The Sylvan god would protect us and tho' the bounties of Ares might not be ours, she could not prevent the smiles of Flora from delighting us—the melody of Apollo or any one of the name—we should have to eat, drink, and sleep upon intellect—You and our sage might like it very well—but as for me, I am not so ethereal and with a trembling wasted body I should soon work out my salvation and reel into an another climate.

---

88. Eliza Kirkland, at "Sylvania," to Sarah (Kirkland) Herring, 19 May 1800, enclosed in T. Herring, in New York, to Smith, in Utica, 15 Aug. 1800, PSP: 1 (transcription courtesy of Hermine Williams); Elizabeth Kirkland, 1778–1819. Kraege, *Kirtland-Kirkland Families*, 92.

Who was this "Plato"? He was more than a mutual male friend of the two sisters; it is likely in fact that he was the "certain company" that Thomas had charged alienated Sally's affection while he was away. According to Thomas, in a note he placed on the letter for Smith, "The wretch dignified with the name of Plato is ye Gods! The detestable Kirkpatrick."

Eliza Kirkland's is an astonishing document in the midst of a no less astonishing situation. She reveals a sensibility formed by the romantic movement of late-eighteenth-century England, nourished by Latin poetry and suffused with subjectivity, all a sea change from that family's Puritan-Yankee past. Quite evidently her sister shared these qualities and was likewise drawn to "Plato" by intellect and feeling. Here was Thomas Herring, from a line of solid farmers who could turn a hand at trade and public service and women capable of bearing and tending children over twenty years or more, attached to someone who valued, indeed required, the expression of feelings, admired sensibility, and who dared to express herself by the public act of leaving her husband.

The "Sylvania" from which Eliza writes was the family home in Paris, Oneida County, that, while no longer a pioneer settlement, was only then experiencing an large influx of settlers. The Rev. Kirkland's daughters had the time and means to read. For them the woods were a place for refreshment and contemplation, not a wilderness to be tamed. Little wonder that a woman with such yearnings for emotional and intellectual fulfillment should choose to leave Thomas Herring, with his mercantile ambitions, one who would "abandon" his new bride for a business trip. Such an open break must have been exceedingly rare among families of "station" like the Herrings and Kirklands. (However, as we shall see, Thomas did indeed have a gentle and aesthetic side and could even be given to expressions of sentiment—traits that may have drawn him and Sally together in the first place.) There was no bridging the cultural clash that drove the two apart. It was the new century, with a new sense of female needs and role.

Here is a sharp break in the Haring-Herring family in the otherwise steady progression of typically life-long marriages producing abundant children. The failure of this marriage, unprecedented in the family, must have left a taint on Thomas within the family and among his Dutch Reformed parishioners that can only be imagined. There is not a hint of this or the financial troubles to come in any of the rare published references to Thomas. He never remarried.

The New York chancery court did not act on an annulment of the marriage (and probably could not), and in 1804 Elbert Herring wrote Smith on his brother's behalf to seek his assistance in preparing a petition for divorce from the Supreme Court of Vermont, which he sent to Smith for Sally to sign, presumably amicably. If the Vermont court took action, no record survives.[89] Divorce in this era was exceedingly rare, and in New York it required an act of the legislature, hence the appeal to Vermont.

The story has a happy continuation for Sarah Kirkland, who four years later married a Boston merchant, Francis Amory, by whom she had four children. Sarah died in Milton, Massachusetts, at the age of fifty. Eliza Kirkland married Edward Robinson, later a noted Biblical scholar and archaeologist. She was thirty-nine, he twenty-four. She died in childbirth a year after their marriage.[90]

As for "Plato," he has yet to be identified. There were no individuals with the surname Kirkpatrick in Oneida County in 1800. There was a James A. Kirkpatrick in New York City at the time, though he was a cabinetmaker—an occupation that does not seem likely to have brought him into contact with the Kirkland sisters.

By July 1802 Thomas wrote that there was the prospect of a "treaty" with the Kirklands. "After that event I purpose associating myself with my Father in Business," Times were good, and Thomas could report in his letter, "Providence has again smiled in our territory—This spring profits add Five Thousand dollars to our Capital."[91] The formal business arrangement linking father and son is born out by the listing in the 1802 directory: "Herring & Son, merchants" at 192 Pearl—also Abraham's address and that of "Herring & Co." That listing continued through 1807. By then Thomas had taken over most contacts with Smith and other upstate trading partners from his father. In 1804, for example, he wrote Smith that "[f]rom 1st to 4th of July we have very considerable payment to make [for which he asks for help, and says he will pay him at Utica or at the

---

89. Elbert Herring, in New York, to Smith, in Utica, 28 Nov. 1802, PSP, reel 1. In a personal communication of 15 Sept. 2002, Paul Donovan, law librarian, Supreme Court of Vermont, confirmed the absence of documents relating to the matter in the court record.

90. Kraege, *Kirtland-Kirkland Families*, 92; Jay G. Williams, *The Times and Life of Edward Robinson: Connecticut Yankee in King Solomon's Court* (Atlanta: Society of Biblical Literature, 1999), 73.

91. T. Herring, in New York, to Smith, in Utica, 17 July 1802, PSP, reel 1.

bank at Albany] . . . should the pestilence [Yellow Fever] [strike?] in the present season, I intend to remove with our goods to Albany, as we have a large & good appointment of goods on hand. I recently made a handsome purchase at 8, 10 & 12 months credit."[92]

In February 1807, as he prepared for the business to come, he wrote, "You can make a purchase of wheat & at Utica or anywhere else, the larger the quantity the better, so as not stand more than half? in Albany and agree to pay for the same when delivered in N York."[93] In September of that year he gave the assessment of the gross business done by the firm, quoted earlier, "my sales in April are $10,000 & by close of the year with life & health & peace will probably make $300,000 [   ]. a small portion of this sum travels the Mohawk, my trade of late has taken another direction."[94]

Perhaps because of the embargo, the war, and his own financial difficulties, there is only one letter from Thomas Herring to Peter Smith between 1809 and 1827. In the dark days for the port of New York in September 1814 he wrote that "ills are now felt, and seen; this city has little activity & apart from what arises from military business, even at this period which in past years exhibiting all the life and bustle of a crowded fair, the stores all supplied & prices high . . ."[95]

Thomas by then had serious ills of his own. The risk-taking merchant had miscalculated and ended up bankrupt and in jail, with creditors hounding him, finally to be rescued by Abraham. The times following the peace that concluded the War of 1812, news of which reached a joyous New York in February 1815, were prosperous for New York merchants as trade across the Atlantic opened up again. Thomas Herring, though, was in deep financial trouble. According to the court record, John Beekman and James Beekman, heirs to Abraham K. Beekman, deceased, claimed that "on or about 1 May 1816 Thomas Herring, merchant having occasion for money and having or pretending to be in fee or in some other good and sufficient estate of inheritance" applied to and received a loan of $7,000. A year later Thomas was unable to repay this debt, and the Beekmans sought to claim the property Herring had mortgaged, at 63 William Street, at the

92. T. Herring, in New York, to Smith, in Utica, 6 June 1804, PSP, reel 1.

93. T. Herring, in New York, to Smith, in Utica, 20 Feb. 1807, PSP, reel 1.

94. T. Herring, in New York, to Smith, in Peterboro, 8 Sept. 1807, PSP, reel 1.

95. T. Herring, in New York, to Smith, in Peterboro, 8 Sept. 1814, PSP, reel 1.

13. *Tontine Coffee House.* Painting by Francis Guy (ca. 1797).

The New-York Historical Society

corner of Cedar Street and William. Other creditors included Jonathan
Fish, attorney for the Southern District U.S. Court, in connection with
customs duties due, Andrew Ogden (for $1,033), and John McDonald
($800 and $35.28 for damages). The legal proceedings forced the appearance of Abraham Herring, who would presumably repay sums owed by
Thomas. (In property transactions in 1816 and 1822 Abraham was identified as "of Elizabeth town, State of New Jersey," but by 1818 he was listed
in the New York City directory without reference to the New Jersey
address. It could be that he chose to be out of town during the tangle of
proceedings involving his son, but he did appear in court.)[96] The master
appointed to schedule the repayment of the debts developed a schedule that
involved auctioning the property at the Tontine Coffee House. The process was completed on 4 December 1819; Elbert Herring represented his
brother.[97] The court record amounts to sixty-four pages. A later Vermont

96. Grantors, 124:174, 3 Dec. 1816, 125:84, 9 Dec. 1816, 162:176, 22 July 1822, microfilm, Office of
the City Register, New York Co., New York, N.Y.

97. "Notice of County Judgments, Court of Chancery at Albany, *Edward Elmendorf vs. Thomas
Herring, John M. Donald, and the United States of America*," CL 53:180–84, CL 111:580–643, New
York Co. Clerk's Office, Division of Old Records, Chancery Court, State of New York.

court case states that Thomas Herring was for a time imprisoned for debt until Richard Riker, Recorder for New York City, directed on 5 April 1817 that he be released from prison, assigning his assets to a master to settle the creditors' claims.[98]

Thomas, after this devastating reverse, was no longer listed as a merchant in the directory. He found some employment from the city from 1826 to 1828, when he served as an assessor to establish new assessments for property holders where streets and sidewalks had been paved or repaved and where wells and pumps had been installed. He was one of the (usually three) assessors appointed on no less than twenty-six projects in those years, a list in itself demonstrating the pace of civic improvements at the time. The projects included the repaving of Wall Street, paving of a portion of Water Street, and paving and sidewalks in Greenwich (near the old family farm property). One project was as far north as Twenty-first Street, which in 1827 was paved from Third Avenue to the Hudson.[99] For many years Thomas shared the same address as his father, who had clearly saved him from total ruin.

From 1822, for the fifteen years that remained of his life, Abraham lived at 45 Hudson Street, on the west side of the city, three blocks north of Chambers Street. Broadway was a short walk to the east, and Greenwich Street and the North River piers were close by to the west—indeed, Thomas knew that it was time to send a letter off when he heard the whistle of the steamboat that would take it. It was a kind of Herring family compound, which Abraham renovated in 1827. "Mother and most of the family are with Elbert on a visit to Albany friends," Thomas reported,

> Our house is undergoing alteration repairs, which caused the leaving home in such a [hurry]. Father remained behind [for] supervisions; but purposes despite of Carpenters, Masons and Painters to take steam about the middle of the week after passing a few hours in Albany, to *hurry* to your mansion and spend a day with you. The prospect of this undertaking already puts him in a

---

98. "Chittenden, December 1826, Thomas Herring, defendant below, vs. David Selding, plaintiff below.—IN ERROR," Asa Aikens, *Reports on Cases Argued and Determined in the Supreme Court of the State of Vermont, Prepared and Published in Pursuance of a Statute Law of the State*, vol. 2 (Windsor, Vt.: Simeon Ide, published for the reporter, 1828).

99. MCCNYC 15:271, 340, 341, 402, 426, 283, 548, 511, 683, 597; 16:151, 281, 274, 306, 330, 349, 355, 398, 422, 340, 485, 486, 512, 589; 17:502, 526.

bustle, and his advanced years do not admit regarding it lightly; was it not to see you, he would not go out.[100]

The house was at the edge of Duane Park, established at the end of the eighteenth century, which was beautified when the wooden fence surrounding it during most of the Herring's sojourn, was replaced by "a stone coping surmounted by an iron railing" at a cost to the city of $1,800 in Abraham's late years, an urbanity consistent with Abraham's renovation of the building.[101] Duane Park was (and is) a patch of green in a densely built up part of the city. As usual, Abraham had invested sagely. Elbert and his wife, Agnes Van Rensselaer, lived in the house with his father and mother until he went to Washington in 1830 to take up a post in the Jackson administration. Thomas is listed at the address in some years, and the affection demonstrated in his letters in references to the unmarried sisters, Harriet and Elizabeth, indicate that they were part of the family circle on Hudson Street. Occasionally Thomas refers to them as away visiting, or with the Smiths in the north.

"Our lives are posting away," Thomas Herring wrote to Peter Smith in Peterboro on New Year's Day 1828, with a wish that they might share on this traditional day for visits among Dutch New Yorkers, "Coffee, Poultry, and other excellent fare . . . and the intellectual banquet of friendly social intercourse." Though only in his late fifties, he was feeling his age—that winter he reported suffering from "rheumatism in the head." Though he would live for another 23 years, on that New Year's he was elegiac to his old friend, reflecting, "It behooves early friends to cling to each other, for new ones scarcely know how to sympathise with the way worn pilgrim."[102] There is more than a hint of disappointment and loneliness in this greeting.

In these years, Thomas, whose commercial activity was minimal, supplied Peter Smith with works of art for his Peterboro "Castle." This involved some discrimination and judgment on Herring's part. "I have now found a head of Washington to please you. The best one extant is about 4 inches by [   ] which if richly framed would value more than any I

---

100. T. Herring, in New York, to Smith, in Peterboro, 19 Aug. 1827, PSP, reel 2.

101. Phelps-Stokes, *Iconography*, 5:1729, approved by the mayor, 13 Oct. 1834.

102. T. Herring, in New York, to Smith, in Peterboro, 1 Jan. 1828; T. Herring, in New York, to Smith, in Peterboro, 30 April 1828, PSP, reel 2.

have seen, no matter what size or how expensive."[103] He bought books, a Bible, engravings from Benjamin West depicting "Alexander the Great & his Physician . . . paired with Leonidas before his departure for Thermopolyae."[104] Another engraving was after Rubens, "I think I could buy for $50 . . . [with] gilt frame [and] . . . figures nearly as large as life."[105] The organ in Smith's house needed replacement parts by a New York craftsman, sent north in the care of Elbert. Thomas was unable to locate a Harmonicon that Smith wanted.[106] He did, however, send a cask of good wine and a buffalo robe from Mr. Klein of New Orleans, and a "Blk Veil and Blk Levantine."[107] Concerning a carpet in a "Bale" sent by the boat under the care of one Crittenden, its skipper, Thomas noted, "[T]here is choice in forming the patterns of the Carpet; the large figures must not lie in juxtaposition abreast of each other, but obliquely."[108] Of one of his purchases he assured Smith that he would find it "genteel and respectable." Indeed what these transactions reveal is that Smith was following others in creating a house with a formal parlor that would display both his "breeding" and his wealth. Smith and his Herring friends were living out Washington's 1783 expectation "of the progressive refinements of Manners, the growing liberality of sentiment."[109] But with liberality there is also money to protect. Smith requested of Thomas to find and send up the rivers to Peterboro "an Iron Chest . . . impregnable . . . of German manufacture."[110]

Thomas also purchased shares of stock for Smith. In 1829 he had been to the "Merchants Bank on your Railway Stock errand," showing the astute Smith had anticipated the next great transportation advance just as

103. T. Herring, in New York, to Smith, in Peterboro, 21 Feb. 1827, PSP, reel 2.

104. T. Herring, in New York, to Peter Smith, in Peterboro, April 1827, PSP, reel 2.

105. T. Herring, in New York, to Smith, in Peterboro, 2 May 1827; T. Herring, in New York, to Smith, in Peterboro, 4 Dec. 1830, PSP, reel 2.

106. T. Herring, in New York to Smith, in Peterboro, 11 July 1827; T. Herring, in New York, to Smith, in Peterboro 19 Aug. 1827, PSP, reel 2. Harmonicon in this context may refer to the "grand harmonicon," a type of musical glasses made by Francis Hopkinson Smith, of Baltimore, from 1824.

107. T. Herring, in New York, to Smith, in Peterboro, 20 Oct. 1828; T. Herring, in New York, to Peter Smith, in Peterboro 20 Oct. 1828, PSP, reel 2.

108. T. Herring, in Albany, to Peter Smith, in Peterboro, 24 Oct. 1829, PSP, reel 2.

109. Washington, Circular to the States, Head Quarters, Newburgh, 8 June 1783, op. cit.

110. T. Herring, in New York, to Smith, in Peterboro, 12 Oct. 1830, PSP, reel 2.

he had the earlier water-borne one. From the city Thomas regularly reported prices from auctions of land as well as Elbert's efforts on legal matters and his lobbying of Governor Clinton and others.[111] His warmth towards Smith, his interest in objects of art, and concern for Smith's daughter, Cornelia, shine through the correspondence. His reveals what Washington termed the "growing liberality of sentiment" that came with the increase of wealth and the spatial mobility that this generation enjoyed.

There was leisure for feelings, as Abraham's wife and Thomas's mother expressed in another of the family's letters to Smith, in which they urged him to behave in a more kindly manner to his daughter, just as Thomas had done years before. Returned to the city after a visit to Peterboro and showing she knew her Shakespeare, Elizabeth in her thanks to Smith expressed her pleasure at nature—and she could have communed with Eliza Kirkland in these sylvan glades.

The same scenes presenting themselves before me, of the same persons acting their different parts, on their stage of life—May heaven preserve them, at least those that move in my little sphere, for they are dear to my heart. Memory frequently brings back to me, the calm retirement & almost uninterrupted solitude of Peterboro—sometimes I [walk] through the majestic woods of our forests—and sometimes with my dear companion, Cornelia.

She asked that the young woman spend the winter in the city, "The spring time of life is the season of pleasure—Why let her beauty bloom in vain, or waste her sweetness on the desert air. I am partial to Cornelia. Why then disappoint the hope of a [ ] or chill with denial the rose of expectancy—but I will not be importunate—" On her way home, reminding of the link between her husband's family and the Smiths, the place to which, however run-down it became, these families continued to return, she added, "We saw your parents at Tappan; they were delighted to hear from you."[112]

Abraham went to considerable effort, though doubtless assisted by young Elbert, to complete the final settlement of the Herring farm. There

111.T. Herring, in New York, to Smith, in Peterboro, 5 March 1829, PSP, reel 2.

112. Elizabeth Herring, in New York, to Smith, in Peterboro, March, PSP, reel 2. Thomas Herring had reported Cornelia Smith's breakdown in 1800, when she was in school, probably thirteen or fourteen years old. If she is now a young woman of twenty or more, this would date the letter to about 1806.

had been ways laid out within the property for streets (Great George, Margaret, Amity Lane) whose lines were provided for on the lots. The city had not accepted these ways as streets—in fact Abraham ceded land to the city to allow Fourth Street to be connected from the Bowery to Sixth Avenue, which conformed to the established grid pattern.[113] He gathered signatures on indentures from all the living heirs of his father, Elbert Herring, releasing their claims on the small portions of lots (few or none of which they now owned—he was simply clearing the title), which had been dedicated to the no-longer-extant ways. In 1822, when he entered these on the city property records only he, Sarah (Herring) Jones and Mary (Herring) Haring survived of old Elbert Herring's children; his sisters Cornelia (Herring) Jones and Elizabeth (Herring) De Peyster had died the previous year—the other siblings had gone several years before. In this legal "gathering" the Herring heirs included grandchildren and their spouses. It was a prodigious effort to clean up the property titles, important, apparently, as much for the family as for any practical purpose.[114] It was a last assemblage—on paper at least—of the heirs of Elbert Herring. It would be Elbert Herring, Esq. who would assemble the remains of many of them when, forty years later, the city that had grown up around required the closing of many churches and their burial vaults in lower Manhattan.

Abraham and Elizabeth Herring enjoyed the fruits of his acumen, living in comfort at 45 Hudson and traveling frequently upriver to his "country estate" and Smith's "Castle" at Peterboro. Their family, however, had been devastated in Elizabeth's childbearing years. Between 1792 and 1799 no less than eight unnamed children of Abraham Herring were buried in the Dutch Church, some of whom may be those in the baptismal register but for whom there is no further record. Their only grandchildren were the children of Cornelia, who married her cousin, William G. Jones. Elbert's daughter died young, Thomas had no heirs, and the other daughters did not marry.

Abraham Herring was the great survivor in his generation. At his death in January 1837 the *New York Evening Post* wrote:

---

113. MCCNYC, 15:10.

114. Grantors, 162:3, 5, 6, 8, 9, 11, 13, 15, 18, 20, 21, 23, micro film, Office of the City Register, New York Co.

This morning, M. ABRAHAM HERRING, 82 years. Born on an estate, owned and cultivated before and for a long time afterwards by his father, spreading from the Bowery across Broadway nearly to Hudson street of which Bond Street was the garden plot, and the site of the University, Washington Square and all the adjacent streets were enclosed fields for tillage and pasture. He had lived to see the almost magical changes the city has undergone, and was a most conspicuous representative of the old Dutch stock, its original founders.

To this elegy for a departed world could be added that Abraham was a witness to the Revolution on Long Island Sound, to the early trade on the Mohawk and its rapid development, as well as to the transformations of the city. The obituary continued:

His funeral will take place on Wednesday at three thirty PM from his late residence, 45 Hudson street, and the friends of the family are requested to attend without further invitation. He will be interred in the family vault, Nassau and Liberty streets.

Elizabeth (Ivers) Herring lived to be 90 and died at her son Elbert's residence at 915 Broadway on 22 October 1845.[115]

Thomas's name disappears from the New York directory after 1841. On 27 August 1851 the *New York Herald* informed readers of the death: "On 20th of August Thomas Herring after a few days of dysentery, an old and respectable citizen, and formerly an eminent merchant of this city." He died at 16 Beekman Street—ironically, named for the family of the creditors who had brought him down in 1816—where friends and relatives were bid to the funeral. "The body will be taken to the family vault at the Reformed Dutch Church corner of Liberty and Nassau streets."[116] (The Beekman Street address was one door from Nassau Street and a short block from Park Row and City Hall Park, a heavily commercial area at a time when most of "society" had moved uptown, indicating Thomas's reduced circumstances.)[117] His remains were placed first at the Old Middle Church. When that burial place was closed, they were removed to Lafay-

---

115. *New York Evening Post*, Barber, 11.

116. *New York Herald*, 27 Aug. 1851; Maher, 2.

117. Perris, *Maps of New York*, 1859, 5. When the map was made the Park Hotel adjoined 15 Beekman.

ette Cemetery and finally to the vault established by Elbert Herring at Green-Wood Cemetery in 1862.[118] Also interred in the Elbert Herring vault at Green-Wood are the remains of Mary A. Moon, who died on 25 October 1851, two months after Thomas, at 16 Beekman Place, his address. She was listed at that address in the 1850 census as aged thirty-five, from New Jersey.[119] She was probably a servant in the household. Charles H. Moon, a widower, and evidently a relative of Mary, who died on 26 July 1870, was also buried in the Herring vault.[120] These are the only two nonfamily members to be installed in the vault, evidence of Elbert Herring's regard for their connection to the family.

Elbert Herring, Esq.

Elbert Herring became the ultimate survivor, one of the few Americans whose lives spanned nearly the first hundred years of the republic. In his lifetime he became a living reminder of the vanished past of the city. He survived all his siblings and through their lifetimes was the counselor when needed. In his late years, he was closest to his sister Cornelia's children, the only members of Abraham's family line to survive into another generation. He was appealed to for support by Samuel Haring's widow, and as head of the family for many years contributed to its preservation in death by establishing a final resting place for his parents, siblings, and their descendants.

Elbert was the first member of the Haring-Herring family to attend college, graduating from Princeton with the class of 1795. Almost eighty years later, when he was the sole surviving eighteenth-century graduate of any American college, the writer of the Princeton alumni report recalled that he "entered college when Mr. Witherspoon was President," and added lugubriously, that he "was present at his funeral the next year, and the impression made by the appearance of that noble form as it lay in the coffin, has never been obliterated."[121]

---

118. Burial Records, Dutch Reformed Church, Collegiate Church, 45 John St., New York, N.Y.

119. 1850 U.S. federal census, Second Ward, New York, N.Y., 301; Green-Wood has Mary A. Moon as aged fifty, unmarried. Internment Certification, Green-Wood, 28 Jan. 2002.

120. Age at time of death 75 years, 9 months; place of death not known. Internment Certification, Green-Wood, 28 Jan. 2002; "At City Island on Tuesday, July 26, of diseases of the heart, Charles H. Moon of this city. The remains were interred in Green-Wood Cemetery." *New York Herald*, 1 Aug. 1870.

After his graduation he studied law with the "father of the New York Bar," Samuel Jones, the able young man whom his aunt Cornelia had married before the Revolution. Jones, well known for his legal ability before the Revolution, had served on the Committee of 100, one of the pre-Revolutionary bodies formed in the city in the uncertain days before a definite break with the Crown. He had sat out the Revolution on the family lands on Long Island, but, as we have seen, though not an active Patriot, dissociated himself from his Loyalist cousin, Thomas. After the evacuation, he swiftly re-established himself in the city and played an important role in creating new municipal statutes from the former English law. He and Cornelia named a son Elbert Herring Jones, and several of their children were baptized in Tappan during the war. As an in-law and counselor, Jones in years past was intimately involved with Herring-Haring-Kip family affairs and the settlement of the Elbert Herring estate.

Like John Haring, Jones early was a supporter of George Clinton. Both men served on the Poughkeepsie convention to ratify the federal Constitution in 1787, and both supported George Clinton in his opposition to ratification. However, when it became evident from the actions of other states that the adoption of the federal constitution was inevitable, Jones and Clinton (but not Haring) bowed to the circumstances, and it was Jones who made the deciding motion in favor of the constitution. Jones became a Federalist in New York politics after the Revolution—which did not deter the Republican young Herring from studying with him.[122] From "Sam Jones" (as he was familiarly called) Elbert gained a knowledge of the bar and of the vanished world of government and litigation in the Province of New York.

Elbert was admitted to the bar in 1799, thus becoming a colleague of famous men, a friend of the man he "always spoke of . . . as 'Colonel' Hamilton." He despised Burr, and "carried to the grave the resentment of

---

121. Samuel Davis Alexander, *Princeton College during the Eighteenth Century* (New York, 1872), text provided to the author in a letter from Margaretta E. Cowenhoven, Office of the Secretary, Princeton University, 14 Aug. 1994.

122. Jones and Haring served together on the Massachusetts Claim and the Cheesecocks Commissions, the first settling the boundaries between Massachusetts and New York, the second resolving contested boundaries between two patents in New York State, west of the river. In 1794, when Jones was controller of the state, living in Albany, Abraham carried a letter to him from Cornelia in the city. Her words reveal the scope some women had in business matters at the time, as she was negotiating the purchase a house for the family entirely on her own.

those earlier days." His strongest political association was with De Witt Clinton, whom he termed "the greatest man known in New York."[123] Over the years Elbert became a master in chancery, judge in the mayor's court, and a practicing attorney. He first appeared in the directory at 28 John Street in 1800, later at 22 Vesey, both off Broadway, close to City Hall Park. For a number of years from 1805 he resided at 35 Wall Street, a center for the law. All of his addresses placed him in the midst of things. He actively practiced law, as we have seen, defended his brother Thomas in bankruptcy proceedings, and performed tasks for Peter Smith.

Elbert was a student of affairs in France from the time of the French Revolution and the execution of Marie Antoinette, which was said to have made a great impression on him.[124] When Jean Moreau (1763–1813), a general under the Directory, banished by Napoleon, came to the United States in the early 1800s, Elbert befriended him, took him hunting for waterfowl on Long Island, and learned firsthand about Napoleon's early campaigns.[125] He became acquainted with Joseph Bonaparte, King of Naples, King of Spain under the Empire (1768–1844), who sought refuge in Bordentown, New Jersey, after Waterloo.[126] Elbert also knew Thomas Paine (1757–1809), the veteran of the American and French Revolutions, when, at the end of his life, he was living in poverty at New Rochelle.

Elbert was appointed a judge to the Marine Court by Governor Morgan Lewis (a Federalist) in 1803. The court was a body "established by the State to give seamen a chance to obtain redress of grievances with jury trial . . . [it also had] a 'small claims' jurisdiction for cases involving less than $100."[127] His support of the Democratic-Republicans was rewarded when Governor Tompkins (certainly with a word from De Witt Clinton, then Mayor of New York) appointed him the first register of New York State in 1812, a position he held for a year. This newly created position

---

123. Elbert Herring obit., *New York Herald*, 21 Feb. 1876.

124. Ibid.

125. Ibid. With the destruction of the Grande Armée in Russia, Moreau returned to Europe and pretended to advise the allies. He died at the side of the tsar at the battle of Dresden. *Enc. Brit.*, s.v "Moreau, Jean. "

126. In America he unsuccessfully plotted to free the emperor from St. Helena. Later he returned to Europe and died in Florence. *Enc. Brit.*, s.v. "Bonaparte, Joseph."

127. Albion, *Rise of New York Port*, 229.

assigned to the appointee the responsibility for recording deeds, conveyances, and mortgages, previously recorded by the city clerk.[128]

In that same year, in Hudson, N.Y., south of Albany, Elbert married Agnes Van Rensselaer, the daughter of Kiliaen Van Rensselaer, of the landowning family on the east bank of the Hudson. She was 24, he 35. A daughter, Elizabeth, was born in 1813 and died in 1831, leaving her parents with no heir.[129]

He early bought land upstate: five lots in the Benson Purchase in 1798 in what was then Herkimer (now Hamilton) County, in the midst of the Adirondacks .(To this day the township where these lots were consists largely of roadless land.) At the same time he bought another 270 acres in Hope Township, part of the Adirondacks wilderness, then and now, due west of Glens Falls. One of Elbert's acquisitions was a ten-acre island in Candarago Lake in today's Richfield, west of Otsego Lake in the county of that name. These lands were not near those that Peter Smith acquired, and to reach them would have required a side trip on any visit to Utica or Peterboro.[130] Such purchases smack of a young man seeking bargains at auction for speculation purposes and possibly never seeing the property.

The most prominent of Elbert Herring's appointments came when, in 1831, at the age of forty-five, he joined the administration of Andrew Jackson as clerk of the Indian Bureau under Secretary of War Lewis Cass. The five years he spent in Washington were the most notable in a career of astonishing length. Elbert's story is entwined with the Jackson administration's controversial Indian removal policy. At the point in his first administration when Elbert Herring took up his position, Jackson had secured congressional support for the removal of the Cherokees, Choctaws, and

---

128. Edgar A. Werner, *Civil List and Constitutional History of the Colony and State of New York* (Albany, 1891), 591.

129. Florence Van Rensselaer, *The Van Rensselaers in Holland and in America* (New York: privately printed, 1956), 30. "In Hudson of the Rev. Mr. Simpson, on the 29th ult., Elbert Herring to Agnes van Rensselaer of Hudson." *New York Herald*, 8 Sept. 1812, in Joseph Gavit, *American Marriages— November 1784–1829*, microfilm, NYGB. Agnes's sister, Margaret, married the Rev. Nicholas Jones, son of Gardner Jones and Sarah Herring, Elbert's maternal first cousin. For Elizabeth Herring, the daughter, see Budke, BC-58.

130. *Military Tract, Index of Patentees,* 23:413–14, 17 Feb. 1796, microfilm, NYSL; 23:431, 5 July 1798; *Calendar of N.Y. Colonial Manuscripts, Indorsed Land Papers, 1643–1803,* comp. E. R. O'Callaghan (reprint, Harrison, N.Y.: Harbor Hill Books, 1987), 135, 140; On 4 May 1796 power of attorney was given from Elbert Haring to Cornelius C. Roosevelt, to take up his land patent 18, ibid., 880; Budke, BC-58:153.

Seminoles who lived in the southeastern states, to lands west of the Mississippi. The administration planned simply to remove them, since squatters, settlers, and state governments were each eager to possess the tribal lands. As the numbers of settlers increased in the southeastern states, the veteran Indian fighter wished to eliminate the great potential for white-Indian conflict. When Elbert Herring joined the department, the president was still engaged in encouraging the tribes to relocate voluntarily.[131]

In his 1833 report to the secretary of war, Herring vigorously supported the evolving policy. He pointed out the "brighter prospects . . . opening to the remnants of nations that were spread over the face of this vast continent." Unlike the "nations" of the northeast, they would not be wiped out but led to "lands distinctly and permanently established as their own" and "protected by the strong arm of government." "Enjoying a delightful climate, and a fertile soil," he prophesied, articulating the Jacksonian position (and betraying ignorance of what would be called the Oklahoma Territory, so different from the forests where these nations then lived), the Indians would "turn their attention to the cultivation of the earth, and abandon the chase for a surer supply of domestic animals." The "transformation from a savage to a civilized condition cannot be expected to be instantaneous, and we therefore hail with satisfaction the first indications that denote a willingness to throw off habits peculiar to the forest, and betake in the kindlier occupations of civilized life."[132]

Herring used the "flourishing condition" of the Choctaw academy as "the best evidence of the sound views and philanthropic motives of those with whom it originated, and leaves the question of Indian improvement in letters and morals . . . no longer doubted." Though in "a refined state of civilization, the mechanic arts sink in appreciation in comparison with letters . . . in the ruder stages of society, and in reference to the actual wants and comforts of life in all its stages, the useful will, in general estimation, take precedence of the ornamental."[133]

---

131. A succinct account of the initiation of the removal policy is found in Robert V. Remini, *Andrew Jackson and His Indian Wars* (New York: Viking, Penguin Books, 2001), 226–38.

132. Office of Indian Affairs, Department of War, 28 Nov. 1833. *Annual Report of the Commissioner of Indian Affairs transmitted with the Message of the President at the opening of the First Session of the Twenty-third Congress, 1833–34* (Washington, D.C.: Gales and Seaton, 1833), 172.

133. Office of Indian Affairs, 25 Nov. 1834, *Annual Report of the Commissioner of Indian Affairs transmitted with the Message of the President at the opening of the Second Session of the Twenty-third Congress, 1834–35* (Washington, D.C.: Duff Green, 1834).

Elbert Herring was appointed the first commissioner of Indian affairs when that position was created in 1832 and served for four years. There is no doubt his views exemplified "the ethnocentrism that characterized Jackson's Indian policy," as a recent study puts it. "Like Jackson and Cass, he equated the removal policy with the preservation of the Indians."[134] Neither Jackson nor Herring expected that the removals would turn out as brutally as they did. Of the 18,000 Cherokees who were routed from their homes by the army in 1838 under President Van Buren, from four to eight thousand are estimated to have died in the stockades, crowded boxcars, and along the eight hundred mile trek, the aptly named "Trail of Tears."[135] Instead of being preserved, these Indian nations were all but destroyed.

The well-meaning New Yorker Elbert Herring, with none of the animus toward the Indians found in the southeast, was deceived by his cultural blinders. His rationale for separating the Indians from rough white settler communities was to preserve them from the baleful influence of "ardent spirits" and the settlers' land grabs. A gentlemanly person like Elbert, much removed from the frontier that had formed Jackson, deemed the separation of these Indians from the settler roughnecks desirable. Later, like many who shared his views, he was probably horrified by the way the removals were conducted and their consequences.

Secretary of War Lewis Cass considered Herring knowledgeable and hard-working but "an inefficient and blundering administrator." An anti-Jackson politician commented, "I never heard Mr. Herring's integrity called in question, yet his want of capacity was admitted by all with whom I conversed." A recent study criticizes Herring for excessive interference in the tribal councils but agrees with the assessment that he was hard working and honest. President Jackson later asserted that he had frequently complained of Herring's "incompetency," but retained him in office at Cass' request.[136] Jackson's dissatisfaction led to Herring's appointment, in 1835, to the less crucial post of paymaster for the U.S. Army in New York City with the rank of major.[137] For his part, Herring

---

134. Indian Bureau, *Annual Reports*, 1832, 163, quoted in Satz, "Elbert Herring," 13.

135. Remini, *Andrew Jackson and His Indian Wars*, 159.

136. Testimony of Hugh L. White, 12 Feb. 1837, *Niles Weekly Register* 32 (6 July 1837); Andrew Jackson to Francis P. Blair, 2 April 1837, *Correspondence of Andrew Jackson*, ed. John Spencer Bassett, 7 vols. (Washington, D.C.: Carnegie Institution, 1926–35), 5:472, ref. in Kvasnicka and Viola, *The Commissioners of Indian Affairs*, 15.

137. Kvasnicka and Viola, *Commissioners*, 13–15.

remembered Jackson "as a man given to bursts of temper, but whose passion was frequently the result of calculation, and not the real, genuine impulse of anger."[138]

Elbert and his wife, Agnes, returned to New York to live with his widowed mother at 45 Hudson Street until her death in 1842. In 1841 he was dismissed from his position of paymaster for an unspecified violation of procedure regarding the disbursement of funds.[139] Whatever the offense, it did not seem to have impaired the affection and respect with which he was held by his colleagues, and he apparently continued to practice law until age slowed him down.

Agnes Van Rensselaer Herring died in 1867, and Elbert, then ninety, lived on alone in the house at 31 East Twenty-eighth Street that they occupied since 1852.[140] Among the New York Bar he had become a venerable figure. He could recount for friends and colleagues his memories of the small city of his youth, of Hamilton and Burr, and of the newly inaugurated President Washington. He could tell of being on Pearl Street with a schoolmate, following Washington and watching him "cross the street, walking alone."[141] In a city conscious that its past was irretrievably lost, he was valued as one of the few witnesses to long gone persons and places. Elbert was virtually the last survivor from the city's Revolutionary past. "He had a mind filled with stories and traditions . . . of the Attorney Generals of the Province and of the State of New York," a judge remembered at his death. "If all that he remembered, and all that he had seen and narrated could be written down it would be one of the most interesting books of reminiscences that his brethren at the Bar today could read. All our histories of today are insignificant compared with the recollections of this gentleman."[142]

The house on East Twenty-eighth Street, where Elbert spent his last twenty-five years, was a four-story brownstone on the north side of the street (others of that vintage remain on the block, but a raw post–World War II building fills in where Elbert's house stood). An attraction to him

---

138. Elbert Herring, obit., *New York Herald*, 21 Feb. 1876.

139. Budke, BC–58:153.

140. New York City directories, 1852–75.

141. Elbert Herring, obit.

142. Judge Curtis, in a motion to adjourn the courts for the day in memory of Elbert Herring and Judge Spaulding, Law Reports, *NYT*, 22 Feb. 1876.

was the proximity of a new Dutch Reformed Church (soon to be called the Marble Church from the material in its façade), which opened in 1854 at 29th Street and Fifth Avenue.[143] It was a short walk from Elbert's house, and a contemporary wrote that his "seat in the church and the prayer-meeting is seldom vacant."[144] He attended the investiture of a new president of Princeton in 1872 and was recognized as not only the sole living eighteenth-century graduate of that college but the last surviving graduate of any college in the country from before the turn of the century.[145]

Elbert's connection to what had become a remote past in the city attracted a reporter whose April 1874 article was entitled "The World's Oldest Lawyer: Hon. Elbert Herring's Remarkable Career; In his Ninety-Eighth Year, Reminiscences of New York in 1790, A Judge in 1805 [1803]."[146] The house was run down, and the visitor observed a drawing on a wall by Elbert's daughter, Elizabeth, who had died at the age of eighteen. The maid told him that the judge usually received no visitors but was "graceful."

Almost two years later the obituarist in the *Herald* based his account on the article and viewed Elbert Herring's life as a reminder of the great changes that had taken place in the city, a favorite journalistic theme in the city, as it had been when his father died almost forty years before.

> When he first remembered New York it was built up only as far as Ann Street. All beyond that was open country, the wealthy citizens lived in Wall Street.... The first Mayor, whose term of office he remembered, was James Duane, who was chosen in 1784 and retired in 1788. The population of the city was then not more than 25,000 [about one million in 1876], and most of the houses were but two stories high; very few were three stories ... the principal theater was on John street. His recollection of the best actors was of Hallam and Hutchinson. Which of the Hallams attracted the attention of the young law student is not known, but it is supposed it was A. M. Hallam, Jr who first made his appearance in 1795. The richest man in New York at that time was Mr. Desbrosses, for Mr. Astor was quietly living at the outset of his

---

143. *Yearbook of the Collegiate Church of the City of New York 1992–1996* (New York: Collegiate Church of the City of New York, ca. 1997), 131.

144. "Elbert Herring," in Samuel Davis Alexander, *Princeton College during the Eighteenth Century* (New York: Anson D. F. Randolph, ca. 1872). The church remains on the site.

145. Ibid.

146. *New York Herald*, 5 April 1875.

mercantile career, and had not become known as the possessor of the stupendous fortune which has become one of the institutions of the country.

He remembered the first steamer that sailed up the Hudson under the command of Commodore Wiswall.

The memorial also struck the note of simpler, more virtuous times, another favorite theme:

> These changes in population were small when compared with the social and material changes in other respects. New York during its earlier days, was little more than a small Dutch settlement, with quaint people and strange fashions, and everybody who could afford it dressed in broadcloth and very few in homespun garments. They were very honest people, he said, in those days, little given to cheating.

According to this memoir, the last twenty years of Elbert's life were

> really spent in silence. He took little interest in modern events, but when questions of circumstances fifty or sixty years old were brought up his mind accepted and discussed them with avidity. He was more familiar with the position of America at the time of Jefferson and Jackson than during the period since intervening. De Witt Clinton was more present to him as an actual positive leader than Lincoln, Seward or Chase.

The vault that Herring established at Green-Wood Cemetery in 1862 lies beneath a flat stone on which "Elbert Herring" is the sole inscription. Beneath that simple marker he had in his lifetime assembled his departed family, moved the remains of his father and mother, of his grandfather Thomas Ivers, Gardner Jones, of his siblings from their resting places in the Dutch Church to the newly laid out and pastoral cemetery across the harbor from Manhattan. In his lifetime Thomas and his sisters, and his wife, Agnes, were laid to rest there. After his death the Gardner Jones descendants became the last to be buried there. The remains of thirty-one family members came to occupy the vault. It was a reunion of the family who had lived in and around New York since colonial times.[147]

After the service at Marble Collegiate Church, it is likely that Jones cousins accompanied Elbert Herring's coffin through the streets and on the

---

147. Herring vault, lot 5392, section 105, Green-Wood Cemetery, Brooklyn. Information provided by Jane Cuccurullo, Secretary, Green-Wood Cemetery, 28 Jan. 2002 and 28 Aug. 2001.

14. Herring vault, Green-Wood Cemetery, Brooklyn, N.Y.

Hamilton ferry to the vault at Green-Wood.[148] The house on Twenty-eighth Street must have had furniture and objects from the Hudson Street house of his parents and papers and books from his long career, but none of these have surfaced in recent times.

Returning to the beginning of the nineteenth century, we find young Samuel and Sarah Haring coming to New York when the Herring uncle and cousin were at the height of their prosperity and Elbert still had seventy-six years to live. Samuel may have been inspired by the examples of enterprise in his family, but he did not remain in central New York, as did his Kip cousin and Smith. He chose rather to pursue his ambition to become a merchant in New York City. There was family precedent for his choosing this path—his father had been prominent in the city, his Uncle Abraham had his prosperous counting house, and Kip, De Peyster, and Jones relatives were also deeply involved in the mercantile arena. Samuel maintained a trading connection with Albany and returned there in later life, but he sought, not so successfully as his Herring uncle, to establish himself in trade in the city. His profession as grocer was a step on the way to the sought-for appellation of merchant that he had given himself in Aurelius.

---

148. Elbert Herring died on 16 Feb. 1876. Death Notice, *New York Herald*, 19 Feb. 1876, Budke, BC-58:153.

Samuel's career provides a counterpoint to that of his Herring relatives in terms of commercial success. He strove and achieved a genteel level of life but did not reach the plateau of financial security that Abraham enjoyed during his long life. Nor, happily, did he suffer the humiliation in business that cut short his cousin Thomas Herring's career as a merchant. Moreover, Samuel's career was interrupted and forestalled by difficult service in the campaigns near Lake Ontario in the War of 1812. He gave part of his life (and his health) to what was seen at the time as the "Second War of Independence." It became a war America wanted to forget because of its apparent lack of accomplishment and the inept performance of American troops in many actions. Samuel served loyally, but the circumstances did not reward him with any honor.

The story of Captain Samuel Haring, as he became known, provides the thread that connects two very different periods in the history of a family, a city, and a country. Two of Samuel's sons achieved the success in the mercantile economy of antebellum New York City that eluded him, and his granddaughter married into the new industrial economy of Connecticut.

III

FINDING A WAY IN THE NEW REPUBLIC

America is a land of wonders, in which everything is in constant motion and every change seems an improvement. The idea of novelty is there indissolubility connected with the idea of amelioration.

—De Tocqueville, *Democracy in America*

The jury rolls in Albany in 1798 listed "Samuel Herron, grocer." Surely this is young Samuel, then twenty-two, with his occupation more appropriately stated than the "merchant" he had somewhat brashly used in Aurelius.[1] The young couple had left Hardenbergh's Corners within a year of their marriage, probably attracted by the potential for trade and choosing built-up Albany. On the Genesee Road heading to Albany they passed a stream of westward-moving emigrants and wagons. On the Mohawk they saw bateaux loaded with grains heading downstream to the Hudson. The river corridor was alive with activity, and they knew that Uncle Abraham Herring and his son in New York City were prospering. It was in the port city that Samuel established his first business, but his personal and commercial life would be lived more broadly in the Hudson River Valley, Albany, and the Mohawk Valley.

Samuel Haring, New York Grocer

After his two or three years at Hardenbergh's Corners, a stay in Albany, and a firsthand look at the emigrants and grain boats making use of the Hudson and Mohawk waterways, Samuel and Sarah returned to the lower Hudson Valley in 1801 and joined the Dutch Reformed Church in Schraalenburgh, Bergen County, New Jersey, where John Haring was a

---

1. Personal communication from Stefan Bielinski, Director, Colonial Albany Social History Project, Cultural Education Center, Albany, N.Y., 14 July 1994.

member. For Samuel, this was a step on the way to a larger ambition; he aimed to emulate his merchant uncle and cousin. His father helped him with the capital necessary to start a business by buying of Samuel 100 acres of the well-placed Lot 47 in Aurelius for $1,230.[2] For the young man this was a fine profit, as he had laid out $425 for the piece; for John Haring it was a way to help his son and make an investment in lands near his friend Hardenbergh. That he could come up with the cash bears out the observation made earlier that his work for the Eastern Proprietors had been lucrative.

Samuel and Sarah moved to New York, where, in 1802, he was in business as a grocer in Manhattan at 74 Vesey, a street that led from Broadway to the North River piers, where sloops from upriver and the ferry to New Jersey docked. It was a good address for a man of twenty-six starting out in business and his twenty-two-year-old wife.[3] (Vesey runs east to west from Broadway at the south end of today's City Hall Park along the north edge of the World Trade Center site. Samuel's shop was between Church and Greenwich Street, the latter soon to be created by landfill that expanded the Manhattan shore.) Thomas Herring noted at the time that Samuel had paid a debt of £53 7s 9d, indicating that he had secured his cousin's help in importing goods that required payment in sterling.[4]

At that time, a grocer was a wholesaler who bought from ships entering the port and usually re-sold in bulk. In October 1802 the *Commercial Advertiser* included a notice that shows how skippers sold consignments and wholesalers learned what was available: "The good brig *Eliza*, Swain [master], 160 tons for West Indies trade," it read, "Has for sale: sugar, Muscovado Sugar, 90 bales Upland Cotton, 32 bales Sea Island Cotton, Hyson Tea, James River tobacco, 10 crates of earthenware assorted."[5] Wholesalers like Samuel would buy what they wanted directly from the master at the dock and have it carted to the shop, usually a short distance away in the compact city of the early 1800s.

---

2. The loan document, dated 10 Oct. 1801, referred to Samuel Haring "presently of Hackensack [near Schraalenburgh] in the County of Bergen, New Jersey." The indenture was signed by John Haring and Sarah Haring and attested by John Suffern of the Court of Common Pleas, Rockland County. Land Records, C:349, C:550–52, Cayuga Co., N.Y.

3. *New York City Directory* (1802).

4. T. Herring, in New York, to Smith, in Utica, 7 May 1802, PSP, reel 1.

5. *Commercial Advertiser*, New York, 1 Oct. 1802.

The wholesale trade had remained much as it had been in colonial times. A grocer handled a variety of goods, not only produce such as grains, sugar, dried peas, but also fabrics, haberdashery ("dry goods") and "those luxuries of diet imported from the West Indies and South Europe, such as lemons, raisins, citron and spices." Many carried wine and rum in addition to sugar. Rarely did a grocer specialize in any one product.[6]

Newspaper notices serve as informative guides to the type and range of goods handled by grocers and available to consumers. 1802 was a prosperous year in the port. Murray & Mumford, at 73 Stone Street, listed "tea, wine, capers, Sweet oil, Red Wine in half Pipes, 4 trunks of silk hose, Mess, prime and cargo Pork, Prime and cargo Beef, 3 boxes dried plumbs, raisins, Figs Roquevaire, silk hose, ribbons, thread, Sheep's Wool, Tallow, Candles."[7] Isaac Moses & Son offered "fabrics, German goods, tea, soap." Samuel Sackett offered "5000 Curacao Cocoa, just landed from Maracaibo, Flotant Indigo."[8] The prosperity of the times can be read in this variety of goods.[9]

The ports from which the ships arrived that October day reveal the range, variety, and intensity of trade at New York. English ships embarked from Liverpool, London, Hull, and Bristol. One vessel came from Leghorn, on the Italian peninsula. Continental Europe was represented by Amsterdam, Bremen, and St. Petersburg. Ships departing from points in

6. Virginia D. Harrington, *The New York Merchant on the Eve of the Revolution* (New York: Columbia Univ. Press, 1935), 61.

7. *Commercial Advertiser,* 1 Oct. 1802. Advertisements from other firms revealed an even greater variety of goods: George Barnewall of 21 Wall Street had for sale "Green Coffee, China Brandy, Jamaica Rum, China Bowls." John Patrick of 4 William Street, east of Broadway, offered fabrics as well as wine and produce: "2 bales British Sail Duck, fancy Wildbores, Bombazetts, striped Calimacoes, and watered Joans, London duffil Blanketing, Wheat Sacks, empty bags, half Pipes Port Wine, New Orleans sugar, Claret Wine of a superior quality, Bandana hdkfs, black Pepper, Havana Segars." Up Vesey Street from Samuel, at number 37, the "NEW-YORK BREAD COMPANY having commenced baking Hard Bread, will have a quantity of Middlings and Pilot Bread of a very superior quality ready for delivery in a few days."

8. Ibid.

9. The record of a court judgment testifies to the fact that Samuel carried a variety of goods as well. In 1811 Charles I. Richardson, "gentleman," had not paid him for "divers quantities of candles, Sugar, Teas, Spirituous Liquors, Groceries, goods, wares and merchandizes." The court awarded Haring the $100/$1,400 cost of these items plus $33.85/$475 damages. *Samuel Haring* vs. *Charles I. Richardson,* filed 17 April 1811, Mayor's Court Records, 1811:310, Office of the New York Co. Clerk.

the western hemisphere originated in Halifax, Surinam, Santo Domingo, St. Martins, Norfolk, and Richmond. The *George Washington* came all the way from Canton, via Providence.[10]

Samuel's occupation was deemed respectable in New York of the day, but he was on a rung of the social ladder below that of his merchant uncle and cousin. When the hero of Washington Irving's *Salmagundi* (1807) mused on social distinctions he noted "some curious speculations on the vast distinction between selling tape by the piece or by the yard—Whole-sale merchants look down upon the retailers, who in return look down upon the green grocers, who look down upon the market women, who don't care a straw about any of them."[11]

Samuel and Sarah's New York

The city in the early 1800s was a busy, rough, freewheeling place, in which money could be and was made and lost in quantity. The population was of an increasingly mixed ethnic heritage: the Dutch and English city was becoming "American." The religious composition of New York was equally heterogeneous. In such a culture there were no central guiding principles by which society at large conducted itself, at least nothing comparable to the legacy of Puritan New England, where an emphasis on social compact, church, and education was palpable. Henry Adams, in his history of Jeffersonian America, acknowledged

> The intellectual and moral character of New York left much to be desired, but on the other hand, had society adhered stiffly to what New England thought strict morals, the difficulties in the path of national development would have been increased. Innovation was the most useful purpose which New York could serve in human interests, and never was a city better fitted for its work.[12]

In 1800 New York City had a population of 60,000, almost double what it had been ten years before, and five times the number that were there at

---

10. Ibid.

11. Washington Irving, *Salmagundi, or the Whim-Whams and Opinions of Launcelot Langstaff, Esq. & Others* (1807–8; reprint, New York: Library of America, 1983), 225.

12. Henry Adams, *History of the United States of America During the First Administration of Thomas Jefferson, 1803–1805* (1890; reprint, New York: Library of America, 1986), 78.

the time of the British evacuation.[13] The fabric of the city was almost
entirely new; little remained of the old Dutch trading city, and most of the
succeeding English city had been destroyed during the fire early in the British occupation or torn down following the evacuation. Visitors commented
on the colorful houses observed in the sparkling air of the harbor. The exterior building material was brick painted "in red, yellow, or light gray enam-
els, which not only acted as a sealant, preventing the clay from freezing and
scaling, but lent 'a cheerful, bright and daylight aspect' to the streets."[14] A
painting by Francis Guy made about 1797 of the Tontine Coffee House at
the corner of Wall and Water Streets, near the East River docks, shows a
number of nearby houses in the Federal style of architecture, derived from
the spare, rational English Georgian style, with large windows to let in
light, necessary when artificial illumination was limited (fig. 13).[15] The
houses lined the streets with little or no space between them, their widths
conforming to city lots twenty-five feet wide or less. "This gaiety of color,
the abundance of windows," writes a modern commentator on the city of
the early 1800s, "and the delicacy of the exterior ornaments suggested to
many the miniature houses with which children play."[16]

Visitors in the early years of the nineteenth century commented on the
quality of the air. There was comparatively little coal burned in New York
at the time compared to Europe, and the prevailing western winds swept
the skies. New York harbor's "singularly bright and lovely" atmosphere
reminded one London correspondent in 1829 "of the sea-bound cities of
the Mediterranean but with more variety of color."[17] According to James
Fenimore Cooper, "The three components of that paradigmatic neatness
and domestic comfort which overspread the native landscape were the

---

13. *Population of States and Counties of the United States, 1790 to 1990* (Washington, D.C.: U.S. Department of Commerce, Bureau of the Census, 1996), 113.

14. Elizabeth Donaghy Garrett, *At Home: The American Family 1750–1870* (New York: Harry N. Abrams, 1990), 17.

15. Charles Lockwood, *Bricks and Brownstone: The New York Row House, 1783–1929* (New York: Abbeville Press, 1972), 7.

16. Garrett, *At Home*, 19. "The common practice is to deepen the colour of the bricks by a red paint, and then to interline them with white, a fashion that scarcely alters their original appearance except by imparting a neatness and freshness that are exceedingly pleasant." Cooper, *Notions of the Americans*, 118.

17. Garrett, *At Home*, 19, quoting "Letters from New York, No. 11," *New Monthly Magazine* 26 (Sept. 1829): 105.

brilliance of the climate, the freshness of the paint, and the exterior ornaments of the houses."[18] The city resembled London, in his view, except
that the houses were painted and there were more trees on the streets.

Bright and cheery though it appeared from afar, a pedestrian experienced the less desirable aspects of the city. There was mud and dust in the
streets, slops and trash thrown out of the houses, standing water, the noise
of the metal wagon wheels, the stench of horse manure, feral pigs and cattle, the cacophony of carts, drays, and the cries of vendors. The dirt that
came in from the streets must have been a perpetual challenge to the
housekeeper. At this period the rough and overcrowded parts of the city
were by the piers, frequented by sailors and other transients. As yet, there
were not extensive slums—a contrast with London and the New York of
mid-century.

In moving to this New York, Samuel and Sarah had made a decisive transition from rural to urban life. They had been brought up in largely self-
sufficient rural households, with animals, crops, home crafts, siblings to
share the chores. Their past, to use the term of a recent study, was in the
"productive household." In the city, theirs became a consuming household, in which most goods and services had to be purchased, requiring a
regular influx of cash from Samuel's business. There was no "productive"
work for Sarah or the children or crops to tend and animals to feed.[19]

The roles of wife and mother also changed. As a town dweller, Sarah
had to purchase food, fabrics, household furnishings, and supervise servants. And it was traditionally the mother who educated children in the
early years. When the family moved to the city, there were three children,
the eldest four years old. Four more would be born in the next ten years. In
addition to minding the small children, Sarah had to keep the house as
clean as possible in the face of dirt, horse, and pig manure coming in on
boots and shoes, and dust and cinders through the windows. Water had to
be carried in buckets from the pump on the street, and cooking was by a
slow fire, requiring wood to be fetched and ashes to be dumped. For Sarah,
even with two servants, there cannot have been much time for reading or

---

18. Ibid., 17, quoting James Fenimore Cooper, *Notions of the Americans Picked Up by a Travelling Bachelor* (1828; reprint, New York, 1963), 1:143.

19. Christine Stansell, *City of Women: Sex and Class in New York, 1789–1860* (New York: Alfred A. Knopf, 1986), xi–xii, 11.

social visits. Hers was a labor-intensive business. The family does not appear to have been rich by the standards of the day, and Sarah had not the leisure time that would be available to middle- and upper-class women later in the century.

Like other Dutch families, the Harings owned slaves; there were two in the household. The custom among Dutch families was for slaves to live with the family, a woman to help Sarah in the household and the children, one or more men in the shop. In late 1807 Samuel did "hereby release and forever set free my Negro man called Tom and my Negro woman called Sarah."[20] When the 1810 census was taken, he held no slaves, though he is recorded as selling a slave to Abraham Herring in 1822 when he was in Albany.[21] Slave owners were a tiny minority by 1820, when there were only 518 slaves in the city.[22]

In New York, Sarah and Samuel lived amongst strangers, on a city street where unknown faces and vehicles passed by—there were neighbors whose names they would never know. Nevertheless, New York was still a relatively small city, and they were only a few blocks from Abraham and most of the other relatives descended from Elbert Herring. It would have been a walk of an hour or so to the site of the family farm, by then broken into lots and owned by the heirs, and perhaps another hour's walk to the cousins at the Kip Mansion, still far in the country (at present Thirty-fourth Street and the East River).

The interiors of all but the houses of the most affluent were sparely furnished. If there was a parlor, steep-backed (and uncomfortable) chairs and drop-leaf tables were set beside the walls, to be pulled out in the event of company. Privacy was limited in most houses, particularly in the cold

---

20. Office of Register of the City and Co. of New York, Liber 78:512.

21. *Index of Conveyances Recorded in the Office of Register of the City and County of New York, Grantors G and H* (New York, 1857), 123–24.

22. In 1820 there were 10,368 "Free blacks" out of a total population of 123,000. Horatio Gates Spafford, *A Gazetteer of the State of New York* . . . (New York, 1824; reprint, Interlaken, N.Y.: Heart of the Lakes Publishing Co., 1981), 44. The importation of slaves into New York State was prohibited in 1785, when an active manumission movement began, and there were legal provisions for freeing slaves. All children born to slaves in New York State after 4 July 1799, by act of the legislature, were to have the status of bondservants to be freed (males at 25, females at 28). It was not until 1817 that slavery was entirely prohibited in New York, with all slaves to be freed within ten years. Ellis et al., *A Short History of New York State*, 185–86.

months, when gathering by fireplaces was necessary for warmth. In the view of a recent account of the development of residential comforts:

> In terms of comfort and convenience the average house of 1805 was not much more advanced than that in the 1600s. People still pumped water from a well [in New York City "tea water" could be delivered on a water wagon for a fee] . . . what they used for cleaning and washing they dumped outside. Cooking was done at the fireplace. Personal washing was performed in the bedroom using a pitcher of water and a basin. For the occasional bath—and usually it was very occasional—they might set up a small portable tub in the kitchen, where they could heat water in the fireplace. Heat was supplied by the inefficient fireplace, occasionally by a stove. And there was that epitome of inconvenience, the outdoor privy.[23]

Fireplaces, the primary source of winter heat, used wood in these years, plentiful but requiring constant replenishment. Until the 1810s, candles required frequent snuffing to trim the wick, and most lamps were simply shallow bowls with a wick floating on fish or animal oil, giving very little light. The Argand lamp, which used a circular wick, was available to the more well-to-do and gave better and surer light.[24]

In a business like Samuel's, the lower floor could be given over to the shop, with the living quarters above. The shop would be fragrant with the odors of the commodities stored in a variety of containers, casks, hampers, baskets, and boxes.[25]

In these years Samuel purchased a flatware service from the silversmith Robert Wilson, at 23 Dey Street, according to the city directory, on the west side of the island, not far from Samuel's business. Serving spoons and a ladle by this maker have come down in the family with the monogram "SH" in an expansive scroll, the S for Sarah (and Samuel), the H for

---

23. Merritt Ierley, *The Comforts of Home: The American House and the Evolution of Modern Convenience* (New York: Clarkson Potter, 1999), 10.

24. Ibid., 56–57.

25. We know from the duties assessed by customs, coffee came in "bags, bales, casks"; sugar ("other than loaf sugar") in "casks, boxes, bags or mals" [Fr. "malle," trunk]; cocoa came in casks and bags; chocolate in boxes; Pimento, cheeses in hampers or baskets ("seroons"); sugar candy, in boxes; glauber salts in casks; candles, soap in boxes; Indigo in barrels, bales or bags; twine, in casks, in bales; "segars" in boxes or casks. "Custom duties by quantity," *Longworth's New York City Directory* (1807), 37.

15. Haring family serving spoons. Made about 1808 for Samuel and
Sarah Haring by Robert Wilson, 23 Dey Street, New York City

Haring. They remind of the modest affluence and gentility the family had
achieved in the city.[26]

Samuel Perseveres

There was no listing for Samuel Haring in the city directory from 1804 to
1806, an unexplained hiatus. Perhaps the family was in Albany (where
there was no directory until later). Perhaps the yellow fever, which Samuel
contracted "for a short period" in New York, compelled the family to seek
a place of respite away from the city.[27] The epidemic of yellow fever in
1805 caused almost half of the population to flee to Greenwich (Village) or

---

26. The ladle and serving spoons from this service are now in the author's possession. The maker's
mark is "RW." Stephen Guerney Cook Ensko, *American Silversmiths and Their Marks IV,* comp.
Dorothea Ensko Wyle (Boston: David R. Godine, 1989).

27. Samuel Haring had "enjoyed good and sound health except for a short period when he had
Yellow Fever in the city of New-York, from which however he recovered perfectly and was
restored to his usual firm health." Deposition of Nicholas Jones, practitioner of physic & surgery,
Buffalo, N.Y., 16 Jan. 1830, file 27931, Veteran, Samuel Haring, Grade: Capt., Service, U.S. Infan-
try, bundle no. 34, can no. 129, Act Mil. Est., 2:170, Pension Application Files, War of 1812 series,
Death or Disability "Old War" Invalid, National Archives, Washington, D.C. (hereafter cited as
Samuel Haring Pension Application.)

other some other country spot.[28] "Heaven preserve this city from like Misfortune," wrote Thomas Herring of an outbreak in Philadelphia, describing the preparations a well-to-do citizen of Manhattan made when a plague threatened: "I have provided myself with boxes and Cartmen convey the same away on the least alarm." he wrote, and "am now [ ] in treaty for a store at Greenwich although without any present prospect of using it & we will therefor rest easy on our Account. Flying reports state it to be sickly in Philadelphia but such reports are often false and I trust so are in the present case." If there was official notice, "the only safety is in flight."[29]

Whatever the reason for the hiatus in Samuel's business, he reappeared again as a grocer at 5 Cortlandt Street. This was even better than his earlier address, being a few doors from fashionable Broadway, again on a street that led down to the North River, and showing that whatever had happened in the intervening years his finances were in good shape. The move was surely in part facilitated by Haring's father, who in 1806 conveyed $3,154 to his son, nominally a loan, but in effect an advance on his inheritance.[30] Another part of their transactions at this time—showing that he did not need this advance to maintain himself and that he could continue to speculate—entailed Samuel purchasing land in Lot 18 in Aurelius from his father and mother for $1,577.[31] It is a curious transaction, receiving from his father on the one hand, and essentially using a portion of it to buy property from him on the other.

The couple's investments in central New York continued to do well for them. Not long after they purchased land from John Haring the couple sold land in Aurelius—possibly the same portion of Lot 18 he had bought from his father—for $2,000.[32] The year before Samuel was becoming fairly affluent in his own right and had purchased from his in-laws, James and

---

28. Spafford, Gazetteer (1824), 248.

29. T. Herring, in New York, to Smith, in Utica, 17 July 1802; T. Herring, in New York, to Smith, in Peterboro [?], 24 July 1807, PSP, reel 1.

30. Promissory note from Samuel Haring to John Haring, 26 June 1806, Budke, BC-34, 108.

31. "John Haring of the Co. of Rockland and Mary his wife to Samuel Haring $1,577 lot 18, delivered in the presence of John Haring, Mary Haring, James D. Demarest, John B. Haring," 26 June 1806, Land Records, C:360, Cayuga Co., New York. The Genesee Trail cut through Lot 18, on the second most northerly tier of lots in Aurelius.

32. Samuel Haring, of the City of New York, and Sally Haring to Benjamin Polk, 18 Aug. 1806 $2,000, recorded 15 Sept. 1806, Thomas Cooper, Master in Chancery [The lot number cannot be deciphered], Land Records, G:363–64, Cayuga Co., New York.

16. *The Foot of Cortlandt Street.* By an Unidentified Artist, 1818–1849.

The New-York Historical Society

Deborah Clark, their remaining portion of Lot 37, on the Owasco Outlet, adjacent to Hardenbergh's mills, for $2,500.[33] In 1809 they sold 150 acres of this lot to Sarah's brother, William Clark, for $2,900, a tidy profit.[34] In these years Samuel was also able to make a substantial purchase in the city. In July 1810 he bought of Morgan Lewis (the former governor) two lots located near Leonard Street in the Fifth Ward of Manhattan for $3,400.[35]

The money to be had in the flourishing port had made it possible for some businessmen to have separate shop addresses, beginning a practice that would become standard in a few decades. Abraham Herring, for one, was at home at 44 Broadway, while Herring & Son remained amidst the

---

33. James Clark, of Aurelius, to Samuel Haring, of the City of New York, 24 Jan. 1805, $2,500, lot 37 to land conveyed by said James Clark to Samuel Banker, north to land of Gideon Tyler, certified 26 Jan. 1805.

34. Land Records, J:344, Cayuga Co., N.Y.

35. Grantors were Morgan Lewis, of Clinton, County of Duchess, and Gertrude, his wife, of Duchess Co., 9 Aug. 1810, indenture, 1 July 1810. Grantors, 88:22, Office of the City Register, New York Co., New York, N.Y.

commercial houses at 192 Pearl.[36] Samuel was not as prosperous, and Sarah and the family continued to live above the shop, but Cortlandt Street was far from shabby. Washington Irving termed it a "famous place to see the belles go by."[37] Further along was the home of Philip Hone, later mayor and one of the great diarists of the city, then head of an auction house, a flourishing business that helped make the city the trading center of the nation.[38] Hoping no doubt to secure his position in the community, Samuel apparently sought, unsuccessfully, a public position. On 22 February 1808 his was one of the names proposed to the Common Council for appointment as city inspector and clerk of the council.[39]

By 1807 the children numbered four. John, nine, bore the name of his distinguished paternal grandfather, Mary, seven, was named for her paternal grandmother, and James Clark, five, was named for his maternal grandfather. The youngest boy, Samuel Kip, three, was named in honor of his Kip uncle-in-law, Samuel, who died the year his namesake was born. Naming a child for her father pleased Elizabeth Kip, the late Kip's spinster daughter, who in her will years later bestowed a building lot from Kip land on any nephew named Samuel.[40] The name of Samuel and Sarah's next child also honored a Kip relative, Catharine Teller (1762–1824), a granddaughter of the Jacobus Kip who had established the family at the bay that bore its name. She was also a spinster and presumably had taken an interest in the Haring family. Later, she lived in Albany when they did, in the 1820s, and died there.[41] The first of the girls with this name died in infancy

---

36. *New York City Directory* (1806); Land Records, F:286–87, Cayuga Co., N.Y.

37. Irving, *Salmagundi*, 223.

38. New York City directories list Philip Hone on Broad St., 1805–8, Greenwich St. (at number 148), in 1809, and 44 Courtlandt, in 1810.

39. He is identified in the minutes as Samuel *Herring*. In fact no one was chosen for these posts in the proceeding. *Minutes of the Common Council of the City of New York, 1784–1831*, 19 vols. (New York, 1917), 5:22.

40. Samuel Kip (1731–1804) married Samuel Haring's maternal aunt, Ann Herring (1744–1801). Will of Elizabeth Kip, 15 Sept. 1817, probated 3 Oct. 1829, Wills, 60:330–36, New York Co. Surrogate's Court, New York, N.Y. Kip and Hawley, *Kip Family*, 402.

41. Kip and Hawley, *Kip Family*, 398; John J. Post, *Abstract of Title of Kip's Bay Farm in the City of New York, also the Early History of the Kip Family and The Genealogy as Refers to the Title* (New York: S. Victor Constant, 1894). Catharine Teller was born on 20 June 1762 and died on 21 July 1824, at Albany, aged 62 years and 1 month. She was the daughter of Catherine Kip, born on 11 May 1730, died 3 Sept. 1771, who married, on 8 Dec. 1759, Peter Teller, son of Johannes Teller of Tellers Point, who died on 20 Aug. 1762. Kip and Hawley, *Kip Family*, 395.

Elbert Herring (1706–73)	=	Elisabeth Bogert (1714–87)
Ann Herring (1744–1801)	=	Samuel Kip (1731–1804)
Samuel Kip (1771–1833)	=	Eliza Howell (1770–1846)
Henry Kip (1807–after 1874)	=	Catherine Teller (Haring) Gates (1802–72)

17. Herring-Kip-Haring relations

in 1807, but the girl born in 1808, the Haring's sixth child, became the longest-lived of the children. She was the "Aunt Kate" who was the last living witness to Samuel's family and in later life married her second cousin, Henry Kip.[42] The New York City–born children were baptized in the old Dutch church on Pearl Street, a quarter mile away, reached through the irregular, narrow and crooked streets that had "little adaptation to the ground, or to the convenience or elegance of the City."[43]

John Samuel Haring, the firstborn, named for his distinguished grandfather and father, died in October 1809, at age eleven. The family placed a notice in the weekly *New York Museum:* "John S. Haring, son of Samuel Haring of this city, died at St. Bartholomew, on the 10th ult., of a malignant fever, after a few days illness in his 11th year."[44] The boy may have been in the West Indies with his father or another relative. Jefferson's embargo was repealed in March of the year, and ships from New York

---

42. Samuel Haring owned a building lot at the edge of the Kip property fronting the Boston Post Road, as shown on a map prepared in 1808 as part of the settlement of the long extant estate of Jacobus Kip (1706–77), who presided over the family from the mansion at Kips Bay until his death during the Revolution. Jacobus was the father of the Samuel Kip for whom the Haring child was named. "Indenture and Map between the descendants of Jacobus Kip, deceased, and Samuel Jones Jr., and Nicholas Stuyvesant of New York, and Showing the Land of Samuel Haring, Surveyed by Charles Coss, City Surveyor," 9 Nov. 1808, Kip Family Papers, 1792–1909, SC16557, Manuscripts and Special Collections, NYSL. The Kip properties lay between the East River and Old Boston Post Road and between Twenty-sixth and Forty-second Streets.

43. Spafford, *Gazetteer* (1824), 247.

44. *Index of Marriages and Deaths in New York Weekly Museum, 1788–1817* ([Worcester, Mass.]: American Antiquarian Society, 1982). The notice appeared on 11 Nov. 1809.

→→ STEAM ←←

During Samuel's years as a grocer in the city the steamboat transformed river travel. Fulton's *Claremont* made its successful maiden voyage in 1807, departing from Paulus Hook (later Jersey City) on a Friday at 8 A.M. to arrive at Albany 9 P.M. the next day, reducing a journey of several days by sloop to a predictable day and a half. It entered dependable regular service at once and was a wondrous apparition at the time. A newspaper report declared that to "see this large and apparently unwieldy machine, without oars or sail, propelled through the element by an invisible agency, at a rate of four miles an hour, would be a novelty in any quarter of the globe."*
The steamboat was immediately accepted as an improved and genteel way to travel, and the expectation that this "aquatic stage" would bring more travelers, trade, and prosperity to Albany was amply fulfilled.

The Herrings were quick to take advantage of it. Thomas wrote Smith in 1808 that his sister Betsy and one of Smith's daughters were to leave "Sunday next . . . in the Steam boat which according to rule ought to land them in Albany the following day."† The Herrings and Harings used the steamers often between the commercial poles of the river—the speed and comfort of the voyage improved as the charges declined.‡

---

* The "accommodation (52 berths, besides sofas, etc.) are said to be equal or superior to any vessel that floats on the river." *Hudson Bee,* June 1808, reprinted in J. Munsell, *Annals of Albany* (Albany, N.Y., 1854), 5:17.

† T. Herring, in New York, to Smith, in Peterboro, 30 May 1808, PSP, reel 1.

‡ The original boat was 100 feet long 12 feet wide and seven feet deep; in 1808 it was lengthened to 150 feet and, widened to 18. In Samuel's children's lifetimes the boats were 400 feet in length, took nine and half hours for the trip at best, and the fare was $1 or less. Benson L. Lossing, *The Pictorial Field-Book of the Revolution,* 2 vols. (New York: Harper and Brothers, 1851), 1:35.

---

were again picking up raw sugar in the Caribbean.[45] There was interest in sugar in the family: Thomas Herring was shortly to go into the sugar business in the city, and Samuel's address at 30 Leonard Street on the west side

---

45. St. Bartholomew was then nominally under Swedish rule but in practice it was dominated by the British navy and was a frequent point of call for American shipping. Amos Kidder Fiske, *The West Indies: A History of the Islands of the West Indian Archipelago, Together with an Account of the Physical Characteristics, Natural Resources and Present Condition* (New York: G. P. Putnam's Sons: Knickerbocker Press, 1902), 304–5.

of the city in 1811 was the same as a "sugar house" of Abraham B. Herring (whose relationship to the other Herrings cannot be determined). Whatever the reason for young John's being in the West Indies, his death was a painful loss in a year that also saw the death of the grandfather for whom he had been named. (The last of the children to be born in the city, John Samuel Haring, was given the name of this deceased older brother.)

An important family link to the Revolutionary War was broken when John Haring, who had a stroke the previous October, died in Rockland County in his seventieth year. "On the last day of March 1809," according to Franklyn Burdge, who must have spoken to descendants, "He was out feeding his horses, when he felt the approach of another paralytic stroke. He walked rapidly into the house and said to his wife, 'Get me to bed as quick as you can.' He died at 6 o'clock the morning of April 1st, 1809."[46] Because of the earlier loan, Samuel, unlike his brothers, did not inherit land, but he did receive his share of the "goods and chattels" and a cash bequest of $504; the "loan" was recognized as part of his inheritance.[47] In the division of the personal effects, or vendue, Samuel received "1 Silver Table Spoon, 1 tea, 1 Table Cloth, 1 sheet, 2 Towels, 2 Shirts, 1 pr. pillow case."[48] According to Fabend, the estate inventory shows that John Haring died, not rich, but "comfortably fixed."[49] His widow, Mary (Herring) Haring remained in Rockland County until her death at seventy-four in October 1825.

Sarah's father, James Clark, the veteran of the evacuation of Brooklyn, died in the city in 1814, after the Samuel Haring family had moved to Albany, and was, surprisingly for a member of an old Presbyterian family, buried in St. Paul's churchyard. Deborah, his widow, was to live many more years, residing principally in Ballston, near Saratoga Springs. She applied for a Revolutionary War widow's pension in 1839, from "Saratoga

46. See Franklin Burdge, *A Notice of John Haring, a Patriotic Statesman of the Revolution* (New York: privately printed, 1878).

47. Haring had a slave at his death: "I give and bequeath unto my wife Mary Haring, One of my Bedsteads with the Beds, Bedclothes and their appurtenances; and my Negro woman slave named Abigail; also the sum of Eight hundred Dollars . . ."; he left lands in Cayuga Co. to his son Elbert. Burdge, *John Haring*, Will of John Haring (appendix).

48. Copy of transcript provided to the author by Firth Haring Fabend, Jan. 1995.

49. Letter from Firth Haring Fabend to Sally Dewey, Tappan Historical Society, 23 July 1987, copy provided to the author.

City, N.Y.," and died in 1843.[50] Their son, William Clark, was, as we have seen, well-off in the city in 1809, when he bought the Aurelius land from his sister and brother-in-law. In 1833 this William, then of Clark & Tallmadge (grocers), guaranteed a loan to Samuel Kip Haring, who had followed his father's profession.[51]

The Clark-Haring connection continued in the next generation, when John Samuel Haring married his first cousin, Mary Clark, William's daughter. Another of the daughters, Helen, married George Alexander Phelps Jr., whose sister was to marry Samuel's son, James Demarest Haring. As we learn from Kate, there were regular contacts with Clark relatives for several decades.[52]

Samuel and Sarah on John Street

The Harings' address in 1811 was 15½ John Street (a shared house), midway on the block next to Broadway, with its smart shops and elegant pedestrians.[53] John Street sloped down past Gold Street to Water Street, ending up at Burling Slip on the East River (within South Street Seaport today) where, according to the guidebook by Horatio Gates Spafford, "the quays and wharves along the shores, are far extended into the original waters that almost surround the Town." The natural unevenness of the original Manhattan had been smoothed, leaving "a gentle ascent from the

---

50. James Clark died in New York City on 13 Dec. 1814 and was buried in Trinity Churchyard. "Trinity Church, Register of Burials," 2 vols., typescript, NYGB, 2:141. A recent inventory of gravestones reveals no stone for James Clark. E-mail communication from Ella Jenness, Parish Recorder, 22 Nov. 2002. Deborah Clark died on 13 April 1843 (JHW MSS). Clark, James; Clark Deborah, pension application file W 16907, Records of the Department of Veterans' Affairs, RG 15, National Archives, Washington, D.C.

51. In 1833 in an action against his partner in a grocery business on the Bowery in New York City, Samuel Kip Haring, son of Samuel Haring and Sarah Clark, refers to a $5,000 line of credit made to his business by his "uncle" of Clark and Tallmadge. BM 540-14, *Samuel K. Haring* vs. *George Colburn*, Feb. 1833, Room 703, 31 Chambers St., Archives, New York Co. Clerk's Office, New York, N.Y.

52. John Samuel Haring married Mary Clark on 12 Sept. 1831, at New York. See "Clark," Genealogical and Biographical Notes in this volume. See also "Phelps I" and "Haring," Genealogical and Biographical Notes in the author's *Hatch and Brood of Time*.

53. This assumes that he lived at this address in the year prior to the publication of the directory as he was in Albany in early 1812. *Elliot's Improved New-York Double Directory Containing Alphabetical List of Inhabitants*, 1812.

Hudson and East Rivers . . . which terminate in a handsome and central elevation [Broadway] that every where overlooks its gently sloping sides, and commands a fine view on the right and left, of the Town, the rivers above named, and their crowds of shipping."[54] Near the juncture of John and Gold Streets was the highest point in the built-up city, called Golden Hill, then highly favored as a residential address.[55] This was a street with well-to-do residents.

Commercial and residential uses were mixed on the street; the Harings lived among tradespeople, craft shops, merchants, lawyers, and gentlefolk. (The same was no doubt true of the Herring residences as well.) Neighbors on the John Street block included merchants, grocers, a baker, a painter, a tinplate worker, a turner, a coachmaker, widows, gentlemen, and a physician. It was a mix sustained by the needs of the cosmopolitan and prosperous seaport.

Surely the most striking sight of the growing city was a short distance up Broadway, at the head of the parade ground: City Hall, eleven years in construction, opened in 1811. Designed by a French architect and built by a Scotsman, its appearance mingled elements of the French Renaissance with the colonial and federal classicism. Spafford termed it "a stately pile of durable architecture," hardly an encomium worthy of a building that continues to grace the city nearly two hundred years later.[56] (A modern appraisal is more enthusiastic. Its design is "[r]eminiscent of the Hotel de Ville of the eighteenth century; the dignified marble structure, chastely embellished with Louis XVI pilasters between arched windows, is notable for its unusual grace and delicate scale. The two wings are balanced on either side by a central portion that is surmounted by cupola.")[57] Its cupola was a landmark visible from Long Island, New Jersey, ships in the harbor, and from the fields in the Bowery, to the north.

---

54. Spafford, *Gazetteer* (1824), 247.

55. I. N. Phelps Stokes, *The Iconography of Manhattan Island, 1398–1909* (New York: Robert H. Dodd, 1918–28), 1:345.

56. Spafford, *Gazetteer* (1824), 248. The building, treasured by later generations as an elegant survival in a city that spared little of the past, was not appreciated by its contemporaries. Cooper, in 1828, considered that "[t]he building is oddly enough composed of two sorts of stone, which impairs its simplicity, and gives it a patched and party colored appearance." Cooper, *Notions of the Americans*, 118.

57. *The WPA Guide to New York City*, rev. ed. (New York: Pantheon Books, 1982), 95.

The opening of the City Hall coincided with the completion of a plan for the city's expansion, embodied in an eight-foot long map of Manhattan on which was superimposed a grid showing streets on the east-west axis and avenues running south-north. Samuel and several of his children would later live within the grid ordained by this 1811 plan—another example of "rationalizing the land," by imposing the will of a technologically adept and intellectually self-conscious society on an uneven topography. The plan was made in the spirit of Simeon De Witt. Avenues and streets on the largely rural island in were laid out in a projection that seemed scarcely believable. The intention of those who devised the plan was to stimulate development by establishing lots of uniform dimensions (eighteen to twenty-five feet wide and usually a hundred and twenty feet deep), which could be developed in predictable ways. The plan allowed no variations for mansions. New streets north of City Hall would be straight, equidistant from each other, accessible from the north-south avenues and allowing "free and abundant circulation of air." The rectangle became the basic design of Manhattan, and New Yorkers would live within the cruciform pattern, with four horizons visible at each intersection.[58]

Captain Samuel Haring in 1812

In early 1812 the Samuel Haring family left John Street and the city for Albany, which became their home for the next eighteen years. It was apparently not the promise of trade that prompted this move, for in March of that year Samuel was commissioned an officer in the regular U.S. army in a unit being formed in anticipation of war with Britain.

Albany had grown mightily in the dozen years since the newly married Harings had passed through it on their way to the lower river. A million barrels of wheat a year were now passing through the city, and Spafford "doubted if there be a place on this continent which is daily visited by so many teams . . ." The Albany dock master told him that there were sixty sloops with regular wharfage at Albany, out of a total of 326 working the river (Maude had reported 90 in 1800).[59] "During the summer of 1811, near 200,000 dollars worth of coarse grain, principally maize and rye, has

58. Edwin G. Burrows and Mike Wallace, *Gotham: A History of New York City to 1898* (New York: Oxford Univ. Press, 1999), 419–20.

59. Spafford, *Gazetteer* (1824), 118.

been brought up in Troy alone, destined for Europe."[60] The quays north of the steam ferry landing extended one mile along the riverbank, along which Spafford "saw from 80 to 200 sloops and schooners." [61]

There were 12,000 people in Albany, living in 1,800 houses. The city was riding a boom that would swell when the canal opened. In 1824 Spafford opined that it "probably possesses greater wealth, more real capital, than any other place in the United States . . . of the same population."[62] He attributed the improvement to the "rapid influx of people from the Eastern States," which stirred the place with "a more enlightened taste." (He blamed "the Dutch character" for favoring "present convenience rather than taste and future elegance.")[63]

Towering over the city was the new state capitol building, placed on the steep hill that rose up from the west bank of the river. There were also "two elegant banking houses," a library, "a theater now a-building, many elegant private mansions and gentlemen's seats."[64] One mansion belonged to William James, grandfather of the novelist Henry James, who made a fortune in trade and land speculation. He was far better known and more prosperous than Abraham Herring, but their activities were akin in that he had offices in New York City and in Albany and bought grains to the west and sold them downriver.[65]

The Haring family's Albany address was 10 North Pearl Street. This may be the same property that the young couple occupied in 1798, as there were no conveyances in the intervening years. Their house was near the recently completed (and still standing) Second Reformed Church, where

---

60. Ibid., 51.

61. Ibid., 120.

62. Ibid., 64, 118.

63. Ibid., 117.

64. Ibid., 118.

65. William James arrived in New York City in 1789 from County Cavan, Ireland, and moved to what he saw as the riper fields of endeavor in Albany four years later. He had the acumen to take advantage of the opening up the agricultural fields to the west whose produce could increasingly easily be brought down the Mohawk River to be transshipped on the Hudson. In recognition of what he had achieved and to celebrate what was sure to bring even greater trade to Albany, James was chosen in 1826 to give the major address at the opening of the Erie Canal. At his death in 1832 his estate was valued at $3 million. Katherine B. Hastings, "William^2 (1771–1832) James of Albany, N.Y. and His Descendants," *Record* 55 (1924): 101. See also Leon Edel, *Henry James: The Untried Years: 1843–1870* (Philadelphia: J. B. Lippincott, 1953), 20.

18. View of Market Street (now Broadway), with Market and Old Dutch
Church, 1805. Watercolor on paper by James Eights, ca. 1850.

Albany Institute of History and Art, Bequest of Ledyard Cogswell Jr.

the last three of Sarah's children were baptized. The more affluent citizens
lived in larger houses on nearby Market Street.[66] A watercolor by the
Albany artist James Eights (1798–1882), based on his memory of conditions as they were in 1805, shows modest wooden houses of one and one-
and-a-half stories near to the old Dutch church, probably like what the
Harings occupied, fitted within the standard lot width of twenty-five feet.[67]

War

Samuel was not to engage in the trade of prospering Albany. Instead he
went to war. In early 1812 the United States moved toward war with Great
Britain. The "war hawks" in Congress in 1811–12, led by Henry Clay, a

---

66. A Thomas Herring of Herring & Walker, merchants, had a house at 54 Court St. As noted earlier, he cannot be the same Thomas as Abraham's son. What connection there is to the Haring-Herring family in this study the author has been unable to determine. Albany Directory (1813), in
Munsell, *Annals of Albany,* 5:53–97.

67. Interview with Stefan Bielinski, Director, Colonial Albany Social History Project, 3093 Cultural Education Center, Albany, N.Y., 14 July 1994.

Jeffersonian Republican of Kentucky, advocated the interests of the frontier and were largely concerned with British impediments to American expansionism in the west. The Jeffersonian Republicans, however, were in the minority in the New York Assembly from 1807 to 1817. The embargo of 1807–9 to protest British violation of the maritime rights of the neutral U.S. was unpopular in the city and in New England for its negative effect on trade. The prospect of war with Britain was so unpopular in New York that in the congressional vote on the declaration eight of the ten Republican congressmen from the state voted "no" with the Federalist minority. Opinion was divided, however, as New Yorkers in 1807 had elected a Republican governor, Daniel D. Tompkins, who was reelected for two three-year terms. Tompkins supported the Madison administration and the war. The New England states, on the other hand, overwhelmingly supported the Federalists and opposed the war.[68]

It was a contentious time in politics. Jeffersonian Republicans, ascendant nationally since 1800, were bitterly opposed by the Federalists, who had strongholds in New England and New York. There is no doubt where the Harings stood. Elbert Herring had spoken out for Jefferson and the unpopular embargo in a speech in New York City commemorating the anniversary of the Battle of Lexington in 1809. With oratorical flourishes, Elbert, thirty-two and a member of the New York bar, equated support of Jefferson's policy with the patriotism of the leaders of the Revolution. "Fellow Republicans," he urged, "I conjure you by the blood of your fathers, which your freedom cost, to guard her hallowed temple with reverential care to transmit the rich inheritance undiminished, to your posterity. I invoke you to preserve her sacred shrine from foreign violence and domestic faction." He charged Federalist critics, that "by encouraging opposition to your laws—by vilifying your administration, and spreading dissentions among the people—[they] have distracted your country, weakened your government, and endangered your constitution." "Resist their distempered efforts," he told his audience, "or they will entomb your liberty."[69]

---

68. "The War of 1812," *History of the State of New York*, Alexander Flick, ed. (New York: Columbia Univ. Press, 1933), 4:217–53. Daniel D. Tompkins (1774–1825) was governor of New York from 1807 to 1817. He was later vice-president under James Monroe.

69. [Elbert Herring], *An Oration of the Anniversary of The Battle of Lexington, Delivered at the Request of "The United Whig Club"* (New York: Southwick and Pelsue, 1809), 12.

The Haring-Herring support for the Republicans had its origins in John Haring's allegiance to George Clinton, later New York's leading Jeffersonian Republican, who was the candidate preferred by New Yorkers for president in 1808 when he was elected vice-president to serve with Madison. When Clinton died in office on 30 May 1812, just before the declaration of war, Elbert Herring was a principal eulogist in New York City.[70]

Samuel Haring left his business well before war was declared. On 12 March 1812 he was commissioned a lieutenant in the Thirteenth U.S. New York Regiment of the regular army then being organized near Albany.[71] Winfield Scott, later the leader of the invasion of Mexico, who served with distinction in 1812 in the campaigns on the Niagara Frontier and along Lake Ontario, recalled the political appointees of 1812 with scorn: "Party spirit of that day knew no bounds, and, of course, was blind to policy . . . the appointments consisted, generally, of swaggerers, dependents, decayed gentlemen, and others—'fit for nothing else,' which always turned out to be *utterly unfit for any military purpose whatsoever.*"[72] Certainly the family affiliation with the Jeffersonian Republicans led to Samuel's commission, but from what we know of his previous career he did not merit Scott's aspersions. His position of quartermaster was appropriate, but as for military experience, it had been confined to militia drills under Col. Hardenbergh in his youth, and, like almost everyone in his regiment (and the hastily expanded U.S. Army), he was an amateur in arms. The anti-British sentiment in the family ran strong; no doubt John Haring's son was imbued from his youth with patriotic resistance to British bullying. (In the last year of the war, when a major British invasion threatened, cousin Thomas in New York City expressed the family belligerence: "We have gained some discipline and are as mad as hornets on account of turning out every day to exercise, if we stand to come in contact with them, many very many will bite the dust.")[73]

---

70. 20 May 1812, in *Constitution and Rules of The George Clinton Society Established 26th July 1812* (New York, 1913); quoted in Kaminski, *George Clinton*, 292–92. In the tangled New York politics of 1812, Herring and New York Republicans supported George Clinton's nephew DeWitt Clinton in the presidential election of 1812 in preference to a second term for Madison.

71. F. B. Heitman, *Historical Register and Dictionary of The US Army from Its Organization September 29, 1789 to September 29, 1880* (Washington, D.C.: National Tribune, 1890).

72. Winfield Scott, *Memoirs of Lieut.-General Scott, LL.D., Written by Himself* (New York: Sheldon, 1864).

73. T. Herring, in New York, to Smith, in Peterboro, 8 Sept. 1814, PSP, reel 1.

The regular army before 1812 was scattered in small units from Florida to the old Northwest, areas where there were conflicts with the Indians. It had also been drastically reduced from 4,000 officers and men under arms at the outset of the Jefferson administration to 2,400 at its end. Army service was ill supported, and few regular officers were capable. President Madison and the war hawks in the Congress who advocated open hostilities with Britain in 1812 were taking on a conflict with a scratch force. The army was beefed up to 6,750 men at the outset of the war, but these were troops who had to learn as they went along, and the first lessons were grim. (As an example of the superannuated officers that abounded in the militia, Sarah's uncle, Samuel Clark, who performed valiantly in the Revolution, rose in rank in the militia during the intervening years and at the age of seventy-three, in the midst of the War of 1812, was promoted to major general.)[74]

The Thirteenth U.S. was a regular army unit, however, and for all its inadequacies its performance was superior to that of New York militia units, which could scarcely cohere as a fighting force in most engagements.[75] Moreover, by war's end the regular army had developed a degree of professionalism, and distinguished military careers were begun, including those of Winfield Scott and of John E. Wool (1784–1869), later a general, who was a fellow captain with Samuel in the Thirteenth.[76]

Samuel was promoted to captain a month after joining the service. The regimental commander was Colonel Peter P. Schuyler, son of General

---

74. Edgar W. Clark, *History and Genealogy of Samuel Clark, Sr. and His Descendants from 1636–1882—256 Years* (St. Louis, 1892), 58.

75. John R. Elting, *Amateurs to Arms! A Military History of the War of 1812* (1991, Univ. of North Carolina Press; New York: Da Capo Press, 1995), 2–3; C. Edward Skeen, *Citizen Soldiers in the War of 1812* (Lexington, Ken.: Univ. of Kentucky Press, 1999), particularly 96 ff.

76. "With the help of De Witt Clinton, [Wool] obtained a commission in the regular army, as a Captain in the Thirteenth, dated from 14 April 1812." He was wounded at the Battle of Queenston Heights in that year. He remained in the army, serving at various times as inspector-general. He was promoted to Brigadier General in 1841 and was cited for meritorious service at the battle of Buena Vista in the Mexican War. He commanded Fortress Monroe at the outset of the Civil War, and though he expected to play a large role in that conflict, his advanced age and the early prominence of McClellan forced him into retirement. *ANB*, s.v. "Wool, John Ellis." See also Louis L. Babcock, *The War on the Niagara Frontier*, Buffalo Historical Society Publications, vol. 29 (Buffalo, 1927), 46; Donald R. Hickey, *The War of 1812: A Forgotten Conflict* (Urbana and Chicago: Univ. of Illinois Press, 1990).

Philip Schuyler, in the regular army since 1798.[77] At thirty-six he and Samuel were nearly exact contemporaries.

The regiment mustered at Greenbush, across the river from Albany, part of a mobilization of 30,000 that Congress authorized in February.[78] The men were recruited locally according to the standards and procedures of the time, with a bounty given to induce enlistment. A notice in the Albany *Argus* for the regiment specified that "Recruits are to be free from sore legs, scurvy, scalled head [a scaly or scabby disease of the scalp] and other infirmities. The age is to be conformable to law, but healthy, active boys, between 14 and 19 years of age may be listed for musicians. No objection is to be made to a recruit for want of size, provided he is strong, active, well made and healthy."[79] The pay scales for officers at the time provided $40 per month for the rank of captain (an increase of $10 for Samuel over his lieutenant's pay) and $75 for colonel.[80]

As quartermaster, Samuel was responsible for supplying the troops by awarding contracts using a "lowest possible" bid, often from corrupt and inefficient suppliers. The results throughout the army were "[l]ate deliveries, short weight, and inferior quality." The troops had to endure fall and winter on the Niagara Frontier with inadequate clothing and bedding because woolen clothing failed to arrive on time. The one piece of adequate equipment was the "musket of 1795," which, thanks to the efficiency of the Springfield Armory, was later termed "lighter and more accurate than its British counterpart."[81]

---

77. *List of Officers of the Army of the United States from 1779 to 1900*, comp. Wm. H. Powell (New York: L. H. Hamersly, 1900; reprint, Detroit: Gale Research, 1967). Peter P. Schuyler was born on 15 July 1776 and died in 1825 at Natchez, Miss., of yellow fever. After the war he immigrated to Mississippi territory, where there was a land boom; he became the first treasurer of the state after it was admitted to the union in 1817. The obituary of Peter P. Schuyler states "he entered the army at the age of 18 and gradually rose to the rank of Colonel and served under General Wayne." Florence A. Christoph, *The Schuyler Families in America Prior to 1900* (Albany, N.Y.: Friends of Schuyler Mansion, [1993]), 2:12.

78. Elting, *Amateurs to Arms!* 3.

79. *Argus*, 2 Feb. 1813, 1:34.

80. "Schedule of the monthly compensation of the troops of the U.S., agreeably to the several acts of Congress in force on the 1st of April, 1813," *The American State Papers, Class V, Military Affairs* (Washington, D.C.: Gales and Seaton, 1832), 1:435–36.

81. Elting, *Amateurs to Arms!* 9.

War was declared in June 1812, but the Thirteenth U.S. New York did not move until the third month of the war. The *Albany Gazette* reported in late September:

> The 13th regiment of United States troops, commanded by Col. Peter P Schuyler of this city, broke up from the camp at Greenbush and passed into this city for Niagara. The regiment consists of 600 men, well clothed, armed and equipped. They made a very martial appearance, which was much heightened by an excellent band of music belonging to the regiment [there was] an excellent stand of colours.[82]

All seemed promising. The general orders given to the Sixth U.S. Regiment, also at the Greenbush camp, expressed the exalted sense of purpose of the day: "We have been assembled Here Not Merely to Enforce Laws But to Revenge Aggressions Heaped upon Our Country by a Nation forgetful of every principle of common and moral Justice," the commander told the troops, continuing:

> The Service We are Called upon to perform Will Require of us the Most perfect Knowledge of Discipline, Obedience and Patience. Our Country Looks up to us for a faithful discharge of Duty. Our Lives are Intrusted and What is More dear to the Breast of a Soldier our Honour is set up a Mark for the Scrutinizing Eyes. Let us Not Therefore disappoint our Country. Nor Tarnish our Honour . . .[83]

Most of the officers in the Thirteenth and other of the hastily assembled regular units were as green as the recruits and had not in any case been chosen for their martial skills. Considering the hapless ensuing campaigns, it is astonishing that the objective was to invade and seize Canada, expected to be not much more than a walk north. John Calhoun, of South Carolina, on the floor of the House of Representatives in March stated his belief "that four weeks from the time the declaration of war is heard on our frontier the whole of Upper Canada and a part of Lower Canada will be in our possession." Thomas Jefferson in Monticello was similarly optimistic and added a larger imperial goal: "The acquisition of Canada this year as

82. *Albany Gazette*, 24 Sept. 1812.

83. Sixth U.S. Infantry Regiment, box 14, folder 167, MS EQ161-222, Regimental Orders, Greenbush, 13 Aug. 1812, Manuscripts and Special Collections, NYSL.

19. The seat of war in the north, 1812

Library of Congress, Map Collection

far as the neighborhood of Quebec, would be a mere matter of marching, and would give us experience for the attack on Halifax, the next and final expulsion of England from the American continent."[84] Many expected the French-speaking inhabitants to be disloyal to the Crown and Americans living in Upper Canada to support the invasion, or at least not to offer resistance. Similar pretensions about an easy foray into Canada had been entertained in 1775.

The lofty sentiments expressed in Albany may have abated during the dusty march of nearly four hundred miles to the Niagara River. The Thirteenth took the Genesee Turnpike following the rutted, pot-holed roads made by the passing troops.[85] Samuel could see how Hardenbergh's Corners had been transformed into the flourishing town of Auburn, with about ninety houses. The early mills, log church, and cabins were only a memory, having been replaced by the courthouse and the county clerk's office. Hardenbergh's widow and his son, named for John Haring, and Jehiel Clark, Sarah's cousin, were prominent and popular citizens. When he visited Auburn in 1810, De Witt Clinton had found it "a fine growing place" and attributed its success to its "hydraulic works"—Hardenbergh's mills had shown this potential—and its role as a county seat.[86] One wonders if Samuel regretted having left when he saw this prosperity.

The Thirteenth U.S. New York moved on to Canandaigua and thence northwest to Fort Niagara, famous for its past role as a bastion of French, and later British, predominance on western Lake Ontario. It commanded the outlet of the Niagara River. The guns of the British Fort George were visible across the water.

It was from Fort Niagara that three hundred men from the Thirteenth, under Captain John E. Wool, went south on a route shielded from sight of the British on the opposite bank to join militia and other regular units. The militia were commanded by Stephen Van Rensselaer, patron of the family that owned extensive lands by the Hudson near Albany and recently appointed a militia general. The force assembled on the American bank of

---

84. Quoted in E. A. Cruikshank, "Battle of Fort George, 27 May 1813" in *Campaigns of the War of 1812–14*, 10 vols. (Niagara-on-the-Lake, Ont.: Niagara Historical Society, 1896–1902), 1:8.; Calhoun ref. dated 6 March 1812.

85. Hall, *Auburn*, 112.

86. William W. Campbell, *The Life and Writings of De Witt Clinton* (New York: Baker and Scribner, 1849), 169–70, quoted in Schein, "A Historical Geography," 319.

20. *Fort Niagara in 1818*. Benson J. Lossing, *Harper's New Monthly Magazine* (June 1861).

the Niagara River facing Queenston and the precipitous cliff above it.[87] On the night of 11 October, men of the Thirteenth were among a party under Captain Wool that crossed the swift-flowing river. They found an unguarded fisherman's path up the escarpment, surprised a British unit and momentarily dominated the heights. They had no backup, however, and a British detachment from Fort George under General Isaac Brock, who was killed in the action, was able to dislodge them, inflicting heavy casualties.[88] Among the Americans captured were young Lieutenant Winfield Scott and Lt. Col. John Chrystie, second-in-command of the Thirteenth.[89] The militia units that should have reinforced Captain Wool on the heights, "not conspicuous for discipline or courage," refused to cross the river into Canada, despite General VanRensselaer's ardent pleas.[90]

---

87. Cruikshank, "Battle of Fort George," 41.

88. Brock was honored by Canadian posterity for his decisive repulse of the invasion with a statue on Queenston Heights that looks steadfastly east to the American shore.

89. Henry Adams, *History of the United States of America During the Administrations of James Madison* (1891; New York: Library of America, 1986), 538–40.

90. Pratt, "War of 1812," 225.

21. *The Heights at Queenston*. Benson
J. Lossing, H*arper's New Monthly
Maga{ine* (June 1861).

The Battle of Queenston Heights was an ignominious defeat for the
Americans and ended expectations of an easy conquest of Upper Canada
or of a revolt by its inhabitants.[91] The idea of conquering Canada was not
scotched, however, and Samuel and the troops would be committed to that
goal in the spring. (Samuel had probably remained with the units of the
Thirteenth posted to Fort Niagara during the Queenston battle and
remained there during the winter.)

The northern campaign of 1812 sputtered to an end with an abortive
foray against Fort Erie at the mouth of the Niagara River. By late November the militia went home, and the ill-equipped and badly led regulars
went into winter quarters. They had to endure the cold without adequate
blankets, knowing that the operations of the autumn had been a costly
fiasco.

The attempt to take Canada in 1813 began in late May with an attack on
Fort George, on the west bank of the mouth of the Niagara River. In a joint
operation planned by the army's Winfield Scott (released by the British in

91. Elting, *Amateurs to Arms!* 38–50; Adams, *History of the United States of America during the
Administrations of James Madison*, 518–40.

an exchange of prisoners) and the navy's Oliver Hazard Perry, the Americans marshaled a flotilla of transports and warships on western Lake Ontario consisting of 4,500 troops (including the Thirteenth U.S. New York and Samuel Haring) and a fleet of armed schooners. On 27 May, under cover of a dense fog, successive waves of Americans landed near Fort George. After a sharp fight (350 British and 140 American dead, wounded, and captured), its defenders left the fort to the attackers. According to a recent student of the war, the amphibious operation was "undoubtedly the best-planned and best-fought engagement of the entire war."[92]

Captain Samuel Haring no doubt shared in the satisfaction from this first apparently decisive victory in the north. However, the triumph was diluted when Morgan Lewis, the former New York governor and a "political general," was unable to sustain pursuit of the British. Despite later attempts to stop and defeat them in engagements at Stoney Creek and Beaver Dam along the northwestern shores of the lake, the British escaped to fight again. They regrouped at York (later Toronto) and, with a small fleet, posed a potentially serious threat to the American camp at Sackets Harbor at the eastern end of the lake. The troops at Fort George that summer were subject to attacks by small units of British and Canadians.

Samuel Haring was among those who spent the hot weather months camped on the flat by the fort. It became a noxious place, with "heaps of rubbish and refuse . . . allowed to accumulate everywhere and a horrible stench arose from the sinks, to the neglect of which the surgeons ascribed most of the ill health of the troops."[93] Weather was an adversary:

> With the exception of a few hot days in the beginning of June, the whole of that month and the first ten days in July had been unusually wet and cool. Then a 'severe and unrelenting drought' set in, which lasted for almost two months. The village of Niagara [Niagara-on-the-Lake] intercepted the breeze from the lake, while the unbroken forest stretching for many miles northward along the eastern bank kept the wind away from those quarters. The pitiless midsummer sun beat down upon their camp until it glowed like a furnace.

92. Elting, *Amateurs to Arms!* 123.

93. E. A. Cruikshank, *Campaigns of the War of 1812–14* (Niagara-on-the-Lake, Ont.: Niagara Historical Society, 1896–1902); "The Battle of Stoney Creek and the Blockade of Fort George," 66.

Dr. Lovell, a medical officer, recalled of the men that

> having been wet for nearly a month, our troops were exposed for six or seven
> weeks to intense heat during the day and at night to a cold and chilly atmo-
> sphere, in consequence of the fog arriving from the lake and river. The
> enemy's advance being within a short distance of the camp, the details for
> duty were large, and skirmishes taking place at the piquet's every morning
> the solders were for a length of time stationed at the several works for several
> hours before daylight, and thus exposed to the effects of a cold damp atmo-
> sphere at the time when the system is most susceptible to morbid impres-
> sions.[94]

By September 1,165 of 4,587 men in the force were sick.[95] Samuel Har-
ing was debilitated by the "lake fever," a dysentery condition. Colonel
John Chrystie, formerly second-in-command of the Thirteenth U.S. New
York and a promising officer, died from it.[96]

By fall most of the army evacuated Fort George and were conveyed in
open Durham boats along the southern shore of Lake Ontario to Sackets
Harbor, where they regrouped. The move was part of a strategy to attack
Montreal from two directions. This army, under General James Wilkinson, was to approach from the west to descend the St. Lawrence. Another,
under General Wade Hampton, was to assemble north of Albany and use
the traditional invasion route through the Champlain Valley. The strategy
made sense, but the execution was a fiasco.

General James Wilkinson (1757–1825) was thought by many to have
plotted against Washington after Saratoga in the course of carrying news
of the victory to the Continental Congress. Recently in the pay of the
Spanish government, he was also the co-conspirator, with Aaron Burr, in
the alleged attempt to create a separate country from Louisiana territory.
Wilkinson's 1813 expedition was the last in "his long-checkered, and on

---

94. Ibid.

95. Testimony of Robert G. Hite, in James Wilkinson, *Memoirs of My Own Times* (Philadelphia:
Abraham Small, 1816), 3:281 (transcript of court marital of General Wilkinson, 1815).

96. Samuel Haring Pension Application. "DIED—At camp by Ft. George, the 16th inst. of a fever,
Col. John Christie, of the 23d Reg. US Infantry, formerly Lt. Col. of the 13th, and one of the
inspectors general of the army—aged about 26 years. By this death the service has lost a valuable
officer, and his acquaintances a sincere friend." *Argus* [Albany], 3 Aug. 1813.

the whole dishonorable career."[97] (The contrary view of himself is enshrined in the three-volume memoir that he published in 1816, including the transcript of the court martial called to try him after the failure of his command.) He was vain and despised his superior, Secretary of War John Armstrong, who had called him back to the service. He treated General Wade Hampton with disdain and was detested to the point that the two men did not communicate. The success of the invasion depended on their cooperation, which the secretary of war could not impose.

Wilkinson arrived at Sackets Harbor to take command at the end of August 1813, already late in the season for carrying out an operation involving thousands of troops. Then there were several weeks of delay, pushing the operation into the fall, with its winds and storms.

Passage in the open boats along almost the entire length of the lake exposed the men to the autumn winds and storms, giving them "a very boisterous passage," according to one participant.[98] Strong winds caused the flotilla to turn back shortly after it left Fort George. There were heavy winds on most days, making for difficult handling of the heavy Durham boats (which were rowed, with, if wind conditions favored, a sail assist), and a storm wrecked a number of them. It took twenty days for the flotilla to reach Henderson Harbor, about 130 miles away, an average of a little over six miles per day.[99] Capt. John Keyes Paige, one of Samuel's fellow officers, characterized what must have been a back-breaking and exceedingly uncomfortable maneuver as "exceptionally arduous . . . especially [for] the platoon officers."[100] Paige, whose affidavit is in Samuel's pension application, had "no certain recollection whether Captain Haring accom-

---

97. Hoffman Nickerson, *Turning Point of the Revolution or Burgoyne in America* (Boston, 1928), 428, quoted in Boatner, 1205. The initial entry in the latter reads: "Cont'l officer, scoundrel." His self-serving account of the action and his subsequent court martial is included in *Memoirs of My Own Times*. See also the account of Henry Adams, *History of the United States of America During the Administrations of James Madison*, 493, which reads in part: "In spite of acquittal, Wilkinson stood in the worst possible odor, and returned what he considered his wrongs by bitter and contemptuous hatred for the President and his Secretary of War."

98. Anonymous Diary, War of 1812, MS 1472, Manuscripts and Special Collections, NYSL.

99. Diary of John Keyes Paige, 13th U.S. New York Regiment, transcribed in *The Documentary History of the Campaigns on the Niagara Frontier*, ed. Ernest Cruikshank, 4 vols. (Lundy's Lane Historical Society, n.d.; reprint, New York: *New York Times*, Arno Press, 1971, 4:149.

100. John Keyes Paige, in Albany, to Mrs. Sarah Haring, 15 Dec. 1829, Samuel Haring Pension Application. Heitman, *Historical Register*, 504.

panied us in the boats, or whether in consequence of his health, he went across the Country, and joined us at Henderson Harbor [adjacent to Sackets Harbor to the west, roughly opposite Kingston]. At this place I well remember that he labored under a severe attack of (I believe) inflammatory rheumatism."[101]

The conditions at the military hospital at Henderson were poor before the onset of cold weather and worsened with the season. Corrupt suppliers of food and clothing were much to blame. Dr. William M. Ross sent a devastating report to the inspector general in mid-September, stating, "Such is the increasing inclemency and severity of a northern climate that the regimental hospital tents are an inadequate protection, and many will doubtless perish." He found the blankets of "inferior quality and of so small a size that it will require three or four to make each patient comfortable." Shirts had not arrived, and "the chocolate, marked 'Smith's fine chocolate, first quality,' is of so inferior a quality, either as an article of diet or medicine, as to be unfit for use." Barley and rice, brandy and rum, had been "lost, or have not arrived." There was no bread for the sick and the flour "is found to contain not only foreign admixture of meal, but to be so sour and damaged, as to prove unhealthy, and from the report of surgeons, has accelerated the deaths of several in his regiment."[102] The hospital patients, he noted, were forced to lie on straw in the absence of bunks.

Fortunately Samuel had a strong constitution. He survived exposure to such rough conditions and was even able to take on some duties, but fitfully. Mary Pratt, the nurse who attended Samuel at Henderson Harbor and whose husband was in the regiment, recalled that he "was exposed several nights to the fall rains especially when Officer of the Guard . . . [and] Caught a Dreadful Cold by which he was Confined to his Bed for several Days During . . . [and] that before Capt. Haring recovered from that Cold he was severely attacked with the Jaundice & a most painful rheumatism—his Color was quite Yellow & he was for several Weeks unable to Join the Main Army . . ."[103]

In late October the fleet of Durhams with the main army began to leave Henderson Harbor. The boats carried about 7,000 men, supplies, and can-

101. Ibid.

102. Letter from William M. Ross, Hospital Surgeon, U.S. Army, Hospital Department, Sackets Harbor to Inspector General, 18 Sept. 1813, in Wilkinson, *Memoirs*, 3: Appendix IX, unpaginated.

103. Deposition of Mary Pratt, Albany, 17 Dec. 1829, Samuel Haring Pension Application.

non. By 3 November the last detachment and General Wilkinson had left, heading for the St. Lawrence through the Thousand Islands.[104] Near Grenadier Island, the flotilla ran into "severe wind, rain and snow . . . a violent wind and snowstorm," and fifteen boats were wrecked and others damaged.[105] On the descent of the river the boats were easy targets for the British regulars on the Canadian bank.

It was a demoralizing passage, and the commanding general was out of control. An officer described his arrival at a camp set up by American troops on foot. When informed that an approaching boat was that of the general, according to one of the officers,

> The major, myself, and others met the General at the water's edge, and asked if he wished to come on shore. Indicating that he did, [Benjamin?] Forsyth and myself took him by the arms to assist him out of the boat, and up the bank. We found him most abominably intoxicated, and hurried him into the house; during which time he was muttering the most desperate imprecations against the enemy—saying that if they did not cease firing, he would blow to dust the whole British garrison, and lay waste their country. After seating him on a chair near the fire, the major and myself retired to consult what was best to be done, under the present situation of the commander-in-chief; when we concluded to detail and post a guard near the door of the house, to keep out both citizens and solders. I made the detail and posted the sentence, and soon afterward perceiving the General to nod, and apprehending that he would fall into the fire, I proposed laying him on something like a bedstead that was in the room, and having done so, he was, in a very short time, in a sound sleep. The time to the best of my recollection, at which we received the General, was about two o'clock in the morning. For some time after this occurrence, he was not very available; it was said he was in very bad health.[106]

Seven days later, about two thousand of the Americans landed at Chrysler's Farm on the Canadian bank of the St. Lawrence to engage the British. They were routed by a force half their number. By then news had arrived that the army under Hampton, intended as part of the strategic plan to join up with Wilkinson's force, had turned back without engaging the enemy.

---

104. References except as otherwise specified from Elting, *Amateurs to Arms!* 140 ff.

105. Diary of John Keyes Paige, in Cruikshank, *Documentary History of the Campaigns on the Niagara Frontier*, 2:149–50.

106. "Major Birdsall's statement," Ogdensburgh, 17 July 1835. Printed in John Armstrong, *Notices of the War of 1812* (New York: Wiley and Putnam, 1840), 2:211.

By 15 November the poorly led invasion was called off. The expedition had started far too late in the fall. Hard work, danger, illness, and deaths had gone for nothing. Hampton's northern army and Wilkinson's army both went into winter quarters already prepared—perhaps in the expectation of such an outcome—at French Mills (now Covington) a few miles from the river. It proved to be another bad winter for the Army of the North. "The incompetence and corruption of the Quartermaster General's Department and the greed and the inefficiency of the supply contractors left American soldiers freezing and half-starved even at French Mills."[107]

Samuel, left behind at Henderson to oversee the sick, was himself ill. When "he was able to ride—[he] hired a horse & started for the Main Army, having previously sent off the Squad of sick that were left with him, under the Care of a Sergeant to the Army . . ." He was "able to travel short journies during the day, but at Night experienced much Pain [so] that it took several Days to reach the Mills. There he was for a long time on the Sick list."[108]

"It was afterwards a subject of general conversation among the Officers," recalled Captain Paige of Samuel, "that he did not [re]join his regiment, in consequence of his health being such as to render him unfit for active service, and that this state of health was produced by his frequent exposure to the severe weather & rains of that fall."[109] In Albany that December, Governor Tompkins was appropriately concerned that because the army was falling apart New York would be exposed to invasion from Canada. "The officers have passed this place in shoals," he wrote Secretary of War Armstrong. "Some suppose they are going to Washington to snort forth their own merits, exploits and claims to promotion, others that they go to expose [sic] the cause of their respective commanders and few believe they are running, or shirking (as they call it) from duty. At any rate, the absence of so many of them at this particular junction creates great apprehension and dissatisfaction in the public mind."[110]

---

107. Elting, *Amateurs to Arms!* 152.

108. Deposition of Mary Pratt, Albany, 17 Dec. 1829, Samuel Haring Pension Application.

109. Samuel Haring Pension Application.

110. Daniel D. Tompkins to John Armstrong, Secretary of War, 24 Dec. 1813, quoted in "The War of 1812" *History of the State of New York*, ed. Alexander Flick (New York: Columbia Univ. Press, 1933), 4:239.

Samuel was not one of those about whom Tompkins wrote, having returned to Albany in February.[111] He was honorably discharged from the army after the war's close, on 16 June 1815.[112] When Mary Pratt saw him two years later in Albany he told her that he "had never recovered from that Henderson Harbor Sickness—but had been lame most of the time since his return." When she visited him in 1829 he told her he "had been a Cripple for the last Ten Years," and was then "so low that he can hardly speak loud enough to be heard."[113] Nicholas Jones, a physician, bore out Mary Pratt's views, albeit in a document that was intended to make the most of infirmities to persuade the pension authorities. He reported that when he saw Samuel "in Albany in April of the year 1814 and then his constitution appeared to be materially impaired in consequence of the cold, wet and fatigue to which he had been exposed in military service; that his disease, in my judgment, was rheumatism which had already affected one ankle-joint and soon extended its effect to the knee of the same limb and rendered him in some degree a cripple . . ."[114]

In New York City, which had not been touched by hostilities but was economically in the doldrums, Thomas Herring reported in September 1814 that the

> ills are now felt, and seen; this city has little activity & apart from what arises from military business, even at this period which in past years exhibited all the life and bustle of a crowded fair, the stores all supplied & prices high and the dealers [   ]. But the great evil now experienced is distrust, partly arising from the chance of invasion, principally from the stoppage of specie issues by the banks. The measure is new here, and the boards of direction without the capacity necessary to the relations it is calculated to introduce in the trading community.[115]

It was the darkness before the dawn. On Christmas Eve 1814 in Ghent, the Netherlands, British and American negotiators agreed on terms that

---

111. Deposition of Mary Pratt, Albany, 17 Dec. 1829, Samuel Haring Pension Application.

112. Letter from John Keyes Paige, Samuel Haring Pension Application.

113. Deposition of Mary Pratt.

114. Deposition of Nicholas Jones, practitioner of physic & surgery, Buffalo, N.Y., 16 Jan. 1830, Samuel Haring Pension Application.

115. T. Herring, in New York, to Smith, in Peterboro, 8 Sept. 1814, PSP, reel 1.

ended the war. The Senate approved the treaty of peace a few days after
the draft arrived. In New York on 11 February 1815 people took to the
streets to celebrate the return of prosperity to the port. No matter how
high their expectations of plenty, the coming reality was to exceed them, as
Samuel's sons would find out.[116] (We have seen that Thomas Herring was
one of those that did not benefit in the peace.)

At the peace, the boundaries in existence before the onset of hostilities
were restored. Neither side had won, but neither side was left with a substantial grievance. The British had learned the cost and impracticality of
war against the United States, and the latter had learned to respect the
integrity of Canada. The stalemate was productive, leading to permanent
peace between the United States and its northern neighbor and to an
increasingly benevolent relationship with Britain. Peace had an immediate
effect on trade between the two countries as manufactured goods flooded
in from England, by the returning ships carried produce and, with time,
cotton, east to Liverpool and other ports. With the Royal Navy enforcing
security on the world's sea-lanes, American shipping and trade flourished.

The difficult and often inglorious actions of the War of 1812 faded from
national memory as commerce expanded and western lands opened up.
The veterans who had suffered in the arduous northern campaign were
not honored, as had been their Revolutionary forebears. No holiday celebrated the end of the war or the sacrifice of the participants. There was a
badge of honor in having been an officer, however, and the family used
"Captain Samuel Haring" in his and other family obituary notices.

In Albany after the War

After his return to Albany, Samuel and his family lived on newly developed Ferry Street, closer to the river than they had been before the war.[117]
This was not a step up in the world, as they again lived in a small, wooden
house.

Postwar Albany shared in the prosperity that came to New York port
with peace and maintained and expanded its role as the gateway to the

---

116. Albion, *Rise of New York Port*, 9.

117. All addresses from Albany city directories by year, various printers. Concerning the type of
housing on the street at that time, personal communication from Stefan Bielinski, Albany, 31 Dec.
1998.

west and the principal transshipping point on the upper Hudson. The state's population grew by an astonishing 413,000 (a 43 percent increase) in the decade of the 1810s, much of it from migration through Albany to settle the lands of the west.[118]

By 1820 construction had begun of a great "hydraulic works" to create a water passage to Lakes Erie and Ontario. This was the beginning of the Erie Canal, which became the principal object of attention for Albany residents in the postwar years. In order to serve the expected increase in traffic they built a new boat basin along the river that would accommodate the canal boats and serve as a station for transshipping cargoes to steamers and sloops. The first segment of the great "ditch" was completed from Albany to Rochester in 1823, the same year the canal was opened to connect the Hudson with Lake Champlain, making it possible to go without portage from New York City via Albany to Montreal and to Lake Ontario at Rochester. On 8 October 1823 Albanians marked the dual canal openings "with great pomp, and grand display of all sorts of pride and 'ceremonies.'" Perhaps with some exaggeration, Spafford reported that the event attracted 30,000 people.[119]

The expanding commercial activity that came with the openings of the canals were the preeminent public experiences during the years that Samuel and the family lived in Albany. Because of the family connection to the Clintons, Samuel must have felt a special pride in the endeavor that owed so much to De Witt Clinton, George's nephew. He and Sarah gave the name of Clinton to the son born in 1817, the same year that De Witt Clinton was elected governor.

Samuel's state of health, however dire the accounts, did not prevent him begetting children. After Clinton came, in 1819, James Demarest, whose given names recalled the family's Tappan connection, honoring the Rev. James Demarest, then a prominent Dutch Reformed minister in Rockland County and the husband of Samuel's sister, Elizabeth. The last of Sarah's children was Sarah Elizabeth, born in 1822, when her mother was forty-two. She was named for her mother and her aunt. Sarah had born eleven children over twenty-four years. Three had died young, and in her lifetime three more would die.

---

118. *Historical Statistics of the United States, Colonial Times to 1970* (Washington, D.C.: U.S. Department of Commerce, Bureau of the Census, 1973), 1168.

119. Spafford, *Gazetteer* (1824), 17.

In 1816 Mary, the eldest child, at sixteen years of age, married Hubbell Knapp, a Connecticut-born boatman and later a skipper and merchant in Albany. They lived near her parents and soon had children who were older than their late-born uncles and aunt. The second of Sarah's children, Kate (Catharine Teller) Haring, fourteen when her last sibling was born, assisted her mother in caring for the young ones, a poignant memory that, a generation later, after their deaths, Kate was to convey to her niece.

In January 1824, Kate, sixteen, married John Gates Jr. at the First Reformed Church of Albany.[120] He had been an ensign in the Thirteenth U.S. with Samuel and was the son of a local hero in Albany, noted for his service with Arnold and Montgomery in the ill-fated attack on the fortress of Quebec on New Year's Eve 1775.[121] Joseph Egbert Gates, their only child, was born eleven months after the wedding.[122] Kate left this marriage for reasons we do not know, and as we shall see, lived in New York City in the difficult role of a separated woman. She had suitors, but because of her scruples, remarried only after Gates's death, when she was middle-aged.

The Albany directory for 1816 listed Samuel Haring as a justice of the peace—a minor judicial office—and master in chancery, a state political appointment that empowered the holder to administer the estates of the intestate and supervise the custody of orphans. It was a prestigious (and lucrative) function. (Elbert Herring, his cousin, was a master in chancery in New York City for many years.) These offices were marks of respect for Captain Samuel, as was his election to the Common Council in 1817, where he served with the Republican-Democrats in opposition to the dominant Federalists. In the same year he was elected charter officer in the Fourth Ward.[123] His war service had won him the support of the Republican political establishment.

---

120. *Records of the Reformed Dutch Church of Albany, New York, 1683–1809: Marriages, Baptisms, Members, etc., Excerpted from Year Books of the Holland Society of New York* (Baltimore: Genealogical Publishing Co., 1978).

121. *List of Officers of the Army of the United States*, 60. John Gates Jr. served in various positions and resigned 5 June 1819. See Heitman, *Historical Register*. John Gates Sr. "ac. Arnold though the wilderness to Quebec, and also a fighter at Saratoga, aged 74, died 9 Sep 1825." *Albany Chronicles: A History of the City Arranged Chronologically*, comp. Cuyler Reynolds (Albany, 1906). No date of death for John Gates Jr. found in Albany or New York City sources.

122. Henry Pennington Toler, *The Harlem Register: A Genealogy of the Twenty-three Original Patentees of the Town of New Harlem, New York* (New York: New Harlem Press, 1903), 139.

123. Joel Munsell, *Annals of Albany* (Albany, N.Y., 1857), 7:125; *Albany Chronicles*, 427

In a deed that was registered in 1820 Samuel was cited as "merchant," but he is not so listed in Albany directories.[124] In any case, he must have had limited resources, as there was minimal real estate activity at the time.

Samuel and Sarah moved frequently within Albany in these postwar years, another sign of their hard times. In 1818 the family was at Lydius (now Madison) Street, the next year at 47 Hudson, a lot that he and Sarah conveyed in 1820 to Hubbell Knapp, husband of their daughter Mary— whether by gift or purchase is not stated in the deed.[125] There were no listings for Samuel in Albany or New York City in 1820 and 1821, but in 1822 and succeeding years Samuel is shown at 51 Hamilton, an address close to the water on an east-west street and the same address as Hubbell Knapp, indicating that the two families, both with young children, shared the same house. (In the 1820s Knapp was a "skipper.")[126] From 1827 to 1830 the family was at 338 North Market, listed as a "boarding house." Sarah, in one of the few occupations open to women at the time, evidently took lodgers so the family could survive. Samuel had no occupation through the 1820s and the source of his support, other than the boarders, is not known. The family was not destitute, however, as there were enough resources for Samuel to make a will at the end of the decade, and there were funds in the estate.

By 1829 Samuel's health had deteriorated. He was, according to his doctor, David M. McLachlan, "in a state of total physical disability constantly confined to bed and has been for several years, incapable of either moving his body or of feeding himself—his complaint is chronic rheumatism amounting almost to universal paralysis." His bedridden condition was affirmed by Lawrence Van Kleeck, a one-time collector of revenue in Albany (1816), shortly to take a position at the War Department in Washington, where Sarah would later appeal for his help. Peter Wendell, a prominent Albanian physician, confirmed Dr. McLachlan's description and wrote that Samuel's condition was a result of "exposure to cold and wet during the war." He and a neighbor, Berent Bleecker (the merchant

124. "Lot 1, NW corner Johnson and Court Streets; Lot 5 N side Johnson St.; lot 1 SW corner Wolf and Robin St., John Willard of the City of Albany, merchant, and Samuel Haring of the same place, merchant," deed of 3 Aug. 1818, recorded 6 Nov. 1820, Grantors, 24:288, Hall of Records, Albany Co., N.Y.

125. Ibid., 24 Jan. 1820, 25: 290.

126. Alfred Averill Knapp, comp., *Nicholas Knapp Genealogy* (Winter Park, Fla., 1958), G-625.

who had dealings with the Herrings and Peter Smith), wrote U.S. Senator Charles E. Dudley on Samuel's behalf. Stephen P. Schuyler, brother of the deceased colonel of the Thirteenth U.S. New York, deposed as to the latter's death and inability to testify.[127] The friendships that are expressed in this support show the Haring family "to have had deep and strong roots in the community."[128] The pension application was successful, and Van Kleeck, in his new position, authorized a payment of $20 a month, which, however, due to a technicality, was never paid.

The debilitated condition of her husband, the many moves, and the maintenance of a rooming house were among the "many trials & much physical suffering" that Kate recalled of her mother to her niece forty years later.[129] Even with limited means, Sarah and the disabled Samuel moved back to New York in 1830. They settled at 53 Chrystie Street, a north-south street one block east of the Bowery, newly developed with modest row houses. (A small, frame dwelling was at the address in the late 1850s, possibly the same house, soon to be torn down to make way for tenements.)[130] The street name had a powerful association for Samuel as it commemorated his fellow officer, Lt. Col. John Chrystie, who had distinguished himself (and been captured) on Queenston Heights and died of fever at Fort George.[131] Nearby streets in this newly opened "uptown" section of the east side were also named for heroes of the war, rare com-

---

127. Deposition of Lawrence L. Van Kleeck, Albany, N.Y., 3 November 1829; Statement of David M. [?] McLachlan, M.D., Albany, 18 Dec. 1829; Affidavit of Peter Wendell, physician, Albany, N.Y., 21 Dec. 1829; Letter to Charles E. Dudley, Esq. from Barent Bleecker (?), Albany, 21 Dec. 1829; Nicholas Jones, practitioner of physic & surgery, Buffalo, N.Y., 16 Jan. 1830, Samuel Haring Pension Application.

128. Interview with Stefan Bielinski, Director, Colonial Albany Social History Project, 31 Dec. 1998.

129. Catharine Teller Haring Kip [CTHK], in Brooklyn, to JPH to Julia Phelps Haring [JPH], in Europe, 18 March 1869. (Unless otherwise indicated, all correspondence is in the author's personal collection, JHW MSS.)

130. William Perris, *Maps of the City of New York, 1859* (New York: Perris and Browne, [1859]), 57.

131. "The names of the streets called First, Second, Third, Fourth and Sixth Sts. on the Commissioner's Map, running north and south in the Tenth Ward, between Division and North Streets are changed, respectively, as follows: First St. to Chrystie St. in honor of Lieut. Col. John Chrystie, Second to Forsythe St. in honor of Lt. Col. Benjamin Forsythe; Third St. to Eldridge St. in honour of Lieut. [Joseph C.] Eldridge; Fourth St. to Allen St. in honour of William H. Allen, USN; and Sixth Street to Ludlow St. in honor of Lieut. [Augustus C.] Ludlow, USN." 17 March 1817, MCCNYC *(1784–1831)*, 9:71–73, quoted in Phelps-Stokes, *Iconography*, 6:1891 (1817).

memorations of a conflict most chose to forget.[132] Within a year young John Samuel Haring opened a grocery business at 75 Bowery, around the corner, and this may well be the reason for the family's move.

Samuel's debility caught up with him. He died in his fifty-fifth year on Chrystie Street on 9 July 1830.[133] His will, made in 1827 in Albany, proved in New York City, made the following bequests: "all my real estate to my children *viz*. Mary, wife of Hubbell Knapp, Samuel [Kip], Catharine wife of John Gates, John [Samuel], Clinton, James, Sarah Elizabeth . . . [and] to my Wife Sarah five hundred dollars to be at her disposal for ever, also all my household furniture so long as she shall remain my Widow and no longer." Sarah and son-in-law Hubbell Knapp were the executors.[134] There were two parcels to be disposed of in Cayuga County. Sarah gave a power of attorney to her son, Samuel Kip Haring, then living in Aurora, N.Y., to dispose of the last pieces of the well-placed Lot 47. She sold 34.5 acres to Abner Beach and Joseph Beach for $486.25, and quitted her "dower and thirds" rights, amounting to 14.5 acres, in the lot to John Herring Hardenbergh (son of John L.) for $36.25.[135]

Samuel Haring was in the first American generation that lived its entire life in the society and polity created by the Revolution. In preceding generations of the family sons followed in their father's footsteps as farmers and stayed near their familial lands to serve as community local leaders. No longer. Samuel had to make his way in a wider world. By his maturity, Tappan, though the spiritual home of the family, was an economic and

---

132. Allen Street was named for Lt. Henry Allen of the U.S. Navy, killed in action.

133. See Genealogical and Biographical Notes. See also Probate file of Samuel Haring, 21 July 1831, New York Co. Surrogate's Court, New York, N.Y.

134. Wills, 68:135, dated (at Albany) 3 Aug. 1827, proved 22 July 1831, New York Co. Surrogates Court, New York, N.Y. In a curiosity connected with the estate, two years after Samuel's death (1833) Sarah sought and received compensation from attorney John W. Cushman, of Albany, who had been the attorney for the estate by reason of "damages which she had sustained as well by reason of not performing certain promises . . ." She was awarded $474.13, which was not forthcoming, and the judge issued a warrant to seize Cushman's property in payment; the lot yielded Sarah only $200. Mayor's Court Minutes, 11 May 1833, Hall of Records, Albany Co., N.Y.; Property conveyed to Sarah Haring by Albert Gallup, Sheriff, 3 Feb. 1833, Grantee List, Albany Public Records; Grantee Book, 48:422, Hall of Records, Albany Co., N.Y.; Sheriff's Certificates, Book 1, 293, Office of the Albany City Clerk.

135. All dated 11 Sept. 1835. Land Records, XX:319–20, 320–21, 321–22, Cayuga Co., N.Y.

political backwater, never to fully recover from the ravages of the Revolution, its society of "yeoman farmers" broken and largely left out of the buoyant economy elsewhere in the Hudson Valley.

The opening up of New York State by the Revolution had given Samuel and the Herrings a greater geographic reach. They lived in a market economy—the Herrings and Peter Smith showed how much money could be made under the right conditions.

There were continuities with the past, notably the way family was tied to business in the extended Haring-Herring family. The Herrings in the 1790s and early 1800s were bigger and more successful merchants, but Samuel was following the same path. Family was important in business relationships in the eighteenth century, and it remained so in these years. Samuel and the Herrings knew personally those they did business with, but this way of doing business would largely disappear after the Civil War.

The inglorious War of 1812 was dubbed by some the Second War of Independence, and Samuel may have thought it so, and in that sense it too provided some continuity with the family's past. The rest of the country concentrated on expansion to the west and building canals, railroads, and cities—things the ailing Samuel could observe in 1820s Albany. His sons would live within the society shaped by these new trends. Samuel's life is a poignant story of striving but unfulfilled ambition, devotion to service in wartime, and the sufferings and frustration caused by the inept leadership of the northern campaign, which broke his health in early middle age.

Sarah Stays On

Sarah lived with the legacy of the fate that disabled her husband and the aspirations to wealth, and probably social position, he did not achieve. This woman, whose fortitude and perseverance can be felt through the spare record, stayed on in New York City for the last ten years of her life, endured multiple moves and the premature deaths of her youngest children, which tested her courage and faith. As Kate later wrote of her, she was "a woman of many trials & much physical suffering." There were supporting pillars: John Samuel Haring, who became a successful flour broker, James Demarest Haring, who joined him, and the sturdy and perceptive Kate, who left her husband and came to New York to be near her mother in these years. This family is the subject of the next chapter. They lived in New York City in the decades of its vigorous self-creation as the leading port and city of the nation.

IV

HEMM'D THICK ALL AROUND WITH SAILSHIPS AND STEAMSHIPS

The Harings in Manhattan and Brooklyn

*The countless masts, the white shore-steamers, the lighters, the ferry-boats,
the black sea-steamers well-model'd;*
*The down-town streets, the jobbers houses of business—the houses of
business of the ship-merchants and money-brokers—the river-streets*
        —Walt Whitman, *Mannahatta, Leaves of Grass*

For the next four decades the destinies of the Haring and Herring families
we have been following were fulfilled in New York City, which provided
opportunity, money, stimulation, comfort—and exposure to fatal disease.
New York merchants and shippers took full advantage of peaceful conditions for world trade secured by Great Britain after its victory over Napoleon. By the later 1820s the city had outgrown all its rivals to become the
most active port on the eastern seaboard. Scheduled freight and passenger
service to and from Liverpool began as early as 1817, meaning that grain
and other commodities from upstate New York could be shipped east
across the Atlantic on a predictable schedule, and metals and manufactured
goods would return from Liverpool. As the population increased in western New York there were more manufactured goods to be sold to families
establishing new homes and more produce to be shipped downstream, all
of which led to increased economic activity in the port. With the opening
of the Erie Canal in 1825, shipping reached even further into the interior,
and the volume of goods and commodities correspondingly increased.

By the 1820s, New York merchants famously came to dominate the
cotton trade, purchasing cotton from the planters, selling supplies to them

22. Bird's eye view of New York City in the middle of the nineteenth century. Engraving, after painting by Heine, J. Kummer, and Döpler (Paris, 1851)

City Hall is at upper center; Broadway passes City Hall Park to the left.

Library of Congress, Prints and Photographs Division

in turn, and transshipping the commodity through New York to Liverpool to be sent to the Lancashire mills, which would transform the raw stuff into fabric, some of which would then return on westward voyages.[1] By the 1830s sail-assisted steamships reduced transatlantic shipping time by a third or more. Soon there were even larger, more reliable ships.

At the turn of the century New York City's population was 60,500. It increased in leaps, to 96,400 in 1810 and 123,000 in 1820, and, more modestly, to 129,000 a decade later, when Samuel and Sarah Haring returned.[2] The city was the "new and ever-changing country" where antiquities and "traditions" could not be found, as Lydia Maria Child wrote on a visit in the 1840s. For its citizens, "Tradition has no desolate arches, no dim and cloistered aisles. People change their abodes so often that, as Washington Irving wittily suggests, the very ghosts if they are disposed to keep up an ancient custom, don't know where to call upon them."[3]

The city was becoming impersonal, but much of it still had a decorous air and had not yet become the broiling assembly of newcomers that it was destined to. In May 1831 Alexis de Tocqueville was puzzled about the lack of what he called "great" buildings such as those found in European capitals. To him, New York had the character of an expanded village: "One sees neither dome, nor bell tower, nor great edifice, with the result," he wrote his mother, "that one has the constant impression of being in a suburb. In its center the city is built of brick, which gives it a most monotonous appearance. The houses have neither cornices, nor balustrades, nor *porte-cocheres*. The streets are very badly paved, but sidewalks for pedestrians are to be found in all of them."[4] The perceptive visitor soon concluded that what had gone on in this raw new world was the unprecedented creation of a middling social class that set the tone of the place:

> What comes clear to me at present is that this country shows the attainment of outward perfection by the middle classes, or rather the whole society seems to have melted into the middle class. No one seems to have the elegant manners

---

1. This process is richly documented in Robert Greenhalgh Albion, *The Rise of New York Port* (New York: Charles Scribners, 1939).

2. *Population of States and Counties of the United States, 1790 to 1990* (Washington, D.C.: U.S. Department of Commerce, Bureau of the Census, 1996).

3. Lydia Maria Child, *Letters from New York* (New York: C. S. Francis, 1843), 125.

4. Alexis de Tocqueville to his mother, May 1831. George Wilson Pierson, *Tocqueville and Beaumont in America* (New York: Oxford Univ. Press, 1938), 67.

and the refined courtesy of the high classes in Europe. On the contrary, one is struck at first by something both vulgar and disagreeably uncultivated. But at the same time no one is what in France one might call *ill-bred*. All the Americans we have encountered up to now, even to the simplest *shop salesman,* seem to have received, or wish to appear to have received, a good education. Their manners are grave, deliberate, reserved, and they all wear the same clothes.

All the customs of life show this mingling of the two classes, which in Europe take so much trouble to keep apart. The women dress for the whole day at seven in the morning . . . Everything bears the stamp of a very busy existence.[5]

It is surely into this mingling that the Harings fitted.

The Widow Stays On

The widowed Sarah moved to 159 Washington Street, close to the west side docks, where she had lived early in her marriage. Washington Street, on landfill, opened in 1808—it did not exist when she and Samuel were first in the city.[6] Because of its proximity to the piers it was a noisy location, crowded with people and wagons. Sarah moved three times in the next three years, undoubtedly a strain.[7] In 1836 she and the still-dependent children lived at 45 Bowery, opposite the Bowery Theater, then running melodramas and spectacles to boisterous crowds—it burned down that same year.[8] The Bowery was "a business street lively and animated in appearance," the main thoroughfare for working people, including the infamous "Bowery b'hoys," gangs noted for swagger, drinking, and class solidarity. It cannot have been a comfortable place for a widow and an adolescent daughter.[9] Sarah and the children's annual ordeal took place on

---

5. Ibid., 69–70.

6. Washington St. was opened in 1808; the lots were numbered in 1816. See Kenneth Holcomb Dunshee, *As You Pass By* (New York: Hastings House, 1952).

7. In 1833 Sarah Haring was at 7 Fourth St., "uptown" and a "good" address because of its surroundings. The next year she was at 67 Franklin, until recently the edge of the city. The next year she returned to Fourth, near the newly created Washington Square, again a "good" address. New York City directories. Fourth was then considered a principal crosstown street, along with Grand, Broome, and Houston. See J. Disturnell, *A Gazetteer of the State of New-York* (Albany, 1842), 272.

8. Founded in 1826, the theater burned and was rebuilt a number of times. *ENCNYC,* s.v. "Bowery Theater."

9. Disturnell, *Gazetteer,* 271; Seth Kamil, "The Bowery: I'll Never Go There Anymore," *New York Chronicle* 6, no. 3 (Fall/Winter 1993): 1–3.

1 May, when most leases in the city expired. "May-day in New York is the saddest thing," Maria Child wrote.

> One house empties itself into another all over the city. The streets are full of loaded drays, on which tables are dancing, and carpets rolling to and fro. Small chairs, which bring up such pretty, cozy images of rolly poly mannikins and maidens, eating supper from tilted porringers, and spilling the milk on their night-gowns—these go ricocheting along on the tops of beds and bureaus—.[10]

Sarah was not without family for support. John Samuel Haring, in his mid-twenties, had established himself as a grocer in the city, and there were the Herrings on Hudson Street, in their seventies by this time. The three children who were minors at their father's death were growing up. Clinton Haring was likely apprenticing in a law office from his mid-teens, and James Demarest Haring began working for John Samuel in those years. Sarah Elizabeth, at the age of fourteen, helped her mother prepare an application for a widow's pension in recognition of Samuel's service in the war.

The War of 1812 was rapidly passing from the national consciousness. The aggrieved spirit of its veterans showed itself in an 1833 petition, which requested that the

> officers of the second war of independence [be awarded] the same munificence which was extended by the United States, and by several of the States, to those of the first. They held the same stake, they exhibited the same valor and love of liberty, and, although as a body, they may not have suffered as much, yet their zeal was not less, nor their exertions less willing.[11]

In 1836 Congress, responding to such pressure, authorized pensions. In June of that year Sarah Elizabeth, having read of the government's intention, wrote on her mother's behalf—perhaps a sign of Sarah's state of health. It is a notably well phrased letter: her neat hand indicates that she had received the foundations of education. She addressed the commis-

---

10. Child, *Letters from New York*, 258.

11. *To the Officers of the Late War, the Following Proceedings Had [ ] to an Application to Congress, for lands, in remuneration for services, are respectfully submitted and recommended to their especial attention, by the Committee in the City of New York* (New York: William A. Mercien, 1833), 5.

sioner of pensions, referring to the "N. Y. Times of 14th inst." concerning the earlier pension legislation and "an act passed in the house of representatives April 16th granting half pay to the widows & orphans of officers & soldiers (in certain wars) who have died, or may hereafter die, of wounds received in the military service of the U.S." She added, "Believing that both these acts apply to my father, I take the liberty of asking attention to it—the very kind answer you returned to my letter of last Winter [not found], encourages me to hope that if any thing can be done in favor of my widowed mother you will readily assist . . ."[12] Sarah Elizabeth elaborated on her mother's "peculiarly trying" situation resulting from her

> father's long continued illness, the melancholy termination of it, left destitute with a family of children, had she not been a woman of uncommon fortitude she never could have risen so superior to the difficulties it has been her destiny to encounter. Should the sum due my father at the time of his death be allowed do you not think it probable that some provision will be made for the future support of Mrs. Haring and if so whether it will not be possible to obtain the back pension also?

The next month Sarah's eldest surviving daughter, Kate (her first daughter, Mary [Haring] Knapp, died in 1833), wrote on her mother's behalf to Lawrence L. Van Kleeck, the one-time Albany resident who had earlier had deposed in favor of Samuel's pension application and who was now in the War Office in Washington. She requested that the matter of "arrears to the United States" be dealt with. (This was the $27.80 claimed by the government to be owed by Samuel at the time of his discharge in 1815, the technicality that had prevented the approval of his pension application and was now an obstacle to the granting of one to his widow.) Kate sought Van Kleeck's help to cut the bureaucratic Gordian knot:

> Presuming that all that is required for the obtaining the amount due my father at the time of his death is to have the enclosed paper presented to the 2d Comptrollers Office, my mother requests a very particular favor that you will hand it in, also will you be so kind as to inform her whether her case does not come under the act recently passed granting half pay to the widows, and if

---

12. Sarah Elizabeth Haring to J. L. Edwards, Commissioner of Pensions, from New York, 11 June 1836, file 27931, Veteran, Samuel Haring, Grade: Capt., Service, U.S. Infantry, bundle no. 34, can no. 129, Act Mil. Est., 2:170, Pension Application Files, War of 1812 series, Death or Disability "Old War" Invalid, National Archives (hereafter cited as Samuel Haring Pension Application).

not, whether, if application were made it is not probable that Government would make some provision for her.[13]

She concluded with a reference to the family's Albany association with the Van Kleeck family: "My mother is very sorry to put you to so much trouble, but the friendship which you have always manifested toward her and her family is her only apology for so doing. She desires to be particular remembered to your self and Mrs. V. Kleeck."

There was no response from the bureaucracy. A month after Kate's letter, Sarah Elizabeth wrote again on her mother's behalf, this time to the prominent New Yorker and former governor, Morgan Lewis, eighty-six years old, who had commanded the northern army in the summer of 1813.[14] "Probably you may remember my father from the circumstance of his being with you in the engagement at Fort George," she wrote. "[H]is subsequent misfortunes are so well known that a repetition of them here would be useless I think, his severe & almost unparalleled sufferings for so many years, the melancholy termination of them together with his having a family so entirely destitute could not but excite the sympathy of all who know them."[15]

Her mother had by then recently paid the $27.80 that Samuel had owed at his discharge in an effort to clear up the matter, but since there had been no response, Sarah Elizabeth appealed to the venerable Lewis to "exert [his influence] in befriending my unfortunate family. My Mother believe me is in every respect worthy and her child would duly appreciate whatever interest you might take in her behalf." The reference she offered to Lewis in confirmation of the family's plight was Elbert Herring, Esq., who had just returned to New York City after five years in the Andrew Jackson administration. He was then the most potentially influential of the family, but he does not seem to have involved himself in the appeal.[16]

---

13. Catharine Teller Haring Gates, in New York, to Lawrence L. Van Kleeck, in Washington, D.C., 7 July [1836], Samuel Haring Pension Application.

14. When Sarah Elisabeth Haring's letter was written he was president of the New-York Historical Society (of which he had been a founder) and a public advocate of pension awards for veterans of the forgotten war. *DAB*, s.v. "Lewis, Morgan."

15. Sarah Elizabeth Haring, in New York, to the Hon. Morgan Lewis, 25 Aug. 1836, Samuel Haring Pension Application.

16. Ronald N. Satz, "Elbert Herring 1831–36," in Robert M. Kvasnicka and Herman J. Viola, *The Commissioners of Indian Affairs, 1824–1977* (Lincoln, Neb.: Univ. of Nebraska Press, 1979). 13–15.

The appeal was for naught. The president of the bank disbursing the pensions wrote, "Upon examination the name of Samuel Haring does not appear upon either of the Rolls of this Agency."[17] Something had gone awry in what would now be called the paper trail, and there was no relief for Sarah.

There was yet a harder blow to come for the widow, however. Sarah Elizabeth, the daughter who had so eloquently and fervently championed her cause, developed consumption and died in July 1839, at the age of seventeen. She returned to Albany in her final illness. Thirty years later Kate wrote of her young sister, "Though it is many years ago, it is only recently that I could talk of her & I cannot bear to hear her spoken of by those who knew her well, in a light or careless manner."[18]

Sarah Haring's last address was 98 Varick Street, near the newly created St. John's Park, above Canal Street, on the west side of the island, "a beautiful green of about four acres, filled with shrubs and flowers, enclosed by a high iron paling" and dominated by an Episcopal church with an impressive two hundred and forty foot steeple. The neighborhood, developed as a speculative endeavor by Trinity Church, had been fashionable in the 1820s and 1840s but was on the decline when Sarah moved there. This was a genteel location, quite unlike her Bowery address of five years before. She was not destitute and was probably supported by her eldest son.[19] The 1840 census shows that the household consisted of five people, the two youngest sons, one of whom was designated as of the "learned professions" (Clinton, then studying to become a lawyer), and in addition to Sarah, a female 30–40 years old (probably Kate), and one 15–20 (possibly a serving girl).[20] In 1841 Sarah died at the Varick Street house in her sixty-first year.[21]

---

17. Letter from John [?] Fleming, Presid. Mechanics Bank, New York to James L. Edwards, Esq., Commissioner of Pensions, 17 Aug. 1836, Samuel Haring Pension Application.

18. Catharine Teller Haring Kip [CTHK] to Julia Phelps Haring [JPH], 18 March 1869.

19. In 1866 the park was converted to a railroad freight yard by Cornelius Vanderbilt, and in the 1930s was paved over to provide access to the Holland Tunnel. *ENCNYC*, "St. John's Park."

20. U.S. federal census, 1840, Eighth Ward, New York, N.Y., 252.

21. *New York Herald*, 12 Feb. 1841. There is no record of Sarah's burial place. Neither hers nor Samuel's names appear in the Dutch Reformed Church burial records, and their remains were not transferred from Manhattan to the vault that Elbert Herring purchased at Green-Wood Cemetery, Brooklyn.

Kate considered her mother's death as "a relief" after much physical suffering.[22] Sarah had endured the long illness of her husband, the deaths of six of her eleven children, the straightened circumstances of her late married life and widowhood, and ill health in a city where she was forced to move year by year. In her lifetime Sarah, too, experienced the impermanence of habitation in a modernizing urban world, the "new and ever-changing country" of which Maria Child wrote.

De Tocqueville mused about the transformation from the wild forest to the settled clearings that he saw, much of which had happened during Sarah's lifetime. He might well have been referring to Col. John L. Hardenbergh when he wrote in 1831 that "the American" gave "his name to a wilderness that none before him had traversed, has seen the first forest tree fall and the first planter's house rise in the solitude, where a community came to group itself, a village grew, and to-day a vast city stretches."[23] Sarah, too, was the representative American. In her lifetime she had seen raw nature tamed and engineered to suit the needs of a young, restless country. She witnessed the independent country defining itself through expansion and knew firsthand the attending uncertainties and tribulations. One wonders how often in her last years did she wonder at the course of her life's journey, taking her from the remote forest clearing where she was married to the crowded city where she spent her final careworn days.

The Haring Brothers in the Flour Business

The Haring brothers were at the height of their careers in the 1840s and 1850s. At their mother's death in 1841, John Samuel Haring, thirty-one, was an established flour dealer, while Clinton, twenty-four, would soon be admitted to the New York Bar. James Demarest Haring, at twenty-two, was shortly to start as a clerk in his brother's flour firm.

Flour had been the family business since their grandfather Elbert Herring was a bolter, over a hundred years before. It was a prime New York City business since the late seventeenth century and was commemorated by a wheat barrel on the official seal. Now the range of wheat growing had been extended by the Erie Canal to the fresh fields of the Genesee valley. The population increase in the city meant an expanding market for bread,

---

22. CTHK to JPH, 18 March 1869.

23. Pierson, *Tocqueville and Beaumont*, 119.

and, when the Corn Laws prohibiting importation of wheat into the United Kingdom were suspended in 1842, the cross-Atlantic markets grew.

New York of the 1840s was a booming, highly commercial place. "Babylon remains the same as then," Maria Child informed her readers:

> The din of crowded life, and the eager chase for gain still run through its streets, like the perpetual murmur of a hive. Wealth dozes on French couches, thrice pampered and canopied with damask, while Poverty camps on the dirty pavement, or sleeps off its wretchedness in the watch-house . . . Sometimes the harsh shouts are pleasantly varied by some feminine voice, proclaiming in musical cadence, "Hot corn! hot corn! Buy my lily white corn!"

With a touch of Bostonian superiority, she added that on "Wall-street and elsewhere, Mammon, as usual, coolly calculates his chance of extracting a penny from war, pestilence, and family; and Commerce with her loaded drays, and jaded skeletons of horses, as busy as ever."[24]

To J. Disturnell, writing in the *Gazetteer* he published in 1842, improvement was everywhere on the land. "Wide and commodious avenues and streets have . . . taken the place of the narrow and irregular thoroughfares of the olden times. Hills have been leveled, rough inequalities in the surface of the ground removed, and bogs and marshes filled up, and the city now presents a uniform grade throughout." The city then extended "about three miles from the Battery toward the north and across the island from river to river." There were improvements too in architecture and the thoroughfares:

> The style of building . . . within the last ten years has reached a high degree of elegance and convenience. The upper or north part of the city has been laid out into spacious streets . . . with wide and convenient *tratoirs* or sidewalks, formed of large flagstones, and the houses, built of brick in uniform blocks, with marble steps (here called *stoops* from the Dutch), span highly ornamented balustrades with cast iron in front, present an imposing and agreeable appearance to the eye.

Above City Hall was "*the fashionable quarter*, the lower part of the city being comparatively deserted even by old residents, whose former man-

---

24. Child, *Letters from New York*, 3.

sions are converted into boarding houses, or have given place to shops or stores." (The Haring firm was in that commercial lower part of the island, and thus distant from "the fashionable quarter.") Broadway was

> 80 feet wide with spacious side-walks that afford a favorite promenade in fine weather for the gay and fashionable. Here are to be found the most extensive hotels, dry goods stores, fancy shops, confectioneries, jewelers, booksellers, grocers, tailors, milliners, and in general all the various establishments that furnish the elegancies and luxuries of life in the greatest perfection.[25]

Early republican simplicity was gone. Opportunity in the variety of occupations devoted to trade and shipping in the port of New York had produced an unprecedented number of the well-to-do and wealthy. There was an abundance of fashionable clothing and home furnishings enticingly displayed in the marble-fronted commercial palaces on Broadway. It was all there for the purchasing. The democratization of luxury had begun.

The City was a noisy and crowded place, but there were improvements. By the 1840s stone had replaced dirt on the avenues and on many streets, which eliminated the nuisances from mud churned up by hooves and wheels after a rain or thaw. Some streets were paved with blocks of wood, which reduced noise and gave a firmer footing.[26] (Gas street lamps had been in use since the 1820s.)[27] A decisive change that made future development possible came in 1842, when the aqueduct that brought water from the Croton River in Westchester County to the city was completed. Walt Whitman considered the aqueduct a "far nobler token for New York than even her steamships."[28] Its construction was an expression of the engineering prowess of the young republic, an emblem of civic pride, a marvel pointed out to visitors in contemporary guidebooks, which encouraged an excursion.[29] With a clean and abundant supply of water available, Manhattan could accommodate hundreds of thousands of new residents. The brownstone houses built by developers in rows cheek-by-

---

25. Disturnell, *Gazetteer*, 271.

26. Ibid.

27. *ENCNYC.*

28. Whitman in 1851, quoted in Gerard T. Koeppel, *Water for Gotham: A History* (Princeton: Princeton Univ. Press, 2000), 287.

29. Disturnell, *Gazetteer*, 136–37.

jowl on streets formerly mere lines on the map were the immediate signs of what this water system had made possible.

Despite improvements, open drains along the streets remained for years to convey vast quantities of horse manure and urine and trash to harbor outlets—the odors permeated the city. Indeed New York was entering the most unwholesome phase of its existence. In 1845 the mortality rate soared to an all-time high of forty per thousand; typhus and tuberculosis were prevalent and hardly confined to the poor, as the fate of three Harings shows. Infant mortality was very high. (Ten of the twelve children of the affluent John Samuel and Mary Haring, died as babies.) "Pulmonary diseases drove the rate to a record high of 166/1000 between 1850 and 1854; between 1850 and '60 half of those under five died each year . . . by 1856 more died than were born, emigration made up growth."[30]

Horse-drawn omnibuses ran up and down the thoroughfares, most originating at the Battery. These provided a comfortable ride at a cost of twenty-five cents from the Battery to Harlem.[31] Businessmen could live "uptown" as far as Forty-second Street and commute to work—few who could afford separate residences lived above their establishments anymore.

The 1840s brought great changes to the way people and goods moved to and from the city. By the early part of the decade, the New York and Harlem Railroad tracks extended from a terminus at City Hall north through the Bowery to join Fourth (later Park) Avenue. Train service to New Haven and points between was begun in this decade. James Demarest Haring, whose father-in-law had a summer retreat in Fairfield on the Sound, frequently traveled on this line. The Hudson Railroad provided service to Albany.[32] And where the Tappan farmers brought produce to the sloops when Samuel Haring was a child, the New York and Erie Railroad built a terminus for a line that ran west through Goshen (whose farmers had once brought their crops to the landing at New Windsor) and along the southern tier of New York State to Lake Erie.[33] The family would make much use of these connections, which were both faster than steamer and more comfortable than stage.

---

30. Edwin G. Burrows and Mike Wallace, *Gotham: A History of New York City to 1898* (New York: Oxford Univ. Press, 1999), 790.

31. Ibid., 565.

32. Disturnell, *Gazetteer*, 287.

33. Ibid., 286.

The crowds of pedestrians and horse-drawn vehicles competed daily for room on the thoroughfares: "Faces and coats of all patterns, bright eyes, whiskers, spectacles, hats, bonnets, caps, all hurrying along in the most inextricable confusion," wrote an observer in 1846. "One would think it a grand gala-day."[34]

In this teeming world, where there was opportunity for progress, there was also overcrowding and disease. Clinton Haring, the young lawyer, second-to-last of Sarah's children, died of tuberculosis at thirty-eight in 1855 in the midst of a promising career.[35] At the age of twenty-seven he was first listed in the directory as a lawyer, and he practiced for eleven years with evident success, as he came to have an office at 18 Wall Street, a prestigious address, close to the Merchant's Exchange.[36] He married Rowena Heywood in 1849, and for two years they lived on elegant Broadway. Kate, his only surviving sister and witness of the family's fate, remembered that Clinton's death left her "dependent as [she] was" without support).[37]

The Haring brothers were among the thousands who flourished in the port economy. They were able to enjoy residences in "modern" areas of the city, clothing that marked them as of the prosperous middle class, comfortable furnishings, capital investments in real estate and—new since their fathers' time—ownership of publicly-traded bonds and shares in banks and railroads.

John Samuel Haring began trade as a grocer at 75 Bowery, near where his parents lived after their return from Albany. Later he was at Ludlow Street, also on the lower east side of the island. By 1843 he had made the big step to 35 Peck Slip, close to the East River Docks, a first class location for a jobber, where "John S. Haring & Co., flour," with James Demarest Haring as partner, remained for another eleven years. Peck Slip was in the midst of the counting houses of merchants who, like the Harings, needed frequent access to the East River docks and the nearby warehouses. By day it was a tumult of cartmen, horse-drawn wagons, clerks, and brokers. (The building at 35 Peck Slip was torn down in the 1850s, and the Harings

---

34. Charles Loring Brace, quoted in Burrows and Wallace, *Gotham*, 692.

35. *New York Tribune*, 5 Jan. 1855.

36. Disturnell, *Gazetteer*, 274.

37. CTHK to Caroline Eliza (Phelps) Haring, 15 Sept. 1868.

23. The East River docks in the middle of the nineteenth century. Engraving, after painting by Heine, J. Kummer, and Döpler (Paris, 1851).

Library of Congress, Prints and Photographs Division

moved to 121 Broad Street. The building that replaced it remains, now a hotel within the South Street Seaport.)

The Harings bought flour and grains from upstate and sold it to bakers within the city. A writer in 1840 reported that over a million barrels of flour had been sold in New York City that year and described the credit arrangements that powered this brisk and extensive trade. The upstate millers raised money by placing in the hands of an agent such as the Haring firm "ample security, by 'mortgages' on the mills and personal security." The security established a credit with the agent, who would "accept drafts for the sum agreed upon, at usually sixty or ninety days, and this before a bushel of wheat is purchased, or a barrel of flour ground. These drafts are made at the pleasure of the drawer, and the internal banks, mostly at Rochester, Buffalo, Canandaigua, Utica and Albany, discount these drafts."[38] With the advance at the harvest the miller bought the farmers' wheat, milled it, then shipped it to the city, where the agent would refund the original advance and, if the retail price was right, make a profit. "The banks are benefited by the circulation of their bills. The miller obtains his wheat. The canals, manufacturers and commission merchants are all benefited, and the consumer is not injured." So began what became the commodities futures market.

Credit was the oil of the system. The agents—or "jobbers," as those who, like the Harings, bought and sold on their own account were called—bought and sold on credit, with notes of thirty, sixty, or more days. "Nearly every one, consequently, had to be granted credit for periods from one month to six months or more; sixty days being the most common term in the major dealings at New York and Liverpool."[39]

It was a high-risk business, subject to local growing conditions, demand, and world commodity prices. The success of a firm depended on the reliability of its credit.[40] By the 1850s, when the first credit evaluations became available, the R. G. Dun Co. (later Dun & Bradstreet), whose innovation it was to make available such intelligence to businessmen, reported of the Harings that "[t]hey have a gd. Custom with Bakers and are in good credit with the trade."[41] In the notes scrawled into the great

---

38. Maryland Pocket Annual for 1840, 75–77, quoted in Charles Byron Kuhlmann, *The Development of the Flour Milling Industry in the United States* (Boston: Houghton Mifflin, ca. 1929), 70.

39. Albion, *Rise of New York Port*, 283.

40. A jobber buys and sells on his own account; a broker or factor is a middleman who acts for others to bring buyer and seller together and usually deals in one line of goods. See Glenn Porter and Harold C. Livesay, *Merchants and Manufacturers: Studies in the Changing Structure of Nineteenth Century Marketing* (Baltimore: Johns Hopkins Univ. Press, 1971), 5.

41. New York City, vol. 370, p. 585, 2 Nov. 1855, R. G. Dun & Co. Collection, Baker Library, Harvard Business School. The following quotations are taken, respectively, from reports dated 2 Nov. 1855, 4 April 1857 (in which the business is referred to as "jobbing"), 14 March 1859, 2 Nov. 1859, and 4 Aug. 1858, and 25 March 1859.

ledger books in his office, the Dun researcher wrote that the Haring partners were "smart active & cautious, understand their business & attend closely to it & in good credit & good credit for contracts." In addition to reporting on the general business character of his subjects, Dun tried to ascertain their net worth from his informants. Of John Samuel Haring there were "various est. of worth," ranging from the "highest 50,000" to "av. 30–40," and he was always "considered reliable for purchases." Dun reported that Haring's wife, his first cousin, Mary Clark, daughter of Sarah's prosperous brother, William, was said to have $20,000 in her own right. He noted of James Demarest Haring ("JD") in 1855 that he was "thought not to have means."

The Haring firm survived the financial panic of 1857–58, and in the midst of the ensuing severe depression, Dun reported that the partners "stand well w. houses in that line."[42] Dun's report was based on information gleaned from the talk of fellow merchants—essentially gossip of the street, based on perceptions of other businessmen rather than hard data, but the existence of such central intelligence meant that a default on debt would be widely known. In the midst of the depression John Samuel had the funds available to buy "the interest of various parties . . . in lot 18, South Street with water rights for $20,000." It was a property near the East River docks and warehouses that had high potential for appreciation when the economy improved.[43] John S. Haring & Co. was consistently in business through the ups and downs of the business cycle and was listed in city directories for nineteen years.

The personalities of both Haring brothers emerge from images taken during this era of inexpensive photographic prints. John Samuel, in an 1850s photo, looks to be a buoyant, energetic man-about-town. Prosperity is evident in his dress—an elegant jacket, shirt with a high wing collar and jeweled buttons, and flowing silk tie. His expression is far from the wooden look of so many who faced the camera at the time and reveals wit and good humor. Yet the confident gaze masked repeated sorrows. Of the fourteen children whom Mary bore between 1833 and 1856, twelve died as infants

---

42. Ibid., 4 Aug. 1858.

43. Ibid., 25 March 1859. J. S. Haring also "bot in Jan 5 2 lots in 132nd Street, east of 6th Ave. and 2 lots in 133rd St. West of 5th Ave. of Clinton Haring for $9 . . ." Clinton Haring, younger brother, died in 1855; the purchase was from the estate.

24. John Samuel Haring (1810–60) and James Demarest Haring (1819–68)

and young children. There is no better illustration of how unhealthy the city had become in the midst of a booming economy. In this family, funerals and burials came with the regularity of births, and only two boys, George Titus and Clinton, lived to maturity. Only George would marry, and both died in young manhood. The widow Mary was sturdy and survived her husband by twenty-two years.[44]

John Samuel and his family moved uptown with the city, from 135 East Thirteenth Street in 1855, then the "heart" of uptown, to West Twenty-second Street, and, by 1860, to the house where he died, at 108 East Thirty-ninth Street, between Lexington and Third Avenues, then the extreme of uptown living. The radiant health he showed in his photograph had deteriorated. Expecting his death was near, in early May 1860 he made his will at his home. It was witnessed by his brother-in-law, William Clark, and his brother, James.[45] He died a month later, on 5 June, of "disease of the heart," according to the notice in the *New York Herald*. "The relatives and friends of the family are invited to attend the funeral services

---

44. Clinton, named for his uncle, died as a youth in 1865. George Titus Haring lived until 1893 but was predeceased by all four of his children. That line of the Haring family came to an end with his death. See "Haring," in the author's *Hatch and Brood of Time*.

45. Probate file of James Demarest Haring, Wills, 138:491, N.Y. Co. Surrogate's Court, New York, N.Y.

this (Wednesday) afternoon, at half-past five o'clock, from his late residence, No. 108 East 39th street, without further invitation."[46] He had just turned fifty. His estate was that of a comfortable and prosperous man. He left to his wife Mary his "household furniture, books, pictures, and silver plate the use of all the rent, residence and remainder of [his] Real and Personal Estate during her natural life." She, the executrix, was empowered to "make an advance to children as they embark on business."[47]

James Demarest Haring continued to do the firm's business at 121 Broad Street for another two years. He had started working for his brother as a clerk at age twenty-seven. At that time he was boarding at 309 Pearl, in the heart of one of the most crowded commercial streets in the city. His life was transformed when he married Caroline Eliza Phelps, the second of George Alexander Phelps's ten children.

Caroline's father was a Connecticut-born fruit importer who lived at 622 Broadway, near its intersection with Bleecker Street—a fashionable uptown address.[48] He also had a modest Gothic revival cottage in Fairfield, Connecticut, on Long Island Sound. By the 1840s Fairfield was a mixture of farms that provided produce to New York and the often fancifully designed country houses of New York merchants. When George Alexander Phelps bought the house in the 1830s the family went there by a steam ferry, which left from the East River docks. By 1845 there were regular trains along the Connecticut shore from a terminus in Manhattan at Canal Street and Broadway; and stops along the line included Thirty-fourth Street.[49] It was in Fairfield that James Demarest and Caroline Eliza were married, on 1 September 1846. Most likely it was a Congregational service, in keeping with the Phelps heritage—the bride was a direct descendant of Rev. John Davenport, a founder of New Haven Colony, and of Rev. Eleazar Wheelock, the founder of Dartmouth College.

The marriage was a union between a handsome young man of distinguished New Amsterdam Dutch stock, with good prospects in business, and a young woman of Yankee-Puritan stock. In the bustle and mixing of the new urban world, Dutch and Puritan Yankee crossed ethnic and

---

46. Death Notice, *New York Herald*, 6 June 1860.

47. N.Y. Co. Wills, 138:491.

48. On George Alexander Phelps, see Judd, *Hatch and Brood of Time*, chapter 5.

49. *The Stranger's Guide around New York and its Vicinity, What to See and What is to Be Seen with Hints and Advice to Those Who Visit the Great Metropolis* (New York: W. B. Graham, 1853), 19.

25. James Demarest Haring and Caroline Eliza Phelps at about the time of their marriage in 1846

denominational lines that would have been forbidding to their grandparents, a sign of the growing mobility and flexibility of American society and of the economic buoyancy of New York, which provided new paths for enterprise that brought these families into proximity. There was a symmetry, too, in the businesses of the two families. The Harings traded in the interior with millers in the Hudson-Erie Canal corridor. Phelps traded across the Atlantic. Both sold in the city. The young people may well have met through a business contact between the elder Phelps and the Harings.

The Phelps family, too, suffered the death of children; four of the ten born to Eliza (Ayres) Phelps prior to Caroline Eliza's wedding died as babies or small children. Eliza was pregnant at the time of the wedding with the long-lived Charles Haring Phelps, whose middle name honored the new in-law. Howard, her twelfth child, would become a favorite uncle—in age closer to a brother—of Julia, the surviving child of the Haring-Phelps marriage. He too would be long-lived.

The photo portrait of Caroline Eliza made at the time of her wedding shows a gentle-looking young woman, reserved, perhaps with a touch of melancholy. A later photograph shows a similar delicacy of mien. In his wedding portrait, James Demarest's face has been smoothed by the artist or photographer, resulting in a charming, if idealized, visage. A later photo shows a hearty person, with an out-going expression that suggests a relish for life. The two seem to have been temperamental opposites.

The couple started married life at 65 Pike Street, a two-story row house on a newly developed street north of the East River docks and a location from which James could walk to the Haring offices on Peck Slip. Pike Street and its neighbors were described at the time as "all handsomely built up with private residences, in the neighborhood of the east River."[50] (A ramp leading from the 1909 Manhattan Bridge covered the site of this house.)

Caroline Eliza did not bear her first child until four years after the marriage. A baby cup and a photo survive this baby, named for her Aunt Kate, who survived less than two years. Julia Phelps Haring was born in March 1851 at 73 Monroe Street, a house around the corner and a hand-me-down from the John Samuel Haring family. It was one of a row of identical two- or three-story frame houses on a residential street; nearby was a large brewery, whose fermenting processes would have added fragrance to the air.[51] Caroline Eliza bore no more children, and Julia—called Julie when she was a girl and young woman as she will be here—remained the precious only child. Her robust health resisted the diseases of the day and brought her a long life and a destiny that could not have been imagined by her parents.

Caroline Eliza and the baby always spent some time in Fairfield at the Phelps's country house, where there were usually aunts, uncles—the youngest of whom were children—cousins, and servants. Julie did not grow up as a solitary child. While James's business address continued to be that of the Haring firm, his home listing for some years was Connecticut. Perhaps health was a motivation, as the country was healthier than the city. James also probably frequently traveled upstate. (On one of these trips he wrote to Julie, "We stopped at every place on the road—I saw many little girls and boys at the depots, and I thought of the danger of children being there. I hope you will be very careful as you are my only Baby. . . Kiss Ma Ma for me.")[52] When in the city they stayed at the elder Phelps's town house at 129 West Fourteenth Street, within an unbroken

50. Disturnell, *Gazetteer*, 272.

51. William Perris, *Maps of the City of New York, 1857*, 12.

52. James Demarest Haring, in New York, to Julia Phelps Haring, in Fairfield, Conn., 22 June 1859.

26. Julia Phelps Haring in 1859

row of brownstones on the north side of the street between Seventh and Eighth Avenues.

In the late 1850s, when Julie was seven to nine years old, the Harings wintered at the Astor Place Hotel at 783 Broadway, where they could be "served with private tables if desired." This hotel had been built in 1853 in the heart of the most elegant residential section of Manhattan at the northern end of the Bowery, where it met Fourth Avenue. It was one of the hotels built at the time "that marked the transition period between the down-town houses, which sought still to make the City Hall Park the hotel centre, and the creation of the vast marble caravansaries beyond the Bowery crossroads."[53] The Astor Place, according to a contemporary account, was a "quiet and very genteel house, kept by Fish & Son mainly as a family hotel."[54] It had recently "been greatly enlarged by an addition, affording many truly elegant suits of rooms [and] . . . a fine carriage house and stable, affording every facility for those keeping their establishment."[55]

---

53. Hines, *A Tour Around New York*, 153–54, typescript, 1845 folder, W. Johnson Quinn Collection, New York Hotels, NYHS.

54. Mower's *Reminiscences of a Hotel Man of Forty Years*, 73, 1852 folder, Quinn Collection.

55. Transcribed from the *New York Herald*, 18 Sept. 1860, 1852 folder, Quinn Collection.

Residence in a hotel meant formality in dress, in dining, and in going and coming. It also would have been costly. James Demarest must have been relatively unscathed by the depression of the late 1850s.

It was in 1859, probably at or before her eighth birthday, that Julie sat for a portrait using a recently introduced process in which a photograph was mounted directly on glass, and colored from behind. The result was a portrait that was intended to rival a painting.[56] Eight-year-old Julie wears an open-necked dress of light purple with puffed sleeves, and holds a fan, her serious expression and poised carriage making her look older, a little lady. This child is the more precious for being the only one of her parents, portrayed in a setting that reveals how treasured she was.

Around the corner from the hotel was the Astor Place Opera House, a handsome theater with a horseshoe-shaped auditorium circled with boxes for its well-dressed patrons.[57] On Lafayette Street, just below Astor Place, was the recently opened library, financed through the will of John Jacob Astor and likewise named for him, the largest and the most luxurious in the city (now the Joseph Papp Public Theater). Nearby was the Cooper Union Foundation building in the Italianate Renaissance style, a four-story building faced with brownstone, completed while the Harings stayed at the hotel, and doubtless a site which drew onlookers during their stay, another object of pride for those concerned with advancement of the city's educational institutions.[58]

---

56. The process was one of those referred to as "ivorytype," even though ivory was not necessarily used. Another contemporary term was diaphonotype. "Because there were several varieties of photographs painted from the back, their descriptions often overlap and fall beneath the heading of ivorytype, which incidentally is occasionally described as being a photograph mounted directly to glass, made transparent and then painted from behind (no space, necessarily or ivory, for that matter) . . . Sutton [a contemporary practitioner] specifically instructs printing through the paper so that even absorbed silver is reduced making for a very 'thick,' saturated negative. Clearly this process required the use of salt prints and would not work with emulsion prints (albumen, collodion)." Personal communication from Heidi Halton, Librarian Assistant, George Eastman House, Rochester, N.Y., 1 Nov. 1999.

57. In May 1849 Astor Place had been the scene of the deadly riot between the supporters of Edwin Forrest, the American actor, and William Macready, his English rival. It was an outbreak of violence that revealed the hostility of the Bowery "b'hoys" for the genteel culture that the opera house represented. *ENCNYC*, s.v. "riots."

58. Cooper Union was one of the first in the city to be framed with steel beams, a particular interest of Peter Cooper, who among other things, was an iron-maker. *ENCNYC*, "New York Public Library," "Astor, John Jacob," "Cooper, Peter"; Norval White and Eliot Wilensky, *AIA Guide to New York City*, 4th ed. (New York: Three Rivers Press, 2000), 163–64.

→→ A FELLOW RESIDENT AT THE ASTOR PLACE HOTEL ←←

Kate recalled "a Miss Mc Bride, an old maid," who lived at the hotel when James and Caroline Eliza did and related an anecdote filtered through her Protestant prejudices. Miss McBride, "who had no settled belief in any creed suddenly [went] over to the Catholic Church—became one of its most devout followers, did all she could to make proselytes, in many ways practicing self-denial, giving up every comfort for the good of the church." New York was no place for her, "She must go to Rome, pass the remainder of her life in the Holy City, so that when she died her bones might rest among the Saints. An intimate friend of hers told me that was her object in going and from her many eccentricities, I did not doubt it."*

---

*CTHK to JPH, 26 April 1869.

By 1860 the family had moved to the townhouse at 98 West Thirteenth Street, near Union Square, which had been occupied by Caroline Eliza's brother, George Alexander Phelps Jr., until he left to open the Phelps office in Palermo, Sicily, the year before. Their experience in the city during the next few years is difficult to surmise. If Julie and the family observed the crowds that surrounded Lincoln when he spoke at Cooper Union that fall, she left no record. Nor do we know what James's position on the issues that led to the Civil War—many merchants in the city did not agree that the North should oppose the secession of the southern states. The draft riots of 1863 in which near-anarchy took over the city took place in July, when the family was probably in Fairfield. Julie could have witnessed the cortege accompanying Lincoln's body on Broadway in April 1865. She was fifteen then and very probably at a New York school. No close Haring relative served in the war and of the two Phelps sons eligible for service in the Union Army, George Jr. was abroad and Frank Phelps bought a substitute.[59]

Julie's great-grandmother Phelps was alive for the first ten years of her life, in a house that George Alexander maintained for her in Fairfield with two unmarried daughters. Their memories and old-fashioned ways put the child in touch with earlier generations. Phebe Phelps (1770–1861) could

---

59. "Frank, 10 years younger, seems to have been drafted and supplied a <u>sub</u> who was killed but Frank died in his 98th year on bought time . . ." Charles Haring Phelps [Jr.] (1870–1944), to "George." Document found with H. W. White papers.

recount a past so remote that a child might scarcely have believed it existed. She was a child of six in Nova Scotia, where her father was a Congregational minister, when the Declaration of Independence was signed. She and her mother crossed the sea to Boston while the Revolution was still on to join her father, who had fled for fear of arrest for his support for the Patriot cause. She died in the year Lincoln was inaugurated, at nearly ninety years of age. A direct connection to America as it had been during and after the Revolution was gone. Julia must have attended Phebe's funeral and followed the cortege the short way to the newly purchased Phelps family plot in Fairfield.[60]

From her father and the Harings Julie learned of the past of her Dutch forebears and their role in the Revolution. Of her great aunt, Maria Haring, who lived in Rockland County, Julie remembered seeing her and learned the account of the execution of Major André "from my father when I was a very little girl."[61] James must have told her about his great uncle, Abraham Herring, that "most conspicuous representative of the ancient Dutch stock" and Judge John Haring of Tappan, the patriot statesman, her great-grandfather. There were other Dutch relatives. "As a little girl I used to visit with my father the home on Twenty-second Street of the Roosevelts and (what seemed to me much finer) the large house at Tenth Street and Broadway. There was an Aunt Margaret (Peggy) Haring Roosevelt, quite old, and of whom my father seemed fond. Also a baby boy I was allowed to hold on my lap, possibly, but not certainly, Teddy."[62]

It was the Kip cousins that Julie knew best—descendants of Ann Herring, her great aunt, and Samuel Kip. "The offshoots of this marriage I knew better and longer than any of the others," she wrote her grandson. "They lived on North Washington Square, New York, and until the older members of the family died I spent many a pleasant day at my Uncle

---

60. See the account of Phebe Phelps and her husband, Eleazar Wheelock Phelps (1766–1818), in the author's *The Hatch and Brood of Time*, chapters 4 and 5.

61. The notebook inscribed "To Elizabeth Wade White, June 8, 1919." JHWMSS. Julia recorded of Maria Haring that "[w]hile an infant she was held in her nurse's arms."

62. JHW MSS. Theodore Roosevelt was born in 1858 when Julia Phelps Haring was seven, quite old enough to hold a baby. Julie's long-lived great aunt Margaret Herring (1722–1821) had married Cornelius Roosevelt (1731–72), but a compilation of the Roosevelt family reveals no Margaret with a Herring/Haring lineage who could have been alive in the 1850s. This charming story has the ring of truth, but Aunt Peggy may have had a different surname. "The Roosevelt Family in America (Part 1)," Timothy Field Beard and Henry Hoff, comp. *Theodore Roosevelt Association Journal* 16:1 (Winter 1980).

Elbert Kip's house."[63] Elbert Samuel Kip was her father's second cousin, his given names honoring his grandfather and father. He probably pointed out to visitors that his house on Washington Square stood on land that had once been the Elbert Herring farm. Julie may well have visited Judge Elbert Herring in his house on East Twenty-ninth Street house with her father, but there is no reference to such a call in her correspondence.

Another Haring relative, Catherine (Knapp) McElroy, lived not far from Kate, in Brooklyn. She was the daughter of Hubbell Knapp and Mary Haring—Samuel and Sarah's eldest child. She was thus Julie's first cousin, though they were twenty-nine years apart in age. Catherine's husband, Samuel McElroy, was the engineer who, in the 1850s, designed the first water supply for the city of Brooklyn using reservoirs in Ridgewood (now in Queens). In 1875 he laid out the street pattern for Kings County, then largely farm land, which provided the basis for its future urban development and, ultimately, to the city's incorporation of the five small villages that comprised the county.[64] One of their sons was named for Samuel Haring. Irving, their eldest, two years older than Julie, recalled to her a visit

63. JHW to H. Wade White (grandson), 29 Oct. 1922. Elbert S. Kip was the grandson of Samuel Kip and Ann Herring, son of Elbert Kip (1769–1827). Kip, *History of the Kip Family in America*, 395, gives the birth year of Elbert S. Kip as 1799, and death year as 1876; however, Elbert S. Kip, then of 373 Lexington Ave., died on 26 July 1874, *New York Evening Post* (Barber), 27 Aug. 1874. See also Emma Howell Ross, *Descendants of Edward Howell (1584–1655) of Westbury Manor, Marsh Gibbon, Buckinghamshire and Southampton, Long Island, New York*, rev. by David Faris (Baltimore: Gateway Press, 1985), 239–40. In this volume the wife of Elbert S. Kip is identified as Nancy Havens Fowler. However, the name of the "widow of late Elbert S. Kip," who died at age 74, was Elizabeth. *New York Evening Post* (Barber), 16 Feb. 1882.

64. Marc Linder and Lawrence S. Zacharias, *Of Cabbages and Kings County: Agriculture and the Formation of Modern Brooklyn* (Iowa City: Iowa Univ. Press, 1999), 141. A statement by McElroy is the epigraph to Part 1 of the book: "If New York is the active elephant's trunk which ministers to a whole nation, these five towns of Kings county lay comparatively supinely on the Bay and Harbor in the form of a huge turtle." Samuel McElroy served as the chief engineer of the Bay Ridge railway. In later life he became an internationally recognized authority on municipal water and sanitary systems. Samuel McElroy, son of Thomas and Margaret McElroy, was born on 4 Oct. 1825 at Albany, New York, died on 10 Dec. 1898, and was buried at Rural Cemetery, Albany. He married, on 4 Oct. 1843, at Albany, Catherine Knapp, who was born on 10 Oct. 1822 and died on 27 Dec. 1878 at Brooklyn. Their son, Irving Mc Elroy, was born on 19 Jan. 1859 [prob. 1849] and died in Jan. 1914. Henry Isham Hazelton, *The Boroughs of Brooklyn and Queens, Counties of Nassau and Suffolk, Long Island, New York 1609–1924*, 6 vols. (Chicago: Lewis Historical Publishing Co., 1925), 6:138–39.

"made at our house in Brooklyn, when you had the Whooping Cough" and remembered fondly his visits to the Fourteenth Street house.[65]

Julie early studied the connections between the Haring-Herring relatives and was later quite interested in genealogy. However, after the death of her Aunt Kate she had little contact with the Haring and Clark relatives, in part because of the decimation in her generation of several of the families by early deaths. That society of Haring Dutch descendants became part of the lost world of childhood for her, recaptured as much as she could in her painstaking lineages and in the naming of her daughter and grandson.

It was her father's sister, Catharine Teller Haring, "Aunt Kate," who succored Julie in her time of need after the death of both her parents. Kate's is a remarkable story, known to us in part through the vigorously affectionate letters she wrote her orphaned niece.

Kate

Kate's marriage in Albany, at the age of sixteen, to her father's comrade in arms, John Gates Jr., led to the birth of a son, Joseph Egbert Gates. However, the last listing for John Gates Jr. in Albany was ten years after the marriage, and there is no record of someone of that name and age in New York City then or later—when Kate was almost certainly in the city attending her widowed mother—a woman of her age was noted by the 1840 census taker in her mother's last New York home, as we have seen.[66] The implication that Kate and Gates had separated is born out by a family

27. Catherine Teller Haring Kip (Julia's "Aunt Kate")

---

65. The Rev. Irving McElroy to JPH, 16 Nov. 1905. He corresponded with Julie about the family history from Bellport, Long Island, where he was priest-in-charge at Christ Episcopal Church from 1902 to 1910.

66. In 1832, eight years after his marriage to Kate, John Gates Jr., was listed at 5 Van Tromp S. in Albany, the address where his mother had lived for many years. The last listing for him in Albany is at that address in 1834. There is no listing for a man of his age in New York City. Gertrude, widow of John Gates [Sr.], his mother, died in 1839. J. Munsell, *Annals of Albany* (Albany, N.Y., 1854), 10:292.

record. A note on a ring passed down in the family reads: "This old ring has a romantic association. It was given to Catharine (Haring) Gates [Kate] by a man who wanted her to marry him. She being a divorcée would not consent because her ex-husband was still living . . . When 'widowed' she married another [Henry Kip, 1859]."[67]

Kate's photo, taken when she must have been in her early fifties, shows another of the open, strong Haring faces, and no stiffness before the camera. There is a hint of a smile, suggesting good humor, a relish of life, intelligence, and wit. She was a good aunt to Julie, as her letters show.

Divorce was rare in this period, and the legal expenses were high. A legal separation could be ordered by the courts after a costly proceeding, which would air details of behavior that many families would not have willingly made public. It seems probable that Kate's "divorce" was in fact a non-legal separation; there is no record of a marital action involving Kate in the records of New York City or Albany. By choosing to end her marriage as she did, Kate put herself in a vulnerable position in polite society at the time. As a woman who left her husband she would have been expected to assume the role of spinster aunt, care for her elderly mother, and later retire to one of her brothers' households. She may well have cared for Sarah Haring in widowhood, but Kate never faded into genteel spinsterhood. In New York City she became involved with at least one man, as evidenced by the ring he gave her, and later she remarried.[68]

This "separated" woman, someone with no evident means, had a passionate affair with a "Langley," and, remarkably, Kate could discuss it confidentially with "Hamilton," a mutual friend:

> Now that there is such a barrier placed between Langley & myself, I cannot refrain from commenting upon the circumstances which have caused this unhappy situation.

---

67. "My mother [Julie] (her niece) adored her and gave me the ring for my fifteenth birthday [1890]. One pathetic case where religious scruples prevailed. C.H.W.G." Caroline Haring White Griggs, probably written in the 1940s, copy of MS in possession of the author. The 1850 U.S. federal census lists a Catharine Gates, 35, born in N.Y., in the Eighth Ward. Kate in that year was 42, but the listed age could conceivably be a census taker's error (or misinformation). Both her brothers were living in the Seventh Ward in that year, according to the directory (but, curiously, they are not listed in the federal census). The others at that address were Elisa Gridley, 28, born N.Y. and Mary Rogers, 18, born in Ireland. U.S. federal census 1840, Eighth Ward, New York City, 38.

68. Kate was the only mature female child to help Sarah in New York with the care of the three minor children after Samuel's death. She wrote in support of he mother's pension application, suggesting that she had left Albany for the city.

To you, in whom I believe Lang ever confided, who have been so familiar with much that transpired between us, I may without hesitation speak, and I truly declare had our would-be friends, mine as well as yours, not interfered, had we been left to exercise our own discretion in affairs that related more nearly to ourselves than all the world, this false position which he has now [been placed will] have been spared him. I know all—everything—he has withheld nothing from me—freely has he discussed this matter, and I say it not to boast, but I do think that even at the eleventh hour, I could have changed the aspect of affairs.

You Hamilton, well know the influence I have ever possessed over Lang, and you also knew that I never exercised the same with a hope to benefit him.

To have insured myself a whole life time of happiness, he never should make one sacrifice for me, and what has been my reward—censorious and ill-natured remarks have been unmercifully bestowed upon me, until my very heart has been made sick & wearied me almost of existence. Poor Lang too—he has been more "sinned against than sinning," and when on Friday night he parted from me, we both of course felt very badly, but what could I do. It was not for me to speak encouraging words to him. Neither could I say—go, be happy. No: it would have belied my woman's nature, as also mocking at him.

Whatever may have happened within the two or three years past, the greater share of blame is mine. I am fully sensible of it. I feel it most keenly and I am most truly sorry but the past is beyond recall. The present is all anguish. The future is with God.[69]

It is clear from this missive that Kate and Langley for "two or three years" past were lovers, that Kate had a strong influence over him, and that as a result of something not specified, individuals in their social circle had "interfered." The result had been to place Langley in a "false position" and treat Kate with "censorious and ill-natured remarks." If it had not been for this unnamed event, there had been the prospect of happiness for Kate, which would not require a "sacrifice" on Langley's part.

This is a tantalizing glimpse of people and a social setting in Kate's New York. Was Langley a married man, compromised by his relation to Kate? Was he well-to-do and Kate suspected by the "friends" as mercenary? Or did family pressures require Langley to reject Kate for someone else, with more social standing or money? Was Kate indiscreet in her attentions, hence her guilt? Was this a genteel demimonde in which someone with Kate's curious unattached status could move freely?

---

69. Catharine Teller Haring Gates, undated letter, no envelope, JHW MSS.

There is no date on the letter—it may be a copy, or perhaps it was never sent. Its text is tantalizing because so much is unknowable—Langley and Hamilton are probably given names, virtually impossible to trace through directories or the census. The letter does, however, put us in the presence of Kate's passionate nature and her independence when dealing with men. She concludes the letter with a finale worthy of the heroine of a romantic tragedy: "I am most truly sorry but the past is beyond recall. The present is all anguish. The future is with God," would not be out of place in the final *scena,* before the protagonist is taken to the executioner, of Donizetti's *Anna Bolena,* an opera familiar on the New York stage in the 1850s.[70] The ethos of New York's genteel middle class did not govern Kate's feelings or her behavior.

Kate left Julie a cryptic token of another social acquaintance during her "separated" years, an envelope marked in her hand, "A keep-sake from Mr. Solkoloff, Nov 29, 1855," Inside was a small unstamped envelope addressed to "His Excellency, Peter Vasilyevich Kazakevich," with a wax seal and containing an 1840 U.S. One Cent coin and a paper folded with the impress of a seal.[71] It appears that Kate had met a Russian gentleman and his nobleman friend and the seal was given to her as a souvenir, indicating that she at one time traveled in circles where she would meet such people.[72]

Kate married for the second time in New York on 20 April 1859. Her new husband, Henry Kip, was also her second cousin.[73] She referred to him as the "old gentleman" in her letters, but in fact, at fifty-one, he was only a year older than she. Henry was the fifth child of Samuel Haring's first cousin, Samuel Kip Jr. (1771–1833) and Eliza Howell (1770–1846), she from a family in Sag Harbor, Long Island, he the son of Ann (Herring)

---

70. See Vera Brodsky Lawrence, *Strong on Music: The New York Music Scene in the Diary of George Templeton Strong: Reverberations 1850–1856* (Chicago: Chicago Univ. Press, 1995), 3–5.

71. Note with date signed "C.H.W.G." (Caroline Haring White Griggs), JHW MSS.

72. Neither His Excellency or Mr. Solkoloff can be identified from a New York City sources, but a possible clue lies in the naming of a child of Kate's grandniece Mary (Knapp) McElroy, daughter of her deceased older sister. Margaret Sikaloff McElroy, was born on 28 May 1857. Samuel McElroy, the child's father, from the mid-1850s was planning the water supply for the city of Brooklyn, a project that could conceivably have drawn a Russian observer, who may subsequently become acquainted with the family. Alfred Averill Knapp, comp., *Nicholas Knapp Genealogy* (Winter Park, Fla., 1958), 289–90; Hazelton, *The Boroughs of Brooklyn and Queens*, 6:138–39.

73. *New York Herald*, 1 Sept. 1859.

Kip.[74] (The Elbert Samuel Kip whom Julie visited in Washington Square was Henry's older brother.) Henry was born in 1807 at Kips Bay and baptized at the New York Dutch Reformed Church, just as Kate was a year later.[75] He grew up as part of the large Old Knickerbocker clan, in an era when their eminence was being overtaken by newcomers to the city; by the 1840s the mansion at Kips Bay was abandoned as the city moved uptown. This marriage of the two middle-aged people—"Darby & Joan" Kate called herself and Henry after a popular song of the day—gave one more twist to the connection between the Harings and the Kip families that was first established before the Revolution.[76]

It was the second marriage for Henry, a widower, whose first wife was Elizabeth Abbatt. The daughters from that marriage, Cornelia and Elizabeth, Kate referred to as "Goneril & Regan" in a letter written when she was awaiting their "august appearance." With a touch of salt she added, "I do not care if I never again see them."[77]

"Henry Kipp" served as one of the harbormasters of the Port of New York for ten years from 1845—the name was occasionally spelled "Kipp." The harbormaster held an influential position, as he was responsible for enforcing the laws of the state and city pertaining to cleaning the docks and "preventing and removing nuisances in or upon them." Harbormasters were the sole judges of infractions, and there were heavy fines for refusal to obey.[78] In the 1850s Henry seems to have been prosperous, living on West Twenty-fourth Street, and for two years having an office at 38 South Street. This generously endowed position was a political appoint-

---

74. Samuel Kip Jr. was the brother of James S. Kip of Utica (see chapter 3). Ross, *Descendants of Edward Howell*, 239–40.

75. He was baptized on 31 Aug. 1807. "Baptisms from 1801 to 1819 in the New York Reformed Dutch Church," 357, MS, NYGB.

76. Darby and Joan were "the type of loving, old-fashioned, virtuous couple. The names belonged to a ballad written by Henry Woodfall, first published in the *Gentleman's Original* in 1735." *Brewer's Dictionary of Phrase and Fable*, ed. Ivor H. Evans (New York: Harper and Row, 1987).

77. On Henry Kip's first marriage see "Haring-Herring," Genealogical and Biographical Notes. CTHK to JPH, 7 May 1869, 29 June 1869.

78. Edgar A. Werner, *Civil List and Constitutional History of the Colony and State of New York* (Albany, 1891), 311–12.

ment, but it was no sinecure. Henry Kip was out of the job by 1855, and the directories for the three subsequent years have no listing for him.[79]

When they married, Kate and Henry took up residence in a newly developed section of Brooklyn, at 222 Clermont Avenue, in what is now the Fort Greene neighborhood.[80] Henry's business address then and later in the 1860s was at 67 Wall Street in Manhattan, his profession "clerk." There was another move in that section of Brooklyn, and two years of no listing, but in 1870 Henry and Kate were living in Brooklyn Heights, first at 116 and after 1871 at 143 Henry Street. By then Henry was listed as "sec." (secretary) at 12 Wall Street.[81] Their house was one of the first row houses to be built in Brooklyn Heights in the 1840s, according to its present owner. Its ground floor and kitchen is slightly below grade, a stoop leads to the entrance to the parlor floor, above which are two upper floors. In contrast to the large town houses built in the heights in the 1850s and after, it is wood-framed and clapboarded, modest in size, with intimate rooms on the parlor floor. What appears to be the original mantle remains in the parlor, over which Henry placed Julie's picture.[82] Kate referred deprecatingly to the house as "the Shanty," probably because it was of wood and smaller and simpler than nearby brownstones.[83] They rented, as there is no record of a conveyance to a Kip for that building or any other on the block.[84]

There were two churches that were then (and now) powerful presences on the block—the First Presbyterian Church, an imposing gothic structure, and the Zion German Evangelical Lutheran Church. They and others nearby added to the dignity of the neighborhood and heightened the contrast with commercial Manhattan. As Henry Stiles declared in his his-

---

79. In 1859–60 there was a Henry Kip at 576 Third Ave. at East Fortieth St. He was a grocer—an occupation at variance with what Kate's Henry did before or later, but it could, of course, have referred to him.

80. Trow, *New York City Directory* (1860–61).

81. In 1871–72 Henry Kip's residence was at 116 in Trow's Manhattan directory, but a Brooklyn directory specifies 143 Henry St. *Brooklyn City and Business Directory for the Year Ending May 1st, 1872* (Brooklyn: George T. Lain).

82. The author is indebted to Mr. Joseph Broadwin, the present owner of 143 Henry St., for permitting a visit the property in April 1999. The reference to Julie's picture is found in CTHK to JPH, 8 Dec. 1868.

83. CTHK to JPH, 19 Nov. 1868.

84. Brooklyn Conveyance Records, Grantor-Grantee, Block 237. There is no Kip listed in any transactions from the initiation of records in the 1830s on this block.

tory of Brooklyn, published when Kate and Henry were living there, "Probably no other city in the Christian world possesses so many places of religious worship in proportion to the population, and certainly it would be difficult to find elsewhere an equal number of church edifices so justly celebrated for their general elegance and beauty of architectural design."[85] Two of the thirteen steam ferries that connected Brooklyn to New York were nearby; the closest was the Fulton Street Ferry (celebrated by Walt Whitman) at the foot of the hill below Henry Street (where James Clark, Kate's grandfather, had awaited rescue in the last minutes of the retreat from Brooklyn in 1776). Henry probably went to and from Wall Street on the Montague Street Ferry.[86]

By the time Kate and Henry lived on Henry Street there was a water main connection to the house whose source was the reservoir that Samuel McElroy had designed. By the 1860s several thousand houses were connected to sewers that drained into the East River. Since the most developed areas were served first, this undoubtedly included the Henry Street houses. Gas light had come to Brooklyn streets in 1848. Thus the Kips had amenities that their parents lacked. The "Shanty" may even have had indoor plumbing.[87]

Henry Kip's frequent changes of address and occupation after the lucrative post of harbormaster suggest that he had come down in the world and, like Mr. Micawber, was waiting for something to turn up. It was a strenuous business. "Nothing yet for Henry," Kate wrote, "He goes regularly every day to the City in hope of hearing something favorable—poor man, he is well nigh discouraged."[88] This was a man aware of a more affluent and engaged past and in late middle age still struggling to find a place.

Young Julie was eight when she acquired this new uncle; she became devoted to him and he to her. When she was nineteen Henry gave her a Kip family keepsake, the silver baptismal cup of his deceased brother, George Washington Kip, made in 1814 by the prominent silversmith Joel Sayre. The inscription he added read, "To Julie from Uncle Henry."[89]

---

85. Henry R. Stiles, *A History of the City of Brooklyn* . . . facs. ed. (Brooklyn, New York: by subscription, 1869; Bowie, Md.: Heritage Books, 1993), 3:504.

86. Ibid., 3:502; the Fulton Ferry House is illustrated on 3:551, the Montague Ferry House on 3:554.

87. Ibid., 3:597.

88. CTHK to Caroline Eliza (Phelps) Haring, 15 Sept. 1868.

89. Silver cup (mark: J. Sayre) with urn marked "George Washington Kip, 1814" and "To Julie from Uncle Henry, 1870," property of the author.

James at the End of His Career

James, in charge of J. S. Haring & Co. at his brother's death, was often away on business, purchasing from upstate growers and millers. By the 1850s, wheat from fields further west began to flow to New York by railroad. Grain boats from Michigan and Ohio transferred their cargoes to grain elevators in Buffalo, where it could be shipped by rail to the city not constrained by the winter's cold that froze the canal. James's estate included a waterfront lot in Buffalo, presumably bought to secure a strategic place on the water in that rapidly growing city.[90] By 1858 there were twelve large grain elevators in Buffalo, a place that owed "its prosperity to the storage facility and to the merchants who handled them."[91] By the 1850s fields even further west were opening up. For James this meant a connection to the small city of Minneapolis, at St. Anthony's Falls on the Mississippi, from which Julie would later unexpectedly benefit.

James had only two or three years as the sole proprietor of the business, however, as the last directory listing for J. S. Haring & Co. occurs in 1862–63, about the time when James began a five-year struggle with tuberculosis. He was forty-nine on 24 June 1868 when he died at the house of his father-in-law, 209 West Fourteenth Street, the third among his siblings to die of the disease.[92] The newspaper notice announced that the funeral service would be at St. Paul's, the Episcopal church near the Phelps house in Fairfield: "The friends and acquaintances of the family are invited to attend, leaving the city by the New Haven railroad, corner of Twenty–seventh Street and Fourth Avenue, at half past eleven o'clock, and can return the same evening."[93] Julie, Caroline Eliza, Kate, Henry, and the Phelpses accompanied the hearse across town to the station and in the train, agonizing experiences for seventeen-year-old Julie. James was buried in the plot where Phebe Phelps and several of George and Eliza Phelps's children and grandchildren lay.

James's death left Kate the sole survivor of Samuel and Sarah's children. Kate wrote Julie that he had been "a good & faithful brother to me.

90. Probate file of James Demarest Haring: Probationary Documents, loc. 09-041719, N.Y. Co. Surrogate's Court, New York, N.Y.

91. Kuhlmann, *Development of the Flour Milling Industry*, 54–60, 61, 69.

92. *Manhattan Deaths*, Index 1868, 10864, Municipal Archives, New York City.

93. *New York Herald*, 25 June 1868.

After Clinton went to his eternal home, James was my sole dependence, the *only one* who took a brotherly interest in the sister left dependent as I was."[94] In the months after his death she looked for a place for the widow and daughter in Brooklyn Heights. It seemed ideal, quieter than Manhattan, with its cultural institutions, and most of all, close to "The Shanty."

"Yesterday I went with Henry to the Mansion House," Kate wrote Caroline Eliza of a visit to a residential hotel in the Heights, "am sorry to say met with no success—I am really disappointed. After it had been spoken of, your coming to Brooklyn, I looked upon it as almost a settled affair & feel my home here would not be quite solitary as it now is—but it is not wise to make calculations—we usually get frustrated." What they were looking for was larger than the "3 or 4 parlors & bedrooms, attached" at Mansion House, "the remainder all taken for the winter. What a nice clean house it is—prices not extravagant as compared with Miss Pearsall, ranging from $55 to 65 per week—a good deal of money though to pay out every few days." Pierrepont House, "now tidy like the others—charges, about the same. Then went to a large boarding house on Montague St. Parlor & bedroom on 3d floor front $36. I do not think it would suit you."[95]

Caroline Eliza was well off. James left an estate with securities and deposits valued at $35,000 to the benefit of his widow, daughter, and sister. It was a goodly sum for a man whom Dun in the late 1850s had considered to have no means. The form of the assets indicated the great changes that had taken place in commerce since his father's day. Securities included the shares of the Corn Exchange Bank, bonds of the Mechanics Bank, the State of Tennessee and the United States, financial instruments that only in his lifetime had become available to people of moderate means. No real or personal property was listed in the initial inventory, but administrative reports in later years included references to the harbor-front property in Buffalo occupied by a lumber yard and warehouse.[96] James's substantial estate showed what capital a man in a middle-rank business in the city had

---

94. CTHK to Caroline Eliza (Phelps) Haring, 16 Sept. 1868.

95. Ibid.

96. Probate file of James Demarest Haring: Probationary Documents (Account and Vouchers, 1881–86, Letters of Administration, 1869–93), loc. 09-041719, N.Y. Co. Surrogate's Court, New York, N.Y., There is no will in these files, but references in the probationary papers specify the legatees.

been able to amass in a working career of about twenty-five years. "[W]hat a consolation it must have been to James to know that he could leave his little family in comfortable circumstances," Kate commented, adding "which he was enabled to do by having practiced through life, the strictest economy himself, ever looking forward to the welfare of those who looked up to him."[97]

Caroline Eliza also had potential support from her father, whose flourishing firm then had overseas offices in Palermo and Liverpool. She was doubtless considering Boston as a place to live, near her eldest sister, Julia Maria Winter, whose daughter Lizzie was close to Julie's age and a firm friend. Fate decreed otherwise. Barely five weeks after the unsuccessful search for a Brooklyn home, Caroline Eliza died of peritonitis in the Fourteenth Street house, on 21 October 1868, after an illness of five days.[98] She lay in the same bed where her husband had died that June. The funeral cortege took the same course through the city, the coffin and the family went on the same train journey, the service was in the same church, and once again Julie attended the burial in the Phelps family plot.[99] Julia was orphaned at seventeen, with her parents' final agonies forever in her consciousness.

Aunt Kate was the counselor to whom she turned. A month after her mother's death, Julie visited Kate in Brooklyn ("a stupid evening in the Shanty" as Kate referred to it, when she learned that contemporaries of Julie's had that same evening called on her in the Manhattan town house where, in Kate's view, she might have had a better time). "You cannot imagine how startled I was this morning on receiving your note," Kate wrote of a gift of money that Julie made.

> [H]aving so recently seen you I feared something had happened, but on opening your dear little missive my alarm was dispelled. Now Julie, my child, this is truly very kind of you but I cannot nor must not allow you to do so. I am now taking from you what I ought not & if by any possibility I could live without I assure you I would not take one penny other than what was set apart for my benefit by your father's will. This little transaction of yours has really made me melancholy. I never thought that anyone would be so thoughtful for

---

97. CTHK to Caroline Eliza (Phelps) Haring, 16 Sept. 1868.

98. *Manhattan Deaths*, Index, 1868, 21197.

99. *New York Herald*, 22 Oct. 1868.

me—and you so young to assume such a task—never can I pay in same my gratitude and everlasting love.[100]

She added that "Uncle Henry has gone to New York," reminding us how separate Manhattan seemed from Brooklyn then. "When he comes home and I tell him this he will be moved as I am & big tears will fill his eyes as he says what he often does, God bless her—"

To spend some time in Manhattan involved an expedition. In that same letter Kate wrote,

> We propose going to see Aunt Mary [probably her ancient aunt-in-law, the widow of William Clark—see below]. The Old Gentleman wants to see Mr. Schevendycke so for that purpose we will go to [   ] Hotel while I take a run down to look in upon you. Don't you think we are going to undertake a great deal in one day, considering that we are the very opposite of what may be called a Juvenile Couple—We shall not start on our journey until Wednesday, probably Thursday, if a fine day, but don't wait in for me, for, as I said before, it will be a call only, and most likely in the morning.

A few weeks later, in response to a despondent Julie's letter, Kate offered her consolation and support. "You have passed through a fearful ordeal, but blessings still are yours. May we think that all things are wisely ordered. The ways of Providence are beyond our ken. God's ways are not as our ways, and we should not with our puny reason attempt to scan his doings." She reflected on how she failed to follow her own advice to abide and hope: "I continually murmur & rebel at the dispensations sent. Mine has been a life of trials. I sometimes take a retrospective view of them & wonder how I ever lived through in all, but yet here I am, fast going the down hill of life. In a few years or months, may be to follow those who have preceded me to the spirit land." Kate gave the eternally valid advice, "Force yourself to take an interest in things around you. I know you can never forget the mournful past, but try not to dwell upon it continually. It will produce a morbid grief which will not only destroy your happiness but injure your health & also would not be an acceptable offering to the loved ones in heaven." She concludes, "I feel, Julie dear, *you will not* forget

---

100. The letter was addressed to 214 West Twelfth St., not the Fourteenth St. house where Julie's parents had died. Presumably she had removed from the associations of that house and was staying with friends. CTHK to JPH, undated, ca. Nov. 1868.

me. Now that your beloved father and mother have gone, I cling to you more than anyone on earth. It seems as if I must have the best claim upon you while I know that others have an equal right, perhaps more, but they cannot love you any better."[101] Kate's loving support to Julie at this time in her life was warmly reciprocated. She saved the letters of "Aunt Kate," told her daughter of her, and gave her a place in the family's history long after her death.

Caroline Eliza left no will. In October, George Alexander, executor of James's estate, filed a statement that Julie would be the beneficiary of her mother's share of his estate. Caroline Eliza had comparatively little money in her own right, less than $4,500. Julie thus inherited two thirds of her father's estate, and when Kate died four years later, she became the sole beneficiary.[102] Seventeen-year-old Julia thus was something of an heiress and promisingly comfortable.

To help Julie overcome her grief, her grandfather sent her and his youngest son, Howard Phelps, on a nine-month tour of Europe, which took them from Sicily to England. Howard was less than two years older than his niece and was a lively companion. They look like brother and sister in a photograph taken in a London photographer's studio. With them is a lady of a certain age, possibly a chaperone. They sailed on the SS. *Calabria*, a sail-assisted steamer and a ten-year veteran of the Mediterranean run.[103] Kate was at the pier with the Phelps relatives to see them off. She sent a letter as soon as she reached home: "I fancy I see you both as you stood on the deck of the steamer watching us on shore. How insignificant we all must have appeared—like atoms. In a little while we all were wending our way home, while you were steaming on the broad Atlantic. How badly I felt & you must have had some regrets, poor child . . ."[104] The Atlantic was rough that December and Julie reported to Kate that she had been miserably seasick.[105]

---

101. CTHK to JPH, 8 Dec. 1868.

102. Probate file of Caroline E. Haring, Letters of Administration, 29 Oct. 1868, Petition of Julia Haring White in the matter of the application of Letters of Administration on the goods, chattels and credits of Caroline E. Haring, 7 Feb. 1897, loc. 90255, N.Y. Co. Surrogate's Court, New York, N.Y.

103. The *Calabria* was built in 1857. See Michael J. Anuta, *Ships of Our Ancestors* (1983; reprint, Baltimore: Genealogical Publishing Co., 1993), 12.

104. CTHK to JPH, 8 Dec. 1868.

105. Ibid.

28. Julia Phelps Haring, Howard Phelps, and unidentified woman.
The party are seated in a mock-up of a railway carriage similar to those
they had used on their nine month grand tour of Europe, 1868.

At Palermo Julia and Howard were welcomed by George Phelps Jr.,
who managed the Mediterranean base of Phelps Brothers, from which he
purchased citrus and dried fruit for shipment to England and America. He
established the office in the late 1850s, at about the time when Garibaldi
ousted the Bourbon monarchy of the Kingdom of the Two Sicilies. Helen
Clark, George Phelps Jr.'s wife, was the youngest daughter of Sarah
Haring's brother, William Clark, thus Julie's first cousin once removed as
well as aunt-in-law.[106]

In those years Palermo had a winter "season," which drew European
nobility and wealth. Howard and Julia arrived when newly married Prin-

---

106. The eldest of the Clark daughters was the Mary Clark who married John Samuel Haring.

cess Marguerite, later Queen of Italy, was on a state visit to the now-Italian city with the prince and heir to the throne of Savoy.[107] She was "a lovely, young bride not more than seventeen—my age," Julie recalled years later, "and with her husband and King Victor Emmanuel—the prince's father—were receiving all the homage the people could shower on them." She recalled, "Uncle George and Aunt Helen Phelps dressed in the most gorgeous apparel starting off for one of the balls."[108]

By March, Julie had visited Naples and was in Rome, which prompted Kate to respond, "Well, have you seen the Pope, for among all the grand sights, I want you to see all the grandest people . . . And if you go to St. Petersburgh, get a peep at the Emperor. They do say he likes the American people." (Mr. Solkoloff may have told her about the tsar's views, or she may have heard of them from the charming Peter Vasilyevich Kazakevich.)

Rome, a small, immensely colorful city, was still governed by the pope at the time. Margaret (Terry) Chanler, an American growing up in Rome in those years, remembered Pio Nono (Pope Pius IX) driving by in a glass coach, on one occasion stopping to greet her and a playmate, and when they told him they were Episcopalians promising that he would pray for them. There was a funeral with "endless processions of monks, Knights of Malta, and diplomatic representatives. The Roman Senate sent three glass coaches with outriders and footmen—real footmen—four walked by each coach, holding long, silken cords, fastened to the top . . . [the senators wore] bright crimson and yellow, footmen in knee breeches."[109] The year after Julie's visit (1870) the Italian government took over the Papal States, ending the colorful era of papal rule and beginning the modern era of the city. This was another soon-to-vanish world that Julie saw, like the antebellum New York of her childhood with its Dutch associations, and, later, Europe before the Great War.

In news from home, Kate reported a visit from Mary, her sister-in-law, John Samuel Haring's widow. "She repeated her former question, how much the Estate amounted to & again did I reply I could not answer. Very

---

107. Margerita Teresa Giovanna, princess of Savoy, daughter of the duke of Genoa, 1851–1926, married on 21 April 1868 Humbert (1844–1900), son of King Victor Emmanuel II of Piedmont (later king of united Italy from 1870). He reigned as King Humbert I (1878–1900). See *Enc. Brit.*, s.v. "Humbert, Hanieri."

108. JPH to Carol White Griggs, 19 Jan. 1926.

109. Margaret Chanler, *Roman Spring: Memoirs of Mrs. Winthrop Chanler* (Boston: Little Brown, 1934), 15.

strange, don't you think so. She said Helen [(Clark) wife of George Alexander Phelps Jr.] had written that you & Howie were enjoying yourselves. Of her husband, she offered, "The *Old Gentleman* is at home. He says tell Julie she must receive my paper kisses. 'till I can give her better.'"

In April, responding to Julie's comments about Rome, Kate was relieved that "there is not much chance of you ever being a convert to Catholicism, and yet we often hear of men, and of women too of superior mind & intelligence embracing the Roman Catholic faith." (She then launched into her story, quoted above, of Miss McBride of the Astor Place Hotel.)

There was news of family. Aunt Martha Clark (in Minneapolis) was going to send her daughter east, and "I have not been to the city since the funeral of Aunt Lydia. Am going soon to see Aunt Mary Clark, poor old soul. [Mary Bogart, the widow of Sarah Haring's brother William.] She must feel very lonely without her almost life companion—they had lived together & been inseparable for *fifty six* years—few sisters-in-law can say as much, a rare occurrence surely." Kate was well aware that she was the last in her immediate family and the last to know these older Clark and Haring relatives.

Kate was also aware of her relative poverty. When Julie's Aunt Harriet (Phelps) Brooke had not come to visit her, she wrote, "I imagine she thinks I am sensitive about my little *Shanty*, and for that reason does not like to come." She added, "Pride and poverty are hard masters. I am their most unwilling slave." The unemployed Henry was "not very well—a sort of blue streak has come over him—occasionally he indulges in such moods, but as a general thing I give him credit for fighting up against fate. He is at home today, sends a deal of love to you & remembrances to Howie."[110]

When she heard from Julie in Venice, Kate reflected,

I used to say if it ever should be my good fortune to go about, I wanted to go to Amsterdam & to Venice. Those two places were the height of my ambition, but now I could not travel a hundred miles without fatigue. To endure all you have would completely use me up. How we do change as we grow old and now years tell upon us in so many ways—but all this is far off in the distant future for you and long before it becomes a reality may you, my dear, see very many years of true happiness.

110. CTHK to JPH, 26 April 1869.

Apparently Julie had been upset by Venice—probably by the extreme poverty she had witnessed there. "Your description of Venice is no longer what my fancy painted it; when reading about it I always thought it one of the loveliest spots imaginable. You have dispelled the illusion, nothing like seeing for one's self. I see through your eyes the charm no longer exists."[111] (In later life Julia would greatly enjoy the city, the centerpiece of the twenty-fifth anniversary trip with her husband.)

Kate gave homely news of her health, which had improved. "By the bye, I had nearly forgotten to tell you. I was weighed the other day and am again getting to be quite a respectably sized woman—113 lbs. My weight last summer was only 98. What if I should grow as enormous as my sister-in-law Mary [Haring, widow of John Samuel]—you would hardly know me I suspect." She added an amusing insight into Henry's former life. "The Old Gentleman heretofore alluded to, is pleased with the improvement. My predecessor, as you know, was a *Mountain* in size. Perhaps he would like a second edition—beg to be excused, can't see it."

In May, along with news of the heat, Kate sent a social comment, as appropriate in New York social circles later as then:

> Hot weather has come upon us, all at once. How I dread the summer. It wilts me down like an old rag. The only thing for me is to keep quiet as I can in my little home—New York [Manhattan] will not be troubled with me very often . . . They who have money are preparing for the watering places. They who have none will seclude themselves in barred doors, closed shutters, live in the rear part of the house and pretend all the while to be out of town— because it is the fashion a few will go for real comfort & change from city life.

After a visit to Manhattan, Kate wrote Julie that "Shoddy is in the ascendant, extravagant dress, handsome laces, expensive jewels & vulgarity are what is now-a-days called the best society. What would such people have been if it had not been for our late Civil War—?" She perceived the social changes that were creating an ever wealthier America as its energies turned to developing its enormous interior, enriching new classes of people who would hardly have known who Kips and Harings were and where they had come from.

On the June anniversary of James's death Kate expressed her sympathy for Julie's loss and reflected once more on her own:

111. CTHK to JPH, 11 May 1869.

My letter today, darling, will not be a cheerful one nor do I believe I can write much. I am dreadfully depressed. You need not ask why. It is, alas, the first anniversary of your father's death, a sad day for us both. Your first real sorrow came that day, but a greater one afterward—mine almost ended, for it left me the last of my generation—but not as I then felt alone—no, while I've *you* & Uncle Henry I cannot say I am alone.

The time seems long and yet how short, only one year. In that brief space how much for us to ponder on. What wonderful changes the two dearest and best loved on Earth have been taken from you. And now you are thousands of miles away from the many who have sincere sympathy & love in their hearts for the poor dear orphan.[112]

Julie clearly became the favored child of the old couple, filling the void in Kate's heart left by the death of her son and in Henry's by the emotional distance of his "Goneril and Regan."

I generally read your letters or a portion of them to Uncle Henry as it pleases him & I do not fancy you object. So after I had read your last he says how singular it is that after hearing one of Julie's letters read it always makes me for a little time feel sad—bless her dear heart, he says, how kindly she speaks of me & always remembers me when writing to you. My children, my children if you were like her, but your aunts have estranged you from me. You are no longer mine save in name—

When he talks in that strain I am sorry but feel provoked. They are no blessing to him, but rather the bane of his life.[113]

Kate and Henry kept a visual reminder of their dear niece in a prominent place in their home, perhaps gazing upon her visage as they read from her letters:

Your picture hangs between the two great statesmen, Clay and Webster. The first thing Uncle Henry does each morning on rising, is, to go to it and say, Good Morning Julie, and now as I am writing, he says, I send her a thousand kisses. God bless her. God protect her—& strange as it may be, I believe you are equal in his affections with his own children.[114]

---

112. CTHK to JPH, 26 June 1869.

113. Ibid.

114. CTHK to JPH, 8 Dec. 1868.

The two statesmen who flanked Julie on the mantel were Henry's heroes. It had been their grand political aim to preserve the Union through compromise. Like many New Yorkers Henry had likely been dismayed by the outbreak of hostilities and less than supportive of the war effort. He probably shared Kate's view that a consequence of the Northern victory was the decline in manners and rise in social ostentation.

Julie wrote in sorrow at the anniversary of her father's death. She knew that in Kate she had someone with whom she could share her grief. Her thoughts evoked Kate's view that "were I a good Christian Woman something no doubt would rise spontaneously in my heart which would meet your requirements—but, alas, like yourself, I see only through an imperfect vision."[115]

What can I say to comfort you my poor Child—. Trials & afflictions may bring some nearer to God, but each one I receive removes me further from grace. Sickness & death have come to those I loved. Poverty & dependence have been my portion & more. Little is left for me when my turn comes but to lie down and die. To go, alas, where—but you my dear one, so young so innocent, so good, a different fate awaits you. Only you must wrestle with yourself—you must try to cast from you this gloomy despondent frame of mind & you will be rewarded. I do not say at once, for it must take time, but eventually you will find you will pass from grief to calmness, to content. to comfort—but you must persevere. . . . I am like you. I would not have the cold pity of the world—but when we feel it is sincere, sympathy is very grateful to the sorrow-stricken heart—

I wept very much over your letter & yet for the sake of sparing feelings I would not you should withhold the truth. I do not want you to write you are cheerful when you are far from being so, but I do want you to say you are not so dreadfully unhappy. You will try to be more reconciled, more resigned, to what was the will of God and may you my darling, ever have an abiding faith in a happy meeting with your beloved parents in a blissful hereafter—

In the same letter Kate opened up the prospect of Julie's living near her:

You are little aware how much Uncle Henry & I talk about you. It is our great pleasure to build Castles—which at once tumble down again. For instance, we say we would like a nice house in New York & everything in it comfort-

---

115. CTHK to JPH, 28 June 1869.

able when Julie comes back, let her alternate between her Grandpa's and our home—how nice it would be. Then I say I would try to be all in all to her till some other supplanted me & Uncle Henry puts in with—dear little Julie, she should reign supreme. . . . Darby & Joan move on just the same as when you came to see us in our little Shanty—comfortable.

Kate promised to visit Julie's Phelps grandmother but, because of the social and economic distinctions between the two, was diffident. "I do dislike to receive hospitalities while we are so circumstanced I cannot return them. It is mortifying to me. Pride & poverty—two such opposites—are hard to contend with—"

By late summer, "Darby & Joan discuss Julie's coming—the time is now rapidly approaching," Kate wrote. "Darby says the 28th will soon be here. Joan puts in with—you forget, ten days crossing—so every day we count & calculate & soon we will count the hours." Kate had visited old Aunt Mary or "what little there is of her—looking as though an ordinary gust of wind might blow her away. Truly it seems as if her time on Earth is short. Were she my Mother I could not leave her knowing to a certainty almost that I should never see her again." (In fact Mary Clark lived for two more years.) Helen (Clark) Phelps had returned from Palermo on a visit, stimulating another of Kate's refreshingly acerbic comments. The writing is worthy of Dickens, a social duet with outward politesse masking inner scorn.

I met my foreign cousin—believe she goes every day to see her mother [the ailing Aunt Mary]—so my chances were slim in avoiding a meeting—would like to have seen [Helen's five-year-old daughter] Nellie, but she was not with her. I agree with you that Helen is quite stylish in appearance, easy in manners but further cannot say—as for her sincerity in the cordial greeting she extended to me I presume it was all assumed and you may be sure that though I appeared to be a little friendly you may be sure I was by no means graciously inclined though was too busy—in bidding her good-by Helen said she would like to have come to see me but her time has been so limited. Pshaw, what was the use of telling such a fib.[116]

---

116. CTHK to JPH, 9 Aug. 1869. As noted earlier, Helen (Clark) Phelps was Kate's first cousin on her mother's side, Julie's aunt by marriage on the Phelps side and her first cousin, once removed. "Nellie" was her daughter, then five years old.

29. The sail-assisted steamship *Russia*.
Julia returned to America on this ship in 1869.

After ten months abroad Julia and her Uncle Howie departed from Liverpool, crossing the Atlantic on the *Russia*. They arrived in New York in September 1869. The grand tour was a formative experience for Julie, one she would repeat throughout her life. Europe, to her mind, became the standard of culture, where there was an elegance and refinement not found at home. She would cross the Atlantic many more times, and her daughter and granddaughter would in their turn be given grand tours at a similarly impressionable age.

Julie had turned eighteen in March while abroad. She was legally a minor, and her funds were doled out by her grandfather. Her city home was with the elder Phelpses on Fourteenth Street, though because of its bitter associations with her parents' deaths, she was more frequently in Fairfield. She also visited her Aunt Julia Maria and Cousin Lizzie Winter in Boston and certainly had a heartfelt reception at the Shanty on Henry Street.

The grandparents were on the verge of retiring from the city. George Alexander Phelps was sixty-six and had put Phelps Brothers in the hands of his four sons (who would continue to prosper). Kate wrote Julia that he had been up the Hudson looking for an estate for his retirement, and that a deal fell through. However, a grand house in the Greek revival style of his youth became available in Fairfield, and the family left the cozy Gothic-revival house that had been the summer retreat for a quarter of a century to move into this magnificent 1820s creation on Main Street. It looked like a temple: Doric columns framed the façade and there were angel wings carved on its pediment. From the porch the elderly owners could watch passersby and be seen through the columns. The acquisition of this house marked George Phelps as a successful merchant, and its architecture was a sign that success was based on the antique values of the republic of his youth.[117] (It was remodeled in the colonial revival style in the early 1900s and still stands at 458 Old Post Road, Fairfield.)

Julie was of marriageable age, an heiress. A young woman in her position had to circulate socially to meet young men and wait to be asked. It was a familiar situation in an era when few daughters of means had occupation or studies after basic schooling. Moreover, Julie had no mother to guide her in society through these waiting years. The grandparents were elderly and retiring, and Aunt Kate was in no position to introduce her to New York society. Julie was hardly forlorn, with the large Phelps family close by, but she was exposed. It was understandable that she spent this period of her life visiting relatives and friends of the family.

In 1872 Julie invited Kate to accompany her to Minneapolis to visit a Clark relation, a prospect that pleased old "Joan" mightily. "Uncle Henry and I have entered into this agreement. I am to go with you to Minnesota if you want me on condition that I come back before extreme cold weather sets in," she wrote.[118] Henry was "to go to Sag Harbor to please me and I shall be better satisfied his being there than alone here." There he would stay with Mrs. Douglas, "a good woman." (Henry's mother, Eliza (Howell) Kip had come from Sag Harbor, and it is likely that there was family there.)[119] "The poor old man says he will miss me sadly but he makes the sacrifice, believing the journey will benefit my health & also because Julie wishes it. You must in consideration of this never scold him or be cross."

Julie offered to pay for a new dress for Kate. "My worry is in it going to be so much expense to you," Kate replied, but then she agreed to accept the favor.

---

117. See Judd, *Hatch and Brood of Time*, 285–87. Marcia Peden Miner, "Metamorphosis par Excellence," *Fairfield Citizen News*, 27 Sept. 1995.

118. CTHK to JPH, Oct. 1872.

119. Ross, *Descendants of Edward Howell*, 239–40. No source or date cited, and there is no death date for Henry Kip.

"As you told me this morning, that is *none of my business*. I know you have the wherewithal to mean it, so go ahead, little lady! to make arrangements yourself. I do not mean you to be ashamed of your auntie's appearance when among your Western friends—therefore I think I had best take the dress I have, for the traveling in, & have the new one be made as [   ] in present style . . . I do not know any dressmaker in Brooklyn, and if you advise it, will go to yours so it can be sent home with your dresses which I believe you mean to send here.

This journey for Kate with her beloved niece was not to be. On the envelope of this letter Julia wrote: "My dearest Aunt Kate died in less than a week after she had sent me this letter."

The Last of the Line

Catherine Teller Haring Kip died in Brooklyn on 12 October 1872, in her sixty-fifth year, deprived of the experience of traveling with her beloved niece that she would have much enjoyed. On her part, Julie was left bereft of her aunt's vigorous support, and the closest connection to her father's Haring and Clark families went with her. Certainly Julie accompanied Henry and the hearse from the house along the road to Green-Wood Cemetery, several miles away, where Kate was buried in a single gravesite.[120]

The "Old Gentleman" continued to live at 143 Henry Street until 1875. He evidently found some work. In the three years after Kate's death he is listed as "asst. sec." and "clerk" in the directory. In the final year the "ins" after his name indicates he was selling insurance at home.[121] The "poor old man" was strong enough to marry for a third time, Geraldine Gardiner, according to a family history.[122]

Kate was the last link to the distant worlds of the New York and Albany of the early decades of the century and, through their recollections, to Hardenbergh's Corners, Tappan, and the Revolution in New York. She was a witness to her father's and first husband's service in the War of 1812.

---

120. Lot 8494, Section 119. Personal communication from Theresa Labianca, Secretary, Green-Wood Cemetery, 12 Aug. 1993.

121. *Brooklyn City and Business Directory* (1872, 1873, 1874, 1875).

122. Ross, *Descendants of Edward Howell*, 240. The surname suggests a connection with the prominent family of eastern Long Island, but there is no confirmation of this. Henry was not buried in Green-Wood, and the author has found no record of his death or confirmation of the third marriage.

She had known the Hudson crowded with sloops, seen Erie Canal boats docking at Albany, ridden the steamboat and railroad when they were novelties. She obviously valued the decorous republican world of her youth. Her secrets, or at least undocumented experiences, are only hinted at in the fragments of letters—the identity of "Langley," and the man (if not he) who gave her the ring and asked for her hand. These secrets died with her, as did the recollections of her years as a once-married woman. For Julie, it was Kate who knitted together the skein of Haring and Clark relatives, giving the child an irreplaceable sense of family, which she maintained throughout her long life and conveyed to her daughter and grand-daughter. Julie was the inheritor and in her time would seek to knit together that same skein of family as her daughter would after her.[123] Her route to matrimony, motherhood, and to Connecticut, surprisingly, went through Minneapolis.

---

123. Kate was survived by her aunt, Samuel Haring's sister, Elizabeth (Haring) Demarest, the widow of the Rev. James Demarest, after whom Julie's father had been named. She lived in Bergen County, N.J., until her death in 1879. Maria Haring, who had seen the execution of André, had pre-deceased her, and died in 1868.

V

FAMILY LIFE AND A MATURING CITY

Julie, the young heiress, found the right social setting in which to meet eligible young men. Surprisingly, it was over a thousand miles from her Fairfield home, in the small city of Minneapolis. There she met a young man from Waterbury, Connecticut, where the two would return to live as man and wife after a season in California and a journey on the new transcontinental railroad.

The flour business is surely what brought Harings west in the late 1860s. Productive grain growing in the Haring brothers' lifetimes had moved from western New York to Michigan in the 1860s and by then was opening up in Minnesota. In 1865 a William Clark was listed in the Minneapolis directory, identified as a grocer and flour trader—occupations in the family tradition. He was probably Julie's first cousin once removed, the son of Sarah Haring's brother of the same name and Rosamond Michael.[1] Julie had visited Minneapolis before her parents' deaths, as we know from Kate's reference in a letter of 1869 to her being, "Off in Minnesota, an immense distance."[2] So flour and family were the connections that allowed the young woman to go west and be "eligible" in a smaller social setting than New York.

The power from St. Anthony's Falls, where the Mississippi River drops sixty-four feet, attracted settlement to what became Minneapolis and its neighbor settlement, St. Paul. In the late 1860s, when Julie first visited, the population of Minneapolis had not yet reached ten thousand, but as a guide book of the time told visitors, the power of the water passing over the falls,

---

1. *A Directory of the City of Minneapolis, August 1, 1869* (Minneapolis: Francis P. Sweet, Tribune Printing Co., 1869). This William Clark, born on 30 July 1822, was the fourth child of Sarah (Clark) Haring's brother, William Clark (1780–1830) and his second wife, Mary Bogart (1793–1871); the younger William married Rosamond Michael on 16 June 1842. See "Clark," Genealogical and Biographical Notes.

2. CTHK, from Brooklyn, to JPH, traveling in Europe, 18 March 1869.

"if economized to the best advantages was sufficient to employ the inhabitants of a large city."[3] The place was well positioned. "The wheat farmer, the flour miller, and the lumberman had a common meeting place in Minneapolis, which, because it lay just south of the great coniferous forest and just north of the principal wheat area, was both a saw-milling and a flour-milling city." Minneapolis thus became "the meeting place of east and west, of urban and rural, of industry and agriculture."[4] The Mississippi was navigable by steamboat to the falls. Soon enough, however, the railroads became the chief means of transporting goods and people to the city.

The presence of a river and several lakes made attractive foci for residential development, and the abundance of lumber made house building inexpensive. (Julie, from a city with paved sidewalks and streets, would have been bemused by the wood frame houses and buildings and the plank boardwalks in Minneapolis in these early years.)[5] Moreover, Minnesota cities were enjoying the prosperity experienced by all the Northern states after Appomattox.

When industrial machinery stopped for the night, a contemporary wrote, "A charm is thrown over the hour of repose by the soft murmur of the falls and the delicious aroma of the air in this elevated region."[6] Since water, not coal-fired steam boilers, provided power, there was none of the smoke and cinders that characterized eastern cities. As an early booster put it, the "pure, bracing, wholesome atmosphere," meant "sound livers and firm muscles." There was freedom from respiratory complaints, and "honest toil [was] not compelled to hobble about through harvest time upon such miserable crutches as calomel and quinine . . . Never has a case

---

3. By the late 1860s a contemporary guide noted a number of industrial activities in addition to flour- and saw-milling: "A large machine shop where locomotives are made and repaired, a paper mill, several pail, tub and barrel factories, carriage shops, iron foundries, planing mills, sash, door and blind factories, eight or ten large grist mills, and a large number of saw mills . . ." The saw mills had much to do. At the falls, the "largest logs are converted into lumber by a gang of saws at a single revolution of the mill carriage, are in operation here. The lumber, when sawed, is conducted over the rapids by long aqueducts, through which it floats to the still water beneath the falls. Here it is made up into rafts and marketed where ever it will bring the highest price on the Mississippi River." Rufus Blanchard, *Hand-Book of Minnesota* (Chicago: Blanchard and Cram, 1867), 16.

4. William E. Lass, *Minnesota: A History* (New York and Nashville, Tenn.: W. W. Norton and the American Association of State and Local History, 1983), 132.

5. Ibid., 147.

6. Ibid., 132.

of fever or ague originated here." When there was disease, it was found in "invalids who come up, pale as a procession of the ghost of Banquo and its attendants, from the damp plains of the South . . ."[7] Easterners living in smoky, damp cities where tuberculosis was prevalent (as Julie well knew) were attracted by the possibility of cure in the clean, northern air.[8]

Easterners were also attracted by a population considered to be "of the better sort." A doctor in 1871 linked the opportunity to regain health with the social standing of those doing so. Minneapolis, he wrote, was "greatly favored in having a society superior to most of the new States, because many families of wealth and high social position are obliged to live in our State on account of ill health . . . Most of our large business men and professional men in St. Paul sought our climate for health."[9] Indeed the young man whom Julie was to marry had come for the dual reasons of health and business.

The influx of well-to-do Yankees provided Minneapolis with a settled, genteel stratum of society fairly early in its history. To some this genteel class represented an improvement over its eastern counterpart, as the expansiveness of the West forced the too rigorous social codes of home to be relaxed somewhat. One reason for this new class organization was the relative ease with which money could be made.

> Easy grades to wealth beget lively social qualities and frequent mingling together in parties, fairs and other gatherings. . . . The restraints of the old established customs of the land of steady habits, are modified to suit the more bountiful allotment in the new home. The old rigid discipline of economy is gradually relaxed. Ambition takes higher flights, and thought a freer range. Sectional prejudices and moral and religious dogmas disappear like the dew before the rising sun.

---

7. *Minnesota Pioneer*, 5 June 1881, from Mary Wheelhouse Berthel, *Horns of Thunder: The Life and Times of James M. Goodhue Including Selections from His Writings* (St. Paul: St. Paul Historical Society, 1948), 86–7; quoted in Lass, *Minnesota*, 116.

8. In 1857 the state was referred to as "one vast hospital. All her cities and towns and many of her farm houses are crowded with those fleeing from the approach of the dread destroyer." Quotation from Helen Clapesattle, "When Minnesota was Florida's Rival," *Minnesota History* 35 (March 1957): 215, quoted in Lass, *Minnesota*, 119.

9. Brewer Mattocks, *Minnesota as a Home for Invalids* (Philadelphia: J. B. Lippincott, 1871), 147.

It was the best of both worlds. Even the cold was an advantage to the proponent of the developing city:

> When Boreas ushers in winter with his whistling voice, activity takes possession of every department of life. Elastic limbs and ruddy faces take an extra stock of strength and beauty. Robes, furs and fuel loom up in every household, and the social winter-evening is inaugurated. Everything Northern is loved.[10]

How did Julie travel to Minneapolis? Mrs. A. A. Colt of Albany suggested the connections in an illustrated travel guide to routes on the New York Central system in 1871. First came an overnight steamer from New York to Albany to change to the newly-formed New York Central. A passenger could leave Albany at 7 A.M. and arrive for "dinner" at Rochester at 2 P.M., re-board the train again and reach Buffalo by evening.[11] Mrs. Colt recommended a steamer from Buffalo to Chicago, but the more probable method was to take the train across southern Ontario to Detroit via Niagara Falls and then west to Chicago.[12] At Chicago "carriages are always to be found" for the transfer to hotel or to another station, so *Appleton's Hand-Book of American Travel* told the traveler. "As is now customary, in all American cities, there are lines of omnibuses connecting with all trains, by which passengers and their luggage are taken to any part of the city at reasonable rates."[13] Julie would have traveled in the newly introduced Pullman cars, either a day coach with swiveling armchair seats or a sleeper with benchlike seats that could be transformed into a lower bunk. (A cabinet above contained the upper bunk, brought down at nighttime.)[14] With

---

10. Blanchard, *Hand-Book*, 38.

11. *The Tourist's Guide Through the Empire State Embracing all Cities, Towns and Watering Places by Hudson River and New York Central Route*, ed. S. S. Colt (Albany: privately printed, 1871), 172, 183.

12. *Appleton's Hand-Book of American Travel: Western Tour* (New York: D. Appleton, 1872), 2–3.

13. Ibid., 11. Travel time between New York and Chicago was thirty-six hours by 1875. By the 1890s the New York Central's best trains took twenty hours for the journey. Peter T. Maiken, *Night Trains* (Chicago: Lakem Press, 1989), 23.

14. "The convenience of the folding berth and the potentialities for the preposterous in their occupancy were of secondary magnitude compared to the over-all intimations of splendor which from the beginning associated themselves with the name of the builder." Lucius Beebe, *Mr. Pullman's Elegant Palace Car* (New York: Doubleday, Garden City, 1961), 17–18. See also William B. Sipes, *The Pennsylvania Railroad: Its Origin, Construction, Condition and Connections* (Philadelphia: The Passenger Department, Pennsylvania Railroad, 1875), illustrations, 27–29.

the slow trains of the time, the need for changes, transfer of baggage and overnight hotel stays, it seems like an arduous journey. It was a great improvement in comfort and speed over pre–Civil War trains, though, and rapidity itself compared to stages and steamboats.[15] Still, it would have been a challenge for Julie, and a woman of her age probably did not make the journey unescorted. A direct rail connection from Chicago to St. Paul had only been opened in the late 1860s—prior there had been a connection to a steamboat on the Mississippi.[16]

For Julie the journey's end was a city built of wood that was changing every day. She joined a social circle of young people in Minneapolis who gathered at the houses of their elders. We know from a reference in a letter that Julie stayed with Mr. and Mrs. Aaron Mulford on her several stays in Minneapolis.[17] They were her hosts for months at a time, and Mrs. Mulford must have acted as her social mentor, but how Julie knew them has not been determined. Aaron Denman Mulford, from Elizabeth, New Jersey, was an easterner who had come to the clean air of the west to find a cure for his hemorrhaging lungs and stayed to make money. The climate did what it was reputed to do, and after five years he was well enough to go into the grain business. He became an exhibit of the Minnesota cure, known in a local history for his "robust form and cheer of face," which indicated "physical health and serenity of mind." His wife, Chiri Morondi, was the daughter of an Italian-born merchant in Boston, whose upbringing and heritage must have added warmth to the society of the western city—and to her advice to Julie.[18] She was Julie's mentor in what was to be

---

15. Commodore Vanderbilt's New York & Harlem connected passengers at Albany with the newly consolidated New York Central (which he did not then control) running from there to Buffalo. The transfer involved crossing the river and "seldom [took] more than three or four hours, at least in clement weather." In order to achieve his aim of through service, Vanderbilt later stopped his trains from crossing the river to the Albany depot, which resulted in "a sharp loss of traffic for the New York Central; the stock fell and he gained ownership and established his dream of a through connection to Chicago." Beebe, *Mr. Pullman's Elegant Palace Car*, 20.

16. Maiken, *Night Trains*, 277.

17. George Montgomery Tuttle [GMT], in Andover, Mass, to JPH, at 31 Dwight St., Boston, [13] May 1873.

18. Aaron Denman Mulford was born on 10 Jan. 1840, at Elizabeth, N.J., son of Benjamin W. Mulford and Jane Baker. He died after 1893. On 17 Feb. 1869 he married Elizabeth Chiri Morondi, daughter of Francis Morondi, of Boston. Isaac Atwater, *History of the City of Minneapolis, Minnesota* (New York: Munsell, 1893), 2:788–90.

a period of "eligibility" lasting little over a year, for she soon attracted an ardent admirer.

George Montgomery Tuttle was the son of a churchman who had come to the city to establish its first Universalist Society.[19] He had just returned from a year in Dresden with his mother, who died there in January 1873. The boy, then sixteen, accompanied her body home for burial.[20] Shortly after this unnerving experience he met Julie. He already had known a number of places—Rochester during his childhood, Chicago, where his father had a church, and Dresden—and had been to school in all of them. He thus had learned something of the world at a young age and acquired a passion for music. He was four years younger than she, but through travel and education more sophisticated.

They must have met early in 1873, as George went east that winter to Phillips Academy to prepare for Yale, with which his family had a long association.[21] The youth was smitten, however briefly he had seen Julie, and wrote from Andover ("Dear Miss Haring"), addressing his letter to the Phelps Brothers office in New York, as she had returned to her grandparents. "I have framed your picture," he wrote, "and it stands on my table before me known as my 'sister' to the fellows who rave over her beauty— waiting for a thought, I look at it, and it sometimes seems as tho' it *must speak* to me, but I start up and find myself gazing blankly out upon the huge, leafless trees, the feeling of despair (or blues)." "The absolute quiet of the village is almost intolerable," he wrote of Andover, "and *unless something* occurs to relieve the monotony, I shall be obliged to succumb. Can you not think what that *something* is?" His great hope was to be able to escort Julie back to Minneapolis in June for the wedding of two of their

---

19. James Hawley Tuttle (1824–?), George's father, was born in western New York. He had led Universalist societies in Rochester and other New York state towns before he went to Chicago in the early 1860s. He moved his family to Minneapolis in 1866 when he became pastor of the First Universal Church. George Frederick Tuttle, *The Descendants of William and Elizabeth Tuttle, who Came from Old to New England in 1635, and Settled in New Haven in 1639* (Rutland, Vt.: Tuttle, 1883), 263; *History of the Class of 1877, Yale, 1877, 1904* (New Haven: Yale Univ., 1904), 138. The Universalist Church, which originated in the late eighteenth century in New Jersey and other eastern states, spread to churches in the Midwest before the Civil War. It was an optimistic religion, free of the Calvinist emphasis on sin and human imperfection. *Enc. Brit.*, s.v. "Universalist Church."

20. Tuttle, *Descendants*, 263.

21. *History of the Class of 1877, Yale, 1877, 1904* (New Haven: Yale Univ., 1904), 138–39.

30. George Montgomery Tuttle
This is the photo he had made for Julia
in 1872.

circle of friends. "I find myself *involuntarily* looking forward to the 7th of June and the bright anticipation connected with that date, cast into insignificance the mountains of Greek and Latin which loom up between it and the present."[22]

In this correspondence we have to imagine Julie's reactions from George's comments, as her letters do not survive. She had given him her photo, and, although sometimes he complained of her tardiness in writing, she kept up the exchange even though George, for all his knowledge of the world, was an adolescent and Julie a young woman of twenty when they met. She surely liked him and was interested in what he reported of music, theater, school, and college, but she must have known that she had to keep a certain distance, as he could not be a suitor with serious intentions. Her tender feelings for George Tuttle—her future husband was named George, too—led her to save his letters all her life. In their mirror we can see that Julie was an attractive woman, attentive to others, and interested in what young Mr. Tuttle had to say, which was considerable when it came to the music and theater of the time.

---

22. GMT, in Andover, Mass., to JPH, c/o Phelps Bros. & Co., New York City, 25 March 1873.

George allayed the damp of late winter with a visit to Boston and a concert. There was intense interest in European musicians in America in those years, as his account suggests.

> Last Sunday I made all my arrangements and on Wed. afternoon I went down to Boston to attend the Peck concert. You remember the list of artists and I think you have heard all except Rubinstein & Wieniawski. For me to attempt to give you an idea of my feelings on that occasion would be more than useless and I can only say, that my conception of what instruments the piano & violin were faint indeed before hearing these great artists. Never did I hear such tones produced... and the audience of some 4000 people fairly screamed with delight. Rubinstein is the same, careless, (almost slouchy) individual that he is represented to be but his mastery over his instrument is nothing short of marvelous. Wieniawski is a very short, fleshy, nervous looking person & this detracts somewhat from the effect—but you forget everything about you & him too when he first draws his bow over his violin. I felt it worth many hundred of miles travel and I thought constantly of how much you would have enjoyed it.[23]

There were studies too, and George was not letting his loneliness get the better of him. "It cost me something of an effort and I was obliged to study until after 1 the night before [the concert]. In fact the only disagreeable thing about my school is the great number of hours which one must study in order to maintain a good standing in the school. However I am getting nicely initiated in my studies & have more leisure than I did at first." In a postscript, George reported, evidently in response to Julie's encouragement, "I am going to have my picture taken next Sat. & will be faithful to my promise, *immediately*. G."

When Julie came to Boston in May to visit her Aunt Julia Winter, George was beside himself, underlining words for emphasis.[24] "My dear Sister," he wrote,

---

23. GMT, in Andover, Mass., to JPH, c/o Phelps Bros, New York City, 13 April 1873. *The New Grove Dictionary of Music and Musicians*, 16:297–300, 20:404–6. This Boston concert by the Russian Anton Rubinstein (1829–94), one of the greatest of the century's pianists, was on the last leg of a long tour with Henryk Wieniawski (1835–80), the celebrated Polish-born virtuoso violinist and composer.

24. Julia Maria (Phelps) Winter (1826–99) was the eldest of the thirteen G. A. Phelps children. The 31 Dwight St. household in 1873 consisted of Julia Maria, her husband, Royal Winter (1818–88), daughters Eliza Phelps Winter (1854–1924), always referred to as "Cousin Lizzie," young Julia's close contemporary and friend), and her sister, Emma (1864–?).

Your letter just rec'd has put me in such a state of nervous excitement and mental disorder that I can scarcely compose myself enough to write these few lines . . . *I am quite delighted beyond measure* to think that I am going to have any opportunity of seeing you so soon, and I can hardly thank Fairfield enough for its intolerable stillness. I have arranged, if it is a *feasible* thing to go to Boston on Saturday and will try and call upon you somewhere about three or four o'clock.[25]

It was too short a meeting, and like many a boarding school boy before and after, he felt imprisoned. (He also kept up the brother-sister fiction of his attachment to Julie.)

Again I am back in this wretched place, and the fact that I have *actually* seen you—even for a few moments is more like a dream than a reality. Some things, I feel I can far better write than attempt to say to you after not having seen you for six weeks. Before I went to Boston I was going to see you, and my hurry and disappointment in the loss of time, together with the aggravation of so short a visit, as you can imagine, did not tend to make it seem any more real. I fear that should I have tried to express to you the delight which I felt at seeing you, I should have been cut short with a request for less hyperbole, but I can write this with perfect safety, with the assurance that I can at least be in ignorance of your opinion until the return of the answer.

The sight of you was actually so pleasant that I felt (in school-girl's language) as tho' I could "eat you up," and I must say that I rarely endeavored to reconcile myself to the fact that I was not your brother (you know a brother's privileges are so numerous & extended).[26]

Then there came a terrible blow. The friends' wedding date was advanced, meaning that Julie must go to Minneapolis without George. *"O luce magis delecta fratri!"* George cried to his "dear Sister." "If you have at any time in your life felt that the force of your own feelings—anger I may say—was something ever beyond your own comprehension—when you felt that you could not restrain yr. wrath but must give vent in some manner—perhaps you may in some small degree imagine the state that yr. brother is now in . . ."[27] Then the lovelorn schoolboy imagines others helping Julie on the trains—incidentally also indicating that she was to

---

25. GMT, in Andover, Mass., to JPH, at 31 Dwight St., Boston, 7 May 1873.

26. GMT, in Andover, to JPH, in Boston, 13 May 1873.

27. GMT, in Andover, to JPH, in Fairfield, 21 May 1873.

travel alone. "I picture you to myself, purchasing R.R. tickets, checking baggage, etc. or having those office which I hoped to perform usurped by some officious 'gray-haired' old fellow and—will—and—You can imagine my feelings."

Some days later George gingerly admitted to more than brotherly feelings and underlined desperately in his response. "In my short acquaintance with you, and very pleasant correspondence following it, I have unconsciously acquired an Unbrotherly *affection* & *interest* in you, at the same time combined with a brotherly *'helpfulness'*. . . .[28] They did meet in Minneapolis that summer, but only a few times, as he reported himself sick.[29] George's lack of push to see Julie more than once on this visit, sickness or no, may be a sign that he implicitly realized the impracticality of his pursuit. However, he remained enamored and continued the correspondence from Yale that fall.

Over the summer the schoolboy seems to have grown into a man. He reported being absorbed in studies and looking forward to college life. His reports give an engaging glimpse of a young life opening out. "I never in my life had so much on my hands as at the present moment," he wrote. "We are just settled in our new rooms and are beginning to look somewhat comfortable having worked a whole day to attain this result." He addresses "My dear Julie" ("Dear sister" is gone) with her picture "on my table looking as calm and dignified as ever." His roommate declared that he had "regular conversations with 'that picture.'"[30] George chides himself for lack of eloquence (or candor) when he had said goodbye to her. "I wanted to say so many things, that now in all probability I may never have an opportunity of saying. I do wish you could tell me what it is that you have done or said that has made it so difficult for me to part with you, far more so than I ever believed it would be to separate from any human being."[31] Unspoken surely was a declaration of love that could have led to a response from Julie. Surely too, his diffidence indicates that with four years of college before him he was aware that he was in no position to make a proposal of marriage.

---

28. GMT, in Andover, to JPH, in Fairfield, 3 June 1873.

29. GMT, in Minneapolis, to JPH, in that city, 3 Aug. 1873.

30. GMT, at Yale College, to JPH, in Minneapolis, 12 Sept. 1873. The roommate was John Birdseye Atwater (1855–1921) of a New Haven family. *Obituary Record of Graduates Deceased during the Year Ending July 1, 1922* (New Haven: Yale University, 1922).

31. GMT, at Yale, to JPH, in Minneapolis, 12 Sept. 1873.

Julie remained in Minneapolis through the fall, defeating George's hope that she would return to her grandparents in Fairfield. Perhaps suspecting something, in a postscript he asked Julie "Has White yet returned?" This is a reference to George White, a young man from Waterbury, Connecticut, in Minneapolis for his health, a bachelor in the social set. If George Tuttle had suspicions, they were justified, for George White was courting Julie.

George Tuttle became increasingly involved at Yale. Only three weeks into his freshman year he was elected to the Delta Kappa Society and was working hard to place in the top half of the class in the forthcoming mid-term examinations. (Later in his Yale career he was elected to Skull and Bones, the most prestigious of the Yale societies.) [32]

That fall the financial markets of the U.S. were in an uproar—the panic of 1873 was in full swing. In September the banking house of Jay Cooke and Co. failed, and other large businesses went under. The New York Stock Exchange took the unprecedented step of closing its doors. "What terrible news about N.Y. failures," George wrote, "I hope sincerely that you have no friends that are in any way injured." The panic became a depression, with factory closings, a cessation of most railroad construction, and bread lines in the cities.[33] However, George's hope was fulfilled, as neither his nor Julie's family finances were destroyed in the crash.

Increasing numbers of European performers were coming across the Atlantic at the time, to be met by a growing number of those eager to hear them. George became acquainted with the finest musicians of the day, important figures in the establishment of European musical culture in the U.S. George announced to Julie—using a term that many of his hearty fellows might have used to describe drinking—that he would "dissipate next week" by going to New York for a concert by the violinist Camilla Urso.[34]

---

32. Unattributed obit., provided by the Archives, New York Academy of Medicine, New York City.

33. Samuel Eliot Morrison and Henry Steele Commager, *The Growth of the American Republic* (New York: Oxford Univ. Press, 1937), 2:75.

34. GMT, at Yale, to JPH, in Minneapolis, 1 Oct. 1873. Camilla Urso (1842–1902) was a violinist and a child prodigy who had come to the U.S. from France at the age of ten. When George heard her she was thirty and in the midst of a concert career that was to last another twenty years. As a child "[h]er face was so solemn that it seemed as if a smile had never visited it," according to George P. Upton, the Chicago music critic. When she was twenty-four, he observed she had "the same pale, serious, inscrutable face, the same dark lustrous melancholy eyes, and the same calm but gracious dignity in manner." George G. Upton, *Musical Memories*, 1902, quoted in *DAB*, s.v. "Urso, Camilla."

A few weeks later he wrote that there were "some splendid amusements to be had here this week. 1st Arbuckle the great cornet player, 2nd Thomas's Orchestra & 3rd Christine Nilsson!!! Is not that an array? I am almost beside myself at the thought of so much & above all *Nilsson*."[35] To be sure, George also went to entertainments of a less elevated sort. "Lydia Thompson is to perform here and I am not quite decided as to that entertainment," he reported. (Lydia Thompson [1836–1908] was the "yellow-haired beauty whose ample proportions pleased an over-stuffed era." It was her London troupe that introduced burlesque to America in 1868 with an enormously popular "leg" show.)[36]

In early December George reported on his admired Nilsson and on the Italian actor, Thommaso Salvini (1829–1916), then on his first American tour, whom George had just been to hear and see in New York:

I have listened to two of the finest entertainments I ever heard in my life this week—Nilsson & Salvini!! I am going to be very cautious what I say about Nilsson lest you should think me crazy and truly I almost believe I am on that subject. I shall never experience the feelings I had at the first tones: all my life I had an ideal voice that every singer that I heard failed to reach, and Nilsson surpassed my imagination even. If you have not heard her you cannot conceive of the purity and sweetness of her voice combined with her remarkable compass, and there is an indescribable factor in her voice that affected me as I

---

35. GMT, in New Haven, to JPH, c/o Mrs. A. D. Mulford in Minneapolis, 13 Nov. 1873. Christine Nilsson, the Swedish soprano, had come first to the U.S. three years before to great acclaim and is best remembered as Marguerite in the first performance at the newly built Metropolitan Opera House in 1883. "Ophelia, Marguerite and Mignon were probably her finest roles," according to Elizabeth Forbes. She had "an attractive appearance and a graceful stage personality. . . . Her voice, though not large, was pure and brilliant in timbre, immensely flexible and perfectly even in scale for two and a half octaves up to top E." *The New Grove*, 13:249. Theodore Thomas (1835–1905) was born in Essen, East Friesland, and emigrated with his family in 1845 to the U.S., where he became the most influential conductor and organizer of symphony orchestras in nineteenth-century American musical life. The Theodore Thomas orchestra toured throughout the country over what came to be called "the Thomas highway," which included cities of moderate size such as New Haven and Waterbury. He was elected music director of the New York Philharmonic in 1877, and in the late 1880s he was invited to Chicago by wealthy citizens and became the founder of the Chicago Symphony, opening Orchestra Hall there in 1904. George Tuttle would have appreciated Ezra Scharas's judgment that "Thomas did more than any other American musician of the 19th century to popularize music of the great European masters. . . ." *The New Grove*, 18:781–82.

36. *Oxford Companion to American Theater*, ed. Gerald Boardman (New York: Oxford Univ. Press, 1984), 655–56; Garff B. Wilson, *Three Hundred Years of American Drama* (Englewood Cliffs, N.J.: Prentice-Hall, ca. 1982), 189–90.

have never been before. Among the whole audience I do not think that there were five who were not crying at the conclusion of some of her songs, and I am not ashamed to say that I cried like a little child. Oh, I could listen to her for years it seems to me without getting satisfied. I cannot compare [Austrian soprano Pauline] Lucca with her & indeed I have almost forgotten her since I heard Nilsson. If I am ever within a reasonable distance of her I shall make every effort to hear her, and I am no rejoicing that she is to come again in February in *Mignon*.

Salvini who has caused such excitement in N.Y. and Boston and who has a wide reputation in Europe is a wonderful actor . . . Did you hear him while you were in Italy?

The play was, of course, in Italian, & altho' I did not understand a word, yet, being well acquainted with the piece, I enjoyed it more than I can tell you.[37]

Was George exceptional at Yale in his love of music and theater and his enthusiasm for the great artists then touring the country? Although he does not mention others, there is nothing in his tone suggesting his were isolated passions. He was joining a great movement of culture, which he would participate in all his life, as a patron and concert- and operagoer in New York City. This exposure to the concert halls and theaters of the old eastern cities was decisive in his own career "How can you remain in Minn. when there are so many attractions in the East?" he asked Julie. "I am afraid I shall never want to live there again unless I change a great deal in 4 years."

Julie remained in Minneapolis for the 1873–74 Christmas and New Year holidays, which George spent in Boston. She was to return east, but not alone, as George Tuttle would have wished. In early January she wrote him that she had accepted George White's proposal of marriage. Tuttle reverted to "My dear Sister" in a sturdy and gentlemanly reply, cut short by "a severe headache."

---

37. GMT, at Yale, to JPH, in Minneapolis, 7 Dec. 1873. Henry James wrote of Salvini's Othello: "He gives his measure as a man, he acquaints us with the luxury of perfect confidence in the physical resources of the actor. . . . His powerful, active, manly frame his noble, steady, serious expressive face, his splendid smile, his Italian eye, his superb, voluminous voice, his carriage, his tone, his ease, the assurance he instantly gives that he holds the whole part in his hands and can make of it exactly as he chooses,—all this descends on a spectator's mind with a richness that immediately converts attention into faith, and expectation into sympathy." "Tommaso Salvini," *Atlantic Monthly*, April 1883, reprinted in Henry James, *The Scenic Art*, ed. Allan Wade (New Brunswick, N.J.: Rutgers Univ. Press, 1948), 170.

Your good letter was very welcome to me, and, altho' I had wondered some-what at having received no word from you for so long, yet, I was confident that you had some excellent reason for not writing.

I cannot hope to express to you the ten thousand kind wishes I have for you in your new relation but let me assure you again and again of my interest in your welfare and of the pleasure the thought of your "happiness" gives me. I wish heartily that I could stand before you and tell you these things that I despair of putting on the paper before me. I cannot make this a simple con-gratulatory letter but I must leave you to imagine all the kindness there is in your brother's heart for you.

I am enjoying college more than ever and now find more time for reading. I had a very pleasant vacation in Boston and Andover. I should enjoy writing a good long letter, but I have a severe headache to day and can hardly see what I am writing so I am compelled to close. I thank you sincerely for your invitation to send your picture and it will give me much pleasure. Again let me assure you of my kind wishes and believe me
Yours very sincerely
Geo. M. Tuttle[38]

George Tuttle's later life was spent in the east, as Julie and George White's lives were to be. He and they were only a two-hour train ride apart, but very differently situated, the one in a profession in New York City, the Whites in the industrial city of Waterbury, Connecticut. Tuttle went on to the College of Physicians and Surgeons at Columbia in New York City. His first appointment was as physician-in-chief of the New York Emigration Hospital, then in thirty or more buildings on Ward's Island in the East River. The buildings were decrepit and unsanitary; the treatments were rudimentary. "Dr. Tuttle was the instrument by which a complete and lasting reorganization of the entire institution, and its practical divorce from politics was effected . . . [an] opportunity that rarely comes to a young man of being the means of bringing great good to a large number of fellow-beings."[39] After residencies in hospitals in Dresden and Prague, he was appointed an assistant to the chair of obstetrics and gynecology at the Col-lege of Physicians and Surgeons and subsequently became attending gyne-cologist at the newly established Roosevelt Hospital.[40]

---

38. GMT, at Yale, to JPH, in Minneapolis, 10 Jan. 1874.

39. Obit., New York Academy of Medicine.

40. *Obituary Record of Graduates of Yale University Deceased during the Year Ending June 1, 1913* (New Haven: Yale College, 1913).

In New York, George was a member of the Century Association and a number of other clubs and on the board of the American Museum of Natural History. He traveled widely, including trips to Japan and Egypt. Not surprisingly, he was known for his interest in music. George did not marry until he was fifty—touching in light of his ardent early love for Julie. His bride at a ceremony at the Palazzo Vecchio in Florence was Mabel (Holden) Kirkbride, a widow.[41] She bore him a daughter in New York City, on whom he doted. He enjoyed the child for only three years before his own sudden death in 1912.

It is a poignant story. The Century remembered the "esteemed member of his noble profession . . . an ennobling influence among his brethren and a benediction to the patient who had the good fortune to be cared for by him."[42] Julie kept his letters in their envelopes in chronological order, the compact pile bound with a lavender ribbon. Beneath the envelope with that last, congratulatory letter, she placed his obituary notice, on which, attentive after thirty-eight years to her one-time admirer's birth date, she corrected his age at death.[43]

George Tuttle was a tender and talented young man to whom Julie surely responded with genuine affection. It must have dismayed her to have the passionate attention of a youth who was in no position to marry her. How different life would have been if she had married a distinguished New Yorker. She shared George Tuttle's interests in opera and theater—as did George White—and regularly attended performances in the city. Surely she read occasional references to George Tuttle in the newspaper. What might have been was surely in her thoughts when she searched out the packet of letters and placed the corrected obituary notice beneath it.[44]

---

41. During World War I, Mabel Tuttle was chairman and organizer of the American Friends of French Musicians in France, which assisted musicians and their families made destitute during the war. In 1923 the French Government conferred upon her the Legion of Honor in recognition of her service in the development of understanding between French and American musicians. She also supported the Fontainebleau School of Music. *NYT*, 4 Nov. 1923, II, 1:6.

42. *Yearbook* (New York: Century Association, 1912).

43. *NYT*, 30 Oct. 1912, 13:5.

44. Julia's daughter, Caroline Haring (White) Griggs kept the packet of letters throughout her life. Evidently Julia had not told her much about George Tuttle, as she could not identify the sender when the author read the letters to her in her 90s.

The Whites

George Luther White was in Minneapolis to heal his lungs and to make a start in business. He had arrived at the age of sixteen and became a member of the same social set as George Tuttle and Julie. He was just of marriageable age when he proposed, but younger than Julie by a year and three months.

George was the second son of Luther Chapin White, an inventor and entrepreneur in the eighth generation of a family whose immigrant ancestor, Elder John White, a founder of Hartford, had come over in the great migration of the 1630s. The son from whom Luther was descended settled on the east bank of the Connecticut River, south of Hartford, on lands that came to be called "Upper Houses." This was the northern section of Middletown (now Cromwell), midway between Hartford and the river's outlet on Long Island Sound. It was an active port in the carrying trade in the eighteenth century.[45] Farmers brought grains and animals there for shipment to New York City, southern ports, and the West Indies. The land by the river in Upper Houses was easily worked and fertile, and the Whites and the intermarried families—Eels, Ranney, Sage, Savage among them—farmed these lands and traded on the river for over two centuries.

Luther's great-grandfather, Jacob, was a privateer on Long Island Sound in the Revolution and a crewmember of the *Trumbull*, the warship built in Middletown as Connecticut's contribution to the first American navy. His son, John—Luther's grandfather—was also a sailor. The tall case clock that celebrated his marriage in 1789 to Ruth Ranney bears the image of a fish on its silver dial; the elegant dial and cherry wood case witnessed the prosperity of the family at that time.[46] John died at sea ten years later, leaving a widow, the grandmother who lived through Luther's young manhood.

Luther's father, Jacob, ventured north and west to Sandisfield, Massachusetts, where he set up a tannery beside a branch of the Farmington River. Here he produced leather to meet the demand for shoes and horse

---

45. In 1851 "Middletown Upper Houses" became the town of Cromwell by action of the Connecticut General Assembly.

46. Clock by Timothy Peck, then of Middletown, owned, in their lifetimes, by John[6] White, Ruth (Ranney) White (his widow), Luther Chapin[8] White, George Luther[9] White, William Henry[10] White, Henry Wade[11] White, and Peter Haring[12] Judd.

tackle for a growing population in the 1820s. It was there that Luther Chapin was born in 1821. Ten years later, Jacob and the family returned to the family farm at Upper Houses, where Luther spent the remainder of his childhood. He was educated at the local schoolhouse and assisted his father on the farm.[47] According to a story handed down in the family, he fell from the roof when he was assisting his brother build a house. His hearing was permanently damaged by the fall, and this forced him into a more sedentary occupation. He was mechanically minded and began to work in metals. Middletown had a number of shops that made fittings for ships, where a young lad could observe and learn.

When he was twenty, in 1841, Luther moved to where his mechanical skills could find greater scope, as many young Connecticut men were doing at the time. An older brother had shown the way to Waterbury, in the Naugatuck Valley, in the west-central part of the state. Over a score of factories had started up there in the previous decade, emerging from a tradition of metal craft shops dating from before the Revolution. In Luther's time, the houses in Waterbury clustered around a town green, away from the nearby flood plain, and continued to evoke the early settlement.

31. Luther Chapin White, 1840s

The meadows by the Naugatuck were not as fertile as they first appeared, and farmers in eighteenth-century Waterbury did not enjoy the prosperity of those elsewhere in the colony, who had surplus crops and animals for export. The Naugatuck was not navigable by anything larger than canoes or small flat boats—its junction with the navigable Housatonic, which led to Long Island Sound, was almost twenty miles south. Another disadvantage of the town's location was that it was far from the main roads along the coast or in the central valley to Hartford.

---

47. This account follows that in Joseph Anderson, ed., *The Town and City of Waterbury, Connecticut, from the Aboriginal Period to the Year Eighteen Hundred and Ninety-Five,* 3 vols. (New Haven: Price and Lee, 1896), 2:425–27, which was written during the lifetime of L. C. White and is presumably based on his submission.

John White (ca. 1597–1683/4)	=	Mary Levit (?–before 1683)
Nathaniel White (ca. 1630–1711)	=	Elizabeth —? (ca. 1625–90)
Jacob White (1665–1734)	=	Deborah Shepherd (ca. 1670–1721)
John White (1712–1801)	=	Elizabeth Boardman (1713–1809)
Jacob White (1737–before 1794)	=	Lucy Savage (1741–1812)
John White (ca. 1766–1799)	=	Ruth Ranney (1776–1862)
Jacob White (1792–1849)	=	Susan Sage (1796–1862)
Luther Chapin White (1821–93)	=	Jane Amelia Moses (1825–99)
George Luther White (1852–1914)	=	Julia Phelps Haring (1850–1928)

32. White descent to George Luther White

Waterbury remained only a local trading center for the first decades of its existence. However, there were a number of sites for grain and saw mills on the Naugatuck's tributary streams, which flowed through the town, and by the last third of the eighteenth century some men began to use water power to fabricate brass buttons using copper stock from discarded ship's sheathing, worn out stills, sugar boilers, and old kettles.[48] The buttons were in demand for uniforms during the Revolution, and it was from these craft shops that the industrial future of Waterbury stemmed. Enterprise began to focus on the opportunities available despite the absence of geographic advantages. The conversion of metal into useful, generally small, objects became the work of Waterbury.

The brass industry in America, which would thrive in Waterbury for more than a hundred and fifty years, is "one of the most striking examples of a localized industry that had not started because of proximity to a natural resource," comments a student of the history and industry of the Naugatuck Valley, who notes that copper and zinc, the principal raw ingredients of the alloy were "not to be found in appreciable quantities anywhere in or

---

48. Ibid., 2:269.

near Connecticut."[49] The reason for the Waterbury's success lies in its advantage in economies of localization. That is, the city happened to cluster trades that used similar and complementary skills, which together created a new industry, "before others got the chance." That it was ingenious and inventive entrepreneurs who overcame the geographical disadvantages of the place gave rise to a prideful self-awareness reflected in the three published histories of Waterbury and the valley.[50]

The industrial processes developed in Waterbury from the 1840s were created by Luther's generation of industrialists:

> By 1840 the business of manufacturing sheet metal and wire had taken the lead of all others. Then began the fostering and development of branches of business, the demands of which would consume this product: pins, hooks and eyes, tubing, brass kettles, clocks, spoons, and forks [to which should be added Luther's lamps]—the thousands of articles which can be made of sheet metal and wire, were added to the list of manufactures, as well as all the incidental industries of machine making, and making, casting, forging, and supplying the other things used and consumed in the various processes of the main production. The effect of all this has been to stimulate in a remarkable degree the mechanical faculty and inventive power of the workmen employed, and indirectly to change by degrees the methods of manipulation, so that every process has a history of development and growth which would need many pages to record.[51]

The men who designed the machines, oversaw production, and marketed the products had grown up on farms. What they accomplished in metals is a prime exhibit of "Yankee ingenuity." On the bench and the factory floor they developed machines that could make objects cheaply and in quantity. It was through the efforts of these men, from country towns, that Waterbury prospered as an industrial city.

Mechanical ingenuity was matched by the Waterbury entrepreneurs' marketing skills. Their ability to find and develop markets and raise capital

---

49. Michael John Everett, "External Economies and Inertia: the Rise and Decline of the Naugatuck Valley Brass Industry" (Ph.D. diss., Univ. of Connecticut, 1987), 3.

50. Anderson, *Town and City of Waterbury;* Henry Bronson, *The History of Waterbury, Connecticut* (Waterbury: Bronson Brothers, 1858); William J. Pape, *History of Waterbury and the Naugatuck Valley, Connecticut,* 3 vols. (Chicago, New York: S. J. Clarke, 1918).

51. Anderson, *Town and City of Waterbury,* 1:263, quoted in Everett, "External Economies and Inertia," 9.

33. Scovill Manufacturing Co., Waterbury, 1850s. From Henry Bronson, *The History of Waterbury, Connecticut* (1858).

were essential to the buoyant growth of Waterbury's industry. The difference between Waterbury and other new industrial centers in New England and abroad at the time was that dozens of small enterprises were involved in making a variety of products. Elsewhere in New England, towns and cities were dominated by one industry—textiles or shoes, for example, and often by one company—Waterbury had a mix of industries and numbers of entrepreneurs. There was not one product, but many, not one "richest man in town," but a number.

When Luther came to Waterbury in the 1840s its population was nearing 5,000, double what it had been twenty years before. (In 1842 the Green, previously common grazing land, was fenced in).[52] Luther worked for what became Scovill Manufacturing, an outgrowth of a button-making factory founded in the early 1800s, later one of the largest of Waterbury enterprises. When he was twenty-four and newly married to a Waterbury-born woman, Jane Amelia Moses, he took a job as foreman with a manufacturer of door trimmings. He worked for this firm for six years, moving briefly to New Haven and Meriden (where George was born), where factories were starting up. In those years his specialty came to be designing and manufacturing parts for oil lamps.

The use of manufactured lamps for home lighting was growing rapidly, as the buoyant national economy gave more households the means to replace inefficient candles with easier-to-use oil lamps, and population growth meant more houses to place them in. (The fuel was changing at that period from whale oil to kerosene.) There were numerous versions of

---

52. Anderson, *Town and City of Waterbury*, 2:63, referring to Frederick J. Kingsbury.

oil lamps in the marketplace, and competition to incorporate improvements was intense.

The adept mechanic working out solutions at the bench can be felt in Luther's description of the device to hold chimneys and control wicks in his successful patent application of 1852. "I claim the method of making lamp stops, stoppers, and other similar articles, from a disc or plate of metal, by bending it, and forming it . . . so that the rim is formed of two thicknesses of metal and the centre and flange, of one thickness."[53] This was invention from the factory bench, worked out by trial and error using steel wire and sheet steel to develop first the device, and then the tools and dies for the machines to manufacture it in quantity.

In Waterbury in September 1853, Luther and a partner (who died within a year) established what became the City Manufacturing Company, with himself as president, offering "Job Work in Metals, Brass Lamps." According to the Dun credit report, the business was a "sml but safe concern" in 1855. The next year Dun considered it "safe and prof[itable]." In this venture Luther had the financial support of Charles Benedict, son of Aaron Benedict, a prominent member of the first generation of manufacturers. The principal business of the younger Benedict's firm, Benedict & Burnham, was producing brass sheets and tubes from its rolling mills.[54] It was the Benedicts' practice to sponsor new businesses, first directly, and, when developed, under a directorship. The investment in Luther's City Manufacturing is a good example of how a young man seen as having potential could be staked to a manufacturing career by a senior. Benedict invested in the company when it incorporated in 1857 with a capitalization of $10,000.[55]

---

53. "Patent Claims to 7 September," *Scientific American* 8, no. 1 (18 Sept. 1852): 6, <htttp://cld.library.cornell.edu/moa/>, accessed 11 June 2001.

54. The company was one of the largest of Waterbury factories at that time. It had a rolling mill that produced brass and copper plate and tubing; its machine shops made metal glides and knobs for furniture, handles, safety pins, rivets, butt hinges, roller bushings, printers' rules and galley plates, lamp burners and trimmings, hard drawn wire for telegraph purposes—the types of diverse, useful products for which Waterbury was becoming famous. Anderson, *Town and City of Waterbury*, 2:298.

55. Reports of 1855, 1856, 1858. The final credit report on City Manufacturing was made in 1868—all reports were favorable. New Haven Co., vol. 32, [no discernible page number], R. G. Dun & Co. Collection, Baker Library, Harvard Business School.

Luther's business was housed in a Benedict & Burnham building and described by Bishop in his *History of American Manufacturers* in 1868 as making "Button Backs, Kerosene Lamp Work, etc." Early button backs had a wire loop welded to their center. As the metal-forming technology evolved, the presses became fitted with tools that could punch out two holes with a strike and raise a portion of the surface to allow the entry of the thread. It must have been Luther who developed the machine that could mass-produce button backs "at the rate of nearly 200 a Minute."[56] In 1868 Luther sold his interest in the City Manufacturing Company to Benedict & Burnham, and the lamps whose manufacture he had supervised were added to its line of products. He kept the button back business for his own L. C. White Co.

The Benedicts had ample opportunity to observe Luther outside of business. Both were members of the First Congregational Church, on whose committees Luther served. Aaron Benedict was the long-serving deacon of the church.

Like his fellow manufacturers, Luther engaged in other businesses. When his brother died, he took over his three quarters of the stock of White & Wells, which made paper and paper boxes, the remaining quarter being held by Alfred Wells. The process used straw as the feedstock for the manufacture of the stiff paper that could hold its form as a box. As straw could also be used for newsprint, White & Wells at one time was a partner in the company that printed the local newspaper.[57] In 1866 Dun considered it "doing well & making money," its owners "smart, good bus men." Four years later Dun deemed Luther's net worth at $40,000. With White & Wells and the L. C. White Co., Luther's worth increased to $100,000 according to Dun in 1877. In 1888, when Luther bought out Wells after George had been working in the firm for some years, Dun

---

56. J. Leander Bishop, *A History of American Manufacturers from 1608 to 1860* (Philadelphia: Edward Young, 1868; reprint, Johnson Reprint Co., 1968), 3:442, quoted in Everett, "External Economies," 125–26. Charles Benedict 1817–1882 was a mayor of Waterbury in addition to being a major manufacturer. Anderson, *Town and City of Waterbury*, 2:306–7.

57. On White & Wells, see Pape, *Waterbury*, 1:71. Cindy Borden, director of the American Museum of Paper-Making, 500 Tenth Street, Atlanta, Ga., in a personal communication of 17 June 1999, notes that straw was widely used for papermaking in Connecticut and Massachusetts in the latter part of the nineteenth century. See also *Paper Making as Conducted in Western Massachusetts* (Springfield, Mass.: Clark W. Bryan, 1874); Clayton Beadle, *Chapters on Papermaking*, vol. 2, *Comprising Answers to Questions on Papermaking set for the Examination to the City & Guilds of London Institute* (London: Crosby Lockwood and Son, 1907), 2:135.

reported that Luther "is considered thoroughly respons. He has a E/W 200 to 300 [estimated worth of $200,000—$300,000] of first class character & high credit."[58]

Luther ran his businesses from a building on Bank Street, in the heart of the commercial district of the town. By 1873 he owned this property clear of mortgage.[59] The buildings were on combined lots at 210–226 Bank, which ran through the block to Cottage Place at the rear, providing room for office and factory and a warehouse.[60] Bank was on a slope that led down to Meadow Street, where the railroad freight and passenger stations were. For Luther to reach the plant it was a modest walk across the Green and through busy commercial streets, to the office.

In 1857, while Luther and the family—then consisting of three young children—were still living in rented quarters, he bought what seems to be a complete set of parlor furnishings from Frederick Thorp of Waterbury. These consisted of "One mahogany parlor table, one sofa, and large Looking Glass, six mahogany upholstered chairs, and one carpet for parlor floor, one parlor Stove and cooking stove and six cane seat chairs, three rocking chairs."[61] In 1860 he bought the property and house that became the family home for his and Jane Amelia's lifetimes. It was on the west side of Prospect Street, at the foot of Hillside, less than 100 yards from the Green. Like many rising in the world at the time and later, Luther financed his initial purchase by taking out a mortgage from the seller—which he paid off in two years—and another from a bank, paid off in eleven years.[62]

---

58. New Haven Co., vol. 33, p. 542, vol. 34, p. 904, R. G. Dun & Co. Collection.

59. The mortgage had been held by Elisha Leavenworth, of an old Waterbury family, who had owned the land. His quitclaim was dated 5 July 1875. Land Records, 92:121, Office of the Town Clerk, City of Waterbury, New Haven Co., Conn.

60. The lots and buildings are portrayed on the insurance map of 1901 which described the businesses (referring to White & Wells) as "mfr. Paper boxes, Glue, Twine, etc." One building was labeled "book bindery." *Waterbury Connecticut, 1901* (New York: Sanborn-Ferris Map Co., 1901), 9.

61. In the transaction, dated 11 April 1857, Frederick Thorp was also required to pay White $20 in compensation for the poor condition of some of the items. Land Records, 67:195, City of Waterbury.

34. 13 Prospect Street, home of Luther Chapin White

When they moved to Prospect Street, Luther was thirty-nine, Jane Amelia thirty-five, William Henry, George, and Harriet, thirteen, eight, and six, respectively.

Living on Hillside

Waterbury's Prospect Street led north up the rise of what came to be called Hillside and had been established as a street only eight years before the Whites' move. The first substantial house on the street was built in 1851, for the young Frederick K. Kingsbury and his wife, Alathea Scovill, a wedding gift from her father, William H. Scovill (1796–1854). "During their engagement," Alice Kingsbury recalled of her parents, they "used often to walk up Prospect Hill, through a red gate into a meadow half way up, from which they had a lovely view of the sunset. All this land . . . was then open country." What became the street was then "a steep, sandy road without any sidewalk, the gutters filled with Sheep's Peeper Grass. On

---

62. The first transfer was from Joseph G. Easton on 31 March 1860. The release by Easton of the mortgage on the property identified as "land and buildings" was 20 March 1862. On 20 July 1873 there was a quitclaim from the Dime Savings Bank. Land Records, 68:528–30; 70:557; 78:134, Office of the City Clerk, City Hall, Waterbury, Conn. The same premises were conveyed to Easton by Wm. K. Scovill by deed dated 16 Feb. 1853.

either side were broad meadows reaching to the bottom of the hill."[63] (These houses from earlier in the century remained during Luther's lifetime and were a reminder of preindustrial Waterbury. His property abutted D. B. Merriman's; on the other side of the street were the greenhouses that provided produce for the Scovill House.) The Kingsbury house, of "the square solid Italian villa type," represented the beginning of the hill's development as the favored place for the residences of the city's manufacturers.[64]

For the next two generations Luther's descendants would live at Hillside, never more than walking distance away from one another and from the men's offices. The house at 13 Prospect Street was in the square and boxy Italianate style, with a suggestion of the Gothic in its decorative peak in the center of the roof. It was large, but not the kind of display piece being built in contemporary Waterbury. Its front porch and tall windows allowed the residents to see and be seen. A house was a retreat and an increasingly comfortable one as the century progressed, but in the porch it had a public face, an observation point on the world outside. Those walking to and from the Green were aware that they were on view and dressed accordingly, as did those who sat on the porch to observe them. In the daily traffic the untoward would be quickly noticed and the habitual expected. If a passer-by was not known by name, he or she usually was by association with a house or a relative. Greetings were expected between sidewalk and porch, porch and sidewalk. Privacy and a public face coexisted.

The second and most distinguished house to be built on the hill and in whose proximity the later generation of the Whites were proud to live was Rose Hill, designed by Henry Austin of New Haven and built in 1852–53 for William H. Scovill, who named the house. Rose Hill, as it was called from the medieval motif incorporated into its façade, was set back from the street on a rise, adding to its unique character. Its first owners enjoyed it only briefly, as both were dead within a year of its completion, and for

63. Alice E. Kingsbury, *In Old Waterbury: The Memoirs of Alice E. Kingsbury* (Waterbury, Conn.: Mattatuck Historical Society, 1942), unpaginated, Research Collection, Mattatuck Museum.

64. "Hillside was the first of the fine residential neighborhoods to emerge in Waterbury, with the building of Buckingham and Prospect Streets by 1853." Ann Y. Smith, Curator, *At Home in Waterbury: A History of the Neighborhoods of Waterbury*, exhibit catalog (Waterbury, Conn.: Mattatuck Historical Society, 1999), 13. *Map of the Town of Waterbury, New Haven County, From Actual Survey by H. Irvine* (Philadelphia: Richard Clark, 1852), Research Collection, Mattatuck Museum.

ten years it remained shuttered, as it was when the Whites moved to their house two doors down the street. It sprang to life as a center for parties and balls in the mid-1860s under the ownership of Joseph Chauncey Welton, who was born on a farm nearby and made good in mercantile New York in the 1830s and 1840s, returning to Waterbury to invest in the Waterbury Brass Co., Holmes, Booth, and Hayden, and the Oakville Pin Company. His wife, Jane Porter Welton, was gregarious and loved entertaining, and gave Rose Hill the first of its periods as a lively center of Waterbury society.[65] Whether or not the Whites were ever in attendance at the Rose Hill parties, they would have seen the carriages pass up and down the hill, hear the music on a warm night, and be well aware of the social tone being set for the street.

The Welton's had one child, Caroline Josephine (1842–84), a great beauty who became the subject of one of the most famous of Waterbury stories, a virtual folk tale. Carrie, as she was called, owned a black stallion, Knight, of whom she was inordinately fond, despite (or as later Waterbury wits had it because of) the fact that her father had been killed by his kick in 1874. She provided Knight "with a velvet-draped stall, special shoes, tack trimmed with lavish silver, and . . . she served him from a bowl and plate of the choicest bone china, hand painted, with pansies and his name in gold to dispel all possible confusion." Carrie Welton, who never married, was adventurous, and died when trapped in a blizzard on Pikes Peak in 1884. A generous portion of her bequest—unsuccessfully protested by relatives who considered her insane—went to the commissioning of a bronze statue of Knight, designed by Karl Gerhardt of Hartford, which still surmounts a horse drinking fountain at the east end of the Green. Few visitors to Prospect Street houses at the time would fail to be told the story.[66]

---

65. William H. Watkins, *Rose Hill* (Waterbury, 1973), unpaginated, Mattatuck Historical Society, Leaflets & Pamphlets, box 1, Research Collection, Mattatuck Museum. Henry Austin (1804–1891), New Haven architect, was the designer there of the city hall and the Greek revival entrance to the Grove Street Cemetery. *ANB*, s.v. "Austin, Henry."

66. Watkins, *Rose Hill*. "Welton's will left $7,000 for the monument and $100,000 to the American Society for the Prevention of Cruelty to Animals; a cause to which she had already given $250,000 in 1874. Relatives thought she was insane and contested the will, resulting in a long trial that was covered by the *New York Times*. Carrie's side prevailed, and the fountain was dedicated November 10, 1888." Silas Bronson Library, Waterbury Landmarks and Monuments, <http://www.biblio.org/bronson/factm.htm>, accessed 8 Dec. 2001.

35. The Waterbury Green in 1851. Painting by Jared D. Thompson.

Mattatuck Museum

Rose Hill briefly became an elegant rooming house, but in 1889 it was purchased by Augustus Sabin Chase—a few years younger than Luther, and like him a country boy come to the city to make his fortune—who became the leading businessman of his day in the city. As will be seen, the impressive ceremony and gathering for his funeral only seven years later had the attention of the Whites as much as the rest of the city. The Chase family occupied the property for a hundred years. The later generation of Whites were always proud of their proximity to these eminent owners of Rose Hill.[67] The differences between it and Luther's house (and later that

---

67. Augustus Sabin Chase (1828–96) was president of a number of companies that under his son became the Chase Brass & Copper Company, one of the three largest factories in Waterbury in the first half of the twentieth century. "Looking up the Hillside with the Mattatuck Museum" (Waterbury, Conn.: Mattatuck Museum, n.d. [1980s]).

36. City Hall and the Scovill House hotel (left) and bank (right), about 1880

Mattatuck Museum

of his son, George) reflected the gradation between the families in terms of wealth, social position, and influence.[68]

The Green, when the Whites moved to Prospect, was shaded by "stately elms" and set off by "a white fence with red-capped posts." It was then a place to play and must have been enjoyed by the White children, as it was by Alice Kingsbury at the time. "Along the north side of the Green was the only paved sidewalk in town—a herring bone mosaic of bricks. It

---

68. Rose Hill remains one of the treasures of domestic architecture in Waterbury, set in a large sur-rounding area and bounded by a cast iron picket fence, "full of Gothic Revival" flavor. The last Chase owner was Lucia Chase, the founder and artistic director of American Ballet Theater, who used it as a retreat for the artists of the company until her death in 1986. In 2000 it was converted to use as a home for girls operated by the Northeastern Family Institute, which has retained its out-ward appearance. "The Hillside, Waterbury, Connecticut: The Architectural and Historic Resources Inventory," Historic Neighborhood Preservation Program: The Waterbury Neighbor-hood Housing Service, xerographic copy of typescript form filed with the Connecticut Historical Commission, 25 Nov. 1886, unpaginated, copy in Silas Bronson Library, Waterbury, Conn.; Peg Ford Pudlinski, "Chase mansion being restored for adolescent girls," *Waterbury Republican-Ameri-can*, 4 April 2000. <http://www.hillsidehistoricdistrict.com/news3.htm>, accessed 19 Nov. 2001.

was known to us children as 'the pavement,' and we would ask permission to go down there and to take our dolls for an airing."[69]

Facing Prospect on the south side of the Green was the Scovill House, hailed at its opening as a "truly splendid and commodious Hotel, which is an honor to our village and a proud monument of the enterprise and public spirit of the Messrs. Scovill." The paper termed it "a noble establishment, acknowledged we believe on all hands unsurpassed by any public house in the state." There was fresh water piped to a sink in each room, an innovation at the time.[70]

Luther and Jane Amelia White were members of the First Congregational Church, the direct heir of the original Congregational Meeting House on the Green, which in mid-century retained some of the severe discipline of the older tradition. The service was plain, the building un-ornamented, baptism was not recognized, Christmas not observed, and there was a strict personal morality. Luther, at twenty-two, was one of those who joined in 1843, inspired by an evangelical preacher who attracted "a great ingathering of converts."[71] (Jane Amelia Moses, whom he married the next year, had been baptized at St. John's Episcopal Church, also on the Green, and maintained an association with it though she joined her husband as a member of the First Church.)[72]

The First Church was a short walk around the corner for the Whites (and its stables abutted his, at the rear of both properties). Luther and the congregation were exposed to the major political issue of the day when, in the 1850s, a southern-born member of the congregation and some others

---

69. Alice E. Kingsbury, op. cit.

70. *Waterbury American*, 20 June 1849, quoted in *The Inns and Taverns in Waterbury*, Part Two (Waterbury, Conn.: Mattatuck Historical Society, New Series No 6, 1945), unpaginated, Mattatuck Historical Society, Leaflets & Pamphlets, box 3, Research Collection, Mattatuck Museum.

71. Anderson, *Town and City of Waterbury*, 3:691. Rev. Joseph Anderson had a nuanced view of the church, terming it rather liberal than conservative. "Like a good many of the 'old First' churches of New England [it] represents the liberal and scholarly reaction against that modern phase of religion which is emotional and impulsive rather than intellectually progressive. There have been various movements and enterprises into which it has not thrown itself but it has worked on diligently in its own chosen way and has identified itself at as many points as possible with the active Christian life of the community." Ibid., 3:623.

72. *Directory of the First Congregational Church*, 1882, MS M-20, box 2, Churches and Religion, Research Collection, Mattatuck Museum.

opposed the Abolitionist minister. Later there were "differences in sentiment in regard to the war itself."[73] Luther certainly knew the learned Rev.
Joseph Anderson, born in the Scottish Highlands, called to the church in
1865, whose ministry extended forty years. (He would preside at the wedding of Luther's granddaughter.) Anderson was an antiquary, historian, and
philologist as well as a minister, a member of the Yale Corporation in the
1880s, and the author of the majestic three-volume history of the town published in 1896, an essential source for research on the town and its families.[74]

Luther was chairman of the committee to select an organ for the new
church building, which replaced the former wooden one in a new and
prominent site overlooking the Green to the north. (Aaron Benedict contributed the huge sum of $30,000 for the new church building, and Luther
probably made a comparatively modest donation.) The building, designed
by Henry Dudley, in "pure Gothic style . . . of the finest pressed brick,
with bands of yellow and brown stone in front, stone arches and lintel,"
was begun in 1873 and dedicated in March 1875.[75] Its spire was nearly two
hundred feet, and it could seat a thousand. The *Waterbury American*
reported that the interior, "with its enriched chancel at one end, and the
immense organ at the other, with the lofty arches of solid masonry in alternate courses of brown and white Ohio stone supported by iron clustered
columns, and the great height of the nave, produces a combination which
is beautiful, grand, and imposing."[76] The handsome new church building
was another sign that Waterbury had arrived at a new stage of urbanity
and, indubitably, of the wealth of its citizens. Doubtless Luther took a
good deal of civic pride in his improving city to George's wedding and the
New York men he met there.

Just as the structure of the church became more elaborate and imposing, so did home furnishings. Probably in the early 1870s Luther and Jane
Amelia purchased a double parlor set in the fashionable Egyptian revival
style, consisting of two settees and four armchairs upholstered in red satin,
and armless chairs in black. The front parlor was thus provided in appro-

73. Anderson, *Town and City of Waterbury*, 3:599.

74. Ibid., 3:316 ff.

75. Ibid., 3:604–5.

76. *Waterbury American*, 24 June 1873, 2, MS M-20, box 2, Churches and Religion, Research Collection, Mattatuck Museum.

priate formality with fashionable matching furniture of the day. There were two works with allegorical subjects and Italian associations on the walls. Horace Johnson's painting *Ceres,* showed a colorfully dressed Italian peasant girl with a radiant expression holding a bowl of fruit, a celebration of the harvest. (This was either a memory of Johnson's stay in Rome or painted there, and it is now on display in a period room at the Mattatuck Museum.) In a handsome gold-edged black frame was a tinted print of Aurora, the dawn, scattering flowers before Phoebus in the Chariot of the Sun, escorted by the Hours, from the fresco by the Bolognese painter, Guido Reni (1575–1642), his most famous painting. While the tinted print does not convey the rich colors of the original, in tasteful show it reminded visitors of Raphael, whose classicism and reserve it emulated, and its allegory gracefully evoked the passage of time. With the richly framed portraits and the echoes of the arts of Europe, there was no mistaking the message of superior cultivation and gentility in the furnishings and art. The lean style of the New England furnishings of Luther's youth had been banished.[77]

Horace Chauncy Johnson was the city's resident artist and portraitist—his career shows how a native-born "fine artist" of the day could support himself in a relatively small and provincial center by patronage from newly prosperous citizens. Johnson was born in rural Oxford, Connecticut, in 1820, making him just a year older than Luther Chapin White, and was, like him, a country boy and one who also early had a mechanical bent—he invented an artesian drill—which he abandoned for an artistic career. He studied in New York City and at Rome. Soon after his return, he opened a studio in Waterbury, bringing his European-trained talents to the service of the newly rich manufacturers and their families.[78] He was a

---

77. One settee, two armchairs, and an armless chair of the Egyptian revival set are in the collection of the Mattatuck Museum and in perfect condition; the other half of the set passed from Harriet to her granddaughter, Katherine Harrison Pillsbury, in Minnesota. *Ceres* is at the Mattatuck Museum; *Aurora* is in possession of the author.

78. Horace Johnson was born on 1 Feb. 1820 at Oxford, Conn., and died on 3 Dec. 1880, at Waterbury. Anderson, *Town and City of Waterbury,* 3:1032–34. He studied painting with A. H. Emmons (1816–?) who practiced in Hartford and later and studied in New York with Samuel F. B. Morse (1791–1872) at the National Academy and in Rome with William Page (1811–85). The latter was referred to by his peers as "the American Titian" because of his emphasis on rich color. See George C. Grace and David H. Wallace, *The New-York Historical Society's Dictionary of Artists in America 1564–1860* (New York: Yale Univ. Press, 1969). On William Page and S. F. B. Morse, see *The Dictionary of Art,* ed. Jane Turner, 34 vols. (London: Macmillan, 1996), 23:765, 22:149–50, resp.

37. Luther Chapin White, 1876.
Portrait by Horace Johnson.

familiar figure on Prospect Street as he walked to and from his studio on
Bank Street from his house at 20 First Avenue.[79]

Luther Chapin White and Jane Amelia sat for their portraits in 1876.
Luther, in three quarter bust, is shown to be a fine figure of a man in his
prime; he has a warm expression with a hint of a smile above a flowing
brown beard. There is a benign, genial look to his expression, and a twinkle in the eyes. Johnson's hand conveys to the viewer through Luther's
confident expression that this man had known what he wanted and how to
get it and had been favored by good fortune. Jane Amelia, in Johnson's
interpretation, is a comfortable, plain woman whose personality is difficult
to discern; she does not have the spark the painter gave her husband. The
portraits are large, about four by three feet, in ornate gold frames adding
to their length and breadth and giving them weight. They must have been
mighty presences in the parlor at 13 Prospect.[80]

---

79. "The house was built around 1860. In 1866 it was purchased by Horace Johnson who . . . made
his home here until his death in 1890. Although the porch has been altered, the house retains its
original classical simplicity." "Looking up the Hillside." Date of Johnson's portraits of Luther
Chapin and Jane Amelia White from H. Wade White to William E. Watkins, Director, Mattatuck
Museum, 8 March 1973.

80. These portraits descended through the family to the author, who donated them to the Antiquarian and Landmark Society, 66 Forest Street, Hartford, in 1998.

38. Jane Amelia (Moses) White, 1876.
Portrait by Horace Johnson.

Luther, with his flowing brown beard in the 1870s and his trimmed, white beard later, was the image of the solid, well-fleshed, even august man of property, forbidding but for the twinkle in his eyes. His grand-daughter had an affectionate relationship with him and recalled to the author how she would sit on his lap and braid his flowing beard.

Jane Amelia (Moses) White was born in Waterbury in a family with roots in colonial Windsor. There is a lack of family anecdotes about her and there are few references to her or her family in letters. It is likely that in her marriage to Luther she came up in the world, and with his prosperity found a social and economic position beyond that of her parents. In her photograph in middle age she appears to be sturdy and confident.

At his death, Luther Chapin White was aptly described as "a notable example of a class of men often met with in our New England business life—men who started in life with nothing but their native ability, pluck and Yankee shrewdness, and by untiring industry, unswerving integrity and sound judgment gained not only a fortune, but the respect and esteem of all who knew them well." In his turn he helped young men rise in business and was "adept at changing the subject to avoid hurting a business associate." He was described as "fond of good company and interested in all that was going on around about him [and] of a cheerful and hopeful nature," qualities than can be discerned in his photos and portrait.[81]

The first born of the White children was William Henry, in 1847, probably named for Luther's elder brothers, William Stocking, a lumber merchant in Hartford, and Henry Sage, who became a manufacturer in Middletown. George Luther, who married Julie, was born five years later, in 1852, the first in the White or Moses family to have that given name. Harriet Sage White was born in Waterbury two years after George. The closeness in age between George and Harriet was matched by their association in later life, when they regularly exchanged visits and often traveled together. Harriet was named after a White great aunt. Her and William's middle name honored their paternal grandmother, Susan (Sage) White. Widowed in 1849, she was probably the sole grandparent alive during the children's childhood and lived on a White homestead in Cromwell (the former Middletown Upper Houses), where she died in 1869 at the age of seventy-three. Clearly the connection with the Sage family was a matter of great pride, judging by the frequency of the use of its name among Luther's siblings and their descendants. The children's names honor only Luther's family line; there are no Moses references.

William Henry White, the eldest son, worked as a bookkeeper at White & Wells in his early twenties, at about the time the much younger George left for the purer air of Minneapolis. In 1871 he was listed as "Sec'y" of the Scovill Manufacturing Company, which probably meant for the twenty-four year old a clerical rather than executive position. He died at twenty-six in 1873 of the tuberculosis that threatened George. In William's memory Luther and Jane Amelia gave a lectern set—a mighty eagle carved in oak atop a tall pedestal on whose back rested the Bible—to St. John's, Jane Amelia's native church. It was in place when the church was re-consecrated in 1873, after a fire five years before (and remains today). Curiously, the author never heard a reference to this short-lived young man in later generations of the family, nor to the superb lectern that remains in use at St. John's.[82]

---

81. Pape, *Waterbury*, 2:58, includes quote from *The Box Maker*, Worcester, Mass., 20 April 1893.

82. The piece is inscribed "In Memoriam WHW, 1873." Waterbury, Connecticut, St. John's Protestant Episcopal Church and First Episcopal Society, Records, 1761–1927, 7 vols., 2:434; *Waterbury American*, 23 Aug. 1873; 3. Anderson, *Town and City of Waterbury*, 3:657. Site visit by the author, 21 Nov. 2001.

The White household was a formal place, on view in the small world of Waterbury society, following the accepted social code in all things. The studio photos of Jane Amelia and Harriet in the elaborate finery of the late 1860s and early 1870s (requiring pins, stays, and buttons that Waterbury made in abundance) show how elaborate that self- and family-presentation could be. There was emphasis on financial prudence too, as George's letters reveal.

George White, the young man who proposed to Julie, had a different background from the cosmopolitan and traveled George Tuttle. He was educated at a proprietary school in Waterbury and for a year boarded at the Gunnery school in the village of Washington, to the west of the city. When, at age sixteen, hemorrhaging in his lungs revealed a tubercular condition, Luther sent him to Minnesota and set him up in business. He was a young lad with a limited education, but as his letters reveal, he was curious about his surroundings and wrote intelligently and clearly. He faced his illness bravely and mostly on his own.

In June 1869 his mother and sister traveled to Minneapolis to visit him. "We have such nice times to-gether," the boy wrote his father, "that, although you, & the rest of our dear ones at home are not forgotten, but are often spoken of and *many more* times thought of, yet, we are aware that we do not write you often enough at least, those are *my* feelings. The week glides swiftly by, and we accomplish little, or nothing. We have made arrangements at the stable, so that we can have a splendid horse and [   ] carriage for four hours or more, for $2.00." The dutiful son was anxious to show Luther that he is managing money carefully.

> So you see by each sharing the expense we can take rides quite often and not feel the expense much. We calculate we can ride certainly three (3) times a week. We take turns about who shall go first. Two of us go before and two after tea. The drives about here are certainly *splendid*. The roads are most of them very hard and in good condition. . . .To day we have been out to lake [   ] (the whole "family") on a picnic. We hired a large Omnibus and piled into it, and rode out in grand style. We had a splendid time. We took out some provisions and had a dinner out there, I, officiating as *cook*. We looked at rooms in farm house situated on the lake. . . . Accommodations about here in the country are very poor, and prices, *very* high. We dislike to pay the same prices which we are now paying for *much* inferior, accommodations.[83]

83. GLW, in Minneapolis, to Luther Chapin White, in Waterbury, 7 June 1869.

George faced the disease with confidence and was objective about his condition and prospects and wanted to move to an even more favorable climate:

> The fact of it is, Father, I feel very unsettled about my *future*, [which] is a subject of a great deal of thought to me, now. Although I have improved greatly in strength and health, yet, there is no *possible* doubt but that my lung is very badly diseased. I am fully satisfied that it will take at least *two* years to cure me if such a thing is possible. Mother while in Chicago consulted with a very excellent Physician, and stated my case to him. He said that change of *climate* & *scene* would be the very best thing that I could do to regain my health & strength. Dr. Willey, looked rather serious the last time we went there, and said "I could not go home yet" as much as to say, your lung is by no means well yet. He also advised a change of climate &c, very strongly and thought that the climate of Denver, would be a good change for me to make now. I do not feel worried but yet I feel that *now* is the time for me to be doing, for it will take but a very little, to [set] me into a condition from which I might *never* recover.

The lad was also thinking of adventure further west.

> Now, I feel as though I must relieve my *real* thoughts to you, and give you my candid feelings. I have been counting and speculating on a large trip. My plans were something like these, viz.—To go from here to Omaha as soon as practicable and remain there a while, and while there find some good opportunity to cross the plains (some 500 miles) to Denver. Spend the Winter at Denver, and perhaps find something to do to pay my way, while there . . . Or, go on to California and Winter there in the very equable climate, of the Southern part of the state . . . Of course I cannot tell now what I would do in California, but I think very probably I could find a place to spend my time on some nice fruit farm and busy myself by working in the soil, which I am convinced would be an excellent thing for me. . . .
>
> Do not think that they are mere "boyish whims" but give them the thought that so serious a subject demands. I *know* you think worlds *of* me, and will do all you can, *for* me. Mother thinks very favorably of them, and will write you about it soon. I really believe such a trip would *cure* me . . . By the way, I wish you would get the Apr, May & June numbers of the Atlantic Monthly, and read the article on the "Pacific Rail Road—open" by Bowles of the "Springfield Republican." They are very interesting and tell all about Colorado, California, &c.

→→ A VISIT TO NORTHERN MINNESOTA ←←

Excerpt from George White's
Handwritten Description, 17 February 1870

A Cabin in a Logging Camp

A suspended kerosene lamp furnishes light for the evening. . . . The living is plain but substantial and consists of pork & beans, warm biscuit, tea with sugar, but no milk, dried apple sauce, mince pie, ginger bread &c &c served on tin dishes.

The men are three fourths of them from Maine, and number some 16 or 18. They are a strong, hardy, looking class and usually pretty rough. They wear very heavy under clothing and work in their shirt sleeves, the coldest days. . . . They arise at half past four and at nine o'clock P.M. are all in bed & asleep. The first dawn of day finds them on their way to the cutting grounds, a mile or two away. They spend their evenings playing cards, grinding axes, telling stories &c &c.

The Process of Logging

After the logging roads are broken, the "axe men," two in number, select, and chop down, the best trees on each side of the road. They fell them parallel with the main road, to make access to them more convenient. They then cut off the top log and measure off the lengths for the "sawyers" who immediately follow them and with long cross cut saws, saw them into the desired length. Then come the "swampers" or road clearers, who clear a road freeing it of all stumps & brush, in order that the two horses may be able to draw the load, consisting of from three to six logs, piled up in pyramid form, and weighing from 7 to 8,000 lbs., including the sled which tracks about 6 ft. It taxes their strength to the utmost. Next after the "swampers" come the "sled tenders" who place chains around the logs & roll them up, on the sleds by means of a block & tackle and a pair of oxen. The logs are then drawn a distance of two or three miles, to the river, or "landing," where they are piled up on the ice, and the "landing man" cuts with a short axe, on each the mark of the owners. Some mark them simply with their initials and others in hieroglyphics perfectly unintelligible to one not accustomed to reading them, but well understood by lumbermen. These logs are all measured or "scaled" (by a man who devotes his time to that alone) every day, to ascertain the number of feet of lumber they will cut. The measure of each log is recorded, and handed to the Surveyor General, who keeps an annual record of them.

George was excited by the opening up of the west. The famous Golden Spike had been driven into the tie at Promontory Point, Utah, earlier that year (10 May 1869), and the transcontinental railroad had become a reality. Samuel Bowles, the author of the article that inspired him, published an account of his journey on the Pacific Railroad, as he called it, from Omaha to San Francisco. In his view the engineering achievement was a sign of the greatness of the America that emerged from the Civil War. The rails made inevitable the movement of empire to the west (and, Bowles—the editor of the *Springfield Republican,* then one of the most influential papers in the nation—foresaw, eventually across the Pacific). It was even a moral instrument in Bowles's triumphant terms. "It puts the great sections of the Nation into sympathy and unity," he proclaimed, "It marries the Atlantic and the Pacific; it destroys disunion in the quarter where it was ever most threatening; it brings into harmony the heretofore jarring discords of a Continent of separated people; it determines the future of America, as the first nation of the world, in commerce, in government, in intellectual and moral supremacy."[84]

Luther, who enjoyed travel and railroads, was doubtless impressed by the prospect laid out by Bowles, but he did not permit his son to go to Denver or further west. George's travel was confined to northern Minnesota that winter. He reported what he saw in what seems to have been intended as a "letter from Minnesota" report for the *Waterbury American.* In two excerpts he described colorful aspects of Minnesota life at the time—logging (the camps, felling the trees, and transporting the cut) and the still numerous Chippewa Indians living in their own camps, clothed in calico and faces painted in bright colors.

What could one predict as a lifetime pursuit for a boy so interested in his surroundings and able to write so clearly? Did he think of himself as a journalist, like Samuel Bowles? This was a possibility, and his letters in later life show similar descriptive abilities. Some of the nervousness, restlessness, and dissatisfaction that appears in his middle age may well stem from the (unacknowledged) path not taken.

---

84. Samuel Bowles, *Our New West: Records of Travel between the Mississippi and the Pacific Ocean* (Hartford: Hartford Publishing Co.; New York: J. D. Dennison, 1869), 71–73. This Samuel Bowles (1826–1878), succeeded his father (of the same name) as editor of the *Springfield Republican* at the age of seventeen. He was a leading abolitionist and his writings on transcontinental railroad travel were widely read. *Columbia Encyclopedia,* s.v. "Bowles, Samuel."

In the early 1870s Luther established his son as a sales representative for "The Victor, the new family sewing machine," as the Minneapolis directory of 1872 listed it under Luther's name. The office was located in the center of the city at 57 Nicollet Ave. (George boarded at Brigham House not far away.)[85] Selling the Victor may have given George a focus for his days, but it cannot have been a consuming pursuit, and he had time for the social gatherings, such as those mentioned by George Tuttle. During the fall of 1873, when the latter at Yale was anxiously awaiting letters from the reluctant Julie, George White was courting her at dances and tea parties. By the new year the match was made.

As Julie's letters do not survive from this courtship, we can only surmise her feelings. As she approached twenty-three, she was surely aware that the time for her to accept a proposal had come. George White was an enthusiastic and reasonable young man, as can be surmised from his letters. He came from a well-to-do eastern family and was attentive and persuasive. Julie accepted.

Once the engagement was announced, George's sister, Harriet ("Hattie") traveled to Minneapolis to help her brother look for a place for the couple to settle after the wedding. In March George wrote from there to Julie in Boston, where she was visiting her Aunt Julia Maria Winter and daughter, Lizzie. George and Hattie looked at rooms that the couple could occupy when they returned west after the wedding. He dreamed of his future bride as an almost ethereal being:

I can redeem my promise today by taking this down to the train and mailing it there as it has closed at the P.O. Hattie & I are just going up to Bedford to look at those rooms and decide which will be the pleasantest . . . I feel pretty happy today for I had another dream about you last night. I thought you were in bed and I was sitting by your side and kissed you oh, *so* hard and long and said to you "my darling, are you still sick?" You said in a very cheerful & happy voice "No my dear, only a little tired" and pointing to a pile of dresses lying near by—see all that I have done since you went away and I am all ready to be married." It is strange I dream of you, and so vivid are they, that they haunt me all day. I never dream of any one else or anything and although I am not at all superstitious, yet dreams of you haunt me. Oh, how I did enjoy those kisses! and how they did linger on my lips. Awfully *sappy*, am I not! Pre-

85. *Tribunes Directory for Minnesota and St. Paul, 1872–73* (Minneapolis: Tribune Publishing Co., 1872).

cious one get well & we will not delay the wedding. Must close for that faith-
ful servant but hard master—the mail
Love & Kisses
Geo.

I must get a letter from you tomorrow morning & expect a telegram from you
when you leave Boston. Also one about post*pone*ment. [86]

A few days later George was full of excitement after a musical church
service and a practical sermon.

My dearest treasure:
Yesterday there being no mail out, I could not write you, and must try and
make up for it today. I have just returned from the Congregational Church
where I heard a most beautiful sermon on "Faith" by Rev. A. D. West. The
music is delightful there now, (Miss Sanderson sustained by a double quar-
tette) and I almost feel like deserting both Episcopal and Universalist &
becoming a full fledged Congregationalist. I shall always incline toward the
Church which furnishes the most simple & *practical* sermons and the best
music, for music is an indispensable part of my worship. [87]

He followed this with what seems in retrospect a period piece about a
man's role. His aspiration to be "patient and loving & devoted," would be
tested in later years, when the mature Julia came to be the one to devote
herself to an often arbitrary husband. Here is his youthful idealism:

I am actually getting nervous over the thought of the ceremony—just a *month*
distant—and awake suddenly, and think it all over, and wonder if anything
will happen to mar its pleasure. I am constantly thinking & figuring & planning—all for you my dear one. Trying to gaze into the future and see if all I
promise and *feel* will be sustained—to see if I will be patient and loving &
devoted to you. To see if I shall be able to supply your every want & if I shall
be blessed with health and strength to battle with the world & make a place &
station that will be pleasing to you. Oh, I do not shrink when I think of it, but

---

86. GLW, in Minneapolis, to JPH, in Boston, 7 March 1874. Return address in envelope: "Coleman
House, 7th and Broadway."
87. GLW, in Minneapolis, to JPH, in Fairfield, 15 March 1874. George's mother was brought up
Episcopalian, his father Congregationalist. In Waterbury he probably attended St. John's Episcopal
and the First Congregational at different hours on a Sunday. Perhaps he had been drawn to the Universalist by George Tuttle's father, then the minister in Minneapolis.

39. George Luther White and Julia Phelps Haring in 1873

on the contrary am filled with courage and almost *conceit*. I feel that beyond our few first years of light enjoyment, we shall find a dear home, filled with comforts—perhaps little ones (with *your* permission)—where we may both live lives of peace and enjoyment. You probably think I am too sanguine! that my thoughts are so visionary. Maybe so; but there is pleasure in possessing them and life never seemed so promising and full of usefulness as it does to me now. But I am constructing more of a sermon than "love letter" for which you must pardon me.

Julie returned to her Phelps grandparents to be married at St. Paul's Church, Fairfield, on 14 April 1874. (Evidently the Phelpses had strayed from the Congregationalism of their forebears.) The bride had just turned twenty-three, and the groom would be twenty-two in July. The wedding took place on a Wednesday evening, the ceremony at 7:30 using the "low church" service in the Book of Common Prayer, which did not include Communion. The reception at the Phelps house a few doors away announced for a half an hour after the service was to begin.[88]

The bridal pair and their well-wishers must have been a stately sight as they proceeded from the tidy Episcopal church to the house with its magnificent pillared façade, their way illuminated by the street gaslights. The house was on display, with lamps in the windows and on the steps, shad-

---

88. Wedding invitation, JHW MSS.

ows on the great Doric columns. It was a handsome stage set with light filtering through the windows. The guests would have been dressed in evening finery, ornaments picked out in the flickering lights.

Grandfather and Grandmother Phelps were then seventy and sixty-five, both grave, reserved figures. The guests probably included Julie's favorite aunt, Julia Maria from Boston, and Lizzie and Emma, her daughters. Aunt Harriet (Phelps) Brooke and her young son would have been there, as well as her brother and Julie's uncle (and trustee of the Haring Trust) Frank Phelps, with his full mutton-chop whiskers. Of the other three Phelps sons, two at least were in the firm's Liverpool office at the time. With the death of Aunt Kate two years before, there was no close Haring relative alive, and there may have been no members of that family present unless curious Mary (Clark) Haring came from the city with her two surviving sons.

The groom's party was far smaller than the bride's and probably less at ease. The Whites may still have been in mourning for their eldest son. Luther would have cut a plain figure beside the worldly Phelps, and his deafness made him awkward at a gathering. As someone who had started out life on the factory bench, he might have seemed rough-hewn beside George Alexander Phelps, the retired New York merchant. However, though eighteen years apart, both men had much in common: each had grown up in small Connecticut towns, been educated in rural schools, and spent childhoods in candlelit houses without plumbing. In their time, the horse was the fastest means of land transportation. Both came of Puritan stock, both were self-made, and both had seen the material world transformed in their lifetimes. Phelps had developed the trading skills of Yankee merchants, knew the ways of the counting house. Luther was skilled with machines and production on the factory floor and knew corporate organization. One represented trade, the other manufacturing, the former and the current drivers of the American economy.

The wedding invitation informed guests that George and Julia would be "At Home after May Fifteenth, Minneapolis, Minn." By the autumn, however, George fulfilled his dream of crossing the continent by rail, now accompanied by a wife. With the opening of the bridge over the Missouri River at Omaha 1872, the iron way was now unbroken.[89] They traveled in a Pullman "Palace Car," whose elegance and comfort had been introduced

---

89. George H. Douglass, *All Aboard: The Railroad in American Life* (New York, 1982), 180.

to the railroads a few years before. "The long lines of travel in our wide and fresh West have given birth to more luxurious accommodations for passengers than exist in Europe or the Atlantic States," wrote Samuel Bowles of "cars that will carry their occupants through from New York to San Francisco, with out stop or change, and with excellent bed and board within them."[90]

After Omaha they entered the Great Plains, and, probably guided by the recently published *Appleton's Hand-Book of American Travel: Western Tour*, enjoyed "the extensive stretch of wide, undulating prairie covered with rich farms." The train moved at about twenty miles an hour, leaving plenty of time for consulting the guide and looking at the view. It stopped every few hours at stations, most of which had been tent and shanty towns for the railroad workers and were wild places of abandoned shacks and streets then inhabited by what the guide called "roughs," faint reminders of the bustling places they had been. The guidebook's mention of "massacres" along the line reminded that Indian threats were only a few years in the past. Still visible by the tracks was the now barely used trail worn by the wagons of westward-bound settlers. The infamous hazards of that more difficult journey were visible from the train: the River Platte spread out in numerous rivulets that had impeded the passage of wagons, the alkali in the waters, poisonous to animals and humans, and the hundreds of miles of inhospitable sage brush. All this was observed from the stuffed armchair of a railroad car gliding by at four times the speed of a horse with (almost) infinitely more endurance.

There were three stops a day for meals where hangers-on and Indians gawked at the exotic travelers from the east. Contrary to Samuel Bowles's account, there was no dining car, and the passengers had to alight to be "herded into station restaurants where unappetizing meals were dealt out to them in countless little bird-bath dishes containing dabs of this and that." The trains departed with little notice and "often" passengers were left behind.[91]

---

90. Bowles, *Our New West*, 46. It was not Pullman all the way; in these early years the Western Pacific railroad required a change to their own "silver cars" at Ogden, Utah for the last days of travel to California. Liston Edginton Leyendecker, *Palace Car Prince: A Biography of George Mortimer Pullman* (Niwot, Colo.: Univ. Press of Colorado, 1982), 103.

91. Margaret Chanler, *Roman Spring: Memoirs of Mrs. Winthrop Chanler* (Boston: Little Brown, 1934), 105 (on a transcontinental trip in 1879).

By the Wyoming plateau, the highest point on the line, the passengers saw bison, antelope, the occasional stage, branch lines to mining camps, and abandoned boomtowns with lurid histories. In Utah Territory they glimpsed the settlements of the Mormons, so different in dress and custom from any of the other European settlers, exotic with their somewhat titil-lating marital practice.[92] All along the route passengers could see the rude settlements at the stops. At Cheyenne and Ogden, the Indians gathered to sell blankets and to look at the strange creatures from the east. It was a col-orful, companionable journey with fellow passengers sharing what was still an exotic experience.

Within the Pullman there was some entertainment—"the special lux-ury of a house organ, and the passengers while away the tedious hours of long rides over unvarying prairies with music and song."[93] After the monotony of the plains the passengers' spirits rose as the trains wound up the mountains of Utah.[94]

Apart from opening up a view of the West, the Pullmans introduced Americans to a level of luxury that few had enjoyed, which doubtless encouraged the introduction of such elaborate comfort at home. There were "window curtains looped in heavy rolls . . . mechanical plate mirrors suspended from the walls . . . beautiful chandeliers, with exquisitely ground shades" hanging from a ceiling "painted with chaste and elaborate design upon a delicately tinted azure ground." The woodwork was of black walnut, and the floors were covered with the "richest Brussels car-peting."[95]

When it was new the Pullman Palace Car . . . was the greatest single agency of urbanity and sophistication available to the American consciousness. In the palace cars for the first time, Brussels carpets, bevel-edged French mirrors, superbly inlaid woodwork and fine linen for bed and table could be experi-enced outside of the private homes of the well-to-do and a very few exclusive hotels patronized by the same society. For the cost of an extra fare of extremely modest proportions Americans who had never before encountered

92. *Appleton's Hand-Book of American Travel: Western Tour* (New York: D. Appleton, 1872), 94–126.

93. Bowles, *Our New West*, 46.

94. Douglass, *All Aboard*, 180.

95. *Illinois Journal*, 30 May 1869, quoted in Joseph Husband, *The Story of the Pullman Car* (Chicago: A. C. McClurg, 1917), 45–46.

anything but the essential elements of shelter and the most primitive décor found themselves part of a midst of velvet portieres, splendid crystal chandeliers, hot and cold running water and at least some of the manners and comportment these amenities imposed or implied.[96]

Comfort was not complete, however. The rail bed cannot have been smooth, there was noise from crewmen talking, and one early traveler complained of the dirt and oil left in the basins after the crew washed up and rinsed out mouths full of tobacco with the common water glass. The berths were three-and-a-half feet wide and there was only enough space to sit up, making it an athletic feat to undress and dress without opening the curtains. And then there were the morning ablutions when "[y]ou see a lady with a sponge and a toothbrush and towel, edging her way along the narrow passage between the curtains, to take her turn at the washstand, where she waits perhaps some minutes for the gentleman to finish who is already in possession. When she gets her turn she is waited for by another gentleman, who is compelled to be an unwilling witness to her ablutions under penalty of losing his place." Such complaints were universal.[97]

For the young couple this crossing of the continent was a treasured experience, which soon became part of family lore. I learned from my grandmother—the child to be born in California—how as a baby she was brought east on the train, held up at the window by Julia, the "white papoose," to be exclaimed over by Indian women, many of whom had never seen one. I realized that distant as it seemed to me, the West of the buffalo and the Indians was less than a lifetime away.

The train left George and Julia at the Oakland Union Pacific station on the San Francisco Bay. From there, probably after a visit to San Francisco, they went to San Rafael, on the Marin Peninsula, north of San Francisco, where they spent the winter of 1874–75. The valley in which the town lay was bounded to the west by hills that separated it from the Pacific fogs and had been known as a healthy place by the Spanish who sent ill sailors there to recover. An article appearing in the *New York Medical Journal* in the early 1870s singled out San Rafael for the tubercular because of its dry climate and even temperature—just what George wanted for his vulnerable lungs.[98]

96. Beebe, *Mr. Pullman's Elegant Palace Car*, 18.

97. Leyendecker, *Palace Car Prince*, 106.

98. H. A. Dubois, M.D., in *New York Medical Record*, 150, 151, May 1872, quoted in *History of Marin County, California* (San Francisco, Alley Bowen, 1880) [no author cited].

San Rafael was about an hour from San Francisco by steamer across the bay and carriage from the landing. (On New Year's Day 1875, the Northern Pacific Railroad opened a line from Sausalito on the harbor to San Rafael and north, another advance of the railroad age that must have pleased George, who likely watched the celebration in town as the first train passed.)[99]

There were then about 900 people in San Rafael, a prosperous place, well served by "three hotels, two livery stables, two general stores, two boot and shoe stores, five Insurance Agencies, three private schools, three blacksmiths, two boarding houses, three water carriers," to which should be added its own newspaper.[100] Nearby Laurel Grove and Ross Drive were favorite locations for carriage drives, where the "beauties of scenery" could be enjoyed. It was a delightful place, whose only problem in November of the fall the Whites arrived was a break from San Quentin prison a few miles south on the bay, a recurring concern of Marin County residents, who feared the roaming escapees. (There was no report of an incident from this escape.)[101]

A photo of the house the Whites occupied, taken a quarter of a century later, shows an open porch and a second story deck and window with a view of the bay through a sumptuous mass of flowering vegetation. In mid-April a notice in the *Marin County Journal* read "WHITE in San Rafael, April 10, wife of George L. White of Waterford, Conn. [sic], a daughter." The baby was Caroline Haring, named for Julia's mother, Caroline Eliza and the Haring family. She came to be called Carrie by family and friends.[102]

With this babe in arms the parents took the transcontinental railroad the full 3,000 miles east that summer to return to George's Waterbury. Carrie was clearly a sturdy baby in the first of her ninety-four years, and her parents were hardy to take such a small child on the seven-day journey. George was never again troubled by his lungs, though he persistently worried about his health.

---

99. Ibid., 333.

100. Clifford J. Flack, *Chronological History of Marin County, 1542–1899*, typescript, n.d., in San Rafael Public Library, listing by date.

101. Flack, *Chronological History*.

102. *Marin County Journal*, 15 April 1875, microfilm, San Rafael [Calif.], Public Library.

40. George and Carrie by the house where she was born,
     San Rafael, California, 1900

When they arrived at New York's Grand Central Station, they changed
to the New Haven line, which Julia knew well from her Fairfield visits.
The route to Waterbury left the shoreline on the east bank of the Housatonic River about three miles from Bridgeport and followed it north to
Derby, situated on high ground overlooking its confluence with the Naugatuck. As neither knew the valley, George having spent his early manhood
in Minneapolis and Julia hardly likely to have visited industrial Connecticut, they might have followed the eastern edition of *Appleton's Hand-
Book,* which described the towns that, together with Waterbury, were
becoming a center of metalworking.

Appleton's told the traveler that the dam under construction at Derby
would "provide the largest water power in the U.S."—a proud claim that
would be quickly superseded. The products made in Derby at the time
were "steel, pins, tacks, hoopskirts, etc."—the last dealing with a fashion
in decline, but reminding that much of the valley business was directed to
products for the apparel trade in New York. Pins and tacks were also made
in Waterbury for a demand that was then virtually insatiable. Two miles
along was Ansonia, which Julia would know was named for her distant
relative, Anson Greene Phelps, the Hartford native who created a business
empire initially out of scrap metal and copper. A factory made hoop skirts
there too, but far more important were "eleven rolling mills, two found-

ries, white-lead works, woolen mills, extensive clock-factories." At Naugatuck, just south of Waterbury, there was an India rubber factory, the
origin of what would grow to become a major rubber manufacturing center.[103] These towns were of small scale, rural in many aspects, some of the
factories still using water for power, the fairly steep hills on either side
shorn of the trees that had been cut to fuel the factory boilers.

The Naugatuck Valley Railroad—essentially a branch from the New
York–New Haven line—was the main route for raw materials to reach the
factories and for the shipment of manufactured goods. That the city's
industrial economy could thrive and grow with such limited access for
materials is another example of its peculiar genius. New York City was the
most convenient destination of the line and most of Waterbury's business
involved sales and financing in that city. All their lives George and Julia
would use the train to take them to the city for business, shopping, theater,
the opera, and to connect with steamships or trains south.[104]

"Its situation is picturesque," *Appleton's* told the traveler about Waterbury:

> The hills, which closely hem in the Naugatuck above and below, here recede
> on the north and east, leaving an irregular triangular plateau, measuring
> about one mile on each side, and on this, and on the adjacent slopes and sur-
> rounding hill-sides, the city is built. A noisy mill-stream called the *Mad River*,
> comes down the east side, and *Great Brook*, another mill-stream, flows nearly
> through the center of the town. The manufactures being mostly on the out-
> skirts of the town, the central part has a neat and tasteful appearance, unusual
> in manufacturing towns.[105]

The city's sense of pride in itself—greatly to expand with its accumulating
prosperity—had been expressed in the construction of a new *"City Hall*

---

103. *Appleton's Hand-Book of American Travel: Northern and Eastern Tour* (New York: D. Appleton,
1873), 150.

104. Ibid. The Hartford, Providence & Fishkill Railway by the early 1870s had developed the eastern connection to Providence and in mid-decade was constructing a line that went west through
Brewster, N.Y., to cross the Hudson on a bridge at Fishkill, thus bypassing New York City and
opening up a direct route to the Hudson Valley and the west. The major route for passenger and
freight to and from Waterbury continued to be through the Naugatuck Valley. By the 1960s rail service in the Naugatuck Valley again terminated in Waterbury, and the east-west rail connections had
long been abandoned.

105. Ibid., 151.

built in 1868, cost of about $140,000, a fine building with brownstone front and clock tower." *Appleton's* may have exaggerated that the "elegant public hall for concerts, lectures, etc.," could hold sixteen hundred, but it did serve for almost forty years as the main place for concerts and theater involving regular appearances by well-known actors, singers, and musicians from New York. The young Whites appreciated music and would attend many of these and also perform there in amateur productions.

Waterbury's leading cultural institution had just been opened, "A public library, free to all inhabitants . . . with a permanent fund of about $200,000 . . . [and] a circulating library of about 10,000 volumes." The library was the bequest of a Silas Bronson in New York, of a family that had been prominent in Waterbury for several generations. He was unknown in the city, however, and his generosity was a surprise. In the 1890s a distinguished new building for the library would be the first of several that would create a more imposing public presence in Waterbury that both Julia and George would enjoy in their lifetimes.

Appleton's called the Green the "*Centre Square,* a small park of three or four acres." On it were the houses from early in the century and the First Congregational Church "of wood" which George remembered from his youth, but which had been replaced in his absence by the English Gothic building on the north side of the Green. St. John's Episcopal Church, the first denomination other than the Congregational in the city, had a prominent position on the west side of the Green; it had been destroyed by fire on Christmas Eve in 1868, and when the young Whites arrived it had been rebuilt "in granite, trimmed with Ohio stone, pointed Gothic style, at a cost of about $150,000."[106]

The Green was the focal point of the city. Luther Chapin and Jane Amelia White lived just a door off it on Prospect Street. Luther and George would pass through it daily on the way to the office and to church on Sundays. In the course of these frequent walks they would see and often chat with the owners of other factories and the factory hands. The grocery and butcher shops that Julia would pass nearly every day to place orders were also near the Green. It was a walking city: owner and worker, lady and maids, would see and greet each other on daily rounds.

Another cultural institution that set Waterbury somewhat above other industrial cities at the time had just been opened on the hillside that rose

106. Ibid.

41. Entrance to Riverside Cemetery

Mattatuck Museum

above the river to the west. This was Riverside Cemetery, dedicated in 1832 and laid out in the romantic manner, with winding carriage paths, copses, and outlooks. *Appleton's* termed Riverside "one of the most beautiful cemeteries in the country," another mark of the distinction that the growing wealth of Waterbury wished to proclaim.[107] The plot that Luther bought was on a rise overlooking a winding carriage path and other graves. The first occupant was George's older brother, and it awaited the rest of the family. If the graves at Riverside could open up, as in *Our Town*, virtually every person in the social stratum that the Whites inhabited in Waterbury for two generations would gather.

The Waterbury that the young couple settled had about 2,300 houses for about 15,000 inhabitants (the population would increase from 12,000 in 1870 to 20,000 in 1880). The assessors reported that there were 678 horses and, curiously, 2,125 pianofortes or other musical instruments, nearly one to a house. A society with which the young Whites would later be part, the Arcadian Drama Club, even had its own office in the center of the town.[108]

---

107. Ibid.

108. *Waterbury City Directory* (1877), 190.

George's bad lung had been cured by Minneapolis and San Rafael air, and he would survive for forty years in the moist and coal-smoke laden atmosphere of Waterbury (albeit with frequent vacations). For him the return to Waterbury placed him in a social setting among the factory owners and their families, where he had a clear view of the social map, and his place in it was implicit. For Julia, however, it was entirely new. Certainly with the social abilities she had acquired in genteel Minneapolis society, not to mention the sophistication that came with a New York upbringing and travel, she had no manners to learn, but she was on her own with no relatives to help her. The Phelps grandparents in Fairfield, only an hour or so away by train, were old; Aunt Julia Maria and Cousin Lizzie, with whom she was closest, were in Boston; Uncle Frank Phelps, the lawyer, in charge of her inheritance, was in New York. She was the wife brought from elsewhere by the son of an already established family, and the life she commenced in Waterbury represented a new start.

As the years passed, her Fourteenth Street childhood, the Clark and Haring relatives and their stories, the warmth and support of Aunt Kate, her parents, Mrs. Mulford in Minneapolis, even the stately house in Fairfield, must have seemed a dream, or a life lived by another person. Years later, when her children were grown, Julia researched her Haring and Clark ancestry to revive her connection with the past and its powerful associations with the Revolution and the state and city of New York.[109] In this new life Julia was far more involved with her husband and children than in society.

Her letters reveal that she lived with emotions close to the surface. She did not have the confidence and outgoing temperament of a social leader, nor did she go in for committee or charity work that would have brought her into contact with her peers. She looked after George first of all, as made clear to her daughter Carrie, who became her confidante and supporter. The youthful George, who vowed to serve his Julia, came to be served by a loyal wife, who shared with her daughter the slings and arrows of an often irascible husband but devotedly carried on, believing that he needed her.

---

109. Julia prepared a notebook, currently in possession of the author, on which she outlined the several lines of descent in the family. She gave it to her granddaughter on the latter's thirteenth birthday, 8 June 1919. In her papers are numerous letters and notes on genealogical questions, largely to do with the Phelps, Clarks, and Haring families.

George and Julia and baby Carrie moved in with his parents at 13 Prospect Street, and remained with them for the next five years.[110] Among their earliest possessions was a bed fashioned of rosewood with a massive carved headboard and a matching bureau. In that bed Julia gave birth to Carrie's two brothers. William Henry White, or Will (named for George Luther's deceased elder brother), was born in the November of 1876, a boy with blond hair and deep blue eyes on whom his mother doted. (His two children would be born in the same bed a generation later.) George Luther Jr. (nicknamed Jimmie) was born in 1878 and became the quiet one in the family. He inherited his father's weak lungs and was often ill. The family was the same size as that of the elder Whites, in both cases relatively small for the time.[111]

George and Julia's first house in Waterbury was at number 7 on the newly laid out First Avenue, where they lived from 1881 to 1888, evidently as renters, as there is no record of a purchase. First Avenue was a short street with about a dozen house lots that ascended the sharp slope between Grove Street and Hillside Avenue. Number 7 was a relatively modest house, built in 1875 by Joshua E. Smith, a carpenter and builder in business with his brother, Floyd B. Smith. First was one of three parallel streets (Second and Central being the other two) that ran up the hill from Grove Street to Hillside Avenue. The 1870s houses that lined them, built by men like Smith, were intended for middle and upper managers and professional people and added diversity (and balance) to what became a neighborhood that mixed a few mansions with more modest family houses. The White's neighbors on First Avenue, for example, included Robert Hill, the architect of the City Hall, Horace Johnson, the painter, E. O. Hovey, a high school teacher, Thomas R. Martin, superintendent of Waterbury Brass Co., and William F. Brett, who had a business on Bank Street. Some of the houses had boarders.[112] The builder Smith's daughter, Florence, the same age as Carrie, was her schoolmate and close friend throughout her life. An architectural survey in 1986 noted that the house at 7 First "contributes to a nearly intact nineteenth century urban residential streetscape, developed

---

110. George L. White is listed at the 13 Prospect St. address in the Waterbury city directories from 1876 to 1878.

111. The rosewood bed is now the property of George and Julia's great-great granddaughter, Comfort Dorn Grandi, of Middletown, Maryland.

112. *Waterbury City Directory* (1889).

for and by Waterbury's upper middle working population." The building is "transitional in style with both Italianate and Queen Anne influences, including a drop pendent peak molding, and bracketed bay window."[113] It was appropriate as a "starter" for the family, and the move gave the children more room (and freedom) than they could have had in the formal environment of the grandparents.

The gabled front of number 7 had a porch, standard at the time, where families could be part of the public social life of the street. Inside there was plenty of room for the children, cook and nursemaid, but the lot was not large enough for a carriage house or stable—a restriction that George must have chafed under, as he later prided himself on his horses. It was served by the public water supply, whose pipes had been laid in 1859, and about the time the Whites moved there, a sewer line was installed. As was every other street in the city, First Avenue was unpaved, and this meant ruts in winter, mud in thaws, and dust in summer. It was not until the 1890s that broken stone was used to provide a firmer surface.[114] It was only about a five-minute walk down the Prospect Street hill to Luther's house, which George and Julia would pass daily on the way to the office or the shops, easy for the children to visit on their own. The family's situation was appropriate to a young heir starting out and, in comparison to the spare accommodations of the families of factory hands, luxurious.

Hillside above First Avenue had been adorned a few years before by the most magnificent of Waterbury houses, which told the world of the success of its industries. Charles Benedict, president of the Benedict & Burnham Manufacturing Company (who had helped Luther start his business) retained Palliser, Palliser & Co., fashionable English architects with offices at Bridgeport, to build a house that would display to onlookers the fruits of what the Benedicts had achieved. The site overlooked First Avenue; indeed, it dominated it, as there was then no surrounding vegetation. It took from 1868 to 1876 to complete it, and Benedict had only a few years to enjoy it, as he died returning from Europe in 1882.

---

113. "7 First Avenue," Historic Neighborhood Preservation Program: The Waterbury Neighborhood Housing Service, "The Hillside, Waterbury, Connecticut: The Architectural and Historic Resources Inventory." Florence Smith married Clarence Merriam, who died soon after the marriage, leaving a daughter, Barbara. No dates have been found for the latter.

114. Anderson, *Town and City of Waterbury*, 2:73, 96, 104.

42. The Benedict House, 32 Hillside Avenue, about 1900

Grove Hall, as he named it, or the Benedict House as it is now called, is a leading example of what the architects termed their "American Cottage Homes." It is a fantastic mélange of architectural motifs in the Queen Anne style that must have looked like a galleon in full sail set on the then treeless hill. A modern guide describes it as borrowing from "many historic traditions without precisely copying any of them. The exterior is an extravagant combination of brickwork, 'stick style' wooden siding, and fish scale shingles accented by a profusion of spindles."[115] Benedict also maintained a large carriage house and had a full working farm on the property with greenhouses and barns. The property included the entire hillside bounded by Pine Street on the west and northwest, Buckingham Street and Prospect Street to the east, and Hillside Avenue (laid out by Benedict) on the south. Only his house and the adjoining one, belonging to his sister, Mary Mitchell, occupied the tract in the early years. Later it was subdivided into large lots, permitting extensive grounds around the

---

115. Ibid., 2:306–7. For the work of the architects, see *American Victorian Cottage Homes, Palliser, Palliser & Co.* Mineola, N.Y.: Dover Publications, 1990), a reproduction of *Palliser's American Cottage Homes*, published by Palliser, Palliser, Bridgeport, Conn., in 1878, a pattern book of houses designed by the firm with illustrations and floor plans.

houses—the ideal setting for the great houses that were built there in the next fifty years.[116]

Mary Mitchell retained Palliser, Palliser & Co. to build on the adjoining lot. Not quite as flamboyant, this house at 54 Hillside Avenue "is a characteristically vigorous composition of intersecting roof lines and picturesquely massed shapes . . . difficult to describe for the many gables, porches and decorative elements."[117] Both it and its neighbor were given a parklike setting, with lawns extending down the hill to the avenue. Carriage access was around the back by a private drive. These houses crowned Hillside and announced to all that Waterbury had entered a new age of affluence and confidence. Carrie, when a young mother, would move into the Mitchell House and live in it for fifty-five years. The house "retains . . . extensive lawns well furnished with trees, and consequently a good share of its original imposing quality."[118]

With the residential display of wealth came social stratification. Luther, by virtue of his position as factory owner and his association with Benedict and others, was in the upper stratum of the society emerging in the city. In the gradations by money and visibility of house and equipage he was somewhere in the middle or lower middle of this upper echelon. It was characteristic of Waterbury, however, that because of its many factories there were many owners, some men recognized as the affluent and influential—Aaron Benedict is the example in Luther's early years in the city—but no one or two families were dominant. Hillside came to display numerous residences that proclaimed their owners status; there were houses on the hill for the wealthy rather than a single "house on the hill."

George benefited from his father's position when he became an officer of L. C. White & Co. and White & Wells. The family circumstances were aided by Julia's inheritance and the regular checks that came from Uncle Frank Phelps, trustee of her father's estate. The investments of the estate had been $50,000 at James Demarest Haring's death, which could yield from $2,000 to $3,000 per year, a comfortable sum, and there was real estate not included in the initial inventory. George had a steady salary, but he had no inheritance and depended on his father for this work and, doubtless, for financial assistance, in buying a house and setting up a household.

---

116. *Atlas of the City of Waterbury 1879.*(Philadelphia: C. M. Hopkins, 1879), Plate P. Research Collection, Mattatuck Museum; *At Home in Waterbury*, 13.

117. "Looking up the Hillside with the Mattatuck Museum."

118. "The Hillside, Waterbury, Connecticut: The Architectural and Historic Resources Inventory."

George and Julia began married life in Waterbury as members of the young married set of this manufacturing upper crust and shared in its expectations, comfort, visible possessions and a love of travel, that successful factory owners enjoyed. The city was provincial and self-regarding—the newspaper's society page reported events as inconsequential as the departure and arrival of locals on vacations, tea gatherings, and "at homes"—but there were frequent appearances by touring musicians and theater companies. New York was two hours away by train, and the Whites were often there for theater and opera and shopping.

Waterbury was evolving month by month. Its population increased exponentially. In the 1850s it doubled, and in the 1870s rose from 13,000 to 20,000. In Julia's lifetime it would be four times that. The post–Civil War growth had transformed to a city into a little New York, with mansions and modest houses, tenements and, ever larger factory buildings (increasingly manned by Irish hands). Extremes of wealth and poverty arose. It was a bustling place, on the move and changing rapidly. As most people walked to work in the morning and evening hours there were troops of pedestrians on the sidewalks, a busy traffic of omnibuses and carriages in the streets. The air was fragrant with coal smoke, the streams tinged by the chemicals used for plating and finishing.

George was not an innovator like his father, nor was he mechanically minded. He slipped into the management of the family businesses and worked under his father for nearly twenty years. He did not found new businesses or take any of his father's into new territory, but he did maintain them and grew wealthy. In an ever growing economy like Waterbury's, his financial position relative to those in the highest levels probably declined, an implication he admits in some letters. In nonrelative terms, his means grew and amply provided for a staffed household and luxurious travel and accommodations.

Julia, the stranger introduced into the society of Waterbury, adapted to life in the same house as her in-laws. She gave her attention almost entirely to her husband and children. However, quite early she independently developed interest and skill in photography. I saw albums, now lost, with her pictures when I was a boy. Those photos of her family in this book that were not taken in a professional studio are hers and show she had a good eye and an ability to handle the awkward cameras of the day. This often diffident woman was thus a pioneer in a new amateur art and developed this interest independently of George and her children.

VI

WATERBURY MATURES

Nineteenth-century Waterbury was an exemplar for American-style factory production. It provided the country, in quantity and at low cost, with items that were once crafted by hand (such as hinges and pins) or not readily available (plumbing fixtures). The city's industry enabled the new communications and electric power technologies to spread economically and quickly. Waterbury factories symbolized the wider phenomenon of the democratization of production.

The energy of most Waterbury residents was devoted to metals—the smelting, rolling, pressing, stamping, bending, extruding, slitting, smoothing, burnishing, plating of metals. As one of the machine makers' cards so baldly put it, the common bond among Waterbury firms was the "manipulation of metals." A look at the "Manufacturer's Cards" in the classified advertisements of the newspaper in the 1880s tells the story. The Scovill Manufacturing Co., for example, offered "Brass: Sheet Brass, Brass Wire, Brass Tubing" from its greatly expanded mill, by then also producing a popular alloy that endowed products with a light, bright finish, "German Silver." Typical of Waterbury factories at the time, Scovill's manufacturing division made small, useful objects: hinges ("Narrow, Middle, Broad, Desk, Ship, Stop, Spring, and Piano Forte"), buttons ("Military, Naval, Livery, Society, Railroad, School, Lasting, Silk and Dress"), German Silver Student Lamps, Kerosene Burners, and Kerosene Lamps.[1]

---

1. *Waterbury American*, 8 Jan. 1885. Waterbury factories also made the machines that fabricated the products of the industries. Farrell Foundry and Machine Company advertised "Patent Power Presses, Drop and Foot Presses, Rolling Mill and Wire Mill Machinery, Rivet Machines, Cartridge Machines, Jewelers Tools, Gang Slitters, Trimming Lathes, Special Machines, and Sheet Metal Working Machinery of every description." The Deming Manufacturing Company on Meadow St. offered "Power Foot and Drop Presses, Rivet and Chain Machines, Tube Machinery, Spinning and Turning Lathes, Slitting Machines, Dies, Tools, etc." and described themselves as designers and builders "of all kinds of special machinery for working all kinds of metals and wire." E. J. Manville could make "Delicate Wire Working Machines, Accurate Gear Cuttings."

43. The Waterbury business district. Landis and Hughes, 1899. The Green and City Hall appear at top right; Exchange Place, where the city's four principal streets meet, is at the lower corner of the Green. The White offices were near Grand Street.

Library of Congress, Prints and Photographs Division

The most recently developed lines included "Camera Boxes" and the metal plates used in the large portrait cameras of the time. In the next century Scovill became a complex that employed thousands and boasted that its products were in every home in America.

The city's small factories made products from the sheets and tubing supplied by the mills. Smith & Griggs—the son of the Griggs founder would marry Carrie—offered "Buckles, Clasps and Slides." Mathews & Willard (where this Griggs would later work) made items for use in the houses and carriages houses of America: "Stove Knobs, Hinge Pins, Urn Tops. Towel Racks, Turnkeys, Saddlery Goods."

While buttons and brass goods were most prominently identified with Waterbury, the factories also worked steel and steel wire, the latter shaped into nails, pins, and later such products as typewriter links, paper clips, decorative furniture nails, and rings to reinforce the bobbins used in New England textile mills. In some operations the wire was fed into a fourslide machine, which, in a sequence of operations, shaped it to make a handle, ring, or link; the machine was Yankee-invented, its name referring to the four operations it could perform to make one part. It would be a mainstay of the last family factory to be owned in the city. Button-makers used mechanical presses to stamp the face of a button, to insert the back of the button with its loops or openings for thread, to affix the head of a decorative nail onto a shaft, and to connect the parts of a buckle or fastener. By the 1870s Waterbury's factories were already using chemical baths to produce a bright finish, and electroplating and heat-hardening would soon follow. The polished steel, brass, copper, and German silver attracted purchasers.

Waterbury benefited directly from leading technological developments of the second half of the century. The telegraph required wire and copper parts; telephones and their interconnections needed more of the same. With the introduction of electricity distribution in the 1880s, a whole new range of products was needed—switches, sockets, connectors, fuses, and wire. Waterbury manufacturers moved energetically into these new markets as they opened up.

The wheels on machines in the factories were connected by leather belts to revolving overhead shafts powered by a steam plant on the premises. Each machine was tended by an operator who, in the din of pounding metal, would watch the operation and release the wheel to re-supply feedstock or stop production of faulty products. Behind that operator was the maker of the tools that tipped the cutting edges of the fourslide machines and presses that created the necessary shapes. A factory needed a wheelwright to maintain the power wheels and mechanics to maintain the belts and power shafts. Waterbury factories typically packaged items, and they had to employ sorters, often women, to pack items in boxes. Management of such factories required the coordination of multiple functions and processes within the plant, and attention to development of new product lines based on assessment of the market.

The mass production of inexpensive clocks and watches involved the most elaborate set of mechanical operations in Waterbury in the post–Civil War years. An 1890s catalog of the Waterbury Clock Company, whose president was the father of the woman who would marry Will White, contained nearly a hundred pages of shelf clocks, alarm clocks, carriage clocks, clocks for offices, pocket watches, and fanciful ornamental clocks. The company had sales offices in New York, Chicago, San Francisco, and Glasgow.[2] The manufacture of clocks and watches was the most complex of the Waterbury industries, involving design, metallurgy, and machine-tooling skills, as well as precision production and assembly. The industry was also intensely competitive nationally; however, aggressive marketing and a steady pace of innovation by Waterbury factories produced attractive and affordable timepieces for a nationwide market.

The post–Civil War Waterbury factory owners showed themselves flexible and responsive to new markets. This led to expansion of existing firms, some mergers, and more and bigger facilities. The economy was extremely dynamic and relentlessly took on new challenges.

George White thus returned to a dynamic and expanding local economy after his California sojourn. A factory owner or investor had abundant opportunities to make money in Waterbury. The fact that his pioneering father could give him the head start he needed to prosper back east probably persuaded him to return to Waterbury rather than settle in Minneapolis or California. George began his business career at age twenty-four as an officer in his father's companies, White & Wells and the L. C. White & Co. For the first thirty years or so of his business life in Waterbury he remained actively involved in the two firms, and, though they remained

---

2. *The Waterbury Clock Company, 1857, 1891, Catalogue No. 131*, introduction by Chris H. Bailey (1891; facs. reprint; Bristol, Conn.: American Clock and Watch Museum, 1982).

small relative to others at the time, he managed them well enough so that his sons could inherit the business from him.[3]

As an investor, George was in a position to learn from fellow Waterbury businessmen, who were doing well, and it was in the stocks of local companies that he put most of his money. He never became as rich as those at the top of the economic ladder in the city, but with his salary, income from investments, and Julia's inheritance, there were ample funds for the family to enjoy a substantial and well-furnished house, horses and carriage, servants, luxurious travel, and to leave a sizeable estate.

The White Companies

George worked alongside his father in the brick building at 156 Bank Street, amid the commercial buildings, which were edging residences out of the area south of the Green, a few doors from the depot of the Naugatuck Railroad. White & Wells was a local pioneer in making pulp-lined straw board, and its business expanded through the 1870s and 1880s. It was a relatively small firm—there were sixteen employees in 1889 in addition to Luther and George, the two officers—but, judging by the Dun reports, a good moneymaker. It was the larger of the two White companies, and the one in which the owners put most effort. The L. C. White & Co., which made button backs (and was also profitable) had only four employees.[4] In the early 1880s Luther purchased the assets of a papermaking company in the town of Southford, about twenty miles to the west, which made strawboard and manila paper. By the 1890s White & Wells had acquired interests in a mill in Piqua, Ohio (on the Miami River near

---

3. Waterbury was his base, but over the years George branched out. In 1911 the list of his business affiliations was diverse: president of the Fuller-Burr Company of New York City; president of the William Van Buren, Inc., of New York City; president of the New England Watch Company of Waterbury; vice-president of the Philadelphia Paper Manufacturing Company of Manayunk, Pennsylvania; director of the Colonial Trust Company of Waterbury; and director of the Dime Savings Bank of Waterbury. In pursuit of these business interests he was frequently on the rails, to New York, Chicago, Ohio, Indiana, Philadelphia and no doubt other places on business. *Genealogical and Family History of the State of Connecticut*, ed. William Richard Cutter et al. (New York: Lewis Historical Publishing Co., 1911), 3:1567–68.

4. *Waterbury, Connecticut, Directories, 1889–91*, online database, <www.Ancestry.com>, accessed 20 June 2001, data from *Waterbury, Conn., 1889* (Waterbury, Conn.: Price, Lee, 1889).

44. White & Wells letterhead, 1900

Dayton, then a center of the linseed oil industry),[5] and another in Bridge-port, Connecticut.

George became president of White & Wells when his father withdrew from active business life in 1892. As many owners were doing with their businesses at the time, he incorporated it three years later with a capitaliza-tion of $50,000. White & Wells then bought and sold "all kinds of paper and paper stock, straw boards, twines, and paper boxes made by hand or machinery" and continued to do so well into the next century.[6]

By the 1880s railroad connections between Waterbury and New York had been established for over thirty years; service was comfortable and frequent—eight trains a day ran to Grand Central Station via Bridgeport. Given the importance of New York as a source of capital and sales, the connection was heavily used. George and other businessmen boarded the through car at 8 A.M., which took just under two hours to reach Grand Central (as it did not require a change at Bridgeport), less than the travel time in the twenty-first century.

By the 1890s the Naugatuck Railroad—"for its length one of the most profitable pieces of road in the United States"—had been incorporated into the New York, New Haven, and Hartford Railroad (NYNH&H).[7] Waterbury was also served by three other lines that provided competition

5. *The Ohio Guide*, Writer's Program, Works Progress Administration (New York: Oxford Univ. Press, 1943), 484.

6. Joseph Anderson, ed., *The Town and City of Waterbury, Connecticut, from the Aboriginal Period to the Year Eighteen Hundred and Ninety-Five*, 3 vols. (New Haven: Price and Lee, 1896), 2:424–25.

7. Wilson Gilbert Lathrop, *The Brass Industry in the United States: A Study of the Origin and the Development of the Brass Industry in the Naugatuck Valley and its Subsequent Extension over the Nation.* (1926; New York: Arno Press, 1972), 82.

and interconnections around the compass. At Winsted, at the north end of the valley, there was a connection to the Central New England, and shipments (and passengers) could proceed west and reach the Hudson and its rail lines at Poughkeepsie. There was a direct connection to New Haven using a branch line from Derby. A line through Bristol and Hartford connected Waterbury with Boston (four hours travel time), Providence, and eastern Connecticut. Another, new line extended over the western hills to connect near the Hudson with the New York Central and Erie lines.[8] This configuration was the high point of rail interconnections. All but a single track along the Naugatuck line to Waterbury were abandoned by the mid-twentieth century, by which time highways reproduced the Naugatuck Valley routes.

The web of rail connections available to the White family in these years meant that Carrie (traveling alone or with Julia) could comfortably visit her Phelps relatives in Boston and Harriet in New Haven. The boys could reach school at Andover and later New Haven and Yale by rail, and Julia and George could move from one northern New England hotel to another by train. When going south, as the elders did every winter, they would transfer across the Hudson to the Pennsylvania Railroad at Hoboken and change to the southern railroads in Washington. (They would not take their first automobile trip until 1906.)

Waterbury had its own dramatic society, the Arcadian Club, which put on plays using local talent. In 1892 Julia and George were featured in *Esmerelda*, set in the eighteenth century. George played the Marquess de Montresor, "a French adventurer," which should have given him opportunities to twirl his fine moustache; Julia was Lydia Ann Rogers, wife of a character called "Old Man Rogers," and doubtless a pillar of virtue in a play that must had its share of intrigue.[9] Waterbury was also benefiting in this period from the expansion of metropolitan culture by touring theater companies and musicians.

---

8. *Waterbury, New Haven County, Connecticut, U.S.A., Its location, Wealth, Finances, Industries, Commerce, and Society; Its Freight and Passenger Facilities, and What it Offers as a Place for Residence or Business* (Waterbury, Conn.: Board of Trade, 1890) Mattatuck Museum, Mss. Collection, 16–18.

9. Among the members of the Arcadian Society at the time were George's sister, Harriet, Professor Francis T. Russell, the elocutionist, and Henry Lawton Wade, whose daughter would marry Will White. The titles of other plays put on by the Acadians evoke the theatrical fashions of the day: *Ici on parle française, A Dead Shot, Turn Him Out, A Rough Diamond, The Loan of a Lover, Married Life, The Lady of Lyons, How She Loved Him, Our Domestics, The Little Treasure, Time Tries All, Money,* and *Love's Sacrifices.* Anderson, *Town and City of Waterbury,* 3:1099–2000.

45. Julia in an Arcadian Club production, 1885

Waterburians celebrated the opening of the new city hall that had so impressed *Appleton's* with a concert by Theodore Thomas and his symphony orchestra—whose playing George Tuttle had enjoyed. Later events at the city hall were organized by a self-trained impresario named Eugene Leslie Jacques (1855–1905). Thanks to his efforts, according to Anderson, "At one time or other most of the principal stars of the country played here."[10] New York troupes presented Shakespeare plays and costume melodramas such as *Sardanapolous* and the popular *Ten Nights in a Barroom*. Among the actors whose names still resonate were Edwin Booth, Joseph Jefferson, and Modjeska.[11] It was the great Booth who figured in

10. Anderson, *Town and City of Waterbury*, 3:2002.

11. Anderson, *Town and City of Waterbury*, 3:1092–94. Even in the dead of winter touring troupes came to Waterbury for one-night stands. In one week in January 1885 Jean Jacques offered at the City Hall "MISS MARGARET MATHER AS JULIANA, in John Tobin's glorious 5 act comedy," 'The Honeymoon,' A New York Play with New York People," "Robert Griffin Morritt's Musical Farcical Comedy, THE KINDERGARDEN, with Billie Graves, formerly at Wallack's Theater, New York," and "Ida Siddons' Female Mastodon & Burlesque Company." *Waterbury American*, 8 Jan. 1895. Edwin Booth (1833–93), was considered the greatest actor of his day, particularly for his Hamlet in New York in 1880. Joseph Jefferson (1829–1905) was famous for his interpretation of Rip Van Winkle. Polish-born Helena Modjeska (1840–1909) was noted for her Rosalind, Mary Queen of Scots, and Camille. *Victorian Actors and Actresses in Review: A Dictionary of Contemporary Views of Representative Actors and Actresses, 1837–1901*, comp. Donald Mullin (Westport, Conn.: Greenwood Press, 1982).

the most exciting event of all when his company arrived at the city hall on 28 November 1881, billed to perform *The Merchant of Venice* and *Richelieu*. Through a mix-up on the railroad, the costumes and settings had not arrived. The Rev. Anderson described the scene. "The curtain rose on Booth and the company in a semicircle, dressed in worn traveling clothes. He announced that anyone could leave, about sixty did, and missed the experience of a lifetime." Booth told those who remained that he and the company would play Hamlet in their street clothes, in effect a modern-dress production well before the fashion. "[T]here were some incongruities," Anderson wrote, "but all was forgotten in the dramatic power and intensity with which Booth delineated Hamlet."[12]

It was the enterprise of Jacques, the young impresario, that gave Waterbury its first real theater in 1886, a small horseshoe-shaped opera house with boxes, said to have cost the proprietor $50,000. The opening of the theater brought out local society, George and Julia likely among them. On the stage was "an elegantly set drawing room . . . [with] richly uphol-stered red furniture, a handsome rug, and attractive bric-a-brac," which imparted "to the stage the appearance of a spacious apartment in a home of wealth." The program included a mandolin quartette playing Granados' "Spanish Concert Waltz." Lizzie C. Gaffney of New Haven sang "My Angel Boy" with a "clear sweet, bird-like voice." Marshall P. Wilder's character impersonations "brought down the house." The drop-curtain showed a scene at High Rock Grove, a private park on the Naugatuck, a favorite place a day's outing by train or carriage.[13] Though it came to be used for variety shows—and later for burlesque—Waterbury then had an opera house complete with boxes.

Harriet

There was an episode in the L. C. White household that shattered its con-ventional calm for a time and about which only the outline is known. Shortly after George's marriage, his sister Harriet abruptly fled the Pros-pect Street house, its furnishings, its routines, and her mother's possibly iron hand. "All" Waterbury would have known about it, her parents would

---

12. Anderson, *Town and City of Waterbury*, 3:1094–95.

13. Unattributed newspaper clipping dated 1882, Jacques Opera House file, MS M-25, Arts & Entertainment Collection, Research Collection, Mattatuck Museum;

46. Harriet Sage White in 1873

have been wild with concern. Harriet, at twenty-one or twenty-two, ran off with a young man, perhaps prompted by the metaphors of fleeting time and succulent abundance in the *Aurora* and *Ceres* on the walls of the front parlor. Needless to say, no word of this appeared in the press, and the affair was never mentioned in the otherwise ample genealogical records of the family. It was only in her old age that Harriet told her daughter about it. "Harriet fell in love with a Jew," is the story that came down to her grand-daughter—"it was quite unheard of in those days for Jews and Christians to marry—and she eloped to Boston."[14]

Word of this, or at least of what Luther had to pay to untangle his daughter, reached the ears of the gossipy Dun credit checker. In February 1877 his report noted elliptically that "White has an expensive family (also a daughter that White was financially embarrassed for in some speculation a short time since but there is no appearance of it outside)."[15] Since it is unlikely that the young woman speculated, this must be code for what Luther had to pay to end the marriage. A property transaction in 1901 involving Harriet as Luther's heir specified she "was married subsequent

---

14. Katherine Clark Pillsbury, *A Cherished Childhood*, ed. Beverly A. Hermes (Wayzata, Minn.: privately printed, 1999), 58–59.

15. New Haven Co., vol. 33, p. 542, R. G. Dun & Co. Collection, Baker Library, Harvard Business School.

to 20 April 1877," presumably a clause intended to protect against a claim from that first husband.

According to her granddaughter, the "marriage was not successful; so, she came back home and was looking for a good divorce lawyer. She went to Hart Lynde Harrison in New Haven, a widower, and he got her the divorce. He fell in love with her, and married her."[16] If she had indeed been married to the man she went off with, attorney Harrison was adept at expunging the record, as she is noted as not previously married on the wedding certificate, and a search of New Haven County Divorce proceedings produced no record of this case in that jurisdiction.[17] The episode, while hidden from view, was evidently not the deepest secret because years later, when Carrie wrote her that she was worried about the expense of her forthcoming wedding, Harriet responded, "Take my advice, the next time you get married, *elope!*"[18]

From the outline of the event we can imagine a young woman desperate to escape the constriction of home and the rules of the society in which she grew up and attracted to a very different kind of man. The photo of her in a long dress in 1873, before the elopement, suggests how elaborate and constricting the conventional presentation of female self was at the time. Harriet also had a streak of independence, which we will glimpse again when, as a widow, after a motor trip across Europe with the Whites in 1906, she chose to remain in Dresden for a time rather than return to New Haven and the society that she and Lynde had been part of.

In her second marriage, Harriet remained close to George and Julia and the family, and as "Auntie" and "Hattie" figures in much correspondence. The children visited her in New Haven—Carrie's charming letters of a visit follow—and in summers they often stayed at the Harrison's house overlooking Long Island Sound at Leetes Island. Julia and George visited the Harrisons a number of times in Thomasville, Georgia, where they had a winter house.

---

16. Pillsbury, *Cherished Childhood*, 58; this version was repeated to the author by Elizabeth Wade White, Harriet's grandniece.

17. Marriage Certificates, 1886, 29 Sept. 1886, Waterbury VS; Divorce Records, Waterbury VS, microfilm, CSL.

18. Harriet (White) Harrison, to CHW, Jan. 1902; Pillsbury, *A Cherished Childhood*, 58.

Children at the Photographer's Studio

The story of the young family in Waterbury is well told in the pictures taken at regular visits to the photographer's studio. Three-year-old Carrie poses in a tightly buttoned winter coat holding in one hand the handle of a small basket, with a determined expression on her face. The photographer used this to prepare a nearly life-sized portrait against a romantic stock backdrop showing a river in a pastel-colored, pleasingly wild valley. Carrie's basket is filled with spring flowers, and the background suggests springtime, despite Carrie's winter coat. Julia placed this hybrid photograph and pastel in a frame worthy of an ancestral portrait, the juxtaposition adding to its charm.[19]

Later photos show Carrie becoming a poised young woman, handsome with her long oval face and regular features. Will is blond with eyes of deep blue, although the black and white photos do not show them. Jimmie is always the little fellow, never as robust as his brother. Judging by their clothes and the care taken to chronicle their growth, the children were made much of and doubtless preoccupied Julia. Disease and early death were still common—Carrie's future husband's family was decimated in the same years—and Julia (whose letters show her to be a worrier) doubtless had many moments of anxiety while the children were growing up. Young George was a concern, in later life tubercular, but he survived childhood without serious illness. It seems a harmonious family, the children handsome and well dressed.

Carrie's Youth

Carrie was educated at St. Margaret's School, under the jurisdiction of the Episcopal Diocese of Connecticut. Its construction (1868) was funded by a subscription from the manufacturers, who desired a school for their daughters. The substantial building was built in the same year as the city hall, another sign of Waterbury's maturing.[20] The school was a "large and

---

19. This portrait hung in the second floor hall of Carrie's house at 54 Hillside Ave. until her death, when it became the property of the author.

20. Robert Wakeman Hill (1826–1909) studied with Henry Austin and was an architect for the state. He was responsible for the Waterbury City Hall and eight public schools in the city. *Waterbury Architectural Survey . . . 1978*. The original school building was for the Waterbury School Association, which was succeeded by St. Margaret's, chartered by the state in 1875 and part of the Episcopal Diocese of Connecticut. Anderson, *Waterbury*, 2:522.

47. The White children, 1878 and 1879
    Carrie poses alone in her best coat and, the following year, with brothers
    Will and George Jr. ("Jimmy")

commodious" presence at the corner of Cooke and Grove Streets as an
early catalog described it, only a short walk for Carrie.[21] It was "lighted by
gas, and heated by steam . . . situated upon a hill-side, overlooking the surrounding country with spacious grounds about it, and there is no danger
from any imperfections of drainage or in the water supply." The Rev.
Francis T. Russell, the principal, and his wife gave boarders and day students alike the "influence of a happy, Christian home." The girls received
"a polite and finished education, and the discipline of the mind in more
rigorous study." They would be prepared for their roles as women, as "the
daily influence of the school will . . . aim at cultivating, as the ideal of
womanly perfection, the graces set forth in the School's motto, chosen
from the Divine Word, 'the ornament of a meek and quiet spirit.'" The
school sought to strengthen in the pupils "all the gentle and loving influences of home, so much neglected in our own day."

The school hosted guest speakers. Mr. F. J. Kingsbury, the attorney and
historian who lived on Prospect Street, spoke to the girls on the "Constitu-

---

21. This and following quotations from *St. Margaret's School for Girls* [catalog], n.d., MS M-17, box
1, Schools & Education, 1709–1906, Research Collection, Mattatuck Museum.

48. George with his children, George Jr., Carrie,
and Will, in 1888

tion of the United States, and the Legal Rights of Women." Other topics
addressed by guests were "Natural Philosophy and Chemistry, with practical demonstrations" (Prof. M. S. Crosby), "Botany and Geology" (Mr.
H. F. Bassett), and "Classical Literature" (Prof. David G. Porter).

The primary academic focus was "the study and expressive use of the
English language"—Latin and Greek had become less important in education at the time). The girls were taught to cultivate the voice with "natural
and expressive renderings of the choicest passages of the English tongue."
Perhaps as a result of this training Carrie had a clear, silvery speaking
voice and was an excellent reader, as the author experienced from countless books read to him by her during illnesses. She became fascinated by
the sounds and meanings of words and the puns that could be made of
them, an interest endured through to her nineties.

Carrie stayed at St. Margaret's through the equivalent of twelfth grade,
her entire formal education. Her schoolmates, Mary Burrall, and her
slightly older sister, Lucy, neither of whom married, and Florence Smith
(later Merriam, but widowed shortly after marriage) lived in Waterbury

and remained her closest friends throughout their long lives.[22] (The St. Margaret's building was demolished after a new campus for the older girls and for boarders was built on the western outskirts of the city. It was replaced on the Grove Street lot in the 1930s by a gas station—the first sign of the change in that section of Grove Street from its once residential and gracious character.

Carrie was a merry and active ten-year-old. "You can not guess how your poor Ma-Ma misses you," Julia wrote her when she was visiting Aunt Julia Maria in Boston. "Papa says the house seems so quiet with out you & Grand-ma asks about you every time I see her."[23]

In 1888 George purchased a house at 114 Grove, at the corner of Prospect Street, for the handsome sum of $30,000; it was the first house he owned.[24] A great advantage was that the lot was large enough to hold a barn for horses and a carriage, for which the First Avenue address was not large enough. The house on Grove Street became the lifetime home of both George and Julia, and it was to be much improved by a renovation at the turn of the century.[25]

Lower Prospect Street began a transformation in the early 1880s with construction of Trinity Episcopal Church on a lot abutting Luther's house. Trinity had been formed by parishioners of St. John's in 1877, encouraged by the rector because the growth of the older parish justified the formation of a new one. Trinity became an Anglo-Catholic parish, with more ceremony than "low church" St. John's, in later years even administering confession. The building was a large Gothic structure made of gray granite from nearby Plymouth. When completed in 1885, it loomed above the elder White's house, a formidable wall of gray stone and Gothic details. Despite the disparity in size, material, and function, the neighbors coex-

---

22. Lucy Beach Burrall (1876–1972), Mary Frances Burrall (1877–1966), and Florence (Smith) Merriam (1873–1954) were born and lived their entire lives in Waterbury, where they died. Social Security Death Index; Connecticut Death Index, 1949–1996, personal communication from Gerald Geci, 24 April 2003.

23. JHW, in Waterbury, to CHW, in Newton, Mass., 1885.

24. Israel Holmes, Administrator, Estate of Calvin H. Carter, to GLW, Property Records, 117:349–51, 28 July 1888, 117:583–584, 28 Aug. 1888, Office of the Town Clerk, City of Waterbury, New Haven Co., Conn. "Estate of George L. White," Inventory, 30 Dec. 1914, Waterbury Probate Dist., file 8742, RG 4, Records of the Probate Courts, State Archives, CSL.

25. In the Waterbury city directories George L. White's address was at 7 First Ave. 1881–88; in 1889 it as at 52 Grove, shortly thereafter renumbered 114 Grove.

isted apparently without irritation during Luther's and Jane Amelia's life-times.[26] (The side façade of the church is now fully exposed by the parking lot on the site of the L. C. White house.)

A Visit to Aunt Harriet in New Haven

Carrie was twelve when she visited the recently married Harriet ("Aunt Hattie") in New Haven, probably her first visit to the Harrison household, in one of the most distinctive houses in New Haven. Harriet's husband, H. Lynde Harrison (1837–1906) came from a venerable Connecticut lineage, was a veteran of the Union Army, a Republican state senator, and a prominent attorney in New Haven. A term of service on the bench led to his later being referred to as Judge Harrison. He represented railroad interests in the state and in the reconstructed South.[27] He had married Harriet in September 1886 at the First Congregational Church in Waterbury. Harriet was thirty-two and became a mother to the last-born of her husband's children, Gertrude ("Truda"), then about thirteen, who became a close friend of Carrie.

The Harrison house was designed by its most famous local architect, Ithiel Town. It was (and is) located on Hillhouse Avenue, north of the Yale campus, with neighboring houses in the same Italianate style and some survivors from the eighteenth century. The three-story Harrison house, an ensemble of two towers, courtyard and a loggia, was a posthumous creation of Town, constructed in 1848–49.[28] For Harriet it was a far cry from her father's Prospect Street house and a grand coming to rest after the turbulence of her elopement and its unhappy resolution. (The house, at

---

26. History prepared by Mrs. C. M. Merriam [Carrie's schoolmate, Florence Smith] and Mrs. Roger Wotkyns, for the sixtieth anniversary of the parish, printed in the *Waterbury Republican*, 30 May 1937, Trinity Church folder, box 2, MS M-20, Churches and Religion, Research Collection, Mattatuck Museum.

27. "Hon. Lynde Harrison," in *Commemorative Biographical Record of New Haven County, Connecticut* (Chicago: J. H. Beers, 1902), 2:688.

28. A description of the house and its owners from 1848–49 can be found in *Pictorial New Haven, Old and New: Its Houses, Institutions, Activities*, ed. Arnolt Guiot Dana, 1913–39, microfilm 32 1/2, 116–18, Dana Collection, New Haven Colony Historical Society. Ithiel Town (1784–1844) was a partner in the 1830s of Alexander Jackson Davis in a firm noted for its Greek revival architecture, including the Customs House in New York and the Ohio State Capitol. Adoption of the Italianate villa style had been encouraged by pattern books published in U.S. by the architect and landscape architect, Andrew Jackson Downing. *ANB*, s.v. "Town, Ithiel."

52 Hillhouse, is now owned by Yale and used for offices, its exterior protected by the Historic District of which it is a part.) Uncle Lynde was later to show Carrie the opulence and influence he enjoyed in Washington, D.C., Aiken, South Carolina, and Tampa, Florida, but this house and the lookout room in its fanciful tower must have enchanted the twelve-year-old.[29]

Carrie enjoyed the ceremonious occasions Aunt Harriet offered her. She learned about "Russian tea," Japanese boxes, Royal Worcester, cut glass and the "lovely dish that Mrs. Hayden" gave (a wedding present from a Waterbury family). At twelve years, she was already well aware how to observe and behave on social occasions. In a letter to Julia she reported the social doings, a charmingly naïve chronicle, with particular observations about accouterments. Julia must have been delighted.

> My darling Mama,
> I suppose you think I am dreadful, but so many things have happened this week that I wanted to tell you in one letter and have it a long one.
> Monday I went calling with Auntie, we called on Mrs. John Alling, she receives on Monday so we had lovely ice cream served on beautiful dark blue dishes of Royal Dresden, and cakes. Auntie had Russian tea but I did not.
> She has a lovely little girl just my age named Agatha, who has a little white rabbit for a pet.
> Tuesday afternoon Auntie took Truda and me to Bushnell Museum, we were too late to see the curiosities but saw the play, which was Muggs Landing; I liked it very well, but Auntie got tired.
> Wednesday afternoon Agatha Alling took Truda and me in a beautiful carriage to the Gymnasium and we found it very interesting.
> Thursday I had a sore throat and was in the house all day. I gargled my throat with clorate of potash and am all right now.
> Friday afternoon Auntie took Truda and me to make our party call on the Mallorys but they were not in.
> Saturday at five o'clock we had a lovely tea. The girls here were May Lewis, Agatha Alling, Kattie Trowbridge and Henrietta Ingersoll. Before tea we played some games. For tea we had first scalloped oysters in little china fishes, and biscuits. I served [   ] in Auntie's beautiful Royal Worcester cups.
> Second course chicken salad and served in Auntie's cut glass bowl and olives in that lovely bourbon dish that Mrs. Hayden gave.
> Third ice cream in the silver dish and cakes, bonbons in the other dish. Just before we were through Auntie came in from the other room and asked each of us which hand we would have, she had, lovely Japanese boxes some with

---

29. See "White," Biographical and Genealogical Notes.

drawers and some long, filled with candies, mine was a long one. After tea we
played some more games.

I am very sorry Miss [   ] has gone away. I am having a lovely time and would
like to stay a little longer, but very anxious to see you and Papa and the rest.[30]

In the weeks around her fifteenth birthday, Carrie accompanied her
grandparents, Luther (then sixty-nine) and Jane Amelia (sixty-five), on a
railroad journey south. In New York they transferred from Grand Central
to the ferry that crossed the Hudson to the Pennsylvania Railroad terminal
on the New Jersey side. From there the first stop was Washington, D.C.
Harriet and Truda were with them much of the journey, Lynde Harrison
in the first weeks.

Carrie again shows herself to be a writer of lively letters. Few visitors
of her age can have been given a private tour of the White House and been
taken for a drive by a senator, as she and Truda were.

You must have thought I was not going to write you, I started to do so yesterday on the tram but could not because it made me very sick. We arrived at
Washington Wednesday evening at 8:40, the car in which we came was very
handsome and comfortable yet I was very glad to get in my little bed at last. It
certainly is the most beautiful city I ever saw. Thursday morning Uncle
Lynde took Truda and me to the White House, we were first ushered into the
East room which is very elegant, then into the Blue Room which was decorated by Tiffany it is perfectly beautiful, then the Green Room which was also
decorated by Tiffany, then Mrs. Harrison's private sitting-room which is red,
and, also the state dining room the man told Truda that as she might someday
be the first lady of land he would seat her in Mrs. H. dining chair but Truda
thought she was rather unlucky, as she sat on a pin, After Uncle Lynde had
made the man happy by a $1 bill he showed us the conservatory which was
like a Tropical garden he gave us a piece of Maiden Lace fern which I have
pressed.

From there we went to that beautiful Capitol, there we met Mr. Platt who
took us into the Senate it was great fun to hear them discuss different things
from there to the House of Repre. (I do not know how to spell it) where they
are always quarreling. The walls of different rooms are hung with large paintings, of course you have seen all these so know how beautiful they all are. In
the afternoon Truda and I were invited to drive by Senators Platt [Sen.
Orville H. Platt from Connecticut][31] and Miles. We went to the National
cemetery at Arlington there are over twenty thousand graves all soldiers

30. CHW, in New Haven, to JHW, in Waterbury, 27 March 1887.

49. Fifteen-year-old Carrie, dressed in
traveling clothes, 1890

killed in the war, and in one grave are buried 2,111 unknown men. The grounds used to be the home of the Lee family and the old mansion is still there where Robert and the rest lived. We went into the house but there was not much to see inside. Coming home we passed the Hill cemetery where is buried the body of the author of "Home Sweet home." In the evening we all, including Mr. and Mrs. Platt called informally on Mrs. McKee and the children. Mrs. is very sweet and pretty, the children are not very handsome but bright. Truda and I played "Hide the handkerchief" in the East room with baby McKee.[32]

---

31. Orville Hitchcock Platt (1827–1905) was a senator from 1879 to his death. An abolitionist before and during the Civil War, Platt became active in Republican politics in Connecticut. As a senator he was noted for "Industry, honesty, sound judgment." He supported protectionism and at the turn of the century supported expansionism. *DAB*, s.v. "Platt, Orville Hitchcock." The *Congregational Biographic Directory* has no reference to a Senator Miles.

32. CHW, in Jacksonville, Florida, to JHW and GLW, in Waterbury, 23 March 1890. Their visit was midway in the term of Ohio-born President Benjamin Harrison (1833–1901), whose single term (1889–93) separated the two of Grover Cleveland. His was the last of the leisured presidencies. He was in his office "only from 9–1 Monday–Friday. After lunch and on weekends he went for strolls and occasionally greeted sightseers taking he White House tour"—but not Carrie and Truda on this visit. Douglas Brinckley, *History of the United States* (New York: Viking-Penguin, 1998), 348. Lynde Harrison had entrée to the White House because of his Republican associations. He was also probably related to the president. The Mr. Platt who took the girls to visit Congress may have been a relative of the senator of the same name, who later took them for a drive.

From Washington the party went south to Jacksonville, where they changed trains to cross the state to Port Tampa. There they would visit Mr. and Mrs. Henry B. Plant, who had built a "cottage" by the water near where he intended to create a resort hotel. Carrie was enchanted.

> This is one of the most beautiful spots I ever saw, it is kind of a large cottage built right on the water. There is water under us and water on every side. Mr. and Mrs. Plant are here and Mrs. Plant has made the house just sweet. Pretty pictures and lovely furniture in every room, she and the maid Fannie made 150 yards of curtain for the doors and windows. The breeze is perfect and I do wish both of you could be with me. I am happy now but if you were here would be perfectly so. In the bay are Gulls and Pelicans. The cooks can fish from the kitchen window and I never knew what fresh fish was till now. One of the cooks threw a decoy into the water one of the Pelicans swallowed it and is now caged up on the verandah. The water is filled with sardines and many other fishes the boys could have a fine time with their new poles.[33]

The host, Henry Plant (1819–99), a multimillionaire and one of the era's "robber barons," was born in Branford, Connecticut, and was the first cousin of Lynde Harrison's first wife. He was an energetic entrepreneur who at an early age developed a successful delivery service called Adams Express. In the 1850s his wife was told to go south for her health, and when visiting the small hamlets in Florida with her, the "shrewd Yankee," as a biographer terms him, saw its potential for development. During the Civil War he handled express service for the Confederacy, and astonishingly, despite being allied with the losing side, acquired bankrupt railroad lines in the south and developed steamship companies, one of the northerners making money by investing in the impoverished states of the old Confederacy. Lynde Harrison presumably did legal work for him and certainly enjoyed his hospitality and services. He himself purchased a house in Aiken, South Carolina. When Carrie and the family visited, the Plant empire included over two thousand miles of railroad lines south of Washington.[34] Plant made a fortune, and his rail lines carried the rich to the lavish Florida resorts then being built, which Carrie would soon see.

---

33. CHW, in Jacksonville, Florida, to JHW and GLW, in Waterbury, 23 March 1890.

34. *DAB*, s.v. "Plant, Henry Bradley." Sarah Frisbie Plant, first wife to Lynde Harrison, was Henry Plant's first cousin, the daughter of Samuel Orin Plant, brother of Anderson Plant, Henry Plant's father. See G. Hutchinson Smyth, *The Life of Henry Bradley Plant* (New York: G. P. Putnams Sons, Knickerbocker Press, 1898), 36.

Port Tampa was the terminus for the Plant steamship lines to Mobile and other Gulf ports, to Key West, and to Havana. The Tampa Bay Hotel that Plant was building was intended to challenge St. Augustine's magnificent Ponce de Leon. These hotels were built at the apogee of the Gilded Age, when the luxury formerly available only to royalty could be purchased by the well-to-do. When the Tampa Bay opened, the "thousand foot long brick structure with Moorish horseshoe-arched windows" caused a sensation. The Moorish design "was repeated in the intricate woodwork of the lengthy veranda. Its silvered domes and minarets, emerging from tropical shrubbery . . . evoked an Oriental quality"[35]

Carrie and her party crossed the state in Mr. Plant's private car to St. Augustine to visit the Ponce de Leon.

> Oh! Oh! Oh!
>
> You never saw such a place in your lives, it is perfectly magnificent I thought I could not express Port Tampa but this is simply impossible. It made one rather mad to have the furniture in my bed room nearly as nice as our parlor home. But, when it comes to the parlor here, The walls are covered with paintings that must have cost $1000 and there is a mantle which was $50,000 it is mostly of onyx with a clock in the top. The floor of the dining-room and hall is mosaic. The dining-room will accommodate 850 persons at one time and the house has accommodations for 750 people. The whole place is said to have cost between two and three millions I can describe it to you better when home.[36]

The Ponce de Leon had been built five years before by Henry Flagler (1830–1913), a rival railroad baron and land developer—and an associate of John D. Rockefeller. Flagler sought to make an American Riviera of Florida's east coast. The Ponce de Leon was claimed as the finest hotel in the country. "At a time when resort hotels, from Maine to California were furnished with a standard brass bed, a rocking chair, a dresser, a wash basin, and a chamber pot, the Ponce offered the luxury of Babylon." The Ponce de Leon was one of the wonders of an age in which the display of wealth had become a condition of its acquisition. Its design "combined

---

35. David Leon Chandler, *The Astonishing Life and Times of the Visionary Robber Baron who Founded Florida* (New York: Macmillan, 1986), 104, 126.

36. CHW, in Jacksonville, Fla., to her "darling parents," JHW and GLW, in Waterbury, 26 March 1890. Unreasonably self-conscious of her penmanship, she instructed them to "Do not let any one see this."

Moorish and Renaissance influences within a Spanish motif for the building's exterior." The structure occupied four and a half acres; the lobby contained a rotunda three stories high. The concrete mix was unique, one part concrete to six parts of local coquina shell, an innovation of which Flagler was proud, as it greatly reduced the need to ship concrete from the north.[37]

Beginning their return trip home, the party stopped at the Highland Park Hotel at Aiken, South Carolina, which Carrie knew her parents had visited when she was a baby.

When we at last arrived here it almost seemed like home. We have two large rooms on the first floor facing the verandah in the long hall. The chamber maid who has lived here ever since the second year the hotel was opened says she remembers you and the babies her name is Sarah, she told me Julia is married and has children.[38]

This place is perfect and I have improved here more than any other place. Auntie and I take long walks together through these lovely forests. Once in a while we stop at some old shanty and have a long conversation with some old member of the family. Down in the grove there is a cabin occupied by an aged couple, we call them Uncle George and Auntie they are very interesting. I bought 3 bottles of blackberry wine of "Auntie" which we all drink and enjoy. This afternoon we are going to bring them some crackers. Granpa has hired a pair of horses, a two seated carriage, and coachman. We drive twice a day and such fun it is to go through the pine woods. Tomorrow morning Truda and I are going out horse-back, with the coachman, he is young [and is going] to get me a riding skirt and Truda is going to wear my red skirt with one of her waists. We are not very stylish, but who cares. Do not worry as we have perfectly gentle horses.[39]

---

37. Chandler, *The Astonishing Life and Times*, 102, 104, 110, 128, 136; Edward N. Akin, *Flagler: Rockefeller Partner and Florida Baron* (Kent, Ohio: Kent State Univ. Press, 1988), 122. The hotel was closed in 1967 and is now the site of Flagler College. Ibid., 234; John D. Rockefeller visited St. Augustine with his ailing wife in the 1880s. In 1885 Henry M. Flagler bought the narrow gauge railroad from Jacksonville to St. Augustine and converted it to standard gauge. He soon after built the Ponce de Leon and Alcazar hotels in that city and in later years extended the railroad south, reaching West Palm Beach in 1894, where he built the Breakers and Royal Poinciana, the last of which Julia and George would later visit. Peter T. Maiken, *Night Trains* (Chicago: Lakem Press, 1989), 135.

38. CHW, in Aiken, S.C., to JHW and GLW, in Waterbury, 9 April 1890.

39. CHW, at the Highland Park Hotel in Aiken, S.C., to JHW and GLW, in Waterbury, 9 April 1890.

Julia sent a loving note on the eve of Carrie's birthday, telling of parties and Easter Sunday Morning when the family went "to St. John's [Episcopal]—The church looked lovely & the music was excellent—Pa-pa said it was the best we ever heard in town. In the evening we went to the First [Congregational]—The music there, was I thought a little worse than usual—" Carrie replied,

> I was so glad to receive your lovely letter as I thought you had given up writing me. I, as well as you, felt rather blue to be away from home on my birthday. I always like to be with Papa and you on such occasions. But I had as happy a day as I could with out you. Auntie and Truda gave me a box of Huyter's mixed chocolates. Grandpa a lovely pine needle basket. Grandma a pair of blue glasses and our wash woman, whose birthday is on the same day, sent me some sweet flowers. I sent her a pretty china pitcher, Auntie also gave Truda and me the treat of a horse back ride. I borrowed a riding habit from a lady uptown which fitted me very well. We went for six or seven miles and today am a little lame but never enjoyed any thing more. I am going again soon. We take the loveliest drives I ever saw through woods and bushes.

Soon it was time to take the train to Washington, New York, and home.

The following summer (1890) George was in Paris (evidently on tour with a group—Julia was at home). He was dazzled by the city, fully restored after its destruction in the Commune and in its *belle époque* as the city of light. Carrie had written him, and his reply showed his affection for her. He was days away from his thirty-ninth birthday when he wrote her from the Eiffel Tower, a wonder of the world, then only one year old.

> Here I am at the summit of this most wonderful structure, and as you were such a good girl as to be the first of my little chicks to write me, I thought this place would be a fitting place to answer it and altho it will be hastily and poorly written, you can keep it as a souvenir of my trip here. I am now 863 feet about the Earth and overlooking one of the most beautiful cities in the world. . . . I have enjoyed my stay here very much and only wish I had a month to stay. I could spend a week in the Louvre and Luxembourg art galleries which Mama can describe to you better than I. The weather has been beautiful. We have had a guide most of the time and find it much the best plan. Yesterday (Sunday) we went by coach to the Castle of Versailles. The 14th of July is a grand fete day in France like our 4th of July, celebrating the formation of the Republic. There was a wonderful review of troops, some 75,000, magnificent decorations, fire works etc. We were sent here to see it, but yesterday the festivities continued at Versailles, and the wonderful Fountains

were all turned on making a grand effect. In the evening at 9 o'clock one of the grandest sights I ever witnessed, was presented. 200 jets of water were let on, and on one side of the Lake a beautiful illumination of orchard colored lights with fireworks of the most expensive and elaborate description was set off. There must have been 500,000 people there. We drove back by star light reaching home at 12 o'clock and so I am jogging about at all hours and in all directions. I stand it pretty well but don't get as much rest as I might.

. . . I think of you so many many times a day, and your sweet faces greet me every time I enter my room, and I am so proud of them that I show them to every one.[40]

The Death of Luther Chapin White

In early April 1893 Luther died suddenly at home, news of which quickly spread. "The public was startled yesterday by the announcement of the sudden death of Luther C. White of the firm of White & Wells, and president of the L. C. White company," the newspaper reported. "Mr. White had partaken of breakfast with the members of his family and had remained in his chair a few moments when suddenly he gasped and almost instantly expired."[41] Dr. Axtelle wrote simply "Apoplexy, Instant death" on the death certificate.[42]

Carrie recalled being called from Grove Street to look at the scene at the breakfast table, with its frozen moment between life and death. In the midst of carving a roast beef Luther's hands gripped his favorite carving knife and fork with handles made of reindeer antler bone. It was a tableau in a Victorian illustration: the body of the patriarch pitched forward onto the table, the widow in tears, his son respectful, and the grandchildren awed and fearful. Carrie was close to her grandfather, as we know from their travels together, and she remembered him fondly to this grandson.

---

40. GLW, at Sommet de la Tour Eiffel, Paris, to CHW, in Waterbury, 17 July 1890. The marvel this structure inspired at the time of George's visit may be intimated by Baedeker's near-contemporaneous description: "The Eiffel Tower was built in rather less than two years (July 1887–May 1889). The enormous structure is the loftiest monument in the world, attaining a height of 954 feet or not far short of twice the height (555 ft) of the Washington Column at Washington (the tower of Ulm cathedral is 528 ft, Cologne 511 ft, Rouen 492 ft, Grand Pyramid 440 ft, St. Paul's in London 404 ft). At the same time it is an interesting specimen of bold and accurate skill in design and of the marvelous scientific precision of modern engineering. . . ." *Paris and Environs, also Routes from London to Paris: Handbook for Travellers* (Leipzig, 1894), 272.

41. *Waterbury Daily Republican*, 6 April 1893, 3.

42. Deaths, 3:302, Waterbury VS.

Luther left an estate valued at $259,247 (equivalent to $4.79 million, modern) but left no will.[43] The real property that passed to his widow, George, and Harriet consisted of the Prospect Street house and several lots in Waterbury. There was land valued at $10,000 in Hartford, "land and stores" in Middletown (where he had worked as a young man) worth $30,000, and a factory and building in Waterbury (used by White & Wells and L. C. White & Co.) valued at $78,000. He had made only a modest investment in stocks other than those of his own companies, 253 shares of Western Strawboard Company being the largest. His horses and carriages were valued at $1,600.

George carried on the management and ownership of L. C. White and White & Wells. Jane Amelia remained in the Prospect Street house until her death six years later. She was cared for by the Irish domestics, Thomas O'Connor, the coachman (who lived above the stable at the back of the property) and the maids, Nora Lahey, and Mrs. Nellie O'Connell, people who meant so much to the lives of those they served, but who are often silent in history.[44]

A Business Trip

In the summer after his father's death, George wrote Carrie, who was visiting the Winter family, now moved to Newton, Mass. (The envelope is edged in black.) He was about to go west on behalf of White & Wells, and, though he does not mention it, the country was in the midst of the "silver panic" of 1893, brought about by a run on the banks by speculators concerned that the country was about to adopt a silver standard. The stock market had crashed in May. The banking crisis was averted in short order, but the economy of the U.S. and Europe languished for the next four years.[45] It was the longest and deepest economic depression of his adult life, but George's finances seem to have weathered it without great strain.

---

43. "Estate of Luther Chapin White," Estate Records, 62:55–56, Inventory, Waterbury Probate Court.

44. Listed in claims against the estate for small sums, presumably for wages due. "Estate of Jane Amelia White," Claims against the Estate, 1 April 1899, Waterbury Probate Dist., file 8749, RG 4, Records of the Probate Courts, State Archives, CSL.

45. Hugh Rockoff, "Banking and Finance 1789–1914," in *The Cambridge Economic History of the United States, The Long Nineteenth Century*, ed. Stanley L. Ingerman and Robert E. Gallman (Cambridge: Cambridge Univ. Press, 2000), 2:643–84, 2:669–70.

In a rare mention of business in the family letters, George revealed he was under pressure:

> Mama is sick abed with a terrible headache—in fact she has been almost sick for a week—and th [large ink blot] (How [   ] like a fountain pen)—to resume—and this fact accounts for my writing you. You know how lazy I am on Sundays and I feel tired out today having had a pretty hard week it including a trip to New York Thursday and Friday. I am about crazed by the accidents to machinery in the mill, and you may consider yourself very fortunate in being away from home. I am too cross and ugly to live with. I am called west to a straw board meeting in Gas City on Thursday next and shall probably leave here on Tuesday. I shall stop at Niagara Falls on my return and may hire a new superintendent there. [Then recently-founded, the aptly named Gas City is in central Indiana (near Marion); sources of natural gas were discovered on farmland there in 1887.][46]
>
> I shall be within 130 miles from Chicago, when in Gas City and I may run out there for a couple of days and look at the buildings. Willie is teasing to go with me, but it would be a foolish waste of money to take him out there for so short a time. Perhaps if my ship comes in we may all be able to go out there in October . . .
>
> You don't know how much we miss you and I know poor Mama is awfully lonesome without you. Aunt Hattie & baby [Katharine White, born 3 August 1892 at New Haven] are quite well. I think she is going to the Cottage [Leetes Island, Guilford, Connecticut] very soon. Truda and Uncle Lynde [Harrison] are there (at the Cottage) today. The boys are both well. Don't wear out your welcome but come home some time to Your loving Pop Ginhwhibi.[47]

George's "look at buildings," meant a visit to the White City of the Columbian Exposition, an "enthralling reality of classical grandeur." Just as he had wanted to travel the intercontinental railroad after its completion, he sought to be one of the tens of thousands of Americans who, after a visit, "proudly felt that their culture had come of age."[48] In subsequent years the City Beautiful movement inspired in part by the Columbian

---

46. After gas was discovered a city of six thousand people grew up in the space of five years, but by the mid 1890s the population declined as the gas supply ran out. *Indiana: A Guide to the Hoosier State,* Writer's Program, Works Progress Administration (New York: Oxford Univ. Press, 1941), 448.

47. GLW, in Waterbury, to CHW, in Newton, Mass., [summer] 1893.

48. Larzer Ziff, *The American 1890s* (1966; reprint, Lincoln, Nebr.: Univ. of Nebraska Press, Bison Book, 1979), 8.

Exposition would influence the construction of several outstanding buildings in Waterbury along classical lines—in George's lifetime a hotel on the Green and a City Hall, part of Waterbury's own "coming of age."

Another glimpse of George's affection for Carrie came in the summer of 1895 in response to a "sweet and very funny letter" from her in Jefferson, New Hampshire, amid the White Mountains, where she and Jane Amelia had gone to escape the pollen in the moist air of Connecticut. Julia and he had been to New York with Aunt Harriet (Phelps) Brooke, and the two ladies had left from there to stay at the Lake Mohonk Mountain House.[49] The boys had that day ridden their bicycles to New Haven, twenty miles away—it was a time when Americans had discovered the pleasures of bicycling, and this must have been a delightful rural journey. George reported that the veterinarian was due to "operate on Ben's hoof and also treat Baldy," the family's prized horses. George himself was going to Southford, Connecticut, where one of the White & Wells factories was located, "to settle matters with my esteemed brother-in-law and hope for success." (A barb at Judge Harrison's amour-propre recurs in George's correspondence.) "Remember me in your prayers to that end," he concludes.[50]

---

49. GLW, in Waterbury, to CHW, in Jefferson, N.H., 23 July 1895.

50. The meeting must have had to do with settling the L. C. White estate and dividing up the properties between George and his sister, the "esteemed brother-in-law" representing Harriet.

50. Looking up Prospect Street and Hillside from the Green, 1899

The George Luther White house is in the upper right, at the corner of Grove (unlabeled, running horizontally across top of image) and Prospect. The Luther Chapin White house is by Trinity Church, on Prospect, north of the Green.

VII

COMING OF AGE

The steamship lines were carrying Americans out of the various ports of the country at the rate of four or five thousand a week, in the aggregate. If I met a dozen individuals, during that month, who were not going to Europe, shortly, I have no distinct remembrance of it now.

—Mark Twain, *Innocents Abroad*, 1869

Waterbury prosperity allowed Carrie to tour Europe for her coming of age; it was an essential rite of passage for well-to-do Americans as it had been for Julia in that very year in which Mark Twain celebrated his travels. European travel was a credential, but for Carrie it was far more—it was a first acquaintance with art, civic and ecclesiastical monuments, and land-scape. She would repeat the trip in later years, probably the deepest enjoyment of her life.

For her twenty-first birthday in April 1896 George and Julia gave Carrie a tour of Europe, for them the preeminent experience in travel and the "finishing" of a daughter who had reached marriageable age. She sailed in June 1896 on the Bremen-based North-German Lloyd steamer, *Kaiser Wilhelm II*, a relatively small ship of recent construction placed in the New York–Mediterranean service that year.[1] Carrie was well aware that she was following in the steps of her mother, who after her parents' deaths effec-

---

1. This *Kaiser Wilhelm II* was one of four express steamers built by North German Lloyd 1887–90. A smaller ship of the same name had foundered in 1873, and the more famous "four stacker" liner of that name entered service in 1902. *70 Years North German Lloyd Bremen, 1857–1927* (Berlin: Atlantic-Verlag, [1927]), 39, 42; William H. Miller Jr., *The First Great Ocean Liners in Photographs* (New York: Dover Publications, 1984), 9, 92.

tively came of age through the experience of the sights and customs of Europe.[2]

Carrie's accounts of what she did and saw are windows into the experience of Americans touring Europe in the high, late afternoon of Victorian peace and prosperity. Every few years more luxurious and faster transatlantic liners were introduced by highly competitive British and German steamship lines. The country's prosperity meant that more Americans could afford what was becoming an obligatory European tour to acquire culture, polish, or, simply, clothes and ornaments for the home. The persistent theme of Henry James's novels, as a recent commentator put it, was that his "characters use Europe to stand for some combination of social distinction, high culture, eroticism and freedom."[3]

As American cities like Waterbury became manufacturing centers, with coal smoke, tenements, and ugly, crowded streets, Europe's beauty spots became a greater attraction—Carrie was breathless at the sight of Lake Como at Bellagio and enjoyed the Warwickshire countryside with its old cottages and romantic associations. There was mass tourism too, not on a later scale to be sure, but "Cook's Tours" had begun and there was an abundance of hotels awaiting tourists and, as Carrie found in Lucerne, "instant" social settings for them.

Woolett in James's *The Ambassadors*, the hometown of the gentle Strether, whose firm manufactured an "unmentionable object," was surely in the author's imagination a place like nineteenth-century Waterbury, whose products formed a spectrum of the mundane. It was in Europe that Strether found complexity, beauty, and a greater depth of experience than at home. Through it he learned the advice given to his young relative, "Live all you can, it's a mistake not to."[4] While Carrie had no such revelation, she deeply enjoyed on this first of several trips to Europe, breathing in its complexity, beauty, and history.

Travelers in this era had an opinionated and highly knowledgeable guide in the "Travelers' Handbooks, compact to hold and to pack," pub-

2. "The whole enterprise of European travel by nineteenth-century Americans was intimately associated . . . with the construction of a privileged bourgeoisie in the context of an ostensibly classless society." William W. Stowe, *European Travel in Nineteenth-Century American Culture* (Princeton: Princeton Univ. Press, 1994), xi.

3. Ibid., x.

4. Henry James, *The Ambassadors*, ed. Christopher Butler, ed. (1903; Oxford: Oxford Univ. Press, 1983), 153.

lished by the firm of Karl Baedeker in Leipzig. The first was produced by the eponymous Baedeker (1804–56) in the 1840s and 50s, and by the 1890s, under his son, there were guides for every region of Europe and much of North America. In densely printed pages Baedeker provided information on transportation, weather, money, local customs, lists of the contents of museums, historical references for monuments (and judgments as to their merits), and advice on dealing with the native inhabitants, toward whom wariness was often suggested, particularly as pertaining to importunate demands. Thoroughness was the publisher's approach, and the same was expected of the traveler. In the guides the middle-class traveler had at hand what only a professional scholar or local guide could have known.[5]

Mary Burrall, Carrie's schoolmate (and intimate friend throughout their long lives), joined her on her journey. "Mary Burrall is a dandy," Carrie wrote her mother early in the trip, "and there is a lot to her. She and I have no fear of not being companionable and it is simply because we are independent and say and do just as we like."[6] She wrote her father that she "keeps me on the laugh most of the time. She is so witty and can recite anything from psalms to Shakespeare."[7] The two young women were escorted by Miss M. L. McKay—we never learn her given name—a veteran chaperone from near Boston, knowledgeable in what to see and in making arrangements. Carrie described her as "really wonderful. She seems so nervous and confused sometimes and talks away to herself and yet, there is nothing she's not equal to, always gets ahead of any man, plans everything to the dot, and is so dear to us all."[8] Miss Leonard, a friend of Miss McKay—again no first name—also accompanied them for most of the trip, attracting admirers wherever the party went.

Schooling done, the young ladies were to be exposed to the artistic treasures of Europe and learn its manners, understood to be more refined than those at home. The exclusive little party traveled in a modest level of luxury: they ate agreeably at communal tables in the hotels, and they

---

5. Karl Baedeker began publishing the guides from his printing shop in Essen, modeling them after those of John Murray of England. His son Fritz carried on the business from Leipzig and developed them over the years to "cover the greater part of the civilized world." *Enc. Brit*, s.v. "Baedeker, Karl."

6. CHW, at the Schwertzenhof, Lucerne, to JHW, in Waterbury, 4 July 1896.

7. CHW, at Hotel Victoria, Interlaken, to GLW, in Waterbury, 20 July 1896.

8. CHW, in Lugano, to JHW, 8 July 1896.

stayed in pensions in London and Paris, but on railways and steamers they traveled first class. They were diligent tourists, attentive to museums, famous vistas and monuments, and spectacles in theaters and opera houses. Carrie shared her reactions with her parents as she went along, just as Julia must have done with her Aunt Kate twenty-five years before (and as Carrie's daughter would with her, thirty years later). Carrie remembered what Julia had told her of her own trip at seventeen and was aware that her parents had visited many of the places she did. There was a sense of shared experience, and she was certainly aware that she was living her own role in a continuing family story.

A century later, coming of age for women younger than Carrie and Mary Burrall meant independent travel with a backpack, frequent moves, usually in mixed company. The scrupulous chaperonage of Miss McKay (who at one hotel would not allow her charges to go to the lobby unescorted) framed the experience. Within that frame Carrie enjoyed a great deal and learned much. She was an attentive, responsive traveler, only occasionally seeming somewhat tired of sightseeing, but for the most part responding appreciatively to the landscape, pictures, buildings that she saw, and places such as the Mme. Laurent's pension in Paris, where she met the son who was an actor and a Japanese diplomat.

The Carrie revealed in her letters is an attentive, affectionate, deeply appreciative person, open to experience, but conservative. She was no future heiress on the lookout or wanting to leap out of the frame. As Julia told her, "There can be no mistake dear—you are not a 'fin de siècle' girl—but one of the good 'old fashioned kind'—dropped in again somehow from the first half of the Century."[9] There is sweetness in her sense of values, love of parents and her brothers, of her country (even when observing less than estimable behavior by fellow American tourists), cooperation with her traveling companions, and good humor.

The voyage across was agreeable in a friendly ship:

We are due at Giberalter at 6 A.M. and it has been reported that we are to remain there for ten hours, but I am not sure of that. I will cable and mail this there.

How many times we have thought of one another and wonder if all was going well. I only hope that you all have been as happy as I. Such a voyage as we have had! I have been perfectly well, slept a great deal and eaten every-

---

9. JHW, in Waterbury, to CHW, in Paris, 28 July 1896.

thing. Everyone says I look like a different person. I have had just a taste of sea sickness. It came on after leaving the Azores and was very rough from Friday night until an hour ago. We have met a great many lovely people and are as one happy family. . . .

The ship is as clean as can be and the table and service fine. I enjoy so much seeing the waiters file in with each course and at the same time the music strikes up. As to the Captain, I have lost my heart, especially with the rear view as he promenades the deck.

Miss McKay is lovely and likes me I think—We are all congenial and are bound to have an ideal trip.[10]

The party and the other passengers enjoyed the familiar shipboard customs. Carrie wrote her father: "The night before reaching Naples, the Captain's dinner was given and we all had the jolliest kind of time. Speeches and toasts were made by several to the Captain, he responded sweetly, and the decorations, music, procession of waiters etc. made us all feel that we loved the *Kaiser Wilhelm II* and his Captain."[11]

Carrie wrote her mother from "strange, mysterious and fascinating" Gibraltar:

We reached the rock about eight in the morning and were on shore from eight-thirty until eleven o'clock.[12] I don't suppose there is another such fortification in the world and R. H. Davis says in his article, that no one but the governor himself, knows all the secrets and arrangement of the underground passages and hidden guns. The streets are filled with English officers and women, Spaniards, Moors and Africans, shouting and pushing to sell flowers, eggs, and fresh vegetables. Tiny donkeys laden with saddle bags, are sliding all over, and I can't begin to describe the effect. The garden is beautiful, with [ ] of purple morning glories and great bushes of heliotrope, [ ] and palms. The streets are very narrow and hilly and are paved with a soft limestone of a whitish color, the houses are stucco with fancy tiled roofs and everything most picturesque and glaring. As we sailed away, the great mountain of rock with the Mediterranean coloured in some places deep blue and in others strips of bright green dotted over with mountainous ships and boats of all kinds, made a picture never to be forgotten.

---

10. CHW, in Gibraltar, on board the *Kaiser Wilhelm II*, to GLW and JHW, in Waterbury, 28 June 1896.

11. CHW, at the Hôtel de Londres, Geneva, to GLW, in Waterbury, 5 July 1896.

12. CHW, in Gibraltar to JHW, in Waterbury, 30 June 1896.

Am I too flowery! But it is all so new and glamorous. The mountains on the coast of Spain and France were distinctly in view until sundown and the sun setting just over the snow capped peaks and pink clouds!!! It is very warm and as smooth as a lake and everyone is well and happy and yet, if you all might be here too, then this would be divine . . .

Waterbury is present in these letters, too—news of friends and family from home, met abroad, and, notably, the death of its leading manufacturer, Augustus Sabin Chase, whose daughter, Alice, had been Carrie's and Mary Burrall's schoolmate and friend.

Death of Augustus Sabin Chase

In Gibraltar Carrie found a letter from Alice Chase, her schoolmate, who had been in Paris with the family when her father, Augustus Sabin Chase, died of a chronic kidney infection at the age of fifty-eight. The loss of one of its most prominent manufacturers in his prime was a major event in Waterbury. Chase, like Luther Chapin White and most of the men who developed the factories that flourished after the Civil War, had come from country towns, in his case, Pomfret, in rural eastern Connecticut. At twenty-one, in 1859, he came to work as a bank clerk in Waterbury. From that lowly position he came, over the next thirty-seven years, to have controlling interests in the venerable Benedict & Burnham, the Waterbury Clock Co., the Waterbury Buckle Co., and the Waterbury Manufacturing Company. He founded the Waterbury National Bank and had his hand in smaller enterprises.[13] The country lad who prospered in the new industrial world of the city had almost epic standing in the Waterbury of his day. In its editorial the *Republican* equated his success not only with native aptitude but with Christianity itself:

> Born on a Connecticut farm and possessing no advantages which are not the property of any country boy who is equipped with a vigorous ancestry and who has a sound mind in a sound body, Mr. Chase was an admirable exponent of the possibilities of Honourable and self-won success under American institutions, and he illustrated the principle of progress, enunciated twenty centu-

---

13. Joseph Anderson, ed., *The Town and City of Waterbury, Connecticut, from the Aboriginal Period to the Year Eighteen Hundred and Ninety-Five*, 3 vols. (New Haven: Price and Lee, 1896), 2:308–310.

ries ago, that he who is faithful over a few things may be made ruler over many things.[14]

Chase was an investor in the *Republican,* and that paper certainly reflected the views of the manufacturers, but it was also re-celebrating the myth of success in Waterbury: the country lad who combined a keen business sense with public spirit—commitment to the public weal of developing Waterbury through charity and help to other businesses. The writer praised Chase's acumen, respect for the many employees, and his charity, "administered with appropriate modesty." "[N]o one was ever quicker than he to recognize and appreciate fidelity and industry and intellectual worth in his subordinates." (One of these was Henry Lawton Wade, another country boy, who, following the myth's outline, had risen to head Chase's Waterbury Clock Company. He had recently built a house on Prospect Street and in eight years his elder daughter would marry Will White.) "To seek office was foreign to his nature, but his interest in public questions, whether local or general, never lagged." The editorial concluded about Chase, "Waterbury he loved; its people he respected; and its possibilities were an article of faith with him." This was the ethos of Waterbury at the end of the century: made by men of native acumen and virtue, public spirited and generous, displaying wealth tastefully, confident of the progress of prosperity and refinement in their city. His sons would bring the New York architect Cass Gilbert to the city early in the next century to design what remains the most distinguished grouping of public buildings in the city.

Augustus Chase and his family were at the top of the local social pyramid. He was a founder of the Waterbury Club ("to promote social intercourse among men of business"),[15] and founder and president of the board of St. Margaret's School. Since 1889, he and his family had lived at Rose Hill, the "Gothic Cottage" (discussed above, in chapter 5) set back on its own large lot on Prospect Street—he expanded the house to closer to its present shape. The younger Whites passed it daily to and from the Green.

Little wonder that his death resonated to the travelers across the Atlantic quite apart from their friendship with Alice. On the day of the funeral the workers in the Chase factories marched to Rose Hill to pay

---

14. *Daily Republican* [Waterbury], 8 June 1896.

15. Organized in 1881. Anderson, *Town and City of Waterbury*, 2:484.

their respects, an example of the almost feudal sense of bond between worker and owner at the time. Julia and George evidently considered it inappropriate to gather with the crowd at Rose Hill, as we learn later, but since they lived only a few doors away, they would have been well aware of the gathering. Julia sent Carrie the newspaper's account of the solemn occasion:

> The residence and grounds were thrown open and there was a large gathering, which included associates in many commercial and manufacturing interests, former employees, their wives and children and residents in general. Many were massed on the lawn, from which point the speakers, standing in the south end of the hall running through the residence, could be heard. A body of former employees of Mr. Chase from the Waterbury Manufacturing company marched to the funeral in a body as a mark of respect. hundreds were standing about the grounds, and the line reached down the walk to Prospect Street, where a considerable body of people had gathered, extending down toward the green, at which place another body of several hundred assembled.
>
> The body rested in the sitting room, on the east side of the house, in front of the fire place. Over the fire place and the casket hung an excellent portrait of Mr. Chase, painted by Mrs. Frederick S. Chase [Elsie (Rowland) Chase, daughter-in-law] while Mr. Chase was abroad, and designed for presentation to him upon his return home. The flowers on the bier consisted of a large and handsome garland of beech leaves, and in addition a few pansies and fleur-de-lis from Rose Hill.[16]

Naples

While Waterbury celebrated its most prominent manufacturer, Carrie was in Naples. She wrote George ("My darling father") about that experience.

> How can I describe the Bay of Naples and the city itself!! We entered the bay about five o'clock on July Second and it is well said "See Naples and Die" or, better, live. It was a little hazy over the top of Vesuvius so that the crater and smoke could not be distinguished but when we sailed away the sight was grand—We were on land for about eight hours and saw in that time much that will never be forgotten. I believe I said that nothing could equal Gibraltar but the general effect of the streets with their pink, white, and green houses with little flower-covered balconies, the terrible looking beggars, the [ ] and

---

16. Clipping, *Waterbury American*, July 1896, JHW MSS.

flower girls, the gaily dressed women all wear their hair exactly as Calvé does, makes a picture that I have often heard and read of but which no one who has not seen can appreciate. . . . [Carrie had evidently seen Emma Calvé at the Metropolitan Opera; Carmen and Santuzza were two of her most famous roles and ones in which her hair style might match that of the colorful Italian women.][17]

I shall always be thankful. For even those few hours at Naples because even though we could not see everything, just to see the streets and people was to me the greatest kind of a truth.[18]

To Genoa

Miss McKay chose not to trust the trains to reach Genoa and booked the party there by steamer, which turned out to be a rough journey of twenty-one hours. Carrie was delighted with the commercial city, not a usual stop on the tourist route of the time. "Its situation, rising above the sea in a wide semi-circle and its numerous palaces, justly entitles it to the epithet 'La Superba,'" declared Baedeker of Genoa. "To the student of art the Renaissance palaces of the Genoese nobility are objects of extreme interest, surpassing in number and magnificence those of any other city in Italy."[19] Carrie found it "so beautiful—This hotel is quaint, our rooms have mosaic floors, beds and Italian windows draped in white muslin and all lighted in the evening by candles in high sticks. It is all such a romance. The [ ] palaces and houses look exactly like stage scenery."

They went by rail to Milan about which Baedeker told them that "[n]o town in Italy has undergone such marked improvement since the events of 1859—In the province of Art it has raised itself to the highest rank in the kingdom . . . Sculpture is carried on to such an extent as to qualify as a

17. The appearances of Emma Calvé (1868–1942) at the Metropolitan Opera House in New York in the 1890s evoked great enthusiasm. "Her voice—a luscious, finely trained soprano, with the addition of strong chest-notes and some very pure high notes (originally extending to high F), the secret of which she claimed to have learnt from Dominico Mustafili, the Italian castrato who became director of the Sistine College Choir—derived a peculiar charm from its combination of absolute steadiness with rich color . . . As an interpreter she was intensely dramatic and impulsive, to the point of capriciousness in later life." *The New Grove*, s.v. "Calvé, Emma" (3:629).

18. CHW, at the Hôtel de Londres, Geneva, to GLW, in Waterbury, 5 July 1896.

19. K. Baedeker, *Northern Italy* (Leipzig, 1892), 60–61.

separate industry..."[20] In addition to visiting the cathedral ("fascinating and inspiring") and the much altered *Last Supper*, Miss McKay took the girls to the Galleria Vittorio Emmanuele, whose urbanity Carrie declared "great fun, so public and so improper!"[21]

Como and the Lakes

After the train ride from Milan to Bellagio on Lake Como Carrie wrote that she was "almost too full for utterance."[22] With a stimulating trip through the railroad tunnels and by stage over the St. Gothard pass, Carrie reached Lucerne, a favorite spot for tourists in this high point of late romantic interest in the Swiss lakes and mountains, which Carrie found "fascinating and cosmopolitan." It was crowded with people from many nations, but Carrie found the Americans there "terrors with only a few exceptions . . . I must confess that I am anything but proud of America's representatives." (Baedeker had a warning for Lucerne visitors. "It must also be admitted that the estimation in which establishments are held varies very much with the temperament of the visitors themselves. Some are more exacting than others, give orders totally at variance with the customs of the country, and express great dissatisfaction if their wishes are not immediately complied with, the unreasonableness of which requires no comment.")[23]

Carrie wished that George Du Maurier, the novelist and illustrator, "would run in for a few days and make some sketches of the mob. My! but they're killing! English, French, German, and the tough Americans. It is almost impossible for me to eat my dinners. There is so much that entertains me at the long tables." Communal meals meant mixing and observing, a pastime lost in the exclusive tables in latter-day hotels. There were limits, however, as "Miss McKay is a careful chaperone here and will not allow us to be alone down stairs."

The veteran chaperone was on look out, doubtless, for adventurers and was put on guard by Le Baron de König of Austria, sixty, with an ad-

---

20. Baedeker, *Northern Italy* (Leipzig, 1913), 92.

21. The Galleria Vittorio Emmanuele, built 1845–47, was "the most spacious and attractive structure of the kind in Europe." Ibid., 93, 95, 159.

22. CHW, in Lugano, to JHW, 8 July 1896.

23. Baedeker, *Switzerland* (1867), xix.

Coming of Age

51. Letterhead of the Hôtel Grande Bretagne, Bellagio, 1896

venurous past and fresh from lion-hunting in Africa when he left flowers
for the McKay party, which led to a further (distant) entanglement for
Carrie.

The day before yesterday in the afternoon, four bunches of lily of the valley
were sent without any name, and the number of both rooms, to Miss McKay's
room. Dr. Carmichael, Miss Leonard's admirer, had been with her nearly all
day but had departed from town. Miss M. thought the flowers were from him
and Miss L. felt sure as in one bunch was a red rose and she had once told Dr.
C. that she was fond of red roses. After a little discussion as to there being no
card, they decided that it had probably been lost. Miss L. gave us each a bouquet and pinned the one with the rose over her heart. I was rather late that
evening and so forgot to wear my flowers to dinner. The others all wore
theirs. Yesterday afternoon someone knocked here. I opened the door and a
package was handed in by a French girl, three bouquets of carnations and one
of roses with the (enclosed) note. Well, I thought Mary and I would die. We
literally shouted, poor Miss L. turned purple, and our chaperone nearly had a
fit. Perhaps I wasn't tickled! Was it not like a book that such good luck as my
not wearing them should have happened!

We all suspect, in fact know who the sender is. No more or less a personage
than Le Baron de König, of Austria. This elegant creature sits directly opposite me at table and I wish I might be able to sketch him. He has large whiskers, very much like Du Maurier's Taffy's, rather good figure, has been an
Austrian officer since eighteen and is now about sixty. From what I have heard
at the table and from a man who sees much of him, his history as he tells it is

most remarkable. At eighteen he went to America and fought on our side in the Civil War, married a Virginia girl who deserted him three weeks after, was disinherited by his father for marrying, is now attempting to get his estate from his brother on friendly terms, has just come from Africa where he hunts lions (and women). Is not this quite enough!

But he is killing, wears a yellow tie with his dress coat etc. That I should resemble any of his dead is sad to say the least. He converses very politely and in broken English but I have never recognized him away from the table and have been no more than civil at it. My position last evening was just a little trying but I acted exactly as though nothing had occurred. Was not that best? Miss M. says she had been suspicious all the time but we feel that we have been very dignified and simply take it as a rich joke.

I hope you will not think it silly of me to write so much about the "Baron" but I would give a good deal if you could see and hear him. He is really very interesting and very amusing. Mary can impersonate him to perfection.[24]

Du Maurier's Taffy, to whom Carrie compared the Baron, "was a very big young man, fair, with kind but choleric blue eyes, and the muscles of his brawny arms were strong as iron hands . . . He was good-looking, but I regret to say that, besides his heavy plunger's moustache, he wore an immense pair of drooping auburn whiskers, of the kind that used to be called Piccadilly weepers. . . ."[25] The baron's beard was not auburn at sixty, perhaps, but if he cut a figure like the tall and emphatic Taffy, he would have made a stir in the hotel dining room.

The Baron's note reads as follows:

You did not wear any bouquet yesterday, although the bouquet with a rose was intended for you. You cannot imagine what pleasure you will give the sender if you will only wear to-night the rose which accompanys this note.

Inasmuch as you will never know who sends it there can be no possible objection to wearing it, as the writer only wishes to recall to his mind the memories of one now long dead, whom you so strikingly resemble.[26]

"You seem to catch the antiques, do you not my dear?" was Julia's comment, terming the Baron's missive at first as a "*pathetic* little note, but soft-

24. CHW, at the Schwertzenhof, Lucerne, to JHW, in Waterbury, 4 July 1896.

25. George du Maurier, *Trilby* (1894; New York: Dover Publications, 1994), 2–3. *DNB*, s.v. "du Maurier, George."

26. The small envelope was not addressed, but an inked notation on the back has "223/229," evidently the room numbers for the party, and the notation in Julia's hand, "Lucerne, July 1896."

ened a bit as she thought of it. "With my *sympathetic* nature, perhaps I should have been tempted to wear the roses, but am glad you have such a sensible little head of your own & such a careful chaperone. Still there is something touching about the note— . . . I will keep the note to be preserved as a trophy by you. I only wish he had put his name & title at the bottom. . . ."[27] Julia added, "Mr. Chase is to be buried to-day. They arrived in Wby Sunday night—(did I write you that before?) It seemed strange that the very paper—*The American*—that announced your & the parties arrival at Gibraltar—had also the announcement of Alice's (or the family's) arrival in Waterbury—it seemed like the 'Irony of Fate'—Poor child—I wrote her just a few lines last evening—They say the family, every one—is braving it so bravely—of course Lucy [Burrall] will write Mary all about it."

Other news from Waterbury was tranquil. Young George, "Jimmy," did well on his Latin and other exams setting him up to go to Yale; "Billie," was another matter—not attentive, not a good student. Julia's evocation of the family on that warm summer night induced a touch of homesickness in Carrie. "We are sitting out on the piazza—It is very warm. George ["Jimmie"] is playing softly on his mandolin. *He does play so well*—& Billie is reading."[28] George Sr. wrote a few days later. He knew Carrie appreciated his waggish sense of humor and affection. Remembering Lucerne as a lively place, he asked Carrie to "jump on the Lion's tail for me, and sing 'America,'" but not to "move into the first "American Bar" she saw.[29]

Carrie responded to her father from Interlaken, approved of by Baedeker as "deservedly a point of attraction to visitors from all parts of Europe . . . many . . . select it as a resting-place for their enjoyment of the magnificent scenery by which it is surrounded, in the intervals between which the strength may be recruited and repose enjoyed."[30]

---

27. JHW, in Waterbury, to CHW, in Paris, 28 July 1896.

28. JHW, in Waterbury to CHW, in Paris, 3 July 1896 (per S.S. *Paris*, addressed to Miss M. L. McKay, Credit Lyonnais, Bd des Italiens, Paris, France 'For Miss White'").

29. GLW, in Waterbury, to CHW, in Paris, 7 July 1896 ("per S.S. *St. Louis*").

30. K. Baedeker, *Switzerland* (Leipzig, 1867), 106. Later he termed Lucerne "a favorite summer-resort, noted for its mild and equable temperature, and is a good starting point for excursions to the Oberland. The chief resort of visitors is the "HOHENWEG, an avenue of old walnuts and planes, extending from the village of Aarmuhle to the upper bridge near the Aare and flanked with large hotels and tempting shops. It commands a beautiful view of the Lauterbrunnen-Thal and the Jungfrau (best by evening light)." K. Baedeker, *Switzerland*, (Leipzig, 1899), 169.

52. Letterhead, Interlaken, 1896

We came on from Lucerne last Friday and were quite brokenhearted to find the weather very disagreeable, cold and rainy. The great question arose, whether to remain for a few days until we should see the Jungfrau and take the time from something else, or go away without having seen the Queen of the Alps. But good luck is with us everywhere, and last evening we walked out from dinner to find the clouds disappeared and the Jungfrau in all the glory of the Alpine glow. Really what could be more divine! It was at first a rose pink, and then, as the light faded, it changed to the purest white, an effect that one might wait for weeks to see and then, not see it. We were all so happy and felt that it was simply for our benefit. Today is glorious and very clear . . .

. . . You would be amused to hear me speak French, German or even Italian (two words) and I am quite surprised at my mathematical ability; it is very easy for me to handle the money though I am not doing so to any great extent.[31]

The party headed north along the Rhine, with a stop in Heidelberg. At the hotel the girls "enjoyed our dinner on our verandah and the beautiful music in the garden nearby," and wondered why such pleasures were not to be had at home. "Why do we Americans never eat out of doors at home? . . . Mary and I have a private verandah in the garden, the dearest garden with beautiful trees, walks and beds of brilliant flowers. We sat out

---

31. CHW, at Hotel Victoria, Interlaken, to GLW, in Waterbury, 20 July 1896.

until late last night in the moonlight, *drinking* [   ] and listening to the
music and all so exclusive that Miss M. sat in her night robe, outside our
door."[32] From Heidelberg the party traveled to Wiesbaden, to Frankfurt,
and by boat down the Rhine to Cologne and, ultimately, to Amsterdam,
where there "so few blue-blooded natives to be seen . . . the larger part of
the population being Jews, and we being there on Sunday, that I met not
one of my ancestors or their relatives. Give me the Hague every time!"[33]

The party traveled via Antwerp to Paris where they stayed at a pension, so there were other guests to meet and observe, and many opportunities to hear French spoken. They stayed longer there than in any other
place on the tour. Within hours of their setting in to the pension, Carrie
concluded that the "living here is to be a great experience for us."

My first meal in the dining room [at the pension, 86 Ave. Klêber, closer to the
Étoile than the Trocadero on that avenue, very much in the new Paris of
Haussmann] was luncheon today. The room is quite small and only one table
at which, besides our party, were Madame Laurent, who runs the establishment, her husband, and daughter. There is a son, age nineteen, very fascinating, a student at Theatre Français, who is to be here for dinner, a German
artist who has had three paintings at the salons, one of which is a portrait of
the daughter, a Japanese, French lady and her son and two American girls.
We are supposed to speak nothing but French (or Japanese) and it's all a
phase of life that I am so glad to know. Our room is large, on the fifth story
and has a balcony over the Avenue from which the Arc de Triumph may be
plainly seen. During the day it is made up as a sitting room and is really very
comfortable and pretty. It is such a delight to unpack everything and really
settle down for what seems a long time.

Like others before and since Carrie considered "this part of the world is
much more attractive and the people all seem happier and not so driven-
to-death." Over the next three weeks in Paris the young women enjoyed
the open omnibuses and the crowds and learned how to shop under their
chaperone's tutelage. ("Miss McKay has started out by teaching us the
general plan of everything so that we may be able to go about without her
if we wish to. We have been to Le Bon Marché once only. I bought a fine
pair of gloves and a lovely light silk petticoat for seven dollars.") She and

---

32. CHW in Heidelberg, to JHW, in Waterbury, 22 July 1896.
33. CHW, in Paris, to JHW, in Waterbury, 30 July 1896.

Mary visited the Louvre twice in that first week and "attended service in the Russian Church in honor of the ex-Czarina, and her brother, the Crown Prince of Denmark was there in full view. . . . When we have any distances to go we ride on the top of a train or omnibus which, though not-at-all elegant, is great fun. And a dandy place from which to observe Vanity Fair. We also walk a good deal and are to take some drives."[34]

At the pension the proprietor's son and a friend who had studied at the Comédie Française after dinner one night gave a recital to the guests.

[A] few evenings ago Miss McKay ordered champagne for all in honor of Jean's winning second prize at the Theatre Français. There was a friend of his for dinner, a little fellow seventeen years old who won first prize last year. After dinner they recited for us and it was perfectly wonderful to see and hear them. Of course it was all in French but their acting is such that it is not difficult to understand. The Prize was won in the Misanthrope which they acted for us. Friday night we are to have a great treat. We are to see Mounet Sully in Oedipus.[35] We have invited M. Jean to escort us.

Wednesday night Miss Leonard, Mary, M. Jean and I heard Faust. We had seats in a loge, where the view of the audience and décolleté gowns was better than of the stage but I saw every thing I cared to. The staging was great and the orchestra of the best but the singing nothing remarkable. The ballet was, as you might imagine, perfectly wonderful and very Frenchy. When M. Jean goes with us we pay the bills for the sake of having a man.[36]

London

Carrie was delighted to see London for the first time and relieved to be where English was spoken. The party stayed at a version of a pension in Bloomsbury with a number of "uninteresting Americans." Soon after they

---

34. CHW, 85 Ave. Kléber, Paris, to JHW, in Waterbury, 4 Aug. 1896.

35. "Mounet-Sully [1841–1916] was the definitive Oedipus of the 19th-century French stage, a gifted tragedian who played all the major roles, including Hamlet and Lear, but who had a deep personal identification with Oedipus. Enc. Brit., s.v. "Mounet-Sully, Jean."

36. CHW, Paris, to JHW, in Waterbury, 14 Aug. 1896. Faust was then at the height of its popularity; Carrie had surely seen it in New York, where it had been the first opera played at the Metropolitan when it opened on 22 Oct. 1883. The Paris production included the Walpurgisnacht ballet, rarely done in New York, and required a running time of almost five hours. The performance was at the Palais Garnier, the Opéra, opened in 1875. The building's richly decorated façade made it immediately one of the symbols of Paris. There was seating for 2,156; grand as it was, the auditorium was slightly smaller than the Metropolitan. See <www.opera-de-paris.fr/>, accessed 27 May 2001.

arrived, she and Mary "took a long ride through the 'West End' on the top of an omnibus. I like London immensely, of course I have seen very little of it but do not think it so beautiful or clean as Paris. Still, I feel more at home. I prefer clean people to clean streets and the French use all this soap and water in their [   ] and streets."[37] The ever-vigilant Baedeker warned visitors that in "point of comfort the vehicles [omnibuses] still leave much to be desired. Those who travel by omnibus should keep themselves provided with small change to prevent delay and mistakes."[38] Carrie and Mary were not deterred by such advice.

"Mary and I go out alone if we care to and feel that we can be quite independent," Carrie wrote George. "It is surprising how soon one gets the run of such immense cities as Paris and London but I am sure I know Paris better than New York." From the top of an omnibus and on their own they visited the slums of East London. "The whole trip was about twelve miles and interesting, but of course did not take us through the vile side streets were the characteristic life really is, still it was enough to glance into them as we drove by. We sat up near the driver and he pointed out all noteworthy objects, his English was simply killing and many of his remarks as well."[39]

With Miss McKay they went to Windsor to visit "the stables and state apartments, but as the Queen is away and nearly all the horses and carriages with her, and the furniture covered and pushed against the walls, I enjoyed much more the exterior of the castle and the chapels of St. George, and Albert Memorial, which is a gem." After seeing the churchyard that was the setting for Gray's *Elegy* at Stoke Poges, Carrie concluded, "It has been hard to realize that we are still far from home. I feel so very much nearer than when on the Continent."

As the trip neared its end Miss McKay took her charges to Leamington Spa in order to show them some of the Warwickshire countryside. At Leamington they stayed at "a very comfortable & select English boarding house," where "The Americans are . . . much nicer, I imagine, than those we met in London and there are also a number of English women, and my! but they are dull . . . old English women and maids at this house and I

---

37. CHW, at 29 Upper Bedford Place, Tavistock Square, London, to JHW, in Waterbury, 21 Aug. 1896.

38. Karl Baedeker, *London and Its Environs, A Handbook for Travellers* (Leipzig, 1892).

39. CHW, at Langton House, Leamington, Warwickshire, to JHW, in Waterbury, 4 Sept. 1896.

think you would smile. Could you see Mary and me taking four o'clock tea and in the evening playing whist with these lace capped and spectacled ladies..."[40]

In the last letter from home that summer, Julia reported that the boys had bought bicycles, which they rode to Aunt Hattie's at Leetes Island in Guilford, about forty miles on the automobile-free dirt roads of the day. The national bicycling craze prompted even George to buy a "wheel," but we do not hear of it again.

Carrie, Mary, and Miss McKay returned on the S.S. *Lahn*, sister ship to the *Kaiser Wilhelm II*, which picked them up at Southampton en route from Bremen and docked at Hoboken on 24 September. George and Julia went to New York the night before to be on hand to greet them, as Carrie learned in a note carried to the ship by the pilot, another ritual of steamship travel.[41] In Europe, Carrie strengthened her love of its places and arts, a lover she would renew on other visits. The destruction of the 1940s deeply grieved her.

It was to the Grove Street house that Carrie returned. Her unstated role from then on was to meet young men and entertain a proposal of marriage. It was expected of her, but it doubtless made her uncomfortable. If there were beaux in the next years, there is no reference in the letters. (A "Mr. Baldwin" who sent flowers to bid farewell to Carrie when she left on the trip may have been an admirer, but nothing later is heard of him.) Waterbury dances were social duties to her, not pleasures in themselves. It is not even certain that Carrie expected to be married; Mary and Lucy Burrall, her closest friends, remained single. Her two unmarried White cousins, Anna and Mary, were teachers, a possible model for a single life, though Carrie never tried it. She chose to help her mother in the household which, with cook, waitress, chambermaid, and in George's sphere, a coachman and gardener, was challenging to manage, and Julia by her own admission was not good at it. Carrie was. George was right about the inter-dependence of mother and daughter. Carrie became Julia's ever-dependable helper and confidant in the next years. But there would be a proposal, and from a quite unexpected direction.

---

40. Ibid.

41. JHW, in Waterbury, to CHW, on board S.S. Lahn, ca. 23 Sept. 1896.

The Family in the 1900s

By the 1900s the White family had become rich. The revenues from L. C. White & Co. and White & Wells—the two companies George inherited from his father—his share of his mother's estate, and the stocks he had acquired, yielded a comfortable income beyond what Julia received from the estate of her father. The family could live as it pleased—first class accommodations for George and Julia on trains and steamers and in hotels, Yale for the boys, a handsome wedding for Carrie, and a house remodeled and modernized. There were no complaints from George about finances and business in these years, as there had been a few earlier. In 1914 his estate amounted to $508,682.[42] He owned shares in prosperous local companies—Scovill, American Brass, and Plume & Atwood—and in nearby Connecticut firms—Stanley Works, American Hardware, Colts Patent Guns. All of these paid good dividends. This family surely could be placed in the 2 percent of the U.S. population that at the time owned 60 percent of the wealth of the country.[43]

Gradations are in order, though. George White's fortune was Lilliputian compared to those amassed at the time by men like Carnegie, Rockefeller, and Mellon. In Waterbury, too, many who had larger assets. However modest George's wealth relative to that of his Hillside neighbors, fellow resort guests, and ocean liner travelers, it did make him and Julia presentable to those in the highest economic stratum of society.

The family's means were visible enough in clothing, in the carriage and horses (later automobiles), in the 114 Grove Street house, in the sons' Yale education, but these were fairly subdued advertisements of wealth compared with the flamboyant expressions of affluence found in mansions in New York. To onlookers, the White's possessions and lifestyle indicated affluence and "station." Their wealth was visible, but tastefully displayed, as befitted an old Connecticut family. It was as different from "old money"

---

42. "Estate of George Luther White," Inventory, 131–357–58, Notes, 129–352–354, Waterbury Probate Court.

43. Referring to an analysis by Willard I. King, in his account of the early 1900s, Cashman observes, "About 2 percent of the population owned 60 percent of the wealth, a middle class of 33 percent of the people owned 5 percent of the wealth. In short two million people owned 20 percent more of the national wealth than the remaining 90 million." Sean Dennis Cashman, *America in the Age of the Titans: The Progressive Era and World War I* (New York: New York Univ. Press, 1988), 203.

plainness, as might have been found in Boston, as "new money" extravagance of the unattractive Americans Carrie found in Lucerne and Paris.

The White house was of sober design and could not be called a mansion. Julia shopped relatively modestly, and she and George sent no cargoes of furniture or abundant *objets d'art* from European travels. We learn of scarves, prints, toys, and clothes purchased abroad. George's most flamboyant acquisition was a set of Bohemian glassware, found in Carlsbad, to furnish fourteen place settings with seven glasses each. (They can hardly have been sported to impress guests at dinner parties at home, as Julia was an uncertain keeper of the house; she dreaded coming home to ill-cooked food. There is no reference in family papers, apart from the weddings, to her ever having entertained other than family.) On the other hand, there was no dearth of the fine material things of life, as witnessed by the fifteen-place silver set later given to Will and his bride, or of the leisure that a cook, waitress, upstairs maid, coachman, and gardener gave George and Julia's, and later, Rob and Carrie's households.[44]

Turn-of-the-century America had become a world power and an empire after the short-lived war with Spain. (Waterbury gave a torchlight procession to welcome home Lieut. Frank W. Kellogg, an officer in Admiral Dewey's fleet when it sank the Spanish at Manila Bay. The reviewing stand was built to resemble the U.S.S. *Baltimore*, on which he had served, and the governor bestowed a medal on the young man.)[45] The national population had grown dramatically in the 1890s from 62.8 to 75.9 million, and it would increase by another thirteen million in the next decade and 20 percent in each of the successive decades. The all-time peak of immigration came in the ten years after 1900. Most years of the decade saw 200,000 Italian immigrants come to America's shores. Waterbury, with its plentiful factory jobs, was a favored destination. About 100,000 immigrated from Russia and Poland every year.[46]

The figures for Waterbury are dramatic. The city's population was 47,000 in 1890, a 17.5 percent increase over the course of the decade, and in the next decade it grew to 74,750, a 57 percent increase. One third of its population in 1910 was foreign born. More striking, and revealing how

---

44. The silver service is now in the Mark Twain House, Hartford, donated by the author.

45. 20 Oct. 1899. Pape, *Waterbury*, 1:212–13.

46. George Thomas Kurian, *Datapedia of the United States, 1790–2000* (Lanham, Md.: Bernan Press, 1994), 5, 52.

small a minority the Yankee factory owners were, less than 2 percent of Waterburians at the time were of English stock. In 1910 the Irish amounted to 21 percent of the population, Italians 14 percent (in 1900 the Irish had been 31 percent and the Italians 5 percent of the population.) Russian immigrants made up about 11 percent of the population in 1910—the third largest ethnic group.[47]

It was an extraordinarily prosperous era for the country. New techniques of industrial organization led to great increases in productivity. This was matched (and made possible by) the rate of capital formation (of which George, in his role as investor, played a part). Net capital formation as a percent of national income was enormous: 13.0 between 1899 and 1908, the highest for fifty years. (By comparison, in the Depression years it was 1.7, and in 1939–48 it was 7.9).[48] The gross national product increased by an astonishing 88.7 percent from 1900 to 1910.[49] It was a fine time to be an investor. For the workers, however, while there were jobs, and better ones than available in the impoverished areas from which many immigrants came, the hours were long—an average of fifty-one hours per week by 1909. The national average weekly wage for a factory worker was low, only $9.74.[50]

New inventions of the preceding decades were affecting the family's life as well as local industry, with new products for Waterbury manufacturers to supply. Electricity was brought into the White's remodeled house in 1900. The connections for its distribution—and appliances that began to infiltrate buildings throughout the country—meant a vast number of new copper products, which Waterbury metalworking plants were in a good position to produce. The telephone came to the house, and its proliferation also provided opportunities for making small parts, for which the copper-working experience of Scovill's and other Waterbury factories were well suited.

The constant arrival of immigrants meant that Waterbury factories could expand production without restraint on the use of low-cost labor.

---

47. *Brass Valley: The Story of Working People's Lives and Struggles in an American Industrial Region,* comp. Jeremy Brecher, Jerry Lombardi, Jan Stackhouse, The Brass Workers History Project (Philadelphia: Temple Univ. Press, 1982), 7–8, tables 2 and 3.

48. Cashman, *Age of the Titans,* 11.

49. The GNP rose from 18.7 billion in 1900 to 35.3 in 1910, current dollars. Kurian, *Datapedia,* 89.

50. Ibid., 79.

The laborers' wooden houses, many of which were of a distinctive three-decker design, allowing one family to a floor, were built in the city's few remaining rural areas. These dwellings were spacious compared to the tenements near the factories, where many lived clustered together in small quarters. Seven thousand of 9,200 dwellings in the city were rented. In 1914 most Waterbury workers exceeded the national averages and put in fifty-four or more hours per week; it was the fortunate who worked the forty-eight to fifty-four hour workweek.[51] The difference was enormous between the mass of workers who rented, lived in cramped housing, and worked long hours and the Whites, who owned property and had the leisure to travel. Indeed it must be in part because the gulf was so great that there is an absence of comment on the poor or the workers in the letters of this family. Charitable causes intended to help the poor at the time in Waterbury were the YMCA, the Boys Club, Waterbury Hospital, Visiting Nurses; these were supported by donations from the well-to-do families establishing a tradition of charitable giving that was carried on by George's children and grandchildren.

Historians call the first two decades of the century the Progressive Era, after the reform-inspired efforts of the Roosevelt and Wilson administrations to develop laws and regulations to improve working conditions, temper the power of industrial combinations, and improve health and housing. There is no trace in the letters of what George thought of Progressive Era politics. He supported McKinley and the gold standard in 1896, we learned from Carrie, but whether he supported the progressive Republicanism of Theodore Roosevelt from 1901 to 1909 or was relieved or dismayed by Taft's more conservative positions is not evident. George did not take part in civic life in Waterbury; unlike other businessmen, he served on no commissions. The one political remark that Julia makes is a scornful reference to the "suffragettes—awful creatures over here—" who prevented entry to London's National Gallery in 1913.[52]

The amalgamations of businesses that resulted in the creation of such giants as U.S. Steel and Standard Oil—and which led ultimately to the Sherman Anti-Trust Act (1890)—were not matched in Waterbury, even though capital invested in manufacturing in the city rose by 50 percent

---

51. *Brass Valley*, 25, 79.

52. JHW, in Munich, to CHWG, in Waterbury, 24 Aug. 1913.

from 1900 to 1905.[53] While the larger companies, such as Scovill and the Chase companies, grew bigger, and several firms were combined to form the American Brass Company, there remained numerous small and medium-sized factories, of which George's two and Henry Lawton Wade's Mattatuck—later so important to the family—were a part. Small and large companies co-existed peacefully and thrived. George's L. C. White Company, for example, made buttons and button backs, as did Scovill, and the larger company could have, but did not, drive the smaller out of business. Similarly, Wade's Mattatuck made many of the same items as Scovill. There was business enough for all. While many may have supported the national movements to break up trusts and monopolies, there seems to have been little concern about monopolies in Waterbury itself.[54]

The only disturbance of industrial growth in these pre–World War I years was the bitter trolley strike of 1903, when cars operated by strikebreakers were attacked, facilities destructed, and a policeman was killed.[55] Labor strife, though, was not to return until after the war.

That these Whites lived in a rapidly changing physical world was obvious to them. Julia's response was largely positive. The ocean liners in which they crossed the ocean in these years were bigger, faster, and far more comfortable than the ships she had known in the mid-1800s. She adored her first ride in an automobile, which added an entirely new dimension to travel. Using the telephone to call home from New York was a pleasure. The hotels they stayed in were comfortably modern, and the Pullman cars where they slept were a far cry from what they had known on their transcontinental journey in 1874, moving at two or three times the speed. What was new was improvement. There is no trace of disaffection from this emerging world.

George gave up his beloved horses for a car in 1907 and thus altered the family budget to include gasoline and metal parts rather than feed and harnesses. (He and Julia found auto-touring so enjoyable in France in 1906

---

53. David Beccia, "Waterbury, Connecticut, in the Progressive Era: 1900 to 1916," 12 May 1964, typescript, 3–4, Histories folder, Research Collection, Mattatuck Museum.

54. Ibid.

55. Ibid., 1–3; Bill Guber, "The Long and Bloody Trolley Strike of 1903," *Sunday Republican Magazine*, 2 Oct. 1988, 5, 11; A. J. Scapino Jr. "Community, Class, and Conflict: The Waterbury Trolley Strike of 1909," xerographic reproduction of an article from an unattributed source, pages 29–42, author identified as from Univ. of Connecticut, Histories folder, Research Section, Mattatuck Museum.

that it compelled them to have a car at home.) The Whites became part of a rapid, nationwide revolution in transportation. The number of passenger cars sold went from 4,100 in 1900 to 181,000 ten years later, when there were nearly three-quarters of a million registered vehicles on the road.[56] The paved roads needed for the automobile, the gas stations, and garages transformed the familiar countryside year-by-year. Frequently visited New York became penetrated by skyscrapers. Cass Gilbert, architect of the Woolworth Building (1913), was commissioned for Waterbury City Hall (1914) and (later) the Chase companies' headquarters.

Urbanity

Within about twenty years from the early 1890s Waterbury was transformed by new building and came to have the characteristics of a modern metropolitan center, where people of all classes and backgrounds mix, where there was ample public transportation, and amenities such as an attractive hotel with a public dining room and bar. The changes can be best seen in the buildings surrounding the Green.

The focal point of Waterbury's settlement from its origin was the common land, Centre Square on nineteenth-century maps, later the Green. It was spacious, about two rectangular acres. By the 1900s it was notable for the gracious shape of its elms, which provided a deep shade in the warm months and a lacy aerial tapestry in winter. At the foot of Prospect Street the white clapboard houses remained from early in the past century. Since the 1850s the gray granite, Gothic St. John's Church stood above the western end of the Green, and in the 1870s the multicolored stone Gothic First Congregational Church replaced a modest predecessor on the Green's north edge. On the south was the City Hall and the Scovill House hotel and houses, the most notable being the Italianate house of Kendrick, a former mayor. Exchange Place, at the eastern end of the Green, was where the east-west and north-south Main streets met and where Bank Street, a shopping and commercial street, began. By the 1880s trolleys ran east and west, north and south along these streets, with an interchange at Exchange Place. It would not have been difficult for Waterbury's citizens to conjure up an image of the Green when thinking about the city.

The appearance and character of the Green began to change when buildings designed by Wilfred E. Griggs were erected. These in turn

---

56. Kurian, *Datapedia*, 267.

53. W. E. Griggs's YMCA Building

Mattatuck Museum

transformed the image of the focal point of the city. His buildings were of different, eclectic styles; there was no master plan or design, but in twenty years the Green looked to be the center of a modern city, no longer a gracious survival from the past. Griggs's YMCA on the Green's north replaced one of the federal era houses as early as 1892. The building was a three-story structure with a portico, meant to be seen and admired—in effect informing viewers that being on the Green in the company of the churches was a place of honor, "a beautiful addition," according to Pape.[57] (In the 1920s it was replaced by the present YMCA building.) That a social service institution took its place so prominently made manifest philanthropy at work. It drew the youths from working families to the foot of Hillside. In 1895 Griggs designed a building in the Venetian Gothic style for the Independent Order of Odd Fellows at the east end of the Green. It was five stories tall, clad in russet brick with fanciful arched windows and with a handsome cornice; a recent survey called it "one of Waterbury's nineteenth-century architectural masterpieces."[58]

---

57. Pape, *Waterbury*, 1:137. This building was demolished to make way in 1922 for a YMCA designed by Richard Henry Dana.

58. "Waterbury Architectural Survey, Waterbury, Connecticut 1978," Ann Y. Smith, Project Director (Waterbury, Conn.: Mattatuck Museum, [1978]), typescript, Research Collection, Mattatuck Museum, 5 (hereafter cited as AYS 1978).

54. W. E. Griggs's Odd Fellows Building, 1895

Mattatuck Museum

The 1902 fire destroyed the Scovill House hotel and the City Hall, which had dominated the south side of the Green since the 1870s. George White joined other businessmen and well-to-do widows in a stock subscription to build a new hotel. Griggs designed a six-story structure in the Parisian Beaux Arts manner. Its first story was clad in stone, and there was a flight of stairs that gave a touch of formality to the main entrance. The tall lobby windows were framed Art Nouveau features. The hotel opened in 1905 and was named for John P. Elton, of an old Waterbury family, who led the subscription to build it. It provided Waterbury with a hotel similar in design to those found in European cities at the time, a facility to be proud of. Its manager put it on the map by joining with hotels as far north as the White Mountains to establish the "Ideal Tour" for the new pastime of automobile touring. The first stop north for motorists to New England was the Elton, and thus for a some years Waterbury became a tourist destination:

> The Naugatuck Valley is dotted here and there with busy towns—whose factories make most of the brass used in the world—yet for many miles at a time one passes though almost primeval forests and the great rocks rising sheer to heights. . . . The very nature of these portions of the valley prohibits the despoliation of man, and so lends the valley in all its wild and rugged beauty to the lover of nature and the motor-car. The Naugatuck Valley Boulevard was opened for 1911 touring travel. It is the widest cement road ever con-

structed in the State. Situated in the heart of the valley is the city of Water-bury, famous for its brass foundries and splendid hotel.[59]

The hotel's stylish dining room and bar were popular meeting places for Waterburians. Visible from the hotel—and completed in the same year—was Griggs's impressive New Haven County Courthouse.[60]

Griggs's Masonic Temple (now the Mattatuck Museum), at the west end of the Green, replaced another of the federal houses in 1911. Adjacent there were (and are) two apartment buildings, designed by Griggs, a sign of the growth of population in the city at the time. The architect's last contribution to the city center was the ten-story Lilley Building (1913), by far the tallest in the city, with a quarter of a million square feet, space for a large store and a hundred and fifty offices, with "its double electric elevator, the most modern of its class of buildings in Waterbury."[61] The economy that had emerged at the beginning of the century needed lawyers, accountants, insurance agents, and doctors and dentists; the Lilley Building, still standing, provided space for them. In an "excellent concentration" of buildings, designed in eclectic styles, Griggs and the investors had created a modern metropolitan center.[62]

Another sign of the modernization of Waterbury was Griggs's handsome Renaissance revival Reid & Hughes department store on Bank Street, which still stands, replacing within a year buildings destroyed in the fire. This brought a handsome version of the emporiums found in larger cities to Waterbury. The most singular of Waterbury's "modern" buildings was the railroad station, opened in 1907, which united the old depots. The president of the New York, New Haven, and Hartford Railroad and his wife were impressed on a visit to Siena by its Torre del Manglia (City Hall), which dominated the central square. The railroad commissioned McKim, Mead, and White of New York to design a station using that model. The result was an elongated version of the tower and a capacious building to house the waiting and baggage rooms. Soon a sign informed

---

59. Almon C. Judd, *Elton Hotel*, "The Ideal Tour" (Waterbury Conn., 1925), 5, Hotel folder, Research Collection, Mattatuck Museum.

60. Pape, *Waterbury*, 1:137. The Elton was converted to an assisted living facility in the 1970s; its exterior remains largely as designed. The Court House was being restored in 2002 for an alternative use.

61. Pape, *Waterbury*, 1:137–39.

62. AYS 1978, 7.

55. George and Julia White, about 1900

arriving passengers that they had arrived in "The Brass Center of the World."[63]

Waterbury had achieved a distinct and modern character in the 1900s. There was a clear visual sense of a place and a distinct and individual identity around the Green. Soon vendors sold tinted postcards so that visitors could prove it to others. Betty White remembered as a child seeing George stride across the Green looking important, presumably with fedora at a slightly rakish angle, cane in hand, gold watch chain across his expansive middle. He would have been proud of the improvements that he had seen in Waterbury in his lifetime. It wasn't Paris, Lucerne, the luxurious steamship *Imperator,* or New York, to be sure—but it was an urbane cityscape with graceful elms, the statue of Knight presiding over Carrie Welton's fountain, and a hotel that could match one anywhere—or so he might have thought. It was a scene involving a convergence of streets and trolley lines, diversity of buildings and functions, bustles of people, stores, newsstands, all which it shared with the metropolitan centers tourists like the Whites had enjoyed abroad. If there were voices deploring the loss of the old colonial Green, they were muted. The new Green showed all that Waterbury was up-to-date.

---

63. AYS 1978, 8.

VIII

TRANSITIONS

Changes in the White family came in clusters in the years around the turn of the century. Jane Amelia died on a visit to Tampa in March 1899. She was seventy-four, the same age as her husband when he died. What had been a regular stop to and from the Green was now an empty house, soon to be sold to Trinity Church to briefly become its Rectory.[1] George, though still in his early fifties, was the patriarch of the family. That summer he and Julia celebrated their twenty-fifth anniversary with a European tour, accompanied by Carrie. George also oversaw a renovation, really a rebuilding and enlargement, of the house at 114 Grove Street—his pride was the new carriage house for his beloved horses, like the house itself, in the currently fashionable colonial revival style. For the first time the household enjoyed the convenience of electricity. Work was completed in time for Carrie's wedding to take place there early in 1902. Will married his childhood sweetheart the next year—Jimmy's marriage followed quietly in 1905. There were now Griggs and Wade in-laws included in the family, all of whom lived nearby, and Julia and George had the house to themselves. Thus over the span of a mere four years the landscape of the family was transformed. For Will there was Yale and a nearly year-long test of endurance and willpower in Yukon Territory, where he entered the new century as a servant of the Crown held by Queen Victoria. For Carrie an unexpected proposal of marriage led her to test her doubts against her feelings for weeks before she assented and received the whole-hearted support of her father.

---

1. Property Records, 166:596, 6 Oct. 1900, Office of the Town Clerk, City of Waterbury, New Haven Co., Conn. The sale was for a "valuable sum." The street number had been changed to 35 from 13.

Colonial Revival at 114 Grove

The securities in Jane Amelia's estate, valued at $52,898, were a substantial legacy. They were divided equally between George and Harriet, who already owned the 13 Prospect Street house from their father's estate.[2] George took on the project of enlarging the Grove Street house and modernizing it with electricity and central heating. The plans were drawn up by Wilfred Griggs, the leading architect in the city, who adapted the house to the popular colonial revival style of the day, intended to remind of the eighteenth century past, restrained compared to the exuberant Queen Anne houses further up on Hillside.

"The *House*—Oh! It is so disheartening that I will say nothing about it except the decorators have begun to get the walls ready for paper, but the delay, and the expense, are something awful," Julia cried to Will. "I sometimes wonder if your father knows what he is doing, but I suppose he does and I am over anxious. He went down to the football game [at Yale] and enjoyed it very much. He seems very well, though nervous and tired over the house, and I think losing interest."[3] For his part George solemnly confessed to his son that "the house remodeling has been a bigger job than I think I ever tackled. Almost everything that I have tackled in the past that has strained my nervous system has been in some way under my control so that I could shape its proceedings and bring them out somewhere near my ideas. This job, however, has been as hydra-headed as any that I have ever tackled and has pretty nearly used me up."[4] Not all of this time was nervous and stressful for George. Julia reported that the "only thing in which he seems to enter heart and soul is the Waterbury Club—*He is President*. I suspect from two or three things that Mr. Rob Griggs [a business friend of George's] has said to me last they may hear it over there as often as we do at home." He basked in the honor that was rotated among the factory

---

2. "Estate of Jane Amelia White," Inventory, 1 July 1899, Waterbury Probate Dist., file 8749, RG 4, Records of the Probate Courts, State Archives, CSL.

3. JHW, in Waterbury, to WHW, in Dawson City, Yukon, 26 Nov. 1900. "How to Win a Wedding Ring: The Correspondence of William Henry White in the Klondike Region of the Yukon Territory, Dominion of Canada, 1900–1901," Elizabeth Wade White, ed., typescript, in possession of the author, 87.

4. GLW, in Waterbury, to WHW, at Forty Mile, Ten Forks, Yukon Territory, 6 March 1901, William Henry White Papers, Western Americana Collection, Beinecke Rare Book and Manuscript Library, Yale University.

56. The White house at 114 Grove, after renovation

owners for a year at time.[5] (The club was then located in a former mansion a few yards from the Green on North Main Street.)

The rebuilding took seven months and bracketed the two centuries. Julia and George moved to the 13 Prospect Street house while work was going on and bad it a last farewell in late February 1900. "I do not think one of us not even your father felt any regret at moving out," Julia wrote Will of the final leave-taking of the house where George grew up and where two of their children were born, "though I did linger with tenderness in the room where you came to bless me and I kissed you first."[6]

After all the strain, the renovation was done, however; new electric lighting animated the rooms and there was the luxury of up-to-date plumbing. Photos of the interior rooms on the ground floor survive, a welcome record of furnishings at the cusp of the new century, when the style of George and Julia's youth had already begun to be overturned. It is a comfortable-looking place, somewhat less cluttered than it would have been a generation before. The number of varied visual experiences being offered in a single space by furniture and decorative objects is familiar from the Victorian past, but there is a greater lightness. Jane Amelia would

5. "Wedding Ring," 87. George was president of the Waterbury Club from 1899 to 1900.

6. JHW, in Waterbury, to WHW, in the Northwest Territories, 25 Feb. 1901, William Henry White Papers.

doubtless have considered it informal and somewhat disorienting. (One of the Egyptian revival settees is in the front parlor, but invitingly placed catty-corner.) Julia's touch allowed the light entering from less constricted windows to bathe the somewhat less formal arrangements of furniture and objects. The dining room can be seen in a photograph of Will's wedding party in 1904; the bridal couple are at the head as the guests sit back during coffee. The built-in cabinet is full of china, a mandatory display of possession and cultivation. "Victoria abhorred a vacuum," and this décor allows no blank spots. The wood is carved and dark and weighty.

The sons had been spending time away from the nest since before its renovation. Will, according to his daughter, had a "rather turbulent pre-university school record." As the local school had not been able to tame this reluctant student, George sent him to board at the Gunnery School in nearby Washington (where he himself had spent a year). The boy then went to Phillips Andover Academy with the expectation that it would fulfill its role and prepare the young man for Yale. "Papa will have told you how miserably I passed my examinations," he wrote Julia soon after his arrival, a homesick lad, but able to report some academic success.[7] Andover managed to get him into the Sheffield Scientific School at Yale in the fall of 1896; he was twenty then, about two years older than the usual freshman.

In the eighteenth century a few young men from Waterbury, a tiny minority, went to the college in New Haven to prepare to be ministers or lawyers. In the mid-eighteenth century, in the era of the first rapid growth of the industries, even fewer of the local youth went to college. Later in the century, however, the well-to-do factory owners chose to send their sons to Yale, expecting that after graduation they would return to take positions in the factories, and they expected that there would be some social polishing to ease their entry into the top of what was becoming a stratified social scene. The factories were larger then and no longer run by farm-boy founders who could work the machines, design the tools, and market the product. The modern college-educated men became a new category of generalists who oversaw engineers, superintendents, and laborers—they were "management." George White saw to it that his sons joined the

7. WHW, at Philips Andover, to JHW, at 114 Grove St., Waterbury, 5 Jan. 1894, William Henry White Papers.

Chases, the Griggs, the Gosses, and other factory-owning families who sent their boys to Yale for four years. The returning graduates quickly became the core of Waterbury society, prominent at the club, and, when the automobile made it possible, the country club. There was a strong tie between Yale and aspiring Connecticut managers in these years. Yale was the college of choice for almost all of the well-to-do. Whether one was an alumnus or not (as with George), the Yale football games were of abiding interest each fall.

Julia's Phelps forebears were prominently associated with Yale in the eighteenth century—Eleazar Wheelock (her four times great grandfather), Alexander Phelps, and Benajah Phelps (her three times great grandfathers) were graduates. To the extent he was aware of this distinguished lineage, it must have made Will, the reluctant scholar, uncomfortable. The Sheffield Scientific School offered a technical education to prepare men for careers in mining and industry. Will stayed the course despite his interest in "parties, athletics and singing."[8]

Will was graduated from Yale in the class of 1900, at the somewhat advanced age of twenty-three. George Jr. completed his undergraduate education a year later. It was an undistinguished period in Yale's history. Brooks Mather Kelley writes that "[i]nterest in scholarly things was just reaching its lowest point in the history of the college . . . years later those who entered in 1900 and 01 would argue which was the worst class to go through."[9] It was a close shave, as he later wrote his mother, "It was such a surprise that I could ever invite you to see me graduate."[10] The only extracurricular activities he listed in the class yearbook were service on the senior dance committee and membership in the Chi Phi fraternity.[11] Before such a category existed, Will was a "gentleman C" student. For all that, he had learned to write clearly, as his reports of the experiences of the next year witnessed.

His father had a rugged challenge for the new Yale graduate. Perhaps he shared the view of self-made businessmen at the time that "higher learning undermined the rugged personal qualities necessary for success.

---

8. Reminiscence of Elizabeth Wade White to the author.

9. Brooks Mather Kelley, *Yale: A History* (New Haven: Yale Univ. Press, 1974), 298.

10. WHW, at Forty Mile, to JHW, in Waterbury, 30 May 1901, William Henry White Papers.

11. Class of 1900, *The Quarter Century Record* (New Haven: Tuttle, Morehouse, and Taylor, 1927), 273.

Success demanded a strong will, diligence, persistence, ambition, good health, and self discipline, qualities which colleges allegedly crippled and dwarfed in their concentration on the development of mental faculties."[12] Because of Luther's support, George himself was not in fact "self-made," but he may have considered himself such on account of his struggle with tuberculosis and his worldly success despite a limited education.

In June 1900 George wrote Will that he was "more than delighted" to learn that he had passed all his exams but German and expected that after "a bit of work on that" it "will be very delightful for me to know that you have been able to secure your diploma, and that your educational career will be ended with satisfaction to all." He laid out an opportunity that he had just learned about at a meeting of the Elliott Mining Company of New York, in which he was an investor. The board had agreed with him that they ought to send someone out to Dawson City in Yukon Territory to assist the firm's representative (a brother of the principal of the firm). George suggested that Will function as an "understudy" to the Elliott at Dawson City and, not incidentally, get the "facts" about an enterprise that was raising some doubts in the home office. If "Mr. Elliott received you properly," George wrote Will, "and you were successful in making a favorable impression on him, and your reports came back in good shape and were satisfactory . . . you would be able to remain there in the service of the company."

George was so enthusiastic about this prospect for his son that after the meeting he stopped at the Canadian Pacific office to get an estimate of the cost of the rail journey to Seattle and the steamer from there to Skagway, Alaska (a four to six day voyage), where there was a rail connection to Dawson. It amounted to $250–$275 "including everything."[13] George clearly wanted Will to be challenged rather than take the comfortable course of returning home after graduation for a job in the family businesses.

The Elliott Mining Company was marketing a portable steam boiler to the thousands of small-stake prospectors seeking riches in the streams and earth of the Klondike, a nearly inaccessible region. When, in 1896, gold was discovered in the gravels of Bonanza Creek, a tributary to the Klond-

---

12. Irwin G. Wyllie, *The Self-Made Man in America* (New Brunswick, N.J.: Rutgers Univ. Press, 1954), 102–3, quoted in Kelley, *Yale*, 279.

13. GLW, in Waterbury, to WHW, at Yale, [June] 1900, "Wedding Ring," 2, 4.

ike, prospectors and adventurers from all parts of the world thronged to the place drained by the Yukon River and the tributary Klondike, Eldorado, Hunker, Dominion, and Gold Run Rivers. Of these, the Eldorado, "for the two or three miles in which it was gold-bearing, was much the richest, and for its length probably surpassed any known placer deposit."[14]

In the first years there was gold to be found in the gravels of the many creeks feeding these rivers. Later the prospectors had to dig into the earth to find veins below the surface. As the ground was permanently frozen in that climate, this required more force than could be exerted by pick and shovel. At first the prospectors used bonfires to melt the permafrost. Soon boilers were developed that could melt the earth more efficiently by pumping steam into the ground through a number of pipes. The units could be assembled and disassembled in the field and were small enough to be transported by pack animal. There was brisk competition among manufacturers and rapid changes in the technology. It was the lack of accurate information about the field marketing of the Elliott boiler that prompted the firm's New York headquarters to support Will's involvement, employing him as the company's eyes and ears.

The Yukon climate was severe, with temperatures as low as -65° F in the winter darkness. In midsummer the mud made traveling difficult, but in the cold months the hardened surface allowed free movement by dogsled. During the spring thaw it was virtually impossible to travel, as the rivers were choked with flow ice and the surface was soft and treacherous.

In the peak year of 1900, $400,000 in gold was extracted in the region, and the population was about 30,000. It had become somewhat easier to reach the fields after a narrow-gauge railroad was built from Skagway in 1899 to near Whitehorse, on the Yukon, whence prospectors could descend the river on steamboats to the gold-bearing creeks near Dawson. According to the indefatigable Baedeker (who included the route in his 1900 *Dominion of Canada . . . Travelers Handbook*), the fare from Skagway to Dawson on the Pacific & Arctic Railway was stiff—about $100 dollars, requiring a considerable sum up front for a prospector. Dawson was then "a bustling little town with about 15,000 inhabitants."[15] It was essentially a

---

14. *Enc. Brit.*, s.v. "Yukon" and "Klondike."

15. Karl Baedeker, *The Dominion of Canada with Newfoundland an Excursion to Alaska: Handbook for Travellers* (Leipzig, 1900), 245.

huge miners' camp, which had expanded from virtually nothing in four years. Although the Fifth Avenue Hotel, where Will put up in August, boasted that it was "strictly first class in every respect," he found Dawson City "a miserable hole."[16] Waterbury and its society were far behind.

In 1895 the first gold commissioner was appointed by the Canadian government, and three years later the part of the northwest where the greatest concentration of gold was located, immediately adjoining the Alaskan border, was established by Parliament as the Yukon Territory.[17] Quite unexpectedly, Will later found himself in the employ of this body, whose authority ultimately was derived from the Crown, then borne by Queen Victoria.

Will reached Dawson in late August. Through his frequent letters to Julia, which display a warm and trusting relationship, we learn something of his personal experience of this rough place. To his father he reported on business matters, always assuring him that he was spending money carefully (just as young George had his father from Minneapolis). The lackadaisical student wrote vivid and well-observed accounts of the scraggly towns and the harsh life of the prospectors swarming to the Klondike. They reveal a young man making difficult decisions and sticking to his course of action, despite setbacks. Will matured quickly, it seems, when he learned from Mr. Elliott that the firm's pipe-boiler had been superseded by what proved to be a more popular type, thus putting him out of a job.[18] Although no comfort at the time, one of the purposes for which his father had sent him there was fulfilled when he reported on the lack of sales and the perfunctory marketing. Go "slow in further investment in the company," he advised his father.[19]

Will resolved to spend the winter in the north, feeling that if he returned at that point it would be in the aftermath of a failure, and he would have gained nothing from the experience. He forced himself to improvise and reported earning $5 as a day-laborer for a man "who decided to move and so I have been carrying the logs which formed his hut, from one side of the gulch down the bank and up the other side, in all

16. WHW, in Dawson City, to JHW, in Waterbury, 20 Aug. 1900, William Henry White Papers.

17. "Wedding Ring," 68, quoting *The Yukon Territory, History and Resources* (Ottawa, Canada: Department of the Interior, 1916), 13.

18. Ibid., 17, 18.

19. WHW, in Dawson City to GLW, in Waterbury, 6 Sept. 1900, "Wedding Ring," 36.

57. Will in front of his cabin at Forty-Mile, 1901

a half mile and all over tailings and loose earth" It cost $3.50 a day to live in that expensive place, $1 for each meal, $.50 for the cabin, and since there was no work or pay Sunday, the net pay for a week of grueling work was $5.50.[20] Will had decided to prove himself without his father's aid.

He did not, as many young men might, hide his feelings from his mother. "Perhaps I am foolish to write you this morning because my mind is naturally filled with the one question as to whether I can make a go of it here," he wrote, and confessed that he was upset, describing it whimsically as wearing a "very persistent pair of blue glasses which cling tenaciously to my nose." He knew that such a confession would agitate the emotional Julia, and so he included details an anxious parent could enjoy—how he found quarters in a bunk house, trekked fourteen miles in the mud from Dawson to a settlement called The Forks, and was planning to rent a cabin

20. WHW, at The Forks, Yukon Territory, to GLW, in Waterbury, 1 Sept. 1900. "Wedding Ring," 26–31.

for $15 a month. He meant it to be a "cheerful letter."[21] For her part, Julia showed her affection for her "Billie" in a birthday letter:

> It is just twenty-four years and two hours since I first had the joy of calling you by so proud a name—"my son." It was in this very room, too, dear that you came to me, and what recollections this anniversary calls up. Our bodies were nearer together then but were our hearts? I loved you—but fear you did not love me as much as you do today though no one else was any dearer to you then. I suppose I had great expectations then, dearest, but whatever they were, they have been more than realized— . . . When I gave you that first kiss, and they laid you on my breast and I knew that I was the mother of a *man.*[22]

Will wrote Carrie with characteristic openness, that

> "[t]his is the kind of a country where you must do one of two things and at the present cheerful writing one of the two is so filled that the other is all that is practically left. You must bring money into the country and be fox enough to invest it well—with results of enormous returns or you must get down to day laborer's work. I have no money to invest and can find no day laborer's work—so there you are. What a kick this is—but I am tired and have no reasons to be writing at all—if I cannot do better than this."[23]

Relief from day labor came when he met Dr. Grant at the Dawson Hospital, who engaged him to do "day duty as nurse in the hospital."

> My salary is the magnificent sum of nothing per minute with my meals and board thrown in and I work from seven a.m. until seven p.m. with an occasional hour and a half off when an easy day comes. Do you think you would care for nursing—If you do you may as well forget the idea. I do nothing but make beds wait on patients, sweep out the wards etc. from morning until night. I was getting along famously at the Forks. My education had gone so far that I could blow my nose as artistically as any of the miners without the use of anything but my fingers and a coat sleeve but if you wish to see a move replete with grace you should see me clean out the bed-pan of a typhoid patient and clean it out with a few scientific moves."[24]

---

21. WHW, at Dawson City, to JHW, in Waterbury, 28 Aug. 1900, "Wedding Ring," 22–25.

22. JHW, in Waterbury, to WHW, in Dawson City, 26 Nov. 1900, "Wedding Ring," 85–87.

23. WHW, at Dawson City, to CHW, in Waterbury, 20 Sept. 1900, "Wedding Ring," 85–87.

24. Ibid.

Then came a stroke of luck. Will found a job that carried him through the winter and allowed him to gain the experience he sought. With the support of Dr. Grant, he applied for a job in the gold commissioner's office. Because it was a position in Her Majesty's Civil Service he was initially rebuffed, "owing to the fact that I was an American." However, there was another advocate, Miss Richardson, "the one pretty nurse" ("I did do the best I could to help her with her work"), whose sister was married to the commissioner who had initially turned him down. Through the entreaties of these ladies the handsome and no doubt charming young man was awarded the position.[25]

It was a great find—a steady job that gave him a good look at the mining activity in the territory. To eliminate the prevalent crime of claim jumping, the gold commissioner oversaw the recording of claims and their subsequent sale.[26] One formality was that Will had to make an oath of allegiance to Queen Victoria. "I asked Dr. Grant's advice in the matter and also Mr. Bell's [the commissioner] and explained to them that so far as I could see from my own interpretation of the oath I might take it freely without cutting myself off in the least from my own citizenship in the States. They both agreed with me in the matter so I took the oath."[27]

Will settled in, found a cabin in Dawson, experienced the onset of the dark and deep cold. He wrote Julia that his salary of $60 a month was "nearly large enough to settle down on at home," but with $50 a month for the cabin and $100 for board there was no chance to save.[28] Julia commented, "If you accomplish little to speak of financially, the experience is worth more than you can appreciate now . . . I am sure you will be broadened and strengthened by this getting out into the world—and such a New World too."[29] By January he had learned the procedures of the office well enough to be sent out on a post of his own, to the Forty-Mile Mining Dis-

---

25. WHW, in Yukon Territory, to JHW, in Waterbury, 30 Sept. 1900. "Wedding Ring," 63–67.

26. The Yukon Placer Mining Act provided that "The Gold Commissioner shall have jurisdiction within such districts as the Commissioner Head of the governing council of the territory directs. Mining recorders shall be appointed tin each mining district and shall possess all the owners and authority of a mining inspector, who shall have jurisdiction within such mining districts as the Commissioner directs." "Wedding Ring," 69, quoting *The Yukon Territory*, 24.

27. WHW, in Dawson City, to JHW, in Waterbury, 22 Jan. 1901, "Wedding Ring," 115–19.

28. WHW, in Dawson City, to JHW, in Waterbury, 23 Dec. 1900, "Wedding Ring," 95–99.

29. Ibid., "Wedding Ring," 99–102.

trict (about fifty miles from Dawson and twenty-three miles from the
Alaska boundary), where there had been a great increase in mining.

> My duties will be varied in the extreme. As one of the fellows put it: "You and
> the telegraph operator will run the town." I am to be, beside Mining
> Recorder, the land and timber agent and in all probability the Postmaster as
> well. In the capacity of Mining Recorder I shall attend to all the business of
> the Department even to the deciding of minor cases of contention which may
> arise among the claim owners in the Division.[30]

Forty-Mile was a camp of about four or five hundred people, a large
percentage being native Siwash. It had been busy, then was partly abandoned, but opened up again as more prospectors arrived. "There are two
stores. . . . two so-called hotels and the police barracks across the river at
Fort Cudahay which contains a detachment of three men and a sergeant."[31] In early February Will reached there by dog team and set up an
office in his cabin.

Because it took three weeks for mail to reach Waterbury from the
Yukon it was not until the end of February that Julia and George learned
about the Forty-Mile posting. They were alarmed at Will's isolation and
the dangers in that rough place and urged him to come home while the
ground was still frozen. "Your mother informs me that she wrote you not
long since to come home," George wrote, "and that she did it with my
approval." He went on to praise his son for passing a test of manhood,
and, as he would do with Carrie later, displayed past criticism in the current praise. "I have watched your career since you left here last August
with a great deal of interest and very much satisfaction. I really did not
think, Will, that you had the snap in you that you have manifested, and am
very much gratified at the effort that you made and the result. You certainly must have done it on your own personality, and it speaks very well
for you."[32]

George went on to give his son an extended paternal compliment:

> I have read your letters with a great deal of interest and have followed the
> trend of your mind from the days when you seemed to think that nothing was

---

30. WHW, in Dawson City, to JHW, in Waterbury, 14 Jan. 1901, "Wedding Ring," 113–15.

31. Ibid.

32. GLW, in Waterbury, to WHW, at Forty Mile, 6 March 1901, William Henry White Papers.

required but a shovel and pick experience, your evident disappointment at not realizing what your day dreams had pictured, your determination not to quit, and to pick up every opportunity you could find for earning a dollar and saving what you had, your gradual development into recognition and a comfortable position.

I have also noted with a great deal of interest your feeling that you were loosing time—wasting fruitlessly your valuable months of early manhood, and you wonder at what the experience is going to amount to. I can see very clearly that you have come through all that I had foreseen and that the experience which you are having will be the best capital of your life if you end it now. There is nothing that you have passed through there that will not apply to some event in your future life practically and thoroughly. One lesson I am sure you have learned, that is, patience. You have found it is one thing to want and another thing to get. In other words, you have been thrown on your own resources among strangers and you had to work out your own ideas in your own way among men of experience. This you could not have gained at home in years. You have further proven to my mind that you are not adapted to the kind of life which you would have to lead in order to reach success in that country. It is against your tastes and you take no evident interest in it. Your interest seems to be entirely centered at home and your goal seems to be your return here, not your success there before your return.

It took a month for the compliment to reach Forty-Mile; by then Will had been carrying out his job, hunting with the dogs and sled, and, at one point, on a "sixty-five mile mush" to gather some information about prospectors and "to tell a few to get off Government grounds."[33] There was no question of a precipitate return.

While Will was on the mush with the sled dogs and dealing with odd characters, Julia and George took their annual end-of-winter trip to the south. At "Uncle Lynde's kind invitation," they accompanied him in his private railroad car in Florida, "a novel and agreeable experience for us." From St. Augustine, where Julia wrote this, they were soon to move down the coast to Palm Beach and stay at Flagler's Royal Poinciana Hotel.[34]

When Will received the letters urging him to come home, he replied jocularly to Julia that where he was a dog team was easier to find than a

---

33. WHW, at Forty Mile, to JHW, in Waterbury, 12 March 1901, William Henry White Papers.

34. JHW, from Private Car 97, R.R. Station, St. Augustine Fla., to WHW, at Forty Mile, 19 March 1901, William Henry White Papers.

private railroad car. He had plenty of work, reports to write, and "[y]ou should see me propounding laws and regulations to four or five sourdough miners each one of my audience ejecting streams of tobacco juice onto the floor while I say weighty things about them to myself."[35] Will did agree to resign and come home, but because it was too late in the season for ice travel he had to wait for the ice breakup and the rivers to clear.[36] Julia wrote that Carrie had become engaged: "I have never said any thing about it because she has thought she was not quite sure—though I have seen her heart for some time. She seems very very happy and you must not think of me being secretive about it. I am so happy for her and I think Mr. [Robert F.] Griggs is just devoted to her and a very fine fellow. He seems to think the world of Caroline—and is fairly brimming with happiness." Of George she wrote that he is "completely delighted," and added, "He has such an absolute belief in matrimony, poor man."

In his solitary cabin Will must have been amused by this flash of wit from his mother. He too was thinking of matrimony. He knew he would propose to his sweetheart of many years, Mary Wade, on his return—indeed the rigors of this northern experience were a test of his resolve, and the separation a test of the ties between them. Julia reported that Mary had just returned from a trip with her parents to California and had won Carrie's heart by visiting her birthplace in San Rafael—she "won mine some time ago."[37] "If I were only home, that is where I want to be *home*," Will wrote in June, and explained that the two weeks that had elapsed between letters was because everything in his cabin was soaked. A newspaper clipping revealed to his parents Will's own role in the crisis at Forty-Mile:

> [O]n the 17th the Yukon broke, a jam occurred at an island below the town, causing both rivers to back up, fast . . . Mrs. E. T. Smith the genial hostess of the Miners House Restaurant, was obliged to climb to the top of the sign board over her boarding house until rescued by her husband and Mr. White, who was giving what assistance they could to the townspeople in a large Peterborough canoe. Mr. White, the mining recorder, was obliged to cut a hole through the roof of his cabin in order to secure important records and papers, the water having risen above the upper limit of his doorway. It might

---

35. WHW, from at Forty Mile, to JHW, in Waterbury 2 April 1901, William Henry White Papers.

36. WHW, at Forty Mile, to GLW, in Waterbury, 7 April 1901, William Henry White Papers.

37. JHW, in Waterbury, to WHW, Forty Mile, 28 April 1901, William Henry White Papers.

be proper to say in this connection that he also spent several hours helping to rescue families from their perilous location and to remove them to higher ground.[38]

It was July before Will could reach Dawson and a steamer to take him south and to the Canadian Pacific Railroad—the fastest route home. "Polly has written me such a sweet letter," he reported to Julia, using Mary Wade's nickname (later it became Molly). "I also told you that, but I did not tell you that she said she cares for me more than she ever has and I— well you know better than she does, how much I care for her and how much I have tried to live as she would have me live and now I am going back to see her."[39]

"Home tonight at eight. Billie," was on the telegram delivered to the Grove Street house at the end of July 1901.[40] Will had enjoyed a unique adventure, proved his manhood to his and his father's satisfaction, and tested the temper of the long-standing attraction between Mary and himself. He brought back gold nuggets for several of the family and one for his watch fob. One of the nuggets later was on his niece's charm bracelet, witness to the author, who played with it as a child, that his great uncle had struck gold in the far-off Klondike. In Waterbury, Will went to work at White & Wells, and soon Mary Wade accepted his proposal of marriage.

Rob and the Griggs Family

When Carrie turned twenty-six in April 1901 she was in the midst of deciding whether to accept a proposal of marriage. The man who perceived the quality of this shy young woman was a business friend of George, Robert Foote Griggs, a widower of thirty-three. Carrie told the author in her old age that Rob, as he was called, frequently came to the house to talk with George—he doubtless paid his respects to the ladies in the parlor between closeted talks over brandy and cigars in the library. Without Carrie being aware of it, so she said, he became attracted to the retiring young woman and—to her surprise—proposed marriage. At first she was not at all sure she should accept.

38. WHW, at Forty Mile, to JHW, in Waterbury, 1 June 1901, William Henry White Papers. Unidentified newspaper, dated 24 May 1901.

39. WHW, at Forty Mile, to JHW, in Waterbury, 30 May 1901, William Henry White Papers.

40. WHW telegram to JHW, in Waterbury, 28 July 1901, William Henry White Papers.

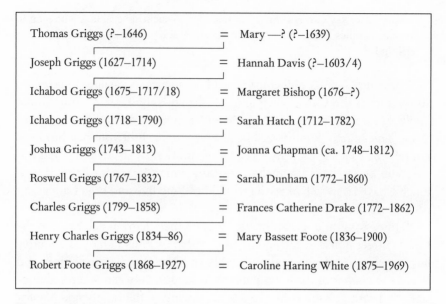

Thomas Griggs (?–1646)	=	Mary —? (?–1639)
Joseph Griggs (1627–1714)	=	Hannah Davis (?–1603/4)
Ichabod Griggs (1675–1717/18)	=	Margaret Bishop (1676–?)
Ichabod Griggs (1718–1790)	=	Sarah Hatch (1712–1782)
Joshua Griggs (1743–1813)	=	Joanna Chapman (ca. 1748–1812)
Roswell Griggs (1767–1832)	=	Sarah Dunham (1772–1860)
Charles Griggs (1799–1858)	=	Frances Catherine Drake (1772–1862)
Henry Charles Griggs (1834–86)	=	Mary Bassett Foote (1836–1900)
Robert Foote Griggs (1868–1927)	=	Caroline Haring White (1875–1969)

58. Griggs descent to Robert Foote Griggs

Robert Foote Griggs's New England ancestry went back to the 1630s. His paternal line stemmed from Thomas Griggs, who arrived at Massachusetts Bay Colony in the 1630s and, with his sons and grandsons, settled in Roxbury, where the family remained for three generations. By the 1740s Ichabod Griggs, in the fourth generation, looked for more fertile fields in Connecticut. After two moves he settled in Tolland, northeast of Hartford, where he and his descendants remained for another three generations. Rob's grandfather, Charles Griggs (1799–1858) was drawn from Tolland and its farms to business opportunities in East Windsor, north of Hartford, and then to Waterbury's factories, just as Luther Chapin White had been. Unlike him, however, he arrived with means, a wife, and a family. In Waterbury he bought from David Prichard, of an old settled family, "a piece of ground . . . about 80 rods southerly from the Congregational Meeting House in the village of Waterbury"—on a street soon to be named Cottage Place—"with a Dwelling House, barn and shop thereon."[41]

Charles's wife was Frances Catherine Drake, from East Windsor, where her family had long been established. She was a descendant of

---

41. Property Records, 50:320, 24 April 1845, City of Waterbury.

59. Charles Griggs and Frances Catherine (Drake) Griggs

Courtesy Thomas Razee

Oliver Wolcott, a signer of the Declaration of Independence and an early governor of the state—a heritage later pointedly referred to in family biographies.[42] At the time of Charles's death, at the age of fifty-nine, in 1858, we know from the estate inventory that the house on Cottage Place (which his son, Henry, Rob's father, would inherit and where Rob was living before he married Carrie) was amply, even elegantly, furnished. The inventory had the detail familiar from the previous centuries and listed pillows, sheets, and an "Eider" for warmth. There were also shares in the recently formed Waterbury National Bank—Charles Griggs had entered the economy of shareholders.[43] Charles was buried in the family plot that he had purchased on one of the slopes at Riverside Cemetery.

Charles left no will, and his estate was divided among his sons and widow. She continued to live in the Cottage Place house, which for the next fifty years remained the family homestead, until it was overwhelmed

42. See "Griggs," Genealogical and Biographical Notes.

43. The sole real property noted in the estate inventory was "5 Acres of Land in South Windsor, Hartford Co, Homestead," "Estate of Charles Griggs," Inventory, 15 Nov. 1858, Waterbury Probate Court Documents to 1881, FHL microfilm 1032499, State Archives, CSL.

by commercial buildings in the early 1900s. A photograph taken later in the century shows a narrow two-and-one-half story building, suggesting an 1820s date of construction, the lot delineated by a picket fence. It was a place with a sense of the rural past near the increasingly busy town center.

Charles and Catherine Drake had come to Waterbury with four sons (a daughter died young), all born in Tolland. For most of the thirty-seven years that remained to her after her husband's death, Catherine shared the house with her son Henry and his family. Two of the sons stayed in Waterbury. Edmund Louis (1838–1904) became a physician, residing and consulting at the Scovill House (until the fire of 1902).[44] Henry Charles Griggs (1834–86), Rob's father, made his mark as a manufacturer, real estate developer, and civic leader. His wife Mary Bassett Foote (1836–1900) was from a Hamden family with an even older Connecticut heritage than the Griggs family's.

With his long, flowing beard and bright, almost wild expression in his eyes, Henry Charles Griggs, in his early fifties, was a dramatic figure, the embodiment of intelligence and energy—qualities that helped him take advantage of the widening opportunities for Waterbury factories during and after the Civil War. He rose rapidly in business, having started as a clerk in a store when he was fourteen, and, at twenty joining the Waterbury Hook and Eye Company, a supplier to the New York City apparel trade. During the Civil War he served as manager of the Waterbury Button Company, which employed about thirty hands and prospered from military orders. In 1865, at the age of twenty-nine, he joined with an older Waterbury businessman, John E. Smith (of the "second rank" of Waterbury businessmen as determined by the historian of the company) in a partnership, Smith & Griggs. It was a small business with sales of about $3,000 per year.[45] The factory developed a line that it advertised as "Vest, Pantaloon, Suspender, Skirt, Shoe, Hat, and Belt, Buckles and Slides; Skirt Trimmings, and a Variety of Small Wares Made from Brass, Tin, Iron, and Steel," items made available to the apparel trade through a sales office in New York.[46]

---

44. Waterbury directories, 1898–1902.

45. Theodore F. Marburg, *Small Business in Brass Manufacturing: The Smith and Griggs Manufacturing Company of Waterbury* (New York: New York Univ. Press, 1956), 4–5.

46. Advertisement, *Waterbury Almanac 1870* (Waterbury, Conn., 1869).

60. Henry Charles Griggs and Mary Bassett (Foote) Griggs with their sons, about 1880

The family is standing before their house on Cottage Place. Left to right are Charles Jared, Wilfred Elizur, David Cullen, and Robert Foote.

In effect the business was sponsored by two of the larger brass manufacturers ("of the first rank"), Israel Holmes and Aaron Benedict. The business historian Mathew Roth points out that these presidents "controlled the stock of Smith & Griggs." A majority of its work "came from customers passed along by a buckle-making company controlled by the large brass firms . . . Smith & Griggs relied on pool agreements among buckle makers."[47] That is, it was not an innovative business, as it made what others were making, but its relatively small size allowed it flexibility, and it was available for work subcontracted by other firms. (We have seen the Benedict sponsorship of Luther Chapin White, whose oil lamps business was folded into the larger firm when it proved itself and White went on to other ventures.) Thanks to Henry's youngest son, David, who preserved its archive, the company is one of the few Waterbury firms of this

---

47. Mathew W. Roth, *Platt Brothers and Company: Small Business in American Manufacturing.* (Hanover, N.H.: Univ. Press of New England, for the Univ. of Connecticut, 1994), 19.

period to have been the subject of a scholarly monograph.[48] From his examination of the records, Theodore Marburg concluded that Griggs "was a thoughtful, careful and considerate person with a somewhat less aggressive manner than Smith, but able to master a situation by strategic compromises."[49]

Henry Griggs left active participation in Smith & Griggs in 1875 and ventured into real estate in the growing city. For $10,000—which was subject to promissory notes to the sellers—he and partners bought farmland a half mile north of the Green, traversed by North Main Street,[50] which he subdivided into building lots. After some lots were sold, in 1880 the project was aided by his agreement with members of the Kingsbury family, who owned adjoining land—where Frederick Kingsbury and his wife, Alathea, would repair for country outings until development ceased to make that attractive—that a road (the future Griggs Street) be cut across a portion of their land. Henry Griggs subdivided the land around this and neighboring Division Street and offered lots for sale. It was well positioned by proximity to expanding factories.[51] By the turn of the century (and after his death), all lots in the "Griggs plot" had been sold. Henry also purchased land on Hillside, off Pine Street, another "H. C. Griggs plot" on the maps, where his son, David, later built houses for himself and his children.[52] (Griggs Street today is pockmarked by vacant lots and some of the remaining houses are close to derelict; by contrast, his former land on Hillside is occupied by substantial houses, some designed by his son Wilfred.)

The most enduring of Henry Griggs' real estate ventures was the commercial building at 221–227 Bank Street in Waterbury. "The Griggs Block" opened in 1884 and remains a notable and well-preserved building on a largely intact commercial block, now protected by its designation as an historic district. It was designed by Robert Hill, the architect responsible for the imposing City Hall (1868), St. Margaret's, and the Hall

---

48. Ibid., 16; Marburg, *Small Business*. Shares remained in the family until its demise in the mid-1930s.

49. Marburg, *Small Business*, 7.

50. Property Records, 33:153, 23 Nov. 1872, City of Waterbury.

51. Property Records, 100:329, 25 Oct. 1880, City of Waterbury. *Waterbury Connecticut, 1901* (New York: Sanborn-Ferris Map Co., 1901), 27, Research Collection, Mattatuck Museum.

52. Waterbury, Conn., *Atlas of the City of Waterbury 1879*. David C. Griggs later lived at 196 Pine St., at the corner of Woodlawn Terrace, in a house designed by Wilfred Griggs; and he built houses for his two children on other portions of what had been the H. C. Griggs land.

61. The Griggs Building at 221–227 Bank
Street (before restoration)

Memorial Chapel at Riverside Cemetery.[53] For Henry Griggs the building
was a commercial venture, and he rented the street front to stores, the
upper stories to a hotel. He lived only a few years after its completion: his
enduring contribution to the city was the building and the support of the
architect's design. (Curiously, this building was never pointed out to the
author by his family, and it was only through researching the present book
that he discovered his great-grandfather was responsible for the building
that bears his surname prominently on a terra cotta emblem. The association of Wilfred Griggs, his talented son, with highly visible buildings,
including those frequently visited by the author as a child, was likewise
never pointed out.) Henry Griggs maintained a small factory on the
Griggs plot off North Main Street; the metal parts for suspenders and
other items were part of his estate.[54]

---

53. The Griggs Building is a "superb example of Queen Anne Revival commercial design," according to a 1980 architectural survey, "a veritable tour-de-force of exquisite craftsmanship in brick and
terracotta, with a fish-scale slate roof, ornate dormers, stained glass borders in the upper sash, and
one of the best cast iron storefronts remaining in this part of Connecticut . . . of the highest historic
and stylistic interest." Maxmillian L Ferro, Arthur L. Brown, Melvin Canzon, and Roger Brevoort,
"Report on Historic Structures in Downtown Waterbury Presently Scheduled for Demolition,"
prepared for Waterbury Action to Conserve Our Heritage (Natick, Mass: Preservation Partnership, [1980]), 39.

54. "Estate of Henry C. Griggs," Inventory, April 1887, Waterbury Probate Dist., file 3275, RG 4,
Records of the Probate Courts, State Archives, CSL.

Griggs moved easily from business to civic affairs. He was an incorpo-
rator of Waterbury Hospital at its formation (but did not live to see it
opened), and he was a member of municipal road and water commissions.
He was elected an alderman and twice as representative from Waterbury
to the Connecticut General Assembly. It was returning from a session of
that body in horse and buggy that signs of what became a fatal illness first
appeared. The stir that Griggs's untimely death caused in Waterbury
could not be anticipated by recounting his business activities alone. There
were obviously personal qualities, some of which can be perceived in the
photographs, of what must have been a powerful and magnetic personality
that endeared him to his friends, neighbors, and colleagues. The account
of his illness and death was front-page news of the *Waterbury Republican*
on Friday, 17 July 1886:

> Representative Henry C. Griggs died at 10 minutes of 3 o'clock this morning
> at his residence on Cottage Place. His sickness had first made itself manifest
> last Sunday, but his condition did not seem critical until Friday, and it was not
> until that afternoon that the indications of fatal results were discernible.
> About the time that the legislature met he suffered from a bilious attack, to
> which he was subject, but seemingly overcame it, and was able to discharge
> his legislative duties as well as those pertaining to his business. But his counte-
> nance did not quite regain its wonted color, and what seemed like a recurrence
> of he trouble began last Sunday, and finally assumed the form of gastroenteri-
> tis. As soon as attacked, he sent for his brother. Dr. Edward L. Griggs, who,
> as the disease progressed, called in consultation Dr. G. L. Platt, and every-
> thing that medical skill or pure affection could suggest was done, but without
> the desired result. Last evening he was conscious and probably without suf-
> fering. All his family were present, including the three sons who are studying
> at Yale College. He spoke to them words of affection, and then, exhausted by
> his long conflict with disease, grew weaker and weaker, until life ebbed away
> as the twilight fades into the night.[55]

The editorial in the same paper praised him as "a gentleman in the
highest and best sense, presuming qualities of mind and heart which made
him welcome wherever he went and obtained for him recognition in public
and private life without self-seeking on his part. Henry C. Griggs excelled,
his character, marked only by virtues, and it is because he thus excelled
that Waterbury mourns him today as only a city can mourn for one whose

---

55. Obit., *Waterbury Republican*, 17 July 1886.

life was a blessing to society individually and collectively." It was a Plutar-chian tribute, much like that later paid to Augustus Sabin Chase, to a man who had contributed considerably to the civic culture. The editorialist emphasized character equally with business ability, both considered to be essential for establishing a standard of behavior for the developing and self-conscious city.

The funeral, at the First Congregational Church, was a civic event, with the printing of the "discourse" by the Rev. Joseph Anderson, as the newspaper termed it, requiring one and a half columns on the front page. There can have few dry eyes as Dr. Anderson spoke:

> Just now, coming in at the gate, an old friend said, "I never expected to attend the funeral of Mr. Henry Griggs." The same might be said of most of us. It was only a week ago, last Friday, that he came home from his place in the leg-islature, wearied and somewhat worn by his official labors, and glad of a little rest; and it was only last Friday that the message went forth from reluctant lips that he must die. How strange it seems to us all that one apparently so full of vigor should be thus suddenly smitten down, and should be lying here today so peacefully in his last sleep, his life's work forever ended.[56]

The pastor went on to describe the deathbed. "He gathered his loved ones around him and spoke to each a word of farewell. And to each he said the right thing." When Dr. Anderson arrived,

> he seemed to be anxiously awaiting me, and at once began to speak of the great change so near at hand. "I am going into the *new world* before," he said, "and ere I go I desire to talk with you about it, and to say to you that it is all right, that it is all right." One who sat beside him, whose heart clung to him, strove to convince him that we should not let him go; but he said, I feel that the time has come. I should have been glad to stay longer, but it is all right, and I am ready to go. I said to him, "To one whose trust is in the mercy and love of God, it need make but little difference whether he go or stay." "It is there," he replied, "that I put my trust," and he added with a gesture which expressed more than words, "I leave all in His Hands. I have tried," he said, after a brief pause, "to live as I ought to live, but I might have done better. "All of us might do better," I replied, " it is not upon what we do that we rely, but upon the grace of God our Saviour." "Yes, that is it," he said. "I leave it all with Him." When I repeated to him some of the sweet promises of God's

---

56. "The Late Henry C. Griggs: Funeral Discourse Delivered by Rev. Joseph Anderson," *Water-bury Republican*, 20 July 1881.

word, he listened with a peculiar earnestness, and now and then uttered some word of response; and when I offered to pray with him he accepted my proposal as with the gladness of a child.

As with Luther Chapin White's passing, this was a scene from genre painting, the dying patriarch attended by four sons, wife, and mother, with the pastor in clerical garb at the bedside.

Henry Griggs left his wife, mother, and the four sons well provided for, though there was no will. The estate amounted to $113,454.36. In the inventory were items in the factory that he ran at the time of his death. He had owned an "open buggy," "business wagon," "business sleigh," and stocks in the Waterbury National Bank, the Waterbury Buckle Co., American Mills, and the Southford Paper Co. (which White & Wells would later buy and George Luther White head for a time). In addition to the house and lot on Cottage Place and the Griggs Block on Bank Street, he left 100 acres in the then rural Bucks Hill section of Waterbury and "1 Factory with Lot and Water Power, 6¼ acres on Pine Street (Hillside, on part of which his son David Griggs would later live).[57]

Carrie's Decision

At the time of his father's death, Rob was eighteen and a sophomore at Yale, which he then left, probably to assist his mother and brothers in settling the estate. (He kept up with Yale in later life, sent one son there, and regularly went to football games.)

Of the eight children born to Henry and Mary Bassett Griggs only four boys survived—a repetition of the experience of the Charles and Catherine Griggs family and another indication of the high childhood mortality in mid-century. Henry recognized the importance of the education he had never had and sent all four of the sons to Yale, one of the earliest of the manufacturers to do so. All had active careers in Waterbury. Charles Jared became a lawyer and was tax collector at his death in 1904. Wilfred Elizur became the architect whose many buildings from the 1890s to 1918 established the essential texture of downtown Waterbury as it emerged in the new century. David, an engineer and manufacturer, was the longest-lived, and died in Waterbury in 1958 at the age of eighty-seven.

---

57. "Estate of Henry C. Griggs," Inventory, file 3275.

Rob, the third of the four boys, grew up well placed in the industrial economy of Waterbury. The inheritance from his father did not temper an eagerness for work and business. When he proposed to Carrie, he was thirty-three and had been for seven years the secretary and general manager of the Mathews & Willard Co. of Waterbury, where he had worked (except for a year at a bank) since he left Yale. The firm manufactured a wide range of metal goods, advertising "Nickel Stove Knobs, Spun metal urns, Covers, Bronze Statuettes, Stove Trimmings, Artistic Brass and Plated Goods, Tubular Lanterns, Carriage Harness and Saddle Trimmings, in Silver, Nickel and Gold."[58] It was a typical Waterbury factory operation, which combined metal forming with plating to create highly finished objects. Rob represented the company for a time in Savannah, Georgia, where he married for the first time. A baby daughter died at a year and a half, and his wife died at age thirty, four years after their marriage.[59] Carrie was thus courted by a man older than she, who had seen more of the world. He was experienced, and sobered by the loss of his first family. His maturity and confidence must have helped him overcome her shyness and reserve.

Rob lived at the Griggs homestead on Cottage Place and was alone after his mother died in May 1900. He proposed to Carrie in early 1901. She, uncertain, told Julia, but asked her to say nothing about it to George until she was certain of her response. Rob, for his part, knew that he must ask the father for his daughter's hand. We can see the engagement emerge in letters between the four of them. In March the elder Whites went south with the Harrisons (on Uncle Lynde's private railroad car, from which she had written Will). On the trip George sensed something was up and pressed Julia to break her confidence. She wrote Carrie that she could not keep the secret from him; Carrie wrote back dismayed, to which Julia replied.

> I have received yours of the Seventeenth. Which of course made my heart glad even if you did grieve me by saying you could not trust me anymore— Carrie dear, I had to use my own judgment in the matter. And you could not expect me to tell your father a deliberate lie. He asked me point blank a question to which I had to say "yes" or "no," and a yes was the truth. I said it. I did not say much else. And he did not say much of anything then. But the next

---

58. *Waterbury City Directory* (1891), xviii. There is no will, or record of one, in the estate papers.

59. *Yale Univ., Class of [18]89 Quarter Centennial Record* (New Haven: Yale Univ. Press, 1914), 287. See also "Griggs," Genealogical and Biographical Notes.

morning he did say a great deal about it. He asked, Carrie, what reason there was that you had kept it all from him. And furthermore, he said of all the men he knew he could think of no one better suited to you. That he was a good all-around fellow, etc. Then I tried to make him see how happy you are. Now for myself dear I must make you see that it was anxiety on my part largely that made me say anything. I was beginning to feel a little frightened. You know how much I like Mr. Griggs. But my judgment is not *always good* when it comes to men. My heart is stronger than my head you know. He is (or has been) the best male-friend of your father's. That is the worst thing I know about him. And as I wrote you before, your father is [   ] as nearly as close to you as I am. Your happiness is my greatest wish. And it is a matter of much moment to him and I felt that I must ask his opinion. You must not blame me, dear. It was no idle desire to tell something. I know that he did not know. It was great that I did not dare keep quiet any longer. The next time you will, no doubt, keep it entirely to yourself—and I shall feel that my reputation as a confidante is gone—but I love you very much—and that is the main reason need my best for being indiscreet . . .

Last night I ventured to put on my black & green gown—the one Mr. G.[riggs] said he liked—When I sat down to dinner your Papa—who sits opposite to me—nodded his head in a doubtful manner that might have meant anything. I immediately commenced to hook up [   ] but found to my great relief he was only expressing admiration. He says it is a "beauty"— What a queer man he is. I have so much trouble with my back fastenings and my back hair—and never feel quite sure how I look without you to give me those affectionate little dabs.

. . . Oh I wish you were with me and not worrying and fussing about the house—We would enjoy the walks here and the chair rides and the beautiful sea. . . .

Nothing from Will [then in Forty-Mile]—I am getting so anxious about him that it spoils everything—but as your Father says How much good does it do me—Uncle Lynde is as nice as he can be and your Father is a model man but not feeling very well—He sends his love with mine—and I send oh so much to you my dear little girl.[60]

The Whites traveled north to Thomasville, Georgia, where Lynde Harrison owned a house. "I am home sick," Julia wrote, "and long to see the pleasant new house again—but it is my duty to stay as long as I am well treated, and I will not stay a minute longer—which I suppose would be just as much, & even more my duty—So far between him and Uncle Lynde there has been every kindness shown me—and I have had a most enjoyable time, but I miss you sadly and long for you every hour." She was relieved to hear from Will but worried about his "big game hunting" (the caribou he hauled back on the dog sled), but the subject of the engagement was dormant for the moment.

On 10 April Carrie, accompanied by her Cousin Lizzie, visited New York City to celebrate her birthday. Two days later—probably when she had already given her formal consent—Rob asked George in writing for her hand, addressing him as "My dear Colonel," evidently a familiar nickname. He couched his request formally, though no doubt well aware that his friend would welcome the request. In terms akin to those that George had expressed to Julia during their engagement, he pledged his devotion to the care of his future wife.

It is a very difficult matter to write you on such a serious subject as I propose to do—more so, I think, because you have been good enough to me to give me your friendship without a thought of the greatest of favors it was destined that I am to ask of you.[61] Although I realize you cannot realize how dear your daughter has become to me and how inseparable from my hopes of happiness, yet I hope you will not be altogether surprised at what I say. As you know, I am not naturally communicative on the subjects nearest my heart and it is hard for me to express myself even to you to whom I know that what concerns so nearly your daughter whom you love anything I may say will be received in the same spirit as I say it. I love her tenderly and truly and in a way that will last and will make it my life's happiness, if it is permitted, to be everything to her and for her to the full extent of my heart and mind and strength. As to this point, please be very sure that I am not impetuous or

---

60. JHW, at the Royal Poinciana Hotel, Palm Beach, Fla., to CHW, in Waterbury, 23 March 1901. The elegance of the Royal Poinciana, razed in the 1930s, and its setting roused the usually terse Baedeker to rhapsodize that it "ranks as one of the most fashionable water resorts in the United States, and in some respects rivals the resorts of the Mediterranean. Unlimited wealth has made of the surroundings of the chief hotels a vast semi-tropical paradise. . . . The cupola of the Poinciana reveals an entrancing view (esp. at sunset) including the entire length of Lake Worth, with the villas on its banks, the narrow peninsula, clad in tropical verdure, between the lake and the ocean, the Atlantic stretching away to thee horizon and the mysterious Everglades to the West. . . ." Karl Baedeker, *The United States, with an Excursion into Mexico: Handbook for Travellers* (New York, C. Scribner's Sons, 1904), 252–53. The fare from New York to Jacksonville was $20, the sleeper an extra $6.50; the dining car meals were $1. The expanding Florida trade had encouraged the railroad to lay on a daily train as luxurious as that to Chicago. It consisted (in 1904) "entirely of Pullman vestibuled cars," with "every imaginable comfort to the traveler. . . . a dining car, a library, a smoking and outlook car, a barber's shop, a bath, a ladies maid, and a stenographer." The trip took from twenty-six to thirty-six hours to Jacksonville. Baedeker, *United States*, 443.

61. Robert Foote Griggs [RFG], in Waterbury, to GLW, at the Highland Park Hotel, Asheville, N.C., 12 April 1901.

uncertain, and I can promise that as far as the faithfulness of my love and devotion can count for her happiness it shall be assured. And she has permitted me to think that this will count a great deal with her—as her love and trust counts as everything with me.

I know how much trust I have asked of her and am asking of you, and perhaps it is folly for me to long for so great and precious a responsibility but the thought of having her love and trust and the hope of having her and her companionship make me feel very strong and that I can surely meet and overcome troubles for her in living.

At any rate I promise you from my heart that if bye-and-bye you can trust her to me in addition to my love, I will do for her everything that my mind and body can and I will count her smallest happiness and comfort before anything in the world . . .

Carrie wrote her father on the same day, explaining that for three months she had been "uncertain," but after "[m]any, many" talks with Rob, she became sure. Some of the uncertainty was the natural hesitation before a decision that would transform her life, part seems to have been due to a sense of inadequacy—she refers to George's past criticism of her abilities and retiring nature.

In this gentle address to her father Carrie's thoughtful, quietly humorous, modest, and affectionate essence is open to us:

Your [birthday] telegram was awaiting me when I returned from New York last evening. It was sweet of you to think of me. Does it not make you feel a little older too, this being the father of a maiden twenty six years old! Well, I hope I may look as young and attractive when I am your age as you are.

Were you here today I should talk with you, but since you are not here I will write a letter of what I would say.

Mother has written me that you asked her a question to which she implied "yes." What the exact question was I do not know, but I do know that had you asked me I too would have answered truthfully.

I have not said anything to you before because you did not seem to be aware of the fact that Mr. Griggs cared for me, and as I have been in a very uncertain state of mind I did not feel that I had any right or that there was any object in talking over so serious a matter. You can understand my feeling, can you not?

Now that I am no longer uncertain, fight against it as I may, I am very much in love, I make my own confession to you, my father.

I hope you know me well enough to believe me when I tell you that I have spent many thoughtful and troubled hours during the past three months. To me it is a very serious questions and I know too much of the bitterness &

62. Rob and Carrie, engaged, 1901

unhappiness to be hasty & careless. Then too, I haven't much higher opinion of my abilities or my disposition than you have (you know you have expressed your self once or twice) but I sometimes wonder if there may not be a better side than the one you have discovered. I pray God it may be so, for this man who loves me is rather blind to my faults and how much I do so want not to disappoint him. I want to be loved and to love and to be able to give happiness and true companionship. Not the immature ideas of a *young thing* for if I ever did have them, which I doubt, they have long since been outgrown.

Rob and I have many many long and serious talks and I think we understand one another as well as two people can in like circumstances.

Oh! This means so much to me and it will mean something to you too. It is all such a responsibility isn't it!

Well, dear, tho' there is more to be said sometime I have told you enough for now and I want you to tell me what *you* feel and think.

I am so glad you are better and I hope you will not hurry home before you are pretty well again. Everything is getting on nicely and I think you will find the house in better order than when you left.

I have just mailed a letter to mother from Will. What an experience he is having!

Of course this is just for *us four* to know for the present. I am very very happy.[62]

In response we see George plain too, all within the one letter—preoccupied with his health ("very bad cold"), missing his helpmate, Julia, who

62. CHW, in Waterbury, to GLW, at the Highland Park Hotel, Asheville, N.C., 12 April 1901.

left for the home she yearned for, forthright about how he had felt with respect to Carrie's apparent retirement from the society of men, affectionate, and wise about what Carrie's prospects would have been without marriage. As he considered Rob one of the "few" honest businessmen he knew—he was delighted with the match. This engagement filled him with pride and relief: a young, admired business colleague would care for his sometime shy daughter. He signed formally with his full name, as did Rob and Carrie in their letters.

> Your lovely letter of the 12th much freighted with such a wealth of information and expressions of love for me as well another, found me miserable indeed. I was feeling miserably when your Mother left me, and while waiting at the R.R. station for her to leave, I contracted a very severe cold and am now just about sick. No wonder then that I have delayed answering both "Babs" letter and your own. The subject is so broad, and I feel the situation so keenly that it seems as though it demanded of me a long, long, letter to each of you. But after all what more is there to be said than that I am delighted?[63]

George had criticisms that he apparently felt should be expressed now that they were no longer necessary:

> It has seemed to me Carrie for a number of years as you have doubtless observed, that your life was incomplete and barren of accomplishment. I saw no future for you. It worried me greatly as many of my allusions to it no doubt revealed to you. The entire and absolute opposition of your Mother and yourself to my views discouraged me. Your attitude to society and all the interest in men which it has always seemed to me was the natural condition of woman worried me. I could see nothing ahead for you but loneliness and a narrowing and contraction of all your mental and physical nature. All would be well so long as your Mother lived and your wants supplied perhaps, but what a dwarfing of nature's design!

"Do you remember my ever having told you that sometime Cupid might throw a little arrow into your heart and change all your ideas and reasoning?" What he hoped would happen had come to be.

> Thank heaven that this time has arrived, and that you have been so fortunate in gaining the love and admiration of so good and true a man as Rob Griggs! As you know for several years he has been my close & warm friend and

---

63. GLW, at the Battery Park Hotel, Asheville, N.C. to CHW in Waterbury, 19 April 1901.

confidant. He has known more of my inner thoughts than you may have known, and after many years of contact with men, I have found few—very few with whom I would share my confidences. There is so much selfishness and dishonesty among them which reveals itself only at a critical moment when you must need them, that I am becoming more and more alone, although as you know I am very fond of men and their society. Again he has had much experience and ought to know himself thoroughly which is so necessary in the selection of a life mate. Perfection is not possible, dear girl, and your ideal must not be too high! Rather fit yourself to the man who has won you, than try and fit him to an ideal. Cater to what you find him to be; not what you wish him to be, and if real instead of fancied love exists he will do the rest.

Yes! my dear, this step means so much to us all. It means an entire change in my future as well as yours. You do not know what an happy man I am. I see before me a silver lining to a cloud which has hung over me for a long long time and unexpected happiness in store for me—happiness in your future; your pleasures and sorrows, and the hope that the development of your nature which comes to all, as personal cares and responsibilities come to them in actual instead of artificial life, will enhance your respect and love for me.

What more can I write, my only daughter—my first born for whom I cherished such a fond love, and built such great expectations for my old age, than to say you have my deepest love and congratulations? I cannot imagine your making a more agreeable choice, and the results all rest with you both.

As stated I have a very bad cold, and the weather is very unsatisfactory here. I am booked to leave here Sunday next but may conclude to remain another week. I am lonely however and may start away Sunday. There is a Golf tournament next week which I am strongly urged to take part in—the "duffers" class.

Tell Rob I have not yet mustered up courage to answer his plea for consent, so beautifully worded. I feel like writing him a lecture on "duplicity." For a time I came near challenging him for such pronounced attentions to my wife. Give him my love and congratulations and tell him when in the mood I will write him.

Rob joined Carrie and the family that summer at a rustic hotel near the Adirondacks.[64] A photo by Julia shows the family enjoying a drink on a rustic porch, another the couple silhouetted against the evening light, posed as though they were looking at their future together. There are, of course, no letters to tell us more, but Julia's snapshots convey the congenial stay they enjoyed at the country lodge.

---

64. The envelope of a letter from Aunt Hattie bears the forwarding address of this hotel. Harriet White Harrison, in Bournemouth, England, to CHW in Waterbury, 14 Aug. 1901.

63. George, Carrie, Rob, and George Jr. at the
Adirondacks, summer 1901

Carrie and Rob Marry

With the renovation done, Julia wrote Will that the "house is lovely, everything is so convenient . . . some of the rooms are quite in order: mine, the parlor and music room, Carrie's and dining room nearly so."[65] Carrie's wedding in February was the occasion to finish everything up and put the house in its new state on display, the product of George's nerve-wracking supervision.

A midwinter wedding can be threatened by ice and snow, but what could not have been expected was a fire that destroyed a large portion of downtown Waterbury only two days before the February 4 wedding date. As the *Waterbury American* described it in a special edition (courtesy of another printer, as the newspaper office had been destroyed), "Thirty-two buildings, among them the finest of the kind in Waterbury, are destroyed. More than 100 business establishments are wiped out."[66] The town's best hotel, the Scovill House [where Rob's physician uncle lived], was no more. Because the wind carried the fire north from Grand Street to the Green, the White & Wells and L. C. White Co. Buildings and the Griggs Buildings were spared. The railroad stations were not in its course, and, as the fire did not cross the Green, Hillside residences were unaffected. There

---

65. JHW, in Waterbury, to WHW, in the Yukon, 24 Feb. 1901, "Wedding Ring," 139–42.

66. *Waterbury American*, 3 Feb. 1902. The newspaper's offices and presses had been destroyed, and this edition was printed courtesy of another printer.

64. Devastation in Waterbury after the fire of 1902

Mattatuck Museum

was no reason, therefore, to cancel the wedding. The bachelor dinner took place as scheduled the night after the fire. Rob, his brother David, Will, and seven other men sat at a round table for a rich meal accompanied by wines and champagne. (Curiously, Rob's older brother, Wilfred, the architect, was not a member of the wedding party, but he and his wife did give the couple the relatively modest present of "Chinese embroidery," as Carrie recorded it.)[67]

The ceremony at 114 Grove began at three o'clock, when, as the newspaper reported, "[d]aylight was excluded, and the house was brilliantly lighted by electricity in all the rooms." The interior was "handsomely" decorated by Dallas, the leading local florist, who provided a floral canopy in the parlor, "the prevailing color of the decorations being pink and white. In the music room the decorations were pink and in the library yellow and white." Carrie wore the dress that her grandmother, Jane Amelia, had worn in 1844, "of white material, covered with Venetian point lace." Mary Burrall, her maid of honor, was "attired in a pretty costume of gray

---

67. CHWG Wedding Book, Carrie's wedding scrapbook, in possession of Nancy Griggs Razee.

crepe de chine." Rob's younger brother, David, was best man. Will White, back from his Yukon adventure, and George Jr. were ushers along with John P. Elton (of Scovill Manufacturing) and Ralph Smith (of Smith & Griggs).

The minister was the Rev. Joseph Anderson, the distinguished historian of the city, and pastor of the First Congregational Church, of which George and his father before him had been members. Although Rob's father had also been a member, he had joined St. John's Episcopal Church—at this point in Waterbury's history St. John's was more "social" than the First Congregational.

Dr. Anderson used the *Book of Common Prayer* for the service. The music was by Fischl, of New Haven—surely a string trio playing salon music such as Julia and George had enjoyed in European hotels. The elegant selection of food was by Delmonico's of New York.[68]

The bride and groom traveled to New York by private rail car, a lavishness that Carrie would laugh about years later. They spent their wedding night at the Hotel Netherlands, one of the "three large and luxurious houses" at the southeastern entrance to Central Park. At two hundred and thirty-four feet, the Netherlands was the tallest hotel in the world when it was built in 1892.[69] The location could not be better for a leisurely visit, with views uptown and down and, a few feet from the entrance, the carriage drives and walkways of Central Park.[70]

In the wedding scrapbook, given to her by Mr. & Mrs. Henry Rowland, Carrie dutifully recorded, on twelve pages, the presents she received. The frontispiece of the book shows a handsome young couple in Regency dress embracing beneath a Gothic arch, with a quote attributed to Dickens, "'Tis love, 'tis love, 'tis love, That makes the world go round."[71] The presents themselves reflected the prosperity that had come to Waterbury, and the country, and the show that wealth was expected to

---

68. Newspaper clippings in CHWG Wedding Book. The headline in the *Waterbury American*, 5 Feb. 1902, was "The Griggs-White Wedding, Well Known Young People Married by Dr. Joseph Anderson."

69. The Netherland's equally luxurious neighbors were the old Plaza, on the site of the present one, and the Savoy. Robert A. M. Stern, Gregory Gilmartin, John Massengale, *New York 1900: Metropolitan Architecture and Urbanism 1890–1915* (New York: Rizzoli, 1983), 261

70. The tariffs were similar to those at the resorts: room and board from $5 a night Baedeker, *United States* (1904), 10.

71. CHWG Wedding Book.

make of itself. Polishing the silver received would have required a maid virtually full time. Carrie listed seven silver lunch dishes, four fancy silver spoons, two silver tea strainers, eight silver candlesticks, two silver bowls, two bon-bon dishes, a card tray, jugs, a coffee pot, tongs, platters—all of silver. There were vases of silver and of cut glass, cut glass glasses, tables, glass bowls, five rugs, and eight "curtain Pieces" (one from Mr. and Mrs. George E. Judd, the parents of a four month old boy who would become the husband of Carrie's daughter). The books included Tennyson's works, a set of the writing of Oliver Wendell Holmes, "Famous Actors and Actresses," and one on famous artists.

The list is a useful record of who was there and what they gave. From George there was a pearl necklace and $500, from Julia silver flatware and bed linens, and from Rob a diamond crescent pin. Aunt Hattie sent a silver tea and coffee set. Two of the Phelps uncles came to the wedding with their families: Charles Haring Phelps, his wife, and their daughter Julie— who kept up with Carrie all her life—and Frank Phelps, then living in Stamford. Cousin Lizzie gave a seven-foot-high hall clock with a rotating sun and moon. There were echoes from the past in the silver and glass "cover" sent by Miss M. L. McKay, the chaperone on Carrie's 1896 tour, and the salad bowl from. Mr. and Mrs. Mulford, Julia's mentors in Minneapolis, quite elderly by then. "Miss McElroy," the daughter of Samuel McElroy, the distinguished engineer married to Samuel Haring's granddaughter, was probably the sole Haring relative to respond to the wedding invitation.[72]

Most of the guests were from Waterbury, and their names constitute a roster of the prominent families of the city: Chases (Alice gave an antique marquetry table, now in possession of the author), Wade, Smith, Miller, Heminway (from Watertown), and Burralls (Mary, Lucy, and their parents). Family names that "everyone" would have known from the men's position in the factories were: Benedict, Goss, Hayden, Elton, Kellogg, Mitchell, and Platt.

Julia wrote only two days into the honeymoon in response to a letter Carrie had sent. She was clearing up after the wedding.

---

72. This Miss McElroy could be either Margaret Haring McElroy (b. 9 March 1854) or Margaret Sikaloff Mc Elroy (b. 28 May 1857). See *Nicholas Knapp Genealogy*, G-625.

To-day has been a busy day too and I am tired but you have been in my mind all the time. My happy child—and I am happy and not at all *weepy*—because I know you are just that. Your telegram was a joy and a comfort—You did not mention Rob—but I suppose he has not deserted—Nellie came up this afternoon and asked when she could put "Mrs. Griggs'" room in order—I fell over in a dead faint—I have sent the flowers to everyone you indicated and wedding cake to those who were not here—I mean to those to whom the flowers went—Mary and Lucy [Burrall] did it all for me—You have had three gifts to-day—a most gorgeous *clock* from Mr. *Jacobs* a small glass & gold vase—I think from Mr. & Mrs. O. D. Seavy—No card but they wrote to announce its coming—and a butterfly—*tinsel* for your hair and a lace end stock from Mrs. Louis F. Cotter who ever she may be—I will leave the cards on every thing. Did you know Mrs.—Dr. Castle sent you a beautiful basket of roses—I did not, until this morning—

. . . Every one is talking about the beauty of the wedding—the charming bride and just *a few* of which I am one—speak of the *fine appearance of the groom*—Give my love to the dear boy—and tell him I bear him no resentment—but am prepared to love him as a son—God bless you both my dear children—The happiness that shone on both your faces as you stood there before me yesterday—dispelled every feeling of doubt or loneliness that I may have had—I love you well enough to be glad in your joy—

I have promised to go down and attend the Opera (Matinee) . . .[73]

From Atlantic City, Rob humorously assured his "mother" that all was well:

I suppose you manage to get along someway but my heart is much touched at your lonely condition, for I positively don't see how anyone who has had Carrie to be able to get along two weeks without her.[74] I was head over heel in love with her before we started on this trip—there is no argument about

73. JHW, in Waterbury, to CHWG, at the Hotel Netherlands, Fifth Ave. and Fifty-ninth St., New York, 6 Feb. 1902. The performance at the Metropolitan Opera that Saturday afternoon was *Die Zauberflöte*, conducted by Walter Damrosch (1862–1950), who then headed the German wing of the company. The German soprano, Johanna Gadski (1872–1932), in the role of Pamina, was in the midst of a brilliant career at the Met, where she became famous for the much heavier roles of Isolde and Brunhilde, which Julia surely later heard. Fritzi Scheff (1879–1954), the Austrian soubrette who had made her debut the year before, sang the small part of Papagena. In 1903 she left the Metropolitan for Broadway and the operettas of Victor Herbert, later for stage plays. See individual entries in *The New Grove*. See also Gerald Fitzgerald, ed., *Annals of the Metropolitan Opera: The Complete Chronicle of Performances and Artists*, 2 vols. (New York: Metropolitan Opera Guild; Boston: G. K. Hall, 1989).

74. RFG, at the Hotel Brighton, Atlantic City, N.J., to JHW, in Waterbury, 16 Feb. 1902.

that—but, mother mine, I will confess to you that it grows—this love—and each day she is dearer an closer to me and my happiness is more than I can tell you. I love her so and she is so sweet to me.

We are both enjoying this place very much. You certainly ought to come here with ~~Dad~~ ["Daddy" inserted in Carrie's hand]. I wish we could all four come down sometime. It is positively unique in its possibilities for fun and all without losing a refined atmosphere in the hotel life. This is Sunday morning and I am waiting for my wife to get ready for breakfast. After that we propose to diligently break the Sabbath steadily from early morn till dewy eve—Concerts—rides, walks vaudevilles and such.

Carrie claims to be feeling well. She has developed since Sunday six different aliments all of them alarming but none beyond possibility of cure. As each required a different specialist, we abandoned the regular paths of medicine and tried Christian Science . . .

Carrie and Rob returned to Waterbury and by fall to a house that George bought for them adjoining the White's house, referred to as the Red House from the color of its paint at 102 Grove Street. Mother and daughter were only a few feet apart. It was a comfortable place with a porch, two stories, and an attic. Carrie's three children would be born in its upstairs bedroom. George paid the goodly sum of $12,000 for it.[75]

That summer Carrie visited her Aunt Harriet at the Harrison summer house, overlooking the Sound on Leetes Island, Guilford, Connecticut, connected to the mainland by a bridge and causeway, and one of the loveliest places on the Connecticut shore. Rob wrote her from the Waterbury Club, where he spent his evenings in a temporary return to a bachelor state. In contrast to the family of prolix letter-writers he had married into, he is spare and direct. "It makes me very blue and lonely to have the evening here and to realize that I am not to see you. I wish I could make you know what a joy and happiness to me you are, and if I can give you a happy life how perfect my life will be."[76]

After looking into other opportunities (one of which was not in Waterbury, to Julia's momentary alarm), Rob settled on stock brokerage and in 1904 opened the Robert F. Griggs Co., with offices on North Main Street above the Green, an easy walk from Grove Street and close to the club. As

---

75. Elizabeth Bronson to GLW, Property Records, 176:624, 7 Nov. 1902, City of Waterbury, cited in "Estate of George L. White," Inventory, 30 Dec. 1914, file 8742, Waterbury Probate Dist., State Archives, CSL.

76. RFG, in Waterbury, to CHWG, at Leetes Island, Guilford, Conn., 21 Aug. 1902.

America's prosperity widened and deepened, more people were able to buy stocks and bonds. Rob rode the business successfully through the 1920s, and his firm became the leading brokerage in the city, eventually with a building of its own.

Will Marries Mary Elizabeth Wade

"Of course your father is completely delighted," Julia wrote when Carrie was engaged. "He has such an absolute belief in matrimony, poor man.— He seems now planning to marry the *whole family off*—though as far as I can see Jimmy is still heart whole."[77] Will was next, a year after Carrie.

Will, Julia's beloved Billee, married Mary Elizabeth Wade, the childhood sweetheart—the girl next door—for whom he proved himself in the Yukon winter. Mary, soon to be known as Molly, was the daughter of Martha Starkweather and Henry Lawton Wade, whose house on Prospect Street the Whites passed daily on their way to and from downtown. (It was designed in 1893 by Wilfred Griggs in the colonial revival style and may well have been the inspiration for George to choose that architect and style for 114 Grove.) It was renowned at the time for the ballroom on its top floor, where the sociable Wades gave parties.[78]

Will was strong and athletic, with a face lit by brilliant blue eyes— "sailor's blue eyes," in the words of an artist who later briefly married into the family.[79] Molly had refined good looks and a love of clothes; her posed photos show an Edwardian beauty, "flirtatious, popular and social," according to her daughter. However, her affections for Will had not been diverted by other suitors while he was at Yale and in the north.[80] The two were deeply attracted to each other, but in temperament and interests, over time, they came to be ill matched. Will was happiest in the outdoors. He enjoyed shooting, camping, and the company of men. He was vigorous, impatient, short-tempered. Molly was drawn to the refined and nuanced,

---

77. JHW, in Waterbury, to WHW, Forty Mile, 28 April 1901, William Henry White Papers.

78. "The handsome house at 101 Prospect that was designed by Wilfred Griggs and built in 1893 is still standing. The house is missing its original balustrade on front and side porch roofs. It retains, however, its fine Palladian window over the columned porch." "Looking up the Hillside with the Mattatuck Museum," (Waterbury, Conn.: Mattatuck Museum [1980s]).

79. Recollection of Patty (Spencer) Day (first wife of Haring White Griggs, who met Will in the years of her marriage to his nephew, 1930–1932), communicated to the author in 1994.

80. Recollection of Elizabeth Wade White, communicated to the author in 1990.

65. Engagement dinner party at 114 Grove, 1904, with Will and Mary at
the head of the table

enjoyed the social round, and was in her element as a hostess. They, their
two children, and their several dwellings, a country estate, town house,
and a South Carolina "shooting camp" became a constellation within the
family galaxy, another part of the future story.

The wedding was in the Second Congregational Church, a massive
building in red stone consecrated in 1895 on land purchased from the
estate of Israel Holmes, the great mid-century manufacturing innovator. It
stood catty-corner from St. John's, its bell tower and imposing presence
proclaiming the position it had established as well as being another indica-
tor of Waterbury's maturity.[81] It had been founded by those from the First
Church who wanted a more liberal order to include the observance of baptism, communion, and feasts such as Christmas—not permitted in the
Puritan tradition. When the Wade family moved to the Second Church,
Molly had to be baptized as an adult before the marriage could take place.[82]

---

81. *The Two Hundred and Seventy-Fifth Anniversary of First Congregational Church of Waterbury,
Corn, 1691–1966,* 22, Research Collection, Mattatuck Museum.

82. Interview with H. Wade White, 1 Oct. 1993.

The pews were arranged in a fan shape around the dais giving everyone a full view; it was a place for the word, not processions. (The building burned down in 1960 and was much regretted by many, including the author; Mr. and Mrs. George E. Judd, Carrie's daughter's future in-laws were devoted members.)

Carrie gave a luncheon for her brother and his bride-to-be the day before, and Rob Griggs entertained the men of the wedding party at lunch on the day itself. In this congregational church the Rev. John Davenport, rector of St. John's, officiated and used the *Book of Common Prayer*—another family wedding with two denominations involved. There was *Lohengrin* for the entrance, Mendelssohn for the recessional, and "arrangements from Dubois and Dudley Bock's arrangement of Annie Laurie." The reception was at the Wade house, where the Fischl Orchestra—which had played at Carrie's wedding—provided the music in the ballroom on the top floor—doubtless where Molly learned her social arts.[83] Julia and George's present to the couple was a flatware in the Paris pattern by Gorham, able to handle up to twenty guests and including seldom-used utensils, such as asparagus and oyster forks and marrow spoons, a material emblem of the life they were now expected to lead.[84] The elder Whites gave the bridal couple a dinner in a richly decorated room at 114 Grove Street.

The bridal pair left Waterbury in a horse-drawn hack in pouring rain, heading east to Meriden to meet the late train on the mainline north to Canada. Instead of supper, according to the family story, to their discomfiture, Sherry, the caterer, had packed only cake and sweets.[85] Their honeymoon was in the Canadian Maritimes. Henry Wade gave the newlyweds the house next door to his, renovated before they moved in. Siblings, parents, and in-laws lived within a few steps of each other.

George shortly "thrust"—as years later his son put it—young Will into the management of the New England Watch Company, a far bigger establishment than the White companies in which he had invested. Will's children, from what they learned in later years, considered that Will had been put in an untenable position by his "almost sadistic" father.[86] At

---

83. *Waterbury American*, 8 Aug. 1903.

84. The service is the "Paris" pattern by Gorham, now in possession of the author.

85. Recollections of H. Wade White and Elizabeth Wade White, 1990, 1 Oct. 1993.

86. Ibid.

George's behest, Will was made secretary of the company. (Will put his profession as "manufacturer" on his marriage license.) New England Watch, the former Waterbury Watch Company, had been reorganized in 1898 with George and other local businessmen participating. The capitalization was $600,000, the products included the "Elfin" watch, the smallest timepiece then made in America ("a Gift of Fairy-Like beauty—the more in good taste, because useful as well as beautiful," read the 1896 advertising copy), and the "Hyde," a dollar watch.[87] However, competition was fierce, and the eminent company was on a downward course. Although in 1904 Baedeker singled it and the output of 60,000 watches per year as the sole Waterbury industry to be mentioned in his guide, it was losing to the stiff national competition for cheap watches, including, significantly, those made by the Waterbury Clock Company, managed by Henry Wade. Thus in his first years in business Will was involved in desperate attempts to survive; through loans and stock offerings the officers increased capitalization in 1906—when George White had become president—to $790,000 and soon thereafter to $1,000,000. According to Betty White, some of the additional capital came from loans for which her father signed, and most was lost. The final humiliation came in 1909, when management applied for receivership, and in 1912 two respected elder members of the business community, Harris Whittemore and John P. Elton, acted as receivers to liquidate the company. By then property taxes were in default, requiring the city to approve the sale of the factory buildings in November 1914. Will had been involved in a shipwreck, and in that close-knit community everyone knew about it.[88] (George's other investments and the White companies maintained the family's prosperity.)

The contrast with Henry Wade's enterprises was galling. In a country in which time-telling was ever more essential for work and transportation, successfully marketing a cheap watch was the grail of many clock firms. Henry Wade, in charge of the Waterbury Clock Company, oversaw the development of a watch small enough "to be put in an overcoat pocket." It bore the attention-getting, deliberately inappropriate name of "Jumbo"

---

87. *Waterbury City Directory* (1896).

88. Baedeker, *United States* (1904), 80. Information in this and succeeding paragraphs on the New England Watch Company and the Mattatuck Manufacturing Company found in Pape, *Waterbury*, 1:194, 221, 224, 226.

and sold for $1.50.[89] It was the key to his success, the result of good management in coordinating the design and the manufacturing process. It took an enterprising marketer from outside Waterbury, however, to make the Jumbo (and other pocket watches produced by the company) a great sales success. When Robert Hawley Ingersoll, who in the 1880s, at twenty-one, started a mail-order business for marketing the dollar watch, learned of the Jumbo, he bought a supply to test its sales potential. He soon marketed it in quantity, and it became one of the soon famous lines of Ingersoll watches. By 1910 Waterbury Clock was making 3.5 million watches a year for Ingersoll, and it was Robert Ingersoll who bought the empty factory buildings of the bankrupt New England Watch.[90]

The Wades

With Will's marriage to Mary Wade, the Whites became connected to another family with deep New England roots. Henry Wade's paternal line extended to Jonathan Wade, who arrived at Massachusetts Bay Colony on the *Lion* in 1632 and settled in Ipswich. His son, Nathaniel, married Mercy, the daughter of Governor Simon Bradstreet and Anne Bradstreet, the poet, who was the daughter of an earlier governor of the colony, Thomas Dudley.[91] Awareness of their distinguished lineage became an integral part of how Mary and her children thought of themselves, and over their lifetimes they maintained a strong interest in family history. Henry's wife, Martha Starkweather Wade, became as involved with genealogical research as did Julia with her family lines and collected early American furniture. Mary (Wade) White was a Member of the Society of Colonial Dames, as was her daughter, Elizabeth (Betty) after her, whose life work was a biography of Anne Bradstreet.[92]

---

89. "In 1887 the Waterbury Clock Company had 300 employees, and in 1889 the management decided to market a watch case with a small escapement lever clock movement in it . . . called 'The Jumbo' designed by Archibald Bannatyne (1852–1931), a Scottish immigrant who had come to work for the company in 1877 and eventually became their master mechanic." *The Waterbury Clock Company, 1857, 1891*, introduction by Chris H. Bailey (1891; facs. reprint; Bristol, Conn.: American Clock and Watch Museum, 1982), 182.

90. Ibid. Robert Hawley Ingersoll (1859–1928) "conceived the idea and commenced manufacture of the 'dollar watch' in 1892, over 70 million sold by 1919." *Who Was Who in America* (Chicago: Marquis Who's Who, 1981).

91. Cutter, *Genealogical and Family History of the State of Connecticut*, 4:2124–25

92. Elizabeth Wade White, *Anne Bradstreet: The Tenth Muse* (New York: Oxford Univ. Press, 1971).

66. Henry Lawton Wade with his granddaughter, Elizabeth Wade White, about 1911

Henry Lawton Wade (1842–1912) was a slender, compact man with delicate features. In photographs his face has a confident, intelligent, and kindly look—his granddaughter remembered him fondly. He neither looked nor apparently was the type of iron-fisted factory manager that might be expected in a freewheeling industrial age. Nevertheless, he was extraordinarily effective as a businessman, proved by the success of the Waterbury Clock. His inner confidence and quiet demeanor contrasted with George White's restlessness and emphatic self-presentation. Although he had substantial securities holdings, acquired from his intimate knowledge of local companies, he was not principally an investor, but a factory manager, responsible for sales, finances, and production of a large, complex, and highly profitable business.

Like Luther Chapin White, Charles Griggs, and Augustus Sabin Chase, he had a country upbringing. His childhood was spent in the hamlet of Williamsville, in eastern Connecticut, where he and his father had settled after leaving Rhode Island. At sixteen he went to work in a cotton mill, proving himself able "in all departments." In 1862 he volunteered for the Eighteenth Regiment of Connecticut Volunteers and served in the army of West Virginia as a messenger, the only member of these immediate Griggs, White, Phelps, and Wade families to serve in the Union

Army.[93] The service left him somewhat frail in later years, according to his granddaughter—though he had an active business career and lived to the age of seventy.[94] In 1866, the year after he was mustered out of the army, Henry Wade came to Waterbury to be a bookkeeper at the Waterbury National Bank, whose president was Augustus Sabin Chase, himself from eastern Connecticut and in the process of developing factories that made him the leading businessman in Waterbury. Wade was an able young man, and in five years Chase appointed him secretary of his Waterbury Clock Company, placing him in charge of the manufacturing division. He was promoted to treasurer, then general manager, bcoming president in 1885, remaining in that position until his death in 1912.

The expansion of the company in the first decade of the new century was phenomenal. The listing of the watches and clocks his company offered required a catalog of over a hundred and fifty pages. Two five story factory buildings were added in 1900, three the next year, four in 1907 and again in 1909. Management coordinated the steadily evolving designs for efficiency, novelty, and lower manufacturing costs. Although the Chase family had a large share of the company, and Irving H. Chase succeeded him as president, the soft-spoken Henry Wade, through innate ability, became one of the leading manufacturers of the time.

Like those of a previous generation, Wade helped younger businessmen. One of these was George Edwards Judd, who also made his start as a clerk in the Waterbury National Bank. By 1888, when he was twenty-seven, he had his own office in the bank building as an insurance agent.[95] Eight years later Wade joined with the younger man to start a metalworking factory, which they called the Mattatuck Manufacturing Company, using the name of a defunct company and the Indian name for what became Waterbury. Wade became president; Judd, secretary and treasurer. The initial capital invested was $30,000, with the stock held in equal

93. Henry Lawton Wade enlisted from a residence in Pomfret, Connecticut, 8 Aug. 1862, served in K Company, Eighteenth Infantry Regiment, and mustered out at Harper's Ferry, W.Va., on 27 June 1865. *Connecticut: Record of Service of Men during War of Rebellion* (Hartford, Conn., 1889), <www.Ancestry.com>, accessed 28 June 2001. EWW believed that her grandfather had been taken prisoner and his health had suffered as a result. Over a hundred men of the Eighteenth were captured during the war, but Wade is not listed among them.

94. Recollections of Elizabeth Wade White, 1990.

95. *Waterbury City Directory* (1888).

amounts.[96] The owners took advantage of a burned out and foreclosed factory on rural land adjoining the Mad River, in the eastern edge of the city. Henry Wade's seniority in the business community gave the venture credibility. Neither man ran the operation on site, nor did either man have mechanical skills. George Judd continued in his office on Bank Street, and Wade was fully occupied with the Waterbury Clock Company. As would be the case for nearly fifty years, the operation was run by a salaried manager, a very different arrangement than what had characterized Waterbury fabricators in previous decades. The Mattatuck, its prospects and fate, became a consuming preoccupation of the later family. Will White represented the Wade shares, and Carrie's daughter married George Judd's son, whose life ambition was to run the factory. The Mattatuck would influence the lives of children and grandchildren in the families for over sixty years.

Henry Wade served on several factory boards that were part of the top business circles of the city. Prosperity allowed him to build an elegant house on Hillside, advantageously placed just up the hill from the Rose Hill estate of the Chases, and near the houses of other factory owners. (The exterior of 101 Prospect Street has now been restored, and the house is included on a self-guided walking tour of historic Hillside suggested by the Mattatuck Museum.)[97] He acquired a shooting camp, called Strawberry Hill, in South Carolina south of Savannah, a place that Will—who never again wanted to spend a winter cold —used when the ownership fell to Mary at her father's death.

His connection with the Chase family through the bank and the clock company brought Henry Wade a wife, Augustus Sabin Chase's cousin, Martha Chase Starkweather (1854–1946). She had been born in Waterville, Ohio, of parents whose families had emigrated from Connecticut to the Western Reserve after the Revolution. The aunt after whom she was named was Chase's wife. As a child she had visited these Chases in Water-

---

96. There were 1,200 shares at $25; held in 400 shares each by Wade, Judd, and George W. Tucker who sold his shares in 1898 to Wade and Judd, who then held 600 shares each. "Records of the Mattatuck Manufacturing Co., 1896–1944: Minute Book," manuscripts property of Gilbert R. Boutin, notes made by the author, December 1994. Tucker is a somewhat mysterious figure. He was first listed and described as "sec." of the Mattatuck in the 1898 Waterbury directory, and in the next year noted as having "removed" to New Boston, probably the small village in New Hampshire. From 1895 to 1899 Henry Green Judd, George's brother, was bookkeeper at the Mattatuck Waterbury city directories, 1895–1899. See "Judd," Genealogical and Biographical Notes.

97. "Looking up the Hillside."

bury, and when her mother died in 1868, the fourteen-year-old girl escaped a harsh stepmother and came east to live with the Chases, where she became the eldest in a household of five other children. Eleven years later, in 1877, she married Henry Wade, Augustus Sabin Chase's promising protégé, which brought him into the Chase social circle. Mary was born the year after their marriage; her sister, Lucy Starkweather Wade, seven years later—still a small child at her sister's wedding.[98]

Both White and Wade families enjoyed being descended from 1630s Puritan immigrants, and both had the comforts and privileges of the wealth that Luther Chapin White and Henry Wade had created in the new industrial economy. The White-Wade marriage brought Will White directly into the Chase orbit. These families were linked in business and were such close neighbors they would see one another every day going to and from the Green or along Prospect Street—it was a walking city, and the owners walked just like the shopkeepers and factory workers from their streetcar stops. And women of all classes shopped in the commercial center.

Henry Wade left an estate of $1.75 million in 1912, consisting of large amounts of Waterbury Clock Company stock, the Mattatuck, and shares from many other local companies, as well as the house and South Carolina camp.[99] Through his wife's inheritance, Will benefited from Henry Wade's acumen. However, the New England Watch experience soured Will on an active business career; when Mary came into her father's estate he withdrew from management and an office routine. He invested money well—notably selling before the 1929 crash—and served on factory boards, but conducted business from his study at home and spent winter months at the shooting camp in South Carolina that Mary inherited from Henry Wade. Will soon assumed the habit of the country squire, donning tweeds, often jodhpurs, and boots. He spent his time overseeing the gardens and grounds of the country estate he developed with that inheritance and on outdoor lei-

---

98. Henry Lawton Wade (b. 24 May 1842, at Harrisville, R.I., d. 31 Oct. 1912, at Waterbury), was the son of Aleph Abby Handel and Lawton Wade. He married, on 20 Sept. 1877, in Waterbury, Martha Starkweather (1854–1946). Their children were Mary Elizabeth Wade (1878–1949) and Lucy Starkweather Wade (1886–1970). The Chase business connection had its unpleasant side. Will and Mary's daughter remembered being told that the Augustus Chase sons were jealous of Henry Wade's success in the family company, and that the Chase son, who succeeded his father, was "mean" to Henry Wade; there was "lots of jealousy." Recollection of Elizabeth Wade White.

99. Will of Henry Lawton Wade, 1913, 122:304–5, Waterbury Probate Court.

sure activities. His temper, legendary in the family, surely derived in part from the frustrations of his early years and the awareness that his way of life depended disproportionately on Molly's fortune.

The autumn of George and Julia's life together had arrived. The next years were filled with travel, to southern resorts at least once and often twice each winter, and in summer Europe or northern New England. Their many bodily complaints were treated with earnest and often rigorous attention at Hot Springs and French Lick in the United States, and Carlsbad, in the Bohemian reaches of the Austro-Hungarian empire in its last flowering as a spa favored by royalty. The population of Waterbury grew rapidly from the influx of immigrants drawn to its expanding factories. The city's physical appearance became gradually altered—for the better perhaps—by buildings designed by Wilfred Griggs that transformed the views from and of the Green. In Carrie and Will's lives it was fruitful summer, with children, her three and his two, born in the first decade of the new century. For George Jr. it was marriage, and a contented one, though not celebrated with the pomp of those of his sister and brother.

67. Waterbury scenes at the turn of the century. Above, a 1904 rendering of W. E. Griggs's Elton Hotel. Below, the Waterbury Green, about 1900.

Mattatuck Museum

IX

BEFORE THE GREAT WAR

George was in his fifties in the new century. In the prime of life, although he may not have acknowledged it, he was preoccupied with his health. With his ample girth, gold watch chain and a stylishly trimmed moustache, he looked the man of property, certainly an urban man, whom one could meet on the streets of New York and in the lobbies of good hotels. However, the turned-up ends of his moustache and the fedora worn at a slight angle also revealed a more debonair, humorous person, found in his jocular letters to Carrie.

In his public persona, cane in hand and gold chain attached to his father's gold turnip-stem watch in vest pocket, George let the world see who he was and where he fitted in the social and economic scheme of things. Through Julia's eyes, however, we also see insecurity, manifesting itself in nervousness and hypochondria.[1] She joked about his tendencies when she reported that the doctor at Hot Springs had given George the "disturbing" news that there was nothing wrong with him. He is "a little chagrined to find he has two lungs—after all these years of interesting invalidism—The doctor's diagnosis is so plausible that we more than half believe he is right—though it is trying, to *give* up that 'Cavity'—The invalid is out golfing now. He goes 'around' twice a day and is making some good scores—"[2] Something deeper was involved, too. In an extraordinary outburst George described his own thoughts on his illness when he was fifty-seven, describing "poisons within me—poisons which are gradually and surely undermining my physical and mental forces . . . Do you think it easy with pains, unstrung nerves, and a muddled brain? The while looking in perfect condition."[3] During the twice-annual visits to southern resorts, extended European sojourns, and jaunts in northern New

1. Conversation with EWW, 1993.

2. JHW, in Hot Springs, Va., to RFG, in Waterbury, 17 April 1903.

3. GLW, in Hot Springs, to CHWG, in Waterbury, 25 March 1909.

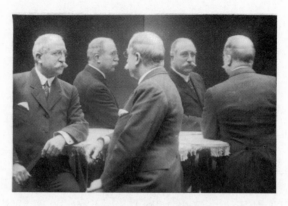

68. George Luther White, Atlantic City, about 1913

England, there was something eating at George from within, undermining that confident-seeming outer frame "in perfect condition." It can be sensed in Julia's reports of his irritability and "nerves," and their joint search for "cures" at spas in these years. Despite financial and familial "success," George seems to have been unfulfilled. Perhaps it was the career in journalism that might have been, or the lack of real challenge at work—the unspoken realization that he was coasting along on what Luther had created with a real entrepreneurial impulse. Whatever the cause, the emptiness or "poisons" within continued to do their work, distractions afforded by wealth and travel notwithstanding.

Julia was a wife freed of manual work, whose role at home was to manage servants, be custodian of the household furnishings, and act the part of emotional anchor to her husband's stormy disposition. House management she dreaded. On the eve of returning from one trip, she lamented to Carrie, "How I hate to go back to 'burned up chops' and 'under done steak' and 'tough chicken'—Alas! I am no home maker."[4] Except for photography, Julia had no other outlets for her energies such as charitable or church work and seems to have had little or no role as a social hostess. Family was all-important. Carrie was her best friend, Cousin Lizzie and Harriet Harrison the only other close female friends we learn of. It was the maternal role that suited her best; she lavished affection on Carrie and Will. She was saddened by the coolness that her daughter-in-law showed. Molly was an adept hostess and social, skilled in those areas where the emotional Julia was not. The result was a more distant and formal rela-

4. Ibid.

tionship with Will (and his children) than she wanted and expected. Looking after George was her first concern. He made the decisions; he could leave a hotel and change travel plans without discussion or prior notice, and she must follow along. "Your father seems pretty well knocked out today but I stood it well and am feeling well," wrote Julia during a tour of southwest England. "As usual he cannot decide where he will be long enough to have his mail forwarded."[5] From Paris she reported, "Your father seems possessed with the 'move on spirit'"; Lizzie wrote her once with characteristic boldness that she allowed George to be her "stage-manager."[6] (Lizzie's sharp tongue not surprisingly made George uncomfortable, and Julia was on pins and needles when the two were in proximity: "This afternoon I sat on the beach a while with Cousin Lizzie while your father played golf—The situation is not pleasant. Coming here places me in a disagreeable position but I shall have to steer through the rapids as well as I can.")[7]

In a letter at the end of what would be their last European trip together Julia managed to put the relationship with George into words. It is a cry of pain mixed with love. "He does not seem any nearer overlooking being called a 'bully,'" she wrote, "than he did a year ago—"

> and if I say a word he tells me I am always against him and on the other side—I hate such things and told him the other day that I 'crawled' after a much worse offence and thought he might give in a little—He will get over it some time. His cold is very much better and he keeps cheerful—Really he has been awfully good and attentive to me the entire trip and he must have been bored to death—but we have seen a lot—both beautiful and interesting—[8]

In these years Julia was a matronly figure, corseted and draped in the style of the times. In her letters she jumbles worries, affection, references to travel, Waterbury news, household concerns in virtually free association. She occasionally makes fun of herself with a reference to "Calamity Julia," and she knows she has a tendency to fear the worst. She writes to Carrie without reserve, as though she can be herself only in her daughter's

---

5. JHW, in Exeter, Devon, to CHWG, in Waterbury, 28 July 1913.

6. "It struck me as being unusually funny even for her—," was Julia's comment. JHW, at Rockland, Me., to CHWG, in Waterbury, 25 Aug. 1905.

7. JHW, in Beach Bluff, Mass., to CHWG, in Waterbury, 31 Aug. 1905.

8. JHW, in London, to CHWG, in Waterbury, 19 Sept. 1913

69. George and Julia aloft in the photographer's
studio, Atlantic City, 1908

company. "Your father still complains of his sore nerves," she wrote
Carrie from Paris, "He had his first colonic this morning and in consequence there is a slight coolness between us—but it will wear off as the
day goes on—It is a nerve racking experience for him and a much worse
one for me—which sounds selfish but isn't." [9]

Julia, too, suffered from "nerves" and was as much committed to the
cures they took as he. In 1913 we learn that she was in New York for
unspecified treatments, which may have been for nerves—serious enough
that Carrie left her family, missing her daughter's eighth birthday, to
attend her.[10] There was melancholy in Julia, revealed by her worrying,
and a loneliness that prompted her to write so expansively to her daughter.

Yet they were fond and close too. Here George described Julia when
they were at Camden, South Carolina:

9. JHW, in Paris, to CHWG, in Waterbury, 13 Aug. 1913.

10. CHWG, in New York City, to RFG, in Waterbury, 2 Dec. 1913.

Your Mother is unusually well. She seems so strong. She walked to the village and back the other day (3 miles) and around the Golf Links with me, and did not seem tired. She is having a pretty hard time of it though with me sticking to her like a plaster. I have just written Auntie about her as follows:—(it is easier to copy than compose something new).

"Julie is having a lovely time cow chasing. She thinks the Camden cows are more polite that the Thomasville cows. She has searched ever since she came here and only discovered one so far, but she *has* hopes. She just shouted 'I'm Mrs. George Luther White of Waterbury New Haven County State of Connecticut' and the cow furled its horns, shifted its (r)udder, dropped a 'heap' turned on its (k)heel and sailed away in an approach direction with Julia following in its wake, safe and sound. She dotes on the *antiquity* of this place and asked the driver the other day innumerable pertinent and important questions. Passing a house with collapsed roof and columns, and crumbled foundations she inquired 'Is this house old?' Going by another she remarked to me, (thinking we had been by there before) 'You just passed that house!' I replied 'that although it hurt me terribly, I *had*.' She is having a fine time, as she is the only one I have to tease, but she says 'I'm the limit.'"[11]

On that same trip when Julia described him as unable to make up his mind where to go next, George gave Carrie a charming picture of her mother in full tourist flight.

Well, we are *here* and every day has brought us nothing but pleasure since we sailed. Mrs. "Barby" [Julia] and her fruit emporium kept her *four* fruit baskets in perfect condition all the way over sorting it night and morning, and making the air *odorous* with over done specimens, and not a kick from her poor suffering *sleepy* room mate. The last Orange was presented to a sweet little English girl today to show her what nice fruit Mrs. "B" grows in her garden at home. But she has thrived over it and is now the busiest mortal in England today. She buys postal cards at every shop she passes—I wait like a dog outside—and immediately rushes to the hotel to write them up, starting usually just at dinner time or bed time. Really, it is remarkable how much pleasure they and her camera afford her. She is literally happy, every minute, and it is a pleasure to watch her. Surely there has been no mistake so far in making this trip. I tell her she must get *fat*, so she has commenced eating *Porridge*. In fact there is mighty little else for her to eat, as meat is the chief dish here. I am in the same boat and am eating too much meat at their miserable never-varying table d'hote English hotel meals.[12]

---

11. GLW, in Camden, S.C., to CHWG, in Waterbury, 12 Jan. 1905.

12. GLW, from Lynton, N. Devon, to CHWG, in Waterbury, 3 Aug. 1913.

And here is Julia describing her husband when they stayed at the Splendid Hotel on the beach at Ostende:

> The whole waterfront being lined with very substantial and handsome hotels and the "Board Walk" is very broad and of cement and blocks of brick or something equally firm—We came through from Munich, twenty five hours of steady travel, arriving at four in the afternoon yesterday—There is a fine balcony outside of our room and we spend hours watching the crowd of promenaders and the bathers. Your father enjoyed it much as it gave him a good chance to follow his life long occupation by watching the human forms divest—If they nabbed the women here for going with skirtless bathing suits there would be none left—Skirts on the bathers and petticoats on the walkers are quite unknown—and as both light and wind is strong the effect is quite startling—
>
> Our night journey was our first experience on a "Wagon Lit" in Europe It was fairly comfortable but your father "took" one of his nervous fits and thought he was *going* crazy—Poor man—the things he "can't stand" are too numerous to mention, though on second thought—it seems as if they always were—He likes it here—and strange to say the sea air seems to have relieved his cough ever so soon—.[13]

There were ups and downs, but the two were inseparable. "I am really feeling quite well acquainted with your father," Julia wrote after some weeks away. "He has not been out of my sight for twenty consecutive minutes since we landed in Carlsbad—hardly during the entire trip for that matter. I should think he would be so sick of me that he would drop me into the ocean."[14] They were not, it seems, miserable, and often enjoyed what they were doing together. On another stay in familiar, "delightful" London, where they were enjoying social pleasures and the theater, Julia writes

> Your father is feeling much better and we are both happier in consequence. It has been a pretty dull trip for him—No males. Either old friends or new since we left the ship—He has not been out of my sights two hours in the past two months—I mean all told—How he stands it "stumps me"—We are doing London rather quietly as far as days go and have been to the theatre every night—Mrs. D'Aubigne invited us to dinner and the play last night—She is a

---

13. JHW, in Ostende, to CHWG, in Waterbury, 7 Sept. 1913.

14. JHW, in Carlsbad, to CHWG, in "Mikado Cottage," Madison, Conn., about 2 Sept. 1906.

70. Letterhead, the Splendid Hotel, Ostende, 1913

very charming woman and lives very *prettily*. We saw "The Great Adventure"—Arnold Bennett "Buried Alive"—It is very good but I think will be better done in New York next winter with Janet Beecher.[15]

There are complaints, but it is real or imagined ill health that makes them miserable, not incompatibility. George and Julia were interested sightseers, who enjoyed what was available to the tourist, the *flaneur* of the Atlantic world. A constant shared pleasure was the opera—four in as many days at Dresden—frequently to the Metropolitan when in New York, in Munich, Bayreuth, Berlin. Wherever there were performances, they would go. (It is a passion that has come down in the family, from Carrie to her daughter, and her son, the author.)

The last of the children was settled when Jimmie married Carolyn Armstrong, from Ossining on the Hudson, on 7 August 1907. It was a

---

15. JHW, in London, to CHWG, in Waterbury, 13 Sept. 1913. The play was adapted from Bennett's novel, *Buried Alive*, and was a comedy about a man whose butler dies suddenly at home. The authorities who arrive on the scene mistake the dead butler for the master, and the latter assumes the role of butler for a time. It was acted by Henry Ainley (1879–1975), the English actor "possessed of a remarkably fine voice and great personal beauty and charm" who specialized in romantic parts. Phyllis Hartnoll, ed., *Oxford Companion to the Theatre*, s.v. "Ainley, Henry." Janet Beecher (1885–1955) was an American actress who took on "leading roles without becoming a star." Gerald Bordman, *Oxford Companion to the American Theater* (New York: Oxford Univ. Press, 1984), s.v. "Beecher, Janet."

quiet ceremony in New York City, a contrast to the lavish displays that accompanied the marriages of Will and Carrie and conveniently timed so the elders could leave a few hours later for Europe. Jimmie, then and for the rest of a life in which he was often ill, worked in the L. C. White Company. He and Carolyn lived in a newly opened part of the city called Overlook, approached by Columbia Boulevard, which, with its parklike median, was an example of planning in the spacious manner encouraged by the City Beautiful movement in the 1890s.[16] Their house, off the Boulevard at 74 Randolph Avenue, was modest in size and appearance, a contrast to those of his siblings. It was about twenty minutes' walk to the Grove Street house, or five minutes by car. Jimmie and Carolyn had no children and perhaps for that reason, they are infrequently (but cordially) mentioned by Julia in her letters.

Resorts

The parlor car on the transcontinental rail journey, with its organ music, garrulous company, and luxurious appointments, provided an experience of the new luxury travel for those with money enough to pay for it. So did the resort hotels where the Whites stayed each winter—The Kirkwood in Camden, the Highland Park in Aiken, South Carolina, the Old Homestead at Hot Springs, the Royal Poinciana at Palm Beach, and the Hotel Mt. Washington, Bretton Woods, New Hampshire. These places offered cosmopolitan sociability as much as fresh air and exercise.

"I like hotel life," Julia wrote from the Hampton Terrace in South Carolina, "with our big comfortable room—fine views and spacious piazzas I should be quite contented if we did not stir off the place—"[17] Table assignments could be stimulating. "You may be interested to know," Julia reported from the Carolina at Pinehurst, "that our table companions are a Mr. & Mrs. Richard Dana—She is a daughter of Henry Longfellow—and he a son of Richard a well known author of the same period [Richard Henry Dana Jr., author of *Two Years before the Mast* (1840)]—I feel quite 'got up'—We met him through the Presberys [friends met at other resorts] and he came to sit with us after they left—She only arrived a few days

---

16. Robert H. Pidgeon, *Atlas of the City of Waterbury, New Haven County, Conn.* (Philadelphia: D. L. Miller, 1896), 4.

17. JHW, in North Augusta, S.C., to CHWG, in Waterbury, 6 April 1904.

71. Letterhead, Hampton Terrace Hotel, 1904

back—and is very simple and nice—"[18] Waterbury acquaintances were visible in a different light at the resorts. "Mr. Earl Smith and Mrs. Smith are here," she wrote from the Hampton Terrace. "It is astonishing how different a person you have known slightly for years will appear, when you meet them in the close friendship of a hotel—I have always rather run away from Mrs. S. in Waterbury—here I find her—what I have always known her to be—a sweet, gentle woman—but also what I never suspected, bright, chatty and *interesting*." (Earl Smith was a neighbor on Hillside and the President of Smith & Griggs and the Waterbury Buckle Company.)[19] Mrs. Whittemore, of the prominent Naugatuck family and her daughter, Gertrude ("poor girl does not grow handsome—") were also there and "[w]e all spent much of last evening together."[20] In Paris, "driving in the Bois [de Boulogne]—we passed a carriage in which were Mr. and Mrs. William Washburn—We all stopped and had a nice little chat—She is such a pretty woman and they are both charming—They

---

18. JHW, in Pinehurst, N.C., to CHWG, in Waterbury, 28 March 1906. Richard Henry Dana III (1851–1931) was a Boston lawyer interested in a number of Progressive causes; quite a different set of concerns than many of the men who must have frequented the resort. At this time he was president of the Civil Service Reform Society, dating from the last third of the previous century, whose purpose was to professionalize appointments to government agencies, a continuing Progressive Era cause. His artistic interests led him to become president of the New England Conservatory of Music. He was a fellow of the American Academy of Arts and Letters. *Who Was Who in America*, s.v. "Dana, Richard Henry."

19. Marburg, *Small Business*, 19.

20. JHW, in North Augusta, S.C., to CHWG, in Waterbury, 6 April 1904.

wanted to know about you and Rob and the children and also about Wilfred and David [Griggs] and their families—Perhaps Rob will be interested to know that they have two grand children—."[21] Abroad was home, and home was abroad.

George waggishly described the social scene at the Mt. Washington Hotel at Bretton Woods, where he hobnobbed with magnates of the day.

> Such a delightful change in the weather came Saturday night, and yesterday and today have been simply *perfect*. Mt. Washington has been cloudless for two days, and this morning *five* trains ascended. Only one has gone up each day before for ten days. My courage has returned, and if this weather continues, and Mr. H. M. Flagler, W. H. Rogers, "Line" Hanna, Curtis Gould and a score of other celebrities & billionaires ask me, I may spend the balance of the time here with them. No one but we have any thing less than a million or two, but as Julia comes from N.Y & lived on 14th St., they don't throw us out. One thing nice about it is they none of them *look* any better than Julia & George, and they don't *behave* as though they had a million. It is very different from Palm Beach. Saturday night the costumes of the ladies were superb, but all *refined*. The Trowbridges (Rutherford) are here from New Haven, Alan A. A. Coles of Ansonia B&C [Brass & Copper] Co. but they are "so near home" it is not to be expected we should know them. However, I played Golf this morning with a Standard Oil magnate and he did not even ask my business, or how much money I had. Thank the Lord I have enough to pay my hotel bills, and that is no bagatelle.[22]

Just as the Ponce de Leon Hotel, which had so delighted Carrie, was the model for the 1890s, so the Mt. Washington at Bretton Woods became the most luxurious of the summer resorts of the 1900s, an instant "city" contained in one rambling building in a design inspired in part by the luxury ocean liner. "This house is the best I think I have ever seen, as a resort house," George wrote. "It is located at the base of Mt. Washington and the whole Presidential Range, about seven miles from Base Station where the road to the summit starts, and overlooks a valley on the West backed by the smaller range of mountains. It is beautifully constructed, furnished and conducted."[23]

---

21. JHW, in Paris, to CHWG, in Waterbury, 13 Aug. 1913. James V. Washburn lived at 56 Kellogg St., on Hillside in 1902—presumably these were relations of that family.

22. GLW, in Bretton Woods, N.H., to CHWG, in Waterbury, 14 Aug. 1905

23. GLW, in Bretton Woods, to CHWG, in Waterbury, 6 Aug. 1905.

The huge wooden structure was festively adorned by flagpoles and had drawn prosperous visitors who, like Julia and George, came by railroad with their trunks. It was just beginning to be a destination for the automobile traveler—Julia reported autos on the roads near the hotel. The cog railway to the summit of Mt. Washington—inspiring Swiss examples—was in operation, thus the pleasures of European mountain resorts could be enjoyed not far from home.

The guests, like the passersby on the Parisian boulevards, were on show. "I never saw such elegant dresses as here—The Hot Springs [the Old Homestead Hotel in Virginia, where he and Julia stayed a number of times] cannot touch it. In fact it is so fine that simple folk do not care what they put on—and I have been about all day in that old crushed white hat—not crushed in packing—which I did not think good enough to wear at home—'Julia' is not in it up here and as your father is 'too nervous' to play maid [button up the back, pull corset strings] my wardrobe is even more limited—."[24] And with a note about the clientele that reminds us that "restricted" policies had begun, George reveals a social anti-Semitism characteristic of the day, "*There is not a hebrew in the house and never has been.* The rates are as high as the mountain it is named after. A fine class of people patronize it—*just my class*, and it is within easy access by team or rail to all the other resort hotels."[25]

It was upon the recommendation of H. W. Flagler, whom George mentioned in his letter, that the owner of the site, Joseph Stickney, chose Charles Alling Gifford as his architect for the Mt. Washington—the same man who designed the entirely different Ponce de Leon in St. Augustine, which had so delighted Carrie. The style for this northern resort, somewhat improbably was, Spanish Renaissance revival, "one of the most lavish and yet among the more orderly of the late-Victorian eclectic styles." The huge structure was built on virgin land and in one piece, unlike many other resort hotels of the era, which had added wings and annexes. The Mt. Washington opened in 1902 and could accommodate six hundred guests, with a staff to guest ratio of three to one. The floor plan was in the shape of a huge Y, with two wings diverging from an octagon. Its "wide, wrap-around (and in some places, two-tiered) piazza" was some nine hundred feet long. The hotel was in effect "a huge luxury ocean liner set upon

24. JHW, in Bretton Woods, to CHWG, in Waterbury, 17 Aug. 1905.

25. GLW, in Bretton Woods, to CHWG, in Waterbury, 6 Aug. 1905.

the land—a small, unified village offering elegance, pleasures, and diversions to an appreciative clientele."[26] (The Mt. Washington, still in operation, has been designated a National Historic Landmark.)

Julia, who loved "hotel life," enjoyed the hotel quite as much as any she had been to. The other, less "modern," resorts certainly offered similar pleasures, though perhaps on not so grand a scale. In any case, George and Julia, veterans of many transatlantic crossings, appreciated the Mt. Washington's resemblance to an ocean liner.

Urban Amenity on the Atlantic

In the early 1900s the competition between German and British shipping companies to build the largest, fastest, and most luxuriously appointed liners mirrored their naval rivalry. Julia and George benefited from this rapidly evolving luxury on successive trips in these years.

In 1907 they crossed on the Hamburg-Amerika line's *Kaiserin Auguste Victoria,* then one year old. It was, according to its sponsors, one of "the great works of steel and power that moved across the sea." The ship was noted for its grill room, managed by the Ritz-Carlton company, in which "[g]old-trimmed menu cards featured such items as whole roast oxen and grilled antelope."[27] (The Whites entertained the captain there for lunch, the menu selection, alas, not noted.) "I wish you could see our rooms," Julia wrote in a note taken off by the pilot at Staten Island. George had insisted on a change in rooms at dockside, and the travel agent "met us at the boat and changed us to a suite Parlor-bed room and bath—among the best on the ship—Your father is feeling more cheerful in consequence—"[28]

"Your father was a perfect wreck for two or three days," Julia reported at the end of the voyage, in a letter taken off at Plymouth, "but is in prime condition now... He is enjoying life and the voyage." (The German line stressed the healthful benefits of ocean travel and would have been pleased by this result.) A "charming man" had helped him recover with a pill and

---

26. Bryant F. Tolles Jr., *The Grand Resort Hotels in the White Mountains A Vanishing Architectural Legacy* (Boston: David R. Godine, 1998), 214–17. Gifford's fluency with Mediterranean styles had been proved in the Ponce de Leon.

27. William H. Miller Jr., *Pictorial Encyclopedia of Ocean Liners, 1860–1994* (New York: Dover, 1995), 35.

28. JHW, on the *Kaiserin Auguste Victoria,* to CHWG, in Pine Orchard, Conn., 7 Aug. 1907.

became a friend for the voyage. Indeed, social encounters were an important attraction of the transatlantic run. Julia reported to Carrie that "on the sun deck—A tall, handsome girl came up and spoke to me—It was Bessie [Heild?] She has changed a lot—a charming, stunning girl as bright as they are made—and makes fun for every body—she has many nice things to say about you and sends you her love says she hopes you will remember her—"[29]

After a trip that took them to Vienna, Dresden, and Carlsbad for a long stay to take the "cure," they left for home via Hamburg on the *Amerika,* another splendid floating palace with wood paneling and a winter garden for first-class passengers.

Two years later they traveled with the British competition, the White Star's *Mauretania* eastbound, its *Baltic* westbound. The *Mauretania* was sister ship to the *Lusitania,* both named in that era of British world hegemony for provinces of the Roman empire, Roman Morocco and Portugal, respectively. The *Mauretania* had taken the Blue Riband from its sister with an average speed of twenty-six knots across the Atlantic and would hold the record until 1920. According to William H. Miller, the interiors were intended to display the "glories of British and European design. The forests of England and France were scoured for the most perfect woods, some of which were exquisitely carved in great detail. The decor themes ranged from French Renaissance to English Country and included lavish lounges, smoking rooms, libraries, salons, private parlors and even an exceptional palm court."[30] From the first landfall at Queenstown, Ireland, Julia reported that "[w]e have been so comfortable not one minute of sea sickness and nothing to complain of but the weather which has been damp and hot—It has been very foggy too—"[31] With them on the ship that summer was George Alexander Phelps Jr., Julia's uncle, then seventy-five, a link to her childhood in New York. It was he whom she had visited in Palermo on her first look of Europe in December 1868. After the Civil War he opened an office for the family firm in Liverpool. He and George got along splendidly.[32]

---

29. JHW, on the *Kaiserin Auguste Victoria,* to CHWG, in Pine Orchard, 13 Aug. 1907.

30. Miller, *Pictorial Encyclopedia,* 17.

31. JHW, from Paquebot Queenstown, R.M.S. *Mauretania,* to CHWG, in Pine Orchard, 19 July 1909.

32. In England they visited a number of times with George Alexander Phelps Jr.'s daughter (and apparently their only surviving child) Helen (Phelps) Ackerley (1864–after 1914), Julia's first cousin, who lived near Liverpool with a daughter.

After touring Ireland, Wales, Scotland, northern England, and "dear old London," they returned via the *Baltic* from Liverpool. When that ship was launched in 1904, it was for a season the largest ship afloat but soon was outclassed in speed and size. It reached New York in seven days—the newer *Mauretania,* which left from Liverpool the same day (with a letter from Julia to Carrie) arrived a day earlier.

The apogee of size, speed, and luxury in transatlantic travel came with the Hamburg-Amerika's *Imperator* and its White Star Line rivals, the *Olympic* and its sister, *Titanic.* In their final crossings together, George and Julia took the *Imperator* outbound, the *Olympic* home. *Imperator* was a colossus of fifty-two thousand tons, launched in May 1912 and intended to be a symbol of Germany's technological prowess in achieving great speed without sacrificing size and luxury. (The launch was just five weeks after the *Titanic's* demise, and publicity stressed the number and capacity of the lifeboats available.)

The *Imperator* had been in service just over a month when the Whites boarded. Jimmie and Carolyn saw their elders off, a ritual of departure with a visit to the cabin, fragrant with fruit baskets, until the announcement that sent visitors to shore. First class was vast, with over 900 berths—"an immense hotel" according to Julia, resembling "an imperial palace afloat." "The first class room on the *Imperator* became the Ritz at sea, incorporating quantities of marble and gilt, to stunning effect."[33] (In Julia's words, *Imperator* was "the liveliest ship we were ever on and the ball room and Roman Bath were fully patronized and each, wonderful creations to be found in mid-ocean.") The swimming pool was modeled on that in the Royal Automobile Club building in Pall Mall and was "literally a marble hall." The Kaiser had charged the German shipping company to build ships to rival the *Titanic,* and this was one result. There was a flaw, however—the ship was known to roll, even in calm seas. Indeed it came to be called *Limperator* by New York wags—not apparently on this trip.[34] "To say the 'Imperator' is a grand ship does not express it," George told Carrie.

---

33. Both Hamburg-Amerika and North-German Lloyd were determined, in an effort backed by the Kaiser, to best British liners in speed and size. The *Imperator* was part of that rivalry, though its particular attraction was luxury (and size) rather than speed, and it never won the Blue Riband. <http://home.pacific.net.au/~bchudso/german.htm>, accessed 8 May 2001.

34. Ibid.

We of course could not experience her sailing qualities as we had a smooth sea all the trip. For three days in the Gulf Stream we suffered terribly from the heat and *humidity*. It reminded me of our West Indies trip [on the Hamburg-Amerika *Blücher* to Venezuela in March 1907]. After this there was not much seen but the sea was absolutely quiet, and there was not the slightest vibration. Fortunately our room, (which was very nice and commodious) had faulty plumbing and we were *requested* to a $1400 suite de luxe of [   ] Bed R & Bath, which proved most "luxe" Our old friend Capt Ruser (now Commodore) invited us to "Tea" in his cabin the second day out but we saw little of him afterward. In fact the ship was so big we did not pass a day without seeing some new faces.[35]

Then there was the cosmopolitan sociality of encountering again those met on other voyages or at the resorts:

We met besides the Presbreys Mr & Mrs Hilms of Phila Mr Schmalke, the former [   ] American conductor of excursions to West Indies, and a Mr Turpin of Mobile, Ala who *all* sat at the same table during our thirty day trip to Venezuela in 1907. Strange wasn't it? Mr & Mrs Fred Upham of Chicago, French Lick acquaintances, were also on board. . . . A nice list of passengers furnished some brilliant dancers and elaborate toilets, low cut above, and high cut below. But Plymouth appeared all too soon for even me, and Friday noon found us docked and located for lunch in the Grand Hotel.

Julia would sail on the ship under different circumstances in 1921, for this pride of the kaiser had been awarded to the British as war reparations and rechristened *Berengaria*, after King Richard's queen, and made the Cunard flagship.

Julia and George returned to New York on the White Star *Olympic*, sister ship of the *Titanic*, whose sinking in April of the previous year was not mentioned by Julia, who surely would have been nervous. The *Olympic* had four stacks, giving it a distinctive profile, and the first class was enormous, with a capacity of a thousand passengers.[36] It departed from Southampton, just then beginning to replace Liverpool as the main English port for the transatlantic passenger service because of its favorable tides.

---

35. GLW, from Lynton, N. Devon, to CHWG, in Waterbury, 13 Aug. 1913.

36. Miller, *Pictorial Encyclopedia*, 86.

The "Cure"

Many of the trips the Whites took in the 1900s included a stay at a spa for a "cure," a rigorous course of hydrotherapy, described in a manual of the day as the "therapeutic use of simple water when taken internally or . . . applied externally in the form of baths [and] douches." In the spas the treatment included diet, exercise, and medical consultation.[37] They both felt the need for periodic relief from "nerves."

A recent study points out how "nervousness" at the turn of the century was considered a symptom of America's emerging culture, one of the effects of attaining an "advanced" stage of civilization, with its concomitant wear and tear on the brain.[38] Neurasthenia, a then fashionable diagnosis, was an advanced form of "nervousness in which a person broke down" and needed rest to "recharg[e] with vital force the nerve batteries," as one authority put it.[39] The symptoms were legion, including dyspepsia, depression, irritability, "fidgetiness," all of which Julia observed in George.

American "nervousness" in the 1890s–1900s was "as much an ideology as an illness—an indication, according to a recent history, of urban middle class and wealthy arrogance and status aspiration. To be agitated with "nerves" was an expected condition for those of wealth and who worked with their brains, deemed to endure more anxiety than laborers.[40] To a contemporary expert, symptoms like George suffered with his "nerves" were conditions of "general debility," caused by "severe nerve shock or chronic mental worry." The condition would reveal itself when "the nervous system and the whole body are . . . in a condition to which the term

---

37. The "internal use of plain water . . . leads to increased urea and the waste products of tissue metabolism, the tissues and the blood being, so to speak, washed out by the treatment." Warm water was recommended for drinking, as it was "more easily spread, without loss of body heat." Hermann Weber, *The Spas and Mineral Waters of Europe with Notes on Balneo-Therapeutic Management in Various Diseases and Morbid Conditions* (London: Smith, Elder, 1896), 1–5.

38. Tom Lutz, *American Nervousness, 1903: An Anecdotal History* (Ithaca: Cornell Univ. Press, 1991), 1–9.

39. *The Household* (1880). The theme of "nervousness" as a symptom of advanced civilization, as stated by George M. Beard in *American Nervousness* (1881), was inspired in part by research published in George M. Schweige's article "Cerebral Exhaustion," *Medical Record* (1876). See Harvey Green, *Fit for America: Health, Fitness, Sport and American Society* (Baltimore: Johns Hopkins Univ. Press, 1986), 138–39 ff.

40. Green, *Fit for America*, 139.

'irritable weakness' has been applied." "Under the influence of mental depression," the description continues, "the breathing and consequently hydration of the blood are minimized: the inclination to take food and exercise is wanting; sleep is disturbed and the nutrition of all the organs and tissues becomes impaired." The supervising physician at a spa must therefore prescribe a suitable "dietetic and hygienic arrangement" for the patient.[41]

The most popular cure was the ingestion of mineral-rich waters and bathing in hot springs, cures that appealed to the affluent, whether afflicted with "nervous" or other ailments. (From Julia's references to indigestion and elimination and George's irritability, the "other ailments" in him may have been brought about by a rich diet and drink. At Hot Springs in 1903 she reported to Carrie, "your father does none of those things that we 'wot of' . . . He talks a little with the men—but he keeps away from their *haunts.*")[42]

Spas were well established, and increasingly large, by the turn of the century on both sides of the Atlantic. A late-nineteenth-century guide to European spas described in jargon-larded terms the treatment as "particularly useful in certain derangements in which gouty persons and free livers are prominent; in cases of 'abdominal plethora,' that is of passive engorgement of the liver and of the intestinal vessels, with a consequent tendency to chronic gastric and intestinal catarrh, with or without diarrhea." The cure was useful for "severe forms of dyspepsia, with much stomach pain and flatulency."[43] In the orotund language of this contemporary guide, the spa waters were "great and powerful purifiers of the body, great eliminators . . . we submit the organism to a threefold purifying influence, for while the hot mineral baths stimulate the excretory functions of the skin, the internal use of the waters greatly promotes the discharge of effete substances through the evacuations of the intestinal canal and the kidneys; in this manner the blood and the tissues of the body become cleansed of retained effete excrementitious substances."[44]

---

41. Weber, *Spas and Mineral Waters*, 289.

42. JHW, in Hot Springs, to CHWG, in Waterbury, 19 April 1903.

43. W. Fraser Rae, *Austrian Health Resorts and the Bitter Waters of Hungary* (London: Chapman and Hall, 1888), 136.

44. Ibid., 137. The description referred to the waters of Carlsbad in Austra-Hungary, where Julia and George would later go, but it applies equally to the Hot Springs.

After their children married, George and Julia became devoted to the rituals of water cures and partook of them at Hot Springs, Virginia, and French Lick, Indiana. Julia described the sociability (with a joke name for their companions) and the rigors of the cure there.

> We have met two or three people—a couple from Chicago at our table are quite pleasant and chummy—and a Mr. Marron (Glacé) who went over on the steamer with us last year and with whom your father became quite intimate is here with his wife. This tends to give a little more amusement to both of us but your father complains of not feeling well—and of the pain in his neck all the time but he keeps partly pleasant and is an angel compared to the last month or two at home. He plays golf a little and has someone besides me to talk to which is somewhat of a relief—to both of us—The baths continue with the same severity—I never had so many things done to me in so short a space of time. And if they are not doing me good, which I hope the are, I at least have the satisfaction of knowing that they make me absolutely clean.[45]

The preeminent place for the cure in that era was Carlsbad, in Austria-Hungary, the watering place of royalty, the "full-blown rose placed upon Austria's bosom to beautify and adorn it."[46] (It is now Karlovy Vary, in the Czech Republic.) Julia and George, veterans of American spas, had treatments there in 1906 and 1907, under the supervision of "Our dear Dr. London."

Carlsbad had become enormously popular and many of its tens of thousands of visitors stayed for three or four weeks, as did Julia and George. By train it was eight hours from Berlin or Vienna, four hours from Dresden or Prague. The reputation of the cure to be had from its waters "was world wide, and it counts among its visitors patients from almost every corner of the globe, especially American, English, French,

---

45. JHW, in French Lick, Indiana, to CHWG, in Waterbury, 15 March 1909.

46. Herr Karl Bottscher, quoted in Rae, *Austrian Health Resorts*, 2. "A celebrated watering-place, with 17,447 German inhab. and upwards of 68,000 annual visitors, is situated in the narrow valley of the Tepl, the wood-clad slopes of which are traversed by paths in all directions . . . The springs rise near the Tepl from the granite rock; the so–called 'Sprudelquellen' . . . The granite part of the town is built upon this crust, under which resides a large common reservoir of the mineral water, known as the Sprudelkessel, fed from fissures of unknown length. The stream of this subterranean cauldron escapes through artificial apertures in the rock, which on account of the incrustations deposited by the water, is required to be cleared and enlarged every year." Karl Baedeker, *Austria-Hungary with Excursions to Cetinje, Belgrade, and Bucharest: Handbook for Travelers* (Leipzig, 1911), 325.

Germans, Africans, Russians, Swedes, Turks, etc." There were gracious surroundings, with about "a hundred kilometers of very pretty walks and drives in the charming woods; the picturesque hills and surrounding mountains have a soothing effect on invalids." (Baedeker devotes three pages of small print to listing these walks.) Health seekers lined up before the spring each morning cups in hand to music provided by "military and private bands composed of celebrated musicians."[47]

There was a social cachet too, as "Carlsbad enjoys the favor of most of the reigning families of the world." A contemporary guidebook evoked the social scene: Early morning where the taps for the springs were set, "reveals a picture which is scarcely seen in any other place of the world. Members of reigning families, princes, statesmen, literary men, merchants from every part of the world and in all possible costumes may be seen at the springs and sometimes eight or ten single file rows are formed to get a cup or goblet of water, but in consequence of the careful arrangements everybody gets his water within a few minutes."[48] The "temperature being 160° F the water is so hot the glasses are filled after being placed in a smaller holder at the end of a long pole."[49] The medically approved dosage was for four glasses per day; eight and more glasses per day were prescribed in earlier years.

"Many persons go to Carlsbad because they have lived too well and grown too stout . . . abstinence should be enjoined." The typical regime for the "patients" was

> to begin the day by rising not later than six and walking to the springs. After drinking at intervals of fifteen minutes, three glasses of the particular water prescribed, and taking gentle exercise for an hour after the last glass, they eat breakfast . . . one to two cups of coffee with milk, chocolate or cocoa, accompanied by two small rolls, cost two kreutzers . . . dinner between twelve and two, three courses allowed: soup, meat, dish of vegetables, or some cooked pudding or fruit for the vegetables . . . soup to be plain, devoid of fat; tender beef, veal, lamb or mutton fowls or game except the skin . . . all pastry is condemned, particularly the Oblaten, or Carlsbad wafers . . . white bread . . . water the best beverage, but limited wines. Vesperbrod, like tea, coffee with

---

47. B. Bradshaw's *Dictionary of Mineral Waters, Climatic Health Resorts, Sea Baths, and Hydropathic Establishments* (London: Kegan Paul, Trench, Trubner, 1904), 69, 71.

48. *Bradshaw's Dictionary of Mineral Waters,* 69.

49. Rae, *Austrian Health Resorts,* 3.

cream and roll may be taken supper a simple meal, a little soup, roll, stewed
fruits or two soft-boiled eggs . . . some like to drink tea, but water is best . . .
    All spare time between meals to be occupied in taking exercise in the open
air . . .[50]

The reward for following the regime was a sense of well-being: "After a
well-spent day during which obedient patients have displayed so great
self-denial and have covered so much ground as if they were in training for
a walking match, and have fared like anchorites, they go to bed between
nine and ten o'clock, there to rest their weary limbs and dream of dining
with Lucullus."[51]

The Savoy Westend Hotel, where the Whites stayed, was "in a quiet
location," which on the map appears surrounded by walks. Baedeker
pointed out that it, like other first-class hotels: "in the chief towns and
watering places in Austria and Hungary," was "generally very good; and
though the charge for rooms is high (5–10 K $1.20–$2.50) the visitor
enjoys freedom from other demands. He may breakfast and dine at the
café and restaurant attached to the hotel, or wherever else he pleases."[52]
The hotel's advertisement promised a "Viennese Orchestra."[53]

"You can hardly imagine 'Pa and Ma'" crawling out of bed at six
o'clock *every* morning," Julia wrote to Carrie,

and walking down to a Spring for three glasses of water but such are our
orders and so far we have obeyed to the letter—Auntie [Harriet] too, but she
is always a little behind us. We carry our little glasses on a strap like old Carls-
baders—and stand in line—a long line it is too no matter how early you get
there.

---

50. Ibid., 13.

51. Ibid.

52. Baedeker, *Austria-Hungary* (1911), 323, xix.

53. Hamburg-Amerika Line, *Guide through Europe* (Berlin: J. Herman Herz, 1911), 379; No doubt
the management of the Savoy Westend had long adopted Baedeker's suggestion—and warning—as
to pleasing Anglo-American clientele: "Hotel-keepers who wish to commend their houses to British and American travelers are reminded of the desirability of providing the bed room with *large*
basin, foot-baths, plenty of water, and an adequate supply of towels. Great care should be taken to
ensure that the sanitary arrangements are in proper order, including a storing flush of water and
proper toilet-paper; and no house that is deficient in this respect can rank as first-class and receive
and a star of commendation, whatever may be its excellencies in other departments." Baedeker,
Austria-Hungary (1911), xix.

Every other day we have lovely pine-needle baths—no massage—The diet is not much more strict that what mine should always be but dinner at noon—no sweets—no soups etc.—I am going to be a fairy when it is over. Your father is very patient about it and adhering strictly to it—I only hope he will keep it up—for the regularity and simplicity of the food and hours will do him good—The same thing might answer just as well at home—We have decided to stay at this hotel—It is very well kept and the location is beautiful—fine views in every direction—I forgot to say that we have to walk a lot—[54]

At the end of the first stay Julia concluded that the "Cure has not been so very hard but we all feel the effects of it and another week would use us up—It takes all the snap out of one—but I am convinced it is a good thing. Your father says he is coming again—That shows what he thinks of it—"[55] A year later when they returned Julia reported that "Our dear Dr. London has put your father and me on peppermint tea instead of our afternoon, delicious coffee—because we are "gas factories" and he wants to make "thunder storms" of us—."[56]

An encounter with royalty was all that could be wished for, and Julia humorously reported her own to Carrie:

Yesterday King Edward came over here—he had a room in our house—and lunched in the public salle a manger with all the rest of us—We were not fifteen feet away from him. He chews his food and drinks wine just like any other mortal but did not eat with his knife—When he left the table every one stood up—but I was so occupied with my food that I failed to see what was going on (or out) until it was over. So *I* sat in the August presence of *Royalty*—He immediately ordered my "head off" but I sent him word that it had been taken off so many times in the past thirty odd years [a reference to her husband's behavior toward her] that I was quite used to it—Well dearie what nonsense this is when there are so many serious thoughts in my head—[57]

It was a vision of the world that vanished in 1914. Those able to discern a cloud on the international political horizon that hot summer day in 1906 would have associated it with the king's host at the Savoy, Admiral Sir

---

54. JHW, in Carlsbad, to CHWG, in Madison, 23 Aug. 1906.

55. JHW, in Carlsbad, to CHWG, in Waterbury, 11 Sept. 1906.

56. JHW, in Carlsbad, to CHWG, in Pine Orchard, 19 Aug. 1907.

57. JHW, in Carlsbad, to CHWG, in Madison, 20 Aug. 1906.

John Fisher (1841–1920), then First Sea Lord of the British Admiralty, a vigorous reformer of the Royal Navy. The previous February he had overseen a triumph of organization and planning, the launch of the battleship *Dreadnought*, four months after her keel was laid. It was a direct response to the increased investment in battleships and cruisers by the German navy under the impetus of the kaiser, which he and others perceived as a challenge to the Royal Navy's ascendancy on the oceans. Launching the *Dreadnought* was a key step in the naval competition between the two countries, year by year each following the other in the construction of battleships and battle cruisers. Edward VII used his influence to support Fisher, who served as his naval aide-de-camp, and his plans for the reform and strengthening of the navy.

On this late summer day at Carlsbad, in the gracious surroundings of the Savoy Westend, it would have been a sharp observer who sensed the British uneasiness at the German challenge—a violent future was just eight seasons away. No doubt the Whites recalled this lunch and the European world it represented when they read the news that Sir John Fisher had been called to command the fleet, under Winston Churchill, at the outbreak of war in August, 1914.[58]

Julia enclosed a clipping in her letter that provided an account of the royal presence, the international nobility, and the cosmopolitan crowd in a prosperous and peaceful Europe. Was it she, who referred to herself as "Calamity Julia," who was involved in the "amusing incident"?

KING EDWARD BREAKFASTS IN OPEN AIR AT CARLSBAD
Sir John Fisher Entertains His Majesty in the Garden of the Hotel Savoy.
(FROM THE *HERALD'S* CORRESPONDENT.)
CARLSBAD, Saturday.—The most glorious weather still prevails, and to-day the heat has been quite tropical. As a result all the dresses of the lightest and daintiest descriptions, concealed so long during the cold summer in trunk and chest, have suddenly sprung into day-light.

On account of the exceptional heat prevailing to-day, Admiral Sir John Fisher decided at the last moment to give his breakfast party in honor of King Edward in the garden of the Savoy Hotel, instead of in the big dining hall, and his decision proved to be very wise, for it was delightfully cool in the shade of the trees.

---

58. *DNB*, s.v. "Fisher, John Arbuthnot."

King Edward, who arrived at about one o'clock, was awaited and escorted into the garden by his host. The Savoy band played better than ever, and King Edward seemed well pleased with the choice of strains from "The Merry Widow" and the "Walzertraum."

The other guests were Lord Chief Justice O'Brien, Mrs. Samuel Newhouse, who sat on the left side of the King and wore a charming toilette of white embroidered chiffon and hat adorned with scarlet roses; Miss Mathilde Newhouse, seated on the right side in a white dress of embroidered muslin and hat with pink roses; Mrs. Townsend, exactly opposite the King, and wearing a handsome dress of white cloth, hand-painted, with violet flowers, and a large violet hat, and on her left Admiral Sir John Fisher. The other guests were the Duque de Alba, Marques de Villavieja, Sir Stanley Clarke and Major Ponsonby. King Edward wore a light gray suit and soft felt hat, and a white flower in his buttonhole, and seemed to be in the best of spirits.

An Amusing Incident

An amusing incident occurred during breakfast. A lady ostentatiously walked past the table with her husband, and was so busy gazing at the King that she marched straight into a tree and embraced it much to her own discomfort and the amusement of all who witnessed it.

After the breakfast was over King Edward drove into town with Mrs. Newhouse and did some shopping on the Alte Wiese. He inspected the famous collection of furs at Grunbaum's and made several purchases. In the meantime the rest of the breakfast party drove in carriages to the Aberg, where King Edward also soon arrived, and the Grand Duke Michael Alexandrovich and his sister, the Grand Duchess Olga Alexandrovna, with her husband, the Duke Pierre of Oldenburg, were also present to take tea with the King. The Savoy band provided excellent music and after sitting there over an hour King Edward drove down again to the Savoy Hotel with Admiral Sir John Fisher, passing along the beautiful Elizabeth and Esterhazy roads.

At five o'clock the King got into his automobile to return to Marienbad with Sir Stanley Clarke and Major Ponsonby. Before he departed he spoke to Herr Aulich, the proprietor of the Hotel Savoy, and praised the breakfast and excellent arrangements, which had in every way met with his entire satisfaction. The visit had been kept so quiet that both on coming and leaving the hotel there was nobody standing about.[59]

The society reporter, giving us a glimpse of the other guests and the flavor of the international gathering (with some apt surnames), "noticed: Mrs. Quadro and her daughter, the latter wearing a smart white coat and skirt;

---

59. Newspaper clipping enclosed in correspondence from JHW, in Carlsbad, to CHWG, in Pine Orchard, 4 Sept. 1907.

Mr. Quadro and Senor de Escandon. At another table close by were the
Duke of Santona and his son and further on were seated Mr. and Mrs.
Clarence Postley and Mr. and Mrs. Sterling Postley, the latter in a beautiful
dainty white dress and large picture hat." Mr. and Mrs. George L. White,
"the latter in pale blue," were mentioned in the same breath as "Mrs. E. R.
Brooks, in a black and white striped toilette and hat draped with a graceful
black lace veil."[60]

The First Tour by Automobile

Julia and George were attended in Carlsbad in 1906 by the magnificent
Thomas 55 HP touring car, in which they had been driven from Le Havre
via Brittany, the Loire, Fontainebleau, Paris, Rheims, the Meuse Valley,
Aachen, Cologne, Munich, and Bayreuth—a stunning stretch of country
on primitive roads. The chauffeur was Paul, a young Frenchman, about
whom Julia wrote that he "drives the car beautifully and carefully—In
other respects your father gets very much out of patience with him—He is
a very uncouth boy—but he understands the car and is not reckless—"[61]
This was their first automobile trip, at the dawn of the age of motor touring, when roads were poorly developed and rough on the vehicles. Julia
took to it immediately: "The motoring is delightful—and aside from
being able to go and come at your own times and convenience it takes you
off of the rail road lines and through a most beautiful country and the
quaintest . . . little towns—It is almost all peasant life that we see as the
large cities are few and far between; but the country folk [in Brittany] are
very picturesque with their caps and coifs—"[62] The vehicle, made by the
E. K. Thomas Motor Company of Buffalo, New York, must have turned
heads wherever it passed. It could seat two in front and five in the rear,
"two revolving seats being detachable and collapsible. . . . The driver and

---

60. Ibid.

61. JHW, in Nantes, to CHWG, in Madison, 22 July 1906.

62. JHW, in Nantes, to CHWG, in Madison, 22 July 1906. Baedeker, who at that time devoted equal
space to cycling, recognized that "[m]otoring enjoys an enormous vogue in France, principally
owing to the absence of police restrictions and to the excellent roads." Karl Baedeker, *Northern
France from Belgium and the English Channel to the Loire, excluding Paris and Its Environs, Handbook
for Travelers*, 4th ed. (Leipzig, 1905), xix. Julia took photographs on this trip, in an album that has
apparently not survived. The author saw the album, featuring the spectacle of the huge touring car
in the countryside, at Carrie's.

72. George in Europe, 1906. Standing with chauffeur, Paul, and the Thomas Touring Car.

a passenger sit in a front, open on the sides, with a windshield. The limousine is electrically lighted, has speaking tubes and toilet sets. It is luxuriously upholstered in leather or broadcloth." The standard color was "royal green." It weighted over two tons, could go from six to sixty miles per hour and cost $4,500.[63] Its arrival in Nantes, Brittany, merited notice in a newspaper:

A NANTES. (Par dépêche.)
NANTES, mardi.—M. White et famille, de New York, sont arrivés à l'hôtel de France sur une Thomas 50 chevaux.[64]

Travel by automobile had its hazards. Tires were punctured frequently (there were five stops for tire repairs between Cologne and Mainz alone), and in Belgium a steering cable broke, pitching the car into a ditch. It was simply too wet for comfortable car travel between Berlin and Hamburg, so the car went with Paul while Julia and George took the train. Their tour-

63. Excerpt from the 1906 catalog of the E. K. Thomas Motor Co., Buffalo, New York, copy supplied by AACA Library and Research Center, Hershey, Pa.

64. Newspaper clipping enclosed in correspondence from JHW, in Paris, to CHWG, in Madison, 31 July 1906.

ing was extensive nevertheless. From Le Havre they went through Normandy and Brittany, taking in Tours and Blois in the Loire Valley, followed by a one-hundred-twenty-mile, one-day run from Tours to Fontainebleau. After Paris they traveled for two days to reach Charleville, near the Luxembourg border, and needed another four days (including two for repairs) to cover the short distance to Aachen and Brussels, then a long haul down the Rhine to Munich and through Bavaria.

At Bayreuth "after much effort and *great expense* we were able to get seats for 'Gotterdammerung'—I never expect to see or *hear* any thing so beautiful in my life again—The orchestra reaches a perfection that is beyond any thing earthly. In Heaven they must have just such music for it raises the soul above worldly things. I have heard better soloists in our Metropolitan Opera House—but they were good enough for *me*—The scenic effect was gorgeous. Too beautiful in fact for one wanted to look but at the same time longed to close the eyes and just *hear*—Do you not think we were fortunate—"[65] (The production was maintained in reverent preservation of her husband's intentions by Cosima Wagner, who was then in her last year as director of the festival.)

George was the leader of this small troupe, in his element as the planner of the itinerary. As usual, however, Julia reported he was occasionally disagreeable, bilious, and "not well." "In Brussels we saw the sights but your father took a day off. He really felt ill—To use a pet expression of Grand-Pa White's 'I think he has bitten off more than he can chew' on this trip and it is beginning to tell."[66] Julia's confiding to Carrie about her husband's down periods doubtless served to relieve her own frustrations. Despite any shortcomings, George effectively led the party on routes that had limited directional signs and where the roads had just begun to be used for auto traffic; it was the most adventurous of their trips.

Lynde Harrison had died in June, and the newly widowed Harriet and her daughter, thirteen-year-old Katharine, accompanied the Whites on this journey—indeed, the trip may have been planned in part to distract her from her grief. Julia reported from Carlsbad that "Auntie is wonderful about the energy she shows in keeping up the treatment. She gets up at six o'clock every morning and walks to the Spring rain or shine—has not missed once—and she takes long, hilly walks. It will do her lots of good if she will

---

65. JHW, in Carlsbad, to CHWG, in Madison, 19 Aug. 1906.

66. JHW, in Bruxelles, to CHWG in Madison, 8 Aug. 1906.

only keep it up—Every thing is serene—and as 'pleasant as pie.' She is like her own cheery self and *Pa* is less nervous—"[67] Harriet's daughter Katharine was a great success on the tour, at least in the eyes of the adults. George doted on her, as Julia reported: "I do not know what he would do without Katharine—I think he loves her better than *any one*—in his immediate family I mean—She is very sweet and affectionate with him—and with every body for that matter and is really a very nice child—"[68]

It is remarkable that a girl of her age could sustain with equanimity a long tour such as this, including a long stay in Carlsbad, where the rituals of the cure could hardly have interested her, in the company of sedate and very senior elders. How welcome it would be to have the child's views of Paul, the chauffeur, the accidents on the way, the dressing for dinner at the hotels, the smell of the Carlsbad waters, George's nerves, bursts of temper, waggish humor and enthusiasm, Julia's emotional volatility and warmth. If she kept a diary, it has not survived. Perhaps she was saved from adolescent fretting by immaturity and the expected social code that governed childish behavior at the time, for Julia commented, "She is a very *little girl* for her years."[69] The grown-ups were fortunate in such a companion, described by Julia at the end of their eight weeks together as "the most affectionate child I ever saw—"[70] (It was Katharine, an only child, who years later learned of her mother's elopement and passed the tale on to her daughter, also an only child.)

From the spa Paul and the Thomas took them to Dresden, where they saw four operas in the Royal Saxon Opera House, designed by Gottfried Semper and entering its second decade (a *Boheme* was "not so awfully good"). About the same time as the White's trip, an American writer—in the aftermath of 1945 this becomes a poignant memory—called Dresden the Fiesole of the North, "essentially a city of pleasure, of fair, wide prospects, of hearty river life, of zest in nature and art. Even the public buildings cluster about the Elbe."[71] It was also hospitable to foreigners, having English and American quarters at the time. It was in Dresden that Harriet decided to remain for a time with Katharine. Julia reported to Carrie, "You

67. JHW, in Carlsbad, to CHWG in Madison, 27 Aug. 1906.

68. JHW, in Carlsbad, to CHWG, in Waterbury, 6 Sept. 1906.

69. JHW, in Paris, to CHWG, in Madison, 31 July 1906.

70. JHW, in Carlsbad, to CHWG, in Waterbury, 11 Sept. 1906.

71. Robert Taylor Schauffler, *Romantic Germany* (New York: Century, 1909), 274, 279.

73. Letterhead, Hôtel Bellevue, Dresden, 1906

may be surprised to learn that she has about decided to remain over here for the winter—It really is a wise decision. She does not know where to go in America, is not sure of her income, and thinks Dresden will be a good place for Katharine to study. I do not blame her for dreading to return to America. Your father approves also of her trying it here."[72] Harriet chose for a time a socially less demanding and physically more inspiring urban setting than New Haven. After a stay in Berlin, where they heard *Carmen*, the Whites sailed from Hamburg, presumably with the Thomas 55 HP stowed in the hold, though we do not hear of it again.

Carrie's Family

During her parent's years of travel Carrie started a family in Waterbury. The first indication that Carrie was pregnant came a year after the wedding, when Rob reported the news to his in-laws at the Homestead in Hot Springs, Virginia. This evoked a humorous reflection by George on his own experience of caring for babies:

---

72. JHW, in Carlsbad, to CHWG, in Madison, 27 Aug. 1906. A full-page advertisement in a contemporary Dresden guidebook showed a female traveler being advised by a genteel representative of an organization called "The Society to Further the Interests of Strangers," which "gives information, either verbally or by letter, without charge, respecting matters of interest to visitors." Hamburg-Amerika Line, *Guide*, 115.

You may imagine your old dad has no interest in events which are now "casting their shadows before" but such is not the case as you will find proven, when you ask me to hold the dear thing while you go out to play golf or to the coming "Assembly" . . .

You know I can do everything required from a first class nurse from getting up on cold nights and starting the alcohol lamp, to nicely adjusting the infantile 'jock strap' (Rob will explain this to you) too! My dear, I have been through it all and although your Mother is too jealous to admit it, stood tall with all my kids—that is up to the time they got able to talk back. Keep up your courage and strength.[73]

Julia was "miserably unhappy" at being away when her daughter was experiencing the sicknesses of early pregnancy. "I think of you every minute and I'm blue and cross and disagreeable," she wrote, which must have upset Carrie.[74] (She later apologized.) Carrie's troubles were, however, more serious and, although the term was never used, she miscarried. Rob and the doctor who attended her sent reassuring letters, but Julia wanted to return to be with Carrie, though she also felt duty-bound to stay with George. When Carrie's recovery was sure, she explained, "[I]t was not dearest that I was so anxious about your physical condition after the first day. I just wanted to take you in my arms and comfort you—My heart ached for you—." She added, with an insight into her own tendencies, "I have no doubt that it really was better for you, that I was away—I am so emotional and have so little self control." There is another reason why she felt compelled to stay in Europe. "If he had gone with me he would had to have given up the treatment, which he had just begun and from which he had great hopes. The look on his face, when, after reading Rob's first letter I said, I must go home—told me, I must stay."[75] George was dependent on Julia and her first loyalty was to him.

All went well with Carrie's next pregnancy, and she was delivered of her firstborn at 102 Grove Street on 16 November 1904. This child was named Haring White for his maternal forebears—Robert Foote Griggs Jr. would come five years later. The naming linked the child symbolically to Julia's vanished and cherished New Amsterdam and New York past. As was often done in "old" families, a surname was made into a given name,

73. GLW, in Hot Springs, to CHWG, in Waterbury, 8 April 1903.

74. JHW, in Hot Springs, to CHWG, in Waterbury, 10 April 1903.

75. JHW, in Hot Springs, to CHWG, in Waterbury, 19 April 1903.

74. Carrie with baby Carol, 1907

to impress the memory of the forebears on the future. Haring told the
author years later that he suffered for it, being called "fish" at boarding
school. He grew to be an intelligent and handsome boy and youth, made
much of by mother and grandmother, expected to live up to the associations they had with the name, an expectation whose failure became a deep
and continuing sorrow in Carrie's life in the invisible future.

With this birth, Julia transformed into a doting grandmother, preoccupied with the health of the baby, attentive to each transformation. "Do you
suppose I will know the dear baby when I go home Rob says he is changing his skin," she wrote while with George on business in New York two
weeks after his birth. "I hope his eyes are not turning blue."[76] The two-
month old baby fell ill in January, news of which had to be sent to Camden, South Carolina, where the elders were escaping the Connecticut winter. The flurry of concern, soon cleared with the baby's recovery. "You
certainly are to be congratulated on getting out of it so quickly and nicely,"
George wrote.

---

76. JHW, in New York City, to CHWG, in Waterbury, 24 Nov. 1904.

Your poor Mother felt as though she alone was needed to bring every thing out right, but the good news being coupled with and following the bad so rapidly, you did not give her time to be rash, or remain in doubt or suspense, so she has taken it quite rationally, and is satisfied now that everything is all right. You are just beginning the worries and anxieties of Motherhood my dear, and before you bring that precious boy up to manhood you will undoubtedly have many more. You must try and take them rationally and not worry yourself into sickness over them. I have seen you and the boys develop a 103° temperature from indigestion many a time which in a grown person would justify doom. But for some providential reason in children they recover as rapidly as they succumb.[77]

Haring was a healthy child, and soon fellow visitors at southern resorts and passengers on the ocean liners came to admire photos of the baby that Julia had ready in her handbag. As she wrote from Hotel Park-in-the-Pines in Aiken, South Carolina. "I look at the pictures every day—and many times a day—Of course Haring is much lovelier than any picture could be because his coloring is perfect and his ever changing expression makes such a difference—I do not mean from smiles to tears. What would not I give to hold him in my arms this minute—My precious little Grandson—"[78]

In April 1906, when the elders were at Pinehurst on their move north with the spring, Rob wrote that Carrie was pregnant again. "It breaks my heart to think of you as suffering from nausea," wrote Julia, "and perhaps fretting about our *first* love and your Mother not there to help you—I am never any use to you when you need me."[79] She did think that it would have been better to have three years between the children, "but really dearest two are better than one and it will be such a good thing for *our* darling boy." Carrie's pregnancy was untroubled, and Carolyn White Griggs, named for Jimmie's wife (and always called Carol), was born on 1 December 1906.

The roughly two-year interval was kept when Robert Foote Griggs Jr., "Bobbie," was born at the red house at 102 Grove Street on 27 January 1908. Carrie and Rob's family was complete, two boys and a girl, the same size and ratio a family as in the L. C. White family.

---

77. GLW, in Camden, S.C., to CHWG, in Waterbury, 12 Jan. 1905.

78. JHW, in Aiken, S.C., to CHWG, in Waterbury, 27 March 1905.

79. JHW, in Pinehurst, to CHWG, in Waterbury, 1 April 1906.

The Griggs Family at 54 Hillside Avenue

Robert F. Griggs, Co., Investments, did well in the 1900s, allowing Rob to purchase the Mitchell house at 54 Hillside Avenue in 1912. The house was a Queen Anne fantasy next to the even more flamboyant Benedict house, built in the 1870s to command a view of Waterbury and evoke wonder from onlookers. These creations, with their multiple gables, steep roofs and visible struts towering over Hillside Avenue, were under construction when Julia began her life in Waterbury. In the intervening years trees and shrubs had made them appear a settled part of the townscape, and houses of comparable size completed a row of six mansions along Hillside Avenue, the most recent of which was a Tudor-style house of brick with formal terraces, next to the Mitchell house. Rob's purchase established for all to see his family's prominence in Waterbury. "Are you not glad that you have moved into a more 'aristocratic' neighborhood?" Julia wrote, in part also reflecting her own dissatisfaction with the Grove Street corner, increasingly busy with auto traffic.[80] The house had ample room for the family and servants, eight bedrooms (three of which were in a servants' wing) and fifteen other rooms.[81]

Rob called in Wilfred Griggs to oversee extensive renovations. Inside he replaced Victorian wood paneling and mantels with lighter, Georgian or colonial revival style details and lighter colors. To give the children their own "world," he added dormers to the third floor, opened up attic space for bedrooms, and created a large central hall there for a playroom. There remained a spacious attic storeroom to hold steamer trunks, clothing, old playthings, and furniture, which became a legacy of the past of the Whites and Griggs families (and the source of properties and costumes for two generations of children).[82] Carrie preserved the artifacts from hers and Julia's lives on that third floor for over fifty years.

After the renovation, the house at 54 Hillside Avenue was no longer a period piece, but a comfortable and functional modern dwelling, though from the outside it retained much of its original fanciful character. Entrance from a carriage—and now car—was beneath a porte cochere into a vestibule, which opened out to a large hall brightened by tall win-

---

80. JHW, in London to CHWG, in Waterbury, 19 Sept. 1913.

81. Assessors' Records, 1023-0-60, City Hall, City of Waterbury, Conn.

82. Based on the author's observations.

75.   54 Hillside Ave., about 1900

Mattatuck Museum

dows over a staircase leading to the second floor, giving a sense of spaciousness and light. Above a black horsehair sofa that Carrie placed against one wall of the hall—perhaps from the L. C. White house—she placed the four oval portraits that evoked the Phelps and Haring past: the 1825 wedding portrait of Eliza (Ayres) Phelps, Julia's grandmother, and the 1859 ivory-types of the wedding portraits of James Demarest Haring and Caroline Eliza (Phelps) Haring and of Julia herself at age seven. "I want you to have your grand-mother's and grand father's pictures," Julia wrote. "It is a comfort to me to know where they are and I am glad you want them. The memory of my beloved parents is none the less dear because the only good portraits of them are in your home instead of mine—Some people could not understand. I know how much they would have loved you and how happy it would have made them both if they could have known that heaven was going to bless my life with such a wonderful and adorable daughter."[83]

Off the hall there was a formally furnished front parlor and a living room with a comfortable sofa and easy chairs. Gone was Victorian wood paneling and the swatches of fabric that darkened windows. It was in a cabinet in the parlor that Carrie kept the ring from Aunt Kate, the lockets with their pictures of Clinton Haring and "Poor Joe," Kate's son, and Samuel and Sarah Haring's serving spoons. From the living room, French

83. JHW, in Southampton, to CHWG, at 54 Hillside Ave., Waterbury, 12 Aug. 1912.

doors led to an enclosed sun porch (part of the renovation) usable when it was too chill to use the piazza. The dining room—with a long oval mahogany table for formal dining—was connected by a swinging door to a butler's pantry and thence to a kitchen, dominated by a huge gas range and oven. This "backstairs" was a world in itself, a maids' dining room off the kitchen, a small back porch where the "girls" could sit on warm days, their sparely furnished bedrooms above. The laundry in the basement had the latest in equipment, a gas-heated drying cabinet and a mangle wide enough to handle a sheet without folding. The laundress aired the wash on a clothesline "tree" hidden from view by a tall lattice fence.

The complement of servants in the early days were cook, waitress, upstairs maid, nurse for the children (all of whom lived in), gardener, laundress and a chauffeur (neither Rob nor Carrie learned to drive). The carriage house, an appropriate distance away on the driveway was now used for the odorless automobile, which made its hayloft redundant.

With this move, Carrie became the manager of a considerable establishment. It was she who saw to it that meals were planned and prepared satisfactorily, the laundry was done, the children were washed and supervised to and from school, and that the servants were content. From the author's observation as a small child years later, it was a smooth operation, with warm-hearted Irish housemaids and friendly male retainers. Julia often mentioned the trials of finding and keeping servants; Carrie was cooler and better organized than her mother, and managed better, it seems.

The front lawn sloped down steeply from the house, shaded by elms and oaks and a great copper beach. The Ralph Millers, owners of the Benedict house next door, had even larger grounds, which included a kitchen garden and greenhouses, adding to the cultivated pastoral setting of both houses. Leading from the Griggs's were stone steps to Hillside Avenue, laid out in an irregular, "romantic" pattern. Rob used these on his way to and from his office, Carrie on her way to place the grocery and other orders at establishments around the Green. Carrie would surely stop in to see her mother, and could nod and say hello if she encountered her sister-in-law, Mary, and her children.

Carrie was to live in this house for the rest of her life, and she died in her bedroom forty-six years later. Two generations of children, including the author, spent their most imaginative hours in that spacious third floor, and it was the repository of the letters and artifacts from which this narrative grew.

The Will White Family

Will and Mary's first child was Elizabeth Wade White, born on 8 June 1906. She was six months older than Carol but would be her classmate throughout their school days. Their son, Henry Wade, named for his maternal grandfather—he always used Wade as a first name—was born on 1 October 1909, about nine months after his cousin Bobbie Griggs. While Julia noted these arrivals in her letters, she found the role of paternal grandmother somewhat distant. Although Will and Mary lived only one door away, next to her parents house on Prospect Street, there was a coolness between Mary and her mother-in-law, and Julia had much less a role with these grandchildren than with the Griggses.

On the last day of October 1912, Henry Lawton Wade, the kindly father and able manager, died at 101 Prospect Street, after a long illness. He left an estate valued at $1.74 million, apportioned between his wife and the two daughters.[84] Mary received the house at 107 Prospect Street that her father had bought and remodeled for her. Her portion also included shares of Waterbury companies—the American Brass Company and the nearly worthless New England Watch Company over which Will was toiling. She and her sister, Lucy, shared the nearly half ownership of the small and profitable Mattatuck Manufacturing Company, which Henry Wade had started with George E. Judd. (Will came to represent the Wade sisters' interest in the Mattatuck, part of a story that extends well into the century.)

An immediate consequence of the inheritance was that Will White, through his wife, was wealthy. This allowed him to leave office work and, except during wartime service, never to have a regular job again. It also allowed Will and Mary to match—indeed, exceed—Rob and Carrie in the vastness of their dwelling. Will followed the lead of Frederick Chase in building a country house in Middlebury to the west, now easily accessible by automobile. These country estates were the harbingers of suburban development to come. The site was Breakneck Hill, overlooking Waterbury to the west, only six miles from Prospect Street.[85] From the hilltop

---

84. Probate file of Henry Lawton Wade, Wills, 122:304–5, 1913, Waterbury Probate Court.

85. "It derives its name from the circumstances of one of the cattle falling and breaking its neck in descending the hill, while employed in transporting the baggage of troops under the command of Gen. Lafayette [In fact, Gen. Rochambeau, leading the French army to Virginia and Yorktown in 1780] . . . the army encamped on the hill, passing eastward to the Hudson River." John Warner Barber, *Connecticut Historical Collections* . . . (New Haven: Durrie & Peck and J. W. Barber, 1836), 229.

76. Will White's Breakneck, Middlebury, Connecticut

the industrial city to the east was on display, but its smoke and grime were distant.

Will took an active part in the design of what might be called a colonial revival-English country house, with wood shingles, and white window-frames, and dormers. It was a rambling structure, with twenty-eight rooms, including a 50-foot-long living room. (Will's son tartly recalled, "Each room was either too large or too small.") There were two furnaces, and it was winterized, but each November the family would return to Prospect Street.[86] The house was begun in 1913 and completed the next year and was always referred to as "Breakneck."

No other houses were visible close by, save a garage with room for eight cars—there was an apartment for the chauffeur on the second story. The chauffeur was the one enduring association from New England Watch, as it was in that factory that Will had spotted a young man still in his teens and hired him to look after his cars. This was George Lombard Bassett, with Scotch and Irish forebears, always known as Curley because of his hair. Curley worked for the Whites all his life, and was referred to by that name even by children in the next generation, including the author. The Whites had a German maid called Lizzie. One day Curley came to Mary and said, "Well, I might as well marry Lizzie," and he did. They moved into the apartment above the garage.

Will was an enthusiast for automobiles and by the 1920s had a yellow Stevens-Duryea to look after. By the 1930s the garage had an ample com-

---

86. Interview with H. Wade White, 1 Oct. 1990.

77. Betty and Wade White at Breakneck, 1915

plement: a family car, spare family car, a car for Will and one for each of the two children. Curley's chauffeuring involved taking Mary about, delivering and returning the maids on their days off, shopping, and errands. He had a lathe in the building and made metal pieces for the gardens that Will built on the estate and created lily pond leaves from copper and a fountain of ironwork.[87] Free of New England Watch, Will supervised the landscaping and ground maintenance of the estate. He kept hunting dogs and had a gun rack in his study. Over the years he came to look the part of the English country squire in tweeds and leather boots, the cosmopolitan urbanity of the privileged rural.

In the house were a cook and two waitresses. The grounds and the extensive gardens designed by Will were tended by Worgan, a Welsh gardener. The estate was not self-supporting except for flowers, herbs, and some vegetables, but there was a touch of the feudal about its relative isolation and the cadre of servants.

87. Interview with EWW, ca. 1990.

1914

"Did I write you that we had a fine view of an air ship crossing the channel the day we came over. It was a beautiful sight but went like the wind (naturally)," Julia wrote from the Carlton Hotel, Pall Mall, of their passage across the channel from Ostende, a foretaste of what was soon to come in travel and in war. Their trip that summer of 1913, which had begun on the *Imperator,* had taken them from rural Devon to Paris, Strassburg (its name under German rule), Munich, Salzburg, and by the Wagon-Lits in the trip that so stressed George. "We spent Sunday afternoon in the national Gallery—It was a great treat after the hundred of modern pictures we looked at on the Continent—Most of them absolutely indecent—What is art coming to?" (Another sign of changes to come.) "I suppose Cousin Lizzie would cut me dead—again—if she saw that we have done no other sight seeing here—Enough is enough."[88] Their return voyage on *Olympic* was their last trip together and the last summer of the Europe that was mobilized for war the next August. If there was a dark cloud to challenge the expectation that Europe and its luxuries would always be there, that life would continue on in the "high, sun-filled uplands of peace," as Winston Churchill would later put it, it was not visible to the Whites.

"Of course it is better for Mother to be left alone some of the time and today she has seemed more tired than any day since I have been here," Carrie wrote Rob from New York in the December after their return. What was wrong cannot be gleaned from her letter, but Julia was obviously ill enough to go to a New York clinic and to require Carrie to be there and away from her family. "Dr. Price says every thing is going nicely with her and that it is perfectly natural she should feel weak and tired. There are so many tiresome treatments too for her that she must rest between times. I cannot but feel however that she is glad to have me near enough to run in to sit with her whenever she is awake."[89] She recovered and returned to Waterbury. She lived for another fourteen years in reasonable health, though she was often depressed. It could be that George's declining health triggered her own distress.

Early in 1914 George became seriously ill with nephritis, severe inflammation of the kidneys—the "poisons" that he had told Carrie about were

---

88. JHW, in London, to CHWG, in Waterbury, 19 Sept. 1913.

89. CHWG, in New York City, to RFG, in Waterbury, 2 Dec. 1913.

78. George with Carol on the piazza at 114 Grove

literally at work. In June he had a stroke. We know nothing of the next months or whether he was aware of the war that had broken out in the Europe he knew so well. The German advance was through the Meuse Valley, in Belgium, which he and Julia had covered in the Thomas 55. The cathedral at Rheims that so impressed Julia was gutted, Belgium was occupied and its people subjected to reprisals, Liege and Namur were damaged, the French countryside was denuded of men, and death was ever present on the lists in London papers. Most of the places that they had visited were not physically destroyed by the war, but had certainly changed in spirit. The kind of sedate travel that Julia and George enjoyed would never be recovered in the quicker social tempo of the 1920s.

George died at home on 2 December 1914 after another stroke.[90] The *Waterbury Republican* gave respectful and detailed coverage of his illness and career:

> Death Overtakes George L. White
> One of City's Most Prominent Manufacturers
> Succumbs to Apoplexy, Aged 62
> WHITE—George Luther White for years one of the business pillars of this city and identified with several of its leading industries, died last evening at his home on Grove Street at 10 o'clock. Mr. White suffered another stroke of apoplexy several days ago and lingered in an unconscious state until death intervened. The deceased was stricken by apoplexy June 1 and had been in

90. Death Certificates, April–June 1928, Office of Vital Statistics, City of Waterbury, New Haven Co., Conn.; *Waterbury Republican*, 2 Dec. 1914.

failing health, since, the last attack being too much for his system. News of his death will be received with genuine regret by his business associates and friends.[91]

A few months later the paper published the inventory of his estate. The type and size of his assets must have impressed the many readers who followed the fortunes of Waterbury families through these regularly published estate inventory reports. The estate amounted to $508,698, which in 2000 dollars would have the purchasing power of $8.72 million.[92] As an investor George balanced his holdings in the two inherited properties, the White & Wells paper board factory and the L. C. White button back factory, with other Waterbury and Connecticut companies: American Brass, Scovill, Colts Patent Gun, Stanley Works, American Hardware, and local banks. He had also invested in the new A.T.&T. In what might be called public service investments, he had stock in the Westover School (which his two granddaughters would attend), the Elton Hotel, and the *Waterbury Republican* shares. Real estate included office and factory properties on Bank Street (from his father) and the Grove Street house and lot on which his and the little red house stood. Investments were his interest, not real estate.

With the exception of $100 to each of the children, the entire estate went to Julia.[93] George's immediate legacy, therefore, was to provide her with the same level of comfort and luxury that she had been used to. Carrie, he realized, was well provided for through her marriage to Rob. Will likewise benefited from the Wade legacy. Jimmie had his position in the L. C. White Company to keep him until such time as he came into an inheritance from his mother. Will had given up any occupation that required him to be regularly at an office, but he represented his mother's shares in the continuing operation of White & Wells and L. C. White— companies that ticked along with moderate returns in the next years. The most important legacy was in securities. When Julia died in 1928 her estate was three times the size of her husband's fourteen years before.

---

91. *Waterbury Republican*, 2 Dec. 1914.

92. "Estate of George L. White," Statement of Account, 23 May 1916, file 8742, Waterbury Probate Dist., RG 4, Records of the Probate Courts, State Archives, CSL.

93. "Estate of George L. White," Will, 2 Aug. 1912, loc cit.

79. Exchange Place, Waterbury, about 1900

Mattatuck Museum

Julia entered the widowhood that Harriet had so feared years before. She made no changes in living arrangements, nor was expected to, and she stayed on in the house, supported by cook, waitress, upstairs maid, chauffeur, and gardener. Carrie doubtless stopped by every day on her way to or from downtown. Carol was close to her grandmother and would pop in after school at St. Margaret's. Julia went regularly to New York with Carrie or Carol for the opera, theater, and shopping. Nevertheless, hers was an existence isolated by money and social position.

Wade White recalled ringing the front doorbell of his grandmother's house when he went for a visit and being told by the maid who answered the door to wait outside while his presence was announced. Julia, at sixty-four, had become a prisoner of the formality and conduct then expected of a respectable and rich widow. She did not become eccentric or difficult as she aged, but as her later letters reveal, she felt herself cut off from life and lived vicariously through her daughter and grandchildren.

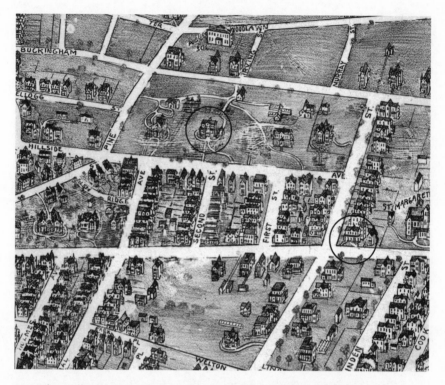

80. The Hillside, Waterbury, at the turn of the century. Landis and Hughes, 1899.

The Mitchell house (circled), at 54 Hillside, occupied by the Griggs family, can be seen in the upper middle portion of the map. St. Margaret's School, which Carol attended, is at the far right. The George Luther White house (circled) was just to its west, at 114 Grove, running almost parallel. The George E. Judd house was at First Street [Avenue] and Hillside, just below number 54.

Library of Congress, Prints and Photographs Division

X

THE TWENTIES

The Griggs sons were too young to be drafted in the war. A family story has it that Haring sold the most war bonds of any Boy Scout in the city, doubtless aided by sales to Julia and his father. Will White was the one member of the family to serve in the military. He was commissioned a major and stationed in an army materials-procurement office in Washington, where his role was to coordinate the output of New England factories in the war effort. Mary and the children were with him during the summer he spent on active duty. A photo of his handsome face, above the wool uniform and tall leather boots of the time, was an icon to his children, a part of family lore.

The Griggs children sat with their parents for periodic family portraits. They are a strikingly handsome group: silver-haired Rob has regular features, bushy eyebrows, and a slightly saturnine expression; Carrie also has regular features, light skin, and fine hair—a handsome woman (the term she would use in preference to "beautiful" or "pretty"), with a composed, reserved expression. Haring had dark, liquid eyes, and slightly dark skin—both he and Bobby favored their father—and had learned to dress smartly at Taft School. Carol is a different type, with her round face and large dark eyes, and her hair always topped by her signature ornament— an outsized bow. They pose as elegantly as they dress, akin to royalty in their self-presentation and doing it well enough not to seem pretentious. The family appears to be Fortune's favorite, and so it was until the late 1920s.

The children came to maturity in a society whose changing temperament and ethos reflected the loosening of old bonds and practices. America's involvement in the European war had relocated over a million men to army camps and depots, hundreds of thousands of them went overseas, most seeing a foreign country for the first time. This mobility heightened personal aspirations and tended to disrupt traditional social frameworks, which were also strained in the immediate postwar years by the influenza

81. The Griggs family, 1912. Rob and Carrie with Haring, Carol, and Bobby.

epidemic of 1919, labor unrest (major strikes in Waterbury required troops to keep order),[1] and the failure of Wilson's internationalism. The rapid proliferation of the automobile, too, played its part in quickening the pace of life and spurring independence and individualism. Now millions could move about with the ease and privacy formerly available only to the very rich.

There were drastic changes in fashion, too, that bespoke another sort of independence. Young women's clothing was no longer drapery equipped

---

1. *Brass Valley: The Story of Working People's Lives and Struggles in an American Industrial Region*, comp. Jeremy Brecher, Jerry Lombardi, Jan Stackhouse, The Brass Workers History Project (Philadelphia: Temple Univ. Press, 1982), 79–89.

with buttons, stays, and hooks from Waterbury factories. It was slighter stuff, revealing more leg and arm, and far easier to move about in.

As though to keep the loosening of society in check, the Volstead Act was passed in 1919, putting teeth in the Eighteenth Amendment to the Constitution, which prohibited the sale of alcoholic drinks. It had the unintended effect of encouraging youths to defy the imposed morality and to drink heavily, as Haring would learn to do at Yale.

Though Carrie's children grew up in a different social environment than their parents, good manners and conventional ways of conducting social and family relationships were still expected. Cracks in the façades were beginning to appear, however, pointed out by Sinclair Lewis, Scott Fitzgerald, and others, who scorned the provincial manners of places like Waterbury. Fitzgerald's *This Side of Paradise* (1920) portrayed the glamorous lives of those who had detached themselves from the restrictions of family and provincial places. Carol, the focus of this chapter, reported evening dances, the attention of "boys," and unescorted shopping on her coming-of-age trip to Europe in 1926. If she was not a woman of the Fitzgerald type, breaking loose from the mores of home and family, her awareness of the potential of sexual attraction was far more sophisticated than had been Carrie's thirty years before. Chaperonage on her journey was considerably less tight, and a stricture such as Miss McKay's to Carrie—to not pass unescorted through a hotel lobby—would have seemed almost ridiculous.

The youthful Haring came close to the literary-minded, sophisticated Fitzgerald hero. He was cynical, world-weary, and self-regarding—with none of the drive his great-grandfathers, grandfathers, and father placed on business and industrial innovation. Lewis's *Main Street* also appeared in 1920, another place-setter for the decade, and its mordant account of the self-satisfaction and provinciality of life in a small city complemented Fitzgerald's view of the more glamorous world of New York, and, eventually, postwar France. At Waterbury dances, one of his contemporaries recalled, "I'd find Haring standing aside making sarcastic and witty remarks, quite funny."[2] Such was the mockery by this new member of the smart set to the eminent in Waterbury society—those very "men" (or their heirs) whom Pape in his 1919 history praised as responsible for

---

2. Reminiscence of Guerin Carmody, Waterbury attorney and a contemporary of Haring's, to the author, 1963.

Waterbury's growth. "[W]ise observers say that Waterbury's success depended on comparatively few men," he wrote, a view that took in Haring's Griggs and White forebears. Such men were "masters of their business, most of whom have been born here, and all of whom prefer to work here."[3] The heroic ideal of entrepreneurs like his grandfathers, L. C. White and Henry C. Griggs, celebrated in the Waterbury of the previous century, had faded in the eyes of sophisticated youth, boosted by the debunking current of the era in which Lewis was joined by H. L. Mencken and many others. To Haring, in the bright-young-thing crowd at Yale, Waterbury, instead of being a place of destiny—as implied by the Rev. Anderson at the Henry C. Griggs funeral—was staid and provincial, a place from which to escape. This is what Haring was to do, with decidedly mixed results.

Connecticut factories provided a large portion of the materials of war used by U.S. forces in the First World War, and Waterbury plants flourished, making shell cases, cartridge clips, buckles, and buttons. Rob's investments in these firms did well, and local people had money to put in the market. In the 1920s he built a one-story building for the Robert F. Griggs & Co. on Leavenworth Street, a few steps from the Colonial Trust Company and in the shadow of Wilfred's County Courthouse. His brokerage office was an innovation. Customers could enter from the street, as easily as they might enter a bank or a store. The door was framed by Ionic pillars, as though a temple lay within. The firm was well poised for the boom in security sales and became Waterbury's preeminent brokerage. With the income from the business and his investments, Rob supported a home establishment with three live-in maids, a chauffeur and car, gardener, and a handyman. The children attended private schools, and the family traveled first-class, making two trips to Europe in the 1920s in addition to Carol's "coming out" tour. Rob provided Carrie with everything that George could have wished for his daughter.

Rob Griggs was a keen businessman, who invested well and built a substantial estate. His personality is somewhat hidden to the historian, though, as Rob confined his letters to a few affectionate lines. "I love you every bit of the time and in spite of the fact that I am having a fine time," he wrote in the midst of a cruise by sailboat in Long Island Sound, one of

---

3. William J. Pape, *History of Waterbury and the Naugatuck Valley, Connecticut* (Chicago, New York: S. J. Clarke, 1918), 1:2.

several he took in the summers, and "I shall have a finer one when I am home with you to talk it over."[4] When Carrie was in Atlantic City with Julia and George, he wrote of the children (and a household without Carrie's experienced hand), "I have just been up with both chicks to the new house [54 Hillside, then being renovated]. They are fine—scrappy at times though—They miss you a lot as I do and you will be mighty welcome when you come back."[5] She remained away for a time longer, and Rob wrote,

You needn't stay down there and try to persuade yourself that I am glad you are away for you know better. I am glad it is good for you all and that things have gone here as well as they have but I long to see you and long to have you with me. I hope all will be just like a story book when you come back and we all of us will be so good that you will never have anything to worry about. There is love in my heart for you every minute and I wish I could have you this minute.[6]

Rob reveals a bit of family life when Carrie was in Boston giving Julia a change of scene six weeks after George's death:

I was very glad to get your letter. I am sure it will do you lots of good to have the change and some amusement. You are certainly entitled to it. I am so glad the change is doing your Mother good too.

You underrate yourself about the children. They talk about you all the time. Only this morning Carol came dancing down and told Bobbie that it was only two days more before you were coming home. When I told her it was three she was quite blue.

They are going to the movies with me to-morrow but they don't know it yet. Haring has gone to Hamilton Park with Phoenix [the chauffeur] this afternoon possibly the others too.

My social life has consisted of dining and playing cards with Haring.[7]

Carrie wrote to "My dear Husband" or to "My dear Rob," he to "My dearest wife." There are only scraps here from a marriage that spanned a quarter of a century, but they betoken affection and respect. On their nine-

---

4. RFG, in Shelter Island, to CHWG in Waterbury, 26 June 1906.

5. RFG, in Waterbury, to CHWG, in Atlantic City, 19 Jan. 1913.

6. RFG, in Waterbury to CHWG, in Atlantic City, 21 Jan. 1913.

7. RFG, in Waterbury, to CHWG, in Boston, 22 Jan. 1915.

teenth anniversary he sent roses: "One rose for every year you had had when we were married, because you seem just as sweet and beautiful to me to-day as you did then."[8]

To Carol, Rob could be humorous. Addressing her as "my dear Chorus Girl," the morning after he and Carrie attended a concert in which Carol sang. "Your mother and I were very proud and happy last night," he wrote, "to learn that the wonderful inheritance of musical ability which you have acquired from us has at last been appreciated. Good for you. I will now sing duets with you. Confidentially I will admit to you that in my youth I was too good a singer to be on the Yale Glee Club but I should love to sing bass on the Westover Club."[9] He was passionate about football, and wanted Carol to accompany him even to prep school games, but those at Yale were a must.

We have far less an impression of Rob's person than we do of Julia and George. Curiously, Carrie told this grandson no stories in which he figured, although, with his portrait in the living room and photograph on her dressing table, he was as virtual a presence in the household as George and Julia. Betty White remembered her uncle as having a sarcastic and mocking sense of humor—Haring apparently acquired this from his father. Given the psychological troubles that each of the children had in abundance, and though there was a genetic origin for some, the family dynamics may have involved paternal disparagement of the sons (Bobby's self-esteem suffered in later life), and over-compensating—perhaps enveloping—maternal affection for Haring and Carol, contributed to later troubles.

In his 1921 inaugural President Harding famously promised "not nostrums but normalcy," the latter tag often used to describe the decade. It was welcomed after the turbulent years at the end of the enfeebled Wilson administration. The Senate had refused to ratify the Treaty of Paris, signed at Versailles by the triumphant president in 1919, and did not permit the U.S. to join the League of Nations. In May 1921 Congress passed a new immigration act that set national quotas and greatly reduced the inflow of Italians, who since the 1890s had been the largest group of immigrants to come to Waterbury and its factories. Republicans expected the new administration in the White House to keep the country out of foreign

---

8. RFG, in Waterbury, to CHWG, in Waterbury, 4 Feb. 1921.

9. RFG, in Waterbury, to CHWG, at Westover, 6 March 1925.

entanglements, settle things domestically, and generally be good for business. A prosperous stockbroker, Robert Griggs was pleased by the prospects for the future. He had done well and would do even better as Waterbury prospered. From the vantage of the brokerage and the number of boards on which he served, Rob had opportunities to observe which firms were doing well, and he chose to invest in them. At his death his portfolio was weighted toward local companies; he had no debt and had not followed the practice of others, doubtless including his customers, of buying on margin.

William J. Pape, the editor of the *Waterbury Republican,* published his history of Waterbury in 1919, its three large volumes meant to echo the 1896 Anderson history. Both works celebrated leading citizens with their biographies to emphasize the role of individual initiative in the city's growth (and not incidentally, assuring a subscription base for the volumes). At the outset Pape reminded his readers that in the 1890s many were pessimistic that industrial growth would continue in the city, as there were then manufacturing centers in the Midwest closer to the sources of iron and copper needed by Waterbury's factories. Such predictions a quarter of a century later were seen to be misplaced; despite comparative remoteness from the Michigan copper supplies, Waterbury's factories had expanded in the 1900s and output jumped during the war, when they supplied a multitude of small items for the armed services.

In the April 1920 fashion shows, hemlines had risen drastically. Women's clothing became slighter and more expensive. The notion of the desirable body changed to the compact and lean from the full bosomed and statuesque. This had its effect on Waterbury, reducing (and ultimately eliminating) the market for most of the stiffeners and fasteners formerly supplied to the apparel industry, but the successful factories had already anticipated this and manufactured other products with more potential for sales. While in Anderson's time someone might foretell Waterbury would merely remain "a small city," it had indeed emerged as "an important manufacturing center," which Pape flatteringly attributed to the activities of the "relatively few men."[10]

The ethic that had built the industrial city and established the wealth of the Griggs and White families was based on "industry, foresight, thrift and personal initiative"—a *production* ethic, as Malcolm Cowley put it in his

10. Pape, *History*, 1:2.

reflection on the twenties. As the 1900s advanced this was giving way to a *consumption* ethic based on purchase and accumulation of goods. The prosperity of the twenty years before the war had weakened the older ethic, and the war accelerated its decline. As Cowley writes, "[P]rohibition came and surrounded the new customs with illicit glamour; prosperity made it possible to practice them."[11]

Such changes can be seen in this family. Rob Griggs devoted himself to the activities of stock trading in which a product need never be seen. He dealt in symbols that were a long way from the bench and factory floor familiar to his forebears. The era's abundance gave him the opportunity to accumulate as well as to spend. His portfolio provided a legacy for Carrie and the children, but he could also consume freely. During his lifetime he was able to purchase, furnish, and staff a mansion-sized house, maintain a car and driver, travel freely, and encourage his wife and children to dress elegantly.

In the 1920s the American cornucopia continued to pour forth to the ever widening American middle class, and Rob and the family partook of its fruits. To Carol and her brothers life was made to seem effortless. There was ample means for most anything, and Carrie ran the household smoothly. Carrie taught the children good manners and refined speech, how to dress in an elegant, non-showy fashion, and to have good taste in surroundings, friends, and travel. There were few challenges to the children as they were growing up, and no reason to expect Carol's mental problems, Haring's drinking, or the changed finances that would come with the Depression.

Elegance, Art, and Battlefields

With Europe at peace, in 1921 Rob took Carrie, the three children, and Julia to Europe. The family was a striking ensemble, father and boys in tailor-made suits, Carrie and Julia in "traveling costume," Carol with her soulful eyes, plump with adolescence, Julia a stately figure in her early 70s. They traveled in first-class staterooms, out on the Cunard *Caronia*, coming back on its *Berengaria*, the former *Imperator*. They stayed at the Carlton in London (where George and Julia had stayed in 1913), the palatial

---

11. Malcolm Cowley, *Exiles' Return: A Literary Odyssey of the 1920's*, rev. ed. (New York: Viking Press, 1951), 61–64, 65.

Crillon on the Place de la Concorde in Paris, and in similar luxury in Switzerland and northern Italy. With the exception of the battlefields, most of what they saw was familiar to Julia and Carrie, and both passed on their memories to Carol. Although the itinerary must have been arranged for them (probably by Raymond & Whitcomb of New York, who did their later trips), they were on their own for sightseeing. It was Rob's first visit to Europe; he is present in Carol's diary, often sightseeing with the boys while she and Carrie and Julia are together, but there is no record of how he responded. He liked the comfort of the hotels and luxurious travel, and in 1926 he returned again with Carrie and Julia, in the hope that his then failing health would improve.

The *Caronia* sailed on 2 July 1921, delayed for three hours so that passengers could receive news of the Dempsey-Carpenter prizefight. Carol found this "ridiculous . . . Sea planes flew out with films of the fight for the *Caronia* to take to England." Carol shared a cabin on the boat deck with Julia, which was supplied with "many tokens of fruit & flowers including orchids from Aunt Hattie Harrison." Julia would have found the ship small compared to the palaces that she had known (and would again on the return journey); there were only three hundred in first class in a ship that held over twenty-five hundred passengers, but the size was just right for Carol, who had a fine time meeting people and playing shuffleboard and tennis.[12] "We have had wonderful weather," she wrote in her diary, "and I was not at all seasick. I just love traveling."[13]

Their stops were in the mainstream of tourism, and the sightseeing was thorough, with some sights particularly attractive to a fourteen-year-old.

---

12. William H. Miller Jr., *Pictorial Encyclopedia of Ocean Liners, 1860–1994* (New York: Dover Publications, 1995).

13. This and subsequent references in CWG, 1921 Travel Diary, a leather-bound notebook, "Carol W. Griggs" in gold letters on the cover, inscribed to her "from Cousin Clara [unidentified], May 25, 1921." It was designed for a record of travel across the Atlantic. On the frontispiece is a sea scene framed by rope held by sea horses enclosing the image of an ocean liner, hull down on the horizon. Several pages of illustrations provide a guide to the stripes and colors on the smokestacks used by the various steamship companies, an aid to passing the time of the voyage by identifying the owners of passing vessels. Tables show the differences in time in European cities, and there is a description of "methods of keeping time aboard ship" (the hours told by the bells), the meaning of "night signals," and the depths of the sea at various points. There is even a plan of a shuffleboard on which Carol wrote, "I played this game often on the boat." The little book is an artifact of the "institution" of the ocean voyage and its rituals.

7/11 London, Hotel Carlton After lunch went to see the parks . . . Saw little dog's cemetery, Hyde Park, went to Kensington Gardens for tea. Saw Peter Pan statue . . .
7/12 Tower of London . . . lunch at the "Cheshire Cheese." went through St. Paul's. Madame Tussaud's . . .
7/13 Old Curiosity Shop. British Museum & saw Elgin marbles, Rosetta stone and Magna Carta. 14, 15, Russell Square, St. Bartholomew's Church. Westminster Abbey. Hampton Court.Kew Gardens. In the evening went to a very funny play called *The Family Man* . . . National Gallery . . .

Carol recorded each day's activity in her diary, a charming mix of sights seen and what appealed to a girl of her age. At Oxford there was "Lunch at Mitre Hotel which was adorably quaint. The boys went in swimming . . . After dinner went paddling & punting on the Thames with Bobby and Haring." The next day it was the Bodleian Library, where she "looked at many of Shelley's possessions & original book of poems written in pencil . . . Went to New College & saw Reynolds window. After lunch walked around town & shopped. Had delicious soda at Fuller's." She experienced the candlelit conditions of a bygone era at the Red Lion in Henley, which had not yet been electrified.

Carol recorded a juxtaposition of experiences in London with the insouciance of a fourteen-year-old. After sleeping "awfully late" and having lunch at the Piccadilly Hotel she visited the Tate Collection, which she "enjoyed very much." After a ride on the embankment she went to a dentist to have her teeth band fixed. This was followed by movies ("Constance Talmadge in *Sally goes down the Road* and Kathryn Mc Donald in the *Turning Point*"). That evening she went to the theater ("*Ambrose Applejohn's Adventure* which was very good . . ."). The next day she was fitted for the new band and went to "Miss Hammond's for shampoo & she nearly killed me." But then there was "great fun with mother looking in the shops. She bought some crystal beads." In the lap of luxury this adolescent did not lack for bounce.

Despite the comforts of the Hotel Crillon, Paris was hot and uncomfortable. It was August, and Napoleon's tomb was closed, but the family "[l]unched at Cafe de Paris. Afterwards went to Brentano's & bought some French war posters. Went to Louvre seeing Venus de Milo & Mona Lisa. Went out to supper to Pre Catelan in the Bois & danced there afterwards with Haring. Received menu souvenirs from the waiter at same place. Drove through lovely places on the way home."

Father, mother, grandmother, and the three children took a touring-car to Rheims to see the shell of the cathedral, which Julia had admired in its glory in 1906. Carol found herself "satiated with horror by the ruined house & trees." At "Fort Pompel which the French captured from the Germans," they saw old tanks on the road & half filled trenches. On the way back they visited wine cellars ("ice-like caves") where refugees had sought refuge. Carol found the drive back to Paris "not so wonderful as now we were used to the destruction."

(The legacy of the Great War was a vivid memory to the author, growing up in the next decade, conveyed initially by Carol. He learned of the horrors of the muddy trenches, trench mouth, trench foot, and above all, poison gas. These became vivid acquired memories. On November 11 the factory whistles blew, and at school we stood silent by our desks to commemorate the Armistice and those who died. A stumbling, staggering figure who walked with the veterans in the Memorial Day parade was identified as suffering from "shell shock." The veterans were accompanied in the parade by a curious vehicle whose "40 et 8" sign referred to forty men or eight horses, the capacity of the French freight car.)

In Lucerne certainly Carol heard the story of the Baron's rose from Julia, and in Venice her grandmother took her into St. Marks, which she had seen first fifty-one years before, and Carol recorded it as "the loveliest cathedral I've ever seen." On the last day of the visit Carol "[s]at and read in the hotel reading room while Mother took Haring to the Doge's Palace. at about six Grandma & I went in a gondola. Our last ride for a long time."

They returned to Paris for a few days by train and in "icy cold" boarded the *Berengaria* from a lighter in Cherbourg, "perfectly enormous, 52,000 tons, elevators, swimming pools, etc. De luxe stateroom with beds and bath room." Julia told them of the ship as it had been on her 1913 voyage. The seas were such that the swimming pool could not be filled. "Not so nice a voyage as coming over. Quite rough weather so much so that there were no deck games. Had more fun on the *Caronia* as it was smaller & met more people and the weather was fine," So Carol put it in the last entry of her trip diary.

The Griggs family, like other rich Americans visiting the newly reopened Europe, saw the notable sights, and enjoyed the urban pleasures of restaurants, drives, and scenery, but their contacts with people must have been confined to hotel staff, drivers, shopkeepers, and gondoliers.

82. Westover School, Middlebury, 1920s

Westover School Archives

Amid this highly privileged touring, Carol reveals herself to be a cheerful and cooperative adolescent, learning the ways of the comfortable world of shopping and touring. She was paying attention to what she saw and wrote about her experiences with care—there are virtually no spelling errors in her diary. Her interest seems to be unflagging and so too her attention to paintings and sculpture, which many of her age would have found boring. She was a sturdy, observant, vivacious traveler and would be again in a grand tour five years hence.

Westover

Later that September Carol entered Westover, a boarding school in Middlebury, about five miles from Waterbury. It had been founded a dozen years before with the backing of several Waterbury businessmen, including Rob Griggs, and was immediately successful in attracting daughters of well-to-do families from the Eastern Seaboard and Midwest.[14] The young women received training in deportment and standards of behavior intended to prepare them to be cultivated wives and mothers. After initial homesickness, Carol was happy and fulfilled in the absorbing structure of

---

14. Curiously, Miss Hillard planned the school to be profit-making and pay dividends to investors. There were shares of Westover stock in the inventories of the estates of George L. White (1914), JHW (1928), and Robert F. Griggs (1928), who was a trustee of the school when Carol enrolled. It subsequently became an eleemosynary institution.

the school. Her cousin, Betty White, entered in the same year and had a similarly rich experience, with friendships and exposure to English literature that helped guide her life's achievement, the biography of the first poet in America, Anne Bradstreet. The academic instruction was excellent, particularly in English, music, and the arts, focusing on the history of European painting from the Renaissance, classical music, and English literature—a curriculum in later years to be called Western civilization. The school was guided in every particular by its founder, Mary Robins Hillard, who believed passionately in the importance of culture and in women's civilizing role in the family and nation.

The motto of the school was "Cogitare, Agere, Esse"—"To Think, To Do, To Be." The knowledge and accomplishment gained at Westover were intended to enrich marriages, husbands, and children. Few graduates went to college in the first decades of the school; however, judging by the quality of Carol's and Betty's knowledge and their ability to write clearly, they would have been suited to it. (Betty White said she never even thought of it; the prospect of what the family offered in travel and a finishing year in Rome was far more interesting to her then.[15] She did, however, earn a B.Litt. from Oxford when she was in her forties.)

The chaplain of the school was Dr. John Lewis, rector of St. John's Episcopal Church in Waterbury (later to marry Carol, baptize her first son, and preside at her funeral). The girls heard passages from the King James Bible read at Chapel on weekdays and Sundays, giving them ample exposure to the language of old England, and as Carrie recalled, Dr. Lewis's sermons left one with the impression that he had been present at the Sermon on the Mount and Crucifixion.[16]

At the end of the school year there was a ceremony at which each girl carried an ancient-looking metal lantern she had made; it was to be kept through her later life as a symbol of the light of knowledge and truth she had received at Westover. At a bonfire at Miss Hillard's nearby farm on a

---

15. Conversation with EWW, 1990s.

16. On Good Friday each year the girls assembled in the hall to hear Miss Hillard read *The Gospel According to St. Luke* from start to finish. She encouraged the exercise of charity. New girls would do chores for the older ones to earn pennies towards a gold piece for each of them, to be given in the collection plate for the poor. On Easter morning Miss Hillard stood at the front door as the girls filed into the chapel. She dropped a coin into the proffered hand, repeating "Blessed Easter" to each girl as she did so. Betty White's imitation made this sound like a parrot's cry. Elizabeth Wade White, in conversation with the author, ca. 1990.

83. Carol (far right) and Betty White (besider her) with Westover classmates, about 1924

June night the girls formed a procession with their candlelit lanterns in
front of the headmistress and the senior teachers. Miss Hillard spoke a
"prophetic word" to each of the new girls as they came up to her to inform
her if the inner light was "burning brightly" or "flickering." In a case
remembered by Betty White, she told one hapless student that her light
had gone out, and that was the end of that student's time at Westover.[17]

The intellectual and moral fundaments of the school were a uniquely
American mixture of New England Calvinism, in its late-nineteenth-century echo, and the ethos of private education as it had evolved in England.
Mary Robins Hillard, daughter of a congregational minister came from a
long line of New England Calvinists. Like her forebears, her life's work
was inspired by the promise of education and its ability to improve individuals and society. The boarding school, however, was an English institution, and for her model Miss Hillard went as far back as William of
Wykeham and the Winchester College he founded in the late 1300s. There
were a few other boarding schools for girls when Westover was founded in
1909, notably Miss Porter's, in Farmington, where Miss Hillard had taught
from 1885 to 1891, but nothing like the number of such that had been
founded for boys. She came to Waterbury and St. Margaret's after her time
at Miss Porter's and was headmistress from 1899 until 1908, when she told

17. Elizabeth Choate Spykman, *Westover* (Middlebury, Conn.: Westover School, 1959), 34.

the startled trustees (according to Betty White) that she was resigning to found what became Westover, four miles away in Middlebury.[18]

Miss Hillard had a partner in her project to create the school, Theodate Pope (1867–1946), the daughter of a Cleveland industrialist. Pope had been a student at Miss Porter's, where she met Mary Hillard. Theodate was fascinated by building and had her apprenticeship in the craft of architecture from Stanford White, with whom she worked on Hill-Stead, in Farmington (now a museum), a house for her parents.[19]

For Westover, Theodate Pope designed one large building in the form of a quadrangle around an inner court. All spaces were connected: the dining hall, study hall, assembly room, and classrooms were on the ground floor; dormitories were on the second floor. From the interior windows the entire building was visible, as in English colleges and medieval cloisters, where the concept originated. The façade's Georgian details, artfully constructed with stucco on wood framing, evoked England and colonial America. Pope placed the building close to the street and the small village green, not set off at the end of a long approach on a hill, as could have been done on the site (and was the practice in many boys' boarding schools). The result is an institutional building integrated into the fabric of the village center.[20] (Westover, considerably expanded with new buildings to the rear of the original, remains a highly regarded school, and the carefully maintained main building is still used.)

Henry James admired the sense of tradition he observed when he visited the school in the company of Theodate Pope in 1911, "[Q]uite right,

---

18. Ibid, 11.

19. The Pope house in Farmington, Conn., on which Theodate worked with Stanford White, is now the Hillstead Museum. According to its archivist there are only one or two letters from Mary Hillard in the Pope archive, and there is no record of Theodate Pope's letters to Mary Hilliard. Theodate Pope married John Riddle when she was forty-nine, after her work on Westover. Personal communication from Sandra Wheeler, Archivist, Hillstead Museum, July 1993.

20. Prominent Waterbury businessmen supported the establishment of the new school by serving on its board, which met for the first time at the Elton Hotel in 1908. They were James Elton, a wealthy businessman, leading citizen of old family, for years senior warden of St. John's; Frederick Kingsbury, a lawyer and local historian from a family prominent in business throughout the previous century; John Goss, president of Scovill Manufacturing, and Archer Smith, an industrialist. The Chairman was J. H. Whittemore, of Naugatuck, from a family that owned a foundry and large tracts of land in that town and adjoining Middlebury. It was he who donated the land on which the school was to be placed for playing fields and walks.

quite right, so civilizing," he commented on the chapel.[21] On this visit to his native country, according to Leon Edel, James "deplored the lack of ritual, the absence of standards. Above all he saw great affluence, great waste, and he was disturbed by the life of the rich who seemed to have no sense of noblesse oblige."[22] These were just the social wants Miss Hillard sought to remedy through her program at Westover.

There was nothing dour about Westover, however strict, and Carol was happy there. She made friends, played field hockey, took singing lessons and sought to qualify for soprano in the Glee Club. She was attentive to her studies, and respectful of her teachers and the school. At the beginning of her junior year she wrote Carrie a report typical of those she sent home. (The telephone had not yet become ubiquitous.)

> Study and then some more is all I have been doing since the day I got here. My subjects are terrific so I have told you before. They are all (except French) very interesting but [ ] notes and History notes take up an awful lot of time. Miss. Clark, a very good but strict teacher, teaches French and English History and so you can imagine why I was pleased when she sprung a test on us in class and I was the only one in her two history classes that got (very good +). Seniors are in both classes. When you get a bit of encouragement like that it pays you to keep going but then there will be a lot of discouragement mixed with it.
>
> My only hope is that I keep well because I have to study in the afternoons after supper and chapel to get all my notes copied and if I was a day behind it would mean studying all night beside.[23]

Westover was only a few minutes from Waterbury by a trolley that had been built for the workers who constructed the school. The girls were allowed to go into the city for church on Sunday, which Carol sometimes extended to visit Julia or Carrie. Other outings required permission from Miss Hillard. Not even a trustee-parent could intercede for an absence, however. "Please ask Miss Hillard if you can get away as early as possible on Saturday and your mother and I will call for you if you are allowed to

---

21. After James had been greeted with applause from the students, he said, "My mind has been undermined . . .," and waved, saying the right word was too difficult. Spykman, *History of Westover*, 43.

22. Leon Edel, *Henry James: The Master, 1901–1916* (Philadelphia: Lippincott, 1972), 251.

23. CWG, at Westover, to CHWG, in Boston, 27 Sept. 1923.

go," wrote Rob. "I want you to go to the Taft-Pomfret foot-ball game next Saturday afternoon. It bids fair to be very exciting because Taft has beaten Hotchkiss and Pomfret has beaten Choate.")[24] Once Carol gave voice to a lament about being so restricted. "Oh I wish that I could come and see you in Boston [where Carrie was attending Haring recovering from a back operation]. It seems *too* unfair that we can't have one little weekend out of this darn place all year." She also found the Will White family more attentive. "Betty [White] has seen her mother four times since she has been here (eight days). She went into town today and to tea one day. Oh these Whites!"[25] That tea was in the long living room at Breakneck with its view of the lawns sloping away beyond the French doors, the chimneys and houses of Waterbury in the distance—Carol's exclamation reflects the Griggs' awareness that the Will Whites were more social and did things in a grander manner.

Carrie spent much of the summer and fall of 1923 and the early months of the next year in Boston with nineteen-year-old Haring, who had an operation on his back followed by prolonged hospitalization and bed rest. As a result, he missed what would have been his sophomore year at Yale, and had to move back a class. Carrie stayed at his side in the hospital and lived in the Hotel Vendome on Commonwealth Avenue during his recuperation. Cousin Lizzie Wetherald, who lived nearby, wrote Carol of the hotel that "I thought all the old women in the world were in Pasadena [where Lizzie also had a house], but not at all, they are here in this hotel with huge double chins, patches on their eyes, every kind of lameness, and one with a swelling on her neck like this. [On the notepaper is a sketch of the front view of a face, with a huge wen sticking out the right side.] They all wear ground grippers or worse, but their bank accounts are enormous so they are tolerated. Money talks but it should not even be heard." She had been working on a portrait of Carol from a photograph: "I want to have a gloss put on it for your mother, but I am afraid of it boring her— she is too polite to say she does not want it." Lizzie's son (Royal Wetherald) had just been divorced, which prompted words of advice: "Take to art Carol dear and do not marry. The novelty soon wears off and then the time is long." She enclosed "a pome." "Why do I send you this little poem, it will not make the slightest impression upon you I'm sure, you are

24. RFG, in Waterbury, to CWG, at Westover, 30 Oct. 1921.
25. CWG, at Westover, to CHWG, in Boston, 27 Sept. 1923.

84. Eliza (Winter) Wetherald in her sudio, Marblehead, 1920s
A sketch of Carol rests on the floor , near the base of the stairway.

so wedded to your shoes, earrings, etc., etc., that it will be forgotten as soon as read, however here is hoping."

> You shall not wear velvet,
> Nor silken broidery,
> But brown things and straight things
> That leave your body free.
>
> Your friends shall be the tall wind,
> The river and the tree:
> The sun that laughs and marches;
> The swallows and the sea.
>
> And you shall run and wander
> And you shall dream and sing
> Of brave things and bright things
> For I will keep you simple
> that God may make you wise.[26]

Lizzie's critique of the focus on marriage and clothing that Carol shared with other young women of similar family and economic status is a breath of the change in the air. Marriage was the only life path that seemed open to young Carol—college was not even considered. In her senior year she noted her unusual single state. "What is becoming of our Waterbury

---

26. Eliza Winter Wetherald, in Boston, to CWG, at Westover, 3 Nov. 1923.

younger set. They are all getting married. Betty [White] and I, we've realized, will be the only unwed, practically, next year."[27] Carol was indeed in love with shoes and clothes, and she recalled Lizzie's characterization in Paris three years later.[28] Betty, however, was an intellectual, committed to literature, and, later, research. She would never marry.[29]

Carol graduated from Westover in June 1925. While most of the girls promptly became engaged—Carol watched closely and marked the names in her yearbook as engaged or married—she had no offers of marriage in the months she spent at home. In December she began her own coming-of-age visit to Europe, a present from Rob in honor of her graduation, continuing the tradition begun by Julia and followed by Carrie and a practice followed by many well-to-do families. For such young women this was the waiting period before the all-important engagement, which could, indeed, come at Carol's age of nineteen but was expected two or three years later, certainly before the mid-twenties. A European tour would add polish by exposure to the society of its elegant hotels with their *thé dansantes*, shops, and museums and historic monuments. Chaperonage was deemed as essential as it had been in Carrie's day, to guard against romantic entanglements with fellow Americans or continental adventurers. The six-month tour began in the Mediterranean, as had the youthful journeys of grandmother and mother, and the party covered Italian, Swiss, Austrian, and French territory familiar to them. Germany, the wartime adversary, was not included. An exotic addition for this trip was a January sojourn in Egypt.

Carol's trip was under the supervision of an experienced chaperone, Miss Adelle Rawson from Brookline, Massachusetts, a veteran of comfortable and proper "continental touring" for young ladies. Miss Rawson knew how to navigate her flock. "In Naples they all cow-towed to Miss Rawson and I thought a Count that was in the American Express office would embrace her on the spot."[30] She had contacts in the larger places,

27. CWG, at Westover, to CHWG, in Waterbury, Sept. 1924.

28. CHWG, in Waterbury, to CWG, 25 April 1926.

29. The Lizzie who tried to put Carol on the path of "art" was then sixty-nine—calculated by Julia in a letter to Carrie, as purportedly she would not tell her husband her age. She was at that time ailing and died within a year. James Wetherald wasted little time after her death and married someone presumably more committed to the institution of marriage.

30. CWG, in St. Moritz, to CHWG, at 54 Hillside Ave., Waterbury, 24 Dec. 1925.

who gave the girls local and often detailed knowledge. In Rome the guide was "the son of a friend of twenty years standing," Miss Rawson wrote Carrie, "a youth who graduated from the University here, then had two years in college in England—a perfect background—and when the girls leave Rome we feel they have material for reading forever after and the happiest memories of a city that can be most depressing if seen through untrained eyes."[31]

Adelle Rawson pointed the girls to suitable tearooms and showed them where and how to shop. The reins were much looser than those of Carrie's Miss McKay, as the girls could shop and visit friends unaccompanied—Westover acquaintances turned up in most places. Miss Rawson gave the girls instructed passage through the treasure house of Europe, with ample time for dining, dancing, and theater-, opera-, and concert-going. A leisurely pace was needed to deal with the time-consuming logistics of travel in those days: getting to trains and boats, passing the time on them, settling into hotels, dressing for sightseeing, changing for tea and then again for dinner. Miss Rawson and friends who accompanied the group for a time, a Mr. and Mrs. Harwood (Mabel Lucasta Harwood, like Adelle Rawson's, a name that might have been chosen by Henry James)—kept watchful eyes as to unsupervised contact with males, but, compared to Westover, the trip was freedom. Carol described Miss Rawson as resolutely cheerful, seeing only the best in people, companionably sharing rooms and suites with the girls. For her part she wrote Carrie that "[b]oth in history and art [Carol] must have worked very faithfully and had unusual teachers. I find her knowledge of both surprising in one of her years."[32] Mrs. Harwood sent Carrie a report that must have delighted her—poignant in light of Carol's severe mental illness a few months later—describing her as "the life of the party with her sense of humor and ready wit and with it all she was so solicitous of us and so thoughtful in little ways constantly thinking our comfort before her own. Thus, she endeared herself very much to us."[33] Carol shared her playful spirits generously in her letters home.

Betty White gave Carol a farewell luncheon at the Will White's Prospect Street house in mid-December, duly noted in the social columns of the *Waterbury Republican*.[34] The party left Boston on the SS *Duilio* of

31. Adelle Rawson, in Rome, to CHWG, at 54 Hillside Ave., 27 Feb. 1926.

32. Ibid.

33. Mabel Lucasta Harwood, in Newton, Mass., to CHWG, 8 April 1926.

34. *Waterbury Republican*, 13 Dec. 1925.

the Navigazione Generale Italiana, which had been in service only four years. Of its fifteen hundred berths, only less than three hundred were in first class.[35] Harriet Hayward ("Hat"), a Westover classmate, was Carol's "partner in crime," as she put it, for the merry time they spent looking (in vain) for eligible young men during the Atlantic crossing. Mary Hayward, her sister, was in the party; so too were Frances and Ruth Norton, the "Misses Nortons [who] are very sweet, very lady-like but with sense of humor enough not to mind how dumb Harriet and I act."[36]

The ship entered the Mediterranean through the Straits of Gibraltar, and the party debarked at Naples in the early morning, allowing Carol to see "the Sun-rise over the bay which was dotted with little fishing smacks and the bare-footed fishermen were dragging in their nets. The trees were heavy with oranges and I thought the streets filled with flower venders was unbelievably beautiful." Perhaps because she had been warned by Julia and Carrie about conditions in the city, Carol reported that there were "a very few beggars in Naples and everywhere one is greeted with smiles and politeness."[37]

Miss Rawson moved the party briskly on by train to Milan, where they heard *Meistersinger* at La Scala. "Most of us didn't know what it was all about because we couldn't get a libretto. To add to the Excitement of the opera, Mrs. Harwood fainted dead away and was carried out of the opera house."[38] (The opera was likely conducted by Arturo Toscanini, then the musical director of La Scala. Wagner's great comedy was the first opera he conducted there in 1898, and his performance of the work was famous in prewar years in New York and at Salzburg. Carol would soon hear two more Toscanini performances.)

Christmas was at St. Moritz. It was an occasion to buy woolens, try out a bit of skiing, and mostly to visit with several Westover girls also there. In Vienna they were entertained by a Baron Fuchs, who termed Carol and her pal, Harriet Hayward, his "dear little gosselets" and exposed them to (no doubt faded) local high society and later sent them postcards.[39] The baron met the party at the train station "and took us immediately out to

35. Miller, *Encyclopedia.*

36. CWG, from the SS *Duilio*, to CHWG, at 54 Hillside Ave., 14 Dec. 1925.

37. CWG, in St. Moritz, to CHWG, at 54 Hillside Ave., 24 Dec. 1925.

38. Ibid.

39. CHW, Travel Diary, 1925–26, 3 Jan. 1926.

85. Carol and Harriet Hayward at St.
Moritz, 1925

see Schönbrunn, one of the many imperial summer palaces of the Austrian
royalty. It was really interesting and very ornate with much gold—and
thousands of pictures of Maria Theresa and her sixteen children. It is
awfully jolly this tramping thru ice-cold palaces and I keep thinking how
Daddy would enjoy it."[40] New Year's Eve was celebrated with *Die Fledermaus* at the opera, and on another evening there was *Aida,* where "I was
terribly thrilled by its spectacular scenes and by the familiar music."[41] At a
performance of *Lohengrin* "Harriet and I got lost between the acts in the
opera house and barely got back for the 3rd act."[42] Carol was delighted by
a tour of the theater a few days later. In Vienna they were guided by Mr.
Salz, who took them to what was still called the Imperial Art Gallery, "and
there to my joy I discovered many familiar paintings—thanks to my education at Westover."[43]

At home Julia overflowed with excitement when Carol's first letters
arrived:

---

40. CWG, in Vienna, to CHWG, at 54 Hillside Ave., 1 Jan. 1926.

41. Ibid.

42. CHW, Travel Diary, 1925–26, 3 Jan. 1926.

43. CWG, in Vienna, to CHWG, at 54 Hillside Ave., 1 Jan. 1926.

If you knew what a state of wild excitement the entire family was in when your first letters arrived you would send one every hour so that they might come in huge bunches and we would telephone the glad tidings from house to house. I had a post-card of "Napoli" and a wonderful letter from St. Moritz in the first haul and then a dear letter written on the *Duilio* later. (I mean it came later) You can form no idea what the wait from December the twelfth until January ninth meant to us.[44]

Carol's trip was a family project. One can imagine Carrie hurrying down the hill to show her mother the latest letter.

Carol and her companions were in Venice briefly before embarking on a steamer to Egypt. Italy's queen mother—whom Julia had seen as a newly married Princess in Palermo in 1868—had recently died, so the museums were closed, but Carol, again on familiar ground, managed to see Tintorettos, Titians, and a Giorgione in the city's churches. They endured a rough and lengthy (five-day) trip to Alexandria on a small steamer, which pitched and rolled across a stormy Mediterranean—they had to stay an extra night on the ship because at Alexandria the pilot "made insulting remarks to the Captain."[45]

In Cairo they stayed at the renowned Shepheard's Hotel where they were taken in charge by their dragoman, Mequid Semeda, "tall, very handsome, fine aquiline features, very white teeth and as straight as an arrow. He speaks English almost as perfectly and he wears beautiful robes."[46] The Tutankamen Tomb had been found and entered by Lord Carnarvon and Howard Carter only four years before, and artifacts were recently put on display in the national museum. The discovery of "King Tut's Tomb" attracted world-wide attention, and the resulting focus on Egypt and its antiquities was doubtless the reason for the presence of the many American tourists that Carol noticed at the hotel and, indeed, for Miss Rawson's inclusion of that destination in her tour.

Carol found Luxor "rather dressy. It must be rather like Palm Beach except that there are not so many people. I met a Marquis last night and have heard from a very cute Scotch boy that I met in St. Moritz. Strange to say he has a very strong English accent. The following sentence is quoted from one of his letters: 'I am keen on you and think that you are a topping

---

44. JHW, at 114 Grove St., to CWG, 14 Jan. 1926.

45. CHW, Travel Diary, 1925–26, 11 Jan. 1926.

46. CWG, in Cairo, to CHWG, at 54 Hillside Ave., 13 Jan. 1926.

86. Carol at the Pyramids, 1926

girl, cheerio and tout a toi, Graham.'"[47] They spent a week in Luxor touring by day, meeting boys. One evening they saw "Karnak by moonlight
via a felucca with Arab musicians, dances & singing. Simply beautiful. Hat
& Teddy Smith [Hat's current flame] sat on a pylon and talked."[48]

Regardless of the social scene, for a person with Carol's devotion to
learning, study remained an important part of her tour. "This Egyptian
history is very difficult for us all, but our dragoman is very conscientious
to explain every symbol on the tombs." Carol went to tea "at Mr. and Mrs.
Whilnlock's house—way out by the Valley of the Kings. They are Boston
people and he has been here for six years excavating with Carter and it was
very interesting to hear him tell of how difficult it was to remove Tut's
Mummy from the Sarcophagus because the oils which were used for preservation had hardened and they had to use a chisel to force out the
Mummy."[49] The great treat of this Egyptian tour was camping out on the
desert near the Pyramids and the Sphinx. "We had real beds in our tents
and the tents were lined very decoratively with appliquéd Egyptian

47. CWG, in Luxor, to CHWG, at 54 Hillside Ave., 20 Jan. 1926.

48. CHW, Travel Diary, 1925–26, 23 Jan. 1926.

49. CWG to CHWG, 20 Jan. 1926.

figures ... Unfortunately the Sphinx had a large framework on it because sands have shifted and all day long the natives carry away sand by hand in small bowls. There are literally thousands of men, women and children who work at the Sphinx all day."[50]

"What a life you are having just now and it will last you always," Julia commented on the news from Egypt. "Fifty years from now you will be telling your darling grandchildren all about that fine trip to Egypt for you will remember the details better than any later experience. You know what a bore I can be—not that you will be—"[51] Carol did not live to be a grandmother, but this visit to Egypt—and a photo of her on a camel— became a vivid part of the wondrous epic her son learned as a small child about his mother in the far-off time before he was born.

Despite the monuments, the education, and the hotel society, Carol was already homesick. "It seems at least a year since I left and just think the trip isn't half over yet ... I love all your letters so and read them over many times."[52] It is a theme that recurs in her letters home. She was dependent on Carrie and wanted her help to buy presents for the relatives and clothes for herself. She urged Carrie to bring Rob over to join her on the continent in the spring. Much to Carol's delight, they shortly decided to do just that. The news reached her in Palermo ("It will be such fun to able to shop with you in Paris and Florence").[53]

The desert and the lush bounty of Sicily in early spring (February) provide a classic contrast of the Mediterranean world, one that delighted Carol.

[A]t the Hotel Politi at Syracuse we used to go out and pick bunches of violets miguorette, narcissus and roses. I am sure that heaven is not half as beautiful as Sicily. The Mediterranean is without a doubt the most beautiful blue that you can imagine—and with the pink houses as contrast—and Mt. Etna snow-capped with the sunrise turning it a soft pink—it is a sight for the Gods. I am not particularly artistic and it is rather cruel not to have the gift to paint such wonders—so I can only rave.[54]

---

50. CWG, in Cairo, to CHWG, at 54 Hillside Ave., 9 Feb. 1926.

51. JHW, at 114 Grove St., to CWG 18 Feb. 1926.

52. CWG, in Cairo, to CHWG, at 54 Hillside Ave., 9 Feb. 1926.

53. CWG, in Palermo, to CHWG, at 54 Hillside Ave., 17 Feb. 1926.

54. Ibid.

In Palermo, Carol noticed a sign of the influence of the latest regime. "It is too bad from the picturesque view-point that Mussolini [called to head the government in 1922] is having all the quaint little cobbled streets repaved and he has forbidden the gay little colored carts in the main streets. In five years Sicily will probably have lost most of its local color but I suppose the renovating of the cities is a great thing for the poor."[55] Julia would have been delighted with this word from this city where she first glimpsed Europe, staying at the same Hotel Igiea on the waterfront with Uncle Howie a lifetime before.

From Palermo via "the horrid little *Catarina*" they went to Naples. Carol's diary entry gives the flavor of the party at play in that city:

> We had breakfast at the Grand. I got some mail and wrote several. A beautiful spring-like day and we watched processions of gay Neapolitans go by. How I love Naples! We went to Zoppa's shop where we bought some coral and tortoise shell things. We were expecting to have tea at Bertolini's Hotel but it was too late so we went there for the view. Very good situation. A tea dance in the ballrooms & we had a gay time and danced with many Italians. All with terrible champagnes.[56]

The party drove to Pompeii by rough roads and had two hours to see the ruins: "very interesting and they were especially so to me after hearing so much about them from you and after reading the "Last Days of Pompeii." They then took the "extremely perilous" Amalfi drive to visit the old Cappuccini monastery, which had a "glorious garden" and view, "familiar to me from Grandma's various post-card albums."[57] "My ship must have come in," Julia wrote,

> because this morning the maid brought me four foreign letters and post cards the most prized of all being yours from Amalfi but it breaks my heart to know the lovely Pergola has been carried away by the land slide. I knew there had been one but thought the damage done was all further to the left from the old monastery. It was charming in the old days. Do you remember the photo I took of your mother sitting in front of the [   ] covered openings. The old monks were so friendly and so interested in everything we did.[58]

---

55. Ibid.

56. CHW, Travel Diary, 1925–26, 21 Feb. 1926.

57. CWG, in Naples, to CHWG, at 54 Hillside Ave., 25 Feb. 1926.

58. JHW, at 114 Grove St., to CWG, 11 March 1926.

The party had two weeks at the Grand Hotel in Rome for what Miss Rawson considered to be a crucial education. After visiting the Forum and the Capitoline Hill, Carol felt "rather sorry that I couldn't find romance in that dry old study of Latin but perhaps if I had such a setting as this to study it I might have found romance in even Caesar instead of worrying about whether I could conjugate the verbs correctly." The hotel did not allow dancing, "which is rather nice after staying up until all hours because in Rome it doesn't do to have one's eye shut while sightseeing."[59] And the sightseeing was intense. After one day's trekking about, Carol reported that she had "only been in the hotel about a half an hour all day and about an hour for lunch so that you can see that we are really doing serious business. I don't think that anyone enjoys it any more than I do. I am the only one that has had art so I don't want to miss a picture and have a wonderful time arguing with the guide. He adores Carlo Dolce who we learnt was the most insipid sentimental painter ever living but whom the Italians seem to love."[60]

On her last day in the Eternal City, Carol visited Betty White, who was spending her "coming of age" year at a school for young women run by a Miss Risser. "There was no telephone at Miss Risser's so I couldn't get hold of Betty until I went there. Harriet and Miss Rawson went with me and we had a great old time all talking (advantage for those who have carrying voices). B. said that her family are now in Sicily." Will, Mary, and Wade were soon to join with the Griggs family and Julia for a time, both families visiting their daughters.

In Florence, Carol enjoyed a day that Carrie found altogether too loose.

I wish you could see me cleaning, washing, steaming, sightseeing, tea dancing, shopping. It would make you quite dizzy. Fortunately the Lord made me quite substantial—but I still do hate to get up in the morning. I tore madly around all yesterday, between sightseeing and looking in shop-windows. I came home at five o'clock quite weary to find an invitation awaiting me for a

---

59. CWG, in Rome, to CHWG, at 54 Hillside Ave., 1 March 1926.

60. Ibid. Dolci (1616–86) was "one of the leading Florentine Baroque painters . . . intensely and neurotically absorbed in religion, . . . specialized in devotional works marked by sweet coloring and enamel-smooth handling. These won him an international reputation in his lifetime, but today usually appear merely sickly." *Random House Dictionary of Art and Artists*, David Piper, ed. (New York: Random House, 1981).

tea dance with *two* boys I had met at Cairo and hadn't seen since then. In spite of being tired I dressed in 15 minutes and tea-danced here in the hotel. I introduced the boys to Harriet and they invited us both out to dinner at Lapis, a typically Florentine restaurant—underground with no windows. We had a very good time and were entertained while we ate by a fat Neapolitan who played a guitar and sang Santa Lucia and other familiar Italian tunes. The boys had to leave at 11.30 for Vienna so they escorted us home in a carriage at 11.15 and tore for the train. There you have yesterday's program![61]

Carrie commented tartly, "I am surprised you went out in Florence without a chaperone. I did not suppose it could be done with propriety."[62]

The party stayed in Florence through Easter, with a steady diet of sightseeing and its attendant lessons every day but Sunday. Miss Rawson made certain that her charges received the education in art and architecture that would cultivate and challenge minds and sensibilities. She also left time for musical performances. Carol had the opportunity to hear a recital by the young Jascha Heifetz at the Pitti Palace, and to attend a performance of *Rigoletto,* which was "a huge success and with Toscanini leading it made it even a greater attraction. Of course I am not a connoisseur on music but I did like it. There was so much familiar music in it. Florence isn't especially noted for its operas but the San Carlo company from Naples came for Easter week."[63] On Easter, Carol had the bewildering experience of many Puritan Yankees confronted with the more elaborate ceremonies of the Catholic Church:

Easter Sunday dawned bright and clear and I took Harriet with me to the Church of Santissima Annunziata. I hadn't been to a Catholic Church in some time so I was a bit confused by the high mass—and wasn't quite sure which altar I should face—but after kneeling for some time we finally discovered the correct place to sit to hear the music—which lasted for about two hours. It was quite an elaborate service with much incense and vestments. I must say I longed for Saint John's with its bank of lilies and the choir singing "Jesus Christ is risen today." The Catholic Church I find is far too diverting to pray in.[64]

---

61. CWG, in Florence, to CHWG, at 54 Hillside Ave., 10 March 1926.

62. CHWG, at 54 Hillside Ave., to CWG, 8 April 1926.

63. CWG, in Montreux, to CHWG, at 54 Hillside Ave., 8 April 1926.

64. Ibid.

After Florence the party went north to the Italian Lakes, which had delighted Julia and Carrie on their visits. In Milan they heard Toscanini again conducting a performance of Arrigo Boito's posthumous *Nerone* in a revival two years after its premiere. Carol commented that it was "[q]uite spectacular but rather long . . . and I was dead sleepy that nothing less than seeing Rome burn would have kept me awake."[65]

After a few days in Switzerland the party arrived in Paris for a stay of several weeks. This was more familiar territory for Carol.

> This morning I ushered Harriet around the city and we walked over to the Place de la Concorde and I looked at the Crillon and it made me homesick thinking of the days we use to spend panting with the heat and sipping lemonades . . . We had lunch today at Henri's and tea at the Parc Catelan in the Bois. I am the only one in the party who can speak any French so I feel quite exhausted having to order for everyone at a restaurant and translate all the menus. It is good practice but rather fatiguing at times.[66]

The girls took in the Bois de Boulogne, races at Longchamps, Millet's studio at Barbizon, the restaurants Pruniers and L'Escargot, and the Bal Tabarin in Montmartre. Carol confessed to her diary, "I am having a hard time resisting the shops but am trying hard to refrain from asking the family for more money, but I hope I may get some clothes when they come over."[67] "Everyone tried to make me bob my hair but I have stood by and kept my tresses long—because I am as Cousin Lizzie once wrote [in her letter of 3 November 1923, quoted above] about me "wedded to my earrings" and I don't think the two go together."[68]

Worry about managing money, strenuous sightseeing, and homesickness began to take their toll on Carol, who was still rather young and somewhat dependent on her mother. "I wept most of the morning being

65. CHW, Travel Diary, 1925–26, 4 April 1926; CWG, in Montreux, to CHWG, at 54 Hillside Ave., 8 April 1926. The posthumous premiere of *Nerone* by Arrigo Boito, Verdi's librettist for *Otello* and *Falstaff* and the composer of *Mefistofele*, took place 1 May 1924. Toscanini was a great champion of the work, though it never entered the repertory, and performances since have been rare. *The New Grove*, s.v. "Toscanini, Arturo," and "Boito, Arrigo." Three weeks after the performance Carol heard, Toscanini led the premiere of Puccini's *Turandot*. In that performance he refused to play the Fascist hymn "Giovinezza" before the opera, resulting in a demonstration by the Fascistii.

66. CWG, in Paris, to CHWG, at 54 Hillside Ave., 11 April 1926.

67. CHW, Travel Diary, 1925–26, 19 April 1926.

68. CHW, in Brussels, to CHWG, in Naples, 25 April 1926.

rather tired from lack of sleep and worried about my finances . . . two wonderful letters from Mother & Grandma got me going." She did manage to pull herself together quickly, however: "Mrs. Hayward took Harriet and me to the Ritz for luncheon. We had a delicious meal. Harriet and I rode around for an hour in the Bois and then came back. Hat slept. I have forgotten what the word means. Mrs. Hayward, Hat, the Nortons & I went to hear Carmen at the Opera Comique. I was mad about it."[69] After that excitement Carol took castor oil (a drastic remedy for what ailment she did not specify) and spent the next three days in bed.

Meanwhile Carrie, Julia, and the ailing Rob were crossing the Atlantic on the *Duilio*, where they sat at the same table as had the Rawson party. The plan was for Carol to meet them in Naples, where they would land. She was ending the Rawson tour in London, then in the throes of a labor strike.

It started with a coal strike and now has reached many forms of laborers. There are millions out of work and no cars are running except by special permission from the government—because they can't get gasoline. I hear that no ships can come into England. It sounds quite serious and there is a talk of a Revolution—but of course we haven't seen many signs of it . . . There are no taxis so one has to hail private cars. Several policemen have been killed.[70]

The Rawson party was in the midst of the General Strike of 1926. Miners walked out on 1 May to protest the end of wartime subsidies. Other unions all over England supported them, bringing about a complete halt to transportation and economic activity. It was the most severe outbreak of class antagonism in modern England, hence the reference to "talk of a Revolution." The strike ended on 12 May, broken by lack of public support and the activities of volunteers who kept essential services going. For tourists and theatergoers, there was no break. "We went to the National Gallery & I enjoyed it tho' not so much as the Tate. Harriet and I went to see *The Sea Wolf*, a movie and heard Paul Whiteman's band. It was marvelous [and may well have included Gershwin's *Rhapsody in Blue*, which Whiteman had introduced two years before] . . . Mrs. Hayward & Fran Norton & I went to the play *The Best People*."[71]

---

69. CHW, Travel Diary, 1925–26, 18 April 1926.

70. CWG, in London, to CHWG, in Paris, 5 May 1926.

71. CHW, Travel Diary, 1925–26, 7 May 1926; *The New Grove*, s.v. "Whiteman, Paul."

Upon arriving in Naples Carrie sent a note to her daughter: "Here we are in fascinating old Naples having landed yesterday morning in a pouring rain. I was thankful I had sailed into the Bay of Bays in clear weather years ago. Uncle Will [White] met us. Was not it dear of him? and such a help to me as Dad leaves practically everything to me . . . We are very anxious over the import of the strike in England and fearful lest it interfere with your comfort and plans."[72] To Carrie, Rob's "leaving practically everything" to her was a sign of his ill health, the chronic nephritis that had settled in (and may not then have been diagnosed). She knew that something seriously was wrong and had written earlier, "You will have to be particularly sweet to him to make up for my nervousness. He is so optimistic about all the benefits he expects to derive from the trip it's pathetic, and I pray his hopes will be fully realized. It makes me so thankful we decided to go."[73] He would make it through the trip, but he did not find the hoped-for benefit.

Carol left Miss Rawson accompanied by a chaperone and, after a six-day journey from London, rejoined her family in Rome. "Happy reunion after five months separation. Days full of delights," Carrie wrote in her small leather travel diary. (On its cover page she wrote, "This 'record' is a bare *outline*, with no details of much interesting and educational sightseeing. I have kept it especially as an itinerary of a trip—hotels, etc. which will bring back to memory things *seen*—and *not forgotten*.")[74]

Riccardo, a chauffeur recommended by Miss Whittemore of Naugatuck, drove the family through Tuscany in a touring car with baggage strapped to its roof. In Florence they met up with the Will White family and with Truda and Edmund Trowbridge and their daughter, Nancy, who had spent the winter in the city. It was a "[g]athering of relations and friends," and Carol's wish had come true. She shopped with her mother and guided her to the sites of the city. "Thrilling week of sightseeing and shopping," Carrie wrote, "Carol familiar with both—a wonderful guide."[75] From Florence they took four days to drive, via Lucca, Genoa, and the Italian Riviera, to Cannes where they spent more than a week. "Hotel Majestic. Luxurious hotel, fine suite overlooking sea, delicious

---

72. CHWG, in Naples, to CWG, in London, 5 May 1926.

73. CHWG, at 54 Hillside Ave., to CWG, 8 April 1926.

74. CHWG, Travel Diary, 1916–35.

75. Ibid, 29 May 1926.

87. Carrie and Carol at Cannes, 1926

food. Here we spent the heavenly days—taking drives—Monte Carlo, lunch at Hotel de Paris. Carol played at roulette. Nice—lunch." A photo of Carol and Carrie (with parasol) in their best daytime outfits on a Riviera sidewalk, shows mother and daughter reunited, having a fine time together, wearing the stylish clothes they had just bought.

Carrie's compact notes recounted the journey to places on this trip that she and Julia had never seen—the Riviera, Carcassone, and the midi—as well as Touraine and Fontainebleau, which held vivid memories for Julia from her first auto trip twenty years earlier.

When they reached Paris they spent five days "principally devoted to shopping. Every thing fascinating and reasonable (with a franc at about three cents). Carol fed up w. six months sightseeing, enjoyed this less uplifting experience." They embarked on the Cunard Line's *Aquitania* in Cherbourg Harbor for the voyage home. It was a huge ship, the last of the four-stackers.[76] They arrived in New York on July 3; Carol had been away almost six and a half months, Carrie and the family two and a half.

The Family Transformed

Seven months later, in December 1926, the lively, articulate young woman who had gone on the grand tour with Miss Rawson vanished forever in the grip of severe mental disorder. Dr. H. G. Anderson, the family physician, wrote that Carol, "after dinner and a dance, abruptly in the night rushed

---

76. First-class held 613 out of a capacity of some 3,200. Miller, *Encyclopedia*.

into her mother's room wildly hysterical with many delusions of stories being told to and about her."[77] Her contemporary, Lucy Templeton, remembered Carol at the dance that evening. There was something off kilter. "She had been dressed in old-fashioned clothes, noticeably so, which seemed odd. We wondered how her mother could let her come looking that way."[78] Dr. Anderson noted a month later that the "first delusions have been replaced by fear and a degree of stubborness." The psychiatrist called in by Carrie termed the condition "exhaustion neurosis."

On 8 February 1927 Carrie and Dr. Anderson, with chauffeur Frank La Chance driving, took Carol to a sanitarium operated by Dr. Clarence Slocum in Beacon, New York. Carol was in poor shape. The attending physician at the sanitarium recorded that she was "in a state of definite distractibility, refused to get out of the car, was taken forcibly to her room at Shadow Lawn by the doctors and chauffeur. When in her room, preparations were made to place her in bed and this was accomplished with a good deal of forced effort.

> During the afternoon she was restless and uneasy, getting in and out of bed, tore her night gown, denuding herself and was in a state of agitation, and at six o'clock was removed by Dr. Slocum and Dr. Yeller to one of the pack rooms in the hydrotherapy building. Once there she was immediately given a forced feeding of four eggs and a glass of half milk and cream, 3 ii castor oil. There was a great deal of resistance, the result of which was that the patient regurgitated the feeding almost immediately.

She was suicidal, and two nurses were assigned to her for the next several days. The staff applied the therapeutic techniques of the day:

> Cold packs are decidedly refreshing and therapeutically valuable. She will sleep for an hour or two after each application. She smiles pleasantly when spoken to but it is apparent that she does not appreciate her environment or the fact that she has been removed from her home. 24 hours after admission temperature dropped to 100 and has been normal since. It was quite evident

77. H. Anderson, M.D., to Dr. Clarence J. Slocum, Beacon, N.Y., 2 Feb. 1927, in "Records in Connection with the Treatment of Carol Griggs at Dr. Slocum's Sanitarium, Beacon, New York, February 1927–March 1929," 18 pp., transcribed by the author from the records of Craig House (the sanitarium's successor), 25 Oct. 1993, MS in possession of the author (hereafter cited as Craig Transcript). All references to Carol's treatment at Dr. Slocum's facility are from this source.

78. Lucy (Templeton) Kellogg, conversation with the author, 7 July 1995.

that it was a temperature due to toxemia. At times she pulls her hair and tries to throw herself off the bed. She is more comfortable in this respect. Inclined to mutilate herself, scratching her face, pulling her hair and quite impossible to keep her in bed. At times there will be emotional outbreaks at which times she invariably calls for her mother.

In the admission that Carrie completed she answered no to the question about a history of alcoholism in the family. The attending physician, however, recorded that she spoke "of her father in a spirit of criticism, says that he is a drunkard and has been a trouble to her mother." This may have been a delusion, or it could be an insight into an otherwise unacknowledged problem in the family. Carol was unwittingly repeating the daughter-mother alliance against the father that characterized Carrie's and Julia's relationship to George. (At the time of her breakdown Rob was a semi-invalid from the nephritis; alcohol would have exacerbated the condition had he consumed any.) The clinic gave Carol no psychoanalytic treatment, and thus there are no further notes about family relationships.

Carol showed some improvement over the next few weeks, but she repeatedly slipped back into violent behavior and delusions, duly reported by the physicians. These conditions continued with diminishing intensity for eighteen months, during which time she was isolated from the family, as was the practice at the time in such cases. The diagnosis by the end of her stay was manic-depressive psychosis, then a fairly well understood condition. It is a recurring illness, characterized by extreme, "bi-polar" mood swings, often with increasing intensity over time. Those with the condition are often highly sensitive individuals, and suicide is a risk. Treatment in Carol's day was entirely institutionalized and consisted of water therapies and sedation. Acute phases of the illness typically abate slowly, as in Carol's case, and there are often periods of remission before a recurrence, which Carol was later to endure.[79]

Unbeknownst to Carol, the family universe that she had known since childhood changed utterly while she was at Dr. Slocum's. A year after Carol's first attack, almost to the day, on 27 December 1927, Rob died at home of a cerebral hemorrhage. He had been incapacitated for months by a deteriorating condition. As had been the case with his father years

---

79. The author is indebted to his friend, Dr. C. Christian Beels, of New York City, for this discussion. Prior to finding the medical records from Dr. Slocum's clinic, Dr. Beels suggested that the illness could be manic-depressive psychosis, born out in the record.

88. Julia with Pierrot, at Pine Orchard, 1926

before, it was front-page news in the *Waterbury Republican*. "The entire business and official family of Waterbury was shocked at the news of the death of Mr. Griggs, who, for years, played a prominent part in the city's affairs . . . Mr. Griggs had been in poor health for the past two years, but recently he contracted pneumonia. The hemorrhage came as a climax to his more recent illness. Today leading manufacturers, business men and bankers of the city joined in expressing their regret at the death of Mr. Griggs."[80] In keeping with the spareness deemed appropriate at their social level, the family "requested that friends omit floral offerings." Dr. Lewis officiated at the service at St. John's. Rob was buried in the empty lot he had purchased at Riverside Cemetery, separate from that which his father had established for the Griggs family.

Four and a half months later Julia died at home from a stroke, at the age of seventy-eight. The death certificate recorded that she too had suffered for a year from the nephritis that had also afflicted George and Rob. Two years earlier she had spent August in a rented cottage at Pine Orchard shore, lonely but content. She had sat for her photograph in the garden there with Pierrot, a magnificent collie, her companion in those years.

---

80. *Waterbury Republican*, 18 Dec. 1927.

"There is nothing else for me to write about," she wrote Carrie in the last of her letters, with its elegiac tone lightened by reference to her "usual uncertainty," and as always she was not one to plunge into a social round.

> I am perfectly healthy and happy, except for the thought that I must leave the ever changing water in front of me and the *(My)* lovely garden in back— When the light is at the most fascinating hour—sun set—I waste my time thinking which I shall watch—water or garden and with my usual uncertainty lose the best of each . . . I made a very delightful call at the Anchorage [the largest of the "cottages" on that shore, its owners the apex of the social pyramid of the summer colony] . . . So my mind is at rest—You see my letter is padded so as to make it worth a two cent stamp which it is not—My world is so small that simple occurrences seem very exciting—[81]

Julia's childhood in New York City and Fairfield before and during the Civil War, her first crossing of the Atlantic in a sail-assisted steamer, Mrs. Mulford and the social scene in Minneapolis, must have seemed impossibly remote in an America swelled by immigration, increasingly urban and industrialized, with electricity, telephone, motor cars, and the faster tempo of the 1920s. The Europe she knew had been transformed by war, little of the New York of her childhood remained, and the Waterbury she had come to with George in 1876 had grown from about 15,000 to nearly 100,000. Her last year was saddened by the disappearance, no doubt incomprehensible to her, of the ebullient granddaughter who had so frequently visited her as a child and had been a faithful correspondent.

Most of the Julia's obituary in the *Waterbury American* was devoted to the lineage she had studied and listed for her grandchildren so carefully. John Haring was there with his eight terms in the Continental Congress as was Eleazar Wheelock, the founder of Dartmouth—key figures in a heritage that she had made part of her identity.[82] Beyond being the widow of George Luther White and a mother and grandmother, it was her connection to these strong eighteenth-century men that readers learned of the lady who had died at 114 Grove Street. Again there was a request from the family that flowers be omitted—no display was to be made. Dr. Lewis officiated at St. John's, and Julia was buried next to George in the L. C. White plot at Riverside.

---

81. JHW, in Pine Orchard, Conn., to CHWG, in Waterbury, 16 Aug. 1925.

82. *Waterbury American*, 14 May 1928.

Will and the family were in Paris when the cable came with news of his mother's death. He took the next boat home, but Mary and the children chose to remain. Wade White remembered how elegant his mother looked in the black and white dress she purchased at Worth's, black with white being then considered appropriate mourning attire for a daughter-in-law, and happily for her, it avoided the dreariness of black in a Paris May.[83]

Carrie was a widow at fifty-two. Within the space of eighteen months she endured the grief that came with the loss of her daughter to mental illness and the deaths of both her husband and the mother with whom she had been inseparable.

Estates

"Amount of Holdings Surprises People of City—$657,322 in Stocks," read the headline in the *Waterbury Republican* to attract readers to the account of Rob Griggs's estate. The total value including real property was $800,000 ($7.53 million, modern). The unnamed reporter commented, "[A]lthough it was recognized that he was a wealthy man, the size of his estate was a surprise to many." Death had made his previously invisible success public, and the editorializing indicates how closely observed business figures were in Waterbury. Almost half of the estate was in the R. F. Griggs Co., much of the rest in local stocks. In real property there was 54 Hillside Avenue and a farm in neighboring Middlebury that he had bought for the boys. The entire estate was left to Carrie.[84]

Julia's estate was valued at $1,667,242 ($16 million, modern), of which $1.1 million was in securities, the balance in the Grove Street properties (114 Grove and the adjoining 102 Grove), the Bank Street lots occupied by the still extant L. C. White Co. and White & Wells, and—a connection with her father—a parcel in Buffalo that had come to her out of trust in 1897. She owned only fifty shares each of the two White companies, the balance of the securities being of local and national companies listed on the New York Stock Exchange. She left $5,000 to each of the five grandchildren, the balance in equal thirds to Carrie, Will, and George Jr. She made three special gifts: to Betty White went a "pear and diamond spray pin" and a solitaire diamond ring; to Carol a silver tea and coffee service, and to

---

83. Conversation with H. Wade White, 1993.

84. *Waterbury Republican*, [1928], clipping in family papers.

Will the grandfather clock made in Middletown by Timothy Peck for the 1789 wedding of John White and Ruth Ranney, his great-great grandparents.[85] Betty wore the diamond ring for the rest of her long life. The silver tea set dated from the mid-nineteenth century and remained with Carol's family until the 1950s, when it was given to Nancy Griggs Razee, one of Bobby's children. Carrie, as daughter, received many other items from Julia's estate not listed in the will. These included the earrings worn by Julia's grandmother, Eliza (Ayres) Phelps in the 1825 wedding portrait, a locket containing Julia's mother's hair, the ring given to Aunt Kate by the unknown admirer, and the letters that form the base of this narrative.[86]

Carrie cleared out the 114 Grove Street house, never again to be used by the family. She distributed the furniture, china, and all else to Will for use at Breakneck, to George Jr., then in a new house (much smaller than those of his siblings), and to 54 Hillside Avenue. She and Will's children, Betty and Wade, later custodians of the family objects, paid close attention to the provenance of objects in the family—the author has a card table given him after Carrie's death as "Julia's table."

The large houses and spacious attics in the family then and for decades allowed the accumulation of objects great and small, a luxury that future generations, living in smaller houses, and often moving to smaller places for retirement, did not have. Carrie had seen her parents clear Luther and Jane Amelia's house and learned the manners of distributing things. The great clearings of houses to come would be after Will's death in 1952, after Carrie's death seventeen years later, and extend to the end of the century, after the deaths of Betty and Wade White. Carrie was a determined pre-server of family objects, and after Carol's death she reclaimed objects from that household—my father deemed her too fond of "things."

An item in the inventory of Julia's estate that Carrie acquired in the division of property was a seven-seat Pierce-Arrow, which Julia had bought the year before her death. It was an "Enclosed Car Limousine" (so termed because of the glass partition separating the driver from the passengers), a stately vehicle. It came to reside in Carrie's carriage house and

---

85. The jewelry that Betty received probably had a family connection, possibly with Caroline Eliza (Phelps) Haring. The clock now keeps time by the front door of the author's apartment.

86. After Carrie's death in 1969, the earrings went to her granddaughter, Nancy Griggs Razee, and were sold; the Haring items remain in her family.

was driven and cared for by La Chance, her last chauffeur, a patient, soft-spoken man from French Canada. The Pierce-Arrow delighted a small child; there were jump seats that could be flipped open, and on cold days there was added warmth from soft gray lap robes, silky on one side. The device to speak to the driver in a pocket by the back seat was of particular interest, but Carrie never used it. To get La Chance's attention she tapped the glass partition with her diamond ring and spoke in her clear, penetrating tones, which carried over any road noise. She was fond of walking, and on occasion La Chance would drive the Pierce-Arrow to a dirt road in the country. Carrie and Jerry, her Airedale, would walk ahead, the great car following slowly, always just out of sight.[87]

The height of the 1920s stock market boom came in 1928. In a year the evaluations in the estates would be sharply reduced and erode further in subsequent years. Briefly, however, the White and Griggs families had the resources to continue their way of life without financial worry.

Carrie chose a positive, life-enhancing response to the sorrows that had come over her family in the space of sixteen months in which Carol's illness forced her separation, and Rob and Julia died. She left Waterbury and its associations for a time to accompany Haring to England, where he successfully sought admission to Jesus College, Cambridge. The handsome Yale graduate was now her great hope for the family.

---

87. Estate of Julia Haring White, Will, 208:418–21, Inventory 208:277–79, 209:512–19, Waterbury Probate Court. The "pear and diamond spray pin" was sold by EWW. The solitaire diamond ring, which she wore until the day of her death, was willed to Deirdre (Judd Lamb) Walsh, her first cousin once removed, and was subsequently sold. The silver tea and coffee set was given by Stuart E. Judd to Nancy (Griggs) Razee, daughter of Robert F. Griggs Jr., in the 1960s. According to Bernie Weis, editor of the Pierce-Arrow Society, Rochester, N.Y., the series 36 was "top of the line, built only in 1927 and 1928." This particular model was called the "enclosed drive limousine." One of the advertisements quoted a price of $5,285 and up for this model. Personal communication, 4 April 2001.

XI

DEATH AND TRANSFORMATION

Haring graduated from Taft in 1922 and went on to Yale as his father and Griggs uncles had done before him, and as did many of his classmates. Julia may have told him of the eighteenth-century men in her Phelps line who attended Yale: John Davenport (the son of the founder of New Haven Colony), Eleazar Wheelock, Alexander Phelps, and Benajah Phelps. He may not have taken this seriously at the time, but the account of his wedding in the *Herald Tribune* eight years later noted he was "of the sixth generation of his family to have graduated from that university."[1]

Boarding school gave a youth a head start in Yale society. "If you came from the big group from Andover," recalled F. O. Matthiessen, of the class of 1923, "you were a college man already and were inflicted almost inevitably with the responsibility of setting the right social tone. You aimed for the right social goals, you wore the right Brooks suit, your soft white shirt had a buttoned-down collar, and you did nothing—except possibly drinking— to excess."[2] Taft, though smaller than Andover, was also a "Yale feeder."

Yale in the 1920s was expanding in size. Its president, James Rowland Angell, had created a departmental system, improved the professionalism of the faculty, and raised academic standards. A construction program was underway during Haring's years that transformed the campus. "Nothing so beautiful as the Memorial Quadrangle, is to be found in any other edu-

---

1. Clipping, *New York Herald Tribune*, 4 Jan. 1930. The paper's reckoning of the family's history at the college is an overstatement. On his maternal side, Haring was descended from Eleazar Wheelock, A.B. 1733, Alexander Phelps, A.B. 1744, and Benajah Phelps, A.B. 1761, all graduated from Yale College. There were no members of his family at Yale between then and 1885, when his father, Robert Foote Griggs, enrolled at Yale for two years. Two of his Griggs uncles, however, were Yale graduates.

2. Paul M. Sweezy and Leo Huberman, eds., *F. O. Matthiessen (1902–1950): A Collective Portrait* (New York: Henry Schuman, 1950), 3. Matthiessen added, "But if you came from a high school or, as I did, from a small prep school that had prepared well for college entrance examinations but had taught you nothing else, you had the giddy sensation of a limitless domain opening out before you."

cational institution," Angell wrote in the 1926 class yearbook of the Gothic buildings in memory of those who died in the war. Of its center-piece, Sterling Memorial Library, with its detailed Gothic styling within and without, he declared, "Yale will have another of the great buildings of the western world."[3] There was pride and a great sense of purpose at Yale in those years.

However, there were also social forces at work that reflected those out-side the university. College life was affected by the loose spirits of the twenties, the reaction against the customs and mores of the recent past (and against Prohibition), and unprecedented national prosperity. Haring was among the undergraduates who carried on a boisterous social life, fueled by affluence that made bootleg liquor and stylish clothes available to many. Students learned to drink and dress in the latest fashions—Fitzgerald portrayed one type in the rough, heavy-drinking, ex-football player, Tom Buchanan in *Gatsby*. Margaret Hockaday, sister of his class-mate, Lincoln, remembered Haring years later as strikingly handsome and witty but so much a creature of the twenties in dress, alcohol intake, and attitude that she could not imagine him out of that period.[4]

In the year Haring entered Yale, there were twelve advertisements for tailors, clothing, and shoe stores in one issue of the *Yale Daily News*, encouraging college boys to shine at the forefront of fashion, with a dis-tinct anglophile bias. D. M. Schwartz—"Tailor and Importer"—pro-nounced itself as "Maker of Distinctive and Conservative Clothes For Yale Men." One shoe store promoted a model made from "Imported Scotch Callikin"; another shop offered "Black Imported Scotch grain." Alderman-Tailors, with "English Accessories" in its logo, requested stu-dents in restrained terms "to inspect our woolens before purchasing your season's outfit." Gunther offered the symbol of the partying Ivy League man in those days: "Raccoon Coats For Motoring And Football Games, $325, Muskrat $350 [about $3,000–$3,250 today])." For music to accom-pany parties, Eddie Wittstein would supply a phonograph for $23.75 and throw in records of "Hot Hits" of the year, *Turly, Grey Moon, Tricks, Dancing Fool, Stuttering, Flapper Walk*.[5]

---

3. James Rowland Angell, *Yale Banner & Pot Pourri 1926* (New Haven: published for the editors by the Yale Univ. Press, 1926), 59.

4. Margaret Hockaday (Mrs. Bancel La Farge) to the author, 1980s.

5. *Yale Daily News*, 16 Oct. 1922, microfilm, Manuscripts and Archives, Yale University Library.

Haring received no academic honors in his years, was not tapped for the secret societies (which generally selected on the basis of achievement), and, despite his later interest in the theater, writing, and literature, took no part in the prominent Yale Dramat and was not elected to the literary Elizabethan Club. In his *Pot-Pourri* (yearbook) entry he noted baseball, though he did not receive the treasured "Y" for varsity play. The only other extra-curricular activity he claimed was the Yale band, which sere-naded the crowds at football games—he did not mention his instrument.[6] He graduated in June 1927, a year after the class in which he entered, because of his long stay in Boston in 1923–24 for the back operation, which caused him to miss an entire academic year.

According to the class history, Haring intended to enter Yale Law School after graduation, but if he did, he did not stay long. Perhaps he was interrupted by Rob's death in December. In any case, by the summer of 1928 he had determined on an entirely different tack. He would study English literature at Cambridge University. (There was no question of his following most Waterbury men who went to Yale and returned to the city to make a career.) He crossed the Atlantic to apply in person, armed with a letter of recommendation from Charles Seymour, Provost of Yale.[7] Carrie, seven months a widow, and with her daughter Carol in enforced isolation at Dr. Slocum's sanitarium, accompanied him. Haring was her great hope; she was thrilled by his plan for more study, and she needed a break from the sadness of recent years.

They left for England on 25 September on the French Line's *Paris*, launched seven years before, another grand, luxurious ship. After two days of fine weather, they ran into a storm that made Carrie so sick she could not leave her cabin, but Haring, apparently a good sailor, enjoyed the company of "young people en route to schools and colleges." He also gained some welcome ready cash, winning four hundred francs in a horse race and $100 in a contest to guess the ship's run. They had to debark at Plymouth at the unearthly hour of 4:00 A.M. and were in London at the Berkeley Hotel by 10:00 that morning. That evening, at the elegant St.

---

6. *History of the Class of 1927, Yale College* (New Haven: Published under the Direction of the Class Secretaries Bureau, 1927), 230.

7. E-mail communication from Frances Willmoth, Assistant to the College Archivist, Jesus College, Cambridge, 7 Feb. 2001. Charles H. Seymour succeeded James Rowland Angell as president of Yale.

James Theatre, they saw *The Return Journey* by Arnold Bennett, starring Gerard du Maurier, then a leading actor-manager in the West End and son of Guy, whose *Trilby* had made such an impression on the youthful Carrie. "Most interesting play with perfect cast," she wrote.[8]

It was easier to get into a Cambridge college in 1928 than it would be a generation later. Haring presented his Yale letter to the head tutor of Jesus College. It took two days for the Master to inform him that he was admitted. Before term began he and Carrie visited the cathedrals at Ely, Lincoln, and York—among the most beautiful in England. Haring left for four days to fly to Paris with a friend, David Graham, also at Cambridge. "I have quiet days in wandering about Cambridge, guide-book in hand, filled with interest and learning my way about," Carrie wrote in her diary, enjoying the comfortable University Arms Hotel. "Sunday morning service at beautiful King's Chapel." When Haring returned, they celebrated by seeing Shaw's *Heartbreak House* at the new art deco Festival Theater, "with many marvelous cubistic decorations."

Jesus was a relatively small college, founded in the late fifteenth century on the spot of a thirteenth-century nunnery, a portion of which is still visible on the site. Haring's tutor was E. M. W. Tillyard, later known for *The Elizabethan World Picture* (1943), an authoritative account used widely in college courses (including those taken by me in the 1950s) and a future master of the college. His comments on Haring ranged from "very fair ability" at the outset, to "might scrape a pass in Tripos" [final examination], later on. This indicates a slacking off, but, as we shall see, Haring did well enough on the examination.[9]

Carrie twice more visited Ely Cathedral, which seems to float above the level landscape of the fens. En route to the steamer home she traveled alone to Southampton. As always interested in seeking out the old and beautiful, from there she took day trips to Winchester ("two interesting

---

8. These and subsequent references from CHWG, Travel Diary, 1928, MS in possession of the author. Gerald Herbert du Maurier (1873–1934), the son of George du Maurier and a leading actor-manager on the London stage, took over the St. James Theatre in St. James Square (demolished 1960s) in 1923. Daphne du Maurier, in her memoir of her father, termed the play, which had a short run, "rather unattractive." Daphne du Maurier, *Gerald: A Portrait* (London: Victor Gollancz, 1934), passim, and 267. Curiously, no play of this title by Bennett is listed in a bibliography of his works. I was informed by the librarian at Stoke-on-Trent that it was unpublished. See <http://www.stoke.gov.uk/council/libraries/infolink/b-plays.htm> accessed 10 May 2002.

9. Willmoth, Jesus College, 7 Feb. 2001.

hours spent at the Cathedral with delightful Verger"), Salisbury and its cathedral, and Stonehenge. She sailed on the White Star Line's *Majestic* (once the *Bismarck*, taken from Germany as war reparations), the largest ship afloat until the *Normandie* was launched in 1935.[10] The luxury was wasted that November as the crossing was rough, and Carrie remained in bed for most of the voyage—a reminder of the frequent unpleasantness of otherwise sumptuous transatlantic travel. At the New York pier she was delighted at a "reception" by her son Bobby, her cousin Mary White (the art teacher at St. Margaret's), and Rowley ("Ray") Phillips, of the R. F. Griggs Co.

There was a reason for Carrie's cheer beyond the satisfaction of seeing Haring settled at Cambridge and being warmly greeted at the pier. She had a letter from Carol. On its envelope she wrote that it was "[t]he first normal letter from Carol after three years away from me. It seemed like a miracle from heaven."[11] (Carol had only been at Dr. Slocum's for twenty-one months at that point, but it must have seemed to Carrie like three years.) "News of Carol's recovery!!" was her heavily inked entry in the travel diary.

Carol's manic-depressive psychosis had followed its expected trajectory: the symptom decreased in intensity over time, and there was a gradual though uneven return to a normal state. In July 1928 the physician noted that there had been signs of improvement, but she remained subject to bouts of psychotic behavior. Over the preceding months Carol had

> shown varied states; has gone from quiet fairly cooperative and improved levels, lasting ten days to two weeks, to extremely disturbed and difficult levels, lasting a week or ten days. During her better periods she still is confused, rather retarded and lackadaisical in her reactions and made many hypochondriacal complaints, mostly of indigestion, headaches and fatigue. During the excited periods she expressed many definite delusions and is apparently hallucinating. Assaultive tendencies developed at these times on the basis of her delusions, such as attempts to escape from her room so she could help a patient in another room who was being tortured. She made several attempts to run away, not with a concerted plan but in a vague, wildly confused

---

10. The *Majestic* was almost 20,000 tons heavier than the *Berengaria/Imperator*. William H. Miller Jr. *The First Great Ocean Liners in Photographs* (New York: Dover Publications, 1984), 96.

11. CWG, at Dr. Slocum's Sanatorium, Beacon, N.Y., to CHWG, in Cambridge, England, 27 Oct. 1928.

manner. In her better times she was able to go driving, take long walks, have golf lessons, play the piano at Tioronda [the main house, once a residence], and was often quite agreeable and social . . ."[12]

The erratic behavior was a setback, and she had to be moved to a more closely supervised setting. There were difficult episodes in September— presumably reported to Carrie before she left for England. However, in October there was dramatic improvement. "During the past week," her physician reported,

Miss Griggs has been extremely well, reaching a true level between excitement and depression, dressing neatly, conducting herself in a most ladylike manner, speaking clearly and rationally about everyone, and participating in the general social and athletic activities of the place without difficulties of any kind. No sedatives have been necessary for some time and her nights have been very good. On the 16th it was deemed advisable to move the patient from the Meadows to new quarters in the Woodbine Cottage, and this pleased her very much and has stimulated her normal behavior. Activities: craft shop, walking, moving pictures, dancing.[13]

"I am perfectly well and have never weighed more because I put on all the pounds I lost," Carol wrote in the letter that so pleased Carrie, adding that she had "no more interesting pallor." That she had been subject to terrible delusions and struggles as recently as the summer would be difficult to suspect from this letter, in which she tells of being sore from horseback riding, taking tea with a fellow resident who was leaving for home, and going to the movies. Calm had returned. "Tomorrow I am going out to a dance with a young man here & we are going to the top of Mt. Beacon which is quite a distance above sea-level." Mary and Lucy Burrall had been to visit, and she remarked that "[a]ll my aunts seem to think it is a Christian duty to write me."[14]

Carol had not been told, however, of the deaths in the family. She knew that her parent's twenty-fifth wedding anniversary had passed in February the previous year, and that "Dad" had given her mother a ring, but not

---

12. "Records in Connection with the Treatment of Carol Griggs," Craig Transcript.

13. Ibid.

14. Carol White Griggs, at Dr. Slocum's Sanatorium, to CHWG, in Cambridge, England, 27 Oct. 1928.

that Rob had died eleven months later. "How thrilled Grandma would be to see Cal. again and of course I am particularly anxious to see your birthplace," she wrote of a possible trip west, unaware that Julia, too, had died. Carrie would have to break some painful news to her.

Dr. Slocum considered Carol well enough for a home visit over Thanksgiving 1928. She tolerated the visit well—especially considering she must have learned of the deaths in her family then. She returned to Beacon briefly, but on 11 December, just after her twenty-second birthday, she was "paroled in the custody of her mother." There is a note of satisfaction in the last entry by the physician in March 1929: "Patient is today discharged from our role having received excellent reports from her mother as to her continued, happy progress."

There is no reason to doubt the Slocum clinic's diagnosis of Carol's condition as manic-depressive psychosis, a disease well recognized then and such would be the diagnosis of a patient with similar symptoms today. At the time, the treatment consisted of wet packs, colonic irrigations, sitz baths, and sedatives. (Today the disease would be treated with drugs that mitigate the intensity of the attacks and shorten their duration.)[15] Carrie told the clinic, according to the record, that there was no family history of mental illness. The only verifiable case that I have found is distant, that of Ralph Wheelock (1742–1817), the son of Eleazar Wheelock, Carol's six times great-uncle through her mother's Phelps line, a man incapacitated by mental disorder that could have been manic-depressive psychosis.[16] As it would with Carol, the disease typically recurs.

Among the wider family Carol's illnesses, then and later, were referred to as "nervous breakdowns." Betty White, her cousin and Westover classmate, told me that she was told "something" was wrong with Carol, but had no knowledge of the symptoms, much less the diagnosis. In later years only the generic "nervous breakdown" was used by anyone to describe her condition. It was not a matter to be otherwise discussed or described—or passed down in the family record. I learned the true nature and extent of her illness by the fortuitous preservation of her medical record, to which I was led after learning of her being at the sanatorium through the return address on Carol's letter; the reference librarian at the Beacon, N.Y., library guided me to what was once Dr. Slocum's clinic.

---

15. The author is indebted to Dr. C. C. Beels for these observations.

16. Judd, *The Hatch and Brood of Time*, 346–47.

In late January 1929 Carrie and Carol left for Florida on the Orange Blossom Special from Pennsylvania Station. The trip was intended to strengthen Carol's return to normal living. At Mountain Lake, near Orlando, they joined Waterbury friends to attend the dedication of the carillon tower donated for public use by the Philadelphia editor, magazine owner, and philanthropist, Edward W. Bok.[17] The main speaker at the dedication was ex-President Calvin Coolidge, in effect a celebration of the culmination of the prosperity of the 1920s, soon to seem an illusion. They visited Palm Beach and spent a week at Ormond (which Carrie knew from Julia and George's stay). They spent a night with Will and Mary White at Strawberry Hill, Henry Wade's "shooting camp" by a tidal creek in South Carolina near the Georgia border, a "delightfully unusual" experience of comfortable roughing it. It was a rustic place that Will loved because he could be out with his dogs all day hunting and fishing. The social Mary sometimes preferred to stay north. When she did stay at the camp, she centered her activities on nearby Savannah.

They joined the Burrall sisters and Miss Edith (Chase) for a tour of the James River plantations. After a stop at the Hampton Institute, which particularly impressed Carrie, they took the train home. Carol had begun to re-enter the world under her mother's guidance.

The wider world on which the family depended was rocked when, after wobbling for weeks, the Dow Jones Industrials had lost a third of its value by "Black Friday," 29 October 1929.[18] Since the family investments were not mortgaged on margin and had not been speculative, there were no failures among the Whites or the Griggs. Of course the value of their stock portfolios was sharply reduced and dividend income would soon follow suit. No one thought then that the Great Depression was at hand. The market was expected to recover and did, to some degree, in 1930, but over the next years portfolios would shrink further. Relative to most, however, the family remained well off. Will White weathered the storm best in the family. He had sold off many stocks in local firms before the crash—for which Waterbury businessmen had criticized him—and thus was in a better position than Carrie in the 1930s when many of these firms were forced

---

17. See <www.bokgardens.org>, accessed 26 April 2002. The tower is located in what is now Bok Gardens, Lake Wales, near Orlando.

18. On 28 Oct. 1929 the loss was 12.8%, on 29 Oct. −11.7%, and on 9 Nov. −9.9%. <http//averagesdowjones.com/djia_fact>, accessed 3 Dec. 2000.

to suspend dividends, and some, like the L. C. White Co., went out of business entirely.[19] Nevertheless, Carrie maintained the same number of staff at 54 Hillside until the late 1930s, and La Chance continued to drive her in the Pierce-Arrow. The two family weddings of 1930 were conducted much as they would have been in previous years, with men in cutaways and top hats, and presents on display. The couples took their honeymoons in choice places.

Haring Marries Patty Spencer

During the summer of 1929 Haring became engaged to Patty Spencer, daughter of a New York lawyer, whom he had met while at Yale. A family story has it that her mother opposed the match, wanting her daughter to choose someone with New York social credentials, evidently deeming provincial the lineage so carefully charted by Julia.[20] Patty was a dark-haired, brown-eyed, vivacious young woman with artistic skills and tastes. She was evidently drawn to the sophisticated and handsome young man with a sardonic wit. The marriage was set for the new year, during the Cambridge Christmas break.

In December Haring returned home on the North German Lloyd *Bremen*, "the fastest liner afloat," which had entered service that year and won the Blue Riband in an early crossing.[21] In the crossing the ship encountered eighty foot waves, and the captain released oil to smooth the waves all the way across and three times stopped the ship to ride out storms. The *New York Telegram* reported of the *Bremen* that "[t]en of her passengers had been severely injured in an uninterrupted crossing of furious gales and giant seas. Forty others nursed bruises and minor discomforts."[22] The fastest ship afloat was two and one-half days late; of the many transatlantic crossings that family members made over the years, this was the worst.

The Spencers gave their daughter a highly visible wedding at Grace Church, New York, whose Gothic façade Julia must have seen often as a child, when it was new and in the heart of the fashionable city. A photo of

---

19. Conversation with Douglas D. Mc Kee, 1990s.

20. Conversation with Comfort (Dorn) Grandi, granddaughter of Haring Griggs, 16 March 2002.

21. Miller, *Encyclopedia*.

22. Samuel Spewack, "Bremen Arrives with 50 Hurt; Fought 80-Foot Waves in Gale," *New York Telegram*, 13 Dec. 1929, front page, clipping in CHWG Wle.

89. Haring and Patty leaving Grace Church, 1930

the couple framed in the doorway of the church accompanied the story on the society page. The *Herald Tribune* reported that Patty, later a skilled clothing designer, wore "a Patou gown of white satin made in the [Empress] Josephine style, with a long train draped from the skirt. Her veil of tulle was studded with tiny silver stars." In the photo she clutches her bouquet of "gardenias, orange blossoms and white orchids" and braces against the cold. Haring, in a top hat, cutaway, and spats, is the epitome of elegance and cants his head slightly toward his bride.[23] For this dashing couple the twenties had not ended with the stock market crash.

Carol was a bridesmaid, who, in keeping with the Napoleonic era style of the bride's dress, wore an empire gown of "yellow satin" and a large

---

23. *New York Herald Tribune*, 4 Jan. 1930, clipping in CHWG file.

picture hat of "brown velvet" and "brown slippers."[24] Bobby was his brother's best man.

One of the ushers was Alfred Bingham, a Yale contemporary (noted by the *Tribune* as "son of Senator Hiram Bingham, of Connecticut"). Sixty-four years later he told me of his part in the wedding and of Haring, whom he knew "only slightly from Yale":

> I was in the wedding for one reason. He was a charming and very intelligent man. He drank a great deal and defied Prohibition. Although I did not agree with the banning of drink, I felt that as a law-abiding citizen that I should follow the law. At a few months before, at the wedding of a man named Holt, I had been the only member of the party to remain sober. After the ceremony and reception, the wedding party went to the bride's parents' house after reception for further partying. It was a dangerous ride. Haring could not be prevented from driving although very drunk. He drove the car on the left hand side of the road and swerved to the right only just in time to avoid an oncoming car. I was very frightened.
>
> Evidently Haring wanted me to be a reliable member of the party at his wedding. I never kept up with Haring after and never knew anything more about him.[25]

Bingham saw the fault line that would soon open up beneath this marriage. The morning after the wedding Patty and Haring left on the *Berengaria* for England and Jesus College, where he would sit for his Tripos examination that spring.

Naples to Cambridge

A month later Carrie and Carol left for a five-month tour of Europe. As Julia and Carrie's youthful trips had done, theirs began in Naples and Sicily. They were joined by Patty and Haring in Spain. Ultimately their aim was to be in Cambridge for Haring's degree-day in late June.

Carol is a silent presence in her mother's notes, closely tied to her "dearest pal." There is no indication that she ever left her mother's side. A latter-day Henry James might have been drawn to this pair, seen in lobbies

---

24. Ibid.

25. Telephone conversation between the author and Alfred Bingham, 4 Aug. 1994. Bingham (1905–98), an attorney and long-time Connecticut resident, was involved throughout his maturity with progressive political causes. Obit., *NYT*, 5 Nov. 1998, D4:1.

and dining rooms of the great hotels—the handsome, reserved widow and the quiet, withdrawn daughter occasionally revealing in her expressions the injuries of her bout with psychosis. Patty Spencer, Haring's wife, was with her a number of times during the course of the trip and remembered Carol as "impulsive" in her eating and shopping, and "immature."[26] Carol needed Carrie's steady presence.

They left New York for Naples on the *Roma* of the Navigazione Generale Italiana, a relatively small ship.[27] Their chief steward had been on the *Diulio* in 1926 and gave them a warm welcome, reminding them, no doubt, of what must already have seemed a remote era. Also on board were Lucy, Mary, and Edith ("M., L., and E."), "a delightfully congenial party." Edith, the only one of the four ladies who could drive, had her car aboard for comfortable touring on the continent.[28] All five shared a table in a dining room that was modeled on an eighteenth-century palazzo, which "had two levels on separate decks . . . capped by a great domed center section. Along the sides were tall windows overlooking the sea." The ballroom onboard recreated one in a baroque palace.[29] After four days of "agitato e grosso" they had a week of calm sailing in which to enjoy the surroundings. "Beautiful ship, delicious food," was Carrie's summation.

In Naples they stayed at Bartolinis Hotel and took day trips in Miss Edith's car to Sorrento, Amalfi, and Benevento (to see Trajan's Arch). At the San Carlo, Giacomo Lauri-Volpi ("Beautiful tenor."), famous for his long, high notes, sang Manrico in *Il Trovatore*. Carrie had heard him at the Metropolitan in his brief career there in the early twenties, and years later she demonstrated to me (with gestures, not voice) how he held his high notes, which he surely did with Manrico's "Di quella pira."

Leaving "M. L. and E.," Carrie and Carol boarded a night boat to Palermo, where they stayed at the Villa Igiea ("Fine room overlooking garden and sea"), familiar to both, and where doubtless they remembered Julia's account of her youthful visit to Uncle George. They stayed in Sicily from mid-February to mid-March and visited the famous sites of Monreale, Segesta, Agrigento ("Hotel dei Tempii. Heavenly spot. View from our

26. Conversation with Patty Day, Nantucket, Mass., Aug. 1991.

27. The *Roma* was launched in 1926 and with only 375 in first class. Miller, *Encyclopedia*.

28. These and the subsequent notes from CHWG, Travel Diary, 1930.

29. William H. Miller Jr., *Picture History of the Italian Line, 1932–1977* (Mineola, N.Y.: Dover Publications, 1999), 15, 17.

room, overlooking landscape of pink almond blossoms through Greek temples."), Siracusa ("Hotel Politi at edge of Latomia, Greek quarry," where the prisoners from Alcibiades' failed expedition had been held).

In Taormina they sought out the brother of Mike, the vegetable deliveryman who daily brought his truck and produce to 54 Hillside, and received a "touching reception by these simple fisher folks." Their hotel was the San Domenico, overlooking the sea, where Carol had stayed with the Rawson party, whose "halls now echo jazz bands." (The famous hotel remains open with its renowned view of the sea and the Greek Theater, and was the setting for memorable scenes in Antonioni's 1960 *L'Avventura*.) With Carrie, Carol visited Mr. Wood the sculptor, another link to the 1926 Rawson trip. On the slopes of Mount Aetna they saw "[a]cres of lava, huge blocks, ashes" as a result of a recent eruption, an awesome sight later described to me when I first learned of volcanoes and the irresistible descent of lava after an eruption.

Returning to Palermo, Carrie bought a chair made by a Sicilian cart maker and decorated with scenes of Orlando's adventures. She would place it on the sun porch at 54 Hillside, where it was a favorite seat for her grandchildren. (I was enchanted with its illustrations as a child, and it is now in my living room.)

From Palermo they returned to Naples to embark on the *Augustus*, "even more beautiful than *Roma*," for "two perfect days" across the Mediterranean. On board were Mr. and Mrs. Frederick Chase, the president of Chase Brass & Copper in Waterbury, no more than Carrie deterred from touring by the stock market crash—and perhaps celebrating the sale of the firm to Kennecott Copper the previous year.[30] With them was their son, Sabin, and his new bride. Carrie found them "delightful companions," and doubtless remembered Julia's friendly encounter with these same Chases while abroad, which Julia had hoped would transfer to friendliness at home. There was an oddness to the Chase party: for Sabin the trip was both a honeymoon and a trip with his parents. He was a U.S. Foreign Service officer who had met his bride in China, where her family had fled

---

30. Chase continued as president of what was still the Chase Brass & Copper Co., but it had been made a subsidiary of the company that supplied the raw material to its mills. American Brass had followed a similar route in 1922 when it became a subsidiary of Anaconda Copper Co. Eduardo F. Canedo, "What is More Enduring than Brass? The Process of Deindustrialization in Waterbury, Connecticut, 1952–1976" (senior thesis, Columbia College, 4 May 1999), 10, Silas Bronson Library, Waterbury, Conn.

from the Russian Civil War—she later indignantly recalled this curious version of a honeymoon.[31]

Meeting Carrie and Carol at the tender in Gibraltar were the Raymond & Whitcomb representative and Ponce, their chauffeur for the next weeks, whose careful driving through Spain came to be much appreciated. "All perfectly arranged. Spent night at unattractive Hotel Cecil."

Ponce drove them to Seville, where they stayed at the Alfonso XII, recently completed for the 1930 Seville exposition. Its elaborate re-creation of Moorish architecture and details and location in Old Seville made it one of the most luxurious hotels of Europe, a distinction it retains today. "Perfectly appointed," was Carrie's comment. Ponce drove the car back to Gibraltar to meet Haring and Patty, who arrived by the Orient Line's *Ormonde,* which stopped en route to Australia via Suez. They arrived for a five-day stay in Seville "looking well and happy." The party attended a bullfight, about which Carrie wrote in her diary, "Cannot explain a certain fascination in watching skill and grace of toreadors and matadors (nor how we were able to sit through it)." On another day "Carol and Patty had photographs taken in Spanish costumes. Very becoming to them." The photo showing Carol in a mantilla and Goyaesque costume became a lodestone to me as a child, a key to my mother's previous existence, like the photo of her on the camel near the Pyramids.[32]

Carrie thought that the eighteenth-century Seville tobacco factory (the setting for the first act of Bizet's *Carmen*) looked more like a "palace" on the exterior, though inside there were "[h]undreds of old women and young women with their babies making cigars and cigarettes." Carrie reminded herself to "[r]emember face (lovely) of old woman" who looked at her closely and told her "'You have known more happiness than I have!' and then laughingly, 'Will you take me back to America?'"

At Granada Carrie found the cathedral like "[m]ost cathedrals in southern Spain too ornate to be beautiful." It was Julia's birthday while

31. Conversation with EWW, ca. 1990. Sabin Chase was one of the "old China hands" of the state department and after Pearl Harbor was interned by the Japanese in Darien, Manchuria, where he had been serving as U.S. consul.

32. In Seville, Carrie purchased two tables with wrought iron bodies and tops of ceramic tiles. She placed them on the sun porch at 54 Hillside with the Sicilian chair. These became heirlooms and are now in the author's possession. The tiles on one display a mounted Don Quixote routing sheep with his lance while Sancho Panza raises his arms in dismay; on the other is an image of Saint Consilio.

90. Carol in Spanish costume, Seville, 1930

they were there, and the day was remembered in a bare note; she would have been eighty.

From Cordoba the two hundred and fifty miles to Madrid took Ponce only from 8 A.M. to the late afternoon, indicating a good road and a skilled hand at the wheel—"Ponce wonderful!" From the "exceedingly comfortable" Ritz, they visited the Prado, with day trips to Toledo and the Escorial. There was another "picturesque and terrible bull fight. Never again! But did not regret seeing the spirit of Spain in their national sport. Not to be understood by us."

Ponce drove them north. In Burgos he joined Carrie and Carol in the cathedral for Palm Sunday service, and with some relief Carrie hailed the "first green" they had seen when they reached the Basque country. At San Sebastian on the border it was stormy, with "magnificent seas—surf driven up over wall and streets," but Ponce managed a drive in the mountains. "One of the most beautiful drives I have ever taken. Thunder storm, hail storm, snow on mountain sides." At Biarritz "Our dear, devoted Ponce, who had so thoughtfully and efficiently guided us for five weeks in Spain (and Marianne, P's wife) bade us farewell."

The leisurely pace of travel continued. Haring and Patty returned to Cambridge, and in Paris mother and daughter "did less sightseeing than usual. Shopping and interesting restaurants, opera, movies, drives in the Bois. One lovely day down to Chartres, my first visit to that wonderful cathedral. Countryside beautiful in spring foliage and apple trees in bloom." En route to the channel crossing at Ostende they visited Ghent to see Van Eyck's *Annunciation of the Lamb*. Bruges in early May (characteristically) was "[v]ery cold and raining much."

On 8 May Carrie entered a cryptic reference. "Crossed from Ostend to Dover. Stuart Judd with us." She offered no words of explanation, and he is not mentioned elsewhere in the diary. The news had great import for the family, however, and reveals that Stuart, the son of the late George E. Judd, of Waterbury, had taken time away from his job as a stockbroker to cross the Atlantic in pursuit of Carol—something I had never learned about my father as a child. At age twenty-eight, and characteristically a man who favored the rational and methodical, he had made a grand, romantic gesture. Did Carrie welcome his arrival? Or does the brevity and terseness of her note mean that she was uncomfortable with Stuart's attention to Carol, perhaps concerned that her daughter remained fragile and dependent? Had he met them in Paris and made his intentions clear only to be put off, deciding then to meet them on the ferry for a second chance? Did he go on with them to London? What is sure is that back home and sometime in the next two or three months Carol accepted his proposal of marriage.

At Dover, Carrie was met by Walter Mears, a chauffeur recommended by Cousin Anna White for the English tour, who turned out to be "splendid."[33] En route to London—with or without Stuart—they visited Canterbury Cathedral ("spiritual" in contrast to the cathedrals of southern Spain) and Knole, the great Sackville house at Sevenoaks, two of the finest sights of England.

Whatever prospects for Carol had been opened up by Stuart's visit were suspended as the two women continued their touring. From London,

---

33. Anna White's note on Mears, preserved with his address (16 Bishop's Road, Paddington W2) in the travel diary, reads: "We wish you could enjoy his services, Lovingly, Anna S. White."

guided by Mears and in the comfort of his car, they undertook a classic tour of Britain, visiting north Wales, Gloucester ("Slept in bed once occupied by Ellen Terry"), the Wye Valley, Tintern Abbey, Bristol, and the coast ("with its hills, moors and sea is enchanting"). Back in London, they had a reunion at Hampton Court with Mary, Lucy, and Edith, themselves doubtless overflowing with tales of their motoring north from Naples since February. These ladies joined Carrie, Carol, Haring, and Patty in Cambridge for a convivial luncheon at the University Arms. This was a send off for Haring, who was about to "sit" his Tripos, the examinations which would determine the level of degree he would receive, from "first" to "third," pass, or failure.

Carrie saved the Cambridge examination papers, thus preserving the formidable questions from which Haring had to choose in May 1930. The students' essays were spun out in intense morning and afternoon sessions of three hours each, and the quality of the degree depended solely on the student's mental acuity, wit, memory, and writing ability as expressed in those six hours. English literature had only been a degree subject for eleven years at that time, and its mentors intended it to be as rigorous as the traditional classics.

Haring's examination results were more than acceptable. Far from "scraping a pass" as Tillyard had prophesied, he received a 2.2 or "lower Second." Carrie was thrilled, and recorded that Haring was "the first American to graduate from Cambridge in this group. Most rewarding!" This distinction became family lore that was proudly handed down to me. In response to a recent inquiry, the university archivist commented that "a 2.2 was an average result: respectable enough, but not especially distinguished," and that it would have been "surprising if no American student had exceeded a 2.2 by 1930."[34] Still, in an era when the concept of grade inflation was not dreamt of, Haring had shown that he could put together an effective essay and had retained what he read. He had more aptitude than required to get a "Gentleman's C" in the Ivy League, of which a "lower third" would be the Tripos equivalent. His achievement at

---

34. There were 41 successful candidates for the second part of the English Tripos in 1930, and the results awarded were as follows—firsts: 3; upper second: 11; lower second: 22; third: 5. E-mail communication from John Wells, Assistant Under-Librarian, Department of Manuscripts and University Archives, University Library, West Road, Cambridge, England, 9 Feb. 2001.

Cambridge makes Haring's subsequent career the sadder and more perplexing.[35]

In the four weeks between the exam and the awarding of the degree, Carrie and Carol left Haring and Patty in Cambridge, and with Mears toured northern England and Scotland, joined at York for a time with the favorite companions, "M., L., & E." as interested in England as they were in Italy. This was ancestral land for them all, with their English Puritan forebears.

It was the season of the long twilight and fair weather, England at its best. In the comfort of Mears's touring car Carrie and Carol had a tour of England and Scotland at a favorable season and at an optimum time in history, when the car and the new roads gave comfortable mobility, but well before the highways became stressed with traffic. Though this was the last visit to England for both, Carrie remained devoted to England, favoring intervention on its behalf in 1940, attentive to Churchill in the war, and keenly aware of the destruction during the Blitz.

They returned to Cambridge, where, on 24 June 1930, Haring received his degree "in old Senate House amid quaint scene." It was a prideful moment for Carrie, and she had the satisfaction of a recovered Carol with her. Carrie and Carol sailed from Southampton on the giant Cunard *Aquitania* (618 in first class), the "last of the four stackers," and a much larger ship than the *Roma*, which had taken them to Europe that year.[36] "Seemed amusing on this fine ship," was how Carrie concluded her record of this trip. Haring and Patty returned later in July and moved to Hartford, where he took up a position in the English Department at Trinity College.

Stuart

A few weeks after the *Aquitania* returned, Carol accepted Stuart Judd's proposal of marriage, and the wedding was scheduled for November at 54 Hillside. The Stuart Judd who met up with Carol and Carrie to travel with them from Ostende to Dover was then twenty-eight years old, a graduate

---

35. Haring's time at Cambridge was in the full tide of English language and literature as a subject for degree examinations, introduced only in 1919 and centered on the great works of its tradition.

36. The *Aquitania* had served as an auxiliary cruiser and troopship in the past war and would serve as a troopship in World War II. It re-entered transatlantic service for Cunard before being broken up in 1950. Miller, *Encyclopedia*.

91. Yale fraternity photo of Stuart
Edwards Judd, about 1923

of the Sheffield Scientific School at Yale in 1924 and the then newly-
founded Harvard Business School in 1927. He had spent a year after Harvard with Western Electric in New Jersey, and in the summer of the
engagement had been for two years with Hincks Brothers, a brokerage
firm in Hartford.[37] His widowed mother continued to live at 37 Hillside
Avenue, which George E. Judd had bought and renovated in 1914. Stuart
stayed there on his frequent visits to Waterbury, and from the house it was
a few minute's walk up the undulating stone stairway to call on Carol,
about the same length of time it would take to drive a car around by the
driveway.

Curiously, Stuart told me little about his childhood, seeming to consider his memories of little importance, compared to the present and
future. The childhood books that his mother saved included those show-

---

37. See "Judd," Genealogical and Biographical Notes.

92. Eloise Judd, Alma (nursemaid), Stuart, and
unidentified child (rear), about 1909

ing how to build things—a log cabin, an ice sailboat, an electric generator, a wet battery. He had inherited the manual skills of the grandfather who died when he was a baby. He also had the series of Tom Swift boys' adventure books. He had been a good student, as I knew because Ms. McMahon in Driggs School first grade taught me as well and spoke admiringly of him. He told me that he often read the dictionary, which I considered strange but impressive. The most distinguishing feature of his early childhood was the photo of him at six, still in a dress, an indication, I was told, of his mother's doting on him. Perhaps that was why he was reclusive about childhood.

In his twenties Stuart was slim, of average height, with dark, wavy hair over a face with its metal-framed spectacles that had a concentrated, intelligent expression. As Betty White remembered, he had an agreeable manner, was polite and pleasant at Waterbury social gatherings—the perfect guest. He dressed meticulously in three-piece tailored suits made by William John Mahon, the leading Waterbury tailor. Stuart conveyed elegance without flash. His fastidiousness and the quality of the materials in shirt, tie, and suit were intended to give the impression of what he himself would later refer to as the "higher type of man," meaning reserved, straightforward, and sound. He clearly had money and used it tastefully, as he had learned to do at Hotchkiss and Yale. While Stuart may have shared Haring's taste in clothes, he was his antithesis in other ways. He was serious without a trace of the sardonic, he was good at numbers and analysis, keen to succeed in the world of finance, unaffected by his contemporaries' disdain for provincial life and steady in habits. That he was not entirely the sobersides is born out by his crossing the seas in pursuit of Carol.

Stuart knew something of the European world that was so much part of the White-Griggs experience. In the summer of 1920, after graduation from Hotchkiss, he toured Ireland and England by car with his two roommates. With an early home movie camera he recorded moments of the trip—the elegantly-suited young men hanging out to kiss the Blarney Stone, visiting with English girls on the terrace of a castle, posing by their car. The jerky images delighted the family in later years. His companions were young men on their way to interesting and creative careers: Day Tuttle (who went to Yale with Stuart) became an actor and theater director; after Harvard, Charles Morgan became an archaeologist, classicist, and a professor at Amherst.

Stuart was too young to be drafted—seventeen the month before the Armistice. He entered Yale in the fall of 1920 just as the institution was beginning its physical transformation under President Angell. Stuart was always proud of the richly Gothic buildings built in that era and identified with the optimism and determination they embodied. He caught the spirit of a dynamic, ever improving institution and was loyal to the college for the rest of his life. Like most of the students and faculty at Yale, he was a Republican and favored a business-friendly administration. He was semi-isolationist, confident that the United States was back on track after having been sucked into Europe's quarrels. (Twenty years later he was a vigorous anti-interventionist, suspicious of England—doubtless from Yale lessons about the origin of the war in European intrigues—and influenced by the post-Versailles reaction against U.S. intervention.)

The requirements of the Sheffield Scientific School in Stuart's years had been broadened to include more liberal arts subjects—he often spoke warmly of the popular Shakespeare course given by William Lyon Phelps. The bulk of his course work, however, was in engineering, physics, and economics. He probably followed the course in "Administrative Engineering," a program for future managers, as he did not graduate as an engineer proper. This concentration suited those who looked forward to a career in business, providing training in calculations and precise record keeping.

His extracurricular activities and achievements at Yale contrast with Haring's lack of involvement. Stuart was a tenor in the Glee Club, continuing an interest in music that had begun at school. He was also elected to the editorial board of the *Yale News*—something he had to work toward and that required a competitive edge and writing ability. In the group portrait of the staff in the *Yale Banner and Pot-Pourri, 1923*, he stands with the other young men, all with serious expressions and wearing three-piece suits—in his case his father's fine gold watch chain visible on his vest. Standing next to Stuart is F. O. Matthiessen (1902–50), who recalled of the spirit that likewise animated Stuart, "About half the class had some service in the war, but we were all young enough to feel the new promise of American life. We even took our cynicism with gusto."

> Yale in those years gave the sense of living on a grand scale through the world that my friends made for themselves and me. We were there just after Archibald MacLeish and Phelps Putnam and Stephen Benét, and could imagine that we too were sharing in what we called with, an inhibiting modesty, "The Yale renaissance." Talk, at the Elizabethan Club, whether it was about Monty Woolley's production of *The Playboy of the Western World* [Day Tuttle, Stuart's former roommate was a "Young Farmer" in that production], or [Edwin Arlington] Robinson's poetry, or the last football game we had lost, was sure to be good talk."[38]

Stuart was not a member of the Elizabethan Club, but he made a collection of first editions of E. A. Robinson.

Stuart was not the beau ideal of a Yale man—winner of a "Y" in sports, hearty in manner, large in build. Nor did he develop in college a dependence on alcohol as many did at that era. He did enjoy football games, owned a raccoon coat and hat, and told his son later about bathtub gin, but moderation characterized him then as later.

Yale was a competitive place, a testing place for the outside world, seen by many students not as a temple in which to learn, but a social setting in

---

38. F. O. Matthiessen, "The Education of a Socialist," in Paul M. Sweezy and Leo Huberman, eds., *F. O. Matthiessen (1902–1950): A Collective Portrait*, 3–20 (New York: Henry Schuman, 1950), 3. Stuart probably did not know Matthiessen well, and I have no memory that he kept up with him in later life.

which to be recognized. According to a recent history of the university, college life was being affected by "the rise of a new, pragmatic, materialistic American culture . . . Many students now came to Yale seeking social prestige or as a route to a business career."[39] Visible achievement meant election to one of the senior societies, of which Skull and Bones was the apex (and to which Matthiessen was elected). For Stuart the editorial board of the *Yale Daily News* was an achievement that set him apart from the majority, though not one to gain him a "tap" into one of the senior societies.

For some, four years of Yale led to brokerage or banking in New York City. For Stuart it was return to his hometown and the family business. George Judd died in Waterbury a few days after his son graduated. Stuart was named co-executor of the estate built up by his self-made father, amounting to $667,167 (equivalent to $6.52 million, modern), including that almost half share in the Mattatuck Manufacturing Company. (William Fielding, the Mattatuck General Manager, and the holder of the balancing 200 shares, was another co-executor.) Stuart became the trustee for his mother's and sister's thirds of the estate as well as his own.[40] He went to work at the Mattatuck for a time as a cost accountant and in sales, but, attracted to its program of teaching business as a profession, he decided to enter the newly founded Harvard Business School in 1925.

It was a "proud and self-confident" era for business, and one of the new Business School professors preached "that the young man who wanted to serve society best would go straight into investment banking."[41] The training stimulated Stuart's intellectual and analytic approach to business, contrasting sharply with his self-made father's pragmatism in insurance, travel, and manufacturing. Stuart liked activities in which he could think through problems and lay out courses of action—not for him the hurly-burly of entrepreneurship or battlefield business.

While at the "B" school he joined the Harvard Glee Club and in later years recalled fondly the experience of singing with the Boston Symphony under Serge Koussevitsky. After receiving his M.B.A. in 1927 he spent a year with the purchasing department at Western Electric in Newark—an

---

39. Kelley, *Yale,* 299.

40. Estate of George Edwards Judd, Wills, 185:23, 692–98; 189:525–26, Waterbury Probate Court.

41. Thomas N. Carver, quoted in Geoffrey Perrett, *America in the Twenties: A History* (New York: Simon and Schuster, 1982), 357.

indication that at one point he thought of a career farther afield. He returned to Connecticut as a broker and "statistician" (securities analyst) for Hincks Brothers, a brokerage firm in Hartford.[42]

Hartford and Hincks Brothers were less than two hours from Waterbury by car or train, and he probably returned to Waterbury on weekends and holidays. A pressing need to return came in early 1928, when his sister, Eloise, then twenty-three, was diagnosed with cancer of the cervix. Nursed by her mother, she died at home after a painful six-month illness, the last phase of which involved the gruesome penetration of her abdomen by the tumor. Her death left a void in the family and all but unhinged the emotionally volatile mother. The future burden for emotional support was Stuart's.[43]

Stuart was the "boy next door" to Carol, on Hillside, but though the Judd house was literally "across the street," in the peculiar geography of the avenue, it was at the bottom of the hill and invisible from the Griggs house because of intervening trees and shrubs. The Judds were below, the Griggs above. To drop in on a neighbor—which in any case was not done in these circles—a Judd would have had to climb the long steps up to Carrie's house, or a Griggs would have had to walk down them (or take the car around by Pine Street and drive half a mile—to arrive at a house three hundred yards away). It was symbolically apt too, for in the Waterbury scheme of things, the three generations in the town's manufacturing elite represented by the Griggs and White families gave them the pride of the place. George E. Judd, Stuart's father, was the first in the family to have made sufficient money to live on Hillside and have a chauffeur and maids. Although the Judds certainly were accepted in Waterbury society—Stuart and his sister Eloise went to parties and dances, and George was a member of the Waterbury Club—they were less established in the industrial economy, and they did not possess the cultural "credentials" conferred by grand tours of Europe.[44]

---

42. Philip W. Pillsbury, ed., *Yale '24–24S: 1934–1955* (New Haven: Yale Class of 1924, Class Officers Bureau, 1955), 197–98.

43. Eloise Elizabeth Judd died on 25 June 1928, three weeks after her twenty-third birthday. Death Certificates, April–June 1928, Waterbury VS.

93. William B. and George E. Judd's advertisements in Waterbury City directories, 1879, 1888

The Judds

George Edwards Judd, Stuart's father, came of Puritan-Yankee stock. His immigrant ancestor was Deacon Thomas Judd, who settled in Farmington after arriving in the Massachusetts Bay Colony from East Anglia in the mid-1630s. Thomas Jr. ("Lieutenant Thomas"), one of seven sons, was in the original "plantation" sent out from Farmington to settle what became Waterbury. His son's descendants down to George moved to better farm-land northwest of Waterbury. George's father, William Brace Judd, was born in rural Bethlehem in 1821 and, like the White and Griggs men of his generation, by the 1850s had been drawn to a manufacturing and commercial center, in his case New Haven. George was born there in 1867.

William was a carpenter and house builder. He moved to Waterbury when George was a boy of seven, concluding that there were prospects for a builder in the rapidly expanding city. In 1884, in his sixties, he advertised from a shop at 19 Meadow Street near the railroad station, "William B. Judd, Carpenter and Builder: All building in my line will receive Prompt

---

44. George and Nina Judd had traveled to Hawaii but not across the Atlantic.

Attention; Jobbing also done at short notice."[45] In the mid-1890s he built a house at 52 Holmes Avenue for George, still a bachelor, an easy walk to the Green and to his office. William moved in with his son after the death of his wife. (The house remains, next to a parking lot used by the Waterbury Club.)[46]

94. George Judd and Nina in the 1920s

George's route to success in Waterbury was in what later came to be called "services." He was a white-collar man, good at figures and money, and did not work with his hands, as his forebears had. As we have seen in connection with his partnership with Henry L. Wade, he began as a bank clerk and soon went into business for himself, selling steamship tickets, insurance, and surety bonds. George's most enduring investment was made in 1896, when he joined with Wade to found the Mattatuck. At his death, over half of the value of the estate ($350,000 out of $671,000) was in 14,000 shares of Mattatuck stock.[47] (His equity in the company when it was founded twenty-eight years before had been $15,000.)[48]

Shortly after George's death the Mattatuck board elected Stuart secretary of the corporation, giving him a salary of $2,500.[49] William Fielding replaced George as president and remained so until after World War II. In 1925 the directors declared a dividend of $30,000 of which almost half went to the Judd interest, thus maintaining the family's prosperity. With this financial support, Stuart resigned as secretary in order "to pursue studies at the Harvard Graduate School of Business Administration," as recorded in the minutes. Nina, George's widow, was elected to the board in 1926 and remained on it for a quarter of a century. There was always a

45. Advertisement, *Waterbury City Directory* (1884), 403.

46. "The Hillside, Waterbury, Connecticut: The Architectural and Historic Resources Inventory," unpaginated, Historic Neighborhood Preservation Program: The Waterbury Neighborhood Housing Service, xerographic copy of typescript form filed with the Connecticut Historical Commission, 25 Nov. 1986, Silas Bronson Library, Waterbury, Conn.

47. Estate of George Edwards Judd, loc. cit., Waterbury Probate Court.

48. Minute Book, Mattatuck Manufacturing Company, 1896–1944.

49. Ibid., 30 June 1924, 170.

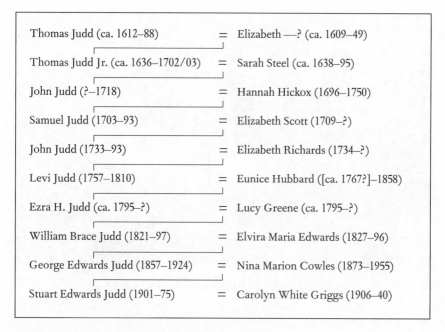

Thomas Judd (ca. 1612–88) = Elizabeth —? (ca. 1609–49)

Thomas Judd Jr. (ca. 1636–1702/03) = Sarah Steel (ca. 1638–95)

John Judd (?–1718) = Hannah Hickox (1696–1750)

Samuel Judd (1703–93) = Elizabeth Scott (1709–?)

John Judd (1733–93) = Elizabeth Richards (1734–?)

Levi Judd (1757–1810) = Eunice Hubbard ([ca. 1767?]–1858)

Ezra H. Judd (ca. 1795–?) = Lucy Greene (ca. 1795–?)

William Brace Judd (1821–97) = Elvira Maria Edwards (1827–96)

George Edwards Judd (1857–1924) = Nina Marion Cowles (1873–1955)

Stuart Edwards Judd (1901–75) = Carolyn White Griggs (1906–40)

95. Judd descent to Stuart Edwards Judd

stir among the clerks and bookkeepers when she arrived for board meetings in her fur-collared coat and richly decorated hat. At the announcement of a dividend she fluttered with pleasure. Apart from offering comments about the employees she met on the way in and out of the general manager's office, she had no role in running the company.

The Mattatuck then employed some five hundred people. In 1919 a new building had been built with the wartime surplus, more than doubling the floor space and adding an office wing (thus physically separating management from the factory floor, as had not been done in the days of Luther Chapin White and Henry C. Griggs). The new building was of steel beam and concrete construction, permitting large windows and open floors free of the numerous columns needed in older buildings. The factory produced parts such as typewriter links, which would be used in products assembled elsewhere. The company also maintained its lines of furniture nails, glides, "fabric," and bobbin rings. Under Fielding's management the Mattatuck had been highly profitable in the war and continued to flourish in the 1920s, when it paid over $20,000 annually to shareholders.[50]

50. Ibid., 1920–29, 141–17.

96. The Mattatuck Manufacturing Company in the 1890s

Mattatuck Museum

In 1914 George purchased the Queen Anne-style house at 37 Hillside
Avenue, built in the late 1860s and early 1870s, as were the Benedict and
Mitchell (later Griggs) houses towering above it.[51] Stuart was thirteen but
was off to boarding school soon after George's renovation (new plumbing, electrification, addition of a glass-enclosed entrance porch, a sun
porch, and refinishing of the interior). It was a capacious house of three
stories with ample room for entertaining. The third floor was for the servants. The Judds lived more modestly than the Griggses and Whites. The
cook-housekeeper in the 1920s was Frieda Ossan, who lived on the top
floor with her husband, a toolmaker; they came from Austria-Hungary,
very different from the Irish "girls" at the Griggs's, who expected to be
single and servants for life.[52] As neither of the senior Judds could drive,
they relied on a chauffeur. While Carrie and Julia rented cottages at Pine

---

51. "This two and a half story three bay Queen Anne House has a T-shaped plan with gabled wings
and a clipped southeastern corner. A central jerkinhead dormer is flanked by gable ends with half-
timbered peak ornamentation and deep, plain large boards with break molded brackets. The arched
windows in gable ends and brackets further articulate the design. The second story windows have
shingled hoods." "The Hillside, Waterbury, Connecticut."

52. "Gocht Ossan, Toolmaker, Frieda Ossan, wife, cook," 1920 U.S. census, Waterbury, E.D. 220:5,
New Haven Co., Conn.

97. The Mattatuck, after 1919 expansion

Mattatuck Museum

Orchard, George bought a summer cottage there in 1919, almost as large as the Waterbury house and a place where Eloise and Stuart could agreeably entertain their friends.

George Judd was struck with a liver infection in his sixty-seventh year, at the high tide of his material success. At the end he was in Waterbury Hospital, the first person in the family not to die at home.[53] The newspaper headline celebrated another Waterburian who had worked his way up from little: "Well Known Banker and Manufacturer Succumbs to Disease; Came Here in 1874, Rose from Bank Teller to Head of Large Concern." The latter was the Mattatuck, to which, according to the obituarist, he "devoted a great deal of his time and strength . . . taking great pride in its growth and prosperity." He was "a man of genial temperament with a large circle of friends."[54]

In the absence of letters or family reminiscences it is difficult to get a sense of his person. The fruits of his career, however, witness an energetic and capable man, and in the years of his success he served on civic and

---

53. Deaths, 10:30, 24 June 1924, Waterbury VS.

54. *Waterbury American*, 30 June 1924, with photograph, scrapbook, Mattatuck Manufacturing Company Archive, Mattatuck Museum.

church bodies. His success in business endowed a far more comfortable and spacious life for his wife and children than any of his forebears had enjoyed—Stuart was the first in the family to receive a college education. His widow was well provided for and until the Depression could maintain the two houses, cook, and chauffeur and shop as she wished. The family had entered the upper middle class.

Nina

Nina (Cowles) Judd, George's wife and Stuart's mother, was a widow at fifty-one. Like Carrie, she had more years of widowhood before her than she had of marriage. In his will George included a clause to protect against fortune-hunters: "To my wife $5,000 and house and property unless she remarry." The use of this once common provision of a husband seeking to control beyond the grave suggests that George may not have completely trusted his wife's judgment. Nina Cowles was twenty-eight, at the edge of female eligibility in those days, when George, a bachelor and householder of 43, married her in 1901. For some years before marriage she was employed by Reid & Hughes, the leading department store in town, and boarded with another family.[55] She caught George's eye with her blonde hair and pretty, rounded face with delicate skin. He was doing well and approaching middle age and doubtless wanted to bring a wife to the empty house his father had built. According to a biographical sketch published in his lifetime, they were married on 18 July 1901, but there is no record of this in Waterbury or neighboring Watertown.[56] If the date is correct, Nina was over five months pregnant with Stuart, who was born on 10 October.[57]

George moved his bride to his 52 Holmes Avenue house, off West Main Street at the foot of Hillside, where he had lived since the mid 1890s. The street was lined with other recently built houses in the Queen Anne style, all with two stories and attic space, most with porches from which to survey the passing scene. A 1986 historic preservation survey of the neighborhood noted that his house contributed "to the Queen Anne streetscape." It has "a simple three bay porch with turned balusters and

---

55. "Cowles, Nina M., Miss, clerk Reid & Hughes, bds 152 Chestnut," *Waterbury City Directory* (1901).

56. Pape, *Waterbury*, 2:86.

57. Births, 5:313, Waterbury VS.

posts, scroll work brackets and rounded ends."[58] I learned of the connection of this house to the family only in the course of research; Stuart never pointed out the house where he had spent his first thirteen years, though it was only a few blocks from where he later lived.

In economic terms, Nina Cowles came from a relatively impoverished background, but her family heritage was much the same as George's Puritan-Yankee Judds. The Cowles had been in Connecticut from the 1630s, and when the Judds were in Watertown in the eighteenth and early nineteenth centuries, they farmed in neighboring Bethlehem. Her paternal grandfather had been the first to break from the rural economy and settled in Poughkeepsie, where Nina's father, Samuel Cowles, was born in 1834. He returned to Connecticut, and in 1880s and in the 1890s lived in the Oakville section of Waterbury, identified as a plater in the Waterbury directories. According to the Cowles family history, in 1894 Samuel was "extensively engaged in the manufacture of the Cowles anti-friction rollers [substitutes for ball bearings] for vehicles."[59] This enterprise, had it been successful, might have made him a millionaire, but it left no trace. It may be that Samuel was quixotic in pursuit of such a project. In any case, the family was impoverished. His wife, Mary Jane Coley, died in 1897 at the age of 64, and he died seven years later at seventy-one of "Old Age & Worn Out," when Stuart was three.[60]

In her marriage, Nina's sphere was the home; she decorated it to her taste (her affection for flowery prints and color a contrast to the dark wood trim and paneling of the interior), supervised the meals, saw to the cleaning, dressed and largely reared the children. George's sphere was business, about which she knew nothing (Mattatuck dividends to her were like manna from heaven), and in evenings George repaired to the Waterbury Club to smoke cigars, play cards, and learn what other businessmen in town were up to.

Carrie lived with her family past about her in pictures and objects and loved to tell stories about herself as a girl, but in Nina's house there were no old pieces of furniture, and most family pictures were of George

---

58. "The Hillside, Waterbury, Connecticut." The house is now used for a law office.

59. Calvin Duvall Cowles, *The Cowles Family in America* (New Haven: Tuttle, Morehouse, and Taylor, 1929), 2:642–43.

60. See "Cowles," Genealogical and Biographical Notes in this volume.

(whom she spoke of with awe) and young Stuart and Eloise. She told no stories to her grandchildren about her childhood. She may have been equally reticent with her son. Stuart put "unknown" for her parents' birthplaces on her death certificate.[61] She never mentioned that she had worked as a salesgirl, as though it was shameful for a woman to have had to work.[62] "Never ask a woman her age" was a humorous axiom of the day, one that she resolutely followed. It was only at her death that I learned that she was two years older than Carrie. This concealment of not only her age but her memories of the family may have hidden humiliation. Her father, with his quixotic notion of cylindrical roller bearings, probably left his wife to scrape by, and the family could have descended into a poverty that Nina could not bear to remember. Whatever its cause, Nina's silence masked something she did not choose to relive.

Nina did relate stories about her own children—how loving Stuart and Eloise were to each other, how one night a year they could stay up as long as they pleased, their having "run away" hand-in-hand to the end of Holmes Avenue (a few hundred yards) and, thinking better of it, turning back, and their happy summers at Mr. and Mrs. Einsen's farm. Nina's photo album showed the children on the farm in summer, wearing smocks and standing on a dirt road near a house untouched by modern development. It was a vision of rural America such as Winslow Homer had portrayed. When they were older, Stuart and Eloise gathered with friends about the piano and sang favorite songs—such was the vanished world that she evoked to me. At Pine Orchard with "young people," they gathered around the upright piano to sing with the warm summer breezes coming in the windows on the porch. It seemed to me impossibly ideal, but probably was not in those days of communal music-making.

No one was more beautiful in the telling than Eloise. To me as a child Nina's aureate accounts seemed unreal but, in retrospect, touching, a glass menagerie of memory. These children grew up in those years where city had not overwhelmed the country with suburbs and before the mechanical amplification of music. Their childhood may have been as favored as Nina described. The death of Eloise led to Nina to her view of God as good, but

---

61. Death Certificates, 27 Jan. 1955, Waterbury VS.

62. It was Carrie who told me of my other grandmother's early employment, in a spirit of regret that she should feel so ashamed of it. (The directory confirms the occupation.)

Nature, quite separate, as cruel—though a pillar of the Second Congregational Church, she did not realize the notion was a Christian heresy.

Nina's emotions erupted on slight prompting. When I stopped in for a visit as a child she exclaimed loudly, covering a reluctantly proffered cheek with kisses. She showered me with this excess of affection in public and in the dancing school line powdered the noses of the other boys as well as mine to stop their shining. On a breezy day at summer camp she instructed the counselors to have the boys put on shirts to keep them from catching cold. This grandmotherly behavior provoked an excess of embarrassment before other boys. When of college age, I was unnerved by Nina staring at me rather than attending to the orchestra and conductor during the closing passages of Strauss's *Death and Transfiguration* at Tanglewood—"I was thinking of you ascending to heaven," she explained. Her emotions betokened needs that had never been satisfied, perhaps too large to be satisfied.

The enchantment Nina conveyed about her children's childhood was juxtaposed to Stuart's inability or unwillingness to recall his. He never spoke of what he had done as a boy. He never spoke of his father, and conveyed no precepts, wisdom, humor, or anecdotes about him. The mother created an idealized past, the son, perhaps in response, avoided it altogether. His mind was on the future, how to be an imaginative businessman and investor, to be a constructive participant in civic life and its boards and associations. If Eloise had lived, she likely would have borne the family memory for the children. The trauma of watching the demise of this attractive and vivacious young woman in the flush of youth doubtless contributed to the near-hysteria of Nina's affections. Stuart's response was to retreat into the measured, rational (or silent) response.

Had Eloise lived, Nina's widowhood would have been softened by her support, and the burden would not have been on Stuart, who could and would not respond in kind. Perhaps Stuart was clam-like because he needed the shell to resist the intrusions of his parent. He was also dutiful, the loyal son, but there was no relaxation between them—his guard was always up. He lost his childhood in the struggle to maintain an identity confronted by neediness that could smother. When I was old enough to notice, I could detect the irony in his replies to his mother's urgings and her "notions." The reflexes he developed influenced his marriages. He was attracted to the needy and wanted to help them, which he surely thought he could do for Carol.

Nina was the soul of propriety and would never have had an affair or married again (in any event, her gushing manner would possibly have put off suitors). She did not drink, and, of course, did not go out to a job. The framework of Nina's long widowed life was staid enough. She was the moving force in a bridge club. Her charity was the Second Congregational Church, to which she was devoted, and her greatest pride was in overseeing its Christmas and Easter decorations.

Some of her emotional needs were fulfilled at the theater. She regularly went to New Haven to matinees of touring shows and tryouts at the Shubert Theater. Her highest praise was that an actor had "dash"—during the war, when the healthiest and handsomest were in the service, she would comment sadly that a leading man "lacked dash." (She would use the bus for the trip to and from New Haven when she could not afford a chauffeur or during the wartime gas rationing.) She subscribed to a ladies lunch program held in the Biltmore Hotel in New York, which brought actors and playwrights to speak—"Book and Play Luncheon"—which she could combine with shopping at Lord & Taylor and B. Altman. It was live theater that she favored; unlike Carrie, she seldom went to the movies. She rarely missed the Second Congregational Church Forum ("The World Comes to Waterbury"), which on Sunday nights presented speakers who gave illustrated talks, allowing Nina to travel vicariously with Burton Holmes. I went with her and was enthralled to hear Osa Johnson in person and see her movies of Kenya and its animals and her "Shangri-La" house by a mountain lake, and Admiral Richard Byrd, with his pictures of the South Pole.

The attic at 37 Hillside was packed with objects—Nina even saved George's gallstones in a jar. There was far too much for a child to explore. In fact it would have been difficult to make a way through the accumulated stuff. Carrie tagged most things in her attic with a note as to its origin, prior ownership in the family, and eventual disposition—which amused and fascinated me as she seemed to live outside of time, and her dying was unimaginable. Nina prepared no such notes. Most of the contents were thrown out after her death, given to Goodwill and the trash collector. Nothing like the record of letters and objects left in the Griggs-White-Phelps families is available for George's Judd or Nina's Cowles families. What may have appeared as junk doubtless contained insights into the past.

XII

MARRIAGE, FAMILY LIFE, LOSS

Carol's Wedding

The *Aquitania* delivered its passengers to New York in early July 1930, and sometime later that summer in Waterbury Carol accepted Stuart's proposal. I have a memory of Carrie reading from a letter in which Carol described how at a meal out Stuart had proposed and she agreed, but it is not among those that survived. He presented her with a handsome ring, with a large diamond set amid small ones.

A prank of Haring's provided a touch of farce the night before the wedding. Victor Coombes, a Russian immigrant, regularly came to the door for a handout from Carrie. Much to her embarrassment, he lavished praise on her beauty and dignity in a thick Russian accent, treated her as if she were a noble lady in prerevolutionary Russia. I remember encountering him seated on the edge of the Pan fountain by the porte cochere; while he dabbled his hand in the water he discoursed on the desirability of the grounds being made a public park for the enjoyment of all. Victor was a ne'er do well and a pest, but an intriguing and sometimes amusing one, and he had a unique skill—he was an expert whistler. Bobby and Haring once persuaded him (and their mother) to present a concert in the house. Carrie told me, with amusement and admiration for Victor's peculiar skill, that the audience she had gathered listened to him whistle famous opera tunes such as "La Donna è mobile," "Vesti la giubba," perhaps the wedding march from *Lohengrin,* and Russian songs.

Because Victor would be hanging about the wedding anyway, Haring gave him a role as guard of the presents laid out in the sitting room, dressed him in his old Boy Scout uniform, equipped him with a flashlight, and commissioned him to guard Carol's treasures. He stationed him within the rhododendron hedge by the porch where, as far as is known, he remained all night. It was a solo version of the watch from *Much Ado about Nothing,* but happily for all no burglar appeared. Despite the long and

475

chilly November night Victor may never have understood the trick that had been played on him and remained proud of his service to the noble lady and her household. He kept up his visits for years to come.[1]

The wedding was at 4 P.M. on 14 November 1930. While the guests waited in the front hall, decorated with palms and chrysanthemums "in the yellow and rust shades," according to the newspaper account of "the season's most prominent wedding," the bridal party processed down the stairway to the strains of the bridal chorus from *Lohengrin*, the tall windows that Carrie and Rob had added to lighten the front hall pale with the November light above them. The ushers in cutaways came first, led by Day Tuttle, Stuart's Hotchkiss roommate.[2] The bridesmaids—including Betty White and the ebullient "Hat" from the Rawson tour—followed "dressed in sleeveless gowns of peach flat crepe made with long full skirts, which flared from the hipline"; their "small poke hats" (bonnets with projecting brims) were of "wine colored velvet." In their hands were "rust colored chrysanthemums tied with wine colored ribbons."

The newspaper permitted fashion-conscious readers to visualize the bride in "a gown of blush panne velvet made in simple but distinctive lines, the skirt being long and terminating in a train." Carol's veil ("of old rose-point lace . . . arranged cap fashion and caught at either side by clusters of orange blossoms") connected three generations; Jane Amelia had worn it at her wedding to Luther Chapin White in 1844, and Carrie wore it when she married Rob in 1902.

Stuart waited in the living room, attended by his best man Charles Morgan, his college roommate. Carrie wore a black chiffon gown with a corsage of white orchids and a black velvet hat—the color of mourning in recognition of the absence of Rob and Julia. Nina, in "Biarritz green georgette," added color. Dr. Lewis, who had known Carol through her school

---

1. Story told the author by Robert Griggs Jr. Victor eventually worked in the WPA. I came across him seated on a child's chair chipping at old paint in Driggs School.

2. Details of the wedding and wedding party from the *Waterbury Republican*, 14 Nov. 1930, clipping, CHWG. The ushers were "F. Day Tuttle of Santa Barbara, Cal., Paul B. Morgan Jr., of Worcester, Mass., Everett B. Merriam, and Edward S. Wotkyns [both from Waterbury], and Robert Foote Griggs, Jr. a brother of the bride." Bridesmaids were "Miss Elizabeth Wade White and Miss Eleanor R. Griggs, cousins of the bride, Mrs. Haring White Griggs of Hartford, a sister-in-law of the bride, Miss Mariette Gilchirst of Cleveland and Miss Harriet Hayward of Boston." The maid of honor was "Miss Martha Wales of Ossining, N.Y., a classmate of the bride at Westover school."

years, officiated using the *Book of Common Prayer;* the Judds' Congregational church was not represented.

Newspaper readers might have thought from the account that it was a decorous and orderly social wedding. In fact it was not. Patty recalled many years later how awkward the occasion was. Carrie and others were concerned that Carol would not be able to hold herself together under the strain. Nina, whom Patty had not met before, "gushed" and "made a display of herself" and was altogether "peculiar," putting some on edge. The Will Whites and David Griggses and other relatives were formal, subdued, and distant—for a reason that will become clear.

There was more than awkwardness. According to the newspaper account the "bride was joined at the foot of the stairway by her brother, Haring White Griggs of Trinity College, Hartford, who escorted her into the reception room and gave her in marriage." Haring was a weaving, sodden figure at that point, his drunkenness obvious to all. Patty told how that morning in their room at the Elton he had ordered champagne with breakfast and, still in his pajamas, donned a top hat to drink the champagne in style. He continued drinking through the day and by the four o'clock wedding was reeling. (The alcohol was, of course, supplied by a bootlegger, as Prohibition had three years to run.) In the photo of the wedding party his figure—blurred because he could not stand still for the photographer—is at the far side of the party, not next to the bride, where he should have been. It was on this day that Patty realized Haring's drinking problem was such that their marriage could not last.[3]

Carrie's feelings can only be imagined. She had to witness the spectacle of her favored son, so recently honored by Cambridge University, too drunk to function in front of family and friends. This surely over-balanced her relief that Carol seemed to be headed toward a settled life.

In one sense, Haring's gesture came from his disdain for conventional society, and he behaved like the "bright young" drunks of the time that Fitzgerald portrayed. However, in this family occasion his behavior was utterly destructive, hurtful to his mother and sister, to his wife, and to himself. He may have thought himself superior to local society and fancied himself as an untrammeled artist. Did he drink to avoid the weight of family and its history? As a riposte to small-town society? To have "fun" and be bright and stylish? Or was this the action of one who had been "spoiled

---

3. Conversation with Patty Day, Nantucket, Mass., Aug. 1991.

98. Stuart and Carol on their honeymoon, 1930

rotten," as Patty also said of him? His behavior can also be clinically addressed: it was compulsive, manic, and could support the view that he had inherited some of the mental illness that afflicted his sister. He may at this point have become addicted to alcohol.

This was Haring's last appearance with the family at any social gathering in Waterbury. It is little wonder that the relatives were frozen and immobile, as Patty had described them. Only forty-two years had elapsed since his grandfather, Henry Charles Griggs, had been the subject of an editorial in the Waterbury paper honoring him at his death for the creativity he brought to developing Waterbury enterprises. Times had changed utterly. Haring actually and symbolically wanted none of that, and in a little over a year he would leave Connecticut for California.

The day after the wedding Carol and Stuart boarded a steamer in New York headed for Bermuda. In a photo taken onboard, Stuart, a proud bridegroom in a tailored dark suit, wears a warm smile; Carol has a hint of a smile and seems content. On Bermuda the photographer catches them as they walk arm in arm, a handsomely dressed couple—Stuart in white plus-fours, dark socks, and two-toned shoes, Carol in a dress. Both are smiling and shyly looking downward. They look well paired, stylish, intelligent, handsome, dignified, and somewhat formal.

Family Life

Carol and Stuart began married life in a rented house in West Hartford while Stuart went to work at the Hartford brokerage of Hincks Brothers. Carol was twenty-four in the December after the wedding; Stuart had turned twenty-nine that October.

A year later, on 3 November 1931, Carol gave birth to a son in Hartford Hospital—with Patty the year before, the first women in the history of the family to have children delivered in a hospital. I was named Peter Haring after the first boy in Julia's Haring family born in America, Pieter Haring, born in Manhattan about 1664. Thus the maternal family line, which Julia had researched and had learned from her father and Aunt Kate, was to be forever associated with the author of this book.

Stuart told me many years later that after I was born Carol had a "nervous breakdown," and the family physician in Hartford recommended that a second pregnancy and child would help her. It was well-meaning but ludicrously ill-informed advice for a woman with her mental history. However, during her pregnancy Carol was cheerful and confident and referred to a "daughter" or "the ping-pong ball" in the spring of 1933.

Carol had sung with a chorus in the Lenten church services that year. She and Stuart had seen *Rasputin and the Empress*, the 1932 film that united all three Barrymores, with Lionel playing the wicked monk, Rasputin: "It was marvelous—wonderful directing & acting." They saw *Of Thee I Sing* with the original New York company, invited Aunt Carolyn White to *Robin Hood*, a revival of the popular 1890 operetta by Reginald De Koven, and looked forward to *Fledermaus*, remembered from Vienna, at the new Bushnell Memorial Auditorium.[4]

A woman named Sally was the cook and looked after "Petie," but she was untidy and let go. "We are getting along beautifully without Sally," Carol wrote. "It is fine not to have a maid for a few days. Stu and I had an asparagus orgy last night which I cooked. When I cook it is a purely vege-

---

4. CGJ, at 42 Concord St., West Hartford, to CHWG, in Florence, Italy, 1 April 1933; CGJ, in West Hartford, to CHWG, in Milan. George and Ira Gershwin's 1931 musical comedy (with George S. Kaufman) about the candidacy of John P. Wintergreen for president. <www.nodanw.com/shows>, accessed 22 June 2002. *Robin Hood*, by the American composer Reginald De Koven (1859–1920), inaugurated in 1890 the era "when American operetta dominated the stage in the U.S.A. . . . a song from it, 'Oh Promise Me,' has remained a popular wedding ballad." *The New Grove*, s.v. "De Koven, (Henry Louis) Reginald."

99. Carol and Peter, 1932

tarian meal & Stuart washes the dishes." There is no suggestion of mental troubles in these letters, which are concerned with practical household affairs, relatives, deaths and illnesses of Waterbury people, and what she and "Stu" were doing.

The pregnancy had indeed given her energy, and for the first time in her life Carol was doing housework. "I have been using a vacuum cleaner (I rented it) in some of the rooms. I enjoy using it except for moving heavy furniture. I have done the 2nd floor thoroughly but am resting now before I continue with the work downstairs."[5] (The appliance was only beginning to be considered essential for the middle-class home. Shortly Nina gave her an extra one from her house—it was a sign of the straightened times that the Judds did not buy a new one.) Carrie praised the development in Carol of an "unusual domestic housewifely side . . . I have a feeling that the separation from your bossy Mother has something to do with your independent spirit. Tho I can hardly believe I am in any way responsible for your urge to use a vacuum cleaner."[6] Carol was "becoming much more independent without 'Mother's advice.'"[7]

---

5. CGJ, in West Hartford, to CHWG, in Milan, 19 April 1933.

6. CHWG, in Milan, to CGJ, in West Hartford, 8 May 1933.

7. CHWG, in Montreux, to CGJ, in West Hartford, 30 April 1933.

Carol enjoyed the fruits of motherhood, and like any young mother reported the incidents of growth. "[L]ittle Petie has gone for a walk looking adorable (sounds like Patty [who favored the word]), in his new blue coat, tam and curls flying . . . He is getting so he repeats many words now. He said 'Anna' and 'good boy' today. It is quite cunning to hear him say 'There you are'—used in the sense of something accomplished—as when we button his coat or tie his shoe."[8]

Most social activity was within the family. "Mrs. Judd came for dinner on Sunday and stayed until six o'clock when she took the bus home. She wrote us a letter after and said that she was the 'happiest woman in the United States' to spend the day with Peter—She is certainly appreciative of small favors."[9] Carol received the *Waterbury Republican* daily and sent reports to her mother (in Italy that summer) on its news of deaths and illnesses in Waterbury, much as Julia and Carrie had, imparting the sense of a self-aware community, where in certain circles "everyone knew of everyone."

A frequent visitor was Aunt Carolyn White, after whom Carol was named, widowed and ever touring, never staying in the same bed two nights in a row, as Carol put it in a later letter. Her husband, George Luther White Jr., "Jimmy," an invalid for the previous six years, had died at the age of fifty-four in their house on Randolph Avenue, in Waterbury, the preceding September. Julia's youngest child, with a delicate constitution and his father's predisposition to tuberculosis, he was the first of the siblings to die. He was affectionately regarded in the family, according to Betty White, for his gentleness and good humor throughout his illness. A benchmark of his quiet life was his presidency of the Waterbury Country Club in the early 1920s. His estate was adequate to keep his widow in comfortable circumstances for the rest of a well-traveled life. Carolyn White was particularly fond of her namesake and was a regular visitor. One evening Carol reported her as making a fourth for bridge with Nina.

Hincks Brothers was struggling in the market downturn. "I am spending this evening upstairs in our sitting room as Stuart, Mr. Speer, and five other Hincks men are bashing over their business troubles," Carol wrote in early May 1933. "They came at quarter of eight—it is now nearly eleven & there is no sign of them leaving. It is h—llish because they make

---

8. CGJ, in West Hartford, to CHWG, in Milan, 3 May 1933.

9. CGJ, at 42 Concord St., to CHWG, in Florence, Italy, 1 April 1933.

so much noise that there is no hope of any sleep for me—so here's hoping they go soon."[10] The times were rough, never more so for the brokerage business. In 1932 the Dow Jones Industrials had dropped to 61 in December from a high of 91. Between 4 and 14 March 1933 the stock market was closed during the bank holiday declared to avert a financial panic. Franklin D. Roosevelt was inaugurated on 20 March with words to hearten the discouraged. The young couple did not then suspect that Stuart's position with Hincks would come to an end during the year, and that they would return to Waterbury.

In the midst of the national crisis Carrie was on the Atlantic, returning to her beloved Italy and France. This crossing was on the *Conte di Savoia*, the new flagship of the Italian Lines, its interior a "tour de force of Italian decorative splendor," with an immense lounge modeled after the Colonna Palace in Rome with a fresco ceiling and with marble walls.[11] Her companion on the voyage was gentle Lucy Burrall. In Rome they joined Mary and Edith Chase.

Carrie reported that when she told her companions she had had a "pleasant voyage," Lucy added "from tuberculosis and related problems"—the former referring to George Jr.'s death, the latter to Carrie's sorrow over the precipitate breakup of Haring's marriage. Patty had acted decisively after finding Haring with another woman. She took Gay, then a year old, and left. Her divorce followed quickly. Haring saw neither of them again and had nothing to do with his daughter.[12] Lucy knew how deeply Carrie was ashamed of her son's actions and how concerned she was for Patty and Gay. She carried this sadness and regret for the rest of her life, compensated in part by a continuing warm connection with the two women.

Haring was not reappointed at Trinity College. He headed west by train, stopping, as the family story has it, in St. Louis to visit his Yale classmate, Lincoln Hockaday, then working for Joseph Pulitzer, to spend evenings drinking at the handsome country club that Pulitzer had helped

---

10. CGJ, in West Hartford, to CHWG, in Milan, 3 May 1933.

11. Miller, *Italian Line*, 50; also see 47–50. She was laid up near Venice when the Nazis sank her in 1943 to prevent her falling into Allied hands. Loc. cit., 59.

12. Conversations with Elizabeth Gay (Griggs) Dorn, 1990s. Gay learned from Patty the account of finding Haring with a woman in their Hartford home, which triggered her immediate departure.

finance. From there he carried on "to rusticate in Tahiti for six months and write a novel" as he reported to his Yale classmates.[13]

Carrie was shocked and ashamed of the divorce and of Haring's behavior that had led to it, a regret that she tried to make up to Patty and her child throughout her life. Patty returned to New York to work for Saks Fifth Avenue. She and Gay regularly visited 54 Hillside and Carrie visited them in Litchfield, where Patty's mother lived. Carrie did her best to make up for her son's repudiation and neglect. When Carol reported that she had heard that four Waterbury couples were about to divorce, she added, "[I]t must make you feel that Haring is not so unusual or disgraced after all—and that Waterbury is getting sophisticated."[14] Carrie would have none of it, and thought of the wives. "What is the trouble with young married people getting divorces? In nearly every case it looks as tho the wives were obliged to 'work for their living.'"[15]

Traveling Companions

Hard times were evident in Europe. "It is not at all gay in these huge hotels now," Carrie reported to Carol from Milan. "You would find it depressing in contrast to what you remember. I wonder, with so little patronage, how they can be kept open. This is so everywhere and it makes me quite happy and reconciled to spending a little cash from our own (poor) country on these shores."[16] In Florence,

> Aunt M. has introduced me to most fascinating antique shops of the highest type where, when times were better, she and Miss Edith bought valuable pieces (and where they are received with *open arms*). The poor merchants feel the depression and lack of American buyers keenly. One, a collector of rare objects, told me that many of the formerly wealthy Italian families frequently come in to him to sell some of their beautiful things which he cannot afford to do. *But* if there are any wealthy Americans left, they certainly are missing the

---

13. *History of the Class of 1927, Yale College, Decennial Record* (New Haven, published with the assistance of the Class Secretaries Bureau, 1937).

14. "I learned of several impending divorces in Waterbury—Bob & Betty Sarkus, Wilton Allerton & wife & Gordon Hurlbut & wife—There are two others which Ed Carmody said are still professional secrets." CGJ, in West Hartford, to CHWG, in Milan, 19 April 1933.

15. CHWG, in Milan, to CGJ, in West Hartford, 8 May 1933.

16. CHWG, in Montreux, to CGJ, in West Hartford, 30 April 1933.

opportunity of their lives to buy for unheard of prices. Please do not think this has led me into extravagances. It's just tempting![17]

In Rome the ladies stayed at the small Windsor Hotel, which charged $3.50 per night for room and bath. "Often Aunt M. & Miss E. do not 'change' for dinner," Carrie reported to Carol, so "you may be consoled for not being with us. Your ideas of a wardrobe trunk full of costumes and dancing with Italian noblemen (?) would be terribly crushed. In fact, we look like a group of school teachers."[18]

Of her companions, Carrie wrote that they "are all great travelers and 'thorough' is my name for it. Besides marvelous memories they read up before and after sightseeing. Also I think they are getting a kick, and are very conscientious as well, in educating 'Mrs. Pipp,'" a self-deprecating reference to herself as Mrs. Pipchin, the "ill-favored widow," in Dickens' *Dombey and Sons*.[19] Carrie was modest about her intellectual abilities and deferred to her companions, but with her silver hair, erect carriage, and wide-awake interest in what she read was far from "ill-favored." Mary Burrall had the identical education as Carrie, but she had an intellectual bent and no household to run, husband to look after, or children to raise.

The ladies were avid and well-informed sightseers. The Roman routine was to leave the hotel at 9:30, return for lunch three hours later, and be out again at 2:30. "It is remarkable to hear how well informed Aunt Mary and Miss Edith are on everything to see. They know the streets and names of all the churches, all the great public buildings, where to go to see the best of every thing and where to eat the best food." Edith Chase knew enough Italian to get around and had an unerring sense of direction. From Venice Carrie reported, "I've never know any one like Miss Edith for finding her way anywhere. The most intricate streets turning and twisting as they do all over Italy but especially here, never fazes her. And she always 'gets there'" "Of course I just lap it up," Carrie added, and "immediately after dinner all of us gather in my small bedroom where we drink Miss E's

---

17. CHWG, in Florence, to CGJ, in West Hartford, 11 April 1933.

18. CHWG, in Rome, to CGJ, in West Hartford, 2 April 1933.

19. CHWG, in Venice, to CGJ, in West Hartford, 23 April 1933. Mrs. Pipchin had qualities that in no sense did Carrie share, including "a mottled face, like bad marble, a hook nose, and hard gray eye that looked as if it might have been hammered on an anvil without sustaining any injury." Charles Dickens, *Dombey and Son* (1848; Harmondsworth, Sussex, England: Penguin Books, 1970), 160.

cointreau and chat until an early bedtime. We never go out in the evening, in fact are usually ready to rest."[20]

L., M., and E.—the Burralls in their mid-fifties like Carrie, and Edith Chase about ten years younger—were in the midst of long lives of untiring enthusiasm for knowledge, for meeting people, and for travel. From childhood I addressed the sisters as "Auntie" and Edith as "Miss Edith." Mary Burrall, the intellectual one, who did most of the talking, was lean and tall and spoke with an upper-class drawl, brandishing a lighted cigarette in its holder as she spoke. She was opinionated and snobbish, balanced, as Betty White observed, by a warm interest in people and events. She was "authoritative, laying down the law, but she also had this manner of being amused."[21] Lucy, her younger sister, shorter, slightly round, with a memorably sweet smile—the homemaker—saw to the meals at the Church Street house. She was a considerate and understanding friend, quietly providing warmth to balance her sister's opinion.

Miss Edith had a round face, which in later years acquired jowls and came to look a little like Winston Churchill's. With her Chase money in the early 1920s she built a house in the style of an English country manor on property in Litchfield, about three quarters of an hour northwest of Waterbury, where the ladies spent the warm months. Many of the furnishings were antiques bought in Lichfield, Staffordshire, England, on various expeditions. A working farm was on the property, and the sow with her piglets delighted me as a small child. Edith was an able investor, served on philanthropic boards and on the board of the Waterbury National Bank. Stuart, who served with her on the bank board, would tell me that she had "a man's mind," the antediluvian sentiment shared by other Waterbury businessmen who regarded Edith's abilities as unusual. All three ladies kept up with the latest books and, as I experienced many times, were keenly interested in those they entertained for tea or had as house guests.

With their independent traveling and self-sufficiency these women lived a life that would not have been acceptable or even possible in earlier generations, and in later generations careers would have been expected. They lived during a brief flowering of New England spinsterhood. No

---

20. CHWG, in Rome, to CGJ, at 42 Concord St., West Hartford, 27 March 1933; CHWG, in Venice, to CGJ, in West Hartford, 23 April 1933; CHWG, in Rome, to CGJ, in West Hartford, 2 April 1933.

21. Conversation with Elizabeth Wade White, 2 July 1993.

longer were single women tied to tending others in the family; rather, they were able to travel as they chose and to maintain independent and hospitable households. Their legacy may be seen in the Litchfield house, with books, furniture, and telephone address book just as they were when the ladies were alive. Edith willed the house and grounds to the State of Connecticut and characteristically provided an endowment for its upkeep.[22]

"You cannot imagine the great changes due to Mussolini since we were here in 1930," Carrie reported to Carol, deeming the Duce responsible for the "most marvelous excavations, opening up great spaces as well as great monuments." Her guides knew "all Mussolini's works and are crazy about him." Carrie was greatly impressed by the new sports stadium being built, then called the Mussolini Forum and considered that it "might well have been built by one of the Roman Emperors."[23] Ten years later, when Mussolini was thoroughly discredited, I remember Mary, no longer defending him, using the phrase of an earlier day, that to his credit he "had made the trains run on time." For those who, like Carrie and her friends, had experienced the poverty and disorganization of Italian cities earlier, the progress seemed promising.[24] Two years hence Carrie would "lap it up" again with M., L. & E. on another well-planned trip in Scandinavia.

There were additions to the family in the fall of 1933. On 1 September Robert F. Griggs Jr. married Annamae (always called Anne) Trankar, from Torrington, Connecticut. They set up house in a recently built colonial-style house at 28 Columbia Boulevard up the hill from 54 Hillside, a walk of about a third of a mile. Bob continued to work as a broker at the R. F. Griggs Company. The first of three daughters, Nancy, was born

---

22. Now Topsmead State Forest in Litchfield. The house is a Tudor Cottage designed by Richard Henry Dana Jr. and built 1924–25, a "fine example of English Tudor." It is surrounded by landscaping, including a garden, and is approached by a drive through rows of apple trees. It is built of masonry and oak and brick, with a slate roof and lead gutters. The brick floors make it cool inside in the hot weather. The living room has beamed ceilings and a large fireplace; a small office looks out into the apple trees. There are four bedrooms, "with horsehair mattresses on the beds." Outside there is a two story dovecote resembling a tower and containing a bedroom. The grounds include a 40-acre wildlife preserve. "Tudor Cottage, built 1924–25, fine example of English Tudor, Estate of $1.4 million" *Waterbury Republican*, 16 July 1981. Edith Chase died in 1972.

23. CHWG, in Rome, to CGJ, at 42 Concord St., West Hartford, 27 March 1933.

24. An early warning of the storm that was to destroy Europe came in February of this year, when President Hindenburg appointed Adolf Hitler to form a government, but there is no mention of the new regime in these letters.

exactly a year after the wedding. Four years later Carrie gave her carriage house to Bob, who replaced it with a sturdy Georgian brick house. It was a few yards to 54 Hillside and closer to where the Judds were soon to move.

Stuart Edwards Judd Jr. ("Tui") was born on 27 September 1933 at Hartford Hospital, named for his father and his long-dead paternal great-grandmother. Within a month the baby was back in the hospital, desperately ill with gastroenteritis. According to his father, he was talked and cuddled through a nearly fatal crisis by a loving nurse. He required mother's milk, which Carol could not supply. It was sent up from donors in New York, and Stuart met the train at 5 A.M. to take it to the hospital. This was a close call. The baby recovered, but the illness riled his system, and he was a colicky infant.

Haring returned from the "spell of creative work" in Tahiti to California, where he settled in Laguna Beach in Orange County, "our most liberal if not our most notorious art colony." Its situation on a long, curving sandy beach at the foot of rolling hills attracted many artists and visitors. There, "after considerable milling around," he became president and director of Laguna Beach Players—so he informed his Yale classmates, and so is it borne out by the records of the present-day Laguna Beach Theater.[25] Haring's first appearances there were in January and February 1934 in vehicles entitled *A Good Woman* and *Night Court*. The leading lady in these productions is listed as Marianne Griggs. Haring married Marianne Kelly in 1942, and it is probably she who was then living with him and assumed his surname—unbeknownst to Carrie or others back home. After her marriage she was a woman greatly respected by Carrie for her positive influence on Haring. He acted in sixteen of the Laguna Beach Players productions, with the last two, *School for Scandal* and *Dracula*, just before the war.[26]

At one point in the thirties he made a try for roles in a more lucrative venue. "What a boy he is," exclaimed Carrie in reporting a birthday cable in Italian from him at a Hollywood office, and Carol mentioned a screen test he had taken.[27] With his looks, he would have been suited to the many

---

25. *Twenty-Five Years Out: History of the Class of 1927, Yale University* (New Haven: Yale Univ., published with the assistance of the Class Secretaries Bureau, 1953), 228–29.

26. E-mail communication from Richard Stein, Executive Director of Laguna Playhouse, 30 Dec. 2000.

27. CHWG, in Venice, to CGJ, in West Hartford, 23 April 1933; CGJ, in Hobe Sound, to CHWG, in Waterbury, 6 April 1937.

movies at the time with upper-crust settings and become something of a Cary Grant.

There was no question of gainful employment for Haring in his Laguna Beach life. He was supported by a monthly allowance that Bobby sent him on their mother's behalf. On his first visit to the family in the east, in 1935, he came by ship through the Panama Canal for $120, cheaper than by rail. Since he was not bringing a car, no more than one month's advance in allowance was needed.[28] This support continued throughout his life, a bitter point with Bobby, who in his old age would not tolerate mention of his brother and cut his photos from the family album.[29] Of writing, which was what Haring meant by "creative activity," nothing came. So was established a legend in the family, the mysterious uncle who had done so well at Jesus College but who lived "on the dole" as Stuart put it. My school theme on the subject had the title, "A Black Sheep."

Stuart left Hincks Brothers in 1934 and the family returned to Waterbury and for a time lived on the third floor at 54 Hillside, well looked after by Carrie's staff. He shortly set up Stuart E. Judd Co., Investments, an office with a secretary and an assistant. From there, in the rough investing climate of the day, he gave investment advice to clients. Betty White appreciated the way he handled her account in the mid-1930s.[30] The largest Judd investment remained in the Mattatuck, which was able to pay some dividends in most years of the Depression. Stuart wanted to have his own business and was capable in investments. Later in the decade, though, he would join the Mattatuck and become part of its management.

In the summer of 1935 Carol and the two boys, then three and almost two, spent July and August at the shore in a small rented cottage a short walk from the beach in Madison on Long Island Sound, along the coast from Pine Orchard, where Carrie and Julia had spent summers. Carrie

28. In 2000 values this $120 was considerably more expensive than an advance purchased airline ticket would be in 2002. Stuart wrote: "I don't think he's bringing his car because he only asked Bobbie for one month's allowance ahead of time." SEJ, in Waterbury, to CHWG, in Gothenburg, Sweden, 16 Aug. 1935.

29. Conversation with George Razee, husband of Nancy (Griggs) Razee, daughter of Robert F. Griggs Jr., 1990s.

30. In 1926 the office was at 100 Grand St., later at 49 Leavenworth in an office where a bay window on the ground floor announced the name. He closed the firm in 1940 after he returned to the Mattatuck.

spent most of the summer touring Scandinavia with M., L. & E., her indefatigable companions. They experienced Sweden and the Gotha Canal in the long nights of early July, traveled up the coast of Norway from Bergen north, and visited Dorothy Phelps Wetherald (Lizzie's daughter) and her friend, Kyllikki Pohjola, a distinguished nurse, and, after the war, delegate to the United Nations. She hosted the ladies in her country house—a high point of their trip.[31]

The full complement of staff remained at 54 Hillside, and Stuart boarded there, well cared for. Sarah cooked for him when Nellie was on vacation, and when Katie, the waitress, went on hers, "Stuart says it is very restful but he does kind of miss her swinging on your chair giving her philosophy on all subjects." Before she went off, "Nellie . . . very kindly sent down cakes, soup and a pie by Stuart at various times. She made my particular favorite, chocolate cake with sliced almonds . . ."[32]

As a child I knew only the first names of these three Irish women whose warmth and loving care animated the household. Nellie, I now discover from the 1930 census was Ellen McCarthy, then fifty-five. She was the round-faced, ample, rosy-cheeked woman, the cook who looked the part. She presided over a great gas range and oven with white enameled doors. On the nearby table she demonstrated to me the use of a rolling pin for making piecrusts and allowed me to taste batter from one of the huge bowls she used. Katie was Catharine Hanahan, three years younger; she wore steel-rimmed spectacles, had graying hair tied in a neat knot, and was a slim figure in her uniform as she passed the food delicately around the table. Her sister Bridget had been the upstairs maid, but when she died her place was taken by Sarah Doyle, forty-six in 1930. Sarah had come as a child from County Wicklow, had a downright manner, openly favored me because I was a boy and would always point out where the butter was in

---

31. As a young woman Kyllikki Pohjola (1894–1979) served as an ambulance driver and nurse in the Finnish and Estonian freedom movements of 1918–19. In 1920 she came to the U.S. as a nurse and trained at Columbia University, where she received her bachelor of science in 1927. It was during those years that she met Dorothy Wetherald. They became friends and exchanged summer visits after Kyllikki returned to Finland. When Carrie and "M. L & E." visited her, she was president of the Finnish Nurses Association, a position she held until 1969. In the late 1950s she was a member of the Finnish delegation to the United Nations, and in the 1960s she was minister of social affairs in the Finnish government. Fact sheet provided by the Finnish Information Service, New York City, translated by Ritva Metso of the Consul-General of Finland in New York City.

32. CGJ, in Madison, to CHWG, in Gothenburg, 5 Aug. 1935.

100. Sarah Doyle in the kitchen of 54 Hillside, 1949

the mashed potatoes when she came to me. She was fervent in her Americanness, scorning my later travel across the Atlantic, where it was "dirty" and not worth bothering about. It was Sarah who stayed on when Carrie had to reduce the staff later in the decade. For years they were an odd couple, often arguing about what should be done, but devoted to each other. Sarah had her own house, and the others had places to go on their days off. The daily social time was in their dining room off the kitchen where they listened to the radio, read the paper, entertained Frank Ray, the handyman, and, occasionally, the maids in the Smith house next door.[33]

If Carol wanted to go to Waterbury, Frank La Chance in the Pierce-Arrow came to fetch; he brought Aunt Carolyn for a day, and he and the car were available to Carrie's friends. "La Chance has been in a constant whirl taking your friends out. He is much busier than when you are home. He says that sometimes three people have called up and want the car the same time so now he has told them to let him know the night before . . . He took great pride in showing me how he painted the wheels of your car but I think I persuaded him not to paint cream colored lines on them which they had when new, because it would look so messy if not done perfectly."[34] While Carol was in Waterbury briefly that summer I remember becoming acutely ill from a luncheon Shepherd's Pie. I desperately longed

---

33. 1930 U.S. census, Waterbury, ED 220:5, New Haven Co., Conn.; Sarah Doyle (1884–1967) is recorded in the SSDI.

34. CGJ, in Madison, to CHWG, in Gothenburg, 5 Aug. 1935.

for my mother and remember the relief when I heard the crunch of tires and saw the hulk of the Pierce-Arrow at dusk. Carol returned thanks to the ever-reliant La Chance.

Nellie and Sarah served on the committee for the Irish cottage at Settler's Village in Waterbury that summer, an involvement of domestic servants in a municipal event that would seem to be unique to America. In Waterbury the tercentenary of the founding of Connecticut Colony by Puritan exiles from England became as well a celebration of the origins of the main ethnic groups in the city. Settler's Village was located in Chase Park on the hill overlooking Waterbury to the west, near where the first the Farmington families had made their settlement. A "sturdy stockade" enclosed a number of buildings, a reconstruction of the early Town Hall and "a series of picturesque little buildings of stone, heavy plank, or logs, each of which represent[ed] one of the national groups which have made definite and important contributions to the city's growth." The Irish House in the international section, which Nellie and Sarah tended, was a "typical Irish stone farmhouse with thick whitewashed walls, two rooms and a large fireplace." There were also French, Italian, German, Polish, Lithuanian, Russian, and Scandinavian houses, reflecting the origins of the Waterbury population.[35] Sarah Doyle was also politically active and loyally attended meetings of the local Democratic party, in winter dressed in her muskrat coat. She was a fervent FDR supporter (Stuart was an equally fervent detractor) and on talking terms with the politicians in the Democratic city administration, several of whom went off to prison at the end of the decade, much to her dismay.

There were intimations of the future that summer. Stuart reported a prescient conversation with a "down-hearted" supporter of the League of Nations in Waterbury. As it became clear that the League could not stop Mussolini from invading Ethiopia, that "as a realist one cannot but realize that if the League cannot effectively stop the war . . . it is all done. He feels that *unless* Italy is stopped in some way by world opinion goodness knows where the conflagration will end."[36] It would take four summers to prove

---

35. "Handbook Number Four: The Connecticut Tercentenary in Waterbury" (Waterbury, Conn.: Mattatuck Historical Society, 1937), 13, 19, 20, Leaflets & Pamphlets, box 1, Research Collection, Mattatuck Museum.

36. Chase Kimball, as reported in SEJ, in Waterbury, to CHWG, in Gothenburg, 16 Aug. 1935. Chase Kimball was a lawyer, the son of the deceased former editor of the *Waterbury Republican*. In 1936 his office was at 193 Grand, his home at 179 Grove. *Waterbury City Directory* (1936).

this man right, and no one could have dreamed of the extent of the conflagration that he foretold.

From Finland Carrie and her companions made a three-day visit to Leningrad. While some had made such a journey and came away thinking that the shape of the future stamped on the Russian population by Lenin and Stalin "worked," Carrie could not agree. In a few sentences she conveyed the perplexing facts:

> Cannot describe my sensations on reaching Leningrad. Crowds of depressing type of peasants. Very disagreeable time trying to get our reservations at Astoria Hotel. Huge Physiological Congress in progress—making everything over crowded and confusing.
>
> The hotel was a wreck of former luxury. Dirty and shabby. Leningrad is the most beautiful city I have ever seen. Magnificent monuments of its past splendor on all sides—unusually wide streets and large squares. And all an incongruous background for the sad, dirty people—it seemed unreal and bewildering. Many groups of children playing happily in Peterhof park and in places of Rest & Recreation. Large groups of people being taken through palaces and Hermitage art galleries by guides lecturing.
>
> Evidence of attempts at education and welfare work and no doubt a great deal has been accomplished already and much is in development. But the general effect to the casual observer is depressing. Impossible for me to *think out* a situation so foreign to an old fashioned New England woman. The future will tell![37]

Their friends told the Leningrad party that they "looked ten years older than when we parted five days earlier." The future took fifty years to mature its story; this New England woman saw the situation more clearly than many others at the time.

In Waterbury

Stuart looked for a house for the family that summer. He was frustrated by the collapse of a handshake agreement for one at $100 per month. He reacted bitterly that the Depression had taught him not to trust the words even of a "gentleman": "In view of what the government has done to money, I am not sure what good any contract is—even when signed." Nina far more than Carrie was feeling the pinch, and he reported she had

---

37. CHWG, Travel Diary, 1935.

101. Lucy Burrall, Edith Chase, Mary Burrall, and Carrie in Finland, 1935

been forced to rent her beloved house at the shore that summer.[38] However, he saw a silver lining—"a very fine rise in the stock market which apparently is foreshadowing better business which means extra or increased dividends and a better living for brokers. And this time it is laid on such a broad and sound base that it ought not to come a bad cropper for quite a while."[39] The dawn of a "broad and sound base" would, however, be five years in coming.

That fall Stuart was successful in finding a house for the family, and it backed onto the driveway of 54 Hillside, making it a short and safe walk for the boys to the kitchen door and the welcomes of Sarah, Nellie, and Katie. The grounds made a parklike space for sledding in the winter and hide-and-seek at other seasons. For Carol it meant that her mother was only a few steps away, which, though, did not encourage the independence that Carrie had been pleased to see in her absence abroad—Stuart told me much later that Carol consulted her mother before every household decision. Carrie's house did also provide Carol a refuge from the often raucous and contentious society of small boys.

38. SEJ, in Waterbury, to CHWG, in Sweden, 10 July 1935.

39. SEJ, in Waterbury, to CHWG, in Gothenburg, 16 Aug. 1935.

For a child the wonders of the great house at 54 Hillside, whose nooks and crannies and objects were already familiar from almost a year living there, were a few skips away. At the back door there were Nellie and Katie to talk to, perhaps a word of sagacity from Frank Ray. Within there was the sound of the Electrolux accompanied by Sarah's wordless singing above it, "did, di, dee, di, di dee." In the early mornings there would be a visit to Carrie in her bedroom while she was dressing, perhaps accompanied by a stick of Beech-Nut gum. The third-floor playroom had Haring's books and curious objects—a mortarboard cap, the brass insignia of his fraternity, and a wooden fox head with a pipe in its mouth and cap that, when lifted, revealed a tobacco jar. With the mysterious attic full of trunks with curving tops, and medical equipment (for Rob), an out-of-tune upright piano, and Carol's dollhouse, it was an inexhaustible playroom for rainy days. The grounds became our outdoor play space, and soon we had a playhouse and a jungle gym. In the winter there was spectacular sledding down Devil's Hill, used by dozens of neighborhood children, leading from an oak tree down the hill across Mr. Goss's property.

For children this spaciousness meant freedom from adult supervision and a world that could be explored on one's own terms. It was full of echoes of the past in its objects and pictures. In two years Bobby would build a house where the carriage house stood, about the same distance from 54 Hillside, and soon he and Ann had three daughters, first cousins and playmates for the Judd boys. Through happenstance and opportunity a family compound had been created.

The house at 111 Buckingham Street that Stuart rented was one of a pair built in 1919 by Carrie's neighbor, John Goss, in red brick with cream-colored wood trim to complement the bricks used in his Tudor-style 1902 mansion, and they provided "excellent background for the grand baroque houses on Hillside."[40] The twin houses were built for his daughters; they faced each other, not the street, and a common pathway led through an arbor at one end to the street and at the other to the driveway to 54 Hillside.

Carrie's and her daughter's households were on intimate relations with each other: comings and goings of the occupants were visible to both—the characteristic tread of Stuart coming home from work in his shoes with leather heels reinforced with metal at one corner, which made decisive taps in his brisk stride, became a familiar and anticipated sound of childhood at

---

40. "The Hillside, Waterbury, Connecticut."

the end of each day. In five years, when the twin at 103 Buckingham became available, Stuart bought it, and the family—then without Carol—moved across the pathway.

The house at 111 was a comfortable place, with four bedrooms and no less than eight other rooms—large by any standards, though modest compared to its Hillside neighbors.[41] Its generous space included an attic, bedrooms for each of the children and for a nurse, a dressing room off the master bedroom, a basement with a coal-fired boiler, coal storage, and laundry room, and porches on two floors. There was no mystery in the house, as there was in 54 Hillside, with its laundry chute and dark recesses. By contrast 111 conveyed solidity and permanence in its hardwood trim within and brick exterior.

The master bedroom had south-facing windows and its own porch; inside it had a fireplace, an adjoining bathroom, and a dressing room, where Stuart kept neatly packed woodworking tools in a lower drawer. In one of the twin beds, the cook of the time (there was a changing cast) brought Carol breakfast on a bed tray, on a set of china specially made for this service, the eggs covered with a domed warmer. This was Carrie's practice too, but in a much larger establishment. Carol did not get up with the family; we had our breakfast and were often off to school before she arose. Through depression or the assumptions she had acquired as Carrie's daughter, she denied herself an active role in the household.

The living room was furnished with a stiff upright sofa, a comfortable wing-backed chair, a round table with a lamp, and a patterned rug. There was a radio in a cabinet in a corner. Unforgettable sounds came from it one day in a high-pitched foreign tongue. It was scary even though at age five I knew nothing of Hitler but the name. The radio station was WOR, which I then associated with war. On the walls there was a Piranesi print of the ruins of a temple and its surroundings, the sole human a shepherd resting on his crook.

There was a library with shelves of stained oak and a large bay window overlooking Miss Florentine Hayden's kitchen and flower garden, where she could often be seen in a floppy straw hat supervising Maurice, the gardener.[42] The shelves were filled with books, including a curious mix of

---

41. Assessors' Records, 235-546-13, City Hall, City of Waterbury, Conn.

42. Florentine Hayden, the unmarried descendant of a pioneer Waterbury button manufacturer, lived at 146 Pine St., a house in the Arts and Crafts style, using "oversize bricks with raked joints." "The Hillside, Waterbury, Connecticut."

102. Carol with Peter and Stuart Jr. ("Tui") at
111 Buckingham Street, Christmas 1936

uniformly bound sets: Thackeray, Anatole France, Hugh Walpole, James
Branch Cabell, and Winston Churchill (the American novelist). Stuart's
first editions of Edwin Arlington Robinson and Walter de la Mare were
slim volumes. When I expressed a wish to read one of a set, possibly the
Thackeray, Carol dissuaded me, as it had "too much description." One
shelf held small ship models that Stuart had made with the finest of the
tools in the dressing room drawer, among them a Chinese junk and a
"China Clipper."

Perhaps it was the strain of dealing with the household that triggered a
recurrence of Carol's psychosis within a few months of the move. Again
she was isolated from her family, given "those horrid wet packs which I
have been having two hours daily and simply loathed." After about six
months of isolation and treatment she returned to a normal condition.
This time she was in the care of Dr. Edward Jackson, a Waterbury psychiatrist, whose sanatorium for a small number of patients—perhaps only
Carol at times—was in a rented house in the village of Washington, about

three quarters of an hour drive from Waterbury.[43] She was looked after by nurses who, as she improved, became her companions, walking and riding with her. "I finished [knitting] a simple bed-jacket and am now well along on a sweater," Carol wrote her mother.

> Mildred Stevens [a nurse] is a wonderful knitter. She made a stunning coat for herself. We all get along very well together and really have rather fun at times. We get rough-housing like boarding-school girls when it is bed-time. It really is surprising that I can endure them after the fiendish things they used to do to me. I used to despise Miss Stevens but think she is a peach now under her somewhat gruff exterior.[44]

Carol looked forward to driving with her when she and Miss Weber, the other nurse, acquired a car. The steps toward recovery were touchingly simple, childlike, and reveal how long she had been incarcerated. "After supper at night we either read, knit, or play some game, soon I am going to be allowed to go the Movies. Today was the first time I have been in a store for almost four months. I purchased this pad." Stuart had been for a visit—the first he was allowed in the four months—but Carol had not seen her boys and would not for some time, in keeping with the then typical procedure of isolating the mentally ill from family. "Dr. Jackson won't let me telephone yet which seems strange as I am as well as I have ever been." She concluded her letter wistfully, "Love to my Judds."

After an interval determined by Dr. Jackson, Carol returned to the family at 111 Buckingham.

The next winter Stuart rented a house for the family in Hobe Sound, north of Palm Beach, a wintering place for rich northerners, but then quite simple and served only by a drugstore and a small market. The gas station was on the other side of a mile-long causeway. The wood frame house was on a lot shaded by palms, and, as Stuart wrote Carrie, with bougainvilleas, hibiscus, and poinsettia in bloom, ripe grapefruit to be picked off the trees, and the yard animated by rabbits at twilight. All of this—and the gas sta-

---

43. Edward J. Jackson had an office at 16 Center St., Waterbury, and a home in Middlebury with his wife, Florence. He is listed as "physician," but it is certainly he who had the sanatorium. It was probably not accepted in Waterbury at that time to term oneself a psychiatrist. *Waterbury City Directory* (1936).

44. CGJ, at Dr. Jackson's Sanitarium, Washington, Conn., to CHWG, in Waterbury, 10 June 1936.

tion, which had the added attraction of "Wild Bill's Animal Farm"—delighted the boys. Carol, who had been in a rocky state after her illness, enjoyed it too. "Was I surprised! and was I happy!" Stuart wrote his mother-in-law, "Carol *really* liked Hobe Sound and also the house I picked out! Believe me I heaved a big sigh when we got here and the place 'clicked.' I was holding my breath every minute."[45] The house was called "The Anchorage," and the rental must have been at Depression-level prices. The stock market had risen from its low point and had done well in 1936, which undoubtedly gave Stuart the extra money he needed for the rental and the boat fares from and to New York (which included shipping Carol's tan Chevrolet).

The "Anchorage" was a short walk to a club overlooking an estuary where the rich and famous arrived in their boats. On one occasion I was shoved forth by my nurse to greet a tall man in white shirt and pants and told to say, "Hello, Gary." Only years later did I realize that I was addressing the future sheriff in *High Noon*.

The Depression was about to deepen, and the stock market again dropped sharply. It had looked as though the nation was climbing out of the trough, and the market had climbed from its low in 1933 to levels in 1936 and most of 1937 double and even triple the low. This steady climb in the broader market could only have been helpful to the family finances and to Stuart's investment business. However, it came to an abrupt halt in late 1937, when the market dropped sharply. The Dow was 30 percent lower at year's end than at the beginning. It was a grim time for an investor—as it was for most everyone else. Despite the efforts of the New Deal, no end to the Depression seemed in prospect.

Carrie's life changed after the Hobe Sound winter as a consequence of the Depression. The full complement of staff, which had lasted so long, could no longer be supported. Sometime in 1938 Nellie and Katie went to other domestic jobs. The Pierce-Arrow was sold to a black church for the minister, and La Chance retired ill and soon died of cancer. I remember going with Carrie to visit an ill-looking man seated in a chair in an open shirt collar—I had only seen La Chance in his uniform. Sarah Doyle stayed on in the great house, cooking as vigorously as she cleaned. As she loved walking, Carrie was not greatly inconvenienced without a car.

---

45. Ibid.

I began school in the junior division of the same St. Margaret's that Carol had attended and Carrie before her (the junior school relocated to a new building on Columbia Boulevard). I moved to public school for first grade and was taught to read by Miss McMahon, who had taught Stuart at the same age. Driggs School was representative of the neighborhood grammar school that then existed throughout U.S. cities. All the children walked to and from school, were assigned a fixed desk in class, sat up straight in their chairs, dressed especially for school, and were (or were made to be) respectful of the teacher. In Miss McMahon's class the children learned from writings and illustrations on rollers that she pulled down. I learned the letter "a" by "Rain, rain, go away, come again some other day." Within a few days I discovered that reading was easy and fun.

At home we were unruly, a changing cast of nursemaids no match for what Stuart called "young hellions." One evening in what was probably 1938 Stuart gathered Carol and us in the book-lined study, the windows black from the night outside, the door closed against eavesdropping by the cook—it was a formal family conference. He told us that he had asked Edna Close, our nurse during the Hobe Sound stay in 1935, to return to Waterbury and take over our supervision. Carol protested that "she is too strict and she cries all the time," and I instinctively took her side. But the decision had been made. Stuart took over the direction of the household, which he apparently considered Carol unable to manage. It set the stage for what was to happen later.

Edna put into effect an orderly, predictable regime. Meals were on a regular schedule, and we were not excused from the table until after dessert and all plates had been cleared. The only radio programs allowed were from 4 to 5 and 7 to 8 P.M. (Saturdays and Sundays excepted). There were set bedtimes with a half hour added at birthdays. Edna was judge as well as rule-maker, not easy with Tui's violent temper. With her late risings, we often did not see Carol until nightfall.

Edna's sense of organization co-existed with emotional instability. One day my seven-year-old self watched from my bedroom window Edna unconscious in a stretcher being carried to a waiting ambulance. In retrospect, I believe she had taken an overdose of sleeping pills, perhaps an appeal for Stuart's attention. In later years she would have severe psychotic episodes.

This curious, stressed, and divided household was short-lived. One of our neighbors was Dr. John S. Dye, Mary White's brother-in-law and a popular surgeon in Waterbury. He lived in the Queen Anne house next to John Goss's Tudor mansion, which shared the same driveway as 54 Hillside Avenue. His appearance delighted children playing in the driveway as he stopped his car, rolled down the window, and with his surgeon's dexterity convincingly extracted a Chiclet from behind the ear of each child. In mid-1939 Dr. Dye removed a malignant tumor from Carol's breast.

Carol

In February of 1940, about four months after the operation, the trunks that Carol and Stuart had packed for their honeymoon trip to Bermuda stood ready in the bedroom. One day I heard voices from my room down the hallway, and for a reason she did not reveal, Edna brought us to the rear of the house, away from the master bedroom. From the window I saw an ambulance beneath the streetlight, and shortly two men appeared with Carol on a stretcher. Edna pulled us from the window, telling us she might cry if we waved to her. It seemed strange, but Carol had been away before, and the order of the household continued with no discussion of what had happened or what was wrong. On a Saturday some days later, I was taken for a drive with Mary and Lucy Burrall. At Waterbury Hospital, Mary went in to deliver a thermos of soup, but I was told not to come because Carol might cry if she saw me. It seemed strange, but I did not question. I liked Auntie Lucy and was content to have a conversation with her as we waited.

Early one Saturday morning—probably a week later—at an hour when Stuart was usually at home, his bed was empty and his car was gone. I noticed that Uncle Bob Griggs's car also was not in its usual place. Neither Edna nor the cook could explain where they were. When Stuart returned for lunch I charged him with being "naughty." During the afternoon an unusual visitor arrived, Dr. Foster, whom I knew as Carrie's physician. Stuart closed the door of the library for their conversation. Tui and I had supper as usual and played in the living room while Stuart and Edna had their dinner in the dining room, talking quietly. A childhood ritual was prayers at bedtime, attended usually by Stuart. This night he brought Tui into my room, both of us in pajamas and bathrobes. He told us abruptly, "God has decided to take mommy to heaven." "You mean she has died?" I said, resolving then and there not to cry.

Stuart and Uncle Bob had been away in the morning, to be with Carol when she died. The news was a total surprise; only in retrospect did the

103. Carol in 1939, a few months before her death

prohibition not to wave at her from the back window, not to be allowed to visit her in the hospital portend what was to come. During the night I awoke from a nightmare, surprised to see Stuart sitting nearby.

The last time I saw Carol was a few days before she was taken to the hospital. She was visiting Carrie at teatime. She was short-tempered and sharp with me, and I decided to steer clear until there was a change, not difficult because the children's household ran on its own schedule. That cannot have been more than two or three days before she was carried from the house.

We boys were kept at home the day of the funeral at St. John's. Betty White remembers the thick, wet snow from the night before that bowed the trees over the Breakneck driveway. Its presence in the city and at the gravesite no doubt matched the gloom that the mourners felt. Stuart told me when he returned that Carol, "looked lovely in a pink dress." She was buried in the plot that George E. Judd had established in Riverside Cemetery. It was many years before I dared to visit the long flat limestone that covered the grave, unique in a plot of upright granite pieces with shiny surfaces.

Fate had created a harsh destiny for the bouncy young woman who had been the wit of the Rawson tour and who so enjoyed the Westover art and history lessons. In a later generation her mental illness could have been alleviated greatly by drugs, and at the time psychiatric counseling could have given her some comfort. Yet there had been some mitigation. It was not in the cards that the young woman who returned from Dr. Slocum's would marry, but she did. She enjoyed doing things with Stuart and had children, and did, indeed, love them.

The child who learned at bedtime that his mother had died faced a cataclysm so mysterious and imponderable that the best course seemed to be keep it to oneself. He could never have expressed what he had lost. Beyond affection, stimulation, and support, there was something else I could never have thought of at the time—Carol's was the closest link to Julia, to James Demarest and Caroline Eliza, to Aunt Kate, Samuel and Sarah, to John and Mary Haring and cousins, uncles and aunts.

In her front-row pew at St. John's at Carol's funeral, Carrie may have thought back to when her family seemed like fortune's favorites—the handsome husband, handsome sons and daughter as they had been on that postwar visit to Paris. In less than twenty years Rob was gone, financial opulence had turned to comfort, Haring had left wife and child and was living on his mother's allowance with no discernible occupation. Carol, with her terrible mental troubles and fast-moving cancer, was the figure in the coffin. Dr. Lewis, who had known Carol from his years as chaplain at Westover and had married her, conducted the service and read from the lectern that Jane Amelia White had given in memory of her prematurely dead son two generations before. When Carrie went home after the burial she was alone with Sarah. There was no reception there or at the Judd house.

Carrie must have wondered what went wrong, what she could have done differently. Could she have made her children less dependent on her? Should she have used a firmer hand? None of that would have saved Carol her most serious troubles, which had a genetic origin, but what about Haring? Had she thrown too much of herself at this firstborn, built him up with her hopes, unwittingly made him too dependent on her, turned his head with excess attention? Rob had immersed himself in business, leaving Carrie to invest in her handsome, apparently scholarly boy what was not fulfilled in her marital relations.

As it happens, the mother who indulges a wastrel or over-dependent son is as familiar in life as in literature. At Cambridge and in his teaching at Trinity, Haring had taken a path that promised to lead him beyond the business interests of Waterbury. This promise was dashed in quick order by his drinking and his marital breakup. Perhaps, without analyzing the situation in this way, Carrie felt guilty. For this reason she never could cut off his allowance, and she took extra care to provide for him and his children at her death. She was probably unaware that this was a factor that wreaked psychic havoc in Bobby, whom she took for granted, but in whom a savage bitterness about his brother welled up in later life.

Perhaps she had "spoiled" this favorite son. Perhaps Rob, with his caustic wit, and concentration on moneymaking, had been a poor influence. The cultural and social changes of the time must of course had an impact on Haring. Youth was beckoned by a looser morality, and fast living was urged by the automobile and the free use of alcohol. Furthermore, belief in the new and modern were widespread as were disdain for the values of the social order that seemed to have perished in the years of the Great War.

The Victorian culture in which Carrie was raised was shattered in the twenties. Certainly, though, the new order was already building a prison of its own, and the quest for self-expression by those not talented or tough enough to create new forms became as strong a trap for the incautious young as the one they were trying to flee.

Carrie held her grief within; she did not allow herself tears or lamentation—at least not in my presence, then or later. In the nearly thirty years that remained to her, she accepted without bitterness what the fates had dealt. And she was grateful for what she had in material comfort, friends, and family. Betty White commented how much more open, warm, and amusing she was in these later years than she had been as Rob's wife and when preoccupied by her children's problems in the 1930s. She found a ready wit and a source of laughter. Her response could have been quite different—she might have retreated into a shell of mournful dignity. The sturdy character whom George had admired in the home and on whom

Julia depended, knew that she could not dwell on her sorrows. She gave her grandchildren a sense of continuity with the past, provided them an example of poise in old age, and maintained in her house the center of family life.

Quiet Years

Carrie was, as she would term it, a person of sentiment, who cherished the memory of her parents and grandparents and of the past she had learned from Julia. The Haring grandparents who died seven years before she was born were present in their oval frames in the hallway. Samuel and Sarah Haring's serving spoons were in the front parlor cabinet along with the earrings that Great-grandmother Eliza Ayres Phelps's wore in her 1825 marriage portrait and the lockets with the indistinct photos of Clinton Haring and Joseph Egbert Gates that Kate had given Julia. This seems to imply that the house was a shrine, and that Carrie's later life had a Miss Havisham-like quality in which the past overwhelmed the present. Not so. While she remained the reserved and dignified lady she was brought up to be, she kept up with books—particularly memoirs—kept informed on current events through the *Herald Tribune* (Walter Lippmann was a favorite columnist), radio commentary (Lowell Thomas and H. V. Kaltenborn) and, later, television news. Just as we watched the news with Huntley-Brinkley in the parlor seated on chairs in the style of Louis XV, so the present co-existed with the past in Carrie's house.

It was then the custom for children to be put to bed for sore throats, colds, and the routinely expected childhood diseases of measles, mumps, chicken pox, and whooping cough. The convalescent sick did have some enjoyable experiences—listening to the daytime breakfast shows and soap operas, for example.[46] But the best possible medicine was a visit from Carrie, who would come for an hour or so of reading. Sometimes she read from one the *Oz* books, which I (and probably she) knew virtually by heart. In the *Picturesque Tale of Progress* volumes (which began with *Neanderthal Man* and went to the *European Middle Ages*), she would laugh at the

---

46. My favorite, because the title promised (but usually did not deliver) an event about the theater, was *Mary Noble, Backstage Wife*. The protagonist was "married to Larry Noble, matinee idol of a million other women." One had to be sick in bed to hear about Mary's ordeals, broadcast in mid-afternoon, during school hours.

Egyptian names as she read of the Dynasties and the terrifying Ramses II, who was then my favorite Pharaoh. Her silvery voice did well, too, with the "quoth he's" and "forsooth's" of Howard Pyle's *King Arthur* books, whose ornate language amused her even as it impressed me. She would place her hand on my brow to check my temperature, and never was a hand so cool, so soothing. She did indeed seem like one who had come from a different place and time.

In her sixties and seventies she seemed not to age between one college vacation and another. She was silver-haired then, with a voice and diction of great clarity, and always curious and interested in the friends I brought. (In her eighties she lost most of this beautiful hair and for a time wore a wig.) She would laugh at herself when she was somewhat heavy that a car sprang up from one side when she got out of it. At Christmas, when it seemed that every grandchild had given her soap, she would laugh that they must think she did not keep clean.

Wartime destruction in Europe preoccupied Carrie. The Winter War between the Finns and Soviets was underway during Carol's final illness—she, like many in America at the time, sent donations and hoped against the odds that the heroic ski fighters of the Finland she had so admired in 1935 would repel the Soviets. After the inconceivable fall of France later that year, she was inspired by Winston Churchill's defiance, supported American aid and donated money and clothing to "Bundles for Britain." When the tide turned and my boyish imagination thrilled at the great air raids over Germany, the invasions at Anzio, Salerno, and Normandy as events that showed we were winning, Carrie would tell me solemnly of the beauty that was being destroyed. She recognized with horror that what had meant to so much to her, to Julia, and to Carol was being ground to rubble. She rejoiced that Rome and Paris were spared.

During the war she moved for a time to a small modern colonial house, deemed more sensible with wartime shortages. At war's end, urged by her grandchildren (who had no idea of the labor and money it took to maintain 54 Hillside), she returned home at the age of seventy and remained there for the rest of her life. Sarah Doyle cleaned and dusted, prepared the meals, and talked and often argued with Carrie—all done with equal vigor—until she retired to a house she had bought with her savings. A quiet Scottish widow came to take her place. Stuart moved to the country from Waterbury in 1950. The center of the family remained Carrie at 54 Hillside.

104. Carrie on her eightieth birthday, 10 April 1965. In the living room at 54 Hillside with Elizabeth Wade White (above) and with Peter Haring Judd (below).

XIII

AN ENDING

The family's involvement in Waterbury manufacturing continued as Stuart took the position of works manager at the Mattatuck and lasted until 1963, when, in awkward circumstances, the plant was sold. In the intervening years Stuart became the sole owner, fulfilling his ambition to exercise his talents as the boss and linking his fate with that of the factory. In the good years, through the early 1950s, he built a small fortune for himself in a profit-making business. He enjoyed the prestige that came with being president and owner of the company, which allowed him to serve on influential charitable boards. The financial fruits permitted vacations in warm climates, a comfortable standard of living, and his sons' educations. However, behind the success of the early years was a strained second marriage, whose stresses grew as the Mattatuck's position deteriorated.

In his prime, the serious young man who had been inspired to go from Yale to the newly-founded Harvard Business School, the diligent husband and father, and the man who had once sung tenor under Koussevitsky, who loved Edwin Arlington Robinson's poems—this man became trapped. The changes in the industrial economy and the caprice of labor-management relations were formidable obstacles, and the social and personal barrenness of his life in the later 1950s was no help. Character is fate too, and a modicum of brutality might have helped him make the wrenching decisions that would have cut his personal and business losses and remain standing. The countervailing circumstances were too much, however, and the trap sprung, literally maiming him. The personal and business circumstances are intertwined.

After Carol's death Edna's presence gave continuity to the household, and she became part of the family. She ate with Stuart in the dining room, accompanied him and the boys on Christmas and Easter visits to New York, to Naples and Miami Beach, Florida, for winter vacations, and in late summer to the Crawford House in the White Mountains to avoid exposure to polio in the cities.

105. Stuart Edwards Judd, about 1939

Despite Edna's intimacy with the family, Stuart's announcement of their marriage in a telegram sent to Tui and me at camp in early July 1944 was a surprise. "Marrying Sam has hitched us," the message read, using a reference to a character in the *Lil' Abner* comic strip to give the news a cheerful informality. It is easy to see Stuart's motivation. It was wartime, and with long hours at the plant, he needed to come home to an orderly household. Their wedding was in New Hampshire and involved none of Stuart's friends and colleagues, none of the Griggs and White cousins, and Tui and I were at camp. Only Edna's relatives attended. Betty White maintained that Stuart had "run away," and by not marrying Edna in front of family and associates in Waterbury put her in an ambiguous position as his wife. In the Buckingham Street house to which they returned—after Carol's death he had bought the twin house across the way—they continued to live in close proximity to the two grandmothers, neither of whom approved of the marriage—Nina by frequent innuendo, Carrie with judicious reserve. Edna had little chance to create a social position of her own as Stuart's wife and eventually cracked under the strain.

In spring 1949 Stuart made an unexpected visit to me one evening in my dorm at boarding school to tell me that Edna had experienced psychotic episodes and had been taken to the Institute for Living in Hartford. There she remained under a legal commitment order for a year and was given electric shock treatments, which she bitterly resented. Stuart once again found himself responsible for a mentally unstable spouse who then and later required major psychiatric intervention.

Upon the advice of Edna's doctor, he sold the Buckingham Street house and bought an eighteenth-century farmhouse in Woodbury, about forty-five minutes west of Waterbury, then only just beginning to be a dormitory suburb. He was delighted with the move—"cities are obsolete" became an oft-repeated refrain. Like most of the other owners of Waterbury factories, he now lived at a remove from the city where the industries had their origin.

The Woodbury house was a pleasantly musty version of a farmhouse that had been altered many times. When Edna returned, she banished the must and opened up the rear of the house with a great picture window. Stuart intended the house to be the setting for her developing a social identity of her own. To acquire friends of a compatible social circle, he joined the Mystic Order of the Shrine, in which Edna's brother was prominent, and they vacationed in luxury hotels in the Caribbean and in Miami Beach, where she could meet people out of the Waterbury context. They both had expensive cars to indicate their wealth. Stuart had no sports like golf or tennis to put him in the company of other social elites in Waterbury. Although he kept in touch with Carrie, he became cut off from the Waterbury social setting in which he grew up, and he did not embrace a new one except as a marital duty.

The change in residence and the different social milieu did not cure Edna. In 1954 Stuart took a week off from work to drive Edna to Texas to spend time with a niece: "I feel this will do the trick and stabilize her again, and I am hoping hereafter to take her off on a long weekend more often so the tensions don't build up to such an explosive point."[1] Three months later he reported, "She wants to live alone and not have anything to do with me." She bought land a few hundred yards down the road and asked him to build a house for her. "She asked me to move out of our room, so I am sleeping in your room." "The plan is that she will live in her new house for a year and at the end of that time will inform me whether she will come back or will part for good!"[2]

---

1. Stuart Edwards Judd, in Woodbury, Conn., to Peter Haring Judd, c/o Chase National Bank, London, 17 Sept. 1954.

2. SEJ, at the Sheraton Astor Hotel, Times Square, New York City, to PHJ, at Magdalen College, Oxford, 1 March 1955.

The way I look at it, maybe it is really all for the best. She does not come from the same background of upbringing, that I do, and maybe the tensions of being Mrs. S. E. Judd are subconsciously greater than she can stand without breaking under it. It is a real outlet for her—a place all her own, no one to account to, no one to imply that she ought to be doing such and such, etc. She and Tui fight continually, and he can be awfully nasty . . . I would rather have her escape to a place a quarter of a mile away than to crack up again ($1000 per week) or go kiting off goodness knows where.[3]

After about five years of declining health, accompanied by what the death certificate termed "cerebral softening," Nina Cowles Judd died at home in January 1955.[4] Stuart wrote me that she "went rapidly when she went, thank goodness, and we gave her the kind of funeral she had asked for, lots of flowers, pink ones, open casket, etc."[5] In a period of truce, he and Edna cleared out the both the Waterbury and Pine Orchard houses. With the level of accumulation that Nina achieved, their instinct was to simply throw out everything, and this they did, as the Woodbury house could only hold so much. If there were clues to Samuel Cowles and her mother's Coley family, and letters from George Judd, they went to the trash collector along with piles of *Good Housekeeping* and *Colliers*. Stuart inherited her Mattatuck shares and became the sole owner in name as well as in fact, as she had always followed his lead.

When Edna's house was completed, she "got a moving van and moved out of this house into her own . . . She took all the best things in this house with her, and what was amazing to me, all of Grammie Judd's [Nina's] best china, knickknacks, chairs, etc. After the things she said about G. J. when she was alive I don't see how she could enjoy using the things."[6] Stuart's toleration—"appeasement" was the word he used—was not helpful, and three months later Edna again had psychotic episodes, briefly alleviated by the new drug Thorazine, prescribed when Stuart, with great effort, persuaded her to see a psychiatrist.[7] In September 1955, however, she took

3. Ibid.

4. Death Certificates, January–April 1955, Office of Vital Statistics, City of Waterbury, New Haven Co., Conn.

5. SEJ, at 37 Hillside Ave., Waterbury, Conn., to PHJ, at Magdalen College, 13 Feb. 1955.

6. SEJ, in Woodbury, to PHJ, c/o Chase National Bank, London, 26 June 1955.

7. SEJ, in Woodbury, to PHJ, in Chaldon Herring, Dorset, 25 July 1955.

"about 10 Seconal tablets, then phoned me." Stuart rushed from work and took her to the hospital where she was pumped out.[8]

In October she escaped briefly from the sanatorium where she was being cared for, but then was legally committed. "It was a difficult decision for me, but I felt I should follow the advice of the medical men and *six* were in agreement so I thought that many could not be wrong . . . She is fighting them every inch of the way . . . She is now madder than a hornet and is all through with me. I believe she has written you about getting a divorce, etc. I wish she meant it."[9]

In late November Stuart went to the Yale-Harvard game in New Haven, where it snowed heavily. He drove back alone in his Lincoln and on a country stretch

> hit an icy part of the road coming around a corner, skidded, tried to get out the way of an on-coming station wagon by going down a side road, didn't make it, got up on a bank alongside the side road—which flipped me over on the road landing top down and wheels to the sky! Luckily I had been travelling with the window in the door open or they would have had to get me out with a torch because both doors were jammed closed and the top was squashed down almost on the top of the seats.[10]

This near-fatal accident was another of the lurid events of the months that followed Edna's stripping of the house of its furniture. In Stuart's professional life a strike threatened, and he was involved in a bitter dispute with his most able assistant at the Mattatuck.

Stuart flew to London for the Christmas holidays 1955–56 where, after an academic year at Oxford, I was awaiting induction into the U.S. Army. Stuart was then fifty-four, energized by his recent decisions at the factory and, so it seemed, by surviving the car accident. He was full of confidence, and in our talks he expanded upon the possibilities for good in technological developments in prospect. He looked like a man enjoying the prime of life. He told me of his confidence that the union would soon settle, that the "cleaned house" at the Mattatuck would put the business back on track, and that divorce would mean a new start. His charitable work with mental health

---

8. SEJ, in Woodbury, to PHJ, at the Adria Hotel, Queens Gate, London, 11 Sept. 1955. The sanatorium was Elmcrest Manor, in Portland, Conn.

9. SEJ, in Woodbury, to PHJ, Woodfall St., London, 30 Oct. 1955.

10. SEJ, in Woodbury, to PHJ, Woodfall St., London, 29 Nov. 1955.

agencies continued to involve him, and during his stay we visited a home for the elderly mentally ill in a former country house, an example of a humane and small-scale facility that could be useful in Connecticut. (He served on the board of the National Association of Mental Health, and later would be its chairman, bringing him to New York City a day and a night a week.)[11]

He was stimulated by my decision to end my student deferment. "I wish I could have learned to stand on my own two feet and make my own decisions after full consideration of but without the dominance of any one else's reasoning as young as you are starting to learn it," he wrote me. "My ability to do it has come far later in life and with far more tragic consequences."[12] We celebrated Christmas Day that year in Stuart's suite in Brown's Hotel.

Stuart's divorce took three years of acrimony and suspicion to be negotiated. Edna received the house Stuart had built for her, a lump sum of $60,000, and $25,000 per year.[13] It seemed like the end to a sordid story.

"I am among people who are my friends and whom I can trust," Stuart wrote me from a cabin at a Connecticut lake, where, in the midst of the divorce battle, he stayed with a bookkeeper in the Mattatuck office, her husband, and a friend. "I am having a pleasant time and getting a much needed rest free from tensions and living outdoors most of the time."[14] These friends became his closest supporters in the struggle to keep the Mattatuck alive.

---

11. The National Association of Mental Health (NAMH) was formed in 1950 from the merger of the nation's three leading voluntary organizations in this field—the National Organization for Mental Hygiene, the National Mental Health Foundation, and the Psychiatric Foundation. Its purpose was to survey conditions in the field and to encourage appropriate funding for and attention to mental health. "Three Groups Join in Mental Health," *NYT*, 14 Sept. 1950, 33:1; "Huge Tasks Noted in Mental Health," *NYT*, 20 Nov. 1951, 51:1; Howard A. Rusk, M.D., "Research in Mental Illness Has Paid a Striking Dividend," with a report on the annual meeting of the NAMH, *NYT*, 31 Oct. 1954, 52:1.

12. SEJ, in Woodbury, to PHJ, c/o Chase National Bank, London, 13 Oct. 1955.

13. Stuart outlined the terms in a September letter. The divorce was effective on 14 Feb. 1958. SEJ, in Woodbury, to PHJ, at 3021 Cambridge Place, Washington, D.C., Sept. 1957; SEJ, at the Mattatuck Manufacturing Co., Waterbury, to PHJ, at General Delivery, Ft. Myers, Fl., 22 Feb. 1958.

14. SEJ, at Bantam Lake, Conn., to PHJ, at 3021 Cambridge Place, Washington, D.C., July 1957. These friends were Doris and Francis Kreiger of Wolcott, Conn., and Susan Bassett, who became the manager of Arrowhead.

The Mattatuck

Stuart had closed Stuart E. Judd Co., Investments, and gone to work in the Mattatuck in 1938. He could not then make a living in investments, and he doubtless felt the first priority was to shore up his and his mother's stake in the factory. It was still run by William Fielding, a hard-boiled manager who ruled by fiat from a front office with a closed door, using a buzzer to summon staff, whom he dealt with in a gravelly voice. *Fortune* magazine at the time ran advertisements showing managers pounding on desks demanding answers. Billy Fielding fitted that mold. He rarely visited the factory floor; some workers had probably never seen him. The superintendent ran the shop like a fiefdom, and in those non-union days an aggrieved employee had no recourse. However, Fielding had guided the firm through the bad times and maintained jobs for several hundred employees. There were small profits in most years of the 1930s, but a large loss in 1938, when the stock market also took a dive. It seemed as if the Depression would never end.

Stuart came on as works manager, but despite the position and the shares he represented, he worked under Fielding—who was supported by the Wade interest—and it took some years before he could fire the superintendent whose autocratic behavior he considered "crooked." (The man became a figure of evil at home, and the first question I asked Stuart when he came when he came home each evening was if he had fired him. It took months.) In 1941 Stuart was elected secretary and treasurer, which solidified his position. He had set his sights on buying out the Wades and having full authority over the operation.[15]

The timing for Stuart's involvement was propitious. In 1939 the plant turned a profit and paid a modest dividend of $3,000. Military orders had begun—the first army order was for links and springs in October 1939, and there were subsequent orders for a primer and screw eyes.[16] The divi-

---

15. The minutes in 1941 cryptically suggest what must have been a clash between the Wade and Judd interests. Fielding was confirmed as president and general manager, "with the full understanding that his time of said office may be terminated at any time at the description of the Board of Directors.' This was a curiously explicit statement and unnecessary; it was probably passed at Stuart's request to make sure that Fielding realized that it was the board who had the ultimate decision—though as we know, he held the balancing shares of stock, and neither the Wades or Judds could act unilaterally. Minute Book, Mattatuck Manufacturing Company, 294, 23 Jan. 1941.

16. Until Pearl Harbor, news of the military contracts was published with the product and the name of the manufacturer. "Supply Contracts of $11,907,560 Let," *NYT*, 21 Oct. 1939, 20:1; "Supply Contracts of $19,662,538 Let," *NYT*, 22 June 1940, 29:1; "Contracts by Army Were $884, 163 in Day," *NYT*, 9 Sept. 1941, 32:1.

dend increased to $22,500 in 1940. In the war years the cash reserve was replenished and the payout was $75,000. With round-the-clock shifts, the work force at some periods numbered 800, almost double what it had been in the 1930s. The navy awarded the Mattatuck an "E" flag for "excellence" to fly beneath the Stars and Stripes.[17]

Wartime success strengthened Stuart's desire to have full control of the plant, but he was opposed by Will White (neither his wife, Molly, or her sister, Lucy Dye, the actual Wade owners, took any interest in the firm). With Carol's death Stuart was, of course, no longer related to Will by marriage, but his sons were Will's grand nephews, and Will's daughter, Betty, was my godmother. The families thus remained intertwined, and discussions between the two men took place as sidebars to social visits.

Molly frequently invited the Judds to tea on Sundays. While Tui and I were entertained by a Sealyham terrier named Giles, who could remain in a begging posture for the course of the tea, Will, in his jodhpurs and tweed jacket, drew Stuart into a small gun-lined room. From the closed door Will's voice was the only one to be heard. Betty White remembered her father complaining after one of these sessions, "Stuart is so stubborn," which amused her, as she had never heard Stuart's voice. According to her, Will opposed Stuart's wish to purchase the Wade shares because he did not think him fitted for the rough and tumble of manufacturing, and at one point (which Stuart later characterized to me as "crooked") he attempted to sell the shares elsewhere.

Will was able and intelligent, but with his sporting interests and his long absences in the south, he acted like a dilettante in business. Stuart resented meddling from this quarter, sheltered from the conditions he had to deal with.[18] Time would show, however, that Will had a point. While Stuart was persistent and eager to take on the task, there was little of the roughness in his makeup that would have been helpful in later difficulties. His gentlemanly exterior and often intellectual approaches to business problems could prevent his meeting critical problems head on.

---

17. Gilbert R. Boutin, president, "Would you drive a car you made the parts for today," letter to employees on the occasion of the nintieth anniversary of the founding of the Mattatuck, 16 Oct. 1986, copy in possession of the author.

18. Years later he let his anger flare in a quite different context. "To me that thinking"—referring to Betty White's effort to get me to avoid the draft—"is right out of the era of Uncle Will and Aunt Mollie and is based on a fundamentally wrong premise—that one in some way should be sheltered from meeting an issue head on." SEJ, in Woodbury, to PHJ, in London, 18 Sept. 1955.

⤝ Toys and Upholstery Nails ⤞

One of the matters that Stuart dealt with early on was the toy business, which had made the Mattatuck a more colorful place in the 1930s. It was the most prominent retail line the company ever offered but proved to be of questionable profitability. In its full flowering, Hoge Toys (sold under the name of that New York distributor, later wholly owned by the Mattatuck) offered a line of inexpensive electric trains, a ferocious-looking Tommy gun (like those used by gangsters in *Dick Tracy*), a wind up "Fire Chief Car" with siren, and target games with pistols that fired darts with suction-cup ends. For girls Hoge offered the "Little Princess Sewing Machine," and a "Busy Betty" washing machine and carpet sweeper.

The train at the top of the line was modeled on the New York Central's *Commodore Vanderbilt*. Hoge also offered a windup "streamline" train with a battery-powered bulb peering from its front end—a "Face that Only a Collector Could Love," as a collector's magazine described it forty years later. The most imaginative set was a circus train that featured color lithography on the thin sheet steel of the car bodies; with transformer it sold for $4.00. The top floor of the 1919 building became the toy room, where a largely female workforce assembled and packaged the toys."[*] It was probably Stuart's analysis that brought this recognizable product line to an end in 1939—to my intense dismay, as I made sensational crashes with the Hoge trains at home.

Furniture nails were marketed under the Mattatuck name, accompanied by an Indian arrowhead logo. The catalogue required fourteen pages to illustrate the models available and included illustrations of nails used in ancient Greece and a Robert Adam chair with a seat elegantly edged with rows of brass nails. The line was remarkably diverse: there were plain brass nails, fancy brass nails with ornamental heads (fleur-de-lys, diamonds, pyramids), each design available in a range of sizes and finishes (brass natural, "leather," "antiqued," etc.), in microcosm an illustration of the ability of the plant to coordinate a number of processes.[†] Furniture nails accounted for only a small share of sales, but they were cherished as the only products specifically identified with the company and remained

---

[*] Bob Hoge, "Hoge: It's All in the Name: A Dedicated Search Yields Classic 1930s Tin Trains, Toys and Ownership of the Companies that Produced Them," *Classic Toy Trains*, Aug. 1991, 40–45. I am indebted to Mr. Hoge for supplying me with a copy of this article and Catalog No. 36. Hoge Manufacturing Company, with a price list dated January 1, 1937.

[†] "Upholstery Nails and Furniture Glides: Mattatuck Products," (Waterbury, Conn.: Mattatuck Manufacturing Co., 1930), in possession of the author.

throughout Stuart's time at the Mattatuck. (My training at the plant at age sixteen was as an expediter for nails, following the progress of orders through the departments and learning the lines.) The other "identifiable" products were furniture glides, binder clips, and thumb tacks, marketed under the name of Hoge and packed in boxes for retail sale by the women in the toy room.[‡]

[‡] "Part 2: Stationery Division" (catalog). The Hoge Manufacturing Co., Inc., 23–25 East Twenty-first St., New York, N.Y., copyright 1931, a copy of which was supplied to the author by Bob Hoge.

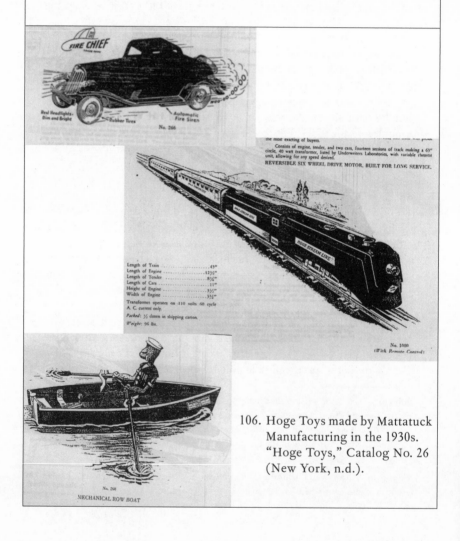

106. Hoge Toys made by Mattatuck Manufacturing in the 1930s. "Hoge Toys," Catalog No. 26 (New York, n.d.).

Stuart persisted, and in 1945 Will let him buy out the Wade interest. Wartime earnings made the Chase National Bank in New York willing to advance a loan for the purchase.[19] Stuart became president and CEO in name when Fielding became chairman of the board at the end of 1950.[20] The Mattatuck was Stuart's baby, and it became his fate.

Stuart had a number of years of success with the company. He soon repaid the Chase loan from earnings and enjoyed his position as manager and overseer of employees. The position helped him with his public service interests as well—he was on the boards of the local Boy Scouts, the local and eventually the National Association of Mental Health, and the Menninger Clinic in Topeka, Kansas. He served for a time as secretary of his Yale class and for years was on the board of the Waterbury National Bank, the most creative member of its investment committee, as I was later told.[21]

The development of a stable management team to assist him in the factory was a goal he never achieved, however. His path became strewn with superintendents, sales and works managers who seemed promising but were found wanting and dismissed. In 1954, despite its being a prosperous year, he wrote me that he was "looking for a good manufacturing manager" and that he intended "to change practically the whole crew. It is an awful job to do."[22] On the departure of one executive the next year he commented that the man would "not be missed by me, anyway. I figure he cost us just about $50,000 between his $1,000 a month salary and the things he got us into that didn't go and will have to be written off!"[23] Stuart wanted a management group to whom he could delegate, allowing and the company to function properly while he was away on his nonprofit business and vacations. The firm was probably not large enough for such a structure, certainly not in the years in the latter 1950s, when sales slipped badly. It was also unreasonable to expect salaried managers to perform with the commitment that ownership brought.

The most able of Stuart's executives over the years was Ervin Schiesel, an ex-navy pilot and an engineer, a graduate of Stevens College of Technology and Columbia University. It was he who helped develop a line of

---

19. Personal knowledge of the author.

20. *Waterbury Republican*, 28 Dec. 1950, Scrapbook, Mattatuck Manufacturing Company, Archive, Mattatuck Museum (hereafter cited as MMC Scrapbook).

21. Harlan Griswold, the bank's president, told me this after Stuart's stroke, fall 1962.

22. SEJ, in Woodbury, to PHJ, at Magdalen College, Oxford, 25 Nov. 1954.

23. SEJ, at 37 Hillside Ave., Waterbury, to PHJ, at Magdalen College, Oxford, 13 Feb. 1955.

connecting rods for automobiles using the company's skills in wire forming, eyelets, and springs. Schiesel also developed a profitable subsidiary
that, by employing handicapped workers, also fulfilled a social need. The
people at Arrowhead—named for the Mattatuck logo—assembled brass
ferrules used by the furniture industry for the feet of tables and chairs.

Schiesel's intelligence and aggressive manners alienated some fellow
employees, and a rivalry grew between him and Stuart—possibly due to
Stuart's refusal to provide his savvy manager a share in the ownership.
Conflict between the two came to a showdown, and Stuart fired Schiesel
from the Mattatuck, rusticating him to the smaller subsidiary.[24] Schiesel
was bitter and was about to sue Stuart when, a few months later, on a clear
day on 16 April 1957, at 1:15 P.M., he rammed his Ford Thunderbird into a
railroad abutment. There were no skid marks on the road, and the inevitable supposition was that he had intended the crash and was a suicide.[25] He
was thirty-five. It was a year after a bitter strike at the plant and was the
most lurid and upsetting event of Stuart's tenure, which was marked by
tensions between him and managers.

The greatest test of Stuart's tenure came in labor-management relations. From World War II through the 1950s labor-management relations
in the U.S. were rancorous. There were frequent highly publicized strikes
in the steel and automotive industries, and federal price and wage regula-
tion added further complexity. There were bitter strikes in Waterbury factories. The largest came in June 1952 when nearly 7,000 employees walked
out at Scovill. The strike lasted four months and resulted in important
gains for the workers, who "were able to establish themselves within the
plants and in the community, as an organized counterpower to management." The role of the union local was solidified—this was the same
union that represented Mattatuck workers, a local of the United Auto
Workers Union (UAW) of the Congress of Industrial Organizations
(CIO), headquartered in Detroit.[26] It was a community-wide event and

---

24. *Waterbury Republican*, 19 Dec. 1955. MMC Scrapbook.

25. The accident occurred on 16 April 1957. Clipping from unidentified Meriden newspaper. Obituary notice from the *American Association for Quality Control Journal*, MMC Scrapbook.

26. *Brass Valley: The Story of Working People's Lives and Struggles in an American Industrial Region*,
comp. Jeremy Brecher, Jerry Lombardi, Jan Stackhouse, The Brass Workers History Project (Philadelphia: Temple Univ. Press, 1982), 190. The UAW-CIO won out over the Mine, Mill, & Smelter
Workers Union, which had initially organized Waterbury plants. The struggle involved charges of
communism against the former union.

set the tone for contention between labor and management in subsequent years throughout the city.[27] Scovill was the Mattatuck writ large, and what happened there had an immediate effect on the smaller plant.

The "organized counterpower" of the union was the reality with which Stuart had to deal at Mattatuck. Temperamentally he was closer to the paternalistic manufacturers of the past, like Augustus Sabin Chase. He was public-spirited and had a sense of shared welfare with the workers. He attended retirement parties, wakes, and funerals, and provided help for alcoholic and mentally ill employees. He was proud of the Mattatuck's independence in the face of the agglomerating trends in industry. To Stuart the rank and file employees were an extended family. Many of them had been with the company for most of their working lives, and he was loyal to them. He was well aware of the new reality, and cooperated in collective bargaining.

The plant was organized in 1941 by a predecessor union to the UAW, and Stuart dealt successfully with the new reality for a decade and a half. In 1951, when the union threatened a strike, Stuart handled the negotiations himself and proactively offered a wage increase, medical benefits, and productivity incentives. He thereby achieved a "unique" four-year contract, which won plaudits from the union and admiration from his peers.[28] His relations with Tim Kearney, chief steward of the shop committee, a tall Irishman who operated nail machines, was so cordial that the next year the two "took the sleeper" to Washington to jointly support the wage agreement with the federal regulators.[29] After this successful result, a real fruit of his role as owner-manager, the salaried employees organized a surprise testimonial, attended by eighty persons, which was written up in the paper.[30] "[W]e are leading the parade again with a 'first,' the increased pension," he wrote me proudly when the contract had received its government approvals.[31]

---

27. *Brass Valley,* 185–90; Eduardo F. Canedo, "What is More Enduring than Brass? The Process of Deindustrialization in Waterbury, Connecticut, 1952–1976" (senior thesis, Columbia College, 4 May 1999), 4, Silas Bronson Library, Waterbury, Conn.

28. *Waterbury Republican,* 21 Oct., 29 Nov. 1951, MMC Scrapbook.

29. SEJ, in Woodbury, to PHJ, c/o Betty White, 32 Park Town, Oxford, 11 May 1952.

30. *Waterbury Republican* (clipping annotated "1952"), MMC Scrapbook. The clippings are not designated as *Republican* (the morning paper) or *American* (evening). Both were published by the same company, and for convenience are here cited as *Waterbury Republican.*

31. SEJ, in Woodbury, to PHJ, c/o Chase Bank, London, 8 Aug. 1953.

107. Inside the Mattatuck in the 1950s

Mattatuck Museum

The contract Stuart had negotiated with such success came to an end in October 1955, when Waterbury was recovering from massive flood damage. After days of rain that August, the Naugatuck, usually a shallow stream, became a torrent, wiping out houses, factories, and commercial buildings, roads, cemeteries, and anything else in its path along the flood plain of the valley. Large units of American Brass and Chase remained closed into the fall. The Mattatuck was on the other side of town and escaped without serious damage. Despite the disastrous conditions and the high unemployment rolls that fall, the union pressed the Mattatuck hard.

There was no contract at midnight on 15 October, when the old one expired. "Negotiations far into the evening, federal conciliator, State conciliator, offers, counter offers, the whole works," Stuart wrote me. "Nasty talk, called me a liar, threats of strike, we made all preparations for a strike." In this standoff, he put in effect the $0.10 per hour wage increase that the union had rejected and announced it in a quarter page ad in the newspaper. "Monday morning came. In came all employees, confused, nervous, leaflets at the gates. We're over the hump. Everybody wants to know how I did it. The employees are working without a contract, and they don't want to strike. They are resigning from the Union all over the plant. I worked seven days last week. Big meeting with foremen Sunday in preparation for expected strike! Wow! I'm bushed."[32] The union charged

---

32. SEJ, in Woodbury, to PHJ, at 6, Woodfall St., London, 24 Oct. 1955.

"failure to bargain in good faith" and wanted a larger increase based on seniority, but the factory continued to operate, and Stuart thought he was again on the way to a mutually beneficial settlement.[33]

However, the union could not tolerate being upstaged by a raise that it had not negotiated, and in February the 369 union employees went out on strike. A prominent issue was the union shop, which Stuart opposed on the principle that no one should be forced to join a union.[34] He was convinced that the strike was not about issues specific to the Mattatuck but was part of a larger UAW strategy to put pressure on Chase, where a long strike was in progress, and on automotive suppliers elsewhere. The day the workers walked out the *Waterbury Republican* ran a four-column story under the front-page banner, "Judd Lashes Union for Strike Action at Mattatuck Co." In "a fiery statement" he was quoted as saying that the shop commit-tee had no real role, that the strike was being called "because Walter Reuther [president of the United Auto Workers Union] says so.[35] The issue, as he saw it, involved the survival of the smaller manufacturer:

> The Detroit leadership seems to be grabbing first for a labor monopoly in the areas served by them, secondly for uniform contract provisions, for all com-panies, large or small, In this policy, the smaller manufacturer and his employees are merely pawns in the big game and in the process are in serious danger of being destroyed, It is to be hoped that the citizens of Connecticut, and particularly the smaller manufacturers and their employees will become aware of what is going on before it is too late.

The spokesman for the local, stung by Stuart's unilateral wage increase, accused him of "imposing an incentive trick on the union." At the plant about fifty of the salaried employees reported for work and endeavored to maintain some production and to ship orders.[36] Stuart was determined to face down the union.[37]

On the picket line the men crowded about cars as they approached the gate, shaking them and mocking the drivers—it was a shock to be jeered at

---

33. *Waterbury Republican*, 17 Oct. 1955, MMC Scrapbook.

34. *Waterbury Republican*, 11 Feb. 1956, MMC Scrapbook.

35. *Waterbury Republican*, 17, 23 Feb. 1956, MMC Scrapbook.

36. *Waterbury Republican*, 13 Feb. 1956, MMC Scrapbook.

37. I was then in basic training at Fort Dix and learned of this strike only from infrequent phone calls.

by someone who a few days before was a friendly fellow worker. The line turned violent after a few days, when men from seven other factories joined it. As they jostled cars, they scraped paint with razor blades and smeared windows—the shaking of the cars and the jeers, now from unrestrained strangers, were fierce. Stuart called for more police to keep the pickets a reasonable distance apart and prevent the threats and harassment. A photo in the paper showed Ervin Schiesel entering the plant flanked by burly policemen after the union charged his car had grazed a picket. The police protection became a political issue, with the union charging that it favored management. After rejecting another offer, the union showed that it was out for the jugular by putting 400 pickets on the line.[38] Men in long overcoats and broad-brimmed hats surrounded the cars of the salaried workers as they entered; the police prevented bloodshed, but not vandalism and bullying.

Theodore Kheel, of New York, the well-known mediator, brokered an end to the strike. The new contract included both an $0.06 hourly rate increase, improved pension benefits, and eliminated a productivity incentive. It did not include a union shop, and in that matter Stuart had won. The union representative praised the workers for "staying the course against an all-out effort by the company."[39]

It was a hollow victory, for employment at the plant steadily declined, and in six years the plant workforce was about half what it was before the strike. Fearing there would be more labor troubles, customers placed their orders elsewhere. By 1960 annual losses were chronic. Both parties were soon aware of the magnitude of the failure. The Mattatuck strike is a tiny blip in the story of the postwar U.S. manufacturing sector, but is surely an example of the most self-indulgent and self-destructive exercises of union action in which local and national leaders brought a company to its knees for negligible gains, which could easily have been negotiated. Stuart's mistakes, if they were such, were the principled stands on the union shop and the expectation that his firm would have any chance against the UAW when it came to a matter of prestige. His cause was just, and the employees were being treated to an industry standard, but his and the firm's self-interests were irretrievably damaged. The result was what he had warned

---

38. *Waterbury Republican*, 17, 23 Feb. 1956, MMC Scrapbook.

39. *Waterbury Republican*, 5 March 1956, MMC Scrapbook.

against in the "fiery statement." The day of the medium-sized manufacturer of the Mattatuck type was dimming fast.

The *Waterbury American* in February 1960 celebrated the Mattatuck in a "Romance of Industry" series focused on Waterbury companies. Readers were told that its "products are used by nearly every industry in the country," including "springs in the millions," such as those used for the cords on the electric iron, springs for toys and electric switches, bed springs ("fabric") for the submarine fleet, perfume sprayers, lipstick containers, inflator needles, and bullets for toy guns. Bobbin rings for the textile industry had long been a specialty, an apparently simple wire ring with an expandable joint whose metal required tempering, hardening, and finishing to survive on bobbins that revolved at great speed; the factory shipped them in the hundreds of thousands. The Mattatuck was the "world's largest maker of binder clips" for the stationery trade and shipped out 30 million thumbtacks a year. About a third of its total sales were accounted for by accelerator rods and linkages for Ford cars. "Management" (meaning Stuart, but not quoting him by name) was optimistic about the future, the newspaper reported, because an exit from Interstate 84, then under construction, would soon be opened, providing shippers easier access to the plant. The company was about to introduce a coaster brake for bicycles. The glowing account concluded that the "Mattatuck is many companies in one" and showed a photo of Ralph Smith, a toolmaker at the plant for forty-one years, to emphasize the continuity of employment and the skills involved.[40]

The article's salute to the plant's multiple capabilities was entirely justified, for its departments retained a wide range of processes to transform and finish metals. The plant could cut and shape steel and brass in wire and sheet form; temper, harden, and provide a range of finishes; and assemble parts when needed. However, optimism about future prospects was whistling in the wind in a Waterbury that, within the decade, would see its industries dwindle and, by the mid-1970s, fade away. The much-anticipated new Interstate would encourage decentralization, and in fact pull commerce away from the city. By the time the article appeared, there had already been a decline of one quarter in manufacturing employment from its postwar height in 1947.[41] The Mattatuck had experienced annual

---

40. *Waterbury American*, "Romance of Industry," 26 Feb. 1960, MMC Scrapbook.

41. Canedo, "What is More Enduring than Brass?," 23.

108. Strike action at the Mattatuck, February 1956

Mattatuck Museum

losses since the strike and was kept afloat only by earnings from its Arrowhead subsidiary.

The coaster brake mentioned in the article was the last hope. In November 1959, I read of Stuart's plan to save the company on the porch of a bungalow in Maiduguri, in the northeast corners of Nigeria, where, in pre-Peace Corps days, I was teaching in the local secondary school. In his usual clear manner he described the venture:

> We have purchased the tools with which the New Departure Division of General Motors made millions of New Departure coaster brakes, and have hired Oscar Liebreich, their production manager, to set it up for us. We have re-designed it to lower the cost without affecting the production of it, and hope to be in production by February 1st. We have already sold out the 1960 production at $2.15 each, so it should come near to doubling our sales and produce a profit of $150,000 and absorb enough of our overhead so that the rest of our business will have an equal profit. My only hope is that our estimates will turn out to be substantially correct. We have placed our all on this

venture, and if it doesn't work out I'll be looking for a job with you in Maiduguri. Everything is going well, and I am very hopeful that this will be the thing that puts the Company back into the profit column. It has been a long, tough haul, and I hope daylight is ahead.[42]

He was supported by the bicycle manufacturers at their convention in Boca Raton. If the price was right, they wanted to buy from an American rather than a Japanese manufacturer. Bendix was the only American competitor, but it was offering brakes at a price higher than Stuart expected the Mattatuck to achieve.[43] By Easter he had a confirmed order of 120,000 out of 600,000 planned for the year. "I go to N Y with Harlan Griswold [a director of the Mattatuck and president of the Waterbury National Bank] week after next to borrow the money to finance it. Looks like $250,000 and I'll have to hock the company. I'm not really afraid, though, as I think it will pay off."[44]

A month later Stuart made another housecleaning of management staff. "The effect of these moves has been like a strong breeze blowing cobwebs away, and I feel they will be the thing that will get us into a non-loss position. I should have done it several years and many dollars ago."[45] The coaster brake was "coming along fine . . . By the end of this month we will have *firm* orders for half our year's production, have completed all shipping schedules on time and have a good backlog for the Fall. Our costs on the brake are as planned and it looks as though it would be profitable." As the New York bankers had turned down the requested loan—an ominous note—he had "nearly worked out a plan to mortgage the company and pledge every single stock I own. If this doesn't work it's liquidation, but I am determined to give it this one more try."[46] (In fact he was able to borrow against the cash value of the insurance the Mattatuck held on his life.)

The last gambit failed. The Mattatuck could not make the brake inexpensively enough to meet foreign competition. By January 1962 Stuart fired Oscar Liebreich, only thirteen months after the agreement to bring him and the coaster brake into the company.[47] There continued to be

---

42. SEJ, in Woodbury, to PHJ, at Maiduguri, Northern Nigeria, 10 Nov. 1959.

43. SEJ, in Woodbury, to PHJ, at Maiduguri, 25 Jan. 1960.

44. SEJ, in Woodbury, to PHJ, at Maiduguri, 17 April 1960.

45. SEJ, in Woodbury, to PHJ, c/o American Express Co., Naples, Italy, 11 June 1960.

46. Ibid.

47. SEJ, in Woodbury, to PHJ, at 1683 Third Avenue, New York City, 3 Jan. 1962.

orders for the brake, but the assembly line in the toy room was mostly quiet. Six months later came a no-nonsense warning from the bankers.

> Clarence Ivy, the banker from Hartford, came over today, and I had a morning with him . . . He is a real nice guy, but no fooling about him. He put it up to me in just so many words. When are you going to be in a profit position? If we are not by the end of 1962 he wants drastic action, and that I promised him. And I agree. I do not intend to go on much longer on a nonprofit or break-even basis. Soooo from here out no quarter to anything. A profit or cut-back to a profit or carve it up or liquidate it.[48]

By August cash was so tight the Mattatuck waited ninety days to pay its bills—any longer would mortally damage already shaky credit. Stuart must have realized that the only way out for him would be to liquidate by the end of the year, a brutal process in which he would have to fire employees who had been with the company for years. He would see the enterprise to which he had dedicated his mature life fail, a fall glaringly visible to the business community in Waterbury and to those on the nonprofit boards that were important to him.

The decision was made for Stuart by that nature whose cruelty Nina feared. On the early morning of the Friday before Labor Day, 1962, alone in the Woodbury house, he became aware he could not pronounce words and that he had lost the use of his right arm and leg. He was unable to use the telephone by his bed to call for help. Somehow he crawled to the bathroom, where the housekeeper found him when she came in. At Waterbury Hospital there was no doubt that he had suffered a cerebral hemorrhage. His doctor told me that it was an incident with severe damage. Stuart had lost the ability to control movement on his entire right side, and he could not formulate words. However, he understood speech and was alert and responsive. After some strokes there is a measure of spontaneous recovery. In this case, unfortunately, there was little, and he lived with the disability for another fourteen years.[49] He turned sixty-one that October.

There is a coda to this last connection of the family with manufacturing in Waterbury. At the time of Stuart's stroke, I had been on the Mattatuck board for years and was nominally its vice-president. The state of the fac-

---

48. SEJ, in Woodbury, to PHJ, c/o General Delivery, Andover, N.J., 13 June 1962.

49. In July he had an operation to repair a ruptured hernia; it is my view that a clot from that operation caused the "cerebral incident." The incident he suffered was unique, not followed by any other in his lifetime.

tory had been the prime topic of my conversations with Stuart for years, and I knew of its plight and many details. When the phone call came to me in my New York City walk-up that Friday morning that Stuart had had a "shock," I had no appointments to cancel and drove right up. In the hospital I encountered a once articulate man who could only make gibberish sounds and who pointed to his right arm and leg to show that he could no longer control them. He was energetic and responsive, but severely maimed. As there was no treatment that the hospital could offer, at Carrie's suggestion, I arranged, some days later, for him to go to the Gaylord Sanatorium in Wallingford, Connecticut, for rehabilitation. There he learned to dress, to walk with support, to swim, to eat. He displayed the purposefulness he always had and a cheer that somewhat disconcerted the staff, who were accustomed to somber responses to such disability.

I sat at his desk when the plant reopened after Labor Day. There remained about 120 employees, but bill payments were at the edge of what was acceptable, and though there was an upturn in the national economy, there was no prospect of profit.[50] Oscar Liebreich, the coaster brake man, had brought a suit against Stuart charging violation of his contract. It was moving through the court system and an award to him could drive us into receivership. (A few days after I settled the claim for a lesser amount out of court, Liebreich dropped dead, another of the lurid happenings that characterized the last years of the family's involvement with the Mattatuck.)

I, too, knew many of the employees by name and shared something of the family sense that Stuart enjoyed. The plant must be saved as a going concern, not liquidated for the value of machinery and real estate. One way out appeared when a delegation from the Bavarian firm, Fichtel & Sachs, came to visit, manufacturers of a competing coaster brake. At a meeting with the visitors it suddenly occurred to me that we might assemble and distribute their brake. The proposal interested them, and in November I visited their plant in Schweinfurt with Vern Barone, our able production manager. There we toured the plant that had been built on the ruins of what had been destroyed in 1944 by American bombers—which doubtless contained parts from the Mattatuck. The machines were new, all with electric drives—unlike the overhead belts at the Mattatuck—and the operators were supervised by "meisters" in long smocks. The brake they

50. The plant at that point needed sales of about $2 million per year to begin to make a profit. As I remember, we were two or three hundred thousand short of that.

produced was elegantly styled, making ours look lumpy by comparison. However, Vern's analysis showed that the production costs would be higher with our plant, so that idea was dead.

Guerin Carmody, who had remembered Haring's trenchant commentary on local swells at youthful dances, was my attorney and noted that the safest course would be to liquidate the company to avoid possible later lawsuits from heirs or from a recovered Stuart himself. Harlan Griswold, the bank president, knew the situation and favored liquidation no more than I did, both of us with an eye on the Waterbury economy as well as the employees.

The solution to the problem began with a meeting by the eighteenth-century fireplace in Griswold's Woodbury house, where he introduced me to Gilbert R. Boutin, then manager of the Chase Brass & Copper Waterville plant. In preference to continuing on the corporate ladder in a large company, Boutin was seeking an opportunity to own a plant of his own. He had an abundance of ability and energy but no capital. If he were to purchase the Mattatuck, we would have to count on his ability to improve the plant's earnings to be paid. It was a long shot, but sale to him, even with "taking back paper" (promissory notes), was the only chance to retain the Mattatuck as a going concern. Because of the losses and the lowering conditions in the metalworking industry, there was no possibility of a market sale except to a liquidator.

It did not take long to develop a sense of trust in Boutin. In a few months he came to the Mattatuck as president and CEO while we negotiated its sale to him, an unusual procedure that could have ended badly but did not. We signed the transfer documents in the offices of Carmody & Torrance in Wilfred Griggs's Lilley Building in late May 1963.[51] The business went at its depreciated book value, a small fraction of what it would have been worth in the early 1950s.[52] For the Griggs, White, and Judd families the year 1963 ended 120 years of involvement in Waterbury manufacturing.

---

51. "Mattatuck Firm is Sold to Boutin by Judd Family. Firm Employs 200 people; Boutin Looks Forward to Record Year in 1963," *Waterbury Republican*, 26 May 1963.

52. The sale of the land and buildings was deferred for Boutin to purchase later, which in some years time he did. The advisers, without whom it would have been impossible to work out this deal, were the attorney, Guerin B. Carmody (1910–87), of the firm of Carmody & Torrance, Harlan H. Griswold (1910–89), president of the Waterbury National Bank, and Ernest Ring, the local partner of Peat, Marwick & Mitchell.

The deal depended on the plant being able to generate earnings in the future and could easily have collapsed with the rest of Waterbury industry in succeeding years, but Boutin was a nimble entrepreneur. He increased the automotive business, bought a number of small shops elsewhere, and employment grew at the Mattatuck over his fifteen-year ownership, one of the few success stories in the city.

It is noteworthy that the enterprise was rescued by a latecomer to Waterbury, a man who, like George E. Judd in the 1880s, had started out in business with no assets but his wits. Boutin's French-Canadian origins, however culturally distant from the Puritan-Yankees who had begun industry in Waterbury, extended back just as far in the new world.

The conglomerate that bought the Mattatuck from Boutin in 1988 could not react to market forces as fast as a single owner, and by 1990 the factory was closed. When I looked at it from the street in July 2001 the buildings remained, sturdy but unkempt, with no window remaining unbroken. A sign proclaimed an environmental clean-up. The Arrowhead logo on the lintel above the second floor office remained, but the winds could blow through Billy Fielding's and Stuart's old office.[53]

109. The Mattatuck in 2002

53. In February 2002 an employee in a successor firm to the purchaser of the Mattatuck from Boutin phoned the Mattatuck Museum in Waterbury. It was his last day of work and the office was being vacated. There were boxes of samples, scrapbooks, and photographs that came from the old plant that should go to the museum. Thus came to be the Mattatuck archive at the Museum that shared its name—the advertising cuts, catalogs, sample boards, and clipping scrapbooks from over 100 years.

AFTERWORD

In the early 1950s Carrie's immediate surroundings altered greatly. In 1952 her neighbor in the Benedict house, the reclusive Sally Miller Smith, died. On a summer day while lunching with Carrie at the small table by the dining room window I heard what sounded like repeated muffled pistol shots coming from the Smith grounds next door. Sarah told us it was Rocco, the gardener, breaking bottles of spoiled champagne. There must have been hundreds of them, as the sounds continued through our lunch, making me think of the chopping of the cherry trees at the end of *The Cherry Orchard*. Stuart had written me that the attorney for Sally Smith's estate was "making plans to dispose of her 16 houses. He tells me she was living so far above her income that she was spending principal like water . . . I am afraid the big house next to G. G. [Grandmother Griggs] will have to be sold immediately."[1]

Demolition of the flamboyant centerpiece of Hillside seemed in prospect, but was averted when preservationists persuaded the University of Connecticut to establish a branch using the house as its center. Shortly thereafter they put up a brick classroom building directly across from Carrie's dining room, transforming what had looked like a gracious park into institutional banality. It was an eyesore, but far from complaining about it (as I did), Carrie accepted it without lament, one of the multitude of changes that she had learned to accept in a life that had begun in a world without cars or electricity.

The house at 114 Grove, which George had so labored over, where Carrie had grown to womanhood and been married, and where Julia had lived until her death, was demolished in the same years, run down and shabby from its use as a rooming house. The little red house next door, where the three Griggs children were born, was also destroyed, both eventually replaced by a commercial office building even more raw in appearance than the classroom on the hill. The Wade house became a nursing home for a time. (Much later it was restored to appear as it might have when Wilfred Griggs completed it in 1893). Its neighbor, the house of Waterbury's hero of Manila Bay, Captain Kellogg, whom Carrie ceremo-

---

1. SEJ, in Woodbury, to PHJ, c/o Betty White, 62 Park Town, Oxford, 23 June 1952.

niously greeted on her morning downtown walk in the 1930s, was demolished after his death and replaced by a government office building. Rose Hill was kept up until well after Carrie's death by Lucia Chase, the director of the American Ballet Theater, who was the last in her family to own her grandparents' house. In the late 1960s, when Carrie was bedridden, a young man appeared at the door and asked to speak to her. He was a member of the ballet company taking a break at Rose Hill, and had heard that there was someone in Waterbury who might remember the original colors of the house. The aged figure in the bed, I was told, was able to tell him, and he left satisfied.

Opposite Rose Hill, the Italianate Kingsbury house with its tower, the gracious place that had been there before Luther Chapin White moved to Prospect Street, had been used for the YWCA since the 1940s. It too was demolished to make way for a more efficient structure. On the Green, the First Congregational Church, where the elder Whites had been members, was gone. The Immaculate Conception Church, in Roman Basilica style, replaced in 1927 the early-nineteenth-century Merriman house that Carrie remembered. She had, of course, been long used to the parking lot next to Trinity Church, where her grandparents' house had been. The Elton had become a residence hotel, with rooms rented by the month or year—Stuart stayed there briefly after rehabilitation. Later it became senior citizen housing. There were no longer grocery stores and butcher shops around the Green, and Carrie's Colonial Trust Company had its handsome stone exterior encased in a glossy steel and glass skin.

It remains possible to sense what the city was in its heyday when Carrie was a young mother and Wilfred Griggs was producing one house and public building after another, when his Elton brought a touch of European urbanity to the Green, when his Lilley Building became the tallest of its surrounding buildings, and when customers could walk off the street to place an order at the R. F. Griggs Co.

The railroad station remained the most distinctive of the city's landmarks, its version of the Sienese town hall tower attracting attention from motorists speeding by on the I-84 overpass; it was saved by the *Waterbury Republican-American*, which located its offices and production plant there. The last time Carrie had taken the train to New York was with me in the late 1940s to see a matinee of *Cavelleria Rusticana* and *Pagliacci* in the early days of the New York City Opera. By then the businessman's 8 A.M. chair car and checked baggage service, which had so often accommodated the family's steamer trunks, was gone. Passenger connections south were reduced to a self-contained Budd car four or five times a day, with fares collected on board.

Carrie saw many of these changes when taken out for drives, and was told about others, but the loss of this physical past was not a recurrent theme with her. She would give a resigned sigh, recognizing that changes must be accepted. The scale of the mammoth high speed highway interchange that was elevated above the flat where the early settlers had started their farms must have been barely comprehensible to someone as at home as Carrie had been in the walking city.

Will White had a disabling stroke in 1946, the year after he had sold the Wade shares to Stuart. It was before the development of rehabilitation procedures for stroke victims, and he remained an invalid in the classic, dependent sense for six years, tended by around-the-clock nurses and wheeled out to the upstairs porch at Breakneck by day. He was a sad, often tearful figure, though his "cerebral accident" had not been as severe as Stuart's would be. Carrie had not often visited Breakneck in the days of his health—the stickiness between Molly and the White in-laws from long past could be the reason—but on her visits to her invalid brother she surely saw behind the gray figure on the porch the handsome young man who had entered the new century in the Klondike. Molly died of cancer in 1949, leaving him and Breakneck in the care of his son, Wade, who maintained the household with three "girls" to run the house, a gardener, and Curley, the chauffeur. It was a thankless and exorbitantly expensive task. After Will died in 1952, Wade unsuccessfully tried to find a use for the place as a school. A local attorney bought it as a land investment and promptly demolished the house. Thirty years later I trekked through woods where the rolling lawns and the formal gardens had been to find the site. In the second-growth scrub I found the contours of the cellar hole, itself returning to forest. The twenty-eight-room country house that was meant to endure for generations, like those in England, had stood forty years.

Neither Betty nor Wade White had children, and their White line ended with their deaths in the mid-1990s. Each followed paths that retained connections to Waterbury and strong attachment to the family past, but they found creative endeavors farther afield.

Betty stubbornly refused the route of the social marriage her mother wished for her. She pursued a variety of interests after Westover, including

110. Elizabeth Wade White, 1935

genealogy, bibliographic techniques, gardening, and herbs. She studied sculpture and art in New York. She enraged Will by supporting FDR and the New Deal. In the mid-1930s she raised funds in Waterbury for children affected by the Spanish Civil War. (Stuart was the treasurer.)

In 1938 in Paris she vainly attempted to volunteer for driver duty with the Loyalist forces through the American Friends Service Committee. After a loss of nerve brought on by this failure, she spent the winter of 1938–39 in England, cared for and strongly influenced by the writer Sylvia Townsend Warner and her friend, Valentine Ackland, both of whom were communists. Valentine became the love of Betty's life, though they were seldom together. In May 1939 Sylvia and Valentine visited her at Breakneck, their political opinions, sexual orientation, cigars, and pants (Valentine) shocking the elder Whites—a unique episode in the history of the family and probably of Waterbury as well.[2] During the war Betty did volunteer work for Russian War Relief and in later years maintained a faith in Stalin and the Soviet experiment despite evidence of cruelty and corruption.

In her forties Betty focused on her academic and genealogical interests and enrolled at St. Hilda's College at Oxford, which awarded her a B. Litt. for a dissertation on Anne Bradstreet, the first poet in the English-speaking

---

2. For an account of EWW's stay in England in 1938–39 see Peter H. Judd, "Letters from Katie Powys to Elizabeth Wade White, 1938–1954." *Powys Journal* 7 (1997): 76–115.

111. H. Wade White at Breakneck, 1934

new world. She turned this work into the biography published by Oxford University Press in 1970. For many years she and her companion, Evelyn Holahan, lived in The Patch, a farmhouse modernized by her grandmother, on the slope of Breakneck Hill; part of each year they spent in Oxford, where Betty also owned a house. In both places they entertained friends from both sides of the Atlantic and of all ages. When in Connecticut, Betty regularly visited Carrie, and family gatherings in her late years were often at The Patch. The political and economic views she had acquired as a thirties silver-spoon radical coexisted with a love of good food, drink, sociability, and devotion to family.

After graduating from Yale in the depths of the Depression, Wade White spent much of his time attending his mother and father until their deaths, but in New York and Gloucester, Massachusetts, he produced paintings in the Precisionist style of the 1930s and 1940s. In the late 1980s one that had been de-accessioned by the Mattatuck Museum surfaced in a New York gallery, whose owner was prompted by the painting's quality to inquire about the artist. Fortuitously, a colleague had known Wade in the registrar's office at Harvard's Fogg Museum, where he volunteered for many years. Janet Marquesee, an art dealer who specialized in 1930s artists, visited his house in Fairfield, Connecticut, to examine his paintings, most of which were rolled up in the attic. She arranged to have them restored and framed, and upon exhibition they sold for sums in the thousands, with some pieces purchased by museums.[3] Seventy-year-old Wade told me it felt like being in a dream. He owned, successively, houses in Gloucester, Boston, Nantucket, and finally Fairfield, Connecticut, which last was remodeled by him and Tibor Kerekes in its original Victorian style.

Neither brother nor sister ever had gainful employment; their parents supported them in their lifetimes, and after their deaths the children had inheritances. For both of them, financial resources were stretched in their last years.

Betty and Wade were custodians of family memory and objects, many of which came to me, most notably more of the silver serving spoons that Samuel and Sarah Haring used in Manhattan in the early 1800s, the baptismal cup of George Washington Kip by the New York silversmith Joel Sayre, which Henry Kip had made over to "Julie" in 1870, and the tall case clock by Timothy Peck from the marriage of John White, the sea captain, to Ruth Ranney in Middletown in 1789.

Stuart valiantly cooperated with the rehabilitation therapists and learned how to walk with a braced leg, to bathe, and to dress himself. However, he remained incapable of independent living and required the attendance of a housekeeper-companion to prepare meals and to drive him. He communicated with gestures and sounds and could do so vividly. It was usually possible to converse with him by asking questions and, once the topic was found, to note concurrence or disagreement by his gestures.

He approved of my sale of what had been his life's work to Boutin, but thereafter set out to reassert absolute control over his affairs, including the still profitable Arrowhead Associates and his investments. Since he could not talk or write, he used the intermediary of a long-time personal assistant, Doris Kreger, who had worked at the Mattatuck.[4] Some months after the sale of the Mattatuck, I was called to Waterbury to take part in a meeting with the attorney, accountant, and Harlan Griswold of the bank to consider what could be done in response to Stuart's reckless and ill-judged actions, carried out by the intermediary. The conclusion was that Stuart was of sound mind and there was no basis for an action to appoint a con-

---

3. "Wade White: 1930's Precisionist," exhibition catalog, Janet Marquesee Fine Arts Ltd., New York, N.Y. [1989].

4. Kreger (1916–93) was then a resident of Wolcott, Conn.

servator. Nothing could be done other than to try to persuade, but when his mind was made up, that was it—he could articulate a forceful "no."

His outlook was clearly distorted by his illness, though not to a certifiable extent. That his single-minded pursuit of what he wanted resulted in the departure of distraught housekeepers and even Doris Kreger, abruptly dismissed after years of service, was a matter of indifference to him. It took me several years to conclude that I could do nothing in response to appeals from those affected by his actions. He was fighting for survival, as I am now aware, and such a fight is not a reasoned venture. He carried on as he had held onto the Mattatuck through its losses. In the event he did not squander all his resources. They remained adequate to support him, the housekeeper, and stays in warm climates over the winters.

In his quest for a continuing involvement with life Stuart got in touch with Edna and married her again. Not unexpectedly this proved disastrous. She filled the evenings with drunken harangues to this man who could not speak, or so I was told by the housekeeper of the day. One day while Edna was out, Stuart arranged for the lock on the apartment door to be changed. When she returned, she found she had to go elsewhere. This resulted in another generous divorce settlement.

Stuart lived for most of the thirteen years of his semi-incapacitation in the penthouse of an apartment building on the site of the demolished E. O. Goss house that matched 54 Hillside Avenue in scale and fantasy and was only four doors away. He was a neighbor of Carrie in her last years, but they never visited. The view from the penthouse showed the new Waterbury in which the highway interchange and the lights of the traffic at night were the most prominent features.

In the early 1970s Stuart hired Polish-born Janina Sofi Wysocka as housekeeper. Jean, as she called herself, told of carrying Jewish children to safety through the Warsaw sewers as a girl. After the war she fled west from the Soviets and in camps for displaced persons won skating contests on iced-over ground. She joined the British Eighth Army and reached the rank of sergeant in two years. How she made her way to America I do not know, but when she went to work for Stuart she had a grown-up son in Hartford. She was highly competent as a driver and as a planner of Stuart's activities. It was her idea for him to get rid of the faithful assistant, Doris, which he did without ceremony or reward. Jean had Polish friends in Modesto, California. The husband was a glass designer for the Gallo Wineries, a veteran of that same Eighth Army, part of a commando team that blew up installations behind the lines in Libya. His wife was the daughter of the last chief of staff of the Polish army before the communist takeover. Jean announced that Stuart would be moving where she could join these hardy survivors. He was pleased because snow and cold were difficult for him in the east. Jean arranged for him to buy a house in a subdivision whose streets were named for characters and locations in the Robin Hood story—the house was on Tuxford Lane. Modesto is a Central Valley town, a center of agribusiness, where the temperature rises to well over 100° F in the summer, not what one would expect of a retirement community. However, Stuart found life on the flat and in a suburb comfortable, Jean appeared to take good care of him, and Jean had the company of congenial friends. About two years after arriving there he died suddenly of an infected pancreas at the age of seventy-five. When I arrived after the night flight west, Jean's friend met me at the house to tell me what I suspected from an earlier visit, that Jean and Stuart had been married. Once again he had not been able to include his son.

Stuart could have sold the Mattatuck in the early 1950s for several times what I was able to get for it ten years later. Had he known what was going to happen, he might have done so, but it is hard to sell at the peak of success, and he had no personal life to fall back on. Though his net worth deteriorated greatly from what it had been, he had not mortgaged his own investments to keep the Mattatuck going, and his stroke occurred just in time for an honorable, if financially diminished, exit. He benefited later from the sale of the Mattatuck land and buildings. He had investments sufficient to make the move, buy the house in Modesto, and provide Jean and himself with a Mercedes sedan. As Stuart's widow, Jean benefited from exemptions and California law, which provides that half the estate go to the spouse. They also had substantial joint savings accounts, which went to the survivor outside of probate. Edna was rewarded as per her divorce agreement. Tui's aggressive behavior on a visit about six weeks before Stuart's death had so alarmed Stuart that he changed his will to create a trust for Tui's four children. I received the identical sum outright.

Jean surely had material interests in mind when she married, and the result was that she could live comfortably for the remaining eighteen years of her life. However, she had taken good care of Stuart, and the move to Modesto gave him his two best years since the stroke. Jean did not become part of the family in any sense. We exchanged a few phone calls in the months after Stuart's death. When, some years later, Tui's ex-wife and her husband, Shilla and William Lamb, stopped in to pick up photo albums and home movies to send to me, they found her disheveled and the house untidy, with "newspapers in the stove."[5] The albums and movies were rescued from Modesto only to be consumed in a fire that destroyed the Lamb house in northern California. An irreplaceable set of family records came close to being preserved, but it was not to be.

There is much that is bizarre about the fate of this New England businessman—the multiple marriages, the tangled relations with assistants at the factory (the most uncanny of which was the apparent suicide of Ervin Schiesel), and his ability to work his will while partly paralyzed and speechless. There were turning points, apart from Carol's early demise. What if his sister Eloise had lived, married and had a stable family that could have given him perspective when a widower? What if he had married a woman less limited and troubled than Edna? What if he had moved from the Mattatuck and returned to investing in the good years of the 1950s? None of these seems plausible, given circumstances and the man's character.

Behind the qualities of intelligence, dedication, vision, and gentility that characterized Stuart when he was well was a flaw that is a fault line through his professional and personal life. Had his own emotions, his wants, and needs been more available to him, he could perhaps have dealt more straightforwardly with others, brought situations to a head instead of letting them simmer, not allow himself to be taken advantage of. His reserve meant that some whom he dealt with did not know where he stood. He had probably learned this reserve early to protect his child self from his emotional mother's intrusions. The "rough" expression of emotion at home and at work (to recall what Will White felt he lacked) might have helped him avoid many of the difficulties he had with subordinates and with his second marriage. Stuart's story is that of an honorable and intelligent man caught in a thicket from which he could not escape. Like the protagonists of tragic drama, he contended with the circumstances of his life.

When she was in her late eighties, it became my pastime to read to Carrie from the letters in the shoeboxes in the third-floor window seat. I had to

---

5. Stuart Jr. (Tui) also had four wives and has spent most of his mature years on the West Coast. His four children by his second wife adopted the surname of a stepfather. This line of the Judd family comes to an end with us.

read loudly as her deafness was far advanced. Perhaps the high pitch increased the drama of Aunt Kate's letters, which she particularly enjoyed.

Carrie's last appearance outside the house was at the funeral of Mary Burrall. The mourners were in their pews at St. John's when she appeared at the door by the chancel; she was too frail to go up the steps to the main door. She wore her light gray winter coat with fur collar, now too big for her diminished and stooped frame. With the almost vacant gaze of extreme old age she concentrated on the task of reaching the front pew, helped by the verger. This was the moment of farewell to her old school friend, with whom she had shared almost ninety years and memorable times in Italy, England, and Scandinavia. Lucy Burrall and Edith Chase survived Carrie. When Edith died, Lucy, who had been bedridden, turned to the wall and died within hours of her friend.[6] Years later, when I visited the house of "L. M. & E." at Topsmead State Forest, I found the furnishings just as they had been, their books by the armchairs in the living room. Next to Edith's bed was her telephone directory; I opened it to "G" and found Carrie's address and phone number neatly lined out.

Carrie was not told when, in the summer of 1969, Haring requested that the ashes of his elder son, Robert Foote Griggs III, twenty-six, be placed in the Robert F. Griggs plot at Riverside. The body of the young man was found in a shack in Florida. The death was recorded as a suicide, but drugs may have been involved. Haring died at eighty-one in Laguna Beach, and though his principal support had been an allowance from his mother and a trust fund after her death, his estate amounted to almost $300,000, which he left to a female friend.[7]

Bobby's wife, Anne, ran the household when Carrie became too frail to come downstairs. Her attention made it possible for Carrie to remain at home, where she died at the age of ninety-four, in the bedroom that she and Rob had first occupied forty-seven years before.[8] As the tiny figure in the bed said herself on her last birthday, "I have lived to a greater age than anyone else in the family." Only Elbert Herring (her first cousin three times removed) in the wider family exceeded this age.

Bob and Anne Griggs soon moved to a condominium in Heritage Village in nearby Southbury, where they lived for over a quarter of a century.

---

6. As reported to me by EWW.

7. See "Griggs," Genealogical and Biographical Notes.

8. 54 Hillside was vacant for about two years before it was bought and restored by neighbors. It remains, with its Benedict house neighbor, one of the most distinctive houses in Waterbury.

By his daughter Nancy's account, in those years Bob was bitter and angry, critical of in-laws, anti-Semitic and anti-black. Alone in his generation in the family he amassed a fortune through investing and left an estate in excess of $4 million. By 1996 all of Julia's grandchildren were gone—a generation that lasted nearly a century had passed. After the turn of the century her great-grandchildren lived in Florida, Oklahoma, Oahu, California—and Connecticut.

Stuart Jr. followed a course akin to Haring's, cutting loose from Waterbury and the east. He early showed a talent for drawing and cartoons, and began to paint in boarding school. He set out to be an artist, which conflicted with what Yale offered, and after a year he chose the bohemian life in Paris and Barcelona. Another try at a conventional college was followed by art school in Boston, where he met the woman who became his second wife and the mother of four children. They joined the cult of a Sikh master with strict dietary laws. From Arizona they moved to Berkeley, where Stuart was the art editor of a newsletter for the California canning industry. In the 1960s the family moved north in California to establish what they expected to become an ashram and a vegetable farm. Both experiments foundered, as did the marriage. When the children's mother remarried, they took the surname of their stepfather. For a time Stuart lived in Vancouver and briefly returned to Waterbury. In another phase of a spiritual quest he was attracted to the teachings of Rajneesh, first at Poona, India, later at Antelope, Oregon, until its notorious collapse. I received word of two more marriages. He settled in Seattle, attracted by the café culture, and there he lives in senior citizen housing and is modestly employed.

His eldest child, the only one of his children with whom he is in contact, is the manager of a rental building in Los Angeles. A second daughter is a professional photographer, and her daughter is an "A" student in a northern California school. A third daughter is the mother of another "A" student in that school, who has been raised by her maternal grandmother. Stuart Jr.'s son was diagnosed with schizophrenia at an early age and is a ward of the state in a halfway house.

Since I write about others, I am obligated to sketch my own path, which also led away from Waterbury. I had literary ambitions from school days, and partly for those reasons—Emerson and Thoreau being my inspiration—chose to break family tradition (though I had no sense then of how deep it was) by choosing Harvard over Yale. There the literary mingled with the theatrical, but neither were strong enough to form the basis of a productive career. In these *wanderjahre* there were two years in the army, an ultimately invaluable experience of fellowship with others beyond expected circles, a year as a teacher in the spare savannah lands of northern Nigeria in what was the last year of the Raj, an exposure to the peace of an imperium that was soon to be shattered all over the world. I had not taken the path that was immediately open to me at the Mattatuck—which Stuart indulged, though he clearly wanted a son's help. Fate put me there at the end of the family involvement, as I have described. That brief reconciliation with what might have been, put me on a new course, one of those second or third choices that American society and its buoyant economy provided—graduate education with a Ph.D. from Columbia that I had initially expected would lead to an academic career. But this was 1968—at one point I taught *Civilization and Its Discontents* on the lawn in a campus that was dominated by buildings "liberated" by students. The academy and society were in disarray, and I had to make another choice. It sprang from the graduate school skills of research and handling information.

I consulted for a time with a government agency and a university and found quite unexpectedly a perch at Northeast Utilities, which supplied most of Connecticut and western Massachusetts with electricity. I was attracted by a brilliant and imaginative man, Peter M. Stern, who with his parents had escaped the Nazis. His role was to help the company move into the then new world of closer regulatory scrutiny and proliferating requirements for reducing the impacts of its facilities on land, air, and water. I enjoyed working with this pragmatic activist and soon grew to value my association with engineers, with their steady view of things and sense of integrity and order. I began to write and over the years became involved in what was then an innovative role for a utility, showing customers how to use electricity more efficiently—it was a turnabout from the former sales ethos. During the twenty years I spent with the company I lived in a house I had worked on along with the carpenters in the February snows. It was in the woods of southern Connecticut, adjacent to a state forest and a mile from a paved road. I had fresh vegetables from my garden and whippoorwills on summer nights.

Then it was a return to the city, to the far larger Waterbury of New York, still, as Waterbury had ceased to be, a city where one walked to do errands and shop, took buses and regularly came into contact with strangers. Because of my interest in energy conservation I was invited to join the

Department of Housing Preservation and Development in New York City to head a small division of dedicated young people seeking to find ways to reduce the enormous costs of excessive fuel use in the stock of thousands of buildings that had been taken by the city in tax foreclosures. For six years I was involved with building superintendents and managers, fraught neighborhoods and buildings in northern Manhattan, the Bronx, and Brooklyn, dealing with the daunting intricacies of city contracting and personnel procedures. This was a time of falling oil prices, and the urgency of the task came to be ignored by higher-ups, but we created a basis for comparison of performance (showing, for example, that a building of the same size and type could be heated with one sixth of the cost of another with due attention to operation and maintenance). There were and are "graduates" of this experience who have gone on to useful careers in energy management.

With retirement while still "whole"—and benefiting from five decades of national prosperity—came the opportunity to get a closer and more personal look at American history from the comfort of an apartment on Riverside Drive that I had been lucky enough to happen on when the price seemed right. And so this book and its predecessor. Absent from the story is marriage, which passed me by in the most possible decades of the 20s and 30s, after which the single life became ingrained.

The future is unimaginable, certainly two generations hence and even, within one life as Julia's, Carrie's, and my experiences (among others in this narrative) demonstrate. Likewise, in the fleeting present of individual lives, the past recedes and becomes remote and itself almost as unimaginable as the future. Thus the antebellum New York City of the Harings must have appeared to Julia in the 1920s, or Waterbury and her young family in their prime to Carrie in the 1950s. Following a strand of family over more than two hundred years links the futures that the individuals could not imagine with what came to be and creates the thread of memory to link the past. Now Alicia Matsumoto, the high-school student in California, Carrie's three times great-granddaughter becomes linked to John and Mary Haring and James Clark and Deborah Denton in the American Revolution, a past that is as remote to her as her life and future would be to them (and is to me).

Carrie preserved the past as she maintained a lively interest in the present. She refused to be turned to bitterness by her disappointment with

Haring and her loss of Carol. Those griefs were contained within by self-discipline and an awareness that she had much to give to the next generation. I am indebted beyond accounting to her presence in my childhood and to the house where my imagination could play. I see now that it is through her that I have come to know the forebears whose memory she kept alive within her—the resolute Sarah Haring, Aunt Kate with her good sense and humor, the shy and retiring Caroline Eliza, and, of course, Julia, to whom she had been so close. Carrie and those ancestors she loved are the heroines of this story.

112. Waterbury in the twenty-first century
    The Green is at the upper right.

Mattatuck Museum

SELECT BIBLIOGRAPHY

Archives and Manuscript Collections

Albany, Albany Co., New York, Hall of Records
    Mayor's Court, Minutes
    Property Records

Baker Library, Harvard Business School, Boston, Massachusetts
    Historical Collections
        R. G. Dun & Co. Collection

Cambridge University
    Department of Manuscripts and Univ. Archives, Univ. Library
    Jesus College Archives

Cayuga County, N.Y.
    Land Records, Auburn, N.Y.

Connecticut State Library
    Lucius B. Barbour Collection, Vital Records
    Hale Headstone Inscriptions Collection
    New Haven County Superior Court, Divorces 1712–1910
    Waterbury, Conn., Probate Court Archives

Mattatuck Museum, Waterbury, Conn., Research Collection
    Churches and Religion Folder
    Histories Folder
    Hotel Folder
    Leaflets & Pamphlets Boxes
    Mattatuck Manufacturing Company [scrapbook, photographs, cata-
        logs, product display boards]

Museum of the City of New York, MSS Collections
    Jones Family Papers 1734–1812

National Archives and Records Administration, Washington, D.C.
    Records of Veterans' Benefits
        War of 1812 series, Pension Applications
        Revolutionary War service series, Pension Applications

New Haven Colony Historical Society, New Haven, Conn.
Dana Collection
H. Lynde Harrison Folder

New York City
Brooklyn Conveyance Records, Grantor-Grantee
Mayor's Court Records
Municipal Archives, Manhattan Deaths
New York County Clerk's Office, Archives
Office of Register of the City and County of New York
New York County Surrogates Court, New York, N.Y.

New York Public Library, Manuscripts Division
Emmet Collection
George H. Budke Collection
Jones Family Collection
Peter Smith Papers, 1767–1851, microfilm (originals at the Special Collections Research Center, Syracuse University Library)

New York State Library, Albany
Anonymous Diary, War of 1812, MSS 1472
Kip Family Papers, 1792–1909, SC 16557, Manuscripts and Special Collections

New-York Historical Society
Johnson Quinn Collection: New York Hotels
New York City Deeds, 1784
Papers of Aaron Burr (microfilm)
Samuel Jones Papers

Orange County, California
Superior Court of California, County of Orange, Probate Records

Yale University
Alumni Archives
William Henry White Papers, Western Americana Collection, Beinecke Rare Book and Manuscript Library

City Directories

Brooklyn
Lain, George T., comp. *Brooklyn City and Business Directory.* 1786, 1872–74.

Minneapolis
Tribune's Directory for Minnesota and St. Paul, 1872–73. Minneapolis: Tribune Publishing Co., 1872.
Minneapolis Directory for the Years 1865–6. Minneapolis: E. P. Shaw.
A Directory of the City of Minneapolis, August 1, 1869. Minneapolis: Francis P. Sweet, Tribune Printing Co., 1869.

New York City Directories, 1800–1880
The American Almanack, New-York Register and City Directory. New York: David Longworth, 1796–1842.
Bode's New York City Directory, 1851–52.
Elliot's Improved New-York Double Directory, 1812.
The New-York Business Directory for 1844 and 1845. New York: John Doggett Jr.
The New York City Directory. J. Doggett, 1842–51.
The New-York Mercantile Register for 1848–49, Containing the Cards of the Principal Business Establishments including Hotels and Public Institutions. New-York: T. Morehead, 1848.
Trow's New York City Directory, 1852/53–1882/83.

Waterbury
Waterbury Almanac 1870. Waterbury, Conn.: American Printing Co., 1869.
Waterbury City Directories, various publishers, 1868–1940.
Waterbury and Naugatuck Directory (including Watertown). New Haven: Price and Lee, 1887.

Abstracted, Compiled, and Indexed Records

The American State Papers, Class V, Military Affairs. Washington, D.C.:
   Gales and Seaton, 1832.
Baptisms from 1639 to 1730 in the Reformed Dutch Church, New York.
   Collections of the New York Genealogical and Biographical Society,
   vol. 2. New York, 1901.
Baptisms from 1731 to 1800 in the Reformed Dutch Church, New York.
   Collections of the New York Genealogical and Biographical Society,
   vol. 3. New York, 1902.
*Baptism Record of the Tappan Reformed Church, Tappan, Rockland County,
   N.Y. 1694–1899,* Arthur C. M. Kelly, ed. and comp. Rhinebeck, N.Y.:
   privately printed, 1998.
Bedford Historical Records. Vols. 4, 9. Town of Bedford, Westchester, N.Y.:
   1975.
*Calendar of Historical Manuscripts relating to the War of the Revolution in the
   Office of the Secretary of State.* Albany, 1868.
Calendar of N.Y. Colonial Manuscripts, Indorsed Land Papers, 1643–1803.
   Compiled by E. R. O'Callaghan. Reprint, Harrison, N.Y.: Harbor Hill
   Books, 1987.
Civil List and Constitutional History of the Colony and State of New York.
   Compiled by S. C. Hutchins. Albany, 1869.
Civil List and Constitutional History of the Colony and State of New York.
   Compiled by Edgar A. Werner. Albany, 1891.
Connecticut: Record of Service of Men during War of Rebellion. Hartford,
   Conn., 1889.
Deaths Taken from the New York Evening Post, *1801–1890.* Compiled by
   Gertrude A. Barber. Typescript, 1933–1941.
*The Debates in the Several State Conventions for the Adoption of the Federal
   Constitution as Recommended by the General Convention at Philadelphia
   of 1787.* Edited by Jonathan Elliot. Philadelphia: J. B. Lippincott, 1881.
The Documentary History of the State of New York. Edited by E. B.
   O'Callaghan. Vol. 3. Albany, 1850.
Documents Relative to the Colonial History of the State of New-York. Edited
   by E. B. O'Callaghan. Vol. 7. Albany, 1856.

Force, Peter. *American Archives, Fourth Series, Containing a Documentary History of the English Colonies in North America from the King's Message to Parliament of March 7, 1774 to the Declaration of Independence by the United States.* Washington, D.C.: St. Clair Clarke and Peter Force, April 1843.

Hastings, Hugh, ed. *Military Minutes of the Council of Appointment of the State of New York 1783–1821.* Albany, 1901.

Heads of Families at the First Census of the United States Taken n the Year 1790, New York. Baltimore: Genealogical Publishing Co., 1976.

Heitman, F. B. *Historical Register and Dictionary of the US Army from Its Organization September 29, 1789 to September 29, 1880.* Washington, D.C.: National Tribune, 1890.

Historical Records, Minutes of Town Meetings 1680–1737. Town of Bedford, Westchester, New York, 1966.

Historical Statistics of the United States: Colonial Times to 1970. Washington, D.C.: U.S. Department of Commerce, Bureau of the Census, 1973.

Historical Statistics of the States of the United States: Two Centuries of the Census, 1790–1990. Compiled by Donald B. Dodd. Westport, Conn.: Greenwood Press, 1993.

Index of Marriages and Deaths in New York Weekly Museum, 1788–1817. [Worcester, Mass.:] American Antiquarian Society, 1982.

Index to Marriages and Deaths in the New York Herald, 1856–1863. Compiled by James P. Maher. Vol. 2. Alexandria, Va.: James P. Maher, 1991.

Journals of the Provincial Congress, Provincial Convention, Committee of Safety and Council of Safety of the State of New-York, 1775–1776–1777. 2 vols. Albany, 1842.

Letters of Delegates to Congress, 1774–1789, August 1774–August 1775. Edited by Paul H. Smith. Washington, D.C.: Library of Congress, 1976.

Marriages and Deaths from The New Yorker *(Double Quarto Edition). 1836–1841.* Edited by Kenneth Scott. Washington, D.C.: National Genealogical Society, 1980.

Marriages from 1639 to 1801 in the Reformed Dutch Church, New York. Collections of the New York Genealogical and Biographical Society, vol. 1. New York, 1890 et seq.

Marriages taken from the New York Evening Post, *1801–1880.* Compiled by Gertrude A. Barber. Typescript. 1933–1948.

Minutes of the Committee and of the First Commission for Detecting and Defeating Conspiracies in the State of New York, December 11, 1776– September 23, 1778 with collateral documents to which is added Minutes of the Council of Appointment, State of New York, April 2, 1778–May 3, 1779. Edited by Dorothy C. Barck. Collections of the New-York Historical Society, vols. 57–58. New York, 1924, 1925.

Minutes of the Common Council of the City of New York, 1784–1831. 19 vols. New York, 1917.

Monroe, Joel H. *Historical Records of a Hundred and Twenty Years: Auburn, N.Y.* Geneva, N.Y., 1913.

Munsell, Joel, comp. *The Annals of Albany.* 10 vols. Albany, 1850–59.

Naval Documents of the American Revolution. Vol. 10. Edited by Michael J. Crawford. Washington D.C.: GPO, 1996.

New York County, New York. County Clerk. *Index to Matrimonial Actions, 1784–1910.* Salt Lake City: Genealogical Society of Utah, 1977.

Obituary Record of Graduates of Yale Univ. Deceased during the Year Ending June 1, 1913. New Haven: Yale College, 1913.

Population of States and Counties of the United States, 1790 to 1990. Washington, D.C.: U.S. Department of Commerce, Bureau of the Census, 1996.

Powell, Wm. H., comp. *List of Officers of the Army of the United States from 1779 to 1900.* New York: L. H. Hamersly, 1900. Reprint, Detroit: Gale Research Co., 1967.

The Public Records of the Colony of Connecticut. Edited by Charles J. Hoadly. 18 vols. Hartford, 1850–1890.

The Public Records of the State of Connecticut. Edited by Charles J. Hoadly, Leonard W. Labaree, Catherine Fennelly, Albert R. Van Dusen, Christopher Collier, Bonnie Bromberger, Dorothy Ann Lipson, and Douglas M. Arnold. 15 vols. Hartford, Conn.: 1894–1991.

Records of the Reformed Dutch Church of Albany, New York, 1683–1809: Marriages, Baptisms, Members, etc. Excerpted from Year Books of the Holland Society of New York. Baltimore: Genealogical Publishing Co., 1978.

Ulster County, N.Y. Probate Records in the Office of the Surrogate and in the County Clerk's Office at Kingston, N.Y. Vols. 1 and 2 combined. New York: Gustave Anjou, 1906. Reprint, Rhinebeck, N.Y.: Palatine Transcripts, Arthur C. M. Kelly, 1980.

Yearbook of the Collegiate Church of the City of New York 1992–1996. New York: Collegiate Church of the City of New York, ca. 1997.

Correspondence, Journals, Memoirs, and Personal Papers

Chanler, Margaret. *Roman Spring: Memoirs of Mrs. Winthrop Chanler.* Boston: Little, Brown, 1934.

Child, L. Maria. *Letters from New York.* New York: C. S. Francis, 1843.

Clinton, George. *Public Papers of George Clinton, First Governor of New York, 1777–1795–1801–1804.* 8 vols. Albany, N.Y., 1899–1914.

Clinton, Henry. *The American Rebellion: Sir Henry Clinton's Narrative of his Campaigns, 1775–1782.* Edited by William B. Wilcox. New Haven: Yale Univ. Press, 1954.

Goebel, Julius, Jr., and Joseph H. Smith, eds. *The Law Practice of Alexander Hamilton: Documents and Commentary.* Vol. 1. New York: Columbia Univ. Press, under the auspices of the William Nelson Cromwell Foundation, 1980.

Hardenbergh, John L. "The Journal of Lieut. John L. Hardenbergh of the Second New York Continental Regiment from May 1 to October 3, 1779 in General Sullivan's Campaign against the Western Indians." Collections of Cayuga Historical Society, vol. 1. Auburn, N.Y.: Cayuga Historical Society, 1879.

Judd, Jacob, ed. *Correspondence of the Van Courtlandt Family of Courtlandt Manor, 1800–1814.* Tarrytown, N.Y.: Sleepy Hollow Restorations, 1978.

Kingsbury, Alice E. *In Old Waterbury: The Memoirs of Alice E. Kingsbury.* Waterbury, Conn.: Mattatuck Historical Society, 1942.

Labagh, James. *Memoir of Rev. James Labagh, D. D., with Notes of the History of the Reformed Protestant Dutch Church in North America.* Edited by John A. Todd. New York: House of Publications of the Reformed Protestant Dutch Church, 1860.

Leggett, Abraham. *The Narrative of Major Abraham Leggett of the Army of the Revolution, Now First Printed from the Original Manuscript.* Edited by Charles I. Bushnell. New York: privately printed 1865.

Martin, Joseph Plumb. *Private Yankee Doodle . . . Joseph Plumb Martin, Private Yankee Doodle: A Narrative of the Adventures, Dangers and Sufferings of a Revolutionary Soldier.* Edited by George F. Scheer. Reprint, New York, 1968.

Maude, John. *Visit to the Falls of Niagara in 1800.* London: Longman, Rees, Orme, Brown and Green, 1826.

Parker, Robert. "Journal of Lieutenant Robert Parker of the Second Connecticut Artillery, 1779." Edited by Thomas Bard. *Pennsylvania Magazine of History and Biography* 27 (1903): 404–20; 28 (1904): 12–25.

Pillsbury, Katherine Clark. *A Cherished Childhood.* Edited by Beverly A. Hermes. Illustrated by Julia Ann Jouker. Wayzata, Minn.: privately printed, 1999.

Scott, Winfield. *Memoirs of Lieut.-General Scott, LL.D.* New York: Sheldon, 1864.

Smith, Richard. *A Tour of Four Great Rivers: The Hudson, Mohawk, Susquehanna and Delaware in 1769.* Edited by Francis W. Halsey. 1906. Port Washington, Long Island, N.Y.: Ira J. Friedman, 1964.

Smith, William. *Historical Memoirs from 16 March 1763 to 25 July 1778.* Edited by William H. W. Sabine. New York: Arno Press, 1969.

Strong, George Templeton. *The Diary of George Templeton Strong: Post-War Years, 1865–1875.* 4 vols. Edited by Allan Nevins and Milton Halsey Thomas. New York: Macmillan, 1952.

Thacher, James. *A Military Journal During the American Revolutionary War, from 1775 to 1783, Describing Interesting Events and Transactions of this Period, with Numerous Historical Facts and Anecdotes.* Boston: Richardson and Lord, 1823.

Trumbull, Benjamin. *Journal, September 15–16, 1776.* In *The American Revolution: Writings from the War of Independence.* Edited by John Rhodehamel. New York: Library of America, 2001.Originally published in *Collections of the Connecticut Historical Society,* vol. 7, 193–96. Hartford: Connecticut Historical Society, 1899.

Washington, George. *George Washington: Writings.* Edited by John Rhodehamel. New York: Library of America, 1997.

Washington, George. *The Papers of George Washington: Revolutionary War Series.* Vol. 5. Edited by W. W. Abbot and Dorothy Twohig. Charlottesville: Univ. Press of Virginia, 1993.

Washington, George. *The Writings of George Washington from the Original Manuscript Sources, 1745–1799, June 12, 1780–September 5, 1780.* Edited by John C. Fitzpatrick. Washington, D.C.: GPO, 1937.

Wilkinson, James. *Memoirs of My Own Times.* 3 vols. Philadelphia: Abraham Small, 1816.

Genealogical and Biographical Literature

Barratt, Albert Gedney. "The Fourth New York Regiment in the American Revolution," *Record* 59 (1921): 219–28.

Beard, Timothy Field, and Henry Hoff, comp. "The Roosevelt Family in America (Part 1)," *Theodore Roosevelt Association Journal* 16, no. 1 (Winter 1980).

Christoph, Florence A. *The Schuyler Families in America Prior to 1900.* Albany, N.Y.: Friends of Schuyler Mansion, [1993].

Clark. Edgar W. *History and Genealogy of Samuel Clark, Sr. and His Descendants from 1636–1882.* St. Louis, Mo.: privately printed, 1892.

Commemorative Biographical Record of New Haven County, Connecticut. 2 vols. Chicago: J. H. Beers, 1902.

Cowles, Calvin Duvall. *The Cowles Family in America.* 2 vols. New Haven: Tuttle, Morehouse, and Taylor, 1929.

Genealogical and Family History of the State of Connecticut. Edited by William Richard Cutter. 4 vols. New York: Lewis Historical Publishing Co., 1911.

Kip, Frederic Ellsworth, and Margarita Lansing Hawley. *History of the Kip Family in America.* Montclair, N.J.: privately printed, 1928.

Knapp, Alfred Averill, comp. *Nicholas Knapp Genealogy.* Winter Park, Fla., 1958.

Krumm, Walter C. "Who Was the Rev. Richard Denton?" *Record* 117 (1986): 163–65, 211–18.

———."Descendants of the Rev. Richard Denton." *Record* 120 (1989): 10–17, 93–97, 159–64, 222–24; 121 (1990): 22–24, 144–49, 221–23; 122 (1991): 37–44, 168–69, 215–28.

Miller, Myrtle Hardenbergh. *The Hardenbergh Family: A Genealogical Compilation.* New York: America Historical Co., 1983.

Post. John J. *Abstract of Title of Kip's Bay Farm in the City of New York, Also the Early History of the Kip Family and the Genealogy as Refers to the Title.* New York: S. Victor Constant, 1894.

Puffer, William Nicholas. "Contributions to the History of the Stagg Family." *Record* 9 (1878): 85–91.

Ross, Emma Howell. *Descendants of Edward Howell (1584–1655) of Westbury Manor, Marsh Gibbon, Buckinghamshire and Southampton, Long Island, New York.* Revised by David Faris. Baltimore: Gateway Press, 1985.

Tuttle, George Frederick. *The Descendants of William and Elizabeth Tuttle, who Came from Old to New England in 1635, and Settled in New Haven in 1639.* Rutland, Vt.: Tuttle, 1883.

Van Renssalaer, Florence. *The Livingston Family in America and Its Scottish Origins.* Arranged by William Beer. New York: privately printed, 1949.

———. *The Van Rensselaers in Holland and in America.* New York: privately printed, 1956.

Weygant, Charles H. *The Sacketts of America, their Ancestors and Descendants, 1630—1907.* Newburgh, N.Y., 1907.

Leisure and Travel Guides

Appleton's Hand-Book of American Travel: Northern and Eastern Tour. New York: D. Appleton, 1873.

Appleton's Hand-Book of American Travel: Western Tour. New York: D. Appleton, 1872.

B. Bradshaw's *Dictionary of Mineral Waters, Climatic Health Resorts, Sea Baths, and Hydropathic Establishments.* London: Kegan Paul, Trench, Trubner, 1904.

Baedeker, Karl. *Austria-Hungary with Excursions to Cetinje, Belgrade, and Bucharest.* Leipzig, London, New York, 1911.

———. *Great Britain.* Leipzig, 1897.

———. *London and Its Environs.* Leipzig, 1892.

———. *Northern Italy* Leipzig, 1892, 1913.

———. *Paris and Environs, also Routes from London to Paris.* Leipzig, 1894.

———. *Switzerland.* Leipzig, 1867, 1899.

———. *The Dominion of Canada with Newfoundland an Excursion to Alaska.* Leipzig, 1900.

———. *The United States, with an Excursion into Mexico.* Leipzig, New York, 1904.

———. *Northern France from Belgium and the English Channel to the Loire, excluding Paris and Its Environs.* 4th ed. Leipzig, London, New York, 1905.

Blanchard, Rufus. *Hand-Book of Minnesota.* Chicago: Blanchard and Cram, 1867.

Bowles, Samuel. *Our New West: Records of Travel between the Mississippi and the Pacific Ocean.* Hartford and New York: Hartford Publishing Co., J. D. Dennison, 1869.

Hamburg-Amerika Line. *Guide through Europe*. Berlin: J. Herman Herz, 1911.

Rae, W. Fraser. *Austrian Health Resorts and the Bitter Waters of Hungary*. London: Chapman and Hall, 1888.

Schauffler, Robert Taylor. *Romantic Germany*. New York: Century Co., 1909.

The Stranger's Guide around New York and its Vicinity, What to See and What is to Be Seen with Hints and Advice to Those Who Visit the Great Metropolis. New York: W. B. Graham, 1853.

The Tourist's Guide Through the Empire State Embracing all Cities, Towns and Watering Places by Hudson River and New York Central Route. Edited by S. S. Colt. Albany: privately printed, 1871.

Weber, Hermann. *The Spas and Mineral Waters of Europe with Notes on Balneo-Therapeutic management in Various Diseases and Morbid Conditions*. London: Smith, Elder, 1896.

White, Norval, and Eliot Wilensky. *AIA Guide to New York City*. 4th ed. New York: Three Rivers Press, 2000.

Studies and Reference Works

Adams, Henry. *History of the United States of America During the First Administration of Thomas Jefferson, 1803–1805*. 1890. Reprint, New York: Library of America, 1986.

———. *History of the United States of America During the Administrations of James Madison*. 1891. Reprint, New York: Library of America, 1986.

Akin, Edward N. *Flagler: Rockefeller Partner and Florida Baron*. Kent, Ohio: Kent State Univ. Press, 1988.

Albion, Robert Greenhalgh. *The Rise of New York Port*. New York: Charles Scribners, 1939.

Alexander, Samuel Davis. *Princeton College during the Eighteenth Century*. New York: Anson D. F. Randolph, ca. 1872.

American Victorian Cottage Homes. Palliser, Palliser & Co. Mineola, N.Y., 1878. Reprint, Dover, 1990.

Anderson, Joseph, ed. *The Town and City of Waterbury, Connecticut, from the Aboriginal Period to the Year Eighteen Hundred and Ninety-Five, 3 vols. New Haven: Price and Lee, 1896*.

Anderson, Scott. "Entrepreneurs and Place in Early America: Auburn, New York, 1783–1880." Ph.D. diss., Syracuse Univ., 1997.

Armstrong, John. *Notices of the War of 1812.* 2 vols. New York: Wiley and Putnam, 1840.

At Home in Waterbury: A History of the Neighborhoods of Waterbury. Exhibition Catalog, Ann Y. Smith, Curator. Waterbury, Conn.: Mattatuck Historical Society, 1999.

Atwater, Isaac. *History of the City of Minneapolis, Minnesota.* 3 vols. (New York: Munsell, 1893.

Babcock, Louis L. *The War on the Niagara Frontier.* Buffalo Historical Society Publications, 29. Buffalo, 1927.

Bagg, M. M., *The Pioneers of Utica: Being Sketches of Its Inhabitants and Its Institutions, with the Civil History of the Place, from the Earliest Settlement to the Year 1825, the Era of the Opening of the Erie Canal.* Utica, N.Y.: Curtiss and Childs, 1877.

Beebe, Lucius. *Mr. Pullman's Elegant Palace Car.* New York: Doubleday; Garden City, 1961.

Bishop, J. Leander. *A History of American Manufacturers from 1608 to 1860.* 3 vols. Philadelphia: Edward Young, 1868. New York: Johnson Reprint Co., 1968.

Bliven, Bruce, Jr. *Battle for Manhattan.* New York: Henry Holt, 1956.

Brass Valley: The Story of Working People's Lives and Struggles in an American Industrial Region. The Brass Workers History Project. Compiled by Jeremy Brecher, Jerry Lombardi, and Jan Stackhouse. Philadelphia: Temple Univ. Press, 1982.

Brewer's Dictionary of Phrase and Fable. Edited by Ivor H. Evans. New York: Harper and Row, 1987.

Brinckley, Douglas. *History of the United States.* New York: Viking-Penguin, 1998.

Bronson, Henry. *The History of Waterbury, Connecticut* (Waterbury: Bronson Brothers, 1858).

Burdge, Franklin. *A Notice of John Haring, a Patriotic Statesman of the Revolution.* New York: privately printed, 1878.

Burrows, Edwin G., and Mike Wallace. *Gotham: A History of New York City to 1898.* New York: Oxford Univ. Press, 1999.

Canedo, Eduardo F. "What is More Enduring than Brass? The Process of Deindustrialization in Waterbury, Connecticut, 1952–1976." Senior thesis, Columbia College, 4 May 1999, Silas Bronson Library, Waterbury, Conn.

Cashman, Sean Dennis. *America in the Age of the Titans: The Progressive Era and World War I.* New York: New York Univ. Press, 1988.

Cerisola Anne-Sophie. "Baedeker City: City Beautiful Planners, Citizens, and Tourists." Ph.D. diss., New York Univ., 1997.

Chandler, David Leon. *The Astonishing Life and Times of the Visionary Robber Baron who Founded Florida*. New York: Macmillan, 1986.

Clarke, T. Wood. *Utica for a Century and a Half*. Utica, N.Y.: Widtman Press, 1952.

Cochran, Thomas B. "An Analytical View of Early American Business." In *Business Enterprises in Early New York*, edited by Joseph R. Frese and Jacob Judd. Tarrytown, N.Y.: Sleepy Hollow Press, 1977.

Cole, David, ed. *History of Rockland County, New York, with Biographical Sketches of Its Prominent Men*. New York: J. B. Beers, 1884.

Conover, George S. *Kanadesaga and Geneva*. Geneva, N.Y.: Geneva Courier, March 1879.

The Constitution of the Reformed Dutch Church in the United States of America with an Appendix Containing Rules and Orders from the General Synod from 1794 to 1815. New York: George Forman, 1815.

Cooper, James Fennimore, *Notions of the Americans: Picked up by a Travelling Bachelor*. Edited by Gary Williams. 1928. Albany: State Univ. of New York Press, 1980.

Cooper, William. *A Guide to the Wilderness*. Dublin: Gilbert and Hodges, 1810.

Countryman, Edward. *A People in Revolution: The American Revolution and Political Society in New York, 1760–1790*. New York: W. W. Norton, 1981.

Cowley, Malcolm. *Exiles' Return: A Literary Odyssey of the 1920's*. Rev. ed. New York: Viking Press, 1951.

Cruikshank, E. A. *Campaigns of the War of 1812–14*. 10 vols. Niagara-on-the-Lake, Ont.: Niagara Historical Society, 1896–1902.

Dailey, W. N. *The History of Montgomery Classis R. C. A.* Amsterdam, N.Y.: Recorder Press 1916.

Diamant, Lincoln. *Chaining the Hudson: The Fight for the River in the American Revolution*. New York: Carol Publishing Co., 1989.

Disturnell, J. A. *Gazetteer of the State of New-York*. Albany: J. Disturnell, 1842.

Douglass, George H. *All Aboard: The Railroad in American Life*. New York, 1982.

Eager. Samuel W. *An Outline History of Orange County. . . .* Newburgh, N.Y.: S. T. Callahan, 1846–47.

Edel, Leon. *Henry James: The Untried Years, 1843–1870.* Philadelphia: J. B. Lippincott, 1953.

Ellis, David Maldwyn. *Landlords and Farmers in the Hudson-Mohawk Region, 1790–1850.* Ithaca, N.Y.: Cornell Univ. Press, 1946.

Ellis, David Maldwyn. James A. Frost, Harold C. Syrett, and Harry J. Carman, eds. *A Short History of New York State.* Ithaca N.Y.: Cornell Univ. Press, for The New York State Historical Association, 1957.

Elting, John R. *Amateurs to Arms! A Military History of the War of 1812.* 1991. Univ. of North Carolina Press, 1991. Reprint, New York: Da Capo Press, 1995.

Everett, Michael John. "External Economies and Inertia: the Rise and Decline of the Naugatuck Valley Brass Industry," Ph.D. diss., Univ. of Connecticut, 1987.

Fabend, Firth Haring. *A Dutch Family in the Middle Colonies, 1660–1800.* New Brunswick, N.J.: Rutgers Univ. Press, 1991.

Ferro, Maxmillian L., and Arthur L. Brown, Melvin Canzon, Roger Brevoort. "Report on Historic Structures in Downtown Waterbury Presently Scheduled for Demolition." Prepared for Waterbury Action to Conserve Our Heritage. Natick, Mass: Preservation Partnership, [1980].

Field, Thomas W. *The Battle of Long Island.* Memoirs of the Long Island Historical Society, vol. 2. Brooklyn, N.Y., 1869.

Fiske, Amos Kidder. *The West Indies: A History of the Islands of the West Indian Archipelago, Together with an Account of the Physical Characteristics, Natural Resources and Present Condition.* New York: G. P. Putnam's Sons, Knickerbocker Press, 1902.

Flack, Clifford J. "Chronological History of Marin County, 1542–1899." Typescript, n.d., San Rafael Public Library.

Flick, Alexander, ed. *History of the State of New York.* New York: Columbia Univ. Press, 1933–37., 10 vols.

Gallagher, John J. *The Battle of Brooklyn 1776.* New York: Sarpedon, 1995.

Garrett, Elizabeth Donaghy. *At Home: The American Family 1750–1870.* New York: Harry N. Abrams, 1990.

Green, Harvey. *Fit for America: Health, Fitness, Sport and American Society.* Baltimore: Johns Hopkins Univ. Press, 1986.

Guber, Bill. "The Long and Bloody Trolley Strike of 1903." *Sunday Republican Magazine,* 2 October 1988.

Guide to the Microfilm Edition of the Peter Smith Papers, 1763–1850. Mimeograph, Glen Rock, N.J. Microfilming Corporation of America, 1974.

Haeger, John Denis. *John Jacob Astor: Business and Finance in the Early Republic.* Detroit: Wayne State Univ. Press, Great Lakes Books, 1991.

Hall, Henry. *The History of Auburn.* Auburn, N.Y.: Dennis Bro's, 1869.

Harrington, Virginia D. *The New York Merchant on the Eve of the Revolution.* New York: Columbia Univ. Press, 1935.

Hastings, Katherine B., "William^2 (1771–1832) James of Albany, N.Y. and His Descendants," *Record* 55 (1924): 101–119.

Hauptman, Laurence M. *Conspiracy of Interests: Iroquois Dispossession and the Rise of New York State.* Syracuse, N.Y.: Syracuse Univ. Press, 1999.

Hazelton, Isham. *The Boroughs of Brooklyn and Queens, Counties of Nassau and Suffolk, Long Island, New York 1609–1924.* 6 vols. Chicago: Lewis Historical Publishing Co., 1925.

"Heading West: 200 Years Ago: Inland Navigation in the 1790s." Albany: New York State Library, ca. 1992.

Heidt, William, Jr. *Simeon De Witt, Founder of Ithaca, N.Y.* [Ithaca:] De Witt Historical Society of Tompkins County, 1968.

Henderson, H. James. *Party Politics in the Continental Congress.* New York: McGraw-Hill, 1974.

[Herring, Elbert], *An Oration of the Anniversary of The Battle of Lexington, Delivered at the Request of "The United Whig Club."* New York: Southwick and Pelsue, 1809.

Hickey. Donald R. *The War of 1812: A Forgotten Conflict.* Urbana and Chicago: Univ. of Illinois Press, 1990.

"The Hillside, Waterbury, Connecticut: The Architectural and Historic Resources Inventory." Historic Neighborhood Preservation Program: The Waterbury Neighborhood Housing Service. Xerographic copy of typescript form filed with the Connecticut Historical Commission, 25 November 1986, Silas Bronson Library, Waterbury, Conn.

History of Marin County, California. San Francisco: Alley Bowen, 1880.

Conover, George S., ed. *History of Ontario County, New York.* Syracuse, N.Y.: B. Mason, 1893.

History of the Class of 1877. New Haven: Yale Univ., 1904.

History of the Class of 1927, Yale College. New Haven: Published under the Direction of the Class Secretaries Bureau, 1927.

History of the Class of 1927, Yale College, Decennial Record. New Haven: Published with the assistance of the Class Secretaries Bureau, 1937.

Husband, Joseph. *The Story of the Pullman Car.* Chicago: A. C. McClurg, 1917.

Ierley, Merritt. *The Comforts of Home: The American House and the Evolution of Modern Convenience.* New York: Clarkson Potter, 1999.

Jackson, J. B. "The Order of a Landscape." In *The Interpretation of Ordinary Landscapes,* edited by D. W. Meinig. New York: Oxford Univ. Press, 1979.

Johnston, Henry F. *The Campaign of 1776 around New York and Brooklyn.* Brooklyn, N.Y.: Long Island Historical Society, 1878.

Jones, Pomroy. *Annals and Recollections of Oneida County.* Rome, N.Y.: privately printed, 1851.

Judd, Peter Haring. "Letters from Katie Powys to Elizabeth Wade White, 1938–1954." *Powys Journal* 7 (1997): 76–115.

———. *The Hatch and Brood of Time: Five Phelps Families in the Atlantic World, 1720–1880.* Boston: Newbury Street Press, 1999.

Kamil, Seth. "The Bowery: I'll Never go There Anymore." *New York Chronicle* (Fall/Winter, 1993).

Kaminski, John P. "New York: The Reluctant Pillar." In *The Reluctant Pillar: New York and the Adoption of the Federal Constitution,* edited by Stephen L. Schechter. Troy, N.Y.: Russell Sage College, 1985.

———. *George Clinton: Yeoman Politician of the New Republic.* Madison, Wis.: Madison House, 1993.

Kelley, Brooks Mather. *Yale: A History.* New Haven: Yale Univ. Press, 1974.

Koeppel, Gerard T. *Water for Gotham: A History.* Princeton: Princeton Univ. Press, 2000.

Kuhlmann, Charles Byron. *The Development of the Flour Milling Industry in the United States.* Boston: Houghton Mifflin, ca. 1929.

Kvasnicka, Robert M., and Herman J. Viola. *The Commissioners of Indian Affairs, 1824–1977.* Lincoln, Neb.: Univ. of Nebraska Press, 1979.

Lathrop, Wilson Gilbert. *The Brass Industry in the United States: A Study of the Origin and the Development of the Brass Industry in the Naugatuck Valley and its Subsequent Extension over the Nation.* 1926. Reprint, New York: Arno Press, 1972.

Leiby, Adrian C. *The Revolutionary War in the Hackensack Valley.* New Brunswick, N.J.: Rutgers Univ. Press, 1960.

———. *The United Churches of Hackensack and Schraalenburgh New Jersey, 1686–1822.* River Edge, N.J,: Bergen County Historical Society, 1976.

Leyendecker, Liston Edginton. *Palace Car Prince: A Biography of George Mortimer Pullman*. Niwot, Col.: Univ. Press of Colorado, 1982.

Linder, Marc, and Lawrence S. Zacharias. *Of Cabbages and Kings County: Agriculture and the Formation of Modern Brooklyn*. Iowa City: Iowa Univ. Press, 1999.

Lockwood, Charles. *Bricks and Brownstone: The New York Row House, 1783–1929*. New York: Abbeville Press, 1972.

Lossing, Benson L. *The Pictorial Field-Book of the Revolution*. 2 vols. New York: Harper and Brothers, 1851.

Lutz, Tom. *American Nervousness, 1903: An Anecdotal History*. Ithaca: Cornell Univ. Press, 1991.

Marburg, Theodore F. *Small Business in Brass Manufacturing: The Smith and Griggs Manufacturing Company of Waterbury*. New York: New York Univ. Press, 1956.

Mather, Frederick Gregory. *The Refugees of 1776 from Long Island to Connecticut*. Albany: J. B. Lyon, 1913.

Matthiessen , F. O. "The Education of a Socialist." In *F. O. Matthiessen (1902–1950): A Collective Portrait*, edited by Paul M. Sweezy and Leo Huberman, 3–20. New York: Henry Schuman, 1950.

Mattocks, Brewer. *Minnesota as a Home for Invalids*. Philadelphia: J. B. Lippincott, 1871.

Meinig, D. W. "The Colonial Period, 1609–1775." In *Geography of New York State*, edited by John H. Thompson. Syracuse: Syracuse Univ. Press, 1960.

Miller. William H., Jr. *The First Great Ocean Liners in Photographs*. New York: Dover, 1984.

———. *Picture History of the Italian Line, 1932–1977*. Mineola, N.Y.: Dover, 1999.

Miner, Marcia Peden. "Metamorphosis par Excellence." *Fairfield Citizen News*, 27 September 1995.

Nutt, John J., comp. *Newburgh, Her Institutions, Industries and Leading Citizens*. Newburgh, N.Y.: Ritchie and Hull, 1891.

Office of Indian Affairs [25 November 1834]. *Annual Report of the Commissioner of Indian Affairs transmitted with the Message of the President at the opening of the Second Session of the Twenty-third Congress, 1834–35*. Washington, D.C.: Duff Green, 1834.

Office of Indian Affairs, Department of War [28 November 1833]. *Annual Report of the Commissioner of Indian Affairs Transmitted with the Message of the President at the Opening of the First Session of the Twenty-third Congress,* 1833–34. Washington, D.C.: Gales and Seaton, 1833.

Orcutt, Samuel. A *History of the Old Town of Stratford and the City of Bridgeport Connecticut.* Fairfield: Fairfield County Historical Society, 1886.

Pape, William J. *History of Waterbury and the Naugatuck Valley, Connecticut.* 3 vols. Chicago, New York: S. J. Clarke, 1918.

Perrett, Geoffrey. *America in the Twenties: A History.* New York: Simon and Schuster, 1982.

Peter T. Maiken. *Night Trains.* Chicago: Lakem Press, 1989.

Pierson, George Wilson. *Tocqueville and Beaumont in America.* New York: Oxford Univ. Press, 1938.

Porter, Glenn and Harold C. Livesay. *Merchants and Manufacturers: Studies in the Changing Structure of Nineteenth Century Marketing.* Baltimore: Johns Hopkins Univ. Press, 1971.

Porter, Kenneth Wiggins. *John Jacob Astor: Business Man.* 2 vols. Cambridge: Harvard Univ. Press, 1931.

Pratt, George W. "An Account of the British Expedition above the Highlands of the Hudson River and of the Events Connected with the Burning of Kingston in 1777." *Collections of the Ulster Historical Society,* vol. 1, 107–174. Kingston, 1860.

The Quarter Century Record [of Yale, Class of 1900]. New Haven: Tuttle, Morehouse, and Taylor, 1927.

Remini, Robert V. *Andrew Jackson and His Indian Wars.* New York: Viking, Penguin Books, 2001.

Reynolds, Cuyler, comp. *Albany Chronicles: A History of the City Arranged Chronologically.* (Albany, 1906).

"Report of Committee of Forfeiture for the Southern Distinct of the State of New York, 24 Dec. 1787." In Alexander Clarence Flick, *Loyalism in New York during the American Revolution.* New York: Columbia Univ. Press, 1901.

Rockoff, Hugh. "Banking and Finance 1789–1914." In *The Cambridge Economic History of the United States, The Long Nineteenth Century.* Vol. 2, edited by Stanley L. Ingerman and Robert E. Gallman. Cambridge: Cambridge Univ. Press, 2000.

Rose, Robert S. "The Military Tract of Central New York." Master's thesis, Syracuse Univ., May 1935.

Roth, Mathew W. *Platt Brothers and Company: Small Business in American
Manufacturing.* Hanover, N.H.: Univ. Press of New England, for the
Univ. of Connecticut, 1994.

Ruttenber, E. M. *History of the County of Orange, with a History of the Town
and City of Newburgh.* Newburgh, N.Y.: E. M. Ruttenber and Son, 1875.

———. "The County of Ulster." In *The History of Ulster County, New
York,* edited by Alphonso T. Clearwater, 17–203. Kingston, N.Y.: W. J.
Van Deusen, 1907.

———. *History of the Town of New Windsor, Orange County, N.Y.* Newburgh, N.Y.: Historical Society of Newburgh Bay and the Highlands,
1911.

Scapino, A. J., Jr. "Community, Class, and Conflict: The Waterbury Trolley Strike of 1909." Xerographic reproduction of an article from unattributed source, 29–42. Research Collection, Mattatuck Museum,
Histories Folder.

Scharf J. Thomas. *History of Westchester County New York, including Morrisania, Kings Bridge, and West Farms.* Philadelphia: L. E. Preseont,
1888. Reprint, Camden, Me.: Picton Press, 1982.

Schein, Richard Huot. "A Historical Geography of Central New York:
Patterns and Processes of Colonization on the New Military Tract,
1782–1820." Ph.D. diss., Syracuse Univ., 1989.

———. "Unofficial Proprietors in Central New York." *Journal of Historical Geography* 17 (1991): 146–64.

———. "Framing the Frontier: The New Military Tract Survey in Central New York." *New York History* 74, no. 1 (1993): 5–28.

Seventy Years North German Lloyd Bremen, 1857–1927. Berlin: Atlantic-
Verlag, [1927].

Sipes, William B. *The Pennsylvania Railroad: its Origin, Construction, Condition and Connections.* Philadelphia: Passenger Department,
Pennsylvania Railroad, 1875.

Skeen, C. Edward. *Citizen Soldiers in the War of 1812.* Lexington, Ky:
Univ. of Kentucky Press, 1999.

Smith, William, Jr. *The History of the Province of New-York, from the First
Discovery to the Year 1732.* Edited by Michael Kammen. Cambridge:
Harvard Univ. Press, The Belknap Press, 1972.

Smyth, G. Hutchinson. *The Life of Henry Bradley Plant.* New York and London: G. P. Putnams Sons, Knickerbocker Press, 1898.

Spafford, Horatio Gates. *A Gazetteer of the State of New York.* Albany, H. C. Southwyck, 1813.

Spafford, Horatio Gates. *A Gazetteer of the State of New York.* . . . New York, 1824. Reprint, Interlaken, N.Y.: Heart of the Lakes Publishing Co., 1981.

Spaulding, E. Wilder. *His Excellency George Clinton: Critic of the Constitution.* New York: Macmillan, 1938.

Stansell, Christine. *City of Women: Sex and Class in New York, 1789–1860.* New York: Alfred A. Knopf, 1986.

Stern, Robert A. M., Gregory Gilmartin, and John Massengale. *New York 1900: Metropolitan Architecture and Urbanism 1890–1915.* New York: Rizzoli International, 1983.

Stiles, Henry R. *A History of the City of Brooklyn including the Old Town and village of Brooklyn, the Town of Bushwick and the Village and City of Williamsburgh.* 3 vols. Brooklyn, N.Y.: by subscription, 1869. Facsimile ed. Bowie, Md.: Heritage Books, 1993.

Stokes, I. N. Phelps. *The Iconography of Manhattan Island, 1398–1909.* 6 vols. New York: Robert H. Dodd, 1918–28.

Stowe, William W. *European Travel in Nineteenth-Century American Culture.* Princeton: Princeton Univ. Press, 1994.

Sweezy, Paul M., and Leo Huberman, eds. *F. O. Matthiessen (1902–1950): A Collective Portrait.* New York: Henry Schuman, 1950.

Taylor, Alan. *William Cooper's Town: Power and Persuasion on the Frontier of the Early American Republic.* New York: Alfred A. Knopf, 1995.

Tolles, Bryant F., Jr. *The Grand Resort Hotels in the White Mountains: A Vanishing Architectural Legacy.* Boston: David R. Godine, 1998.

Twenty-Five Years Out: History of the Class of 1927, Yale Univ. New Haven: Yale Univ., published with the assistance of the Class Secretaries Bureau, 1953.

The Waterbury Clock Company, 1857, 1891, Catalogue No 131. Introduction by Chris H. Bailey. Reprint, Bristol, Conn.: American Clock and Watch Museum, 1982.

The WPA Guide to New York City. Rev. ed. New York: Pantheon Books, 1982.

Wade White 1930's Precisionist. Catalog, Janet Marquesee Fine Arts. New York, [1989].

Ward, Christopher. *The War of the Revolution*. Edited by John Richard Alden. 2 vols. New York: Macmillan, 1952.

"Waterbury Architectural Survey, Waterbury, Connecticut 1978." Ann Smith, Project Director. Typescript, Waterbury, Conn., Mattatuck Museum Research Collection, [1978].

Waterbury, New Haven County, Connecticut, U.S.A., Its location, Wealth, Finances, Industries, Commerce, and Society; Its Freight and Passenger Facilities, and What it Offers as a Place for Residence or Business. Waterbury, Conn.: Board of Trade, 1890.

Watkins, William H. *Rose Hill*. Waterbury: Mattatuck Historical Society, 1973.

White, Elizabeth Wade. *Anne Bradstreet: The Tenth Muse*. New York: Oxford Univ. Press, 1971.

White, Elizabeth Wade, ed. "How to Win a Wedding Ring: The Correspondence of William Henry White in the Klondike Region of the Yukon Territory, Dominion of Canada, 1900–1901." Typescript, collection of the author.

Who Was Who in America. Chicago: Marquis Who's Who, 1981.

Wood, Gordon S. *The Radicalism of the American Revolution*. New York: Alfred A. Knopf, 1992.

Wyckoff, William. *The Developer's Frontier: The Making of the Western New York Landscape*. New Haven: Yale Univ. Press, 1988.

Yale '24–24S: 1934–1955. Edited by Philip W. Pillsbury. New Haven: Yale Class of 1924, Class Officers Bureau, 1955.

Yale Banner and Pot Pourri. New Haven, 1923, 1926.

Yale Univ., Class of '89 Quarter Centennial Record. New Haven: Yale Univ. Press, 1914.

Ziff, Larzer. *The American 1890s*. Bison ed. Lincoln, Neb.: Univ. of Nebraska Press, 1979.

INDEX

Prepared by Thomas Kozachek

Design & Typography by Thomas Kozachek